Handbook of Short Selling

Handbook of Short Selling

Greg N. Gregoriou

Editor

AMSTERDAM • BOSTON • HEIDELBERG • LONDON
NEW YORK • OXFORD • PARIS • SAN DIEGO
SAN FRANCISCO • SINGAPORE • SYDNEY • TOKYO

Academic Press is an imprint of Elsevier

Academic Press is an imprint of Elsevier
225 Wyman Street, Waltham, MA 02451, USA
The Boulevard, Langford Lane, Kidlington, Oxford, OX5 1GB, UK

Notices

Knowledge and best practice in this field are constantly changing. As new research and experience broaden
our understanding, changes in research methods, professional practices, or medical treatment may become
necessary.

Practitioners and researchers must always rely on their own experience and knowledge in evaluating and
using any information, methods, compounds, or experiments described herein. In using such information or
methods they should be mindful of their own safety and the safety of others, including parties for whom
they have a professional responsibility.

To the fullest extent of the law, neither the Publisher nor the authors, contributors, or editors, assume any
liability for any injury and/or damage to persons or property as a matter of products liability, negligence or
otherwise, or from any use or operation of any methods, products, instructions, or ideas contained in the
material herein.

Library of Congress Cataloging-in-Publication Data
Gregoriou, Greg N., 1956-
  Handbook of short selling / Greg N. Gregoriou.
    p. cm.
  ISBN 978-0-12-387724-6
1. Short selling. 2. Speculation. 3. Risk-taking (Psychology) I. Title.
  HG6041.G725 2012
  332.64'5–dc23   2011020284

British Library Cataloguing-in-Publication Data
A catalogue record for this book is available from the British Library.

For information on all Academic Press publications
visit our Web site at *www.elsevierdirect.com*

Typeset by: diacriTech, Chennai, India

Printed and bound by CPI Group (UK) Ltd, Croydon, CR0 4YY

Transferred to digital print 2012

Contents

Section 4 Emerging Markets

Section 5 Portfolio Management and Performance

Preface

This handbook differs from other edited books because on a global scale it addresses new rules and regulations about short selling. Quantitative papers in this book use the latest data available, but more importantly, the papers are written by well-known academics and money managers.

Many investors believe that short sellers are responsible for market downturns, but academic theory does not suggest this. Instead, short sellers create liquidity in markets and are the best at spotting overpriced stocks as well as making markets more efficient through the aid of price discovery. This short selling handbook comes at a time when financial markets worldwide are recuperating from the credit crisis and the global carnage of 2008. It can assist investors, hedge fund managers, investment analysts, research analysts, lawyers, accountants, endowments, foundations, and high net worth individuals to better understand short selling during and after the crisis of 2008.

The 39 chapters in this handbook will be a valuable source of information to anyone interested in short selling. Among its most exciting subjects are views of what the regulators temporarily did to ban short selling in order to prevent markets from further collapse. Contributors look both at developed global markets and emerging markets. They also take up naked short selling, the ethics of short selling, and other important issues.

The first section of the book is devoted to regulation in the United States with a chapter for Canada. The second section examines both eastern and western European markets, while the third focuses on Japan, China, and Australia. Section four investigates short selling in Russia and in emerging markets such as in Latin America and South Africa. The fifth section examines portfolio management and performance of short biased hedge funds, short selling by portfolio managers, and more. The last section addresses modeling, earnings, announcements, and term structure in a short selling framework. In short, the book does a tour of every continent to investigate short selling during the recent market meltdown.

For more information see the companion site at http://www.elsevierdirect.com/companion.jsp?ISBN=9780123877246.

Acknowledgments

I thank the handful of anonymous referees during the selection process. In addition, I also thank J. Scott Bentley, Ph.D., executive finance editor at Elsevier, for his helpful suggestions to ameliorate this book, Kathleen Paoni, editorial project manager as well as Heather Tighe, associate project manager at Elsevier. I also thank Sol Waksman, president at Barclay Hedge, for supplying hedge fund data for Chapter 29. In addition, we thank PerTrac for the use of PerTrac Analytics which enabled critical parts of our analysis in Chapter 29. Each contributor is responsible for his or her own chapter. Neither the editor nor the publisher is responsible for chapter content.

About the Editor

A native of Montreal, Professor Greg N. Gregoriou obtained his Joint Ph.D. at the University of Quebec at Montreal (UQAM) in Finance which merges the resources of Montreal's four major universities UQAM-McGill-Concordia-HEC. He is Professor of Finance at State University of New York (Plattsburgh). He has published 43 books, 60 refereed publications in peer-reviewed journals, and 20 book chapters since his arrival at SUNY Plattsburgh in August 2003. His books have been published by McGraw-Hill, John Wiley & Sons, Elsevier-Butterworth/Heinemann, Taylor and Francis/CRC Press, Palgrave-Macmillan, and Risk Books. In addition, his articles have appeared in the *Review of Asset Pricing Studies, Journal of Portfolio Management, Journal of Futures Markets, European Journal of Operational Research, Annals of Operations Research, Computers and Operations Research*, etc. Professor Gregoriou is hedge fund editor and editorial board member for the *Journal of Derivatives and Hedge Funds*, as well as editorial board member for the *Journal of Wealth Management*, the *Journal of Risk Management in Financial Institutions, Market Integrity, IEB International Journal of Finance*, and the *Brazilian Business Review*. Professor Gregoriou's interests focus on hedge funds, funds of funds, and CTAs. He also is Research Associate at the EDHEC Business School in Nice, France.

Contributor Bios

Paul U. Ali is an associate professor in the Faculty of Law, University of Melbourne, and a member of that law faculty's center for Corporate Law and Securities Regulation. Prior to becoming an academic, Paul was, for several years, a lawyer in Sydney. Paul has published widely on banking and finance law, derivatives, securitization, and structured finance, including, in 2009, a book on credit derivatives. Paul has also recently participated in Joint India-IMF and Malaysia-IMF training programs as part of an IMF project on derivatives in emerging markets.

David E. Allen is a professor of finance at Edith Cowan University, Perth, Western Australia. He is the author of three monographs and over 70 refereed publications on a diverse range of topics covering corporate financial policy decisions, asset pricing, business economics, funds management and performance bench-marking, volatility modeling and hedging, and market microstructure and liquidity.

Jørgen Vitting Andersen, Ph.D., is a physicist and a senior researcher at CNRS, University of Nice (France). He has broad international experience and has worked at the following universities: Paris X (France), McGill (Canada), Nordita (Denmark), and Imperial College (UK). Over the last 10 years he has published a series of seminal papers in the new domain of econophysics, applying ideas from complexity theory to financial markets.

Paul Brockman is the Joseph R. Perella and Amy M. Perella Chair of Finance at Lehigh University. He holds a B.A. degree in international studies from Ohio State University (*summa cum laude*), an M.B.A. degree from Nova Southeastern University (accounting minor), and a Ph.D. in finance (economics minor) from Louisiana State University. He received his certified public accountant (CPA) designation (Florida, 1990) and worked for several years as an accountant, cash manager, and futures and options trader. His academic publications have appeared in such journals as the *Journal of Finance*, *Journal of Financial Economics*, *Journal of Financial and Quantitative Analysis*, *Journal of Banking and Finance*, *Journal of Corporate Finance*, and the *Journal of Empirical Finance*, among others. Paul has served as a member of the editorial board for the *Journal of Multinational Financial Management* and the Hong Kong Securities Institute's *Securities Journal*.

Soufiane Cherkaoui awaits admission to practice law in the state of New York and is presently an LL.M. degree candidate in the Fordham University School of Law Corporate, Banking and Finance Law program. He holds a *Juris Doctor* from Pace University Law School and a B.A. from New York University.

Graciela Chichilnisky has worked extensively in the Kyoto Protocol process, creating and designing the carbon market concept that became international law in 2005. She also acted as a lead author of the Intergovernmental Panel on Climate Change, which received the 2007 Nobel Prize. A frequent key-note speaker and special adviser to several UN organizations and heads of state, her pioneering work uses innovative market mechanisms to reduce carbon emissions, conserve biodiversity and ecosystem services, and improve the lot of the poor. She is a professor of economics and mathematical statistics at Columbia University and the Sir Louis Matheson Distinguished Professor at Monash University. Her most recent book is *Saving Kyoto*, coauthored with K. Sheeran.

Stefano Corradin is an economist at European Central Bank, research division. He earned his B.A. in economics from the University of Verona (1998), his M.Sc. in economics from CORIPE (1999), and his Ph.D. in business administration from the University of California at Berkeley (2008). From 2000 to 2004 he worked in the risk management department of Cattolica Assicurazioni and Allianz-RAS.

Jeannine Daniel is an investment analyst at Kedge Capital. Prior to joining Kedge, she worked at Ivy Asset Management, a fund of hedge funds, where she was charged with coordinating the firm's European research efforts, which included the sourcing and investment due diligence of managers across the various hedge fund strategies. Prior to Ivy, Jeannine worked at Barclays Global Investors and JP Morgan Chase. She holds a B.Sc. (Hons) in business management from the University of London.

Miguel Díaz-Martínez holds an MBA from the University of Bath and was a Senior Consultant of the National Planning Department of Colombia where he analyzed the financial strategies of public companies and advised the National Government in external debt topics. He has also held positions as trader and financial analyst in firms such as Banco Santander and ICAP. Miguel holds a Bachelors Degree and a Specialisation Degree in Finance and International Affairs from the Externado University in Colombia, and an International Degree in Political Science from the Institute of Political Studies in Paris.

Elena Dukhovnaya is a consultant at Ernst & Young in Moscow, one of the leading international audit and consulting companies. She graduated from Plekhanov Academy of Economics (Moscow, Russia) with a degree in economics and mathematics in 2005, and also successfully completed 1 year in the University of Konstanz (Germany) on an exchange program. She specializes in business, accounting, and regulatory advisory services to telecommunication and media companies.

Mohamed El Hedi Arouri is currently an associate professor of finance at the University of Orleans, France, and a researcher at EDHEC Business School. He holds a master's degree in economics and a Ph.D. in finance from the University of Paris X Nanterre. His research focuses on the cost of capital, stock market integration, and international portfolio choice. He published articles in refereed journals such as *International Journal of Business, Applied Financial Economics, Frontiers of Finance and Economics, Annals of Economics and Statistics, Finance,* and *Economics Bulletin.*

Wei Fan obtained his Ph.D. from the University of Electronic Science and Technology of China, Chengdu Nankai University, Tianjin. He is senior vice-president of the fixed-income department at Hong Yuan Securities Co. Ltd. in Beijing and is in charge of interest-rate derivatives pricing. He has authored more than 10 academic papers in the *International Financial Review, Journal of Financial Transformation, New Mathematics and Natural Computation, Journal of Management* (Chinese), and *Operation and Management* (Chinese). In addition, he has been in charge of two National Natural Science Foundation projects and one Securities Association of China project. His research focuses on asset pricing.

Sihai Fang obtained his Ph.D. in Economics from Naikai University in Tianjing, China. He is a Professor of Finance at the University of Electronic Science and Technology in Chengdu, China. He is a well-known economist in Mainland China and has published over 100 articles. He is Managing Director and Chief Economist of Hongyuan Securities, Co. Ltd., in Beijing. His research area focuses on asset pricing.

Dean Fantazzini is an associate professor in econometrics and finance at the Moscow School of Economics–Moscow State University and visiting professor at the Higher School of Economics, Moscow. He graduated with honors from the Department of Economics at the University of Bologna (Italy) in 1999. He obtained a master's in financial and insurance investments at the Department of Statistics–University of Bologna (Italy) in 2000 and a Ph.D. in economics in 2006 at the Department of Economics and Quantitative Methods, University of Pavia (Italy). Before joining the Moscow School of Economics, he was research fellow at the Chair for Economics and Econometrics, University of Konstanz (Germany), and at the Department of Statistics and Applied Economics, University of Pavia (Italy). He is a specialist in time series analysis, financial econometrics, and multivariate dependence in finance and economics. The author has to his credit more than 20 publications, including three monographs. On April 28, 2009, he received an award for productive scientific research and teaching activities by the former USSR president and Nobel Peace Prize winner Mikhail S. Gorbachev and by the MSU rector Professor Viktor A. Sadovnichy.

Emmanuel Fragnière, Ph.D., CIA (certified internal auditor), is a professor of operations management at the Haute Ecole (HEG) de Gestion de Genève. He is also a lecturer in management science at the University of Bath's school of management. His research interests are modeling languages, energy and environmental planning, stochastic programming, and services pricing and planning. He has published several papers in academic journals, such as *Annals of Operations Research, Environmental Modeling and Assessment, Interfaces,* and *Management Science.* Before joining HEG, was a commodity risk analyst at Cargill (Ocean Transportation) and a senior internal auditor at Banque Cantonale Vaudoise (risk management and financial engineering).

Giampaolo Gabbi is a professor of financial investments and risk management at the University of Siena and a professor at the SDA Bocconi School of Management, where he is a risk management unit leader. He coordinates the M.Sc. in finance at the University of Siena and holds a Ph.D. in banking and corporate management. He has published many books and articles in refereed journals, including *Journal of International Financial Markets, Institutions & Money, Journal of Economic Dynamics and Control, European Journal of Finance, Managerial Finance,* and *Journal of Financial Regulation and Compliance.*

Paola Giovinazzo is a Ph.D. candidate in finance at the University of Siena. She studies the regulatory framework of financial markets and the impact on microstructure.

Russell B. Gregory-Allen is an associate professor of finance in the school of economics and finance at Massey University, where he has been since December 2004. Prior to coming to New Zealand, he was a portfolio manager for a large pension fund in New York, and before that an assistant professor of finance at Rutgers University. His research interests are in issues in portfolio management and performance measurement.

(Grace) Qing Hao is an assistant professor in the finance department at the University of Missouri. She is a CFA (chartered financial analyst) charter holder. She holds a M.S. degree in business from the University of Kansas and a Ph.D. in finance from the University of Florida. She also holds a bachelor of art, a bachelor of engineering, and a master of engineering from Tianjin University (China). Grace has published in the *Journal of Financial Economics* and won the Fama-DFA first prize for the best paper published in 2007 in the *Journal of Financial Economics*. She has served as an ad-hoc reviewer for the *Journal of Finance, Journal of Financial and Quantitative Analysis, Journal of Banking and Finance, Journal of Corporate Finance, Financial Review, Journal of Multinational Financial Management, International Review of Economics and Finance,* and *Research in International Business and Finance.*

Chinmay Jain is a doctoral candidate in finance at the University of Memphis. His research interest areas are market microstructure and international finance. He has a book chapter in *Project Manager's Handbook* published by McGraw Hill in 2007. He and his coauthors have presented his research papers in conferences such as the Academy of International Business and Midwest Finance conference.

Pankaj K. Jain is the Suzanne Downs Palmer associate professor of finance at the Fogelman College of Business at the University of Memphis. Previously he worked in the financial services industry. He has published award-winning research on financial market design in leading journals such as the *Journal of Finance, Journal of Banking and Finance, Financial Management, Journal of Investment Management, Journal of Financial Research,* and *Contemporary Accounting Research.* He has been invited to present his work at the New York Stock Exchange, National Stock Exchange of India, National Bureau of Economic Research in Cambridge, and the Capital Market Institute at Toronto.

Vicente Jakas is a vice-president in finance global markets at Deutsche Bank AG, Frankfurt am Main. He holds a M.Sc. in financial economics from the University of London (London, UK), a B.A. (honors) in business administration from the Robert Gordon University (Aberdeen, UK), and a B.Sc. in business economics from the Universidad de La Laguna (La Laguna, Spain).

He has more than 10 years' experience in the banking industry and has worked for the Big Four audit and consultancy firms in the area of banking and finance. His main areas of research are institutions and capital markets, as well as macroeconomic policy and the financial markets.

Fredj Jawadi is currently an assistant professor at Amiens School of Management and a researcher at EconomiX at the University of Paris Ouest Nanterre La Defense (France). He holds a master in econometrics and a Ph.D. in financial econometrics from the University of Paris X Nanterre (France). His research topics cover modeling asset price dynamics, nonlinear econometrics, international finance, and financial integration in developed and emerging countries. He has published in international refereed journals, such as *Journal of Risk and Insurance, International Journal of Business, Applied Financial Economics, Finance,* and *Economics Bulletin,* and several book chapters.

Meredith Jones is a managing director at PerTrac Financial Solutions. Prior to joining PerTrac, she was the director of research for Van Hedge Fund Advisors. Her research has been published in a number of books and periodicals, and she is a frequent lecturer on a variety of hedge fund topics.

James Kozyra holds a master of science in management, with a concentration in finance, and is currently a level III candidate in the CFA (chartered financial analyst) program. He also earned a honor's bachelor of commerce degree, with majors in accounting and finance. His research has been published in both academic and practitioner journals.

Akhmad Kramadibrata holds a postgraduate diploma in finance from Edith Cowan University and a bachelor of commerce in accounting from Curtin University of Technology, Perth, Australia. He currently works as a research assistant in the School of Accounting, Finance, and Economics at Edith Cowan University.

Alexander Kudrov is a researcher at the Higher School of Economics (Moscow, Russia), where he obtained his Ph.D. in economics in 2008. His main area of research is extreme value theory with applications in economics and finance, and he has to his credit many publications in Russian mathematical journals.

Camillo Lento is a Ph.D. candidate in accounting at the University of Southern Queensland. He received both his master's (M.Sc.) degree and undergraduate degree (HBComm) from Lakehead University. Lento is a chartered accountant (Ontario) and a certified fraud examiner. His Ph.D.

research investigates the capital market implication of earnings management and earnings quality of firms that meet or beat their earnings expectations. His research interests also include technical trading models, and he has published his research in both academic and practitioner journals. Lento is a contributing editor for *Canadian MoneySaver* magazine and has authored numerous articles on personal tax planning matters. Before embarking on his Ph.D., he worked in a midsized public accounting firm. He was involved in various engagements as part of both the assurance and business advisory services group and the specialist advisory services group.

François-Serge Lhabitant, Ph.D., is currently the chief investment officer at Kedge Capital. He was formerly a member of senior management at Union Bancaire Privée, where he was in charge of quantitative risk management and, subsequently, of quantitative research for alternative portfolios. Prior to this, Lhabitant was a director at UBS/Global Asset Management, in charge of building quantitative models for portfolio management and hedge funds. On the academic side, Lhabitant is currently a professor of finance at the EDHEC Business School (France) and a visiting professor at the Hong Kong University of Science and Technology. His specialist skills are in the areas of quantitative portfolio management, alternative investments (hedge funds), and emerging markets. He is the author of several books on these subjects and has published numerous research and scientific articles. He is also a member of the scientific council of the Autorité des Marches Financiers, the French regulatory body.

Abraham Lioui is a professor of finance at EDHEC Business School and a member of the EDHEC Risk Institute. He has taught in several institutions, such as the University of Paris I Sorbonne, ESSEC Business School, and Bar Ilan University where he was vice chair of the economic department before joining EDHEC. He has published widely in academic journals in fields related to portfolio choice theory and asset allocation, derivatives pricing/hedging, and asset pricing theory.

Marco Lo Duca is an economist at European Central Bank, International Policy Analysis Division. He earned his B.A. in economics from the University of Ca' Foscari, Venice (2002) and his M.Sc. in economics and finance from the Venice International University (2004). He has been working at the European Central Bank since 2004.

Christopher Lufrano is a third-year law student at Pace University Law School and a student intern for the nonprofit Investor Rights Clinic. Prior to attending law school, he was an analyst and fixed income trader with Morgan Stanley. He holds a B.S. in business from Boston University.

Andrew Lynch holds a master's degree in economics from the University of Missouri and a B.A. in finance and communications from Southwest Baptist University (*summa cum laude*). He is a Ph.D. candidate (emphasis in econometrics) in the finance department at the University of Missouri. He has several working papers in the areas of short selling, mutual funds, and asset pricing and has presented them at the Southwestern Finance Association and the University of Missouri.

Mario Maggi is an assistant professor of mathematical finance at the University of Pavia. He holds a M.S. in economics from the University of Pavia and a Ph.D. in mathematical finance from the University of Brescia. He has held positions at the Universities of Insubria (Varese), Piemonte Orientale (Alessandria), Bologna (Rimini), and Bocconi (Milano). His research interests are mathematical finance, decision theory, and numerical methods. He is author of numerous research papers published in international reviews and textbooks.

Iliya Markov has a M.Sc. in operational research with finance from the University of Edinburgh and a B.A. in mathematics and economics from the American University in Bulgaria. His research interests include the financial and commodity markets, financial modeling, and optimization and risk management. He is a recipient of numerous awards and distinctions, including an Outstanding Achievement in Mathematics at the American University in Bulgaria and a full scholarship at the University of Edinburgh.

Peter D. Mayall is a lecturer in finance in the School of Economics and Finance at Curtin University of Technology in Perth, Western Australia. His primary qualification was in chartered accounting and he worked in this capacity in his early career in Africa, the Middle East, and the United Kingdom. He then moved to Australia and changed to the finance industry, being involved in the assessment and funding of capital projects. He joined academia in 1993 and lectures in corporate finance, mergers and acquisitions, and financial decision making. His research interests include topics of mergers, agency issues, and the teaching of finance. He has published in the area of the teaching of finance.

Stuart McCrary is a director and principal at Navigant Economics. His consulting practice involves traditional and alternative investments, quantitative valuation, risk management, and financial software. He was president of Frontier Asset Management, managing a market-neutral hedge fund. He held positions with Fenchurch Capital Management as senior options trader and CS First Boston as vice-president and market maker of over-the-counter options. Prior to that, he was a vice-president with the Securities Groups and a portfolio manager with Comerica Bank.

Thomas H. McInish is an author or coauthor of more than 100 scholarly articles in leading journals such as the *Journal of Finance, Journal of Financial and Quantitative Analysis, Journal of Portfolio Management, Review of Economics and Statistics*, and *Sloan Management Review*. Cited as one of the "Most Prolific Authors in 72 Finance Journals," he ranked 20 (tie) out of 17,573 individuals publishing in these journals from 1953 to 2002. Another study ranked him as 58 out of 4990 academics in the number of articles published during 1990–2002. His co-authored, path-breaking articles on intraday stock market patterns originally published in the *Journal of Finance* was selected for inclusion in (1) *Microstructure: The Organization of Trading and Short Term Price Behavior*, which is part of the series edited by Richard Roll of UCLA entitled *The International Library of Critical Writings in Financial Economics* (this series is a collection of the most important research in financial economics and serves as a primary research reference for faculty and graduate students), and (2) *Continuous-Time Methods and Market Microstructure*, which is also part of the *International Library series*.

Qingbin Meng obtained his Ph.D. from Nankai University. He is an assistant professor in the finance department, School of Business, Renmin University of China, Beijing. He has authored eight academic papers in *SIAM Journal of Control and Optimization, Applied Mathematics Computation*, and *Statistics and Probability Letters*. He is a member of the AFA and was in charge of two National Social Science Foundation projects and one Natural Science Foundation project. His research focuses on financial engineering.

Maryam Meseha is a third-year law student at Pace University School of Law, anticipating a *Juris Doctor* in May 2011. She received a Bachelor of Science in international relations from Seton Hall University *magna cum laude*. Her professional interests include international business law and commercial arbitration.

Duc Khuong Nguyen is an associate professor of finance and head of the department of economics, finance, and law at ISC Paris School of Management (France). He holds a M.Sc. and a Ph.D. in finance from the University of Grenoble II (France). His principal research areas concern emerging markets finance, market efficiency, volatility modeling, and risk management in international capital markets. His most recent articles have been published in refereed journals such as *Review of Accounting and Finance, Managerial Finance*,

American Journal of Finance and Accounting, Economics Bulletin, Applied Financial Economics, and *Bank and Markets.*

Andrei Nikiforov is an assistant professor of finance at Rutgers School of Business Camden. He holds B.A. and M.A. degrees in geophysics from Perm State University in Russia (*summa cum laude*), an M.B.A. degree from the University of Missouri (*summa cum laude*), and a Ph.D. in finance from the University of Missouri. Prior to pursuing his academic finance career, he worked for several years as a geophysicist modeling and simulating geophysical fields generated by oil and gas deposits. He published four research articles in geophysical industry journals. He has presented at FMA and has several working papers investigating the role of earnings seasons on financial markets.

Mehmet Orhan is an associate professor at the economics department of Fatih University, Istanbul, and vice dean of Faculty of Economics and Administrative Sciences. He obtained his Ph.D. from Bilkent University, Ankara, and graduated from the industrial engineering department of the same university. His main interest includes both theoretical and applied econometrics, and he has published in *Economics Letters, International Journal of Business, Applied Economics,* and *Journal of Economic and Social Research,* among others. His theoretical research interests include HCCME estimation, robust estimation techniques, and Bayesian inference. He is presently investigating the performance of IPOs and hedge funds, value-at-risk, tax revenue estimation, and international economic cooperation as part of his applied research studies.

Razvan Pascalau joined the school of business and economics at SUNY (State University of New York) Plattsburgh in 2008. He graduated with a Ph.D. in economics and a M.Sc. in finance from the University of Alabama. He also holds a M.Sc. in financial and foreign exchange markets from the Doctoral School of Finance and Banking in Bucharest, Romania. In 2004, he worked full time for the Ministry of Finance in Romania as a counselor of European integration. His primary field of interest is applied time series econometrics with an emphasis on modeling nonlinear structures in macro and financial data. His research interests also include topics related to financial risk management, international finance, and managerial finance/economics. He has published in *Applied Economic Letters, Managerial Finance, Journal of Derivatives and Hedge Funds, Journal of Wealth Management,* and *IEB International Journal of Finance.*

Edward Pekarek, Esq., is a visiting professor at Pace Law School and the assistant clinic director for the nonprofit Pace Investor Rights Clinic of John Jay Legal Services, Inc. He is a former law clerk for the Hon. Kevin Nathaniel Fox, USMJ, of the U.S. District Court for the Southern District of New York. Pekarek holds an LL.M. degree in corporate, banking, and finance law from Fordham University School of Law; a *Juris Doctor* from Cleveland Marshall College of Law; and a B.A. from the College of Wooster, all of which were awarded with various honors. As a law student, Pekarek coauthored and edited the Respondents' merit brief in the U.S. Supreme Court matter of *Cuyahoga Falls v. Buckeye Community Hope Foundation* and an *amicus* brief in *Eric Eldred, et al. v. John Ashcroft, Attorney General*. He is the former editor in chief of a specialty law journal and a nationally ranked law school newspaper and is the author of numerous academic writings that analyze various financial topics, such as securities trading, broker–dealer and hedge fund regulation, initial public offerings, banking mergers, and corporate governance issues. His scholarly work has been cited by former Securities and Exchange Commission (SEC) Director of Enforcement Linda Chatman Thomsen, as well as the Levy Economics Institute of Bard College regarding the banking policy doctrine of "too big to fail" and by the RAND Institute for Civil Justice in a report commissioned by the SEC regarding broker–dealer and investment adviser regulation.

Jack Penm is currently an academic level D at the Australian National University (ANU). He has an excellent research record in the two disciplines in which he earned his two Ph.D.'s, one in electrical engineering from the University of Pittsburgh and the other in finance from ANU. He is an author/coauthor of more than 80 papers published in various internationally respectful journals.

Robert J. Powell has 20 years of banking experience in South Africa, New Zealand, and Australia. He has been involved in the development and implementation of several credit and financial analysis models in banks. He has a Ph.D. from Edith Cowan University, where he currently works as a researcher and senior lecturer in banking and finance.

Mathew J. Ratty is a final year honors student in the School of Economics and Finance at Curtin University in Perth, Western Australia. He is also a research assistant in the department of banking and finance. His honors dissertation examined Western Australian stock market data and investigated the effect of director decisions to buy or sell shares on cumulative abnormal returns.

Simonetta Rosati is a principal market infrastructure expert at the European Central Bank, based in Frankfurt am Main, Germany. She has contributed to central banks' working group in the field of securities settlement systems, cross-border collateral arrangements, and repo market infrastructures. She has carried out research in the field of determinants of large-value cross-border payment flows, the role on nonbanks in retail payments, comparative analysis of prudential and oversight regulatory requirements for securities settlement, and the securities custody industry.

Daniela Russo is the director of general payments and market infrastructure at the European Central Bank (ECB), based in Frankfurt am Main, Germany. She chairs or participates in several working groups or committees working in the field of payment and settlement systems, both at European and global levels. Some of these groups involve only central banks (e.g., PSSC, CPSS, CLS, and SWIFT Oversight). Other groups involve central banks and securities regulators (ESCB-CESR, CPSS-IOSCO, T2-S Oversight and Derivatives Regulators Forum). Other groups also involve participation of the industry (COGEPS, COGESI, CESAME, MOC, SEPA High Level Group, and EPC).

Houman B. Shadab is an associate professor of law at New York Law School and an associate director of its center on financial services law. He is an internationally recognized expert in financial law and regulation and is the author of several academic articles on hedge funds and credit derivatives. He has testified before Congress on the role of hedge funds in the financial crisis and also on the compensation of public company executives. Governmental bodies have recognized his research, which has been cited by the Delaware Court of Chancery and in studies published by the U.K. House of Commons and the European Parliament's Committee on Economic and Monetary Affairs.

Kym Sheehan, Ph.D., came to the law after a varied career in human resource management, where she worked for private sector organizations in Australia in executive search, as well as working in the IT and mining industries. Her primary areas of research interest are the regulation of executive compensation via "say on pay" and institutional investor activism.

John L. Simpson is an associate professor in the School of Economics and Finance at Curtin University in Perth, Western Australia. His Ph.D. from the University of Western Australia researched international banking risk models and his research areas remain in international banking, finance, and economics and in international business risk management. More recently, research interests include the financial economics of energy. John is well published in book chapters and internationally referred journals.

Abhay K. Singh is an integrated postgraduate with Btech in information technology and has a M.B.A. in finance from the Indian Institute of Information Technology & Management, Gwalior, India. He currently works as a research associate in the School of Accounting, Finance and Economics at Edith Cowan University.

David M. Smith is an associate professor of finance and director of the Center for Institutional Investment Management at the University at Albany (State University of New York). He currently serves as associate editor—finance and accounting for the *Journal of Business Research*. He received his Ph.D. from Virginia Tech and holds the CFA and CMA designations.

M. Nihat Solakoglu is an assistant professor in the banking and finance department of Bilkent University in Ankara, Turkey. Previously he was an assistant professor in the Department of Management at Fatih University. Before joining Fatih University, he worked for American Express in the United States in international risk management, international information management, information and analysis, and fee services marketing departments. He received his Ph.D. in economics and master's degree in statistics from North Carolina State University. His main interests are applied finance and international finance. His papers have been published in *Applied Economics*, *Applied Economics Letters*, *Journal of International Financial Markets, Institutions & Money*, and *Journal of Economic and Social Research*.

Cristina Sommacampagna is an economist in the risk management division of the European Central Bank. She holds a Ph.D. in mathematics for economic decisions from the University of Trieste (2005), a M.Sc. in finance from CORIPE (2002), and a B.A. in economics from the University of Verona (2001). From 2006 to 2008 she worked in the financial engineering practice of Duff & Phelps, LLC, in the San Francisco office. In 2009 she worked in the risk management department of Commerzbank AG in Frankfurt.

R. Deane Terrell is a financial econometrician and officer in the general division of the Order of Australia. He served as vice-chancellor of the ANU from 1994 to 2000. He has also held visiting appointments at the London School of Economics, the Wharton School, University of Pennsylvania, and the Econometrics Program, Princeton University. He has published a number of books and research monographs and around 80 research papers in leading journals.

Peter T. Treadway is the chief economist of CTRISKS, an Asian-based risk ratings agency. He had a distinguished career on Wall Street and with major American financial institutions. In 1978–1981 he served as chief economist at Fannie Mae. In 1985–1998, he served as institutional equity analyst and managing director at Smith Barney following savings and loans and government-sponsored entities. Treadway was ranked an "all star" analyst 11 times by *Institutional Investor Magazine*. He holds a Ph.D. in economics from the University of North Carolina at Chapel Hill, an M.B.A. from New York University, and a B.A. in English from Fordham University in New York. He served as an adjunct professor of City University of Hong Kong and Shanghai University of Economics and Finance.

Nils S. Tuchschmid is currently a professor of banking and finance at Haute École de Gestion (HEG), University of Applied Sciences, in Geneva, Switzerland. He's also an invited professor of finance at HEC Lausanne University and a lecturer at the University of Zurich and ULB in Bruxelles. Tuchschmid is the author of books and articles on traditional and alternative investments, on portfolio management, and on the optimal decision-making process. Up until 1999, he was a professor of finance at HEC Lausanne. Prior to joining HEG in 2008, he worked for various financial institutions, among others BCV, Credit Suisse, and UBS.

Erik Wallerstein is a research fellow at Haute École de Gestion (HEG), University of Applied Sciences, in Geneva, Switzerland. He holds a M.Sc. in applied mathematics from Lund University, Sweden, and a master of advanced studies in finance from Swiss Federal Institute of Technology Zurich (ETH) and University of Zurich. At HEG he is working with Professor Nils Tuchschmid on several research projects on hedge funds.

Mark Werman is a Senior Tutor at Massey University and has taught there for the past 15 years. From 1994 to 2003 he taught constitutional law, contract law, and commercial law, and for the past 6 years he has been teaching finance. Mark has been living in New Zealand for the past 20 years, having moved to New Zealand from New York. In New York he practiced law with his wife, Audrey J. Moss. While living in New York, he was a member of the board of directors at a local hospital, a performing arts organization, and nationally recognized philharmonic orchestra. He has a BA in History from SUNY at Stony Brook, a JD from Union University Albany Law School, and an MBA from Auckland University. He is fascinated by financial crises and scandals and he has been studying the current crisis since 2006.

Michael C.S. Wong is a professor of City University of Hong Kong, specializing in bank risk management, risk process reengineering, and risk modeling. From 1998 to 2002 he served as a member of the Education Committee and FRM Committee of Global Association of Risk Professionals, pacing the foundation for the success of FRM examination in the globe. He is also a founder of CTRISKS Rating, a credit rating agency for

Asia. Dr. Wong graduated from University of Cambridge, University of Essex, and Chinese University of Hong Kong. Prior to his academic and consulting career, he spent 7 years on investment banking, specializing in currencies, precious metals, and derivatives trading. He mainly teaches MSc, MBA, and DBA students at the university, with "Teaching Excellence Award" and "Doctoral Dissertation Award" granted. Dr. Wong has published more than 50 journal articles and book chapters in Finance and Risk Management and authored 6 professional books.

Lingqing Xing obtained her master of financial engineering from New York University. Her area of research is asset pricing. She has published several academic papers and has presented at numerous international conferences.

Liu Yang obtained her master of business administration (major in finance) from the Renmin University of China located in Beijing. She is a member of the treasury system construction team at the headquarters of the China National Petroleum Corporation. Her research centers on financial management.

Sassan Zaker is a manager of alternative investments at Julius Baer. He joined Bank Julius Baer & Co. Ltd. in 2004 as head of alternative products and advisory. Before joining Julius, he worked for Swissca Portfolio Management, Finfunds Management AG, and UBS. Zaker has 17 years of business experience in quantitative analysis, portfolio management, and private and institutional client experience. He holds master's and Ph.D. engineering degrees from the Swiss Federal Institute of Technology (ETH) and is also a CFA charter holder.

Kaiguo Zhou is a deputy head and associate professor of the Department of Finance of Lingnan (University) College of Sun Yat-Sun University in China. He graduated from City University of Hong Kong with a Ph.D. degree in finance in 2003 and served as visiting fellow of Sloan School of Management at MIT in 2006. Zhou has published more than 15 journal articles on China's financial markets and was granted numerous outstanding researcher awards by the university.

Andrew Zlotnik is a private asset management consultant in emerging markets investments. He started his career as an intern utilities analyst in the research department of the leading Russian investment bank Troika Dialog. After this he was a leading economist and a leading risk manager at Moscow Interbank Currency EXchange. He is a postgraduate student at the Central Economics and Mathematics Institute of the Russian Academy of Sciences. He holds a B.Sc. degree in economics from Lomonosov Moscow State University.

Goldman Sachs and Regulation in the United States and Canada

Short Sales and Financial Innovation: How to Take the Good While Avoiding Widespread Default

Graciela Chichilnisky

CONTENTS

ABSTRACT

This chapter examines the functioning of a market with short sales and provides necessary and sufficient conditions for avoiding volatility and default. When traders are sufficiently diverse, a market with short sales generally fails to reach equilibrium, trading can grow without bounds, leading to volatility and eventually traders default on their contracts. Financial innovation makes things worse because it increases the exposure to default by creating system-wide risks through a cascading effect where default by one trader leads to default by all, (Chichilnisky and Wu, 2006). We show that graduated reserves dampens limits volatility and restores market equilibrium. With the appropriate system of reserves, which are an increasing proportion of the value of trades, traders, by their own choices, limit their positions with respect to each other even though unbounded trades are, in principle, available to them. Graduated reserves can resolve runaway volatility and default in markets with short sales.

KEYWORDS

Default; Financial innovation; Gains from trade; Global cone; Graduated reserves; Limited arbitrage; Market cone; Social diversity; Volatility.

1.1 INTRODUCTION

Short sales can enhance market performance and improve a trader's ability to allocate resources. This is their good aspect, and it is known that the welfare gains can be considerable. But increased gains often mean increased risks. Short sales can also lead to market volatility and increase the risk of widespread default, as recent experience has shown as was predicted earlier by Chichilnisky and Wu. This chapter explains the mechanism by which all this happens and shows a practical way to avoid increased volatility and defaults in markets with short sales such as those observed in the US financial crisis of 2008–9.

First we show analytically how volatility and widespread default arise in markets with short sales. When traders are sufficiently diverse, as is rigorously defined here, a market with short sales creates incentives for increasingly long and short trading positions, a situation that can continue unchecked and without limits (Chichilnisky, 1994b). As trading can indeed increase without bounds in a market with short sales, this leads to situations where short sales widely exceed available stocks, for example, where traders leverage 30 or 40 times the value of underlying assets, as occurred recently with CDSs. Therefore, if called, traders cannot cover their positions and have an increasing likelihood of defaulting on their contracts. To add to all this, financial innovation makes things worse by creating systemic risks that magnify individual risks. This was shown rigorously in Chichilnisky and Wu (2006) just prior to and anticipating the 2007 financial crisis—they showed that financial innovation increases market interconnectedness and creates a cascading effect where default by one trader leads to default by many or eventually default by the entire economy. The solution proposed here is an introduction of an appropriate system of graduated reserves that reduces the likelihood of default and restores the market equilibrium in markets with short sales. We show rigorously how graduated reserves dampen the incentives for taking large short-term positions and help stabilize short sales.

Markets with short sales as defined here differ from Arrow–Debreu markets in that traders have no bounds on short sales (Chichilnisky & Heal, 1998).

Elsewhere we identified one condition on the diversity of traders' preferences—or expectations—that is necessary and sufficient for the existence of market equilibrium where the invisible hand delivers consistent and efficient solutions (Chichilnisky, 1991, 1994b, 1995; Chichilnisky & Heal, 1998). This chapter goes a step further and shows in practice how the diversity of traders in markets with short sales can undermine market equilibrium, inducing volatility and default that worsen with financial innovation. We also show that through the creation of a graduated reserves system the problem is resolved and equilibrium can be restored. With such reserves systems in place, by their own choice traders take bounded positions with respect to each other even though unbounded short sales in principle are available to them. The German government has recently banned short selling, a policy that is somewhat extreme and, as shown here, may not have been necessary. The conclusion derived here is that short sales can work well, provided graduated reserves are required—a simple strategy that can prevent runaway volatility and default and restore market equilibrium. The results reported here are based on prior work by the author and others, Chichilnisky (1993), Chichilnisky and Heal (1984, 1997), Chichilnisky and Kalman (1980), Debreu (1954), Lawuers (1993).

1.2 MARKETS WITH SHORT SALES

A competitive market has $H \geq 2$ traders and $N \geq 2$ commodities that are traded over time $t \in R_+$. The consumption of commodities yields utility $u(x(t))$ at each period of time t^1 and creates utility paths over time $f(t)$. In this context, a *preference over time* is a real valued function $U : X \to R_+$ ranking utility paths within the space of trading paths available that we take to be a Hilbert space X as in Chichilnisky (2009a, 2009b, 2010a, 2010b). The vector $\Omega_h \in X$ represents trader h's property rights, and $\Omega = \sum_h \Omega_h$ represents society's total resources over time.^{2} A market has *short sales* when the *trading*

---

[1] $u(x(t)) \in R^N$, and $u(x): R^N \to R_+$ is a concave increasing real valued function that represents instantaneous utility in period t. Following Chichilnisky (1996a, 1996d, 2009a, 2009b), one views utility paths over time $f(t) = u(x(t))$ as elements of an appropriate Hilbert function space $X = L(R)$.

[2] We consider general preferences where normalized gradients to indifference surfaces define either an open or a closed map on every indifference surface, namely (i) indifference surfaces contain no half-lines, for example, strictly convex preferences, or (ii) normalized gradients to any closed set of indifferent vectors define a closed set, for example, linear preferences (e.g., Chichilnisky, 1995). The assumptions and results are ordinal and therefore, without loss of generality, assume $U_h(0) = 0$ and $\sup_{x \in X} U_h(x) = \infty$. Preferences are increasing so that $U_h(x(t)) > U_h(y(t))$ when for all t, $x(t) \geq y(t)$, and for a set of positive Lebesgue measure, $x(t) > y(t)$. In addition, we assume the traders' preferences are uniformly nonsatiated, which means that they can be represented by a utility U with a bounded rate of increase: for smooth preferences, which are Frechet differentiable, $\exists \varepsilon, K > 0 : \forall x \in X, K > \|DU(x)\| > \varepsilon$. If a utility function is uniformly nonsatiated, its indifference surfaces are within a uniform distance from each other: $\forall r, s \in R, \exists N(r,s) \in R$ such that $f \in U^{-1}(r) \Rightarrow \exists y \in U^{-1}(s)$ with $\|f - g\| \leq N(r,s)$; see Chichilnisky and Heal (1998). Preferences satisfy either (i) or (ii).

space is the entire space X: therefore by definition, traders can trade any positive or negative positions without bounds on short sales (Chichilnisky, 1991, 1995; Chichilnisky & Heal, 1998).

The following concept of a global cone[3] contains global information about a trader: a *global cone* $G_h(\Omega_h)$ is the set of directions with ever increasing utility according to trader h[4]:

$$G_h(\Omega_h) = \{f : \sim \exists \, Max_{\lambda \in R} U_h(\lambda f)\}$$

A *market cone* $D_h(\Omega_h)$ is the set of all prices that assign strictly positive value to net trades in the global cone[5]:

$$D_h(\Omega_h) = \{p \in X : \forall \{g\} \in G_h(\Omega_h), \, \exists \, i : \langle \lambda g, p \rangle > 0 \quad \text{for all} \quad \lambda > i\}$$

1.3 GAINS FROM TRADE

This section defines a concept of limited arbitrage and provides an intuitive interpretation in terms of gains from trade, establishing its role in the existence of a competitive equilibrium. This is based on Chichilnisky (1991, 1994a, 1994b, 1995, 1996b, 1996c, 1998) and Chichilnisky and Heal (1998).

Gains from trade are defined as

$$G(E) = \sup \left\{ \sum_{h=1}^{H} (U_h(f_h) - U_h(\Omega_h)) \right\}$$

where $\forall h, f_h$ satisfies $\sum_{h=1}^{H} (f_h - \Omega_h) = 0$ and $U_h(f_h) \geq U_h(\Omega_h) \geq 0$.

---

[3] The global cone was introduced in Chichilnisky (1991, 1994a, 1994b, 1995, 1996b, 1996c) and in Chichilnisky and Heal (1998).

[4] We assume that $G_h(\Omega_h)$ has a simple structure, which was established in different forms in Chichilnisky (1991, 1994b, 1995, 1998) and in Chichilnisky and Heal (1998): when preferences have half-lines in their indifferences, then $G_h(\Omega_h) = A_h(\Omega_h)$ and are both convex, and when preferences have no half-lines in their indifference surfaces, then $G_h(\Omega_h)$ is the closure of $A_h(\Omega_h)$.

[5] We assume the results of the following proposition, which was established in different forms elsewhere (Chichilnisky, 1991, 1994a, 1994b, 1995, 1996b, 1996c, 1998; Chichilnisky & Heal, 1998) and is used in proving the connection between limited arbitrage and the existence of a sustainable market equilibrium:

Lemma
If a utility $U : X \to R$ is uniformly nonsatiated, then the following cones

(i) $A(\Omega) \neq \varnothing$
(ii) $C(\Omega) = \{\{f\} \subset X : \lim_{j \to \infty} f^j = U(j^{j_0}) \text{ for some } j_0\}$

as well as the cones $G(\Omega)$ and $D(\Omega)$ are convex and uniform across all vectors Ω in X. For general preferences, $G(\Omega)$ and $D(\Omega)$ may not be uniform (Chichilnisky, 1998; Chichilnisky & Heal, 1998).

The economy E satisfies *limited arbitrage* when traders are sufficiently similar that

$$\bigcap_{h=1}^{H} D_h \neq \emptyset$$

which means, geometrically, that the traders' directions of ever increasing utility (or global cones) are close to each other in particular they can all be restricted to the same half space. Observe that the diversity of traders increases gains from trade and the tendency of traders to trade unbounded amounts with each other. For example, if one trader is certain that a price will increase and another trader is certain that the price will drop, these two traders have incentives to continue trading short and long with each other without bounds. With short trades this is possible—without short selling, the trading stops naturally when stocks run down. This is a very simple example, but the situation is completely general, as Proposition 1 shows. The tendency to ever increasing short trading is checked off if eventually the traders agree in their expectations. This is what limited arbitrage measures. In that sense, limited arbitrage limits *social diversity* as defined in Chichilnisky (1991, 1994a, 1994b, 1995, 1996b, 1996c) and bounds the trades that traders wish to enter with each other. Proposition 1 shows that even though the market allows unbounded short sales in principle, *limited arbitrage* bounds the trades that traders wish to enter with each other by limiting the utility gains that can be achieved through trading. The limited arbitrage property is essential: it implies compactness of the set of efficient trades. This is shown to be sufficient for the existence of a competitive equilibrium without requiring bounds on short sales.

■ **Proposition 1**

An economy E satisfies limited arbitrage if and only if it has bounded gains from trade, namely $G(E) < \infty$.

Proof

See Chichilnisky (1991, 1994a, 1994b, 1995, 1996b, 1996c).   ■

Proposition 1 applies in case (i) when normalized gradients of indifference surfaces define a closed map. The proof of sufficiency in Proposition 1 is valid for all preferences; therefore, in economies with uniformly nonsatiated preferences, limited arbitrage always implies bounded gains from trade.

1.3.1 Market Equilibrium

In a market with short sales, a competitive equilibrium is defined as a standard equilibrium of an Arrow–Debreu economy, except that short sales are allowed in this case. Consider a market economy $E = \{X, U_h, \Omega_h, h = 1, \ldots, H\}$.

A competitive market equilibrium is defined as a vector of net trades, $x_1^*, \ldots, x_H^* \notin X^H$ satisfying $\sum_{h=1}^{H}(x_h^* - \Omega_h) = 0,$ and a price $p^* \in X',$ where for each $h = 1, \ldots H,$ trader h maximizes utility $U_h(x)$ at x_h^* within his or her budget set $\{x \in X : \langle p^*, x - \Omega_h = 0\}.$

■ Theorem 1

Consider a market economy $E = \{X, U_h, \Omega_h = 1, \ldots, H\}$. Then economy E has a sustainable market equilibrium if and only if it satisfies limited arbitrage and the equilibrium is Pareto efficient.

Proof

See Chichilnisky (1991, 1994a, 1994b, 1995, 1996b, 1996c).   ■

1.4 SOCIAL DIVERSITY, VOLATILITY, AND DEFAULT

The link among social diversity, volatility, and default is a direct consequence of the results presented earlier. *Social diversity* was defined as the failure of *limited arbitrage* (see Chichilnisky, 1991, 1994a, 1994b, 1995, 1996b, 1996c). Proposition 1 establishes that it means that traders have sufficiently different preferences or expectations (in the case of expected utility) that they develop an incentive to take increasingly long and short positions with each other to and continue this process unchecked without limits. This is indeed the scenario that leads to nonexistence of a competitive market equilibrium in economieswith short sales. As established in Proposition 1, gains from trade become unbounded in such a situation and therefore larger and larger gains can be realized through short selling. Under the reasonable assumption that the probability of an adverse material effect—or mistrust and attendant requirements to deliver—increases with the scope of the trades in the economy, we have the following.

■ Proposition 2

In markets with short sales, social diversity leads to an increasing probability of default as the scope of trading increases.   ■

Empirical observations show that in markets with short sales, lack of equilibrium or default is accompanied by spikes of large short and long positions, which are generally identified with volatility. The next section explains the role of financial innovation in increasing individual uncertainty and creating aggregate or systemic risks.

1.5 FINANCIAL INNOVATION CREATES SYSTEMIC RISKS OF WIDESPREAD DEFAULTS

The situation described in the previous section is significantly worse in markets with financial innovation and short sales. As shown rigorously in Chichilnisky and Wu (2006), financial innovation increases the interconnectedness of traders throughout the economy and precipitates cascading effects by which default by one trader leads to defaults by many others—in some cases, default by one leads to default by all traders in the economy. This occurs because an individual trader's default cascade throughout the system, magnifying individual risks into systemic or aggregate risks of widespread default (Chichilnisky & Wu, 2006).

The implication is that in markets with short sales and financial innovation, volatility and default are more frequent than in markets without short sales, and their scope is system-wide rather than individual. This explains the impact of short selling in the current crisis that started in 2007 [a year after our article with Chichilnisky and Wu (2006)], following a period of intense financial innovation in the U.S. economy and worldwide.

The following section defines the concept of *graduated reserves* and explains how this helps overcome the worst risks in markets with short sales and financial innovation.

1.6 INTRODUCING GRADUATED RESERVES

In our context, reserves mean that the purchasing of a short sale contract requires the deposit of part of the proceeds of the sale into a third-party institution—limiting accordingly by use of income from the short sale. We assume that reserves are returned to the short seller at the equilibrium as appropriate. One way to visualize a reserves ratio is therefore as a change in relative prices between the good (or security) that is traded short and any other goods (or securities) that the trader produces with the income it receives from the short sale, effectively decreasing the trader's income from short sales and the attendant utility he or she gains from short selling. For simplicity, in a two good economy, the reserves ratio can be visualized as a shift in the relative prices of the good that is sold short with respect to all others. Figure 1.1 illustrates a market with unlimited short sales and without reserves, while Figures 1.2 and 1.3 illustrate the same market when reserves are in effect. They illustrate the reserves as a shift in relative prices.

Graduate reserves are defined as a system whereby the reserves ratio increases with the size or value of the short trade. This means that the relative value to the trader of selling short decreases the larger short sale.

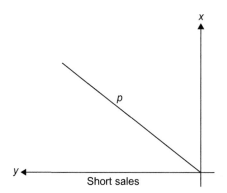

FIGURE 1.1
Short sales without reserves.

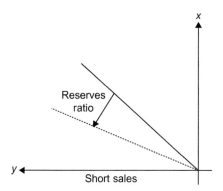

FIGURE 1.2
Short sales with fixed reserves ratio.

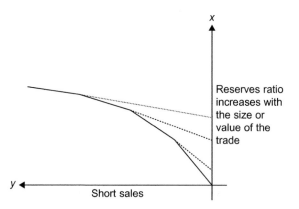

FIGURE 1.3
Short sales with graduated reserves.

1.7 GRADUATED RESERVES RESTORE STABILITY AND PREVENT DEFAULT

How do reserves—and graduate reserves—improve the stability of the economy and help prevent widespread default? The following proposition establishes the main result in this direction.

■ **Proposition 3**

An appropriate system of reserves can restore limited arbitrage and therefore the existence of equilibrium ensuring that traders have no incentives to engage in increasingly larger trades with each other. A system of graduate reserves can achieve the same effect with less reserve requirements by small traders.   ■

Figure 1.3 illustrates how this happens. Formally, the global cones "shrink". Larger trades are increasingly less desirable, checking each trader's wish to take large short positions. Eventually the global cones become empty as reserves ratios increase and therefore limited arbitrage as defined above automatically satisfied, leading to the existence of competitive equilibrium.

By restoring limited arbitrage, the existence of a competitive market equilibrium is ensured by Theorem 1 and the tendency toward increasingly larger short selling is checked. The reserves required to restore equilibrium are smaller in the case of graduate reserve policies.

1.8 CONCLUSION

When traders are sufficiently diverse, a market with short sales may fail to reach equilibrium: trading grows without bounds, leading to volatility. Eventually, traders default on their contracts, with the likelihood of default growing with the size of short trading. Financial innovation can make things worse. It increases the exposure to default by creating systemic risks through a cascading effect where default by individual traders leads to default by all (Chichilnisky & Wu, 2006). The introduction of appropriately graduated reserves checks volatility and restores the conditions needed for market equilibrium. With the appropriate system of reserves, traders, by their own choices, limit their positions with respect to each other, even though unbounded short sales are available to them. Graduated reserves can thus resolve runaway volatility and default in markets with short sales.

ACKNOWLEDGMENTS

This research was conducted at the Columbia Consortium for Risk Management (CCRM) and directed by the author at Columbia University in New York and its Program on Information and Resources. We gratefully acknowledge support from Grant No. 5222-72 of the U.S. Air Force Office of Research and its officer Professor Jun Zhang (Arlington, VA). CCRM Web site: http://columbiariskmanagement.org/.

REFERENCES

Chichilnisky, G. (1991, 1995). Limited arbitrage is necessary and sufficient for the existence of competitive equilibrium with or without short sales. Discussion Paper No. 650, Columbia University Department of Economics, December 1991. Later published in *Economic Theory, 95*(1), 79–108.

Chichilnisky, G. (1993). The cone condition, properness and extremely desirable commodities. *Economic Theory, 3*(1), 177–182.

Chichilnisky, G. (1994a). Limited arbitrage is necessary and sufficient for the existence of a competitive equilibrium and the core, and it limits voting cycles. *Economics Letters, 46*(4), 321–331.

Chichilnisky, G. (1994b). Social diversity, arbitrage and gains from trade: A unified perspective on resource allocation. *American Economic Review, 84*(2), 427–434.

Chichilnisky, G. (1996a). An axiomatic approach to sustainable development. *Social Choice and Welfare, 13*(2), 231–257.

Chichilnisky, G. (1996b). Limited arbitrage is necessary and sufficient for the non-emptiness of the core. *Economic Letters, 52*(2), 177–180.

Chichilnisky, G. (1996c). Markets and games: A simple equivalence among the core, equilibrium and limited arbitrage. *Metroeconomica, 47*(3), 266–280.

Chichilnisky, G. (1996d). What is sustainable development? *Resource Energy Economics, 73*(4), 467–491.

Chichilnisky, G. (1998). *A unified perspective on resource allocation: Limited arbitrage is necessary and sufficient for the existence of a competitive equilibrium, the core and socialchoice.* Mathematical economics. Chestershire, UK: Edward Elgar.

Chichilnisky, G. (2009a). The limits of econometrics: Non-parametric estimation in Hilbert spaces. *Econometric Theory, 25*(04), 1070–1086.

Chichilnisky, G. (2009b). The topology of fear. *Journal of Mathematical Economics, 45*(12), 807–816.

Chichilnisky, G. (2010a). The foundations of probability with black swans. *Journal of Probability and Statistics, 2010*, 1–11.

Chichilnisky, G. (2010b). The foundations of statistics with black swans. *Mathematical Social Sciences, 59*(2), 184–192.

Chichilnisky, G., & Heal, G. M. (1993). Limited arbitrage is necessary and sufficient for the existence of a competitive equilibrium with or without short sales. *Journal of Economic Theory, 59*(5), 364–384 (1993). Initially circulated as Chichilnisky, G., & Heal, G. M. (1984). Existence of a competitive equilibrium in L_p and Sobolev spaces. IMA Preprint series #79, Institute for Mathematics and Its Applications, University of Minnesota, Minneapolis, MN.

Chichilnisky, G., & Heal, G. M. (1997). Social choice with infinite populations. *Social Choice and Welfare, 14*(2), 303–319.

Chichilnisky, G., & Heal, G. M. (1998). A unified treatment of finite and infinite economies: Limited arbitrage is necessary and sufficient for the existence of equilibrium and the core. *Economic Theory, 12*(1), 163–176.

Chichilnisky, G., & Kalman, P. (1980). An application of functional analysis to models of efficient allocation of economic resources. *Journal of Optimization Theory and Applications, 30*(1), 19–32.

Chichilnisky, G., & Wu, H.-M. (2006). General equilibrium with endogenous uncertainty and default. *Journal of Mathematical Economics, 42*(4–5), 499–524.

Debreu, G. (1954). Valuation equilibrium and Pareto optimum. *Proceedings of the National Academy of Sciences, 40*(7), 588–592.

Lauwers, L. (1993). Infinite Chichilnisky rules. *Economic Letters, 42*(4), 349–352.

CHAPTER 2

The Goldman Sachs Swaps Shop: An Examination of Synthetic Short Selling through Credit Default Swaps and Implications of *Securities and Exchange Commission v. Goldman Sachs & Co., et al.*

Edward Pekarek and Christopher Lufrano

CONTENTS

ABSTRACT

This chapter examines the prospect of civil and criminal liability for an investment bank that structured a collateralized debt obligation (CDO) that referenced residential mortgage-backed securities instruments at the behest of a client who sought to short the same instruments synthetically. The prospect of regulatory reform is also considered relative to its expected impact on a bank's ability to maintain proprietary trading in over-the-counter derivatives such as those used in the ABACUS 2007-AC1 CDO and related credit default swap transactions, which prompted the filing of civil enforcement litigation by the Securities and Exchange Commission and a parallel criminal probe by the U.S. Department of Justice.

KEYWORDS

ABACUS 2007-AC1; Asset-backed securities; Collateralized debt obligations; Credit default swaps; Dodd–Frank Wall Street Reform and Consumer Protection Act; Exchange Act; "Financial weapons of mass destruction"; "Granddaddy of all bubbles"; Over-the-counter derivatives; Residential mortgage-backed securities; Securities Act; *Securities and Exchange Commission v. Goldman Sachs & Co., et al.*; Tranches.

2.1 INTRODUCTION

Collateralized debt obligations (CDO) and credit default swaps (CDS) are derivative instruments widely believed to have caused the seizure of global credit markets from 2007 through mid-2009. This chapter summarizes various aspects of CDO and CDS and explains how they contributed to the recent financial crisis. This chapter focuses on one derivative transaction in particular, known as ABACUS 2007-AC1 (ABACUS), created by Goldman Sachs & Co. (Goldman) in 2006 and 2007, as part of an examination of the regulatory dearth in the derivative market and how lawmakers and regulators are seeking to reform the way derivatives are structured, bought, and sold.

The CDS was originally devised in the mid-1990s as a means for commercial banks to transfer or "hedge" loan origination credit risk and employ capital otherwise reserved to meet minimum standards established by banking regulations. Because CDS are not viewed as assets (or liabilities) for accounting purposes, they are typically not depicted on banks' balance sheets. Early CDS development can be traced to transactions involving municipal and corporate debt in which the purchaser of the instrument also held the underlying credit asset (often a loan or bond) on its balance sheet.

At the onset of the 2000s, this then nascent financial industry segment, known as "structured finance," necessitated the expanded use of CDS to hedge investment bank underwriting activity for other structured products, such as CDO.

Later that decade, CDS trading mushroomed into a so-called "dark" secondary market for parties who sought to hedge, and/or speculate, by selling these derivative products to other investors. Roughly $615T worth of interest rate, foreign exchange, and credit default swaps trade in mostly unregulated over-the-counter (OTC) markets, which lack the transparency and oversight provided by exchanges or centralized transactional clearing facilities. Today, financial and nonfinancial companies alike use CDS for traditional hedging purposes, akin to bond insurance, as well as for speculation when the buyer does not own the underlying asset. In this sense, CDS purchasers are much like "short sellers" who expect the value of a security to decline. Due to this lack of regulation, and the blossoming use of CDS for speculation, these instruments are the source of populist and political scrutiny from Athens to Berlin to Chicago to the District of Columbia.

The CDS swap dealer market is presently dominated by the five largest U.S. banks: Goldman, Morgan Stanley, JPMorgan Chase, Bank of America/Merrill-Lynch, and Citigroup. This chapter chronicles aspects of the CDS market in general, and the ABACUS transaction in particular, and evaluates many of its associated prospective liability issues, primarily through analysis of the Securities Exchange Commission (SEC) civil enforcement litigation captioned: *Securities and Exchange Commission v. Goldman Sachs & Co., et al.,* civil case no. 1:10-cv-03229 (BSJ).

2.1.1 Collateralized Debt Obligations

The CDO is a structured product, a derivative investment customized to match investors' specific risk tolerance(s), which typically raises capital through the issuance of debt and/or equity securities and invests the funds in pooled credit assets. The underlying assets are often bank loans, corporate bonds, or asset-backed securities (ABS), such as residential mortgage-backed securities (RMBS), and structured using a cash or "synthetic" basis. Payments on component CDO securities are generally derived from the revenue streams generated by their underlying assets. A typical CDO is composed of multiple layers, or classes, of component securities, generally known as "tranches." These tranches may vary in terms of seniority, interest rate (coupon), and relative credit quality.

Subordinate tranches provide credit support to those that are senior to them. A typical CDO contains four types of tranches, distinguished by credit risk, and commonly classified as senior debt, mezzanine debt, subordinate debt, and equity. The three largest U.S. credit rating agencies—Standard & Poor's, Moody's, and Fitch Ratings—assign debt tranches with credit ratings and serve a vital role in the functioning of the derivatives market. The senior debt tranche is structured with component securities, which are typically awarded the highest credit rating, and subordinate debt tranches are structured with securities designated successively lower credit ratings.

Risk of loss on CDO assets is divided among the tranches in reverse order of seniority. Senior debt, the highest rated tranche, is exposed to the lowest credit risk, yields the lower relative returns, and is the last tranche to experience losses when the underlying securities decline in value. In contrast, the equity tranche is typically the highest risk layer, designed to yield the highest relative returns, and is the first tranche to experience losses. A significant aspect of *SEC v. Goldman Sachs & Co., et al.* is the allegation that Goldman misled the CDO portfolio selection agent, ACA Management LLC (ACA), to believe that Paulson & Co. (Paulson), a hedge fund client of Goldman, took an interest in the riskiest tranche of the deal—the equity tranche. Paulson was synthetically short the ABACUS CDO through a CDS intermediated by Goldman, after allegedly selecting the underlying assets it expected to decline in value.

A CDO is often distinguished by the composition of its underlying portfolio assets.[1] One that holds the underlying assets, bonds, loans, RMBS, or other collateral directly is referred to as a "cash" CDO. Other CDO are known as "synthetic" because they are not supported by cash assets, but rather gain exposure to reference assets indirectly through one or more derivatives such as CDS. In a synthetic CDO, banks typically sell notes to investors for the equity, single-A tranche, double-A tranche, and a portion of the triple-A tranche, thereby leaving the highest quality loans behind, referred to as the "super senior tranche." Funds derived from the sale of these lower tranches are then often used to pay CDS credit protection premiums on the higher quality super senior tranche.[2] The CDS manager traditionally collects a fee for arranging the transaction. For example, Goldman structured the ABACUS deal, a synthetic CDO, by selling Class A-1 and Class A-2 notes to the IKB bank and subsequently entered into CDS with ACA for the super senior tranche, which referenced a Triple B ("BBB")-rated RMBS portfolio.

---

[1] The following is a nonexhaustive list of the various types of CDO defined by portfolio composition. For example, a CDO composed of a bond portfolio is often called a "collateralized bond obligation." A CDO consisting of pooled corporate loans is called a "collateralized loan obligation." CDO with underlying portfolios composed of structured finance products, such as ABS or mortgage-backed securities (MBS), are called "structured finance" (SF) CDO. A hybrid CDO composed of a combination of any or all these assets is sometimes called a "multisector" CDO.

[2] The subsequent "write downs" of assets on bank balance sheets refer primarily to the result of a number of banks maintaining their super senior tranche CDO exposure unhedged.

2.1.2 Credit Default Swaps

A CDS buyer or holder, through a bilateral contract with the seller, obtains a future right to be compensated upon the happening of some credit or "trigger" event(s) that is generally of a binary or "zero-sum" nature, meaning that if the predetermined credit event(s) is not realized during the CDS contract term, no compensation is paid to the holder and the CDS expires worthless, not unlike put-and-call options.

Credit events are contractual conditions typically negotiated between counterparties prior to the transaction and often include one or more such events, including (i) full or partial default of the reference asset(s) or entity's financial obligations; (ii) a bankruptcy petition for debtor protection (for nonsovereigns); (iii) material adverse restructuring or repudiation of debt; and (iv) debt moratoria (relevant only to sovereigns). The happening of a contractual credit event triggers the payment obligation(s) owed by the seller to the holder, or a third party if the risk has been shifted yet again, which calls for "settlement" via the "swap" mechanism, as defined by the original counterparties' contract. In some CDS transactions, the amount that must be paid to the CDS holder is determined by a predefined correlation to the value of the reference asset (or entity's) debt obligation(s) that follows the triggering credit event(s), a function that mirrors losses incurred by the reference entity's creditors following a credit event. Paulson's ABACUS CDS carried a 1:1 inverse correlation, creating a zero-sum dynamic between Paulson's economic interests and that of ABACUS CDS sellers in the event of a decline in the value of the CDO super senior tranche.

In a simple risk managed transaction involving, for example, a bank loan, such as a mortgage, the holder of the promissory note (who may also be the mortgagee) might synthetically short the loan's performance by acquiring CDS exposure that references that same loan. The benefit to the buyer of the CDS is protection against default and/or diminution in value. Thus by purchasing so-called "credit protection," a mortgagee could effectively offset the risk of a nonperforming loan loss and reduce or, depending on the terms of the CDS, altogether eliminate that negative credit exposure, without necessarily removing the asset from its balance sheet. Such a mortgagee would typically pay a modest premium to the CDS seller in exchange for the possibility of a substantial gain, in the event of a credit event, which would effectively offset any loss on the underlying asset(s). The downside CDS risk to the buyer is relegated to the premium paid. Conversely, a CDS seller, via the swap function, is effectively "long" the performance of the mortgagor's obligation and partially offsets exposure to capital loss on the CDS through a stream of risk premium payments received from the buyer.

In the context of CDS linked to residential mortgages, home prices had rarely declined on a historical basis, and the housing market was the beneficiary of substantially accommodating fiscal, monetary, and legislative policies during recent decades. As a result, CDS sellers were able to reap lucrative profits for years by taking in the premiums and rarely paying for defaults. However, as what was learned when the recent financial crisis unfolded, an issuer of numerous CDS instruments with default exposure concentrated in one sector, for example, subprime RMBS, might experience catastrophic losses if that sector were to fail. The following section analyzes how CDS exposure in RMBS CDO helped precipitate a credit crisis that endangered the entire financial system.

2.2 "WEAPONS OF MASS FINANCIAL DESTRUCTION"

As the domestic housing bubble inflated in 2004 through the first half of 2007, "naked" CDS became increasingly favored for speculation by buyers and sellers, neither of whom held any interest in the underlying reference asset(s). The CDS market swelled so swiftly that by some estimates, it exceeded $60T in mid-2007, nearly doubling the capitalization of the entire U.S. equities market.[3] Roughly $20T of the CDS market was reportedly speculation on the possibility of various credit events for specific assets. While many sectors of the economy well beyond derivative trading certainly do share in the blame for the resulting financial crisis, the enormous size of the unregulated CDS market, and its extensive influence in the seizure of credit, was perhaps the most consequential. According to Alan Greenspan, former Federal Reserve Bank Open Market Committee Chair, financial services firms flirted with disaster and "risked being able to anticipate the onset of crisis in time to retrench. They were mistaken." Greenspan has identified the CDS as "the most sensitive measure of the probability of bank default...."

Credit rating agencies became a target for regulatory reformers due to the influence these firms wield in the derivatives market, and because these ratings were the *sine qua non* of many of the most controversial ABS derivative deals that precipitated the bubble. Warren Buffet, iconic leader of the conglomerate holding company Berkshire Hathaway and an "angel" investor to Goldman during the depths of the market decline, famously referred to these derivative instruments as "weapons of mass financial destruction" in Berkshire's 2002 annual report. Berkshire owns companies involved in bond insurance, and it recently lobbied, albeit unsuccessfully, to relax proposed new legislation aimed at increasing required minimum capital reserves held by derivatives traders. Berkshire is also the largest stakeholder of the

---

[3] One cannot gauge the size of the OTC market for CDS with certainty due mainly to its lack of regulation, transparency, and centralized clearing.

troubled credit ratings agency Moody's, which, in addition to being the target of a separate SEC probe, is also one of the troika who dominate derivative credit ratings and provide the credit rating services for ABACUS.[4] Buffet acknowledged during a CNBC interview, conducted just moments prior to his Financial Crisis Inquiry Commission (FCIC) testimony, an appearance compelled by subpoena, that Berkshire had reduced its Moody's stake by almost 40% in the last year. During his FCIC testimony, Buffet also maintained that no one, including himself, could possibly have seen the "granddaddy of all bubbles" about to pop.

According to an admission made by Moody's CEO, Raymond McDaniel, during his FCIC testimony, performance of its "credit ratings for U.S. residential mortgage-backed securities and related collateralized debt obligations over the past several years has been deeply disappointing." A former Moody's employee, Eric Kolchinsky, has publicly accused the firm of violating federal securities laws by knowingly providing "incorrect" credit ratings, a contention that Moody's denied. According to *The New York Times*, citing notes taken by an unidentified Wall Street investor during a May 2005 telephone call with Fabrice Tourre and an unidentified Goldman employee, Goldman traders described their efforts to persuade analysts at Moody's Investors Service "to assign one part of an ABACUS CDO a higher rating but were having trouble."

In addition to the many failings of credit rating agencies, excessive leverage in the U.S. economy is widely believed to have been a key catalyst for the 2008 financial meltdown. As borrowers of domestic residential mortgages, primarily those with credit below prime, began to default on debt service and the derivative ABS started to decline in value, CDS sellers faced a cascade of collateral demands and settlement liabilities that could not be settled. Only adding to already excessive systemic leverage and multiplying the destructive effect of derivatives, the same subsets of risky subprime mortgage loans were packaged repeatedly in numerous different structured products. For example, a $38M Baa2 Moody's-rated subprime mortgage bond, among the riskier tranches of the Soundview Homeloan Trust 2006-OPTS (MBS), was referenced by more than 30 different structured debt pools, including Goldman CDO products Hudson Mezzanine Funding 2006-1 ("Hudson") and ABACUS. The RMBS ultimately caused roughly $280M in losses to investors by the time the bond's principal was exhausted in 2008.

Leveraged CDS exposure, and a lack of sufficient collateral, brought one of the most prolific CDS issuers, American International Group (AIG), to the

---

[4] Moody's, Standard & Poor's, and Fitch are the three dominant credit rating agencies for derivatives, as well as for a host of other credit rating functions in the United States and abroad.

precipice of bankruptcy before it received roughly $182B in federal funds to stave off its collapse. In return, U.S. taxpayers assumed a substantial equity stake in the beleaguered Wilton, Connecticut-based, multinational monoline insurer.

AIG's credit rating was downgraded in September 2008 from AA to A, an event that caused AIG's counterparties to demand 100% collateral for many of its open CDS contracts. AIG reportedly lacked sufficient capital, by a wide margin, to satisfy mounting CDS claims for instruments it had originated throughout the first half of the decade, and it effectively received a massive margin call from one or more of its counterparties, which threatened the stability of global credit markets. In its weakened state, AIG was unable to satisfy the margin calls.

The Federal Reserve and U.S. Treasury offered unprecedented assistance to AIG commencing in the fall of 2008 to "backstop" this major participant in the "shadow banking" system. On September 16, 2008, the Federal Reserve extended an $85B credit line to AIG, charging an interest rate of the 3-month London Interbank Offering Rate (LIBOR) plus 8.5%, in exchange for warrants to purchase approximately 80% of AIG common stock. On October 8, 2008, the Federal Reserve authorized the Federal Reserve Bank of New York (FRBNY) to "borrow" $37.8B in illiquid securities from AIG. On November 10, 2008, the U.S. Treasury invested $40B from the Troubled Assets Relief Program (TARP) funds and infused AIG with fresh capital (some of the $40B was used to pay down the $85B loaned on September 16, 2008). By some estimates, prior to the controversial government "bailout," AIG was reportedly exposed to aggregate CDS settlement liability of approximately $440B, much of which referenced various CDO tranches of RMBS.

The historic bailout spared a number of domestic and western European money center banks from the near certain consequences of an AIG bankruptcy, an event that would have likely resulted in material write downs of the value of the CDS exposure each held with AIG, followed by significant net operational losses. On November 10, 2008, the FRBNY created an entity called "AIG CDO LLC" with $5B from AIG and $30B from the Federal Reserve. The special purpose vehicle (SPV) was designed to acquire CDO from third parties who had purchased CDS from AIG and require the third parties to close the CDS contracts. The SPV used $20.1B to purchase so-called "toxic assets" with an aggregate notional value of greater than $53.5B. The assets were later deposited, surreptitiously, into another FRBNY special purpose vehicle known as "Maiden Lane III," where they reportedly still remain. The entity is presently administered by the BlackRock hedge fund, acting as an agent for the FRBNY.

It is widely believed that many of these toxic assets were purchased at or near face value, despite substantially deteriorated quality. According to a November 2009 report issued by the Office of the Special Inspector General for the Troubled Asset Relief Program (SIGTARP), the price paid for the assets was "an amount far above their market value at the time." The SIG-TARP noted further that "there is no question that the effect of FRBNY's decisions—indeed, the very design of the federal assistance to AIG—was that tens of billions of dollars of government money was funneled inexorably and directly to AIG's counterparties." Despite congressional hearings and public ire, concerted efforts were reportedly made to conceal many pertinent details of these dealings from the public eye until sometime in 2018.

A substantial portion of the unprecedented federal largess was destined for three major banks: Merrill-Lynch (now a Bank of America subsidiary); the French financial services conglomerate Société Générale; and Goldman. Each of these mega banks was an AIG CDS counterparty. Goldman reportedly received approximately $14B in federal assistance passing through AIG for CDS that were reportedly worth only $6B. Without the historic taxpayer-funded bailout of AIG, Goldman and others would have realized "untold billions in crippling losses." While bailout negotiations were under way, Goldman CFO, David Viniar, maintained publicly that Goldman's exposure to AIG's imminent collapse was "not material."

FCIC Chairman Philip N. Angelides asked Viniar during the commission hearings, "You guys are net short and you're driving down prices, are you creating a self-fulfilling prophecy? Were you in fact pushing the market down?" Goldman rebutted the accusation with documents posted on its Web site that detailed its valuations of AIG transactions. The documents noted that "a certain degree of judgment was necessary" in appraising AIG's obligations to Goldman, and the bank was "able to access the best available market information to price these CDO securities and to ensure that our pricing represented actual fair market values at the time."

Until recently, U.S. taxpayers possessed scant information regarding the names or values of the assets purchased by Maiden Lane III. AIG sought to disclose some of this information publicly through SEC filings, but the attempt at transparency was thwarted by the FRBNY in December 2008. Then FRBNY president, Timothy Geithner, assumed the helm of the U.S. Treasury Department just 1 month later. A September 2009 government audit revealed that the U.S. Treasury anticipated a $30B loss on TARP-related purchases from AIG.

As America careened toward financial collapse and the AIG controversy festered, populist outrage fomented, later manifesting itself as public protests and even threats of violence to AIG employees at their homes. Even Federal

Reserve Bank Chairman Ben Bernanke lamented, "Of all the events and all of the things we've done in the last 18 months, the single one that makes me the angriest, that gives me the most angst, is the [government] intervention with AIG." President Obama reportedly put it more pointedly during an emergency meeting with the heads of the nation's 13 largest banks, warning them, "My administration is the only thing between you and the pitchforks." Many members of Congress derided the government's intervention, deeming it a "backdoor bailout" for the world's biggest banks. The perception of Goldman's extensive political influence, particularly due to its many "alumni" who work at high government ranks, has fostered even greater public suspicion of the bank. The U.S. Senate and House of Representatives each established investigative bodies to probe erstwhile derivatives transactions as part of a wider inquiry into the causes of what has come to be known as the "Great Recession."

2.2.1 Credit Default Swaps and the Sovereign Debt Crisis

Credit default swaps have been used increasingly to speculate against government debt default rather than as an innocuous hedge to manage investment risk, as the instrument was first envisioned. Sovereign debt default swaps have been blamed for exacerbating the European Union's (EU) debt crisis. It is widely believed that speculators, such as hedge funds and investment banks not exposed directly to eurozone debt, employed CDS as a mechanism to wager on the probability of Greece and other European states, derisively known as "PIIGS," being unable to satisfy various sovereign debt obligations. The worst of these speculators have been dubbed "empty creditors." For example, if Greece were to default on its sovereign debt obligations, these speculators stood to realize substantial profits as CDS holders.

The swaps market has become so influential that CDS rates now act as an indicator of the fiscal health and creditworthiness for sovereigns and corporations alike. Market observers compare the difference in interest rates, known as the "spread," between a proxy such as the LIBOR and the sovereign debt interest rate. A higher spread differential implies a greater perceived risk of default. Political leaders have even cited CDS rates in public remarks when addressing the issue of a nation's fiscal health.

Burgeoning CDS exposure against a sovereign's debt obligations can create the impression, especially if shorting a particular sovereign's debt becomes a "crowded trade," that the target country's credit worthiness is perhaps more impaired than it might otherwise appear. A crowded CDS trade tends to exacerbate negative perceptions and increase relevant sovereign bond yields, making it increasingly daunting, and expensive, for the targeted sovereign to raise capital in the bond market or refinance its debt, which may itself precipitate a self-fulfilling prophecy of default. This phenomenon is especially criticized when CDS holders do not own the underlying government bonds. These so-called "naked" CDS holders are believed to have contributed greatly to private sector credit contraction, and consequently to the demise of shadow banking participants such as Bear Stearns and Lehman Brothers. In the sovereign debt context, such a "domino effect" is feared as it may present the risk of global contagion.

As Greece and other eurozone states experienced worsening financial conditions, a number of major derivative dealers, including Goldman, began to draw criticism from politicians and the media regarding their roles in concealing the true degree to which some of the eurozone members were indebted. The countries have a large incentive to conceal pernicious debt levels because, since 1999, rules of the Maastricht Treaty threaten to impose substantial fines on eurozone member countries that exceed a budget deficit limit of 3% of gross domestic product.

In 2002, Goldman entered into a series of cross-currency swaps with Greece's debt managers, in which the Greek government issued debt in U.S. dollars and Japanese yen in exchange for euros. The cross-currency swaps are to be exchanged back into the original currencies at a later date (10- to 15-year maturities). It was alleged that Goldman used fictional exchange rates that enabled Greece to receive a far greater up-front sum, by some accounts an additional credit of $1B, beyond the actual $10B market value of the exchange. Goldman received hefty commissions for these seemingly nefarious deals and then unloaded the swaps to a Greek bank in 2005.

A London firm known as Markit Group, owned in part by Goldman, JPMorgan Chase, and roughly a dozen other swaps dealer banks, established an index that lets traders wager on whether and which eurozone sovereigns might default. The swaps-based iTraxx SovX Western Europe index was created in September 2009, at the cusp of the Greek debt crisis, and provides speculators easy access to bearish positions on western European sovereign debt.

The ease with which traders can take synthetically short positions against sovereign debt arguably fueled a self-fulfilling prophecy, prompting bond investors to eschew European debt, which necessarily increased the at-risk nations' costs to issue bonds. Goldman banking analyst Charles Himmelberg advised the firm's clients in the spring of 2010 to adopt CDS exposure to southern European banks in Portugal, Spain, and Italy, hedged by selling "protection" against the relevant Markit iTraxx index. Not surprisingly, the price of CDS keyed to the iTraxx SovX soared shortly after the index was introduced. The crowded CDS trade can also potentially contribute to the destabilization of a nation's banking system by way of collateral effects, such as a depositor "run," which had been anticipated in the Spanish banking sector and could conceivably threaten the very fabric of the EU.

Concerns over the role of bearish trades against eurozone sovereigns and informational asymmetry of a "dark" market composed of bilateral contracting parties prompted the Committee of European Securities Regulators (CESR), in part, to recommend an extensive "Model for a Pan-European Short Selling Disclosure Regime." Germany went beyond the CESR-suggested disclosure model and unilaterally banned naked short selling of CDS referencing sovereign debt.

The stern German policy was initially designed to prohibit anyone from acquiring CDS exposure that referenced sovereign debt unless the CDS buyer used the derivatives to hedge a concurrent "long" position in government bonds. As the eurozone debt crisis escalated further, the German Finance Ministry unilaterally opted, without any extra-territorial effect, to propose an expanded and highly controversial ban to include any naked short sales of "all stocks and euro-currency derivatives not intended for hedging." As a result, it risked disregard by foreign speculators and the perception of concealment of other fiscal problems that could be met with further CDS short seller attacks conducted off-shore, evading the unilateral ban. French officials have also recently warmed to the German notion of expanding the ban throughout the EU.

Ironically, investors of securities listed in the United States voiced concerns years earlier about suspected naked shorting of domestic issues by way of exchange listings in Germany. The belief among many U.S. investors at the time was that listing a target security on the Berlin bourse was a method to evade U.S. securities laws by using an international arbitrage exception to manipulatively naked short-sell battered issues traded primarily in the United States, many of which were fixtures on the Regulation SHO list of securities due to "persistent failures to deliver."[5]

German officials could be quick to note that its ban on short selling is hardly without precedent, as U.S. officials imposed a similar ban on short selling for a variety of common stocks in the fall of 2008, particularly benefiting a number of so-called "too big to fail" financial institutions. The policy decision was made at the behest of outgoing U.S. Treasury Secretary Henry

---

[5] It was widely believed that a Berlin bourse listing for stocks present on the Regulation SHO list was indicia of "naked" short selling where common stocks are not tendered after the shares have been sold short. The reason for this belief was that Regulation SHO permits certain arbitrage exceptions. While many of these issues experienced little, if any, bona fide trading in Berlin, the exchange listings seemed to serve as a basis to circumvent the spirit of Regulation SHO [see Regulation SHO, Rules 200(d) and (e); 201(d)(4)].

Paulson to then SEC Chairman Christopher Cox. Paulson (no immediate relation to John Paulson) urged Cox to implement the ban rapidly because, "if you wait any longer, there won't be any market left to regulate." The U.S. short-sale ban was met with sharp criticism and was perceived as unjustified meddling with laissez-faire capitalism, much like Germany's ban was more recently received.[6]

The use of naked CDS speculation extends beyond sovereign and corporate debt. California Treasurer Bill Lockyer called for substantial securities law reform, including a prohibition of all naked CDS targeting municipal debt, similar to the German ban, and urged regulators to adopt minimal capital margin requirements with an aim toward reducing leverage and preventing perceived abuses. According to information provided to Lockyer, Goldman purchased a $35M CDS against California's debt, despite underwriting various California bond sales. In addition, although the transaction constituted the largest such trade recently, Goldman noted that the CDS purchases it made against California, by comparison to its overall California debt exposure, were relatively small. As of the publication of this text, the growing credit crisis in European sovereign debt, and in an increasing number of states, including California, appears far from resolved.

2.2.2 The Paulson "Put"

Financial industry nomenclature often characterizes the CDS as a form of "insurance policy" or "credit protection," as these instruments can be used to shift credit risk from one party to another. However, this terminology is perhaps something of a misnomer because a bona fide insurance policy holder must typically hold an insurable interest in whatever property is covered, pursuant to state insurance laws [see, e.g., *Warnock v. Davis*, 104 U.S. 775 (1881); McKinney's Insurance Law §3401 (2007)]. In contrast, under the current state of U.S. securities and banking law, one can presently obtain "naked" CDS exposure, known as such because its holder lacks any financial interest in the reference asset(s) or its credit obligations, or so-called "skin in the game." AIG, once one of the world's largest insurers, often maintained the sell side of these CDS transactions—an error rooted in hubris that ultimately led to its near demise.

In transactions such as the one contemplated in this chapter, Paulson had no ownership interest in the referenced ABACUS assets. In such instances, the CDS is more akin to a put option than insurance coverage because it functions to give the holder a short interest against the performance of the

---

[6] Please refer to Chapters 9, 11, and 12 for additional discussion and analysis of European short-sale policies, including pertinent regulations and restrictions.

reference assets with a finite downside risk. This differs from the traditional short sale in which one sells a borrowed security with an implicit obligation to replace the loaned securities subsequently, known as "covering" the short, which completes the transaction. The goal of the traditional short sale is to capture the difference between the price at which the short sale was affected and a lower price at which the short is later covered. In contrast, a cover in a rising market for the subject security results in a loss to the short seller, which in theory is maybe without limit.

It has been widely reported that John Paulson and his hedge fund lieutenants, quite correctly, adopted a pessimistic "wipeout" forecast for the prospects of the domestic housing market. Prior to the financial crisis, Paulson contacted a number of banks specializing in structured finance, such as Bear Stearns, Deutsche Bank, and Goldman, and requested they create mortgage-based CDO portfolios to sell to investors. In one such transaction, Deutsche Bank reportedly lost approximately $500M when they failed to sell all of the CDO deals packaged for Paulson. Through two credit funds, the first created in 2006, Paulson obtained strategic naked CDS exposure referencing ABACUS, and other similar derivative instruments, in order to effectively short sell the underlying RMBS reference assets and profit from the toppling of a vastly overleveraged and teetering "house of cards." In 2007, Paulson generated an estimated $15B in profits by short selling the "granddaddy of all bubbles," primarily using CDS that referenced RMBS, especially subprime mortgage obligation, using, among other things, MARKIT's ABX.HE 06-2 minus index.

2.3 KEY SOURCES OF RELEVANT U.S. SECURITIES LAW

Securities regulation in the United States is a mosaic of federal and state statutes enforced by numerous agencies that function to protect the interests of a diverse group of issuers and stakeholders, with an aim toward ensuring fair, efficient, and transparent capital markets. Federal law comprises the bulk of securities regulation in the United States. In response to the 1929 stock market crash, Congress enacted two "New Deal" statutes named the Securities Act of 1933 (Securities Act) and the Securities Exchange Act of 1934 (Exchange Act), referred to collectively as the "Acts."[7] These laws are supplemented by a host of rules and releases issued by the SEC, as well as judicial interpretation of the Acts found in case law.

---

[7] The Investment Company Act of 1940 is not discussed in this chapter because hedge funds typically structure holding entities to advise a limited number of limited partner "clients," which presently affords funds a "safe harbor" from investment company registration requirements (see Pekarek, 2007).

The SEC was established to administer the comprehensive regulations found within the Acts and was empowered to initiate civil and administrative proceedings, as well as investigate, rectify, and prevent violations. When warranted, the SEC collaborates with the Department of Justice (DOJ) on potentially criminal securities law violations. Many federal prosecutions result from SEC investigations and subsequent referrals to the DOJ. Following the filing of the SEC enforcement complaint against Goldman and Tourre, the assistant U.S. attorney for the Southern District of New York, Preet Bharara, announced a parallel criminal probe of swaps dealers following an SEC referral.

The DOJ investigation overseen by Bharara has reportedly cast a "wider net" than that of its SEC counterpart. The *Wall Street Journal* predicted that the DOJ probe was likely to be "long, complicated and contentious." The assistant U.S. attorney for the Eastern District of Virginia has also recently established the interagency Virginia Financial and Securities Fraud Task Force to investigate securities violations. The task force maintains jurisdiction because publicly held issuers file periodic SEC reports and other disclosure documents within that judicial district, making it a "major battleground" for the Obama administration's campaign against financial fraud.

In addition to civil and criminal federal securities laws, each state has promulgated its own statutes governing the purchase and sale of securities, commonly referred to as "blue sky laws," which regulate the offering and sale of securities in that particular state. Although federal law and the SEC serve a prominent and often preemptive regulatory role, any securities law issue must also be analyzed in conjunction with applicable state "blue sky" law. For example, the New York state legislature passed the Martin Act in 1921, granting broad antifraud investigatory powers to the New York attorney general (NYAG). Today, the Martin Act serves as a powerful enforcement tool for NYAG Andrew Cuomo and, before him, former NYAG Elliott Spitzer who resurrected the dormant Martin Act to police-suspected Wall Street malfeasance. The Martin Act is a substantial departure from the state securities laws of the other 49 states because it lacks any private right of action for securities fraud claims.

Following the initiation of SEC enforcement proceedings against Tourre and Goldman, NYAG Cuomo announced a sweeping state regulatory probe of Goldman and seven other major CDS dealers, including Morgan Stanley, Bank of America/Merrill-Lynch, Citigroup, UBS, Credit Suisse, Deutsche Bank, and Crédit Agricole S.A., pursuant to the powers of the Martin Act. NYAG Cuomo's inquiry focuses on suspected misconduct in connection with the structuring of derivative offerings, specifically the possibility that dealer banks duped or somehow otherwise manipulated ratings agencies to provide false and inflated opinions regarding the creditworthiness of derivative reference assets.

2.3.1 Derivatives Regulation—CDO and CDS

Through the broad authority conferred by the Exchange Act, the SEC is primarily responsible for three key administrative functions: rule making, adjudication, and enforcement. The Exchange Act's broad scope encompasses all aspects of secondary market securities transactions and the securities markets in general. By comparison, the Securities Act is decidedly narrower and covers security offerings that have yet to trade in the secondary market. The Exchange Act governs day-to-day secondary market securities transactions and empowers the SEC with regulatory oversight of securities dealers and other market professionals, national securities exchanges, and self-regulatory organizations, such as the Financial Industry Regulatory Association (FINRA), which supervises broker–dealer member firms and their associated persons. The Exchange Act, through promulgation of Section 10 and Rule 10b-5 thereunder, grants expansive authority to the SEC to investigate and enforce prohibitions against civil fraud in connection with all secondary market securities transactions.

The SEC's authority to regulate CDO and CDS is narrow, conditioned upon the term "security" as defined in the Securities Act and its application within the Exchange Act. Section 2(a)(1) of the Securities Act enumerates various types of financial instruments deemed securities for the purposes of the Acts (e.g., stocks, notes, commodities, options, futures, variable annuities, certificates of deposit, and certain real estate interests).

As a function of the deregulation legislation known as the Commodities Futures Modernization Act of 2000 (CFMA), Congress amended the Securities Act to expressly exclude swap agreements, such as CDS, from the definition of "security" and from the requirement for the public filing of a registration statement with the SEC in connection with an offering. Nonetheless, securities-based swap agreements are still subject to the Acts' broad antifraud provisions: §17(a) of the Securities Act and §10(b) and Rule 10b-5 of the Exchange Act. Former U.S. President Bill Clinton reflected recently on the push for derivatives deregulation during his second presidential term and how former Treasury Secretaries Robert Rubin and Larry Summers both urged him to support an easing of derivatives trading rules:

> I think they were wrong and I think I was wrong to take [the advice] because the argument on derivatives was that these things are expensive and sophisticated and only a handful of investors will buy them and they don't need any extra protection, and any extra transparency. The money they're putting up guarantees

them transparency. And the flaw in that argument was that first of all sometimes people with a lot of money make stupid decisions and make it [*sic*] without transparency.

One result of this relaxed regulatory structure was an exploitable void in CDS regulation and oversight, contrary to the very foundation of U.S. securities law, which is rooted in transparency and disclosure. This $60T global market, which dwarfs the stock market by an order of magnitude, utilizes Rule 144, an exception to the Securities Act, for the sale of trillions of dollars worth of derivatives products without the public filing of registration statements. Among those who would benefit from the CFMA registration exemption, as well as the overall lack of meaningful regulation and oversight, was Goldman through the offering undertaken by a Cayman Islands limited liability entity known as ABACUS 2007-AC1, Ltd.[8]

In the absence of specific laws regarding CDO and CDS, the SEC can rely on a broad application of §10(b) to assert Rule 10b-5 enforcement claims in connection with the purchase (or sale) of derivatives in myriad circumstances in which oral and/or written misrepresentations and/or omissions are made. The five elements required to plead a cause of action for securities fraud properly, pursuant to §10(b) of the Exchange Act and Rule 10b-5 thereunder, are (1) a misrepresentation or omission of material fact; (2) by any person; (3) in connection with; (4) the purchase or sale; (5) of any security.[9] In addition, because a Rule 10b-5 claim sounds in fraud, the elements of common law fraud, specifically scienter, reliance, causation, and damages, must also be pleaded with particularity.

2.3.2 "Short Sale" Definition Excludes CDS

Collateralized debt obligations and CDS are excluded from the term "security," as well as from the definition of a short sale. Exchange Act Rule 3b-3 defines a short sale as "any sale of a security which the seller does not own

---

[8] Goldman also relied upon the "safe harbor" registration exemption found in Regulation S, which applies to offerings made to foreign persons, such as IBK, with respect to the ABACUS CDO offering.

[9] The pertinent Exchange Act antifraud rule reads as follows:

> Rule 10b-5 – Employment of Manipulative and Deceptive Devices
> It shall be unlawful for any person, directly or indirectly, by the use of any means or instrumentality of interstate commerce, or of the mails or of any facility of any national securities exchange,

a) To employ any device, scheme, or artifice to defraud,

b) To make any untrue statement of a material fact or to omit to state a material fact necessary in order to make the statements made, in the light of the circumstances under which they were made, not misleading, or

c) To engage in any act, practice, or course of business which operates or would operate as a fraud or deceit upon any person, in connection with the purchase or sale of any security.

or any sale which is consummated by the delivery of a security borrowed by, or for the account of, the seller" (17 C.F.R. §240.3b-3). As discussed earlier, swaps such as CDS are not deemed "securities" pursuant to the CFMA amendment to the Securities Act. Therefore, this statutory language necessarily excludes synthetic short CDS positions by negative implication. Moreover, because it involves the *purchase* of an instrument that is not borrowed, a CDS position is a synthetic short that is not within the ambit of the existing restrictions generally enforced by the SEC.

When one sells securities short, the brokerage firm typically locates and loans the securities to the seller, who owes an obligation to later return a like number of the borrowed securities. The shares of the security sold short are located from the firm's own inventory, the margin account of another customer, or some other brokerage firm. In contrast, the CDS buyer either owns the underlying reference instruments or is naked, and the transaction calls for no "physical" exchange of instruments. The CDS seller is merely obligated by contract to pay the buyer a predetermined amount upon the happening of a defined credit event. Ultimately, due to the gaping void in CDO and CDS regulation, the SEC must resort to its broad antifraud enforcement powers.[10]

The following sections analyze the application of federal antifraud prohibitions with respect to materially misleading statements and omissions allegedly made by Tourre and Goldman, one of the most prominent financial institutions in the world and reportedly the fifth-largest U.S. bank in terms of total assets, in connection with the purchase and sale of synthetic CDO and CDS created during the crescendo of the subprime mortgage lending boom.

2.4 *SEC v. GOLDMAN SACHS & CO., ET AL.*—THE COMPLAINT

The SEC initiated a civil securities fraud action against Goldman and Tourre for allegedly making materially misleading statements and omissions in connection with the purchase and sale of ABACUS. Goldman structured the controversial ABACUS to reference various RMBS and marketed the CDO to a variety of institutional investors, known in the industry as qualified institutional buyers or "QIBs."

Even the very filing of the complaint to initiate civil enforcement proceedings was not without controversy; the five-member commission was evenly split along political party lines. The two members appointed by former

---

[10] Please refer to Sections 2.1, 2.2.1, and 2.3 for additional discussion and analysis of foreign and domestic short sale policies, including regulations and restrictions.

U.S. President George W. Bush both voted against commencing the action. Newly appointed SEC Chairperson (and former FINRA chief executive officer) Mary Shapiro cast her vote in favor of pursuing the enforcement litigation. Chairperson Shapiro's decisive ballot followed a closely watched internal proceeding in which SEC Enforcement Division attorneys presented the commission with the evidence then gathered against Goldman and Tourre. SEC attorneys filed pleadings on April 16, 2010, in the U.S. District Court for the Southern District of New York to initiate the civil litigation. The matter was assigned to U.S. District Judge Barbara S. Jones.[11]

The SEC complaint alleges that Paulson, reportedly the second-largest hedge fund in the world at the time of the action, approached Goldman and expressed its desire to purchase bearish CDS exposure against synthetic CDO referencing subprime RMBS. Paulson sought to participate in selecting the portfolio of reference instruments and synthetically short the same portfolio it helped select by entering into CDS transaction(s) intermediated by Goldman.[12] Ostensibly to market ABACUS more effectively, and enhance the credibility of the CDO offering to potential investors, Goldman recruited a well-known third-party CDO collateral manager, ACA Management, LLC, to analyze and select reference assets for the CDO portfolio.[13] ACA's involvement was critical, based on the SEC theory of the case, because fractures in the subprime mortgage market were beginning to surface that could have alerted prospective investors to increased risk. Another CDS portfolio selection agent and a former unit of Travelers Insurance, GSC Group, Inc. (formerly Greenwich Street Capital Partners, Inc.), previously rejected ABACUS. According to an email written by Tourre in early 2007, GSC "declined given their negative views on most of the credits Paulson had selected."

---

[11] Early in her career, Judge Jones was an assistant U.S. attorney assigned to the DOJ organized crime and racketeering task force in the 1970s, a unit she led in the mid-1980s. The 1995 Clinton judicial appointee is no stranger to high-stakes securities fraud litigation; among the cases over which she presided was the securities fraud conviction of former WorldCom CEO Bernard Ebbers, sentencing him in 2005 to an effective life sentence of 25 years, the longest sentence ever meted out to a chief executive in the United States.

[12] Paulson created two "contrarian" funds, known collectively as the Paulson Credit Opportunity Funds, designed to implement strategies consistent with a bearish "wipeout" view on subprime domestic mortgage loans. The funds achieved this primarily through CDS, which referenced RMBS securities.

[13] It was reported in early January 2011 that the bond insurer arm of ACA initiated litigation in New York state court regarding the ABACUS transaction, seeking $30M in compensatory damages and $90M in punitive damages. According to ACA, it was "misled by Goldman's fraudulent activities," and in a statement following the filing, an ACA representative stated that the ABACUS "was worthless" when Goldman marketed the CDO. The ACA representative also stated that "had Paulson's true role as a short investor selecting the portfolio been known, neither ACA nor anyone else would have taken a long position in it" (Moyer, 2011).

Tourre's email reveals that at least one other CDO portfolio agent was uncomfortable with the portfolio selected by Paulson and/or its involvement in the deal. In addition, through congressional testimony offered by Goldman's mortgage trading desk executives in 2010, we know that Goldman soured on the subprime mortgage market prior to issuance of the ABACUS deal in May 2007. According to the SEC, the head of Goldman's Structured Product Correlation trading desk wrote to Tourre on February 11, 2007, just as the ABACUS deal was being made, "the cdo biz [*sic*] is dead we don't have a lot of time left." These acknowledgments by Goldman employees, coupled with GSC's refusal to participate in the offering, reveal a potential motivation for omitting any reference to Paulson's involvement in the portfolio selection process and its aggressive short interest.

The SEC maintains, among other things, that Goldman and Tourre (1) misled ACA by misrepresenting that Paulson was a "transaction sponsor"; (2) failed to disabuse ACA of its misapprehension that Paulson would take a long position in ABACUS equity; and (3) misled CDO and CDS investors by misrepresenting, in a host of communications, by way of deceptive omission, Paulson's true role in the ABACUS portfolio selection process, kin the offering's term sheet, a "flip book" sales presentation, and the offering memorandum. The ABACUS offering memorandum was not filed publicly with the SEC, but was circulated to institutional investors pursuant to Rule 144 safe harbor provisions.

The ABACUS offering memorandum makes frequent mention (44) of "ACA," yet excludes any reference whatsoever to Paulson. The February 26, 2007, "flip book" sales presentation, entitled "ABACUS 2007-AC1 $2 Billion Synthetic CDO Referencing a static RMBS Portfolio Selected by ACA Management, LLC," prominently displays a green ACA logo on each of its 66 pages. The "flip book," like the offering memorandum, omits reference to Paulson altogether, and key portions of the presentation touted ACA's CDO expertise.[14]

In all, nearly half of the "flip book" sales material was dedicated to extolling the virtues of ACA as the ABACUS portfolio selection agent. The conspicuous emphasis Goldman and Tourre placed on the role of ACA in the transaction

---

[14] Among the "flip book" sections that touted ACA's ability to manage ABACUS were the following: (1) executive management biographies; (2) business strategy; (3) equity and ownership structure; (4) capital strategy; (5) business mix (in terms of contribution to ACA net income); (6) senior management team highlights; (7) investment philosophy, as well as (8) ACA's "alignment of economic interest"; (9) its "investment philosophy"; (10) "deep expertise"; (11) "track record"; (12) "assets under management"; (13) "core competencies in analyzing credit risk"; (14) a résumé of CDOs under ACA management; (15) details of the ACA credit analysis process; and (16) an elaborate "CDO asset management organization chart."

throughout its marketing and disclosure documents necessarily begs questions regarding its motivation to omit all public reference to Paulson, the supposed "transaction sponsor." If the matter proceeds to trial against Tourre, it is likely the SEC will make an exhaustive evidentiary showing the extent he communicated the role of ACA and the dearth of disclosure regarding Paulson.

There can be no question that Paulson representatives were actively involved in the ABACUS portfolio selection process. Through late 2006 and early 2007, Paulson selected 123 subprime RMBS rated Baa2 to be included in ABACUS. The Paulson-selected portfolio featured a high concentration of adjustable rate mortgages, with relatively low borrower credit (FICO) scores. The highest concentrations of mortgaged properties were located in Sunbelt states such as Arizona, California, Florida, and Nevada (all of which experienced higher mortgage default and foreclosure rates and steeper subsequent property value declines). ACA rejected nearly half of the RMBS selected by Paulson. Thereafter, Paulson, ACA, and Goldman representatives, including Tourre, held a series of meetings and discussions, the result of which was a mutually agreed upon portfolio consisting of 92 RMBS rated Baa2.

According to the SEC, ACA was unaware of Paulson's motivations, interests, or incentives when the ABACUS CDO was structured and marketed in early 2007. Moreover, it alleged Tourre and Goldman misled ACA, causing it to believe Paulson was the "transaction sponsor" and that the hedge fund did or would acquire an equity interest in ABACUS, thereby creating the misapprehension that Paulson's economic interests were closely aligned with ACA and potential CDO investors.[15] According to SEC allegations, the exact opposite appears to have been true, because Paulson was predicting a subprime mortgage "wipeout scenario" and synthetically shorted the ABACUS CDO based on that prescience.

The ABACUS CDO resulted in nearly $1B in losses for investors and CDS sellers. Goldman sold a portion of the CDO to IBK, a German commercial bank, who purchased $50M of Class A-1 notes and $100M of Class A-2 notes, all at face value. Within just a few months, consistent with Paulson's "wipeout scenario" prediction, those ABACUS Class A-1 and A-2 notes were virtually worthless. ACA's parent company, ACA Capital Holdings, Inc. (ACA Capital) sold the CDS protection, meaning it assumed the credit risk of the performance of the ABACUS super senior tranche.

---

[15] The equity tranche of a CDO is generally the first tranche to experience losses associated with a decline in the performance of the underlying portfolio; therefore, equity investors have perhaps the most acute economic interest in successful performance of the RMBS portfolio. According to a cooperating witness, widely believed to be Paulson lieutenant Paolo Pelligrini, the SEC alleged that Paulson was anticipating a "wipeout scenario" in the subprime mortgage market.

The super senior transaction was intermediated by ABN AMRO Bank N.V. (ABN), formerly one of Europe's largest banks, and subsequently acquired through a merger of necessity by the Royal Bank of Scotland (RBS) during the market meltdown in late 2007.[16] A series of CDS contracts, initially between ABN and Goldman, and then between ABN and ACA Capital, led to ABN assuming the full credit risk associated with the super senior tranche, in the event ACA Capital was unable to satisfy the obligation. Subsequently, ACA Capital experienced severe financial difficulties and was unable to satisfy its CDS obligations, leaving ABN (now RBS) obligated to "unwind" the CDS agreement and pay Goldman $840,909,090. Most of this money was eventually paid to Paulson, according to the SEC complaint, in what has been immortalized by *Wall Street Journal* reporter Gregory Zuckerman as supposedly the "Greatest Trade Ever."

2.4.1 Securities and Exchange Commission Antifraud Enforcement Theories

The theory behind the SEC's enforcement action is twofold. The complaint's first claim was asserted pursuant to Section 17(a)(1), (2), and (3) of the Securities Act and alleges Goldman and Tourre knowingly, recklessly, and/or negligently (1) misrepresented in the marketing materials for ABACUS that the reference portfolio was selected by ACA without disclosing Paulson's role and (2) misled ACA into believing Paulson invested in the equity tranche of ABACUS by representing it was the "transaction sponsor." The second claim, asserted under §10(b) of the Exchange Act and Rule 10b-5 thereunder, alleges Goldman and Tourre knowingly or recklessly (1) misrepresented in the ABACUS marketing materials that the reference portfolio was selected by ACA, without disclosing Paulson's role, and (2) misled ACA into believing Paulson invested in the equity of ABACUS. A key distinction between the two antifraud counterparts is the requisite level of culpability for liability to attach.

In order to constitute an actionable violation(s) under Section 17(a) of the Securities Act, the defendant(s) must have acted merely with negligence, a lower level of culpability, when making any false and/or misleading statement(s) and/or omission(s) of material fact in connection with a securities offering. However, a §17(a) claim is limited in scope because it can only be brought by a purchaser of the registered security (or by the SEC). However, a 10b-5 claim is broader and can be brought by a purchaser or seller of "'*any* security' against '*any* person' who has used '*any* manipulative or deceptive device or contrivance'" [*Herman & MacLean v. Huddleston*, 459 U.S. 375, 381 (1983)].

---

[16] For additional analysis of bank mergers, those borne out of necessity and otherwise, see Pekarek and Huth (2008).

While broader in scope, a 10b-5 claim imposes a substantially higher burden on a plaintiff (or the SEC) to establish what is known as scienter, which generally means the intent to deceive, manipulate, or defraud [see *Ernst & Ernst v. Hochfelder*, 425 U.S. 193, 197 (1976)].

As filed, the SEC enforcement action focused on Goldman and Tourre's alleged misrepresentations to ACA, as well as omissions in the relevant marketing materials to potential investors in connection with ABACUS. Due to the SEC's focus on disclosure, other potential parties, such as various credit rating agencies who might otherwise face liability, have escaped regulatory scrutiny and prospective civil liability, if perhaps only for the moment.

The fate of a number of the third parties involved in the ABACUS transactions, at least in terms of private civil liability, may well hinge on whether Congress overturns the effect of *Stoneridge Invest. Partners, LLP v. Scientific-Atlanta, et al.* At present, *Stoneridge* precludes investors from suing actors who allegedly participated in a scheme to violate Section 10(b) of the Exchange Act and SEC Rule 10b-5, provided the plaintiffs did not rely directly on any alleged misleading statement(s) and/or omission(s) attributable to the third party actor(s) [552 U.S. 148 (2008)]. Unlike private parties, the SEC has a multitude of available laws and regulations to prohibit manipulative primary offerings, marketing, and short selling despite the preclusive effect of *Stoneridge*.

Some commentators, such as former CIBC Oppenheimer analyst Henry Blodget, himself the target of a 2003 SEC enforcement action, which led to his lifetime industry bar, opined initially with a view that the SEC case against Goldman and Tourre was "weak." However, perhaps naysayers such as Blodget have underestimated the significance of a lower culpability threshold found in the antifraud provisions of Securities Act §17(a) and the impact the lower standard has in the outcome of an enforcement proceeding.

2.4.2 The Goldman Settlement

The SEC and Goldman submitted settlement papers to Judge Jones jointly on July 15, 2010. Goldman agreed to settle the SEC charges for $550M, the largest settlement in SEC history by a financial firm. The settlement amount includes disgorgement of $15M of fees and commissions Goldman received for structuring and selling the ABACUS deal and a civil penalty in the amount of $535M. The agreement provides that $300M will be paid to the U.S. Treasury, while $150M and $100M will be paid to IKB and ABN, respectively. The amount Goldman agreed to pay to the U.S. Treasury to resolve the enforcement action equates to roughly 97¢ for each American; nearly 3.6% of the roughly $14B it received in the AIG bailout; less than

3% of its annual bonus and compensation pool; or roughly 4 days' worth of Goldman revenues. Goldman also agreed to undertake remedial actions over the course of the next 3 years that require audit, review, and reform of its business practices, as well as additional education and training for Goldman employees with respect to residential mortgage-related securities. The settlement did not compel the resignation or termination of any Goldman officers or employees.

In addition, Goldman consented to the entry of a final judgment, without admitting or denying the fraud allegations of the Complaint, that provides for a permanent injunction from violations of §17(a) of the Securities Act. The settlement is silent with respect to enjoining Goldman from future 10b-5 violations, which, as discussed earlier, would require a higher standard of culpability than negligence. The agreement included the following acknowledgments by Goldman:

> Goldman acknowledges that the marketing materials for the ABACUS 2007 AC1 transaction contained incomplete information. In particular, it was a **mistake** for the Goldman marketing materials to state that the reference portfolio was 'selected by' ACA Management LLC without disclosing the role by Paulson & Co. Inc. in the portfolio selection process and that Paulson's economic interests were adverse to CDO investors. Goldman regrets that the marketing materials did not contain that disclosure. (emphasis added)

The SEC's inclusion of a 1933 Act §17(a) claim allowed Goldman to admit it was merely negligent in connection with the incomplete and "mistaken" marketing materials. Thus, Goldman was able to negotiate a settlement that minimizes reputational damage and reduces prospective liability because it did not acknowledge that it intentionally or recklessly violated the law or materially misled investors. In addition, the settlement all but eliminates the risk of criminal liability to Goldman as a result of the DOJ referral relating to ABACUS.

It is this lower level of culpability that likely served as the key incentive for Goldman to settle the SEC enforcement action while avoiding any admission of intentionally fraudulent conduct. Goldman's seemingly innocuous admission that it erred in its ABACUS nondisclosures was a source of "regret," according to the Consent Judgment approved by Judge Jones. Although it seems Goldman was spared from the worst possible outcomes, the SEC seems quite satisfied with its "victory." Robert Khuzami, director of the SEC's Division of Enforcement, pointed to the size of the settlement in subsequent public appearances and characterized the settlement as "a stark lesson to Wall Street firms that no product is too complex, and no investor too sophisticated, to avoid a heavy price if a firm violates the fundamental principles of honest treatment and fair dealing." Similarly, SEC Enforcement Division Deputy Director Lorin L. Reisner added that "half-truths and deception cannot be tolerated and that the integrity of the securities markets depends on all market participants acting with uncompromising adherence to the requirements of truthfulness and honesty." It appears that Wall Street has been placed on notice that a reinvigorated SEC will not be deterred by the size of the target or the extent of its political capital.

As evidenced by each side's rhetoric, both seem to claim victory, although the truth is likely somewhere in between. Tourre was not a party to the settlement agreement, reportedly by his choice, and must wait to learn his fate with respect to the continuing enforcement proceeding. The following section analyzes Tourre's Answer.

2.4.3 Fab Fights Back during His 15 Minutes of Fame—The Answer

Tourre answered the Complaint on July 19, 2010, 4 days after Goldman settled due to its "mistake." Tourre denies nearly every SEC allegation and refutes specific allegations on the basis that certain emails and documents are only "partially-quoted." He asserts this denial nearly 20 times throughout the responsive pleading. Importantly, he does admit Paulson approached Goldman through a "reverse inquiry" and that he knew Paulson intended to purchase a synthetic CDO from Goldman in order to gain exposure to the BBB-rated RMBS in the ABACUS deal.

The Answer sets forth several general arguments in opposition to the Complaint. First, he was only one of several Goldman employees, lawyers, and ACA representatives involved with and/or responsible for ABACUS. Second, the SEC mischaracterized Goldman's and Paulson's role in the transaction because, according to him, ACA selected the portfolio and exercised its own judgment with respect to the component securities. Third, he did not mislead or misrepresent Paulson's role as "transaction sponsor" to ACA, IKB, or ABN because, according to him, the marketing materials stated no one owned the equity interest. Fourth, he did not conceal Paulson's involvement or interest in ABACUS to ACA with intent to mislead, for the purpose of retaining it as the ABACUS portfolio selection agent and enhancing the credibility and marketability of the CDO offering to investors such as IKB or ABN. Finally, he implies there is more evidence and factual information available that was not presented by the self-serving SEC Compliant, which utilized "partially-quoted" emails and documents.

Tourre asserted eight affirmative defenses in his responsive pleading. The first, third, and fifth ostensibly assert the defense of "failure to state a claim upon which relief can be granted" pursuant to Rule 12(b)(6) of the Federal Rules of Civil Procedure (FRCP). The second and sixth defenses essentially contend that the Complaint fails to "plead fraud with particularity," as required under FRCP Rule 9. The fourth defense states "neither Mr. Tourre nor Goldman Sachs had a duty to disclose any allegedly omitted information." The success of this defense is among those that will depend ultimately on the analysis of materiality by the court and jury. The seventh defense asserts the general proposition that he cannot be held liable for any misrepresentation or omissions that he did not make. Tourre's eighth defense advances the theory that because he relied reasonably on Goldman's "institutional process to ensure adequate legal review and disclosure of material information," he therefore cannot be found liable for "any alleged failings of the process."

Federal law provides scant precedent for a "reliance" defense as it relates to a registered representative's duties with respect to disclosure in sales literature concerning ABS; however, generally, "an experienced professional has an independent duty to use diligence 'where there are any unusual factors'" [*SEC v. Graham*, 1998 WL 823072, at *6-7 (2000); quoting in re *Alessandrini & Co., Inc., et al.*, 45 S.E.C. 399, 406 (1973)]. The reliance on counsel defense may be raised to negate certain violations, particularly those that require proof of intent to deceive, manipulate, or defraud (see, e.g., *Ernst & Ernst*, 425 U.S. at 197). For successful assertion of the advice of counsel defense, a defendant must demonstrate the following: (1) a request for advice of counsel regarding the legality of the proposed action, (2) full disclosure of all relevant facts to counsel, (3) assurance by counsel of the action's legality, and (4) good faith reliance on counsel's defense [*Markowski v. SEC*, 34 F.3d 99, 104-05 (2d Cir. 1994)].

A defendant's reliance on other internal employees and even outside legal counsel will depend on whether "red flags" existed or suspicious events created reasons for doubt [see, e.g., *Wonsover v. SEC*, 205 F.3d 408, 411 (D.C. Cir. 2000); *SEC v. Steadman*, 967 F.2d 636, 642 (D.C. Cir. 1992) (holding mutual fund directors had not been reckless in relying on legal opinions from outside counsel and a disinterested independent auditor when there were no "red flags" and no suspicious events causing doubt)]. As a result, Tourre's reliance defense may depend on the court's review of information he conveyed to Goldman's counsel in light of possible concerns and other seemingly suspicious events surrounding the ABACUS deal.

The SEC Complaint alleges facts and circumstances, sufficient, if true, to constitute the type of "red flag" or suspicious events contemplated earlier. The interactions via email and telephone among ACA, Tourre, and an unidentified Goldman sales representative suggest that ACA was confused with respect to Paulson's status in the transaction. In particular, an ACA staffer stated to the Goldman sales representative in a January 8, 2007, email that "it didn't help that we don't know exactly how they [Paulson] want to participate in the space." Two days later, Tourre sent an email to ACA, which communicated a "Transaction Summary" that identified Paulson as the "transaction sponsor" and included a description of the capital structure.

According to the SEC, ACA reasonably believed Paulson would purchase the equity tranche based on Tourre's email. On January 12, 2007, Tourre spoke by telephone with an ACA representative about the proposed deal, and ACA sent a subsequent email to the Goldman representative, once again expressing confusion about Paulson's interest in ABACUS. This email was forwarded to Tourre shortly thereafter. From the allegations of the SEC complaint, apparent confusion at ACA may suffice to constitute "red flags" and/or suspicious events that may bar the use of a reliance defense (*Wonsover*, 205 F.3d 408, at 411).

In addition, according to the SEC, Tourre knew that the identity and experience of the portfolio selection agent were critical to the marketability of the transaction to investors. IKB revealed to Tourre and an unidentified Goldman sales representative in late 2006 that the selection of CDO portfolios was an important investment factor for IKB. A Goldman sales representative emailed IKB on March 6, 2007, and represented, "this is a portfolio selected by ACA...." Subsequently, Tourre sent an internal email that represented the portfolio was selected by ACA/Paulson.

The facts and circumstances given previously demonstrate that Tourre was aware of at least some "red flags" and suspicious events, especially as he was the Goldman employee with the most amount of information related to the ABACUS deal and had direct contact with ACA, IKB, ABN, and Goldman internal departments. Tourre and at least one other Goldman executive "were aggressive from the start in trying to make the assets in A[BACUS] deals look better than they were," according to *The New York Times* citing an anonymous prospective ABACUS investor.

One could reasonably maintain that Tourre was in a position to inform any one of the transaction participants, especially those within Goldman, of ACA's apparent confusion and could have ensured that adequate disclosure was included in the ABACUS marketing materials. These factors, when viewed as a whole, arguably give rise to an independent duty on Tourre's part to conduct a duly diligent inquiry as an experienced professional (see, e.g., *Graham*, 1998 WL 823072, at *6-7). This independent duty necessitated full disclosure by Tourre to his legal department, as articulated by the *Markowski* court, irrespective of his French citizenry[17] and engineer training (34 F.3d at 104-05).

---

[17] A detailed analysis of Tourre's motion for judgment on the pleadings, based in part on his foreign citizenry, may be found in Pekarek and Cherkaoui (2011).

As a result, if the matter is not settled, the SEC will likely be positioned to rebut his reliance defense sufficiently.

2.4.4 The Key Legal Element: Materiality

Although arriving at vastly different conclusions about prospective liability, many commentators agree that resolution of the issue of materiality will likely be a determining factor in the continuing litigation against Tourre. As a result, a number of key questions loom. Was Paulson's involvement in the portfolio selection process, and its bearish CDS position against ABACUS, material? Would the aggrieved investors (IKB, ACA, ACA Capital, and ABN) have been influenced significantly by Paulson's role in the transaction when coupled with its adverse economic interest? How might the "reasonable investor" view the import of this information within the context of all other facts? This section analyzes materiality with respect to the antifraud claims asserted in the SEC enforcement proceedings.

The SEC alleged the defendants misled ACA with respect to material information concerning Paulson's interest in the portfolio selection process and failed to disclose material information in their marketing materials to IBK, ACA Capital, and ABN. In the seminal U.S. Supreme Court case of *TSC Indus. v. Northway, Inc.*, Justice Marshall opined on behalf of the court, determining "the question of materiality, it is universally agreed, is an objective one, involving the significance of an omitted or misrepresented fact to a reasonable investor" [426 U.S. 438, 445 (1976)].

The context in which the *TSC* court defined materiality was with regard to proxy statement disclosures under §14(a) of the Exchange Act. It stated that a misrepresentation or omission is material if there exists a "substantial likelihood that the disclosure of the omitted fact would have been viewed by the reasonable investor as having significantly altered the 'total mix' of information made available" [426 U.S. 438, at 449-50445 (1976)]. The Supreme Court later applied the *TSC* materiality standard to §10(b) and Rule 10b-5 actions [see *Basic Inc. v. Levinson*, 485 U.S. 224, 232 (1988)]. The "reasonable investor" is a legal fiction, an abstract concept, for which one must presuppose an objective standard for the resolution of whether certain information present within the "total mix" of all other available information would have strongly influenced, or "significantly altered," that mix.

The SEC must establish that this fictional "reasonable investor" would have considered Paulson's involvement in selecting the RMBS portfolio, as well as its adverse economic interests to ABACUS, to be significant within the context of the "total mix" of all available information related to the offering [see *Basic Inc. v. Levinson*, 485 U.S. 224, 232 (1988)]. Whether a particular misrepresentation or omission is "material" is a mixed question; one composed of law, (decided by a judge); and of fact, (determined by a jury). (*TSC*, 426 U.S. 438, at 450). Judge Jones must resolve whether the information is relevant to the issue of materiality and, if so, the jury will then determine whether a "reasonable investor" would have deemed the information material (*TSC*, 426 U.S. 438, at 450).

The SEC maintains that Paulson's adverse economic interest and its role in the portfolio selection process was material. The Complaint alleged "IKB would not have invested in the transaction had it known that Paulson played a significant role in the collateral selection process while intending to take a short position in ABACUS 2007-AC1." As a result, the SEC contends that one or more of the participants would have considered the information significant *and* would have acted differently with the benefit of the information. In addition, the SEC has reportedly elicited pretrial testimony from one or more GSC representatives, including the portfolio selection agent who worked previously with Goldman on prior synthetic CDO transactions and refused to act as an agent for the ABACUS CDO, out of apparent reputational concerns, apparently due to the poor quality of the reference RMBS selected by Paulson.

The SEC can conceivably make a compelling presentation that representatives from at least one entity, experienced in the derivatives market, viewed Paulson's involvement, at least in terms of the portfolio it selected, as material and objectionable. The SEC need not present a parade of actual and/or potential investors who can testify regarding the perceived materiality of the information regarding Paulson. Nonetheless, SEC attorneys do appear to have at least one possible materiality witness available.

It is not unreasonable to anticipate that representatives from IKB and ABN, now afforded the clarity of hindsight, might testify that the alleged misrepresentation(s) and/or omission(s) would have indeed significantly altered the total mix of information available. In fact, a former ACA executive, Joe Pimbley, has alleged publicly that

> there was a passive deception, which means ACA asked "what exactly is this person's role?" and instead of giving the clear, concise answer of "he's the short side" which by itself would be fine but instead it was a vague response back . . . *We were misled and led into a deal we otherwise would not have done.*

The testimonial evidence that the SEC may elicit from the GSC representative(s) could be rather damaging to any defense(s) Tourre might assert regarding the question of materiality, provided the jury is influenced in its evaluation of how the "reasonable investor" might have interpreted GSC's rejection of ABACUS. However, Tourre might object to the introduction of any evidence regarding GSC's rejection of ABACUS as presenting a greater risk of prejudice than probative value, and as such, lacking relevance. Nonetheless, *The New York Times* reported that Tourre was among those at Goldman who were allegedly "trying to make the assets in A[BACUS] deals look better than they were," and the SEC may well have identified the anonymous prospective investor who provided that information and compel that person to testify. Such testimony seems unlikely to be excluded on relevance grounds.

2.4.5 "Doing God's Work"—Factual Rebuttals and Legal Defenses[18]

Although Goldman did not respond to the SEC complaint prior to reaching a negotiated resolution to the enforcement litigation, Goldman representatives, among them CEO Lloyd Blankfein and Tourre, revealed potential defenses during congressional hearings held on April 27, 2010. Goldman insisted it owed no duty to disclose the "transaction sponsor" because inherent in every CDO is a portfolio selection agent, as well as at least one long and one short investor. According to Goldman, it is not industry practice for a market maker, such as Goldman, to disclose the identity of the parties on either side of a transaction. In other words, breaching the confidentiality of the transaction participants would undermine its role as a market maker.

Paulson's short interest, albeit allegedly misrepresented by omission, should be immaterial to IKB, ACA Capital, and ABN based on Goldman rhetoric. This argument is flawed in a number of key respects because (i) a transaction sponsor typically invests in the CDO equity tranche and maintains a long economic interest, which is aligned with "long" synthetic CDO investors; (ii) it would be antithetical to the role of transaction sponsor to maintain a short position in any CDS referencing the super senior tranche of the synthetic CDO; and (iii) it is the market maker, at least initially, who maintains short side exposure of a synthetic CDO transaction—*not* the transaction sponsor.

Goldman representatives further maintained that IKB, ACA, and ABN are "sophisticated investors" and, as such, should have been aware of market practices and attendant CDO and CDS risks. The sophisticated investor defense is often used by the financial industry in securities cases, albeit with varying success. Prior to the SEC charges, a Goldman spokesperson told *The New York Times* "investors could have rejected the CDO if they did not like the assets." However, the sophisticated investor defense is likely unavailing

---

[18] See Arlidge (2009).

because the antifraud provisions of the Acts are construed objectively and, "as a general matter, the securities laws do not distinguish between sophistication and unsophisticated investors; both are entitled to protection, of disclosure and antifraud provisions" [in re *Scientific Securities Litigation*, 71 F.R. D. 491, 512 (S.D.N.Y. 1976)]. In addition, "the Act[s] does not speak in terms of sophisticated as opposed to unsophisticated people dealing in securities. The rules when the giants play are the same as when the pygmies enter the market" [*Scherk v. Alberto-Culver Co.*, 417 U.S. 506, 526 (1974)] (Douglas, J., dissenting).

Federal courts are likely to disregard the "sophisticated investor" defense and instead apply the overall materiality standard of the "reasonable investor." It is worth noting that UBS, Merrill-Lynch, and, to a lesser extent, JPMorgan Chase have all had recent success defending actions in New York state courts involving derivatives through use of a so-called "caveat emptor" defense. However, Tourre is defending himself against federal securities law claims in a federal forum. The "sophisticated investor" theory may have been foisted simply for consumption by the "court of public opinion," which would presumably include the pool of prospective jurors.

Among the strongest materiality arguments Tourre might advance is that Paulson's role in selecting reference securities is immaterial because ACA was also involved in the process. According to the SEC complaint, the portfolio selection process was iterative and involved Goldman, Paulson, and ACA. Thus, Paulson was not solely responsible for selecting the portfolio of subprime mortgages. For example, Paulson representatives initially selected 123 subprime mortgage positions and ACA ultimately included less than half (55). However, according to the SEC pleadings, ACA actually "sought Paulson's approval" to make any changes to the RMBS reference asset portfolio, which, if proven, may undermine Tourre's defense substantially.

Tourre might also contend Paulson's economic interest was immaterial because, as Buffet maintained when he spoke in support of Goldman after the filing of the Complaint, there is always at least one counterparty who is short in every bond transaction. According to Buffet, it is incumbent upon the buyer to conduct sufficient due diligence, a necessary component of which is obtaining appropriate credit rating analysis. The "Oracle of Omaha" is certainly not alone as a detractor of the SEC theory of the case on this point, although a so-called "due diligence" defense seems inapplicable and without apparent legal support.

Finally, and perhaps most convincingly, Tourre can assert that the majority of all domestic subprime mortgages, regardless of credit rating, were ultimately downgraded after ABACUS was created. Thus, irrespective of who made the RMBS selections, 93% of all AAA-rated subprime RMBS issued in

2006 were eventually downgraded to "junk" status. As a result, Tourre might maintain that composition of the selected RMBS reference portfolio was not material to the overall performance of the synthetic CDO and subsequent CDS exposure.

Overall, the prospect of a negotiated resolution between the SEC and Tourre remains. It remains to be seen whether Tourre's counterarguments and defenses will succeed if he does not settle and litigation continues. However, he is unlikely to prevail by motion for summary judgment, which is an application to a judicial officer seeking dismissal of some or all of the litigation. Motions for summary judgment are typically made at the conclusion of the discovery phase of pretrial activities. Pursuant to Fed. R. Civ. Pro. 56(c), a two-part standard must be satisfied for the grant of dismissal by summary judgment: (i) there is no genuine issue as to any material fact and (ii) the movant is entitled to judgment as a matter of law [see generally *Celotex Corp. v. Catrett*, 477 U.S. 317 (1986)]. The former prong is likely impenetrable in this matter and such a motion is probably futile as a result. Goldman cogeneral counsel, Greg Palm, noted the probability of this disputed fact recently to reporters, "It's all going to be a factual dispute about what he remembers and what the other folks remember on the other side." Therefore, jury verdict or settlement is the more likely path to resolving what remains of this litigation. At this juncture, despite Goldman's settlement, uncertainties remain, regarding, for example, what collateral consequences Tourre's pending litigation might have on Goldman's future business and reputation.

2.5 VAMPYROTEUTHIS INFERNALIS—COLLATERAL CONSEQUENCES

The foundations of a robust and well-functioning capital market are confidence, certainty, transparency, and trust. These cornerstones are eroded severely when executives from the world's most prominent banks, credit rating agencies, financial institutions, and hedge funds are all haled before congressional committees and various regulators by subpoena and compelled to answer for alleged transgressions, much like a modern-day Pecora Commission. In particular, Goldman has long been heralded as one of the world's preeminent financial institutions, attracting the best and brightest minds in the industry. Perceptions of Goldman became decidedly negative following the SEC action, as evidenced by the 83% of participants to a June 7, 2010, *Bloomberg News* survey who responded that their views of Goldman's reputation have been tarnished over the prior 6 months. Despite rampant public mistrust, as "the bank Americans love to hate," Goldman's employees remain "enamored" with the firm while continued calls for

Blankfein's resignation as a result of the regulator scrutiny echoed in the financial media.

Goldman may encounter far-reaching collateral consequences due to the SEC investigation and civil action, irrespective of the settlement. A prospective loss in confidence and the escalation of uncertainty quickly impacted Goldman's share price, which shed nearly 25% in market value in the month following the announcement of the SEC civil action, compared to a decline of 5% for the S&P 500 during the same time period. Ironically, the uncertainty surrounding Goldman's future also precipitated a steep increase in Goldman CDS rates. Nonetheless, in the days following the SEC settlement, Goldman's market value increased nearly $5B—a substantial short-term win when compared to the $550M settlement.

The incalculable damage to its reputation and brand has resulted in popular culture and media disdain, suspicion, and scrutiny. *Rolling Stone* characterized the bank as a "great vampire squid wrapped around the face of humanity, relentlessly jamming its blood funnel into anything that smells like money." Goldman's presence in a popular culture publication that recently featured a scantily clad "Lady Gaga" on its cover demonstrates one effect of the financial crisis on broader society: ordinary citizens are more attuned to how the financial markets affect their lives than perhaps ever before. The loss in public trust may drive away current and future clients, which, together with increased broader financial regulation, may further compress Goldman's market capitalization and operating profits, despite its surging stock price during the broad market rally that followed the settlement. A number of European governments, including Greece, Spain, France, and Italy, have all refused Goldman the lead role in sovereign bond offerings, and one French treasury source noted that "French people would riot in the streets if we chose Goldman [as an investment bank]."

In addition to the many potential collateral consequences stemming from the SEC enforcement proceedings, even after it reached a settlement accord, Goldman could still encounter further legal consequences. For example, it may face additional regulatory risk of fines and sanctions through FINRA, which commenced an inquiry into the firm and Tourre following the SEC action. Moreover, Goldman could potentially face additional private civil actions brought by clients, counterparties, and shareholders and might be found liable for Tourre's alleged misconduct, under the legal theory *respondeat superior*.

Among the types of potential lawsuits it may yet have to defend against are ERISA claims, shareholder derivative actions, individual state and federal claims, and international cases, as well as state and federal shareholder class actions. Many of the potential claims may involve Goldman's failure to disclose immediately that it received a "Wells Notice," an SEC notification informing the bank of the regulator's ABACUS investigation, in September 2009, as well as for the CDO deals named "Hudson Mezzanine" and "Timberwolf."[19] In fact, just 2 weeks after the SEC filed the ABACUS complaint, no less than seven separate shareholder derivative[20] and class action claims were asserted against Goldman regarding the synthetic CDO. More recently, ACA initiated litigation against Goldman in New York state court maintaining that it was "misled by Goldman's fraudulent activities" related to ABACUS.

Investors in Goldman common stock who purchased shares between October 15, 2009, and April 16, 2010, quickly filed a putative class action against Goldman, asserting claims pursuant to §10 of the Exchange Act and Rule 10b-5 thereunder, for nondisclosure related to ABACUS in various periodic reports filed with the SEC. The putative class period commences with filing of a Form 10Q, Goldman's quarterly report for the third quarter of 2009, in which Goldman allegedly omitted its receipt of the September 2009 Wells Notice issued by the SEC informing the bank of its ABACUS investigation.

Goldman was also named in a $1B claim by another former client, Basis Yield Alpha Fund (Master), a Cayman Islands fund. Basis filed a securities fraud action in the Southern District of New York in which it maintains it was forced into insolvency after buying RMBS within the Timberwolf 2007-1 CDO that Goldman created and which Goldman executive Tom Montag, now famously remarked to his colleague, Daniel Sparks, in an email cited repeatedly by Senator Carl Levin during an April 27, 2010, Congressional Committee hearing, "[B]oy, that timeberwof [sic] was one shitty deal." Goldman has reportedly implemented a communications filter to prevent its employees from making similar remarks via company email in the future.

Although it is too soon to determine the long-term effects of these and other potential collateral consequences, it is clear, at least in the short term, that Goldman's reputation has been diminished greatly. The bank has taken some remedial steps to recast its image, although some, such as developing a documentary film about itself, have been met with rebukes and ridicule. However, despite the expanded first amendment rights for corporate political speech resulting from the recent Citizens United decision, Goldman has vowed to "not spend corporate funds directly on electioneering communications" [see *Citizens United v Federal Election Commission*, 558 U.S. 50 (2010)].

---

[19] The synthetic Hudson Mezzanine 2006-1 CDO reportedly contained CDS that referenced $2B in subprime, BBB-rated RMBS.

[20] For additional analysis regarding shareholder derivative litigation, see Pekarek (2010). See also http://www.mhprofessional.com/handbookoftrading.

2.5.1 One Costly Debate—No Shortage of CDS Critics and Advocates

The general consensus among voters, politicians, economists, and members of the international community appears to be that derivatives must be regulated in some meaningful fashion to prevent future market meltdowns. Buffett's reference to OTC derivatives as "financial weapons of mass destruction" crystallizes populous sentiment that these products, mostly in the form of swaps, helped create, or at least exacerbated, the global financial crisis, in large part due to the multiplier effect of the numerous wagers that were made on the prospects of subprime RMBS. However, derivatives are not without proponents, who maintain that they serve a vital role in the functioning of modern capital markets and that another crisis would ensue if their use was curtailed sharply or if they were altogether abolished.

Swaps critics contend that the bilateral nature of the contracts, formed in "dark" markets, creates unacceptable opacity, risk, and uncertainty. The term "systemic risk" has been used to describe a host of contributing factors to the current financial crisis (e.g., "too big to fail" financial institutions, excessive leverage, proprietary trading); however, the term remains largely undefined in the abstract. One must look to the underlying characteristics of the CDS market to unravel a key source of systemic risk.

Most commentators agree that a major source of underlying risk is the lack of CDS market regulation. As mentioned in earlier sections of this chapter, the Securities Act expressly exempts swaps from regulation, while the Exchange Act only provides regulation of CDS with respect to fraud. Thus, it is plausible that a comprehensive provision in the Securities Act regulating CDS issuance may have prevented the alleged abuses that spawned from the creation and solicitation of ABACUS. It was this lax regulatory approach to CDS issuance, pursuant to the "safe harbor" of Rule 144, that allowed Goldman to disseminate "incomplete" information in the marketing materials for ABACUS by "mistake." Industry-wide, the largely unregulated purchase and sale of OTC CDS obscured the full extent of potential damage as the crisis unfolded due in no small part to a dearth of aggregate data.

Proponents of an orderly and regulated CDS market, primarily through the use of clearinghouses and/or exchanges, argue that centralization offers many benefits, including decreased risk, increased transparency, and greater liquidity. Clearinghouses function at the center of other derivative trading, like commodities, acting as the buyer to every seller and vice versa. A central clearinghouse requirement may reduce the risk that failure of one or more market participant(s) could conceivably trigger "domino-effect" losses on counterparties because it would end the opaque bilateral relationships between the derivative contract counterparties. Thus, clearinghouses, instead of U.S. taxpayers, would assume the risk of CDS contract default, in the event that a counterparty could not satisfy its contractual commitment(s). Exchange trading could further reduce risk with greater transparency through the propagation of real-time derivative contract volume and pricing data. Moreover, this increased transparency would likely narrow trading spreads. Another benefit exchange trading would offer is centralized record keeping and a host of oversight functions undertaken in cooperation with the SEC and the Commodity Futures Trading Commission (CFTC).

Clearinghouses may also dampen systemic risk by requiring CDS purchasers and sellers to pledge collateral in the form of margin requirements. Similarly, requiring derivatives traders to contribute a predetermined percentage of capital to a reserve fund and subject their trading books to inspection and risk assessment procedures would represent significant reform. A standardized central clearinghouse system may also reduce the customization of derivatives. Parties often refine their hedges to the specific financial risks they encounter, and some may contend that lessening the ability to tailor bilateral instruments to narrowly defined risks will stifle innovation. Although one might certainly question the value of the last era of "innovation," which led the world to a precipice of financial collapse.

Credit default swap critics argue that the bilateral nature of CDS transactions, without the use of clearinghouses or exchanges, created a lack of market liquidity. Sell-side participants must typically pay what is known as an "unwinding fee" to close out any CDS position(s) prematurely, causing participants who seek to avoid such costs to enter into offsetting contracts with different counterparties that negate the effects of the previous CDS position(s). This facet of the current derivatives market structure and related trading strategy(ies) effectively multiplies aggregate counterparty exposure. The phenomenon is repeated throughout the market, to such an extent that the recent net exposure of CDS dealers totaled $3T, compared to a gross "notional" total of $23T in dealer-to-dealer transactions (and a $28T notional total for global CDS liabilities) by June 2009. As stated earlier, a centralized CDS clearing system would provide increased liquidity and lessen the need for sell-side participants to establish offsetting positions.

Finally, critics deride the purely speculative nature of naked swaps trading where CDS market participants lack any genuine ownership interest in the underlying securities or collateral. There can be little debate about whether the aggregate value of the CDS that referenced subprime RMBS dwarfed the actual indebtedness of subprime mortgagors exponentially. Many detractors have questioned whether leveraged swaps exposure involving insufficiently capitalized participants, such as AIG, who nonetheless originated trillions of dollars worth of CDS, holds any redeeming social value whatsoever, especially when one considers the systemic risks.

Financial institutions and their lobbyists pushed back against so-called "overregulation" and contended that swaps, even when held "naked," serve a vital function in a modern financial and economic system. They have argued that swaps provide efficient ways for financial and nonfinancial users to hedge a variety of risks (i.e., interest rate, foreign currencies, and loan defaults) and, if not permitted in the United States, trillions in transactions will simply migrate offshore. In response, naked swaps proponents argue the following: (1) speculators enhance market liquidity by providing a counterparty for hedge transactions, (2) speculators improve CDS informational value (which is often more price sensitive than equities) and enhance market liquidity, (3) naked CDS are similar to an option contract because an option holder *often* does not own the underlying security, and (4) the options market is not widely criticized.

Critics of swaps cite the failures of "shadow banking" institutions such as Bear Stearns, Lehman Bros., and AIG, as well as the sovereign debt crisis experienced by eurozone members such as Greece and the other so-called "PIIGS," as examples of short interest derivative speculation seemingly run amok. However, naked CDS advocates contend that speculators are exposing essential truths about what is happening, or likely to happen, to a target company or country with solvency issues. Short sellers have a long history of presciently exposing malfeasance and fraud; perhaps among the most notable is James Chanos, who correctly identified the Enron accounting scheme well before regulators. Similarly, when one sets aside moral judgments and legal arguments, there can be little debate that Paulson correctly predicted the "granddaddy of all bubbles," the same one Buffet proclaimed that no one could possibly envision. A careful balance must be struck between "overregulation" and unfettered market autonomy so as to not stifle innovative free markets, while simultaneously guarding against "systemic risk."

In response to many of the perceived risks associated with CDS described in this chapter, the Obama administration and both houses of Congress identified key areas in the CDS market they sought to recast, and some pundits attributed the path to regulatory reform as nothing more than "a concerted effort by the Obama administration and the Democratic-controlled Congress to demonize Goldman Sachs." Key proposed reforms included (1) induce or require "standardized" derivatives to be cleared on exchanges and/or central clearinghouses; (2) establish conditions to induce derivatives trades already cleared centrally to be traded on exchanges or an equivalent transparent platform, much like commodities and futures now trade; (3) ensure that adequate reserves, in the form of capital or margin equity, are held against all OTC trades that are not centrally cleared; (4) require margin or collateral to support derivatives positions, held either in segregated accounts or by third parties; and (5) for derivatives that are both centrally cleared and traded on exchanges, regulators should ensure that the transaction prices (pretrade and post-trade) and volumes are posted promptly using the equivalent of a ticker symbol.

During a televised interview, Gary Gensler, CFTC CEO, said that in our "dealer dominated world," clearinghouses and exchange-based derivatives trading are not in Wall Street's pecuniary interest because the firms simply "make more money in a 'dark' market." According to Gensler, the only acceptable outcome is "transparent trading venues" brought by "broad comprehensive reform." Gensler was clear to support the bill that later became the Dodd–Frank Wall Street Reform and Consumer Protection Act (Dodd–Frank) without dilution. However, according to critics, including UniCredit SpA, new rules forcing CDS contracts to be backed by clearinghouses may hike hedging costs and make derivatives trading more difficult.

Most of the proposed CDS market reforms were incorporated into Dodd–Frank. However, Senator Blanche Lincoln's controversial amendment, known as "Section 716," which would have banned swaps trading by commercial banks, was eventually removed from the bill. As a compromise to the Lincoln Amendment, which would have severely impacted Wall Street's profits, Congress included a provision that will force banks to move nonbusiness- or nonhedging- related swaps to a subsidiary, coined a "swap execution facility" (SEF), the aim of which is to reduce systemic risk to depository institutions that enjoy access to the Federal Reserve's discount window.

In an effort to curb some of the questionable business practices of investment banks such as Goldman, Senators Merkley and Levin introduced legislation designed to prevent firms that underwrite an ABS from other transactions that would create a conflict of interest. Another provision will force lenders, with the exception of some mortgage providers, to retain at least a 5% stake in securitized debt the firm packages or sells. Less than 1 week after President Obama signed Dodd–Frank, mandating that substantially more of the $615T market for privately negotiated derivatives be cleared by SEFs or clearinghouses, Goldman announced it had launched a clearing unit to capitalize on the new regulation for OTC derivatives, products that include interest rate and currency swaps, credit derivatives, and some commodity-related contracts. Dodd–Frank also includes an altered role for the Federal Reserve, strong consumer-protection laws, procedures for unwinding "too big to fail" financial institutions facing insolvency in an orderly fashion, limitations on proprietary trading, and a new

"Financial Stability Oversight Council." Overall, it remains to be seen how well Dodd–Frank will ultimately achieve its goal of regulation, but it is clear that the Obama administration and Congress were intent on at least creating the appearance of vigilant action.[21]

The SEC has increased its enforcement activity on the heels of sharp criticism regarding Bernard Madoff's fraud, while ignoring Harry Markopolous, who was shouting from the rooftops to just about anyone who would listen. In fact, just after settling with Goldman, the SEC reached a settlement with Citigroup for $75M in connection with its failure to disclose "vast holdings of subprime mortgage investments that crippled the bank during the financial crisis," according to *The New York Times*. The SEC action alleged that the Citigroup subsidiary, Citi Markets & Banking, had $50B in subprime RMBS exposure, while it claimed to have only $13B and omitted from disclosure numerous subprime derivatives to which it was exposed. The SEC reportedly singled out Citigroup's former CFO and head of investor relations for concealing material information from shareholders as part of the agreement. Like Goldman, Citigroup was afforded the light slap of §17(a)(2) of the 1933 Act in its settlement accord, which, as discussed earlier, requires merely negligent conduct to constitute a violation of federal securities law.

2.6 CONCLUSION

The probability of Tourre prevailing in motion practice is quite low as the pleadings sufficiently allege the requisite elements of fraud with particularity and there appear to be substantial disputes of material fact, factors likely to deter the Honorable Barbara Jones from granting summary judgment.[22] Tourre's two main options for resolution of the SEC civil enforcement litigation remain settlement and trial. The prospect of settlement likely exists in the Securities Act claim, which requires negligence, a lesser degree of culpability. However, some market observers have opined that any settlement may call for a lifetime industry ban, perhaps an unpalatable condition for Tourre as he endeavors to "clear" his name.

A trial could pose significant risks for Goldman, Tourre, and the SEC, especially if a jury deems the alleged misrepresentations and omissions to be "material." At a minimum, Goldman may face the prospect of extensive discovery, which would potentially distract the bank from its daily operations

---

[21] An examination of the full extent of Dodd–Frank exceeds the scope of this chapter.
[22] A detailed analysis of Tourre's motion for judgment on the pleadings may be found in Pekarek and Cherkaoui (2011).

and a media circus during courtroom proceedings that reminds the public of its role in ABACUS. However, the SEC would face the risk that a fact-finder would reject its theory(ies) of liability, much like the jury did in the attempted prosecution of two Bear Stearns executives in 2009, accused of somewhat similar conduct in the Brooklyn federal court.

While one certainly cannot predict the next crisis with prescience, appropriate reform measures in the credit, derivatives, and equities markets are all clearly warranted and history will likely place AIG and Goldman at the forefront as companion catalysts for such reform. At times, prospects of a financial bill passage seemed bleak, with both Congress and the public losing interest in reform due to the protracted and partisan effort at health care reform earlier in 2010 and a significant market rally in the second half of 2010, fueled substantially by accommodative Federal Reserve Bank policy aimed in part at ginning up stock prices. However, perhaps the environmental disaster in the Gulf of Mexico at the British Petroleum drilling platform, "Deepwater Horizon," stoked renewed support for sweeping reform and an increased appetite for greater government regulation in a seething public's collective consciousness.

Goldman's alleged misconduct served as the catalyst for financial regulatory reform as few politicians were willing to risk the public perception of defending Wall Street after it appeared to have again run amok in avarice. The often sensationalist vilifying of short sellers is, however, somewhat misguided as it is among the private market forces that provide more accurate price discovery and has historically revealed a number of frauds that may have remained undetected absent a profit motive to discover corporate malfeasance. One perfect example of this function is that Paulson uncovered an enormous portion of the U.S. economy that was rife with fraud. Unfortunately, far too few were willing to rein in the excesses of an unregulated and obscenely leveraged mortgage market before it was far too late.

Canada weathered the global economic crisis with comparative aplomb, far better than other developed nations, including the United States. In fact, the 10 provinces and three territories to the north did not experience a single major financial institutional failure, nor was there a mortgage meltdown or anything even resembling a banking crisis. A key difference between the two countries was the extent of what was perceived as appropriate regulatory oversight. In fact, the Canadian government recently strengthened its residential mortgage rules in anticipatory prevention of a real estate bubble, possibly fueled by the low interest rates of the global recession and the "easy money" policies of the current Federal Reserve Bank.

Regarding the alleged misconduct, which is the focus of *SEC v. Goldman Sachs, et al.*, had an enforcement action of this sort been initiated in Canada by the Ontario Securities Commission (OSC), the outcome(s) may not have depended so heavily on an issue of materiality. In fact, had the charges been made pursuant to Canada's "public interest jurisdiction," which affords OSC staffers great latitude in determining how they enforce securities laws, OSC officials would not have been constrained with the need to prove, or even allege, a breach of any specific securities law(s). Perhaps we have much to learn from the ways of our northerly neighbor?

ACKNOWLEDGMENTS

The authors thank Pace Investor Rights Clinic Director Professor Jill I. Gross for her tireless and sage counsel and 2010 Pace Law School graduate, Braem Velo for his meaningful contributions to the research and writing of a portion of this chapter.

REFERENCES

ABCNews. (2010, June 16). *Bigger villain: BP or Goldman Sachs?* Retrieved from http://blogs.abcnews.com/nightlinedailyline/2010/06/bigger-villain-bp-or-goldman-sachs.html. (Last visited June 29, 2010).

ABCNews. (2010). *Clinton: I was wrong to listen to wrong advice against regulating derivatives.* Retrieved from http://blogs.abcnews.com/politicalpunch/2010/04/clinton-rubin-and-summers-gave-me-wrong-advice-on-derivatives-and-i-was-wrong-to-take-it.html. (Last visited July 22, 2010).

Adelson, M. (2004). *CDOs in plain English.* Nomura Fixed Income Research. Retrieved from http://www.vinodkothari.com/Nomura_cdo_plainenglish.pdf. (Last visited May 31, 2010).

Balzli, B. (2010, February 8). *How Goldman Sachs helped Greece to mask its true debt.* Der Spiegel. Retrieved from http://www.spiegel.de/international/europe/0,1518,676634,00.html. (Last visited June 5, 2010).

Barnett, G. (2008). *Nuts & bolts of financial products 2008: Understanding the evolving world of capital market and investment management products.* Practicing Law Institute, 1653 PLI/Corp 449, 453.

Barnett-Hart, A. K. (2009, March 19). *The story of the CDO market meltdown: An empirical analysis.* Harvard College. Retrieved from http://www.hks.harvard.edu/m-rcbg/students/dunlop/2009-CDOmeltdown.pdf. (Last visited July 8, 2010).

Basis yield alpha fund (Master) v. Goldman Sachs group, Inc., et al., Case No. 10-cv-4537 (BSJ) (DCF) (complaint).

Bituin, A. (2010, February 15). *Defusing "financial weapons of mass destruction." Polifinancial Times.* Retrieved from http://www.polifinance.com/2010/02/15/defusing-financial-weapons-of-mass-destruction/.

Blake, R. (2010, August 2). *eBay for Swaps.* Reuters Hedgeworld. Retrieved from http://www.hedgeworld.com/blog/?p=1103. (Last visited Aug. 3, 2010).

BrandIndex. (2010, April 26). *Fraud allegations cause Goldman Sachs scores to fall.* Retrieved from http://www.brandindex.com/content/news-2010-main.asp?aID=32. (Last visited June 29, 2010).

Bryan-Low, C., & Luchetti, A. (2010, July 29). *George Carlin never would've cut it at the New Goldman Sachs: Firm bans naughty words in emails; An 'Unlearnable Lesson' on Wall Street? The Wall Street Journal.* Retrieved from http://online.wsj.com/article/SB1000142405274870 4895004575395550672406796.html. (Last visited Aug. 3, 2010).

Buffet, W. (2010, June 2). *Buffett to face crisis commission.* Televised interview, CNBC. Retrieved from http://www.cnbc.com/id/15840232?video=1511142188&play=1. (Last visited June 4, 2010).

Bullock, N. (2010, June 5). *Goldman bet $35M against California. Financial Times.* Retrieved from http://www.ft.com/cms/s/0/75b12d70-703a-11df-8698-00144feabdc0.html. (Last visited June 5, 2010).

Carney, J. (2010, May 26). *Goldman Sachs girds for battle with the SEC over fraud case.* CNBC.com. Retrieved from http://m.cnbc.com/id/37362236/Goldman_Sachs_Girds_for_Battle_ With_the_SEC_Over_Fraud_Case. (Last visited June 2, 2010).

Chanos, J. (2002, February 6). *Anyone could have seen Enron coming.* Prepared witness testimony given to the House Committee on Energy and Commerce. Retrieved from http://www.pbs .org/wsw/opinion/chanostestimony.html. (Last visited Feb. 16, 2010).

Code of Federal Regulations, 12 CFR §§ 201-33.

Cohan, W. (2009). *House of cards: A tale of hubris and wretched excess on Wall Street.* New York: Doubleday.

Cohan, W. (2010, July 6). *Let Goldman be Goldman. The New York Times* Opinionator (blog). Retrieved from http://opinionator.blogs.nytimes.com/2010/07/06/let-goldman-be-goldman/. (Last visited July 8, 2010).

Committee of European Securities Regulators. (2010). *CESR proposal to the European institutions for a pan-European short selling disclosure regime* (March). Retrieved from http://www.cesr.eu/ data/document/10_088.pdf. (Last visited June 6, 2010).

Cronin, J., Evansburg, A., & Garfinkle-Huff, S. (2001). *Securities fraud. Am. Crim. L. Rev. 1278,* 1321 (2001).

Dash, E., & Story, L. (2010, July 29). *Citigroup Pays $75 million to settle subprime claims. The New York Times.* Retrieved from http://www.nytimes.com/2010/07/30/business/30citi.html.

Davidson, A. (2008, September 18). *How AIG fell apart.* Reuters. Retrieved from http://www.reuters .com/article/idUSMAR85972720080918. (Last visited May 19, 2010).

Eder, S. (2010, July 30). *Goldman employees still enamored with firm and CEO,* ABCNews. Retrieved from http://abcnews.go.com/Business/wireStory?id=11289277 (Last visited Aug. 2, 2010).

Faber, D. (2009, June 4). *House of Cards.* CNBC Documentary. Retrieved from http://www.cnbc .com/id/15840232?video=1145392808&play=1. (Last visited July 11, 2010).

Federal Reserve Bank of New York. (2008, December 3). *AIG CDO LLC facility: Terms and conditions (effective 2008).* Retrieved from http://www.newyorkfed.org/markets/aclf_terms.html. (Last visited June 5, 2010).

Federal Rules of Civil Procedure, Pleading Special Matters, Rule 9(b). Fraud or Mistake; Condition of Mind.

Federal Rules of Evidence, Rule 401. Definition of "Relevant Evidence."

Gallu, J., & Harper, C. (2010, June 10). *Goldman Sachs Hudson CDO said to be target of second SEC probe.* Bloomberg. Retrieved from http://www.bloomberg.com/apps/news? pid=20601208&sid=aSNYXMe69Kh8. (Last visited June 19, 2010).

Gasparino, C. (2009). *The sellout: How three decades of Wall Street greed and government misman-agement destroyed the global financial system.* New York: HarperBusiness.

Gillies, R. (2010, June 1). *Canada becomes first G-7 country to raise interest rates since the global financial crisis.* Associated Press (AP). Retrieved from http://finance.yahoo.com/news/

Canada-raises-interest-apf-459245508.html?x=0&sec=topStories&pos=8&asset=&ccode=. (Last visited June 1, 2010).

Goldfarb, Z., & Markon, J. (2010, May 1). *Justice probe of Goldman goes beyond deals cited by SEC. Washington Post.* http://www.washingtonpost.com/wpdyn/content/article/2010/04/30/AR2010043001336.html. (Last visited June 19, 2010).

Goldman, S. (2010, August 2). *Valuation & pricing related to transactions with AIG, submitted to the FCIC 2010.* Retrieved from http://www2.goldmansachs.com/our-firm/on-the-issues/valuation-pricing-doc.pdf. (Last visited Aug. 2, 2010).

Greenspan, A. (2010, March 9). *The Crisis.* pp. 8, 23-25, *n.*39, 44, Working Paper, Brookings Institution: Brookings Papers on Economic Activity. Retrieved from http://www.brookings.edu/~/media/Files/Programs/ES/BPEA/2010_springbpea_papers/spring2010_greenspan.pdf. (Last visited July 8, 2010).

Grocer, S. (2010, July 29). *The SEC's Citi complaint: When $13 billion should have been $50 billion. The Wall Street Journal Deal Journal* (blog). Retrieved from http://blogs.wsj.com/deals/2010/07/29/the-secs-citi-complaint-when-13-billion-should-have-been-50-billion/. (Last visited Aug. 2, 2010).

Gross, D. (2010, April 21). *The rise of the 'Empty Creditor.' Newsweek.* Retrieved from http://www.newsweek.com/id/194820. (Last visited May 17, 2010).

Gross, D. (2010, July 16). *Goldman's best trade ever. Newsweek.* Retrieved from http://www.newsweek.com/2010/07/16/goldman-s-best-trade-ever.html. (Last visited July 19, 2010).

Harper, C. (2010, May 5). *Goldman Sachs said to be late to report SEC probe to FINRA. Bloomberg.* Retrieved from http://www.bloomberg.com/apps/news?pid=20601110&sid=a4lnTH5KviGQ. (Last visited June 19, 2010).

Harper, C. (2010, August 2). *Goldman Sachs provides examples of how it priced AIG mortgage derivatives. Bloomberg.* Retrieved from http://www.bloomberg.com/news/2010-08-02/goldman-sachs-gives-examples-of-how-it-priced-aig-securities-to-u-s-panel.html. (Last visited Aug. 2, 2010).

Harper, C. (2010, July 27). *Goldman Sachs unit to offer OTC derivatives-clearing service. Bloomberg Businessweek.* Retrieved from http://www.businessweek.com/news/2010-07-27/goldman-sachs-unit-to-offer-otc-derivatives-clearing-service.html. (Last visited Aug. 3, 2010).

Hazen, T. (2002). *The Law of Securities Regulation.* St. Paul, MN: West Group.

Henning, P., & Davidoff, S. (2010, July 16). *Weighing the trade-offs in the Goldman settlement. The New York Times,* DealBook (blog). Retrieved from http://dealbook.blogs.nytimes.com/2010/07/16/weighing-the-trade-offs-in-the-goldman-settlement. (Last visited July 19, 2010).

Hernandez, J. (2010, August 2). *Political Ads off limits, Goldman promises. The New York Times.* Retrieved from http://www.nytimes.com/2010/08/03/nyregion/03goldman.html. (Last visited Aug. 3, 2010).

Hintze, J. (2008, September 29). *Placing blame on naked shorts, SEC overlooks reg SHO issues.* Securities Industry News. Retrieved from http://www.securitiesindustry.com/issues/19_76/22843-1.html. (Last visited June 19, 2010).

Howard Sorkin, et al. v. Goldman Sachs Group, Inc., et al., case co. 10-cv-3493 (PAC) (MHD) (complaint).

International Swaps and Derivatives Association, Inc. (ISDA) (2010). *CDS marketplace: About the CDS market.* Retrieved from http://www.isdacdsmarketplace.com/about_cds_market. (Last visited May 31, 2010).

Jamieson, D. (2007, April 23). *SEC seen shy on naked shorting; Agency called reluctant to take on hedge funds and their prime brokers. Investment News.* Retrieved from http://www.investmentnews.com/article/20070423/FREE/70423007. (Last visited June 19, 2010).

Jawoski, M. (2010, May 28). *Berkshire Hathaway's (NYSE: BRK-B) Warren Buffett subpoenaed by FCIC*. American Banking and Marketing News. Retrieved from http://www.americanbankingnews.com/2010/05/28/berkshire-hathaways-nyse-brk-b-warren-buffett-subpoenaed-by-fcic/. (Last visited June 7, 2010).

Johnson, S., & Kwak, J. (2010). *13 Bankers: The Wall Street takeover and the next financial meltdown*. New York: Pantheon.

Jones, A. (2010, July 20). *Fabrice Tourre not only 'Fabulous,' but also a fighter. The Wall Street Journal*. Retrieved from http://blogs.wsj.com/law/2010/07/20/fabrice-tourre-not-only-fabulous-but-also-a-fighter/. (Last visited Aug. 2, 2010).

Klassen, S. (2000). *JP Morgan risk metrics group: Guide to credit derivatives*. Retrieved from http://www.investinginbonds.com/assets/files/Intro_to_Credit_Derivatives.pdf. (Last visited Aug. 3, 2010).

Kwak, J. (2009, March 11). *AIG in review*. The Baseline Scenario (blog). Retrieved from http://baselinescenario.com/2009/03/01/aig-bailouts-1-2-3-4/. (Last visited June 5, 2010).

La France a-t-elle manipule les autorités américaines dans l'affaire AIG? Le Monde, January 19. Retrieved from http://finance.blog.lemonde.fr/2010/01/19/la-france-a-t-elle-roule-les-autorites-americaines-dans-l%E2%80%99affaire-aig/. (Last visited May 31, 2010).

Leising, M., & Frye, A. (2010, June 2). *Moody's chief says CDO ratings 'Deeply Disappointing.' Bloomberg Businessweek*. Retrieved from http://www.businessweek.com/news/2010-06-02/moody-s-chief-says-cdo-ratings-deeply-disappointing-update1-. (Last visited June 3, 2010).

Lenzner, R. (2010, June 2). *Buffett didn't foresee granddaddy of all bubbles. Forbes*. Retrieved from http://www.forbes.com/2010/06/02/warren-buffett-testimony-markets-streettalk-lenzner-angelides.html. (Last visited June 4, 2010).

Litan, R. (2010, April 7). *The derivatives dealer's club and derivatives market reform: A guide for policy makers, citizens and other interested parties*. The Brookings Institution. Retrieved from http://www.brookings.edu/papers/2010/0407_derivatives_litan.aspx. (Last visited June 17, 2010).

Maastricht Treaty. (1992, February 7). *Provisions amending the treaty establishing the European economic community with a view to establishing the European community*. Retrieved from http://www.eurotreaties.com/maastrichtec.pdf. (Last visited June 19, 2010).

Marois, M. (2010, June 4). *California's Lockyer seeks curbs on 'Naked' swaps. Bloomberg Businessweek*. Retrieved from http://www.businessweek.com/news/2010-06-04/california-s-lockyer-seeks-curbs-on-naked-swaps-update2-.html. (Last visited June 5, 2010).

Martin Act, N.Y. Gen. Bus. Law §§ 352-359-h; Fraudulent Practices in Respect to Stocks, Bonds and Other Securities (2010).

Matheson, A., & Michael, N. (2010, August 2). *SEC v. Goldman Sachs: Issues in focus*. McCarthy Tétrault research. Retrieved from http://www.mccarthy.ca/article_detail.aspx?id=5019. (Last visited Aug. 3, 2010).

McGee, S. (2010). *Chasing Goldman Sachs*. New York: Crown Business.

McGroarty, P., & Kissler, A. (2010, May 26). *Germany proposes wider ban on naked short selling. The Wall Street Journal*. Retrieved from http://online.wsj.com/article/SB100014240527487040262045752662124882968502010850.html. (Last visited May 30, 2010).

McQuillen, W., & Hurtado, P. (2010, April 21). *Goldman's caveat emptor defense mirrors UBS, Merrill. Bloomberg Businessweek*. Retrieved from http://www.businessweek.com/news/2010-04-21/goldman-s-caveat-emptor-defense-mirrors-ubs-merrill-lawsuits.html. (Last visited June 19, 2010).

McTamaney, R. (2003, February 28). *New York's Martin Act: Expanding enforcement in an era of federal securities regulation*. Legal Backgrounder. Retrieved from www.wlf.org/upload/022803LBMctamaney.pdf. (Last visited May 7, 2010).

Mollenkamp, C., & Ng, S. (2010, May 2). *Senate's Goldman probe shows toxic magnification. The Wall Street Journal.* Retrieved from http://online.wsj.com/article/SB1000142405274 8703969204575220300651236446.html. (Last visited June 30, 2010).

Morganson, G., & Story, L. (2009, December 23). *Banks bundled bad debt, bet against it and won. The New York Times.* Retrieved from http://www.nytimes.com/2009/12/24/business/24trading.html. (Last visited June 19, 2010).

Morrissey, J. (2008, March 17). *Credit default swaps: The next crisis? TIME.* Retrieved from http://www.time.com/time/business/article/0,8599,1723152,00.html. (Last visited May 18, 2010).

Moscovitz, I. (2010, June 15). *The coming financial meltdown. The Motley fool.* Retrieved from http://www.fool.com/investing/general/2010/06/15/the-coming-financial-meltdown.aspx. (Last visited June 17, 2010).

Moses, A. (2010, August 3). *Credit-default swaps regulation to increase hedging costs, UniCredit says. Bloomberg.* Retrieved from http://www.bloomberg.com/news/2010-08-03/credit-default-swaps-regulation-to-increase-hedging-costs-unicredit-says.html. (Last visited Aug. 3, 2010).

Moshinsky, B., & Viscus, G. (2010, June 9). *Sarkozy, Merkel urge faster EU curbs on speculation. Bloomberg Businessweek.* Retrieved from http://www.businessweek.com/news/2010-06-09/sarkozy-merkel-urge-faster-eu-curbs-on-speculation-update1-.html. (Last visited June 19, 2010).

Moya, E. (2010, February 15). *Calls to curb CDS gamblers as Greek crisis continues. The Guardian* (UK). Retrieved from http://www.guardian.co.uk/business/2010/feb/15/credit-default-swaps-regulation. (Last visited May 19, 2010).

Moya, E. (2010, July 18). *Europe freezes out Goldman Sachs. The Guardian* (UK). Retrieved from http://www.guardian.co.uk/business/2010/jul/18/goldman-sachs-europe-sovereign-bond-sales. (Last visited Aug. 3, 2010).

Moyer, L. (2010, July 30). *Goldman Sachs in the clear? Goldman Sachs pays the SEC less than 3% of its bonus pool.* Forbes Video Network. Retrieved from http://video.forbes.com/fvn/business/goldman-sachs-settlement. (Last visited Aug. 2, 2010).

Munchau, W. (2010, February 28). *Time to outlaw naked credit default swaps. Financial Times.* http://www.ft.com/cms/s/0/7b56f5b2-24a3-11df-8be0-00144feab49a.html. (Last visited May 20, 2010).

Nolan, G. (2010, May 24). *CDS report: More pain in Spain. Financial Times.* FT Alphaville (blog). Retrieved from http://ftalphaville.ft.com/blog/2010/05/24/241171/cds-report-more-pain-in-spain/. (Last visited June 19, 2010).

O'Dell, L. (2010, May 21). *Task force in Virginia to target financial fraud. Bloomberg Businessweek.* Retrieved from http://www.businessweek.com/ap/financialnews/D9FRC6FO2.htm. (Last visited June 19, 2010).

Orol, R. (2010, June 7). *FCIC issues subpoena to Goldman Sachs. MarketWatch.* Retrieved from http://www.marketwatch.com/story/fcic-issues-subpoena-to-goldman-sachs-2010-06-07. (Last visited June 7, 2010).

Paletta, D., & Patterson, S. (2010, April 27). *Bill deals Buffett a setback. The Wall Street Journal.* Retrieved from http://online.wsj.com/article/SB3000142405274870344140457520625225 2365076.html. (Last visited May 30, 2010).

Patterson, S., & Holm, E. (2010, May 1). *Buffett defends Goldman; Berkshire posts profit. The Wall Street Journal.* Retrieved from http://online.wsj.com/article/SB100014240527487046 0810457521807102922354.html.

Paulson, J. (2008, November 13). *Statement of John Paulson, U.S. House of Representatives Committee on oversight and government reform. Financial Times* (Hearing Transcript). Retrieved from http://media.ft.com/cms/a1d35562-b192-11dd-b97a-0000779fd18c.pdf (Last visited June 5, 2010).

Pekarek, E. (2007). *Pruning the hedge: Who is a "Client" and whom does an adviser advise?* 12 Fordham J. Corp. & Fin. L. 913. The Investment Company Act of 1940 is not discussed in this chapter because hedge funds typically structure holding entities to advise a limited number of limited partner "clients," which presently affords the funds a "safe harbor" from investment company registration requirements.

Perez, E., & Craig, S. (2010, May 1). *U.S. faces high stakes in its probe of Goldman. The Wall Street Journal.* Retrieved from http://online.wsj.com/article/SB1000142405274870409320457 5216613173555050.html. (Last visited June 19, 2010).

Petruno, T. (2010, July 15). *Goldman's $550 Million SEC settlement: Who gets the money?* Los Angeles Times Money & Company Blog. Retrieved from http://latimesblogs.latimes.com/money_co/ 2010/07/goldman-sachs-sec-settlement-550-million-subprime-ikb-royal-bank-scotland.html. (Last visited Aug. 2, 2010).

Phillips, M. (2008, September 27). *The Monster that ate Wall Street. Newsweek.* Retrieved from http://www.newsweek.com/id/161199. (Last visited May 19, 2010).

Pimbley, J. (2010, July 30). *Ex-ACA Exec. on Goldman deal. FoxBusiness.* Retrieved from http://video.foxbusiness.com/v/4298572/ex-aca-exec-on-goldman-deal-/. (Last visited Aug. 2, 2010).

Pozsar, Z., Adrian, T., Ashcraft, A., & Boesky, H. (2010, July). *Federal Reserve Bank of New York staff reports: Shadow banking. Staff Report No. 458,* (pp. 59-64). Retrieved from http://www .newyorkfed.org/research/staff_reports/sr458.html. (Last visited July 22, 2010).

Prial, D. (2010, June 7). *Goldman slapped with subpoena by crisis commission. FoxBusiness.* Retrieved from http://www.foxbusiness.com/story/markets/goldman-slapped-subpoena-crisiscommission/ ?utm_source=feedburner&utm_medium=feed&utm_campaign=Feed%3A+foxbusiness%2Flatest +%28Text+-+Latest+News%29. (Last visited June 7, 2010).

Pulliam, S., & Perez, E. (2010, April 30). *Criminal probe looks into Goldman trading. The Wall Street Journal.* Retrieved from http://online.wsj.com/article/SB1000142405274870357 2504575214652998348876.html. (Last visited May 4, 2010).

Sabry, F., Sinha, A., Mark, J., & Lee, S. (Nera Economic Consulting). (2010, June 17). *Credit crisis litigation revisited: Litigating the alphabet of structured products. Mondaq Finance and Banking.* Retrieved from http://www.mondaq.com/unitedstates/article.asp?articleid=102298. (Last visited June 19, 2010).

Sanati, C. (2010, May 13). *Cuomo and the broad power of the Martin Act. The New York Times,* DealBook (blog). Retrieved from http://dealbook.blogs.nytimes.com/2010/05/13/cuomo-and-the-broad-power-of-the-martin-act/. (Last visited May 15, 2010).

Schoetz, D. (2010, June 16). *Bigger villain: BP or Goldman Sachs?* ABCNews, Nightline's Daily Line. Retrieved from http://blogs.abcnews.com/nightlinedailyline/2010/06/bigger-villain-bp-or-goldman-sachs.html#tp. (Last visited June 29, 2010).

Schwarz, N., & Dash, E. (2010, February 24). *Banks bet Greece defaults on debt they helped hide. The New York Times.* Retrieved from http://www.nytimes.com/2010/02/25/business/global/ 25swaps.html. (Last visited May 31, 2010).

SEC Litigation Release No. 21592/July 15. (2010, July 15). *Securities and Exchange Commission v. Goldman, Sachs & Co. and Fabrice Tourre,* Civil Action No. 10 Civ. 3229 (S.D.N.Y. filed April 16, 2010), *Goldman Sachs to pay record $550 million to settle SEC charges related to subprime mortgage CDO.* Retrieved from http://sec.gov/litigation/litreleases/2010/lr21592.htm. (Last visited June 24, 2010).

SEC Press Release 2003-56 (2003, April 28). *The Securities and Exchange Commission, NASD and the New York Stock Exchange permanently bar Henry Blodget from the securities industry and require $4 million payment.* Retrieved from http://www.sec.gov/news/press/2003-56.htm. (Last visited June 7, 2010).

SEC Press Release 2010-123 (2010, July 15). *Goldman Sachs to pay record $550 million to settle SEC charges related to subprime mortgage CDO. Firm acknowledges CDO marketing materials were incomplete and should have revealed Paulson's role.* Retrieved from http://sec.gov/news/press/2010/2010-123.htm. (Last visited June 22, 2010).

SEC v. Citigroup, civil case no. 1:10-cv-01277 (ESH) (complaint). Retrieved from http://www.sec.gov/litigation/complaints/2010/comp21605.pdf. (Last visited Aug. 2, 2010).

SEC v. Goldman Sachs & Co., et al., civil case no. 1:10-cv-03229 (BSJ) (Goldman Consent of Defendant Goldman, Sachs & Co). Retrieved from http://sec.gov/litigation/litreleases/2010/consent-pr2010-123.pdf. (Last visited July 24, 2010).

SEC v. Goldman Sachs & Co., et al., civil case no. 1:10-cv-03229 (BSJ) (proposed judgment against Defendant Goldman, Sachs & Co). Retrieved from http://sec.gov/litigation/litreleases/2010/judgment-pr2010-123.pdf. (Last visited July 24, 2010).

SEC v. Goldman Sachs & Co., et al., civil case no. 1:10-cv-03229 (BSJ) (complaint). Retrieved from http://sec.gov/litigation/complaints/2010/comp21489.pdf. (Last visited July 24, 2010).

Sloan, R. (2009). *Don't blame the shorts: Why short sellers are always blamed for market crashes and how history is repeating itself* (pp. 97–114). New York: McGraw Hill Professional.

Son, H., & Moore, M. (2010, January 21). *AIG took four tries on filing as Fed asked to withhold data. Bloomberg.* Retrieved from http://www.bloomberg.com/apps/news?pid=20601087&sid=aRexIMpLtIL4&pos=.

Sorkin, A. R. (2009). *Too big to fail* (pp. 175, 382). New York: Viking.

Stoneridge Invest. Partners, LLP v. Scientific-Atlanta, et al., 552 U.S. 148 (2008).

Story, L. (2010, May 13). *Prosecutors ask if 8 banks duped ratings agencies. The New York Times.* Retrieved from http://www.nytimes.com/2010/05/13/business/13street.html. (Last visited June 8, 2010).

Susanne, C. (2010, July 24). *Goldman, the movie. By Goldman. The Wall Street Journal.* Retrieved from http://online.wsj.com/article/SB10001424052748704249004575385471576237734.html. (Last visited Aug. 2, 2010).

Taibbi, M. (2009, July 9–23). *The Great American bubble machine. Rolling Stone.* Retrieved from http://www.rollingstone.com/politics/news/12697/64796.

Tavakoli, J. (2009). *Dear Mr. Buffett: What an investor learns 1,269 miles from Wall Street* (p. 167). New York: Wiley.

Thompson, M., Keiser, R., & Albanese, G. (2010, April 19). *Credit market commentary: Market derived signal: SEC charges trigger wider CDS spreads at Goldman Sachs.* Standard & Poor's. Retrieved from http://www.standardandpoors.com/products-services/articles/en/us/?assetID=1245210322801. (Last visited June 19, 2010).

U.S. v. Stout, 965 F.2d 340 (7th Cir. 1992).

U.S. Senate Committee on Banking and Currency (2010). *Stock exchange practices: The final report of the Pecora commission.* CreateSpace.

Vekshin, A., & Mattingly, P. (2010, June 26). *Lawmakers reach compromise on financial regulation. Bloomberg News.* Retrieved from http://www.bloomberg.com/news/2010-06-25/lawmakers-reach-compromise-on-financial-regulation.html. (Last visited July 2, 2010).

Walker, M., & Shah, N. (2010, May 19). *Germany to ban some naked short selling. The Wall Street Journal.* Retrieved from http://online.wsj.com/article/SB10001424052748703957904575252611852571860.html. (Last visited May 20, 2010).

Wenzel, R. (2010, June 16). *Bank run in Spain and its destabilizing ramifications for the entire EU.* EconomicPolicyJournal.com (blog). Retrieved from http://www.economicpolicyjournal.com/2010/06/bank-run-in-spain-and-its-destabilizing.html. (Last visited June 19, 2010).

Whitehouse, M. (2010, May 22). *Number of the week: 75% chance of Greek default. The Wall Street Journal*, Real Time Economics (blog). Retrieved from http://blogs.wsj.com/economics/2010/05/22/number-of-the-week-75-chance-of-greek-default/. (Last visited June 17, 2010).

Wyatt, E. (2010, July 20). *S.E.C. Pursuing more cases tied to financial crisis. The New York Times.* Retrieved from http://www.nytimes.com/2010/07/21/business/21sec.html. (Last visited Aug. 2, 2010).

Yerak, B. (2010, July 29). *Goldman Sachs swears off swearing. Chicago Tribune.* Retrieved from http://www.chicagotribune.com/news/opinion/ct-talk-swearing-at-work-0730-20100729,0,3256026.story. (Last visited Aug. 2, 2010).

Zuckerman, G. (2009, October 31). *Profiting from the crash. The Wall Street Journal.* Retrieved from http://online.wsj.com/article/SB10001424052748703574604574499740849179448.html. (Last visited June 5, 2010).

Zuckerman, G., & Ng, S. (2010, April 28). *SEC questions 'Not Us' firm.* Retrieved from http://online.wsj.com/article/SB10001424052748703648304575212641381556412.html. (Last visited May 3, 2010).

Zuckerman, G. (2009). *The Greatest trade ever: The behind-the-scenes story of how John Paulson defied Wall Street and made financial history.* New York: Broadway Business.

BIBLIOGRAPHY

Arlidge, J. (2009, November 8). *I'm doing 'God's work.' Meet Mr Goldman Sachs. The Sunday Times* (UK). Retrieved from http://www.timesonline.co.uk/tol/news/world/us_and_americas/article6907681.ece. (Last visited June 19, 2010).

Basic Inc. v. Levinson, 485 U.S. 224, 232 (1988).

Celotex Corp. v. Catrett, 477 U.S. 317 (1986).

Citizens United v. Federal Election Commission, 558 U.S. 50 (2010).

Commodities Futures Modernization Act of 2000, Ch. 38, Title I, § 2A, as added Dec. 21, 2000, P.L. 106-554, § 1(a)(5), 114 Stat. 276 (May 27, 1933).

Dodd-Frank Wall Street Reform and Consumer Protection Act, P.L. 111-203 [HR 4173](July 21, 2010).

Ernst & Ernst v. Hochfelder, 425 U.S. 193, 197 (1976).

Herman & MacLean v. Huddleston, 459 U.S. 375, 381 (1983).

In re Alessandrini & Co., Inc., et al., 45 S.E.C. 399, 406 (1973).

Markowski v. SEC, 34 F.3d 99, 104-05 (2d Cir. 1994).

McKinney's Insurance Law §3401 (2007).

Moyer, L. (2011, January 6). *UPDATE: ACA financial sues Goldman for alleged ABACUS-related fraud. The Wall Street Journal.* Retrieved from http://online.wsj.com/article/BT-CO-20110106-713760.html. (Last visited Jan. 17, 2011).

Pekarek, E. (2007). *The Due Diligence Defense and the Refco IPO* (Working Paper). Retrieved from http://ssrn.com/abstract=1145930. (Last visited Aug. 2, 2010).

Pekarek, E. (2010). In G. N. Gregoriou (Ed.), *Shareholder demands and the Delaware derivative action. Handbook of trading: Strategies for navigating and profiting from currency, bond and stock markets* (pp. 171–185). New York: McGraw-Hill Financial Education Series (2010). Retrieved from http://www.mhprofessional.com/handbookoftrading.

Pekarek, E., & Cherkaoui, S. (2011). Off-shore short sales after Morrison: Will the SEC be emboldened or constrained? *The short seller handbook.* Elsevier Publishing.

Pekarek, E., & Huth, M. (2008). *Bank merger reform takes an extended Philadelphia national bank holiday*. 13 Fordham J. Corp. & Fin. L. 595.

Regulation SHO, 69 FR 48008, 48030 (Aug. 6, 2004); 72 FR 36348, 36359 (July 3, 2007); 72 FR 45544, 45557, (Aug. 14, 2007); 73 FR 61690, 61706 (Oct. 17, 2008); 75 FR 11232, 11323 (Mar. 10, 2010).

Scherk v. Alberto-Culver Co., 417 U.S. 506, 526 (1974) (Douglas, J., dissenting).

SEC v. Goldman Sachs & Co., et al., civil case no. 1:10-cv-03229 (BSJ) (Tourre answer).

SEC v. Graham, 1998 WL 823072, at *6-7 (2000).

SEC v. Steadman, 967 F.2d 636, 642 (D.C. Cir. 1992).

Securities Act of 1933, ch 38, Title I, § 1, 48 Stat. 74 (May 27, 1933). 15 U.S.C. § 77a *et seq.*

Securities Exchange Act of 1934, ch. 404, Title I, § 1, 48 Stat. 881 (June 6, 1934). 15 U.S.C. § 78a *et seq.*

TSC Indus. v. Northway, Inc., 426 U.S. 438, 445 (1976).

Warnock v. Davis, 104 U.S. 775 (1881).

Wonsover v. SEC, 205 F.3d 408, 411 (D.C. Cir. 2000).

CHAPTER 3

Off-Shore Short Sales after *Morrison*: Will the Securities and Exchange Commission Be Emboldened or Constrained?

Edward Pekarek and Soufiane Cherkaoui

CONTENTS

ABSTRACT

This chapter examines pending litigation between the Securities and Exchange Commission (SEC) and Goldman Sachs & Co. executive Fabrice Tourre and analyzes the viability of the SEC legal theories against Tourre through a review of his motion for dismissal. The discussion considers how the court might interpret and apply the recent U.S. Supreme Court holding in *Morrison v. National Australia Bank Ltd.* and reconciles *Morrison* with provisions of the newly enacted Dodd–Frank Act as it relates to enforcement actions involving foreign participants.

KEYWORDS

ABACUS 2007-AC1; Collateralized debt obligation; Credit default swap; Dodd–Frank Wall Street Reform and Consumer Protection Act; *Morrison v. National Australian Bank Ltd.*; Residential mortgage-backed securities; Securities and Exchange Commission; *Securities and Exchange Commission v. Goldman Sachs & Co., et al.*

3.1 INTRODUCTION

The casual channel surfer is often overtaken by generic (often meaningless) nightly news references to what has been dubbed the worst financial meltdown since the Great Depression. Segments typically include commentators positing as to the causes of the economic downturn and, in the process, singling out key participants—namely the dominant Wall Street banks. The conversation frequently turns to the inefficacy of the present regulatory framework, focused squarely on the Securities and Exchange Commission (SEC or Commission). However, the discussion becomes stale without an appreciation for the scope of powers granted to the SEC by congressional fiat through the Securities Act of 1934. To be sure, the particular challenges facing the current securities enforcement regime are tied directly to the extent of SEC adjudicatory authority. More importantly, recent securities enforcement developments have raised questions concerning SEC enforcement activities and general efforts to regulate the U.S. securities markets.

This chapter does not pretend to resolve the ongoing dispute over what is the appropriate role for the SEC in administering and enforcing the federal securities laws. Instead, it reflects on domestic enforcement in the face of increasing securities markets globalization. This trend invites the SEC to revisit its enforcement functions and reconsider its regulatory reach, especially in the shadow of *Morrison v. National Australian Bank Ltd.*, the most recent and relevant word from the U.S. Supreme Court on the topic.

The pending litigation against Goldman executive Fabrice Tourre[1] portends a changing focus of regulatory activity. As the Commission asserts a more

---

[1] *Securities and Exchange Commission v. Goldman Sachs & Co., et al.*, 10 Civ. 3229 (BSJ) (S.D.N.Y. filed April 16, 2010).

prominent role in enforcement actions, it has also resisted some pushback effect from regulated entities. The ultimate outcome of the case against Tourre, therefore, is likely to inform future SEC enforcement strategy. Through an examination of the documents filed by the respective parties in the Tourre matter, this chapter addresses questions regarding the appropriate scope (and direction) of SEC enforcement activity. The discussion is three-fold: the first part is devoted to a recitation of the relevant facts giving rise to the civil securities fraud action against Tourre; the second part analyzes the parties' moving papers, together with the arguments made therein, guided in large measure by *Morrison*[2] and its progeny; and the third part explores the impact of the Dodd–Frank Wall Street Reform and Consumer Protection Act of 2010 (Dodd–Frank)[3] in terms of extraterritorial application of federal securities laws.

3.2 GOLDMAN AND PAULSON ENTER INTO A MARRIAGE OF CONVENIENCE

Despite its serious overtone, the Commission's civil suit against Goldman and Tourre has at times turned farcical. At the center of the controversy is the longstanding investment banking and securities firm Goldman Sachs. The supporting cast includes Paulson & Co., a hedge fund and Goldman client, and Fabrice Tourre, a 31-year-old bombastic executive who entertainingly holds himself out as "Fabulous Fab." As described in far greater detail throughout Chapter 2, the plot involves the structuring and marketing of a collateralized debt obligation (CDO)—a complex derivative instrument—labeled ABACUS 2007-AC1 (ABACUS). The overriding theme is one of duplicity whereby Goldman and Tourre allegedly misled investors by failing to disclose Paulson's directly adverse economic interest in the ABACUS transaction.

Toward the end of 2004 or beginning of 2005, Goldman created its structured product correlation trading desk, with the ultimate aim of synthetic CDO structuring and marketing.[4] A CDO is a derivative instrument composed of underlying assets that most often include corporate bonds, bank loans, or asset-backed securities (ABS). It is typically divided into several

---

[2] 561 U.S. ___; 130 S. Ct. 2869 (2010).

[3] Dodd–Frank Wall Street Reform and Consumer Protection Act, Pub. L. No. 111-203, 124 Stat. 1376 (2010).

[4] An internal Goldman memorandum dated March 12, 2007, makes apparent the bank's nefarious objectives, stating in relevant part that "[e]xecuting this transaction [ABACUS] and others like it helps position Goldman to compete more aggressively in the growing market for synthetics written on structured products." Pl. Compl. ¶10.

classes (or tranches), all of which present varying levels of credit risk.[5] The synthetic CDO—unlike its cash counterpart—does not hold the underlying assets. Rather, credit exposure is determined indirectly by reference to the performance of a portfolio of debt obligations.

In structuring the ABACUS transaction, Goldman issued Class A-1 and Class A-2 notes to IKB Deutsche Industriebank AG (IKB), a foreign commercial bank. Payment on the notes was derived from revenue generated by the underlying assets—in this case, residential mortgage-backed securities (RMBS). With the funds earned from note sales, Goldman then executed a credit default swap (CDS) with ACA Management, LLC (ACA) for the most senior CDO tranche, which referenced a portfolio of RMBS, largely backed domestic subprime mortgages. All in all, Goldman expected to earn between $15 and $20 million for structuring and marketing ABACUS.

A CDS is a contractual obligation between the seller and the buyer, with the latter obtaining a right for future compensation conditioned on the happening of a credit event at a later date. In exchange for payment of a premium, ACA—through a wholly owned subsidiary—provided a hedge against default on the home mortgages, which were referenced by ABACUS. The downside risk to ACA totaled $909 million (representing the most senior ABACUS debt tranche) and was partially offset by a regular stream of premium payments approximating 50 basis points per year. As the CDS seller, ACA effectively bore the risk associated with RMBS default at a time when the housing market showed signs of distress. Considering that home prices had proven remarkably stable over time, though, ACA had the misapprehension that it stood to reap a handsome return as a CDS seller.

The forecast, however, was not nearly as ebullient as ACA believed. At around the same time, a historic housing bubble faced an ever-increasing prospect of bursting. In truth, housing prices were inflated artificially. Credit was easily obtainable and financial institutions employed relaxed lending practices. Savvy market participants, as a result, monitored the subprime RMBS sector closely. The following excerpt by a Paulson employee incisively describes the fragility of the domestic housing market as ABACUS was structured:

> It is true that the market is not pricing the subprime RMBS wipeout scenario. In my opinion this situation is due to the fact that rating agencies, CDO managers and underwriters have all the incentives to

---

[5] Generally speaking, a CDO is composed of four tranches: senior debt, mezzanine debt, subordinate debt, and equity. Correspondingly, the senior debt tranche would include securities awarded the highest credit rating (as attributed by the credit rating agencies), whereas subordinate debt tranches would include successively lower-rated securities.

keep the game going, while 'real money' investors have neither the analytical tools nor the institutional framework to take action before the losses that one could anticipate based [on] the 'news' available everywhere are actually realized.[6]

Still, without more, the aforementioned facts do not necessarily implicate wrongdoing, let alone civil or criminal securities fraud. Enter Paulson and Tourre, whose controversial involvement in the ABACUS deal raised a host of worrisome conflict of interest issues.

Paulson, a Goldman hedge fund client, had adopted a particularly bearish position on subprime mortgage loans. Through two of its funds (namely, the Paulson Credit Opportunity Funds), Paulson developed a strategy to sell short the RMBS referenced by ABACUS. Accordingly, it purchased so-called "credit protection" by way of a CDS, serving as counterparty to ACA's long position. Paulson partook in the structuring of ABACUS and carefully selected RMBS reference assets it believed were likely to experience full or partial default. This opposing economic interest was unknown to ACA. That Paulson would profit from its aggressive short sale tactic was, at this stage, a *fait accompli*.

Paulson methodically handpicked RMBS bearing strikingly similar characteristics. For example, the hedge fund heavily favored those mortgages carrying so-called "teaser" rates for homebuyers with low FICO scores. It goes without saying, then, that the odds were skewed disproportionately in Paulson's favor. The difficulty lay in soliciting sufficient interest in the ABACUS transaction. As is often the case, time was of the essence. In a partially translated email to a friend dated January 23, 2007, Tourre appreciated the evident constrictions in the CDO market and revealingly stated:

> More and more leverage in the system. The whole building is about to collapse anytime now....Only potential survivor, the fabulous Fab[rice Tourre]...standing in the middle of all these complex, highly leveraged, exotic trades he created without necessarily understanding all of the implications of those monstruosities!!! [*sic*][7]

In this display of hubris, Tourre reported that the CDO market was inching ever closer to collapse, soon to be enveloped in losses. Undeterred, Goldman nevertheless proceeded to solicit interest in ABACUS.

In an effort to shroud the deal with the cloak of legitimacy, Goldman approached ACA, a respected collateral manager, to serve as portfolio selection agent. ACA boasted vast experience in analyzing credit risk associated

---

[6] Pl. Compl. ¶17.
[7] Pl. Compl. at ¶18.

with RMBS. By the end of 2006, it had completed 22 CDO transactions, representing $15.7 billion in aggregate assets. For Goldman, it became imperative to lure ACA into the ABACUS transaction, especially after a rival collateral manager has rejected ABACUS. In a February 7, 2007, internal Goldman email, Tourre noted astutely:

> One thing that we need to make sure ACA understands is that we want their name on this transaction. This is a transaction for which they are acting as portfolio selection agent, this will be important that [*sic*] we can use ACA's branding to help distribute the bonds.[8]

Goldman deftly recognized that investors—in particular, IKB—would likely decline to participate in the ABACUS transaction absent the inclusion of a collateral manager to vet the reference portfolio.

At all relevant times, however, Goldman, and Tourre, allegedly failed to disclose Paulson's materially adverse interest in the transaction. ACA was unaware that Paulson was synthetically short selling the ABACUS RMBS reference portfolio. It is safe to add that ACA likely would have been discouraged from participating in the transaction had it known of Paulson's bearish position in anticipation of a "wipeout scenario" of the domestic housing market. For this reason, the SEC alleged the defendants misrepresented Paulson's economic interest in ABACUS, characterizing it as being in alignment with ACA's. According to the pleaded allegations, Goldman spuriously informed ACA that Paulson had invested in the equity tranche of the synthetically structured CDO, the first to experience losses in the event of a decline in the performance of the underlying RMBS. Tellingly, ACA acceded to the ABACUS transaction with the apparent understanding that "the hedge fund equity investor [Paulson] wanted to invest in the 0–9% tranche of a static mezzanine ABS CDO backed 100% by subprime residential mortgage securities." Nothing could be further from the truth.

Having secured ACA's services, Goldman launched an aggressive marketing campaign targeting investors, according to the SEC. In a 9-page term sheet, the investment bank described ACA as the portfolio selection agent for ABACUS and went so far as to represent that the reference portfolio of RMBS had been selected by ACA, not Paulson.[9] Equally disturbing, Goldman finalized a 65-page marketing "flip book" in early 2007 that falsely claimed the party selecting the portfolio (i.e., Paulson) had "an alignment of economic interest"

---

[8] Pl. Compl. at ¶22.
[9] Paulson had initially selected and submitted a list of 123 subprime RMBS to be included in ABACUS, none of which enjoyed a credit rating greater than Baa2. ACA, in turn, accepted 55 of the original Paulson submissions. Following a series of meetings and discussion, relevant parties agreed that ABACUS would reference a portfolio of 90 subprime RMBS.

with potential investors. Importantly, Tourre was responsible for allegedly preparing both documents, neither of which adequately disclosed the extent of Paulson's involvement in the structuring of ABACUS. An internal Goldman memorandum, circulated at around that same time, meanwhile was ominous in its declaration that "Goldman [was] effectively working an order for Paulson to buy protection on specific layers of the [ABACUS 2007-] AC1 capital structure."[10] This language dispels any doubt surrounding the closeness of both parties' working relationship.

Following an investigation into the aforementioned alleged facts, the Commission commenced an enforcement action against Goldman and Tourre. Accordingly, the following discussion addresses the substance of the SEC's claim against Goldman and Tourre, together with any legal underpinnings. The focus, in turn, rests on the cases supporting the respective parties' positions.

3.3 THE SECURITIES AND EXCHANGE COMMISSION CHARGES GOLDMAN AND TOURRE WITH SECURITIES FRAUD IN CONNECTION WITH ABACUS STRUCTURING AND MARKETING

In its April 16, 2010, complaint, the SEC alleged that Goldman and Tourre violated U.S. securities laws—specifically §17(a) of the 1933 Securities Act and §10(b) of the 1934 Securities Exchange Act. Following a series of discussions with Goldman executives, the Commission entered into an agreement with the firm for $550M, the largest settlement in SEC's 76-year history. Goldman consented to disgorgement of ill-gotten gains ($15M) and payment of a civil penalty ($535M). However, since entry of the judgment against Goldman, the legal landscape has undergone significant change, spurring Tourre to vigorously contest the charges against him.

3.3.1 *Morrison* Curbs Extraterritorial Application of Federal Securities Law

The Supreme Court's recent *Morrison* decision engendered much discussion regarding SEC authority in enforcing transnational fraud cases. In *Morrison*, foreign investors commenced a putative class action under §10(b) of the Exchange Act against National Australia Bank ("National"), an Australian banking corporation. National's shares traded solely on foreign exchanges. National acquired a majority interest in HomeSide Lending, Inc., an

---

[10] Pl. Compl. ¶43.

American mortgage company, in February 1998. Between 1998 and 2001, HomeSide and its senior officers touted the company's supposed profitability. As it turned out, however, the mortgage servicer had computed its profits based on a flawed model, resulting in an overstatement of balance sheet assets. HomeSide subsequently wrote down the value of its previously vaunted assets by a reported $2.2B, precipitating a decline in its stock value. The plaintiffs in *Morrison* alleged that HomeSide (together with senior officers) had manipulated its financial models to perpetrate a fraud on investors.[11]

National, in response, moved to dismiss for lack of jurisdiction under Federal Rule of Civil Procedure ("FRCP") 12(b)(1) and FRCP 12(b)(6) for failure to state a claim for relief. The district court, in an opinion rendered by Judge Jones (who also presides over the enforcement action against Tourre) granted National's motion to dismiss under FRCP 12(b)(1), concluding that subject matter jurisdiction was lacking. The U.S. Court of Appeals for the Second Judicial Circuit affirmed Judge Jones' jurisdictional reasoning, citing the absence of "any allegation that the alleged fraud affected American investors or America's capital markets."[12] The court based its conclusion on the longstanding "conduct and effects" test, explaining further that the plaintiffs "do not contend that what [National] allegedly did had any *meaningful effect* on America's investors or its capital markets."[13] Thereafter, the U.S. Supreme Court granted *certiorari* to "decide whether §10(b) of the Securities Exchange Act of 1934 provides a cause of action to foreign plaintiffs suing foreign and American defendants for misconduct in connection with securities traded on foreign exchanges."[14] The Supreme Court's answer to that question produced profound reverberations.

Justice Antonin Scalia wrote in a 5-4 opinion that the Supreme Court set out to "correct a threshold error in the Second Circuit's analysis."[15] The question certified for review, he continued, was not one of jurisdiction. Rather, the focus rested squarely on whether the plaintiffs' allegations entitled them to relief under the securities laws. In a sweeping fashion, the

---

[11] Robert Morrison—the named petitioner—was a U.S. investor who had purchased National's American deposit receipts (ADRs). ADRs purchased by Morrison represented an ownership interest in National shares on deposit with the New York Stock Exchange (NYSE). His claims against National, however, were subject to dismissal for failure to allege damages, a required element of §10(b). By the time the Supreme Court granted *certiorari*, there remained only foreign plaintiffs who had purchased National shares on foreign exchanges.

[12] *Morrison*, 547 F.3d at 176.

[13] Id. (emphasis added).

[14] *Morrison*, 130 S. Ct. at 2875.

[15] Id. at 2876-77

Supreme Court resolved the jurisdictional question by pointing to 15 U.S.C. §78aa, which provides, in relevant part, that

> The district courts of the United States … shall have exclusive
> jurisdiction of violations of the [Exchange Act] and the rules and
> regulations thereunder, and of all suits in equity and actions at law
> brought to enforce any liability or duty created by the [Exchange Act]
> or the rules and regulations thereunder.

Having resolved the jurisdictional issue, the Supreme Court turned next to the merits of the case, determining "what conduct §10(b) prohibits." The majority opinion held that §10(b) does not provide a foreign plaintiff with a viable claim for relief in connection with alleged misconduct involving foreign securities transactions. In so doing, the *Morrison* court noted that "it is a longstanding principle of American law that legislation of Congress, unless a contrary intent appears, is meant to apply it only within the territorial jurisdiction of the United States."[16] It further observed that "unless there is the affirmative intention of the Congress clearly expressed to give a statute extraterritorial effect, we must presume it is primarily concerned with domestic conditions."[17] The Supreme Court did not detect any such legislative intent regarding extraterritorial application of §10(b).

In an abrupt break with the Second Circuit's longstanding embrace of its "conducts and effects" test, the Supreme Court fashioned a new two-prong "transactional test" to determine the applicability of §10(b) in any given context. Accordingly, plaintiffs must establish that the purchase or sale of securities (1) "is made in the United States" or (2) "involves a security listed on a domestic exchange." Applying the transactional test, the Supreme Court concluded that the *Morrison* plaintiffs did not demonstrate the relevant transactions were made in the United States or, alternatively, the securities at issue were listed on any domestic exchange, and as a result, it affirmed dismissal and, in doing so, it seemingly dispensed with the Second Circuit's "conducts and effects" test. The watershed decision in *Morrison* would have immediate implications for so-called "foreign-cubed" cases.[18] Importantly for the purposes of this chapter, *Morrison* provided Tourre with a potential lifeline in the pending enforcement litigation.

---

[16] *Morrison*, 130 S. Ct. at 2875 (internal quotations omitted).

[17] *Morrison*, 130 S. Ct. at 2875.

[18] *Plumbers' Union Local No. 12 Pension Fund v. Swiss Reinsurance Co.*, ___ F. Supp. 2d ___, No. 08 Civ. 1958, 2010 WL 3860397, at *7 (S.D.N.Y. Oct. 4, 2010), citing and quoting *Morrison*, 130 S. Ct. at 2875. ("The suit resolved in Morrison was a 'foreign-cubed' action: it involved 'foreign plaintiffs suing foreign and American defendants for misconduct in connection with securities traded on foreign exchanges.'")

3.3.2 Tourre Sought Judgment on the Pleadings Based on *Morrison*

In light of the developments in *Morrison*, Tourre moved to dismiss the complaint against him for failure to state a claim for relief.[19] He maintained that the commission—contrary to the dictates of the Supreme Court—had not been able to show that any ABACUS-related transaction took place in the United States. The sole investor identified in the SEC complaint was IKB, a German-based bank. According to the remaining defendant, IKB purchased ABACUS notes outside the United States pursuant to Regulation S (Reg. S). In an attempt to characterize the ABACUS transaction as not falling within the purview of federal securities laws, Tourre noted that "Regulation S is available only for offers and sales of securities outside the United States."[20]

In support of his position, the defendant cited a string of post-*Morrison* opinions that applied the new transactional test. In *Cornwell v. Credit Suisse Group*, for instance, plaintiffs alleged that the defendants, CSG, made material misrepresentations concerning risk management practices during the collapse of the domestic housing market.[21] The case involved American investors who purchased shares of a foreign entity on a foreign exchange— that is, the archetypal "foreign-squared" claim. The plaintiffs advocated a narrow reading of *Morrison*, limiting its holding strictly to so-called "foreign-cubed" cases. In a derisive opinion, however, Judge Victor Marrero of the Southern District of New York stated unequivocally that he was "not convinced that the Supreme Court designed *Morrison* to be squeezed, as in spandex, only in the factual strait jacket of its holding."[22] He lauded the transactional test as "embodying the clarity, simplicity, and consistency that the tests from the Second and other circuits lacked."[23] Carving out an exception for foreign-squared cases would dilute the *Morrison* holding.

The gravamen of Tourre's motion is what he maintains is the preclusive effect of *Morrison* in connection with ABACUS structuring and marketing. Tourre contended, somewhat persuasively, that "[a]s the [ABACUS] notes were not listed on any exchange, the SEC cannot carry its burden of proving that the conduct alleged in the Complaint violated the federal securities laws unless it can prove, *inter alia*, that the transactions alleged in the

---

[19] Parenthetically, the defendant's motion to dismiss for failure to state a claim was treated as a motion for judgment on the pleadings under FRCP 12(c)—reason being that an answer had already been submitted to the court.

[20] Pl. Mem. at 12.

[21] ___ F. Supp. 2d ___, No. 08 Civ. 3758 (VM), 2010 WL3069597 (S.D.N.Y. July 27, 2010).

[22] Pl. Mem. at 4.

[23] Pl. Mem. at 3.

complaint took place in the United States."[24] While the defendant also relied on other contemporaneous securities litigation matters, none seem to provide as staunch a defense of the *Morrison* ruling as *Cornwell*. However, *Cornwell*, as well as the other cases Tourre cited, spoke directly to the second prong of the transactional test (i.e., whether the purchase or sale at issue involved a security listed on a domestic exchange). Tourre therefore placed undue emphasis on cases involving foreign exchange-traded securities. For this reason, there is conspicuous dissonance between the defendant's dispositive motion argument and the supporting case law.

3.3.3 The SEC Opposition Advanced an Expansive and Malleable *Morrison*

As the SEC noted correctly in its reply brief, the authority on which Tourre relied is inapposite. Indeed, those cases "involved securities traded on foreign exchanges, rather than non-exchange transactions like those in [the present] case."[25] The Commission, in response, developed two lines of attack and in the process buttressed its case factually. First, the SEC called the court's attention to those post-*Morrison* cases involving *nonexchange* transactions, advancing the position that the "sale" of securities [as required under Section 10(b)] encompassed the "entire selling process." Second, it argued in favor of a narrow reading of Regulation S, limiting its scope only to the registration requirement—not to the antifraud provisions—of the federal securities laws.

The Commission first invited the court to consider the broad definition of "offer."[26] It then asserted that, consonant with *Morrison*, courts must review the "entire selling process" to determine whether any given transaction(s) occurred in the United States, a faint echo of the now abandoned "conduct and effects" test. Taking an expansive approach, the SEC argued that numerous circumstances demonstrated that IKB's purchase took place in the United States. It highlighted that, when the ABACUS deal was being finalized, Goldman was a U.S. broker–dealer headquartered in New York City. Further, Tourre—Goldman's employee who was primarily responsible for structuring the transaction—also worked at the same New York office. The SEC buttressed its case factually to place ABACUS within the definitional mould of an offer. According to the Commission, for the purpose of satisfying the minimal federal pleading requirements, it was sufficient to show that Tourre (1) sent false and misleading marketing and offering

---

[24] Def. Mem. at 9.

[25] Pl. Opp. at 10, n. 2.

[26] Under §2(a)(3) of the 1933 Securities Act, the definition of a securities offering is "every attempt to offer or dispose of, or solicitation of an offer to buy, a security or interest in a security, for value." 15 U.S.C. §77b(a)(3).

materials (e.g., term sheet, flip book, and offering memorandum) to IKB, (2) maintained contact with IKB to negotiate and finalize ABACUS, and (3) met with an ACA representative to promote the transaction. In the SEC's view, these factual predicates, *in toto*, established that Tourre "attempt[ed]," "offer[ed] to dispose," and "solicit[ed] an offer to buy" securities. Together, the events confirm that the ABACUS transaction occurred in the United States.

As mentioned earlier, Tourre sought the refuge of Reg. S in his legal reasoning. The SEC, meanwhile, maintained that his reliance on Reg. S was misguided. According to the SEC, that provision of the 1933 Securities Act operates merely as a safe harbor from public registration requirements for certain offerings are "deemed to occur outside the United States."[27] The SEC advanced a narrow reading of Reg. S, relating only to the registration requirements under Securities Act §5, but not of any federal antifraud provision. In support of its position, the Commission relied on a statement to that effect found in the preliminary notes to Reg. S.[28] The only case cited on this point is the Supreme Court decision in *SEC v. National Securities, Inc.*, where the defendant tried to constrict the scope of the antifraud provisions. In *National Securities*, the plaintiff–shareholders were misled into approving the merger of insurance companies. Tourre invoked Rule 133 of the Securities Act, which provides that no sale or offer shall be deemed to be involved in connection with certain corporate reorganization. The Supreme Court, however, rejected the defendant's argument and held that Rule 133 had no bearing on the antifraud provisions:

> The rule is specifically made applicable only to cases involving §5 of the 1933 Act; this case arises under §10(b) of the 1934 Act. Although the interdependence of the various sections of the securities laws is certainly a relevant factor in any interpretation of the language Congress has chosen, ordinary rules of statutory construction still apply. The meaning of particular phrases must be determined in context. Congress itself has cautioned that the same words may take on a different coloration in different sections of the securities laws.[29]

Drawing on the Supreme Court's excerpted language stated earlier, the SEC contended that an issuer who offers securities under the Reg. S safe harbor cannot elude the sweeping reach of §10(b) based merely on availing itself of an exemption from registration requirements.

---

[27] 17 C.F.R. §230.903.

[28] The relevant text reads: "The following rules relate solely to the application of Section 5 of the Securities Act of 1933…and not to antifraud or other provisions of the federal securities laws."

[29] 393 U.S. 453, 466 (1969).

3.3.4 Tourre Retreats from *Morrison* and Colorfully Attacks the SEC Position as Encouraging "Judicial-Speculation-Made-Law"

Tourre filed a reply memorandum on October 25, 2010, in support of his motion for judgment on the pleadings, chipping away at the Commission's original complaint. The ensuing contest centered on the sufficiency of SEC allegations in the face of the *Morrison* holding. Tourre maintained in his reply that the SEC had not satisfied the so-called "transactional test," thereby warranting dismissal. He also cautioned against accepting the Commission's subtly disguised invitation to revive and expand the previously discarded "conduct and effect" tests. To do so, he maintained, would ignore the *Morrison* precepts.

According to Tourre, the SEC complaint identified only two transactions in connection with the marketing of ABACUS, neither of which could be described credibly as domestic for *Morrison* purposes. The first transaction involved the German bank IKB as purchaser of the CDO. Specifically, IKB purchased ABACUS notes outside the United States pursuant to Reg. S. Tourre attacked the SEC position that Reg. S did not "purport to limit the territorial scope of the antifraud provisions of the federal securities laws."[30] In doing so, he explained that the SEC impermissibly expanded the application of the antifraud provisions to Reg. S in reliance on the since discredited "conduct and effects" test.[31] The second transaction involved the Dutch bank ABN AMRO as a CDS counterparty. That bearish swap, however, was executed by London-based Goldman Sachs International and ABN AMRO, operating through its London branch.

Tourre next challenged the SEC iteration of the *Morrison* transactional test, that is, the "sale" of securities encompasses the "entire selling process." The Commission, he contended, sought to resuscitate the "conduct and effects" test, yet "*Morrison* [made] clear that allegations of securities-related conduct in the United States [were] insufficient to invoke the antifraud provisions of the federal securities laws."[32] To be sure, such a departure from *Morrison*'s bright-lined rule has been met with strong opposition.[33]

---

[30] Def. Reply at 3.

[31] *Offshore Offers and Sales*, Securities Act Release No. 33-6863, 1990 WL 311658 (Apr. 24, 1990). ("While it may not be necessary for securities sold in a transaction that occurs outside the United States, but touching this country through conducts and effects, to be registered under United States securities laws, such conduct or effect have been held to provide a basis for jurisdiction under the antifraud provisions of the United States securities laws.")

[32] Def. Reply at 6.

[33] But see J.P. Elwood, *The Supreme Court and Extraterritoriality: Yesterday's Decision in Morrison v. National Australia Bank.* The Volokh Conspiracy (blog), June 25, 2010. Available at http://volokh.com/2010/06/25/the-supreme-court-and-extraterritoriality-yesterdays-decision-in-morrison-v/.

For example, in *Plumbers' Union Local No. 12 Pension Fund v. Swiss Reinsurance Co.*, the court ruled that "a purchase does not occur when and where an investor places a buy order."[34] There, a pension fund plaintiff made a series of purchase orders for shares of Swiss Re domestically, with its orders placed by traders located in Chicago. However, those orders were routed through electronic connections for purposes of matching buy and sell orders. The plaintiff's trades were ultimately executed in transactions on the SWX, a stock exchange based in Switzerland.[35] The court, in an opinion sharing the concerns expressed by Judge Marrero in *Cornwell*, neatly concluded:

> As the Supreme Court emphasized in *Morrison*, where a security is traded only on a foreign exchange, the adoption of a clear test that will avoid interference with foreign securities regulation is of paramount concern. This could not be accomplished if every security traded on a foreign exchange were subject to section 10(b) whenever an investor located in the United States placed an electronic order.

The plaintiff's claims against Swiss Re were dismissed with prejudice. If anything, *Plumber's Union* suggested that post-*Morrison* courts have been remarkably rigid when considering the pleadings of §10(b) claims. It remains to be seen whether Judge Jones is persuaded that the broad reading of the terms "offer" and "sale," as advanced by SEC lawyers, comports with *Morrison*.

3.4 CLIMAX: DODD–FRANK AFFORDS THE SECURITIES AND EXCHANGE COMMISSION EXTRATERRITORIAL JURISDICTION

In *Morrison*, the issue presented before the Supreme Court was whether a private litigant could state a claim for extraterritorial application of the U.S. securities laws. The Supreme Court's answer was a resounding "no" because Congress did not express an affirmative intent to give §10(b) any extraterritorial effect. Interestingly, one member of the *Morrison* court presaged attacks on the SEC's ability to invoke §10(b) in transnational fraud cases. Justice John Paul Stevens included a cautionary footnote in his concurring opinion, advising that *Morrison* does not "foreclose the Commission from bringing enforcement actions in additional circumstances, as no issue concerning the commission's authority is presented in this case."[36]

---

[34] ___ F. Supp. 2d ___, No. 08 Civ. 1958, 2010 WL 3860397 (S.D.N.Y. Oct. 4, 2010).
[35] Additionally, stock market transactions in Swiss Re common stock were executed, cleared, and settled on a trading platform that was a subsidiary of the SWX Swiss Exchange based in London.
[36] *Morrison*, 130 S. Ct. at 2894, n. 12.

Because §10(b) covers private litigants *and* government enforcement agencies, however, the transactional test could conceivably apply with equal force to limit transnational enforcement activity by the SEC. *Morrison* did not establish any extraterritorial jurisdiction for government agencies pursuing fraud cases under §10(b), although Justice Stevens made sure to note that the opinion rested on its own facts, pertaining to the implied *private* right of action for shareholder litigants. Nonetheless, the decision presented the potential to severely curtail SEC enforcement powers, in particular, its ability to pursue transnational cases. The following section addresses how Congress used legislative fiat to restore SEC extraterritorial enforcement authority.

3.4.1 Dodd–Frank as *Deus ex Machina*

The House–Senate Conference Committee passed the Dodd–Frank Act on June 25, 2010.[37] Almost without question, Congress was responding directly to the Supreme Court's *Morrison* ruling by empowering the SEC to pursue offshore securities fraud cases. Section 929P(b) of Dodd–Frank, for example, resurrects the "conducts and effects" test and creates express extraterritorial jurisdiction over actions brought by the SEC where (1) "conduct within the United States…constitutes significant steps in furtherance of the violation, even if the securities transaction occurs outside the United States and involves only foreign investors" or (2) "conduct occurring outside the United States…has a foreseeable substantial effect within the United States."[38] The legislative text noticeably strays from Justice Scalia's new transactional test, at least with respect to SEC enforcement activity.

Curiously, Dodd–Frank approached the issue of extraterritoriality as one of jurisdiction. The *Morrison* court, however, had decided summarily that federal courts enjoyed jurisdiction over cases involving foreign securities transactions. Moroever, the SEC (together with the solicitor general) maintained in its opposition of the *Morrison certiorari* petition that extraterritoriality raises a question of substance, not jurisdiction: "If a particular suit is otherwise an appropriate means of enforcing a 'liability or duty created by' the Exchange Act or rules promulgated thereunder by the Commission, Section 78aa unambiguously vests the district courts with jurisdiction to resolve it."[39] Some commentators contend that Dodd–Frank did nothing more than

---

[37] Dodd–Frank was passed 1 day after *Morrison* was issued.

[38] Title IX, Subtitle B, Increasing Regulatory Enforcement and Enforcement, section 929P.

[39] Brief of the United States as Amicus Curiae, *Morrison v. National Australia Bank* on Petition for Writ of Certiorari (Oct. 2009), at 9.

confer jurisdiction on the U.S. courts without addressing the substantive reach of §10(b). In a published memo to clients, George T. Conway III—counsel for National Australia Bank—contested the view that Dodd–Frank provided the SEC extraterritorial jurisdiction:

> In *National Australia Bank*, the Supreme Court reiterated the longstanding principle that the territorial scope of a federal law does not present a question of 'jurisdiction,' of a 'tribunal's power to hear a case,' but rather a question of substance—of 'what conduct' does the law 'prohibit'? The new law [Dodd–Frank Act] does not address that issue, and accordingly does not expand the territorial scope of the government's enforcement powers at all.[40]

Accordingly, the statute's extraterritoriality provision (as a result of oversight) leaves the *Morrison* holding unchanged. Dodd–Frank, after all, did not amend the text upon which the court based its transactional test.

To intimate that Dodd–Frank did not augment the substantive scope of §10(b) would ignore legislative intent. The statutory language relating to extraterritorial jurisdiction was first inserted in the congressional record shortly following the oral arguments in *Morrison*. It would make sense then that Congress—like the Second Circuit—tackled the issue as a question of jurisdiction.[41] More revealing still are the comments in the congressional record by Rep. Paul Kanjorski who contributed to the legislative drafting:

> This bill's provisions concerning the extraterritoriality, however, are intended to rebut [the] presumption against extraterritoriality [in *Morrison*] by clearly indicating that Congress intends extraterritorial application in cases brought by the SEC....

> Thus, the purpose of the language of Section 929P(b) is to make clear that in actions and proceedings brought by the SEC...the specified provisions of the [U.S. securities laws] may have extraterritorial application, and that extraterritorial application is appropriate, irrespective of whether

---

[40] Wachtell, Lipton, Rosen, and Katz, "Extraterritoriality of the Federal Securities Laws after Dodd–Frank: Partly Because of a Drafting Error, the Status Quo Should Remain Unchanged," June 21, 2010 (authored by George T. Conway III). Available at http://www.wlrk.com/webdocs/wlrknew/WLRKMemos/WLRK/WLRK.17763.10.pdf; George T. Conway III, Extraterritoriality after Dodd–Frank (Aug. 5, 2010). Available at http://blogs.law.harvard.edu/corpgov/2010/08/05/extraterritoriality-after-dodd-frank/.

[41] Prior to the scheduling of oral arguments in *Morrison*, however, the SEC (in its brief opposing the grant of *certiorari*) did frame the issue as one going to the substantive scope of Section 10(b)—not one of jurisdiction.

the securities are traded on a domestic exchange or the transactions occur in the United States, when the conduct within the United states is significant or when conduct outside the United States has a foreseeable substantial effect within the United States.[42]

Thus, Dodd–Frank expressly extended the application of §10(b) (and, more generally, the antifraud provisions of federal securities laws) extraterritorially. Courts, in turn, are unlikely to frustrate congressional intent concerning extraterritorial application of federal securities laws, particularly as the record indicates that the measure was a direct legislative response to the *Morrison* rationale.

3.4.2 Dodd–Frank Codifies the "Conduct and Effects" Test and Gives Shape to an Expanded Enforcement Regime

With Dodd–Frank, the focus shifted anew to pre-*Morrison* jurisprudence and articulation of the "conduct and effects" test, primarily the watershed case of *Bersch v. Drexel Firestone, Inc.*,[43] decided by the Second Circuit. The threshold inquiry in *Bersch* was "whether Congress would have wished the precious resources of United States courts and law enforcement agencies to be devoted to [foreign transactions] rather than to leave the problem to foreign countries."[44] Courts faced this same issue with some frequency and eventually developed a two-prong test to guide the pertinent analysis. Accordingly, jurisdiction would be found when (1) "the wrongful conduct occurred in the United States" and (2) "had a substantial effect in the United States or upon United States citizens."[45] The Second Circuit's conjunctive test became the focus of increasing scrutiny, primarily because it was not anchored in any statutory text and could yield inconsistent results. It also underwent several permutations, causing the Seventh Circuit to sardonically remark in a leading opinion that "[a]lthough the circuits…seem to agree that there are some transnational situations to which the antifraud provisions of the securities laws are applicable, the agreement appears to end at that point."[46] Still, pre-*Morrison* juridical commentary regarding the breadth and scope of the "conduct and effects" test has reemerged with fresh relevance, with courts expected to reconcile these cases with the new statutory text.

---

[42] 156 Cong. Rec. H5235 2010 (June 30, 2010).
[43] 519 F.2d 974 (2d Cir. 1975).
[44] Id. at 985.
[45] *SEC v. Berger*, 322 F.3d 187, 192-93 (2d Cir. 2003).
[46] *Kauthar SDN BHD v. Sternberg*, 149 F.3d 659, 667 (7th Cir. 1998).

The SEC, for its part, is expected to advocate for a broad formulation of the test. The Third, Eighth, and Ninth Circuits have employed the least restrictive standard. In *Continental Grain Pty. Ltd. v. Pacific Oilseeds, Inc.*, for example, the Eighth Circuit required only that a pleading allege domestic conduct "was in furtherance of a fraudulent scheme and was significant with respect to its accomplishment."[47] More permissive still, the Third Circuit asserted jurisdiction "where at least some activity designed to further a fraudulent scheme occurs within this country."[48] These formulations permit the Commission to test statutory limits, while continuing to pursue transnational enforcement aggressively. To be sure, the newly emboldened SEC would be remiss not to push for the adoption of the "direct cause" standard it advanced in *Morrison* which would find jurisdiction exists "if significant conduct material to the fraud's success occurs in the United States." It remains to be seen how the Commission will litigate cases under the disjunctive Dodd–Frank variation of the conduct and effects test. For now, SEC investigations and settlements in connection with transnational fraud cases may offer insight into the agency's likely approach in the future.

3.5 CONCLUSION—TOURRE AND HIS COHORTS CELEBRATE A PYRRHIC VICTORY

Under Dodd–Frank, the SEC benefited from an express expansion of its regulatory authority. In the context of the Tourre matter, however, it stands to suffer a short-lived defeat if the court rules in favor of the defendant on the basis of *Morrison* and declines to apply Dodd–Frank §929P(b) retrospectively. Excepting some mild form of embarrassment, the SEC's enforcement program will emerge generally unscathed, if not more robust in the aftermath. In fact, arguments raised in the parties' filings could conceivably be relegated to the legal dustbin. Following the enactment of Dodd–Frank, the Commission may resume enforcement litigation against alleged transnational fraudsters, whether the subject transactions are "long" or "short." As it does so, courts will commit themselves to reworking the "conduct [or] effects" test, mindful of "the difficulty of applying such vague formulations."[49] *Morrison*'s strict, bright-line rule has given way to an amorphous test under which the SEC is expected to increase its regulatory reach with new vigor.

---

[47] 592 F.2d 409, 421 (8th Cir. 1979).
[48] *SEC v. Kasser*, 548 F.2d 109, 114 (3d Cir. 1977).
[49] *Morrison*, 130 S. Ct. at 2879.

BIBLIOGRAPHY

Bersch v. Drexel Firestone, Inc., 519 F.2d 974, 985 (2d Cir. 1975).

Brief of the United States as Amicus Curiae. (2009). *Morrison v. National Australia Bank* on Petition for Writ of Certiorari (2009, October 27). Retrieved from http://www.sec.gov/litigation/briefs/2009/morrison1009.pdf.

Code of Federal Regulations, 17 C.F.R. § 230.903 (2008).

Cont'l Grain Pty. Ltd. v. Pacific Oilseeds, Inc., 592 F.2d 409, 421 (8th Cir. 1979).

Conway, G. T. (2010, August 5). *Extraterritoriality after Dodd-Frank.* Retrieved from http://blogs.law.harvard.edu/corpgov/2010/08/05/extraterritoriality-after-dodd-frank/.

Cornwell v. Credit Suisse Grp., 779 F. Supp. 2d 620, 624, 625 (S.D.N.Y. 2010).

Dodd-Frank Wall Street Reform and Consumer Protection Act § 929P, Pub. L. No. 111–203, 124 Stat. 1376 (2010).

Elwood, J. P. (2010, June 25). *The supreme court and extraterritoriality: Yesterday's decision in Morrison v. National Australia Bank,* The Volokh Conspiracy (blog). Retrieved from http://volokh.com/2010/06/25/the-supreme-court-and-extraterritoriality-yesterdays-decision-in-morrison-v/.

Kanjorski, Rep. Paul E. (2010, June 30). 156 Cong. Rec. H5233, H5237 (statement). Retrieved from http://www.gpo.gov/fdsys/pkg/CREC-2010-06-30/pdf/CREC-2010-06-30-pt1-PgH5233.pdf#page=1.

Kauthar SDN BHD v. Sternberg, 149 F.3d 659, 667 (7th Cir. 1998).

Morrison v. Nat'l Australia Bank Ltd., 561 U.S. ___, 130 S. Ct. 2869 *passim* (2010).

Plumbers' Union Local No. 12 Pension Fund v. Swiss Reinsurance Co., 753 F. Supp. 2d 166, 176, 177 (S.D.N.Y. 2010).

SEC v. Berger, 322 F.3d 187, 192–93 (2d Cir. 2003).

SEC v. Goldman Sachs & Co., No. 10 Civ. 3229 (BSJ) (S.D.N.Y. filed April 16, 2010) (complaint).

SEC v. Goldman Sachs & Co., No. 10 Civ. 3229 (BSJ) (S.D.N.Y.) (plaintiff's opposition).

SEC v. Goldman Sachs & Co., No. 10 Civ. 3229 (BSJ) (S.D.N.Y.) (defendant's motion for judgment on the pleadings).

SEC v. Goldman Sachs & Co., No. 10 Civ. 3229 (BSJ) (S.D.N.Y.) (defendant's reply).

SEC v. Kasser, 548 F.2d 109, 114 (3d Cir. 1977).

SEC v. Nat'l Secs, Inc., 393 U.S. 453, 466 (1969).

Securities Act Release No. 33-6863, 1990 WL 311658. (1990, April 24). *Offshore offers and sales.*

Securities Act of 1933, ch. 38, tit. 1, § 1, 48 Stat. 74. (1933, May 27). 15 U.S.C. § 77a *et seq.*

Wachtell, Lipton, Rosen, & Katz. (2010, June 21). *Extraterritoriality of the federal securities laws after Dodd-Frank: Partly because of a drafting error, the status quo should remain unchanged.* Retrieved from http://www.wlrk.com/webdocs/wlrknew/WLRKMemos/WLRK/WLRK.17763.10.pdf.

CHAPTER 4

Regulating Short Sales in the 21st Century

Houman B. Shadab

CONTENTS

ABSTRACT

This chapter provides an overview of how the short selling of securities is regulated by the U.S. Securities and Exchange Commission (SEC). Existing regulation of short sales prohibits any party from short selling stocks that display significant price declines and, consistent with the SEC's approach toward self-regulation, requires private "trading centers" to implement and enforce the regulation. Several transactions are exempt from the regulation, and the SEC has reserved the authority to make additional exemptions. Current short sale regulation is a result of the Dodd–Frank Act of 2010 and a flurry of temporary and experimental SEC rule making during the financial crisis of 2008, which had its roots in the June 2007 repeal of short sale price restrictions—the first significant change to short sale regulations since their inception in 1938.

KEYWORDS

Dodd–Frank Wall Street Reform and Consumer Protection Act; Naked short selling; Regulation SHO; Rule 10a-1; Rule 201; Securities and Exchange Commission; Tick test; Trading centers; Uptick rule.

4.1 INTRODUCTION

The sale of a security by the owner of the security is a "long" sale. The sale of a security that is borrowed or otherwise not owned is a "short" sale. Short sales are undertaken in order to profit from a price decline, hedge risk, or engage in arbitrage. This chapter provides an overview of how short selling is regulated by the U.S. Securities and Exchange Commission (SEC). Short selling is regulated under the SEC's authority to prohibit fraud and insider trading and requires disclosures of positions in publicly traded securities by institutional investment managers. Short sale regulation is also a product of rules that have the goal of preventing market manipulation that artificially depresses stock prices or results in or exacerbates significant price declines.

For nearly 70 years, the SEC's regulatory framework applicable to short selling remained unchanged since it was first enacted in the 1930s. This framework prohibited fraud in connection with short sales and imposed a price test that permitted short sales only at a price equal to or above the previous market price at which the security was sold. But the early part of the 21st century put an end to the SEC's original short sale regulatory framework and the dormancy of short sale regulatory actions. In response to market developments and a growing recognition of the ineffectiveness of the price test, in 2007 the SEC adopted a new framework in the form of Regulation SHO. At first, Regulation SHO eliminated the short sale price test and imposed new rules to prevent failures to deliver securities resulting from manipulative naked short selling. However, after taking a series of emergency short sale actions in 2008 in response to the dramatic price declines associated with the financial crisis, the SEC amended Regulation SHO in 2009 and 2010 with stricter rules to prevent failures to deliver and also introduced a new price test that currently prohibits short sales if a 10% 1-day price decrease has taken place unless the sale is higher than the best available national bid. Regulation of short sales also stems from the Dodd–Frank Wall Street Reform and Consumer Protection Act (the Dodd–Frank Act), which was enacted on July 21, 2010. The Dodd–Frank Act requires disclosure of short sale positions by institutional investment managers, broker–dealer communications to customers regarding certain aspects of securities lending activities, and the SEC to conduct and report to Congress on certain short sale-related studies.

4.2 U.S. SHORT SALE REGULATION BACKGROUND

4.2.1 The Tick Test

In 1934, the Securities and Exchange Act (Exchange Act) gave the SEC the power to regulate short sales pursuant to its mission to protect investors and maintain market efficiency and integrity. The Exchange Act broadly authorizes the SEC to regulate the trading activities of market participants, including brokers, stock exchanges, and investors. In particular, Section 10(a) of the Exchange Act makes it unlawful for any person to directly or indirectly use the means of national commerce to engage in short sales in violation of SEC rules and regulations. The first official restriction on short selling activities came in 1938 when the SEC adopted Rule 10a-1. The rule placed a floor on the price at which securities were permitted to be sold short and applied only to exchange-traded securities. Subject to certain exceptions, Rule 10a-1 prohibited short sales at a price lower than the previous market price at which the security was sold. In what later came to be known as the "tick test," Rule 10a-1 specifically prohibited short sales unless the sale was for a price above that of the immediately preceding sale or the same as the last sale price if that last sale price was higher than the prior different price. Limitations on short selling were generally intended to prevent the manipulation or artificial depression of share prices regardless of whether short sellers intended such outcomes. The tick test was specifically meant to further the policy objectives of permitting robust short selling activity during market upswings, while at the same time preventing short sales from causing or exacerbating market price declines. Rule 10a-1 remained in effect and largely unchanged for approximately 70 years.

During its existence, however, the Rule 10a-1 tick test was slowly eroded by a series of additional legal exemptions that came about in response to several governmental inquiries into short selling and also changes in market practices and infrastructure. In 1963, the SEC conducted a study that concluded that existing short sale rules failed to prevent manipulation or depression of stock prices, but it did not take any regulatory action. In 1976, the SEC sought to reexamine its short sale restrictions comprehensively and proposed three different rules that would have had the effect of suspending the tick test temporarily. Due to the overwhelming majority of comments filed in opposition to the proposed rules that would have suspended the tick test temporarily, including opposition from the major stock exchanges, the SEC withdrew the proposed rules. In 1991, the U.S. House Committee on Government Operations issued a report generally supportive of the role of short selling in financial markets and critical of much of the opposition voiced against short sales. The 1991 report was nonetheless supportive of the restrictions imposed by the tick test. It recommended mandatory reporting of large short sale positions, that data on weekly short selling be collected systematically, and that the NASDAQ system should also regulate short sales (which the NASDAQ eventually did in 1994 in what came to be known as the "bid test"). In October 1999, the SEC issued a concept release with eight proposed changes to its short sale rules, including making an exception for hedging transactions and even eliminating Rule 10a-1 entirely. Market developments that eroded the need for the tick test included decimalization of U.S. stock prices in 2001, automation of market trading, and increased transparency and regulatory surveillance by national securities exchanges allowing them to monitor trading in real time. One result of such developments, for example, is that the SEC in 2003 exempted alternative trading systems from the tick test. In addition, the SEC recognized that the growing use of trading strategies involving short sales may have caused its existing regulation of short sales to undermine beneficial trading activities.

4.2.2 Tick Test Elimination and 2008 Temporary Emergency Rules

Due to the SEC's ongoing uncertainty regarding the effectiveness of the short sale restrictions of Rule 10a-1 and recognizing the need to update its rules, in 2004 the SEC adopted Regulation SHO and created a new framework for short sale regulation. Rule 201 of Regulation SHO temporarily suspended the tick test and the price test of any national securities exchange. The purpose of the suspension was to allow the SEC to conduct a study to determine the tick test's effectiveness in achieving its policy goals in regulating short sales in light of governmental studies and market developments that had taken place since Rule 10-a1 was originally adopted. SEC's data gathered during the temporary tick test suspension were mixed. The SEC found that its short sale regulations did not have a significant impact on the daily volatility of actively traded stocks and effectively reduced short sale volumes. However, the SEC's report also found only limited evidence that the tick test distorted prices and that it actually increased quote depths. Nonetheless, in response to the SEC's own report and other staff analyses, and after considering market developments and numerous studies conducted by independent researchers on the impact of short sale price restrictions, effective July 3, 2007, the SEC completely eliminated the tick test and prohibited any exchange from adopting restrictions on short sales.

In addition to eliminating any short sale price tests, Regulation SHO also created a new framework to prevent abusive naked short selling. In contrast to "covered" short sales, a naked short sale takes place when a short seller does not borrow the security and fails to deliver it within the standard 3-day settlement period (also referred to as "T+3"). As initially adopted, Regulation SHO required broker–dealers to reasonably believe that a security could be borrowed so as to be delivered timely before affecting a short sale and also required broker–dealers to correct certain failures to deliver that persisted for 13 consecutive settlement days.

In 2008, in response to concerns about abusive short selling exacerbating the declining share prices of publicly traded companies due to the then ensuing financial crisis, the SEC issued several temporary rules to prevent panicked selling and sharp price declines. In July 2008, the SEC temporarily effectively banned naked short selling by instituting a "hard T+3 close-out requirement." This requirement prohibited a broker–dealer from affecting short sales in the stock of certain financial firms unless the seller would be able to borrow the security and deliver it on the sale's settlement date (i.e., 3 days after the transactions date). Due to ongoing concerns about manipulative short selling, on September 17, 2008, the SEC adopted a new rule that broadened the temporary hard close-out requirement to the shares of all public company securities, which remained effective until July 31, 2009.

On September 18, 2008, the SEC, acting in cooperation with the U.K. Financial Services Authority, also issued a temporary rule that prohibited short selling the shares of nearly 800 financial firms, including major banks, broker–dealers, and insurance companies (the rule expired in October 2008). Several other leading financial jurisdictions such as France, Germany, and Australia in September 2008 also instituted their own temporary bans on short selling the shares of financial companies. In addition, from October 2008 to August 1, 2009, the SEC issued new temporary rules that required institutional investors owning public shares having at least $100 million in value to confidentially disclose to the SEC short sale positions exceeding stated thresholds. Although now all expired, these and other temporary rules shaped the SEC's current approach to short sale regulation.

4.3 CURRENT SECURITIES AND EXCHANGE COMMISSION REGULATION OF SHORT SELLING ACTIVITY

The current U.S. federal short sale regulatory regime is made up of five components. The first finds its root in antifraud provision Exchange Act Rule 10b-5 and other antifraud laws. These laws prohibit misrepresentations and insider trading in connection with short selling and the use of short sales to implement a scheme of market manipulation such as through abusive naked short selling that drives down market prices. Second, short sales are regulated by a price test that prohibits sales below the national best bid when there is a 10% or greater daily price decline in an exchange-listed equity security. Third, short sales are subject to disclosure requirements. Securities exchanges, in their capacity as self-regulatory organizations subject to SEC regulation and oversight, must publicly disclose aggregate short sale volume for each security daily and individual short sale transactions monthly. Certain institutional investment managers, under rules to be promulgated by the SEC pursuant to the Dodd–Frank Act, will also be required to publicly disclose information relating to their short sales. In addition, the execution of short sale trades are governed "locate" and "close-out" requirements that place relatively stringent requirements on certain market participants for failing to timely deliver equity securities to purchasers by the standard 3-day settlement date. Finally, registered broker–dealers must notify customers that they may choose to disallow lending of their fully paid securities in connection with short sales and also that the broker–dealer may receive compensation from lending customer securities in connection with short sales.

4.3.1 The Rule 201 Price Test

In response to increased market volatility and the sharp decreases in public share prices that took place after Regulation SHO eliminated short sale price tests in 2007, in February 2010 the SEC amended Regulation SHO and introduced a new short sale price test that would be triggered by a significant share price decline. Amended Rule 201 of Regulation SHO combines a "circuit breaker" approach with an "alternative uptick" rule: if the price of an exchange-listed equity security declines by 10% or more in 1 day, absent an exception Rule 201 prohibits a national securities exchange, alternative trading system, or other "trading center" from affecting a short sale unless the price is above the current national best bid (i.e., the highest available bid price). The alternative uptick rule generally places long sellers ahead of short sellers when a security's price is in substantial decline with the goal of stabilizing share prices and maintaining investor confidence. The SEC's view is that creating a 10% price decline trigger strikes the appropriate balance between minimizing impediments to the price discovery and liquidity providing functions of short selling, while at the same time preventing market manipulation and the exacerbation of price declines.

Rule 201(b)(1) contains the text of the price test and states that

> [a] trading center shall establish, maintain, and enforce written policies and procedures reasonably designed to: (i) Prevent the execution or

display of a short sale order of a covered security at a price that is less than or equal to the current national best bid if the price of that covered security decreases by 10% or more from the covered security's closing price as determined by the listing market for the covered security as of the end of regular trading hours on the prior day; and (ii) Impose the requirements of paragraph (b)(1)(i) of this section for the remainder of the day and the following day when a national best bid for the covered security is calculated and disseminated on a current and continuing basis by a plan processor pursuant to an effective national market system plan.

"Covered securities" for the purposes of Rule 201 mean any national market system stock and generally include all securities listed on a national securities exchange regardless of whether they are traded on the exchange or over the counter. Rule 201 does not apply to securities listed on the OTC Bulletin Board system or elsewhere in the over-the-counter market. Nonetheless, in adopting Rule 201, the SEC indicated its willingness not only to extend the rule to cover over-the-counter stocks, but also to equity derivatives and synthetic short positions. In addition, the SEC did not specify how far above the current national bid test a short sale price would have to take place at to be permitted when a circuit breaker is triggered, so long as the sale is in compliance with minimum price increment rules. The short sale price test would apply through the end of the day on which it is triggered and on the following day.

Trading centers are required to have written policies and procedures to ensure compliance with Rule 201. Trading centers must also be able to determine when the short sale price test is triggered and are allowed to reprice impermissibly low short sale prices upward to ensure compliance with the alternative uptick price test. A trading center whose policies and procedures are not in compliance with Rule 201 may be subject to SEC enforcement action and liability for aiding and abetting the violation of Regulation SHO or federal prohibitions of fraud and market manipulation. Rule 201 only applies to short sales executed on U.S. domestic trading centers. However, U.S. brokers are not permitted to transmit orders to offshore centers to avoid application of the rule once a customer has agreed to a transaction.

Under Regulation SHO, broker–dealers must mark all equity trades as "long," "short," or "short exempt." A trade marked "short exempt" must be permitted by a trading center to be executed or displayed even if the order is at a price that is less than or equal to the current national best bid. Once a 10% price decline triggers the Rule 201 short sale price test, a broker–dealer affecting trades in compliance with the price test (i.e., above the national best bid) may mark the order as "short exempt" pursuant to Rule 201(c)'s broker–dealer exception. This provision places a compliance burden on brokers seeking to prefilter customer orders before they are transmitted to trading centers, while at the same time allowing brokers to manage their order flow more effectively. In addition, Rule 201(d) contains several general exceptions to the price test that also permit a broker–dealer to mark the following types of short sale orders as exempt:

- short sales of "deemed to own" securities that owners intend to deliver as soon as restrictions on delivery are removed;
- short sales of a security by a market maker to offset customer odd-lot orders;
- certain arbitrage transactions involving domestic securities convertible or exchangeable into the securities sold, or international transactions involving cross-border price differentials;
- short sales by an underwriter or member of a syndicate (or other group) related to either an overallotment of securities or a distribution of securities through a rights or standby underwriting commitment;
- short sales by broker–dealers that facilitate customer purchases or customer long sales on a riskless principal basis;
- short sales that meet specific volume-weighted average price criteria.

The SEC is also empowered to grant additional exemptions from the Rule 201 price test as it deems necessary to further its policy objectives. Pursuant to the Dodd–Frank Act, the SEC is required to conduct a study by July 21, 2011, on the merits of a voluntary pilot program in which the trades of public companies' shares would be reported in real time through the consolidated tape and marked "short," "market maker short," "buy," "buy to cover," or "long."

4.3.2 Public Disclosure by Institutional Investment Managers

Section 929X of the Dodd–Frank Act orders the SEC to promulgate rules for institutional investment managers to disclose their short sale positions. Institutional investment managers that own $100 million or more in publicly traded securities must disclose such holdings on a quarterly basis on Form 13F. Pursuant to rules the SEC must promulgate, institutional investment managers must also publicly disclose information relating to their short sale positions, including the issuer and aggregate amount of each security sold short. These short sale disclosures will have to be made on at least a monthly basis. By July 21, 2012, the SEC is also required to conduct a study on the feasibility of mandatory real-time short sale disclosures, either to the public or only to the SEC and the Financial Industry Regulatory Authority.

4.3.3 Borrowing and Delivery Requirements

Regulation SHO also seeks to reduce failures to deliver securities within their standard 3-day settlement period and to undermine abusive naked short selling. Regulation SHO's "locate" requirement from Rule 203 generally requires that prior to accepting a short sale order in an equity security, a broker–dealer (and not the seller) must have actually borrowed the security, arranged to borrow the security, or at least have reasonable grounds to believe that a security can be borrowed so as to be delivered on time. Exceptions to these requirements include short sales in securities subject to certain restrictions on delivery and short sales by a market maker undertaking market-making activities for the security sold short. On October 14, 2008, the SEC adopted a new antifraud rule (Rule 10b-21) specifically prohibiting short sellers from misrepresenting to broker–dealers the source of their borrowable shares or whether they own the securities being sold short. This antifraud rule is targeted directly at what the SEC views as abusive naked short selling—a seller's intentional failure to deliver securities in time for settlement by misrepresenting the source of the securities or their ownership.

On July 27, 2009, the SEC adopted Rule 204 of Regulation SHO to reduce persistent failures to deliver by clearing brokers with a relatively strict "close-out" requirement. Rule 204 generally requires a clearing broker (i.e., a "participant of a registered clearing agency") with a failure to deliver position in any equity security to purchase or borrow the security and immediately close out the position. An "immediate" close-out must take place by the beginning of trading hours on the settlement day after the trade's settlement date. Exceptions to this rule include failures to deliver that result from long sales, which permit the clearing broker to purchase or borrow the security and close out the position by the third day after the settlement date. In addition, a failure to deliver a security that a clearing broker is "deemed to own" may be closed out 35 calendar days after the trade through a purchase of the security and so long as the participant intends to deliver the security as soon as delivery restrictions are removed. Finally, a failure to deliver resulting from certain market-making activities permits the clearing broker to purchase or borrow the security to be closed out by the third consecutive settlement date following the original settlement date.

Failing to comply with these close-out requirements will subject the clearing broker *and* any broker–dealer sending trades to the clearing broker to a "preborrow" requirement. Until the clearing broker has closed out the fail to deliver position by purchasing the security, the preborrow requirement prohibits the clearing broker, and any broker–dealer sending them trades, from short selling the security unless they have already borrowed or arranged to borrow the security. Rule 204 attempts to encourage broker–dealers to close out early (i.e., prior to the close-out date) when a clearing broker has failed to deliver by allowing a broker–dealer to claim a "prefail credit" from closing out early. The credit prevents the broker–dealer from being subject to the next day close-out and preborrow requirements if the following conditions are met: the purchase or borrow is bona fide, executed after the trade date but no later than the settlement date (i.e., the purchase or borrow is executed on T+1, 2, or 3), and is sufficient to cover the failure to deliver position, and the broker–dealer has a net flat or net long position in the security on the day it is purchased or borrowed. Clearing brokers may also allocate a failure to deliver position to the broker–dealer actually responsible for the fail, thereby relieving other broker–dealers that send trades to the clearing broker from the preborrow requirement.

Pursuant to the Dodd–Frank Act, the SEC was required to conduct a study by July 21, 2012, on the impact of the foregoing rules on the incidence of failures to deliver and delivery of shares on the fourth day following the short sale transaction.

4.4 CONCLUSION

Although U.S. regulation of short sales remained fundamentally unchanged for nearly its first 70 years of existence, it is unlikely that another several decades will pass before fundamental changes are again introduced into the way the SEC regulates short sales. Developments in market microstructure now happen at a faster pace than in the 20th century, which makes it more likely that any particular regulatory framework will be rendered ineffective, counterproductive, or even obsolete in the near future. In addition, ongoing efforts at financial reform under the Dodd–Frank Act and other initiatives will likely keep the technicalities of short sale regulation permanently unsettled.

Differences in opinion among the SEC's body of five commissioners responsible for approving any new rule making may also keep short sale regulation an area that is revisited relatively frequently. For example, the most recent alternative uptick rule price test was approved by a vote of 3-2, with Commissioners Kathleen Casey and Troy Paredes issuing strong dissents. Among other concerns, the dissenting commissioners questioned the empirical basis for the price test based on academic studies, whether the test would actually achieve its intended goal, and whether the overall benefits outweighed its costs. These types of divisions among commissioners indicate that any particular short sale regulation may be amended if the rules are revisited once the makeup of the commissioners changes. Indeed, in their release adopting the alternative uptick rule, even the three approving commissioners noted with respect to particular exceptions and other rules that alternative approaches could also likely achieve their stated goals in regulating short sales and that they were exercising their collective judgment in choosing a particular approach and not another.

Accordingly, although the SEC has recently returned to its original approach to short sale regulation in implementing a price test, market participants should be aware that there is no guarantee that a price test or any of its particular exceptions or approaches will remain in place for an extended period of time. Rules with respect to locate and close-out requirements in particular may be amenable to change to the extent that the SEC is influenced by economic studies specifically analyzing naked short sales. A study by Fotak and colleagues (2009), for instance, found that naked short sales generally contribute to price quality, which may undermine the rationale for relatively strict locate and close-out requirements. The studies that the SEC must conduct pursuant to Dodd–Frank may also call aspects of the current short sale regulatory regime into question. In short, market developments, differences in opinion among commissioners, an extended period of share price volatility or stability, and continued governmental and academic research into the impact of short selling and its regulation are all factors likely to cause change to any particular short sale regime.

ACKNOWLEDGMENT

The author thanks Gloria Keum for her invaluable research assistance. Any errors are the author's alone.

REFERENCES

Fotak, V., Raman, V., & Yadav, P. (2009). *Naked short selling: The emperor's new clothes?* Working Paper, University of Oklahoma, Oklahoma City, OK. Retrieved from http://ssrn.com/abstract=1408493.

U.S. Securities and Exchange Commission, Office of Inspector General. (2009). *Practices related to naked short selling complaints and referrals.* Washington, DC: Author.

U.S. Securities and Exchange Commission. (2008, October 14). *'Naked' short selling antifraud rule; final rule* (Release No. 34-58774). Washington, DC: Author.

U.S. Securities and Exchange Commission. (2009, July 27). *Amendments to regulation SHO; final rule* (Release No. 34-60388). Washington, DC: Author.

U.S. Securities and Exchange Commission. (2010, March 10). *Amendments to regulation SHO; final rule* (Release No. 34-61595). Washington, DC: Author.

CHAPTER 5

Evolution of Short Selling Regulations and Trading Practices

Chinmay Jain, Pankaj K. Jain, and Thomas H. McInish

CONTENTS

ABSTRACT

This chapter provides a detailed historical account of the evolution of short selling regulations and trading practices during both normal and crises periods. Certain aspects of short selling restrictions, such as the uptick rule and limitations on short selling by mutual funds, hamper the price discovery process. In contrast, the Regulation SHO curb on naked short sales and the recent short selling ban on a subset of financial stocks did not diminish the overall market-wide price discovery process. The level of outstanding short positions was very high just before the recent financial crisis. The Securities and Exchange Commission's response in form of bans and stricter restrictions against naked short selling was quite effective in reducing both short selling and delivery failures. We also test Miller's (1977) hypothesis by comparing abnormal returns surrounding the short selling rule change for groups of stocks with different levels of divergence of opinion. We find that stocks having a higher dispersion of opinion showed more positive abnormal returns after the short sale ban than those with lower dispersion of opinion and no ban.

KEYWORDS

Bear raids; Cross-autocorrelation; Investment Act of 1940; Microscopic analysis; Naked short selling; Price tests; Regulation SHO; Short selling ban; Uptick rule.

5.1 INTRODUCTION

Short selling enables a trader to borrow and sell a stock today without actually owning it. To close a short position, the trader must buy back the stock in the future and realize the gains or losses based on the difference between selling price and buying price. Whether or not short selling is a desirable market feature is a question that has always generated controversy. Proponents of short selling cite several benefits. Short sellers contribute to efficient pricing in stock markets by allowing negative information to be incorporated easily in prices as traders can sell an overvalued stock even when they do not own it. In the absence of short selling, at least some traders with negative opinions about overvalued stocks are unable to act on that information. As a result, optimistic investors can push stock prices above fundamental values in markets where short selling is not allowed.

Bris and colleagues (2007) propose that negative public information can be incorporated faster in the presence of short sellers and provide empirical evidence to that effect, in recent periods. Short sellers are viewed as sophisticated traders who can align a stock's price with its fundamental value. For example, by analyzing accounting information rigorously, short sellers can overcome the inertia of existing shareholders who may continue to hold a stock due to endowment effects and other behavioral reasons. Therefore, one can expect to see speedier and more immediate price adjustment instead of a prolonged drift in prices after negative news such as announcements of poor earnings. Short sellers also provide very substantial additional liquidity in the stock markets. In the year 2005, short sales represented 31% of share volume for NASDAQ-listed stocks and 24% of share volume for NYSE-listed stocks (Diether, Lee, & Werner, 2009a). Another benefit of short selling is that it makes index arbitrage possible and helps in linking derivatives and cash markets.

Critics of short selling argue that short sellers may hammer a stock's price below its fundamental value by engaging in predatory short selling practices.

Bear raids were common in the early 1900s. In a bear raid, short sellers identify a target stock in which long investors have already fully utilized their margin accounts. Then they aggressively short the stock. The stock price declines due to the short sales and potentially unauthentic rumors spread by the bear raiders. This price decline triggers a margin call for long investors, causing some of them to sell as well, resulting in a further decline in stock prices. The NYSE prohibited short selling on downticks in 1931, and the Securities and Exchange Commission (SEC) introduced an uptick rule later in 1938 to prevent such bear raids. The uptick rule specifies that a stock can only be shorted at a transaction price that is at least one tick higher than the price of the most recent trade with a different price. Over time, regulators have often imposed restrictions on short selling in reaction to steep declines in stock prices. Recently, the SEC and the U.K. Financial Services Authority placed restrictions on short selling after the financial crisis in 2008, and their action was followed by regulators in countries such as Australia, France, Germany, Switzerland, Ireland, and Canada, among others.

This chapter discusses briefly the literature dealing with changes in short selling regulations. It provides historical background for short selling regulations in the United States since the 19th century. It also measures price discovery around these regulatory changes and tests whether short selling contributes to a more efficient price discovery, taking a long-term perspective. The chapter then focuses on the short selling rules in place at the time of major crises in U.S. stock markets. It also takes a microscopic look at short selling around the recent financial crisis by using several data sets containing information about outstanding short interest, fails to deliver, and returns.

5.2 LITERATURE REVIEW

Several studies have examined the impact of short selling regulations on the stock market using short horizon event studies around rule changes. Jones (2008) examines several discrete changes in short selling regulations that made shorting more difficult during the 1930s. He finds that the average return associated with these events is positive. He also finds that the rule requiring all brokers to obtain written authorization from customers before lending their shares caused a decline in market liquidity. In contrast, short sale restrictions on downticks in 1931 and the uptick rule in 1938 caused an increase in liquidity. Alexander and Peterson (1999) demonstrate that quality of the execution of short sell orders is affected unfavorably by the uptick rule, even when stocks are trading in advancing markets. Thus, the uptick rule hinders the price discovery process in all states of the market. Diether and colleagues (2009b) study the effect of the temporary removal of short sale price tests on designated pilot stocks under Regulation SHO. They find that the short sales relative to share volume increased for pilot stocks relative to control stocks and suspension of the price tests makes short selling easier. They do not find evidence of changes in daily returns or daily volatility of the pilot stocks. In addition, the authors argue that the effect of the price tests on market quality can likely be due to the irregularity in order flow influenced by the price tests themselves. Therefore, they conclude that price tests can be removed safely. Boehmer and associates (2009) study the impact of the short selling ban for 797 financial firms in 2008 on their market quality. They find that the ban caused degradation in their market quality as measured by spreads, price impact, and intraday price volatility. Their findings suggest that the boost in prices of the banned securities may have been due to the TARP program, which was announced at the same time and not necessarily due to the ban on short selling.

Kolasinksi and colleagues (2009) confirm the findings about degradation in market quality and also find that the SEC's June 2008 emergency order to ban naked short selling in 19 financial firms had a similar effect on market quality. Beber and Pagano (2009) examine this issue in an international context and find similar results about the ban's effect on market quality. They find that "imposing bans or regulatory constraints on short selling diminishes market liquidity, especially for stocks with small market capitalization, high volatility, and no listed options." They also find that bans slow down the price discovery process and fail to hold up stock prices, with the exception of U.S. financial stocks. Aromi and Caglio (2008) study short selling during the 13-day period preceding the short selling ban on September 19, 2008. They find that, on average, the short sale volume is higher for positive return periods compared to negative return periods. They also find the average price aggressiveness of sellers owning stock to be higher than the price aggressiveness of short sellers. We complement this literature in two ways. First, we provide a broad historic perspective of short selling rules and their impact on the price discovery process. Second, we conduct a microscopic analysis of several aspects of short selling activity surrounding recent regulatory changes.

5.3 HISTORICAL BACKGROUND ON SHORT SELLING

Perhaps one of the first formal regulations against short selling was enacted in January 1610 after a group of Dutch businessmen indulged in short selling of East India company stock. In 1733, naked short selling was banned in Britain after the market collapse following the South Sea Bubble of 1720. In the United States, the practice of short selling was banned in 1812 by New York State. The ban remained in place until 1858, when it was repealed. Reacting to a decline in stock markets, the NYSE imposed special short selling regulations during World War I in November 1917. The NYSE required all brokers to provide a list of speculators every day by noon and threatened to disclose their identity in case of unusual price behavior.

Following the Wall Street crash of 1929, many new laws were passed to restrict short selling. On October 6, 1931, the NYSE prohibited short selling at a price lower than the previous sale price. On February 18, 1932, the NYSE announced that all brokers were required to obtain explicit written authorization from their customers before lending their shares. A short-short rule was introduced in the Taxpayer Act of 1936 to discourage active trading and short selling by mutual funds. The rule required mutual funds to derive less than 30% of their gross income from the gains on positions held for less than 3 months or from short sales. After a steep market decline in 1937, the SEC adopted an uptick rule in 1938. The Investment Company Act of 1940 placed severe restrictions on the mutual funds' ability to short. This law was lifted in 1997. In the same year, the Taxpayer Relief Act of 1997 repealed the "short-short" rule. The market timing ability of mutual funds increased significantly after the repeal of this rule (Bae & Yi, 2008).

In January 2005, Regulation SHO established "locate" and "close-out" requirements for broker–dealers in an effort to curb naked short selling. The locate rule obliges a broker–dealer to have rational grounds to consider that the security is accessible for borrowing and delivery on the settlement due date before initiating and executing a short sale. The close-out requirement imposed additional restriction for short sales in securities where there has been a considerable number of delivery failures at a registered clearing agency.

> For instance, with limited exception, Regulation SHO requires brokers and dealers participating in registered clearing agency to take action to "close-out" failure-to-deliver positions (open fails) in threshold securities that have persisted for 13 consecutive settlement days. Closing out requires the broker or dealer to purchase securities of like kind and quantity. Until the position is closed out, the broker or dealer and any broker or dealer for which it clears transactions (for example, an introducing broker) may not effect further short sales in that threshold security without borrowing or entering into a bona fide agreement to borrow the security (known as the pre-borrowing requirement) (SEC, 2008).

These changes were followed by a period of market strength and rapid trading that allowed for some relaxation of short selling restriction. Under the Regulation SHO pilot program, 1000 stocks started trading without short sale price tests (i.e., without an uptick test for the NYSE and bid price test for the NASDAQ) beginning May 2, 2005. The suspension of price tests was originally set to expire on April 28, 2006, but was extended to August 6, 2007. The SEC concluded from the pilot program that price tests diffidently decrease liquidity and likely do prevent manipulation. The SEC removed the uptick rule in July 2007.

There was a 180-degree reversal in this policy within a year's time. In response to the financial crisis, the SEC issued a temporary emergency rule to stop naked short selling in 19 major financial firms on July 15, 2008. The rule required any person making a short sale in the listed securities to borrow the securities before the short sale is initiated and deliver the securities on the settlement date. On September 17, 2008, the SEC added new temporary rule 204T to Regulation SHO. The temporary rule imposes a penalty on any participant of a registered clearing agency, and any broker–dealer from which it receives trades for clearance and settlement, for having a fail-to-deliver position at a registered clearing agency in any equity security. The SEC also repealed the exception for options market makers from short selling close-out provisions in Regulation SHO. Another rule called the "naked short selling antifraud rule" became effective the same day. It covers short sellers who deceive broker–dealers or any other market participants about their intention or ability to deliver securities in time for settlement. After normal trading closed on that day, the SEC initiated a ban on short selling for 797 financial stocks. The short selling ban expired on October 8, 2008. On February 24, 2010, the SEC adopted a new rule to put restrictions on short selling when a stock is experiencing significant downward price pressure. This alternative form of the uptick rule restricts short selling from driving down the price of a stock when the stock has already declined more than 10% in 1 day. This rule will put long sellers in front of the line and will enable them to sell shares before the short sellers.

Table 5.1 lists major changes in short selling regulations and changes in price discovery around those changes. We follow Bris and associates (2007) to compute our price discovery measure and compute cross-autocorrelation between lagged value-weighted market return and contemporaneous individual stocks returns for the day. In particular, we calculate $\rho_{iT} = corr(r_{it}, r_{mt-1})$ for all NYSE-listed stocks using daily observations for each period T and then average the cross-autocorrelation across N sample stocks to calculate the measure of price discovery. We compute cross-autocorrelation separately for periods 1 year after (ρ_A) and 1 year before (ρ_B) each regulation change and report the difference between the two:

$$\rho_A = \frac{\sum_i^N (\rho_{iT,A})}{N}, \quad \rho_B = \frac{\sum_i^N (\rho_{iT,B})}{N}, \quad \rho_\Delta = \rho_A - \rho_B \tag{5.1}$$

Table 5.1 Efficiency of Price Discovery around Short Selling Regulation Changes[a]

Date	Rule Change	Expected Change in Cross-Autocorrelation	Actual Change in Cross-Autocorrelation
10/06/1931	NYSE prohibited short sales on a downtick	+	+0.0133
06/22/1936	Short-short rule was introduced in the Tax Payer Act	+	+0.0182
02/01/1938	The NYSE's tick test was tightened to require all short sales to take place on a strict uptick and was extended to all exchanges	+	−0.0094
08/22/1940	Investment Act of 1940 restricted short selling by mutual funds.	+	−0.0134
08/05/1997	Short-short rule was repealed.	−	+0.001
01/03/2005	Regulation SHO established "locate" and "close-out" requirements for broker–dealers, in an effort to curb naked short selling.	+	−0.0325
07/03/2007	Uptick rule was removed by the SEC.	−	−0.0975
07/21/2008	The emergency rule to stop naked short selling in 19 major financial firms becomes effective.	+	−0.0312
08/12/2008	The emergency rule expires.	−	−0.0242
09/17/2008	After normal trading closed, the SEC initiated a ban on short selling for 797 stocks. The SEC issued new and temporary rule 204T, which imposes a penalty on any participant of a registered clearing agency, and any broker–dealer from which it receives trades for clearance and settlement for having a fails to deliver position at a registered clearing agency in any equity security. The SEC also eliminated the options market maker exception from Regulation SHO's closeout.	+	+0.0967
10/08/2008	Following the 10/03/08 announcement, the short selling ban expires.	−	−0.0700
02/24/2010	Effective from May 2010, the SEC approved alternative uptick rule (Rule 201) designed to restrict short selling from further driving down the price of a stock that has dropped more than 10% in 1 day. The full-compliance date for Rule 201 was February 28, 2011.	+	+0.0196

[a]Major short selling regulation changes and associated dates are listed in columns 1 and 2. Price discovery is calculated by computing the average of cross-autocorrelation between lagged value-weighted market return contemporaneous individual stocks returns for the day. A higher cross-autocorrelation implies slower price discovery. The expected change in cross-autocorrelation is provided in column 3. The actual change is reported in column 4 based on the difference between cross-autocorrelation 1 year before and 1 year after the event. For the last four events, change is calculated as the difference between the cross-autocorrelation 1 month before (or from the date of previous change in regulation) and 1 month after (or until the date of next change in regulation) the event.

Bris and colleagues (2007) use weekly returns, whereas we use both daily returns and weekly returns. Because the results are similar, we report results based on daily returns. Daily returns capture the effects of events that are very close to each other. We compute cross-autocorrelation between lagged value-weighted market return and contemporaneous individual stocks returns for the day.

For events that occurred very close to each other, we use the period of 1 month before (or from the date of previous change in regulation) and 1 month after (or until the date of next change in regulation) instead of 1 year. A higher cross-autocorrelation signifies slower price discovery. The third column in Table 5.1 shows the theoretically expected change in the sign of cross-autocorrelation for each regulation change. The last column shows the actual observed empirical change in autocorrelation.

Long horizon empirical results indicate that the predicted relation between short selling rules and price discovery holds true in the univariate analysis only for some sample periods. Nevertheless, we formally test this relation in the multivariate regression framework where we control for other potential determinants of price discovery. We compute yearly time series of average cross-autocorrelation across stocks from 1926 to 2009. Table 5.2 reports results of the regression estimation for cross-autocorrelation. Specifically, we look at the effect of tick restrictions, the Investment Act of 1940, Regulation SHO, and short sale ban on financial stocks during the financial crisis in 2008 on cross-autocorrelation. We find that the speed of price discovery as measured by cross-autocorrelation is significantly related to these short selling rule changes. Some aspects of short selling regulations such as the tick restrictions and the Investment Act of 1940 hampered the price discovery process as evidenced by increased auto-correlations. In contrast, other aspects of short selling, such as those in the curb on naked short selling by Regulation SHO and ban on a subset of stocks during 2008, do not appear to diminish the overall price discovery process, as autocorrelations do not increase.

We define variables for short selling regulation changes as follows. Tick restrictions take the following values: 0.5 from 1931 to 1937 when downtick restriction was in place; 1 from 1938 to 2006 when uptick restriction was in place and 0 for the remaining period. The Investment Act of 1940 equals 1 for a period from 1940 to 1997 and 0 otherwise. Regulation SHO equals 1 for a period from 2005 to 2009 and 0 before. A ban on a subset of stocks (Financials) equals 1 for year 2008 and 0 otherwise. Models 1–4 use a negative return as a dummy variable, which is 1 for years with a negative return and 0 otherwise. A negative return dummy has a positive and significant coefficient, implying a slower price discovery during periods of negative returns.

Table 5.2 Price Discovery Regression[a,b]

	Model 1	Model 2	Model 3	Model 4	Model 5	Model 6	Model 7	Model 8
Intercept	0.0432**	0.0333***	0.08***	0.0725***	0.8634***	0.5936***	0.3897***	0.4891***
Tick restrictions	0.0329*				0.0843***			
1940 Investment Act		0.0545***				0.0535***		
Regulation SHO			-0.1194***				-0.0097***	
Ban on a subset of stocks (Financials)				-0.1771***				-0.1353***
Negative return	0.0353***	0.0387***	0.0308**	0.0411***	0.0264**	0.0299***	0.0251**	0.0316**
Ln (No. of stocks)					-0.1285***	-0.0831***	-0.0479**	-0.0634***
Risk-free rate					0.0113***	0.0075***	0.0074***	0.0085***
Adjusted R^2	0.0744	0.2529	0.3107	0.1601	0.3845	0.4127	0.4023	0.2941
No. of observations	84	84	84	84	84	84	84	84

[a]Yearly time series of price discovery measure are computed using daily returns of all NYSE-listed stocks and value-weighted market returns for the period from 1926 to 2009. Price discovery is calculated by computing the average of cross-autocorrelation between lagged value-weighted market return contemporaneous individual stocks returns for the day. A higher cross-autocorrelation implies slower price discovery. We estimate the regression with the cross-autocorrelation as our dependent variable and short selling regulation changes separately in each model as the independent variable. Models 1 and 5 look at the effect of tick restrictions, which take the following values: 0.5 from 1931 to 1937 when downtick restriction was in place; 1 from 1938 to 2006 when uptick restriction was in place; and 0 for the remaining period. Models 2 and 6 look at the effect of the Investment Act of 1940, which equals 1 for a period from 1940 to 1997 and 0 otherwise. Models 3 and 7 look at the effect of Regulation SHO, which equals 1 for a period from 2005 to 2009 and 0 before. Models 4 and 8 look at the effect of the short sale ban on financial stocks in 2008, which equals 1 for year 2008 and 0 otherwise. Models 1–4 control for negative return using a dummy, which is 1 for years with negative market return and 0 otherwise. Models 5–8 also control for number of stocks and risk-free interest rate along with a negative return dummy. Number of stocks is the number of firms with available stock price in the CRSP database. The risk-free rate for the period before 1954 is from Siegel (1992). For the period after 1954, we take the risk-free interest rate from the Federal Reserve Web site.[1]

[b]Symbols ***, **, and * indicate significance at the 1, 5, and 10% level, respectively.

---

[1] http://www.federalreserve.gov/releases/h15/data.htm.

Models 5–8 use a risk-free interest rate and log of a number of stocks as additional explanatory variables and find qualitatively similar results.

5.4 SHORT SELLING AND FINANCIAL CRISIS

Since the 1600s, short selling and regulations restricting short selling have been topics of debate and controversy, particularly in periods surrounding financial crisis. Regulators are quick to blame short sellers for steep declines in valuations and sometimes allege they manipulate stock prices. In the United States, there were relatively few restrictions on short selling during the 1920s.

Brokers could borrow stocks from their customers or other brokers. Alternatively, stock lending could be done through a centralized market on the floor of the NYSE (Jones & Lamont, 2002). Many argue that short selling was responsible for the market crash of 1929. After a big fall in the markets during 1937, an uptick rule was implemented to restrict short selling in 1938. Apparently, the uptick rule exacerbated the market decline during the crash of 1987. The uptick rule makes index arbitrage more difficult, as arbitrages have to wait before they can short sell a stock on an uptick. This resulted in an uncoupling of equity and future markets on October 19, 1987, resulting in a crash (Macey, Mitchell, & Netter, 1989). During the dot-com bubble in the late 1990s, there were substantial short sale restrictions on Internet stocks (Ofek & Richardson, 2003), which further supports the argument that prices can go above fundamentals in the absence of short sellers.

Short selling regulations have been at center stage during the recent financial crisis. While the SEC relaxed the short sale constraints in September 2007 by removing the uptick rule, it reversed its stance during 2008 and took several measures to restrict short selling. The SEC banned naked short selling in 19 financial firms in July 2008, followed by a short selling ban for 797 financial firms in September. In an interview with the *Washington Post*, SEC Chairman Christopher Cox said that agreeing to the 3-week ban on short selling of financial companies in September was the biggest mistake of his tenure. He acknowledged publicly that this ban was not productive and said that he was under intense pressure from Treasury Secretary Henry M. Paulson Jr. and Fed Chairman Ben S. Bernanke to take this action and did so reluctantly. They "were of the view that if we did not act and act at that instant, these financial institutions could fail as a result and there would be nothing left to save."

More recently, European authorities have responded to the Greek debt crisis by imposing bans on short selling. The Capital Market Commission of the

Greek Market decided to ban short selling on the Athens Stock Exchange on April 28, 2010, effective until June 28, 2010. In a similar move, Germany's market regulator, BaFin, announced a ban on naked short selling of eurozone government debt and shares of 10 major financial companies on May 18, 2010. The ban runs through March 31, 2011, and also applies to naked credit default swaps involving eurozone debt.

5.5 A DETAILED ANALYSIS OF SHORT SELLING IN RECENT TIMES

We perform a detailed analysis of short selling in recent times using data from shortsqueeze.com,[2] CRSP, and the SEC Web site.[3]

5.5.1 Descriptive Statistics

We use short interest data from www.shortsqueeze.com for the sample of 797 financial stocks that had a short sale ban in 2008 and a matched sample of stocks that did not have a short sale ban. These are fortnightly data with information on the number of shares short, shares float, total shares outstanding, trading volume, and institutional ownership, among others. We access these data for the period from November 2007 to October 2009. We create a matched sample of stocks with no short sale ban based on market capitalization, trading volume, listing exchange, and option listing status. Table 5.3 presents descriptive statistics of our sample data. The mean value of short shares as a percentage of float for short sale ban stocks is 3.81%; the corresponding number for the matched sample has a mean value of 3.27%.

Next, we plot the time series of value-weighted short interest as a percentage of float for stocks with a short selling ban and matched sample of firms with no such ban in Figure 5.1 for the same period. The short interest as percentage of float for stocks with a short sale ban became much higher than the matched sample before the short sale ban implementation. We see a dramatic decrease in short interest of financial stocks after the SEC's short selling ban on 797 financial stocks and a curb on naked short selling on September 17, 2008. We also see a decline in the matched sample in which there was no such ban, although for these stocks the decline is not as severe as the sample of stocks that had a short sale ban.

---

[2] Shortsqueeze.com is the premier source for short interest data for U.S. stocks.

[3] Available at http://www.sec.gov/foia/docs/failsdata.htm.

Table 5.3 Descriptive Statistics[a]

	Short Sale Ban Stocks			Stocks with No Short Sale Ban		
	Mean	**Median**	**STD**	**Mean**	**Median**	**STD**
Short interest[b]	39.4	0.41	26.6	40.9	0.40	18.4
Short as % of float[c]	3.81	2.26	7.33	3.27	2.20	8.57
Days to cover[d]	3.12	4.30	16.9	3.17	3.60	15.0
Trading volume[e]	34.5	0.04	20.5	19.0	0.06	6.91
Market capitalization	53.3	0.16	11.2	67.8	0.20	18.0
% institutional ownership[f]	64.2	29.3	26.3	66.1	43.5	33.7

[a]Descriptive statistics are presented for the sample of 797 financial stocks that had a short sale ban and a matched sample of stocks that did not have a short sale ban for a period from November 2007 to October 2009. Short interest and trading volume are in million units, and market capitalization is in billion units. All mean values are value weighted.

[b]Total number of outstanding shorted shares for each stock.

[c]Short interest divided by number of shares float.

[d]Number of days required for cumulative daily trading volume to equal the current number of shorted shares outstanding.

[e]Specified in terms of number of shares.

[f]Percentage of shares held by institutional investors such as mutual funds, hedge funds, and pension plans.

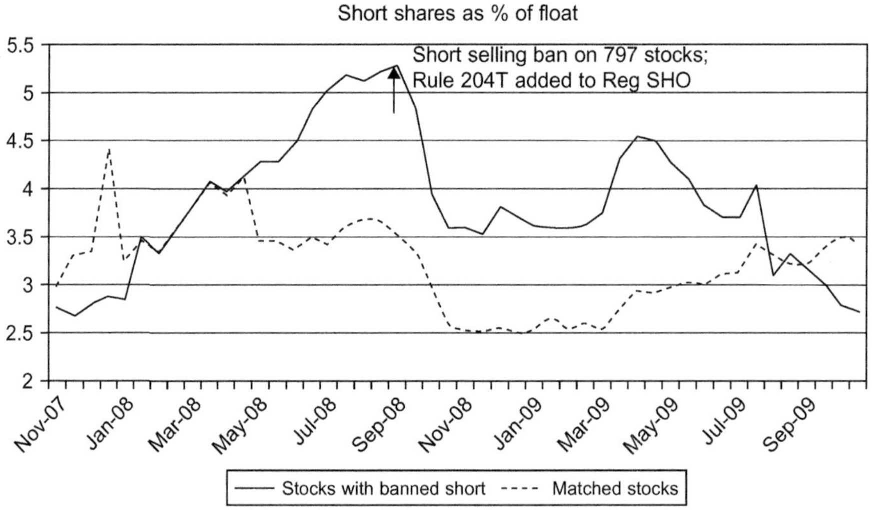

FIGURE 5.1

Short shares as percentage of shares float for the two subgroups.

We also look at another important aspect of short selling where some market participants choose not to deliver the security on the due date even if it is available to borrow. They may be doing so specifically to avoid the borrowing cost for hard-to-borrow stocks (Evans, Geczy, Musto, & Reed,

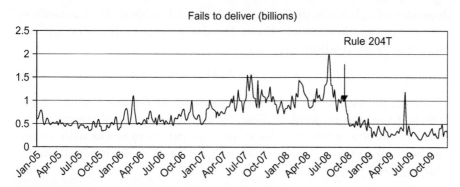

FIGURE 5.2

Five-day moving average of aggregate fails to deliver quantity for all stocks.

2009). With the primary motivation of avoiding these fails to deliver practices, regulators introduced the T+3 closeout rule (204T) on September 17, 2008. Fails to deliver shares represent the aggregate net balance of shares that failed to be delivered as of a particular settlement date; these data are available from the SEC Web site. The SEC adopted the 204T temporary rule and eliminated Options Market Maker exception from Regulation SHO on September 17, 2008. The commission made the Rule 204T permanent as Rule 204 in July 2009.

Figure 5.2 plots the 5-day moving average of aggregate fails to deliver shares for all stocks from 2005 to 2009. We find the SEC's rule to be effective in reducing aggregate fails to deliver quantity.

5.5.2 Divergence of Opinion

Miller (1977) hypothesizes that short sale constraints cause stock prices to be overvalued in the presence of dispersion of opinion among investors. Short sale constraints prevent traders with a negative outlook on the stock from selling that stock if they do not own it. Boehme and associates (2006) test this hypothesis indirectly using short stock rebate rates, the relative short interest level, and the presence of exchange-traded options as a proxy for short sale constraints. They find evidence of significant overvaluation for stocks that have short selling constraints and higher dispersion of opinion, although there was no explicit ban on short selling in their sample. The recent short sale ban in 2008, when the SEC placed short selling restrictions on 797 financial firms, presents an ideal scenario to test Miller's theory more directly. We use the CRSP data set to form quintiles based on dispersion of opinion for stocks with a short sale ban and matched sample of stocks with no bans. Following Chang and colleagues (2007), we measure dispersion of opinion as the standard deviation of residuals from an ordinary least squares market model using a 250-day preevent estimation window preceding the short selling ban:

$$R_{it} = \alpha_i + \beta_i R_{Mt} + \varepsilon, \text{ and Dispersion} = \sigma_\varepsilon \qquad (5.2)$$

We divide the sample into five quintiles of stocks ranging from lowest to highest dispersion of opinion. Next, we calculate abnormal returns for N_q stocks in quintile q for each day of the ban period in stocks with a short sale ban and compare them with abnormal returns in the matched sample with no ban:

$$AR_{t,q} = \sum_1^{Nq} (R_{it} - \hat{\alpha}_i - \hat{\beta}_i R_{Mt})/N_q \,|\, i \in q \qquad (5.3)$$

Table 5.4 reports the abnormal return on September 18 and September 19, and the cumulative abnormal return during the ban period for stocks with a short sale ban and for a matched sample. For stocks with a short sale ban, we find that the abnormal return for stocks with the highest dispersion of opinion in quintile 5 is higher by 3.80% and statistically significant as compared to stocks with lowest dispersion of opinion in quintile 1 on September 18, while this difference for matched stocks is only 0.04% and insignificant. On September 19, the corresponding numbers are 2.11 and 0.89%, although insignificant. The cumulative abnormal return during the ban period for quintile 5 is higher by 18.58% for stocks with a short sale ban.

These findings support the theory that stocks with a high dispersion of opinion become overvalued under short sale constraints. For the matched sample, we have the opposite findings. The abnormal return for quintile 5 is

Table 5.4 Abnormal Return in Dispersion of Opinion Quintiles[a]

RSTD Quintile	#Obs	Stock with Short Sale Ban			Stock with No Short Sale Ban		
		18-Sep	19-Sep	Sep 18–Oct 8	18-Sep	19-Sep	Sep 18–Oct 8
1	130	1.86%	2.38%	3.79%	−0.14%	−0.98%	−3.40%
2	127	4.43%	2.11%	9.75%	−0.98%	0.32%	−9.08%
3	130	3.13%	1.68%	10.4%	0.57%	−0.38%	−11.6%
4	129	4.47%	3.12%	10.4%	0.55%	0.17%	−7.99%
5	127	5.66%	4.49%	22.4%	−0.10%	−0.09%	−19.7%
p value (Diff 5-1)		<0.0001	0.1934	<0.0001	0.9682	0.3655	<0.0001

[a]Quintiles of stocks with a short sale ban and matched stocks based on dispersion of opinion were formed. Dispersion of opinion was measured by standard deviation of residuals (RSTD) from the market model for the 250-day preevent estimation window (−280, −31) preceding the short sale ban. Next, abnormal returns in these stocks were calculated for each day during the ban period. Equal-weighted abnormal returns for each quintile are presented.

lower by 16.25%. Thus, matched stocks with a higher dispersion of opinion perhaps become the new target of short sellers.

5.6 CONCLUSION

The role of short sellers in stock trading and efficient pricing is a hotly debated topic. This chapter presented a historical background on the evolution of short selling regulations and the specific rules in effect at the time of major financial crises in the United States. Most restrictions on short selling are triggered by a sharp decline in the stock market. Nonetheless, short selling is considered an essential tool of efficient markets and therefore the restrictions are usually lifted after market recovery. This chapter looked at the quality of price discovery in the stock markets before and after each major change in the short selling regulations.

Short selling restrictions have several formats and can affect the trading process in general, a set of stocks, or a set of market participants. We find that the tick restrictions implemented in the 1930s and short selling restrictions on mutual funds implemented in 1940 both hamper price discovery. In contrast, the Regulation SHO's curb on naked short selling implemented in 2005 and SEC's temporary short selling ban on financial stocks in 2008 do not hamper the overall price discovery in stock markets. On February 24, 2010, the SEC approved a variation of the "uptick rule" to place curbs on short sales. This rule applies to stocks that decline at least 10% in a single day. For such stocks, short selling will be allowed only if the price of the sale is above the highest bid price nationally. In other words, short sellers cannot automatically execute a marketable sell order against the best bid price in the limit order book as they can under normal circumstances. This curb will be in place for the remainder of the day when stock falls 10% and the next trading day. The nature of this rule makes it similar to the trading halts commonly adopted by exchanges around the world. We conjecture that this rule will prevent abuse of short selling, but not at the cost of severe deterioration in the price discovery process.

This chapter studied in detail several aspects of recent short selling regulations in 2008. We found that the outstanding short interest levels were very high before the SEC banned naked short selling in 19 stocks in July 2008 and then banned short selling in 797 financial firms in September 2008. We found that the measures taken by the SEC to curb naked short selling and to reduce fails to deliver in securities were very effective in achieving their respective purposes. Also, we tested Miller's (1977) hypothesis by looking at the effect of a short selling ban on groups of stocks with varying degrees of dispersion of opinion. Stocks with a high dispersion of opinion and a short sale ban generate a high abnormal positive return after the short sale ban consistent with the hypothesis. We found diagonally opposite and interesting findings for a matched sample of stocks with no short sale ban. In that no-ban sample, stocks with a high dispersion of opinion generate a negative abnormal return, implying that short sellers begin to target alternative firms with similar characteristics after a short selling ban on financial stocks.

Future research can characterize the dynamics between short selling restrictions and price discovery in an international context. In particular, the recent Greek crisis and the naked short selling ban implemented by the European authorities, which requires preborrowing of securities, present a fertile ground for further research on the nuances of short selling regulations.

REFERENCES

Alexander, G. J., & Peterson, M. A. (1999). Short selling on the New York Stock Exchange and the effects of the uptick rule. *Journal of Financial Intermediation, 8*(1–2), 90–116.

Aromi, D., & Caglio, C. (2008). *Re: Analysis of short selling activity during the first weeks of September 2008*. Office of Economic Analysis Memorandum. Retrieved from http://www.sec.gov/comments/s7-08-09/s70809-369.pdf.

Bae, K., & Yi, J. (2008). The impact of the short-short rule repeal on the timing ability of mutual funds. *Journal of Business Finance and Accounting, 35*(7–8), 969–997.

Beber, A., & Pagano, M. (2009). *Short-selling bans around the world: Evidence from the 2007–09 crisis*. Working paper, Center for Studies in Economics and Finance, University of Salerna, Fisciano, Italy.

Boehme, R. D., Danielsen, B. R., & Sorescu, S. M. (2006). Short-sale constraints, differences of opinion, and overvaluation. *Journal of Financial and Quantitative Analysis, 41*(2), 455–487.

Boehmer, E., Jones, C. M., & Zhang, X. (2009). *Shackling the short sellers: The 2008 shorting ban*. Working paper, Cornell University, Ithaca, NY.

Bris, A., Goetzmann, W. N., & Zhu, N. (2007). Efficiency and the bear: Short sales and markets around the world. *Journal of Finance, 62*(3), 1029–1079.

Chang, E. C., Cheng, J. W., & Yu, Y. (2007). Short-sales constraints and price discovery: Evidence from the Hong Kong Market. *Journal of Finance, 62*(5), 2097–2121.

Diether, K. B., Lee, K., & Werner, I. M. (2009a). Short-sale strategies and return predictability. *Review of Financial Studies, 22*(2), 575–607.

Diether, K. B., Lee, K., & Werner, I. M. (2009b). It's SHO time! Short-sale price tests and market quality. *Journal of Finance, 64*(1), 37–73.

Evans, R. B., Geczy, C. C., Musto, D. K., & Reed, A. V. (2009). Failure is an option: Impediments to short selling and options prices. *Review of Financial Studies, 22*(5), 1955–1980.

Jones, C. M. (2008). *Shorting restrictions: Revisiting the 1930's*. Working paper, Columbia Business School, NY.

Jones, C. M., & Lamont, O. A. (2002). Short-sale constraints and stock returns. *Journal of Financial Economics, 66*(2–3), 207–239.

Kolasinksi, A. C., Reed, A. V., & Thornock, J. R. (2009). *Prohibitions versus constraints: The 2008 short sales regulations*. Working paper, University of Washington, Seattle, WA, and University of North Carolina, Chapel Hill, NC.

Macey, J. R., Mitchell, M., & Netter, J. (1989). Restrictions on short sales: An analysis of the uptick rule and its role in view of the October 1987 stock market crash. *Cornell Law Review, 74,* 797–835.

Miller, E. M. (1977). Risk, uncertainty, and divergence of opinion. *Journal of Finance, 32*(4), 1151–1168.

Ofek, E., & Richardson, M. (2003). DotCom Mania: The rise and fall of internet stock prices. *Journal of Finance, 58*(3), 1113–1137.

SEC. (2008). Retrieved from http://www.sec.gov/comments/s7-20-08/s72008-566.pdf.

Siegel, J. J. (1992). The real rate of interest from 1800–1990: A study of the U.S. and the U.K. *Journal of Monetary Economics, 29*(2), 227–252.

CHAPTER 6

Financing Techniques for Short Sellers

Stuart McCrary

CONTENTS

ABSTRACT

Traders can easily create short positions in an extensive list of over-the-counter and exchange-traded derivatives markets. Creating short positions in cash securities and commodities is somewhat harder. However, traders may prefer to create short positions in cash instruments for regulatory reasons because the pricing is advantageous or as part of a market-making function. Technical factors in financing markets can influence the pricing of cash instruments. In many instances, the economics of financing short positions determines the fair value of derivative securities.

KEYWORDS

Coupon payment; General collateral; Gold leasing; Haircut; Rebate; Repo trade; Reverse repo market; Sale–repurchase trades; Substitute payment; Warehouse receipt.

6.1 INTRODUCTION

Traders that own securities and other assets (i.e., long positions) can use the lending market to finance part of the value of that position. Alternatively, traders can fully pay for the asset. However, traders that sell securities or commodities that they do not own (i.e., short sales) must borrow the securities or assets to make delivery on the settlement date. This chapter explains how lending markets allow traders to finance both long and short positions.

6.2 INTRODUCING THE REPO MARKET FOR FIXED INCOME SECURITIES

Traders may wish to borrow cash to finance a long security position. The seller delivers the borrowed security to the buyer on the settlement date. The value of the bonds purchased secures the loan of cash used to pay for the position. Eventually, the trader must repay the loan and the lender will return the securities to the owner.

Traders need to borrow a security when they sell short. The short seller delivers the borrowed security to the buyer on the settlement date. The proceeds of the short sale provide cash to secure the loan of the bonds. Eventually, the trader must buy back the security and return the security to the lender.

The "sale–repurchase" (repo) creates a credit-enhanced loan to fund a long position in a bond. Assume that a trader bought a $10 million position in Bond A at $98.25. The trader pays that price plus $1.25 in accrued interest for a total purchase price of $9.95 million (98.25 + 1.25 = 99.5; 99.5% of $10 million face amount is $9.95 million) to settle on the next business day. The trader will use $9.95 million cash to buy the bonds. Suppose, however, that on the settlement date, the bond is worth $98 plus accrued interest. The trader creates a repo loan by structuring a sale of Bond A at $9.925 million (98 + 1.25 = 99.25; 99.25% of $10 million is $9.925 million) and a repurchase (hence the name of the lending transaction) a week later at $9.925 million plus interest at 3%.[1]

---

[1] Interest on repo is Actual/360 so that interest on a 7-day repo at 3% equals $9.925 million × 3% × 7 ÷ 360 = $5,789.58. The resale price is $9.925 million plus $5,789.58, or $9,930,789.58.

Because the purchase and the sale are created at the same time but settle 7 days apart, it constitutes a lending trade, not a risk-reducing sale of security.

T-accounts like those used in an accounting textbook document the details of the sale–repurchase trades involving Bond A:

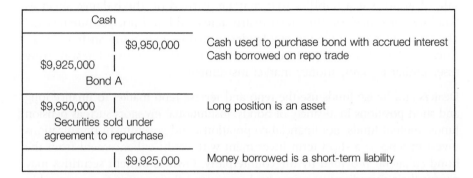

The accounting treatment highlights an important legal point. The repo market creates a financing trade when the owner sells the bond and later buys the issue back. The trader, the accountants, and the risk managers of the firm recognize that the trader retains all of the risks of owning Bond A. Despite the sound of the name of the account carrying the repo trade, it is actually the balance of the repo loan.

The trader could have borrowed the bond in much the same way using the reverse repo market. Assume that the trader sells $10 million of Bond A at 98.25. If the trader can deliver the bond to the buyer, the trader will receive $9.950 million on settlement, as in the previous example. The trader finds a holder of Bond A that is willing to lend the issue. The reverse repo creates a purchase of Bond A on the settlement date for $9.925 million and a sale a week later for the purchase amount plus interest.

T-accounts detail the reverse repo trades involving Bond A:

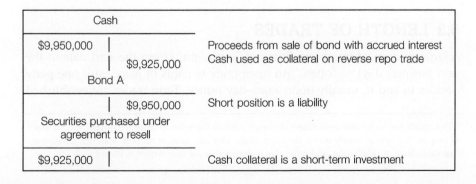

Note that all of the dollar amounts are identical to the repo trade except that the roles of the counterparties reverse. The trader delivers cash to the securities lender and earns interest on that collateral. The lender delivers the bond to the trader but retains all of the risks of owning Bond A. Similarly, the accountants reverse the debit and credit entries. In particular, the short sale of Bond A is a liability that may get carried on the balance sheet as "trading liabilities" or "financial instruments sold and not yet purchased." The cash delivered to the security lender carried in an account such as "securities purchased under agreement to resell" is a short-term interest-bearing asset similar to many money market instruments.

Dealers and hedge funds use the repo and reverse repo market to finance long and short positions in a variety of bonds. Institutional investors such as pension funds, mutual funds, nonfinancial corporations, and government organizations invest in repo as a short-term investment with credit enhancement from the bond collateral provided by the counterparty. Owners of debt securities may permit their custodians or prime brokers to lend their securities to earn additional income. Central banks use repo markets as an important tool for their open market operations that are used to fine-tune the money in circulation.

Dealers and hedge funds use the repo market to a limited extent to finance long positions in mortgages and mortgage-backed securities. However, these securities are somewhat difficult to settle because the face value of the assets can change from month to month. Traders rarely use reverse repos to borrow mortgage securities. It is often risky to sell short specific pools of mortgages or even mortgage-backed securities because these loans or pools of loans are uniquely identified and the floating supply of the particular assets is frequently very small. Because many mortgage products trade in a well-defined forward market, a dealer can instead buy specific assets from a customer and sell back similar assets in the forward or TBA[2] market. The combination resembles a reverse repo but is not deemed to be a financing trade because the securities delivered do not exactly match the securities returned. The terms of the TBA market permit the short seller to close out the short by delivering similar but not identical assets to the customer.

6.3 LENGTH OF TRADES

A large amount of bonds are financed "overnight" (from the start date to the next business day) or "open." An open trade remains in place until one party decides to end it, usually upon same-day notice. Term trades are established

[2] TBA stands for "to be arranged" where the buyer permits the seller to delay identifying specific assets as long as they approximately match the terms of the TBA sale, such as coupon, maturity, remaining face value, time of origination, and other characteristics that the counterparties identify.

at a fixed rate and for a specific maturity. The bond that serves as collateral will not change for a special trade but traders may be willing to accept substitutions of general collateral (see next paragraph).

6.4 SPECIAL RATE

Repo and reverse repo transactions appear to be identical except that a repo trade involves a trader borrowing money in the lending market, whereas a reverse repo involves a trader borrowing securities in the lending market. When a trader borrows money, the bonds that serve as collateral are not in high demand and the repo rate reflects the general level of interest rates and is called the "general collateral" (or "GC") rate. However, if the trader needs to borrow a bond that is scarce or in high demand, the reverse repo rate gets set below the GC rate. In this way, the lender of the bond is compensated by getting access to the cash collateral at a below-market rate called a "special repo" rate.

If the short trader fails to deliver the bond issue on the settlement date, the buyer holds onto the cash value of the trade beyond the settlement date. The buyer is able to invest this cash for additional time and keep the interest. The effect is the same as if the buyer borrowed money equal to the value of the settlement from the seller at a repo rate of zero. For this reason, the special rate has historically been bounded by zero. Beginning in May 1, 2009, the Treasury Markets Practice Group and the Security Industry and Financial Markets Association established that failing sellers pay a 3% fails charge (Treasury Markets Practice Group, 2009), which can lead to traders negotiating negative special financing rates.

6.5 THE REPO MARKET IN BANKRUPTCY

As described earlier, generally accepted accounting principles accounting describes repo and reverse repo transactions as financing transactions. These transactions are treated more like true purchases and sales when a counterparty fails to close out a trade and under bankruptcy. Following the bankruptcy of Lombard–Wall in 1982, bankruptcy judge Edward J. Ryan froze all assets, including repo and reverse repo collateral. Congress later exempted such repo transactions from the general provisions of the bankruptcy code. The court handling the bankruptcy of Bevill, Bresler, and Schulman further ruled in 1986 that the courts should respect the market custom and practice that treats the financing trades as purchases and sales by recognizing them as secured financing trades (Lumpkin, 1998).

6.6 HAIRCUTS AND MARGIN MAINTENANCE

The repo example showed the trader buying at one price and financing the position at the updated value on the settlement date. In fact, the short selling trader may have to overcollateralize the reverse repo trade by depositing cash in excess of the value of the bonds. This excess amount is called a "haircut." The excess collateral provides some protection if the borrower fails to return the security at the end of the financing trade. The haircut amount is very small for highly liquid assets but may be 25% or more for illiquid issues or when the value of the issues is uncertain.

The difference between the value of the bond and the value of the loan principal creates an unsecured credit risk. As prices change, firms find that some repo and reverse repo transactions may become overcollateralized and others undercollateralized. The International Securities Lending Association recommends that lending counterparties calculate the net difference on all the lending trades and usually adjust the pricing of those transactions daily.

6.7 FINANCING EQUITY SHORT POSITIONS

The stock loan market closely resembles the reverse repo market. In the United States, traders must "locate" or find a willing lender before short selling a stock. Stocks that are hard to borrow are described as hard to locate. The equity version of the reverse repo rate is called a "rebate." Like the special repo rate, the rebate rate is set below prevailing interest rates. In fact, this rate can be negative, in which case the borrower of the stock deposits cash that does not receive interest and also pays a fee or rebate.

Most stock loans are collateralized with cash but some 2% are collateralized with U.S. Treasury Securities (D'Avolio, 2002). Stock lending trades are typically collateralized with cash equal to 102% of the value of the stock loaned for U.S. issues and 105% of the value of international stock issues (Duffie, Garleanu, & Pedersen, 2002). Stock loans may be subject to recall, where the lender of a stock may demand return of the security.

6.8 IN LIEU PAYMENTS AND OTHER RIGHTS

When a repo trade extends over a bond payment date, the holder of the bond receives the coupon payment. Because the bond is being held as collateral, the true owner receives a substitute payment from the holder. At the same time, the value of the collateral decreases by the amount of the coupon payment, as accrued interest is now zero. As a result, the repo trade is repriced and the difference roughly equals the substitute coupon payment.

When a stock loan extends over an ex-dividend date, the holder of the stock receives the dividend on the dividend payment date. The original owner receives a substitute payment from the holder. Because the ex-dividend price of the stock is lower, the stock loan will be repriced.

Substitute coupon payments and substitute dividend payments may not be treated exactly like an actual coupon or dividend payment. The substitute payment of a corporate coupon is taxed the same as a coupon on a corporate bond for most taxpayers but a substitute payment of U.S. Treasury interest may not be exempt from state income tax. Likewise, a substitute payment in lieu of a dividend may not qualify for exclusion for U.S. corporate income tax. In contract, the United Kingdom has rules designed to treat substitute payments the same as actual dividends (Bank of England, 2010). Market participants should be aware of the differences and take steps to avoid unfavorable differences in tax treatment.

Holders of stock may temporarily acquire voting rights. Traders may use the stock loan market to affect the outcome of shareholder voting. Likewise, shareholders should exercise care if a company will pass through tax effects during the time of a stock lending transaction because companies have found themselves in litigation over such tax rights. Lenders of stock positions may need to recall shares to be certain of their shareholder rights on key dates.

6.9 FINANCING CURRENCY SHORT POSITIONS

The foreign exchange market is primarily an over-the-counter market called the "interbank market," which includes active trading in the spot currencies of many countries and extensive trading for forward delivery. In addition, several futures exchanges have contracts that permit trading of foreign exchange with the protection of a clearing corporation and on an organized exchange. Because of the depth of these markets, traders do not generally rely on financing markets similar to repo or stock loan.

6.10 FINANCING COMMODITY SHORT POSITIONS

Much of the trading in gold and silver worldwide occurs over the counter such as traders of the London Bullion Market Association consisting of spot and forward trading and a lending (leasing) market. Central banks have long used gold swaps (sales and repurchase transactions closely resembling repo transactions), which lend gold as part of their open market operations. Today, similar trades are generally described as gold leasing and are loans secured by assets. Like a bond repo, the true owner of the gold should carry the asset on the balance sheet while the position is out on lease to someone else. Because gold forward rates are generally close to Libor, holders of gold are not well compensated for lending spot gold. While the leasing market is most liquid for gold and silver, the technique is used for many metals.

Gold loans represent a longer term variation on the short-term financing described throughout this chapter. A mining company borrows gold, usually from a bank, which, in turn, may have borrowed the gold from a central bank. The mining company then sells the gold and uses the proceeds to develop a new mining operation. The mining company uses the gold output to repay gold to the bank over time.

Many agricultural commodities can be stored in elevators in exchange for a warehouse receipt. Warehouse receipts document the ownership of a specified quantify of the commodity of a particular grade. Elevators and warehouses commingle the commodities and promise to return the stated amount of a grade of the stored commodity, not the specific lot delivered to the elevator. Warehouse receipts issued in the United States under the protection of the U.S. Warehouse Receipts Act of 2000 are generally nego-tiable. They can be sold, used as collateral for loans, or lent to traders that must make deliveries.

6.11 TRADING IN THE LENDING MARKETS

Large dealers have security-lending departments both to finance dealer positions and as a profit center. Dealer financing desks seek to run a matched book of borrowing and lending trades to assist trading for their customers and to make profits for the dealer. Prime brokers provide turnkey access to the lending markets, combined with delivery and custody. A prime broker will finance long positions, locate and borrow short positions, and guarantee delivery of clients' purchases and sales.

Brokers facilitate lending participants by matching buyers and sellers, main-taining a marketplace for term trades, and providing a degree of anonymity to potential traders. These brokers have begun to create electronic market-places to execute repo trades and negotiate stock lending transactions. Electronic trading of repo has been growing in importance for almost a decade. ICAP, one of the world's largest interbroker dealers, has created a screen-based market for Japanese and major European shares. Eurex Repo had capitalized on the size of their derivatives exchange to cross-market a repo financing platform that offers anonymity by passing trades through to a clearing corp.

6.12 CONCLUSION

Most futures contracts and many derivatives contracts permit traders to buy or sell a wide range of financial assets and commodities. These instruments are convenient, usually create leverage, often are very liquid, and are usually insulated from counterparty risks. Still traders that can trade the underlying assets may have advantages over traders not familiar with the underlying cash markets or not in a position to finance long and short positions in the underlying assets.

The repo market permits traders to finance both long and short positions in a wide variety of bonds. The stock loan market similarly provides access to financing of long and short stock positions. Finally, leasing and other negotiated financing provide financing of long and short commodity positions.

REFERENCES

Bank of England. (2010). *Securities lending: An introductory guide.* Retrieved from http://www .bankofengland.co.uk.

D'Avolio, G. (2002). The market for borrowing stock. *Journal of Financial Economics, 66*(2), 271–306.

Duffie, D., Garleanu, N., & Pedersen, L. (2002). *Securities lending, shorting, and pricing.* Retrieved from http://papers.ssrn.com.

Lumpkin, S. A. (1998). Repurchase and reverse repurchase agreements. *Instruments of the Money Market.* Retrieved from http://www.richmondfed.org/publications/research/special_reports/ instruments_of_the_money_market/pdf/chapter_06.pdf.

Treasury Markets Practice Group. (2009). *Claiming a fails charge for a settlement fail in U.S. Treasury securities.* Retrieved from http://www.newyorkfed.org.

BIBLIOGRAPHY

Szabo, T. (2007). *Gold and silver 'leasing' examined.* Retrieved from http://www.silveraxis.com/ commentary/gold_silver_leasing.pdf.

CHAPTER 7

A Survey of Short Selling in Canada

Camillo Lento and James Kozyra

CONTENTS

ABSTRACT

The purpose of this chapter is to provide insights into the nature of short sales in Canada. More specifically, the chapter summarizes the regulatory framework that governs short sales, taxation of short sales, and trends and patterns of short sales. It highlights important short sale trends from the recent 2008–2009 credit crisis, as well as consequences of the 2008 short sale prohibition. This chapter can benefit both investors and regulators in Canada and abroad as it provides pertinent information regarding the nature of short sales in Canada.

KEYWORDS

Exchange-traded funds; Insider short sales; Investment Industry Regulatory Organization of Canada; Naked short sales; Universal Market Integrity Rules; Uptick rule.

7.1 INTRODUCTION

The purpose of this chapter is to provide a brief survey of short sales in Canada. As such, the chapter provides insights into the regulatory framework that governs short sales, the taxation of short sales in Canada, and recent trends in short selling activity in Canada. The regulatory framework discussion is based on a review of the Universal Market Integrity Rules (UMIR) sections that apply to short sales. The regulatory framework discussion begins with a definition of short sales and then provides a general discussion of the governing bodies and important regulations dealing with the uptick rule, naked short sales, and insider short sales.

The taxation treatment of short selling transactions in Canada provides a discussion of the tax consequences of realized versus unrealized gains/losses on short sales by reviewing Canada Revenue Agency pronouncements and documents. In addition, a discussion regarding the nature of the gain/loss (i.e., on account of capital or income) is provided. Recent trends of short selling activities in Canada provide insight into the impacts of the recent short sale prohibition and also sheds light on overall short selling activities in Canada (e.g., short selling as a percentage of trading activity, short exempt as a proportion of short sales, prevalence of short sale reporting). Overall, this survey is intended to provide insights for both investors and regulators regarding short selling activities in Canada.

7.2 CURRENT REGULATIONS

The recent volatility in equity markets led to a variety of responses by regulators. A common international response was the introduction of limits to short sales of securities. Limiting short sales was intended to ease some of the downward pressure on the equity markets. For example, in late 2008, the Securities and Exchange Commission (SEC) prohibited short selling financial firms' stocks. In Canada, the Ontario Securities Commission (OSC) made a similar move by restricting short selling activity on any interlisted companies that were on the SEC's restricted list. Although these short selling restrictions were later removed, they provided an impetus for Canadian regulators to revisit the regulatory environment for short sales.

In Canada, the Investment Industry Regulatory Organization of Canada (IIROC) governs most of the activity related to equity short sales through the UMIR. Part 1 of the UMIR provides the following definition of a short sale: "a sale of a security, other than a derivative instrument, which the seller does not own either directly or through an agent or trustee..." (IIROC, UMIR Part 1, 2010a).

Part 3 of the UMIR deals specifically with short selling and provides detailed guidance on the restriction of short sales and outlines the uptick rule (Part 3.1) and prohibition on the entry of orders (Part 3.2). The following is a brief discussion of some of the key aspects of the regulatory landscape that governs short selling in Canada, including (1) the uptick rule, (2) naked short sales, and (3) insiders and short sales.

7.2.1 The Uptick Rule
An uptick rule implies that any short sale transaction must be entered into at a price higher than the price of the previous trade. The intention of the uptick rule is to help alleviate downward pressure on stock prices. Part 3.1 of the UMIR deals with restrictions on short selling activities and begins by outlining the uptick rule as follows:

> Except as otherwise provided, a Participant or Access Person shall not make a short sale of a security on a marketplace unless the price is at or above the last sale price (IIROC, UMIR Part 3.1, 2010b).

On July 6, 2007, the uptick rule was eliminated by the SEC. As such, Canadian regulators moved in the same direction by repealing the uptick rule for companies interlisted in the United States to allow for a consistent treatment of interlisted securities. In addition, a proposal was put forward in 2007 to repeal the uptick rule in Canada altogether. However, the market turbulence of 2008 led the IIROC to defer the proposed removal of the uptick rule (Romano, Colangelo, & Grewal, 2009).

7.2.2 Naked Short Sales
The UMIR does not make a distinction between naked and covered short sales. However, naked short sales that fail to settle may violate other provisions in security legislation. For example, Section 126.1 of the Securities Act (1990) and Part 3 of the National Instrument 23-101 Trading Rules have been interpreted to be provisions that may restrict naked short sales (Romano et al., 2009).

7.2.3 Insiders and Short Sales

Although it is not part of the IIROC's UMIR, some short selling activity is prohibited by certain insiders by the Canada Business Corporations Act (CBCA). Paragraph 130(1) of the CBCA outlines the following regarding short sales:

> An insider shall not knowingly sell, directly or indirectly, a security of a distributing corporation or any of its affiliates if the insider selling the security does not own or has not fully paid for the security to be sold (CBCA, 1985).

There are some exceptions to this prohibition, as outlined in Paragraph 130(3), that allow insiders to sell short under certain conditions if they own another security convertible into the security sold or an option or right to acquire the security sold.

7.3 TAXATION OF SHORT SALES

Although short sales in Canada are a fairly common transaction, a search of the *Income Tax Act* or any other Canada Revenue Agency (CRA) documents provides very little guidance on the taxation of short sales. The CRA's *Income Tax Interpretation Bulletin 479R—Transactions in Securities* (IT-479R) provides some guidance on the taxation of short sales. IT-479R does not provide explicit guidance on short sales but suggests that the realization principle, which applies to the long position, also applies to the short position.

In essence, a short sale becomes taxable when the borrowed shares are repurchased and returned to the original owner. At this point, the transaction is complete and any gain or loss has been realized. Therefore, a short sale creates a tax implication when the transaction is completed and any gain or loss is realized. Unrealized gains and losses do not create any tax implications until they are realized.

In addition to the tax implications of realized versus unrealized gains/losses, IT-479R also provides guidance on whether the gain or loss from a security transaction is on the account of capital or income. The CRA guidance explicitly states that "the gain or loss on the 'short sale' of shares is considered to be on income account" (CRA, 1995, IT-479R, Paragraph 18).

Investors do have an alternative against the taxation of the short sale on the account of income. An investor can elect to have all Canadian securities transactions, including short sales, on account of capital going forward. The election will shelter all Canadian short sales as capital gains treatment. However, U.S. security transactions are not included under this election. Note that a more complete and detailed discussion of the taxation of short sales can be found in Lento (2010).

7.4 RECENT TRENDS IN CANADA

Recently, the IIROC conducted an investigation of trends and market activities, including short selling, for the period spanning May 1, 2007, to September 30, 2008 (IIROC, 2009a). The study reviewed trading data from the following seven marketplaces: (1) Toronto Stock Exchange (TSX), (2) TSX Venture Exchange (TSXV), (3) Canadian National Stock Exchange (CSNX), (4) MATCH Now, (5) Pure Trading, (6) Omega, and (7) Chi-X.[1] The study was conducted in hope of being able to better protect investors and the integrity of the capital markets, particularly during times of market turmoil.

This study is the most comprehensive research paper that deals with recent trends for short sales in Canada. As such, a brief discussion of this study is provided and organized into the following five sections: (1) short selling as a percentage of trading activity, (2) attributes of short sales, (3) short exempt as a proportion of short sales, (4) prevalence of short sale reporting, and (5) the relationship between rates of short sales activity and market stress.

7.4.1 Short Selling as a Percentage of Trading Activity

The level of short selling activity was fairly constant during the May 2007 to September 2008 period, with a slight increase in the percentage of trades made in interlisted securities. Overall, short sales as a percentage of total trades on the TSX increased from 24 to 26.1%. The increase is likely a result of the aforementioned exemption to the uptick rule. Results were consistent across the majority of marketplaces studied, with the exceptions being Pure Trading and Chi-X marketplaces, both of which saw a decrease in short sales as a percentage of trades when comparing the beginning period to the average for the overall period.

Another notable finding was that short selling was generally more prominent in newer marketplaces (e.g., Pure Trading, Omega, and Chi-X) with the

---

[1] MATCH Now is an alternative trading system for dealers and their clients to trade Canadian-listed equity securities. MATCH Now provides fully automated order matching and trade execution. No pretrade information on participants, order sizes, or pricing is displayed publicly. Access vendors only receive indicators of the stock symbol and side. Pure Trading is a distinctly branded facility operated by CNSX Markets Inc. for dealers trading in Canadian-listed securities. Securities listed on other Canadian stock exchanges are posted and available for trading on Pure, which provides visible, fully automated order matching and trade execution. Omega ATS is an alternative trading system providing registered dealers with fully automated order matching and execution of trades in TSX-listed equity securities. Order price and volume information is available, while orders and trades are anonymous. Chi-X Canada is an ATS providing registered dealers with fully automated order matching and execution of trades in TSX-listed equities. Order price and volume information is available, while orders and trades are anonymous. These definitions are reproduced from http://www.iiroc.ca/English/About/OurRole/Pages/MarketplaceWeRegulate.aspx.

assumption being that these marketplaces were used for arbitrage via algorithmic trading. During their first month of operation, Pure Trading, Omega, and Chi-X saw short sale levels as a percentage of trading activity of 45.7, 47.5, and 71.4%, respectively. On average, numbers for Pure Trading and Chi-X declined as time went on, while Omega saw an average of 56.3% (compared to 47.5% in the initial period).

A negative relationship was found between the level of short sales made on a security and the level of liquidity of that particular security. Finally, results indicated that the repeal of price restrictions did not have a major impact on the level of short selling activity on the TSXV and CNSX, the junior marketplaces under study. Increased volatility was found to reduce the level of short sales on the junior marketplaces, while having little effect on the number of short sales on the TSX.

7.4.2 Comparative Trade Attributes of Short Sales

Short sales typically have volumes lower than that of the opposing long position in a given security. Short sale volume consisted of 78% of the average trade volume for the TSX as a whole comparable to the 83% on the TSXV. Short sale volume for interlisted securities on the TSX hovered slightly under the 100% of that of the opposing long position for the majority of the study period, while the short sale volume of exchange-traded funds (ETFs) on the TSX was approximately 123%, or 23% greater than that of the respective long position in such securities. The high volume of short sales on ETFs was due to the hedging of derivative transactions in order to qualify as a "program trade" under UMIR.

Finally, the lowest level of short sale volume relative to long positions was seen on the CNSX, with an average rate of 52%. It was revealed that, during periods of market stress, those in which the level of volatility is increasing, the volume of short sales decreased by 3 to 5% when compared to the average for the period for securities traded on the TSXV and CNSX. There was a 15 to 17% decrease in the volume of short sales for both interlisted and other securities on the TSX during market stress periods. Unlike the other securities, ETFs experienced an increase, rather than a decrease, of 8% in the volume of short sales when market stress was present.

Further analysis identified that the value of the average short sale, on a relative basis, was nearly identical to that of the average trade in securities for the TSX as a whole, as well as for interlisted and other securities on the TSX. In relative terms, short sales on the CNSX were lower in value than the average trade, with the exception being the first 2 months during our investigation period (May–June 2007). TSXV and TSX ETFs saw short sale values greater than those of the average long transactions on the respective securities.

Short sale values on the TSXV ranged from 130^2 to 150% of the average trade value for most of the study, while the short sale value was most volatile on the TSX ETFs, ranging anywhere from 100% to approximately 230% over the period of study.

7.4.3 Short Exempt as a Proportion of Short Selling

With the exception of the TSXV and CNSX, the marketplaces recognize use of the short exempt marker.[3] Short sales for arbitrage purposes are exempt from restrictions on pricing, and the recent decision to grant exemptions on interlisted securities has led to exemptions occurring at a more frequent level.

The short exempt as a percentage of short sale trades figure for the TSX was 32.5% at the beginning of the period, with an average of 54.5% for the duration of our examination period. Less than 50% of short sales on ETFs were marked as short exempt, even though all such trades are eligible for the exemption. Similarly, while all securities that trade on Omega are eligible for the exemption, only 25.5% of the short sales made were marked as such.

7.4.4 Prevalence of Short Position Reporting

Universal Market Integrity Rules requirements make it necessary to periodically report the short position held in each security on an account-by-account basis. This requirement allows for an analysis of the rates of turnover of short positions and the percentage of securities on a given marketplace that a short position has been undertaken in.

On average, during our examination period, the turnover rates were 0.76, 0.38, and 0.63, respectively, on a monthly basis for the TSX, TSXV, and CNSX. These numbers indicate that the short positions were held, on average, for 15.96 trading days on the TSX, 7.98 trading days on the TSXV, and 13.23 trading days on the CNSX. The quick turnover rate, such as that on the TSXV, is typically an indication that there are temporary price dislocations the investor is trying to take advantage of. However, higher numbers indicate a more long-term position, with the investor undertaking a short sale position for purposes of betting against the prospects of the particular security.

An average of two-thirds (66.5%) of securities listed on the TSX were reported as having an open short position during the course of our study.

---

[2] A value of 130% indicates that for every $1.00 invested in a long position, $1.30 was invested in the respective short position.
[3] The "short exempt" marker allows for short sales to be made even in absence of compliance with the uptick rule (UMIR Rule 3.1) in certain situations. The short exempt marker is supported by the TSX, Alpha, Chi-X, Omega, MATCH Now, and Pure Trading, while the TSXV and CNSX do not support the marker.

The TSXV and CNSX saw short sales opened in roughly one-quarter (26.2%) and one-fifth (18.49%) of their securities on average, with the figure ranging from 20.5 to 31.4% on the TSXV and from 12.3 to 29.7% on the CNSX. The numbers remained fairly constant for the TSX, while TSXV and CNSX figures appeared to be on a downward trend over the course of the study period.

7.4.5 Relationship between Rates of Short Selling and Market Stress

Statistics were indexed to analyze both market stress and short selling to determine if there was an identifiable relationship between the two. Indexing was done by taking the overall period average for a given measure and comparing the monthly statistic as a percentage of the overall period average (e.g., when the monthly average is equal to the overall average, the score will be 100% for the given month). The level of short sales on the TSX experienced a slight increase in indexed terms throughout the duration of the study period. The slight increase in the level of short sales is explained by the fact that interlisted securities became short exempt in July 2007, which was partway through the period of study. There was seemingly no link between this and the level of market stress, as the level of market stress ranged from roughly 60 to 250% in indexed terms throughout the entire period.

A more evident pattern was observed for the TSXV measures, as the level of short sales and the measure of market stress had a negative relationship. This relationship held regardless of whether the market was trending up or down.

7.5 IMPACT OF RECENT SHORT SALE PROHIBITION

On September 19, 2008, the OSC instituted a temporary prohibition of short sales for certain securities until October 8, 2008. The securities impacted were those of financial issuers that were listed on the TSX and were also interlisted on only the U.S. exchange. These measures were taken with the intent of ensuring that a fair market remained, as well as preventing regulatory arbitrage from occurring, based on the actions of the SEC.

The IIROC increased surveillance during this time period, compiling their findings into what was referred to as the "short prohibition study" (IIROC, 2009b). The study spanned from August 1, 2008, to October 24, 2008, with subperiods being used to distinguish among the preorder period, the preorder week, the order period, and the postorder period. Results of the study are summarized here by reviewing (1) effects on price levels, (2) trading rates, (3) volume rates, (4) short selling rates, (5) effect on market quality, and (6) changes in short positions.

7.5.1 Effect on Price Levels

During our entire examination period, S&P/TSX composite index price levels were down by an average of 11%. Restricted financials and nonrestricted financials averaged much smaller losses, as they were down 2.6 and 3.4%, respectively. On the first day of the postorder period, the price of restricted financials dropped by over 9%. Interestingly, the number of short sales on this day was 20% less than the historical average, implying that the drop in prices was not due to excessive amounts of short selling, but possibly due to excessive amounts of short selling, which caused "long" investors to sell. Overall, following the prohibition of short sales, restricted financials outperformed nonrestricted financials, albeit by a small margin.

7.5.2 Trade Rate Review

Trading activity was up across the board during the preorder week, as the number of trades was up 50% from the preorder period. Trading activity continued to rise for the market as a whole over the remainder of the study period, while restricted and nonrestricted financials saw moderate declines in trading activity during the order period.

The proportion of trades in restricted financials compared to overall trades in the TSX remained in the 8 to 12% range for the preorder period. This number jumped into the 12 to 18% range during the preorder week before dropping into the 6 to 8% range during the order period. Trading activity settled back into the 8 to 12% period during the postorder period. Meanwhile, nonrestricted financials also peaked during the preorder week. This trading activity accounted for 4% of the entire TSX, up from its normal level of 2 to 3%.

7.5.3 Volume Rate Review

The volume of trades in restricted financials as a proportion of volume on the overall market was in the 3 to 7% range for the majority of the study period, with the order period being the exception. During this time, the volume in restricted financials peaked between 8 and 20% of the overall trade volume. Nonrestricted financials followed a similar pattern, with proportional volume levels in the 1 to 4% range for the majority of the study, with peak levels of 4 to 6.75% during the preorder week.

7.5.4 Review of Short Selling

During the preorder period, short sales were in the 27 to 40% range as a proportion of trades in restricted financials. Following lifting of the prohibition order, this figure dropped to the 19 to 29% range. From May 2007 through September 2008, the proportion of trades that were short sales for interlisted securities was 30.3%. Nonrestricted financials also experienced a drop in the number of short sales during the order period on a relative basis, even though there was no prohibition on such trading activity.

7.5.5 Effect on Market Quality

One measure used to measure market quality was comparison of the bid/ask spread of restricted financials to that of nonrestricted financials. From the preorder period to the order period, the spread on nonrestricted financials increased by slightly over 50%, while the spread on restricted financials increased by more than 300%. A second measure, volatility, was also used to determine the effect on market quality. Volatility was up across the board during the preorder week, with restricted financials being the most volatile. During the order period and postorder period, the TSX was more volatile than both restricted and nonrestricted financials, while restricted financials were slightly more volatile than nonrestricted financials.

7.5.6 Changes in Short Position

The TSX saw a constant decline in short positions during our examination period. At the beginning of the period, 0.956% of shares on the TSX were held in a short position, a number that fell to 0.810% by the end of the period (a 15% decline). Restricted financials followed a similar pattern, with 0.872% of shares being held in a short position at the beginning of the period and 0.695% of shares being held in a short position to end the period (a 20% decline). Nonrestricted financials saw an increase in the percentage of shares held in short positions, much of which can be accounted for by an increase in short sales during the early stages of the order period. For the period as a whole, nonrestricted financials saw a 5% increase in short positions.

7.6 CONCLUSION

The paper summarizes the regulatory framework that governs short sales, and also offers insight into the taxation of short sales in Canada. In addition, important short sale trends from the recent 2008–2009 credit crisis are highlighted, along with a discussion of the consequences of the 2008 short sale prohibition. Both investors and regulators will find this chapter useful in terms of providing pertinent information on short selling in Canada.

REFERENCES

Canada Business Corporations Act. (1985). R.S.C., c. C-44.

Canada Revenue Agency. (1995). IT479R—Transactions in securities. Retrieved from http://www.cra-arc.gc.ca/E/pub/tp/it479r/it479r-e.txt.

Investment Industry Regulatory Organization of Canada (IIROC). (2009a). *Recent trends in trading activity, short sales, and failed trades.* Retrieved from http://docs.iiroc.ca/DisplayDocument .aspx?DocumentID=DE2E6F9F4AE442F5BC0AE75A9E812FE5&Language=en.

IIROC. (2009b). *Study on the impact of the prohibition on the short sale of inter-listed financial sector issuers.* Retrieved from http://docs.iiroc.ca/DisplayDocument.aspx?DocumentID=3B4FDC12E 7AA4177890D0170914D5D7A&Language=en.

IIROC. (2010a). *Universal market integrity rules, part 1—definitions and interpretations.* Retrieved from http://www.iiroc.ca/English/Documents/Rulebook/UMIR0101_en.pdf.

IIROC. (2010b). *Universal market integrity rules, part 3.1—restrictions on short selling.* Retrieved from http://www.iiroc.ca/English/Documents/Rulebook/UMIR0301_en.pdf.

Lento, C. (2010, June). *CRA's short of information on short sales.* Canadian MoneySaver, p. 26.

Romano, S., Colangelo, A., & Grewal, R. (2009). *Short sales in Canada: Current regulations and recent changes.* Unpublished working paper. Retrieved from http://www.stikeman.com/cps/ rde/xchg/se-en/hs.xsl/12516.htm.

Securities Act. (1990). R.S.O., Chapter S.5.

SECTION 2

European Markets

CHAPTER 8

Are Restrictions on Short Selling Good? A Look at European Markets

Mohamed El Hedi Arouri, Fredj Jawadi, and Duc Khuong Nguyen

CONTENTS

ABSTRACT

This chapter proposes to reassess the accuracy of policy decisions imposing short sales constraints on equity trading activity during the ongoing global financial crisis of 2007–2010. We analyze the changes in trading volume and volatility of short selling-banned stocks in France and Germany where transactions resulting from short positions are prohibited during both the global financial crisis and the Greek crisis. We then provide a concise response to the model for a pan-European short selling regime, proposed by the Committee of European Securities Regulators, which aims at reducing harmful impacts of short sales actions, and point out some implications for market efficiency and professional equity investments. Our intuition is that no regulation might be better than regulation, but some transparency requirements for excessive short selling operations are indeed needed.

KEYWORDS

Committee of European Securities Regulators; Credit default swaps; F test; Federal Financial Supervision Authority for Germany; Rolling standard deviation; Short sales ban; Volatility; Volume behavior; Z test.

8.1 INTRODUCTION

Short selling consists in arbitrage and/or speculative strategies often carried out by investors and traders using options and other derivatives. Investors sell assets generally borrowed from a third party with the intention of buying identical assets back at a future date. A short sell position normally does not exceed 10 days, whereas a buy position has a term of 1 year (Lioui, 2009). The short seller hopes to profit from a decrease in the price of the assets between the sale and the repurchase. According to Diether, Lee, and Werner (2009), short sellers include a large majority of financial institutions and only a few individual sellers, but together they are responsible for 25% of daily trading in stocks subject to short sale price tests.[1]

We should also note that short selling is often viewed as a contributing factor to undesirable stock market volatility, especially in extreme market conditions. Indeed, speculators use short selling not only to bet on a declining trend in the stock prices, but also to influence and even help determine that trend by selling large quantities of shares of a targeted company. Thus, short selling can force stock prices to fall below what is justifiable by fundamentals and destroy market and public confidence in a company that may collapse, but would have survived without the short selling activity. However, some researchers consider that short sellers contribute to market efficiency by eliminating price differences and arbitrage opportunities, as well as increase market liquidity, price discovery, facilitate hedging, and help mitigate market bubbles, as well as other risk management activities. In other words, the impact of short selling on stock markets is a crucial question that needs to be examined empirically.

More interestingly, during the global financial crisis of 2007–2009, several stock markets declined dramatically and many stocks moved below their fundamental values. To stop the effects of the financial crisis, financial market authorities in several countries decided to restrict and/or impose conditions on short selling activity. The restrictions took effect in September 2008, but the length of the restrictions varied from country to country. Some countries, such as the United Kingdom and United States, removed them in 2009, whereas other countries (Austria, France, Germany, and

---

[1] Price tests refer to the uptick rule for NYSE stocks and the bid price test for the NASDAQ.

Portugal) kept them in place until the time of this writing. Moreover, these restrictions generally took various forms across countries in that some imposed restrictions on all short selling of specified shares or specified categories of shares, whereas other countries restricted naked short selling and some also introduced disclosure obligations of different sorts.[2]

The objectives of banning short sales were to diminish drop stock prices and to stabilize stock markets. This decision has, however, addressed a pessimistic message for small investors particularly because financial market authorities have not explained the reasons of this action. Consequently, it seems that restrictions on short selling produce negative effects on stock markets through implying a significant rise in stock market volatility and idiosyncratic risk. Options trading is also affected, and the gap between stock price and fundamental value would become important.

In order to provide insights about the impacts of short sale restrictions on stock market behavior, we analyze the changes induced on return volatility and volume transaction of a sample of 10 banned stocks in France and Germany by distinguishing the ban period from the normal period. Our findings suggest that restrictions on short selling did not permit deemphasizing the market nervousness.

The remainder of this chapter is organized as follows. Section 8.2 empirically investigates the reaction of stock markets to short selling bans. Section 8.3 discusses the Committee of European Securities Regulators (CESR) initiative and its impacts on professional equity investments.

8.2 SHORT SELLING BANS AND ANALYSIS OF MARKET REACTIONS

To reduce the harmful impacts of the global financial crisis sparked by the U.S. subprime crisis, the Federal Financial Supervision Authority for Germany (BaFin) prohibited naked short selling in shares of 11 financial companies by its decree dated the 19th and 21st of September 2008. Accordingly, all transactions that result in a short position or in an increase in a short position in the shares issued by the said companies are banned. Restrictions were intended to expire on December 31, 2008, but were eradicated on January 31, 2010. Recently, BaFin has, in the wake of the Greek crisis, prohibited temporarily naked short selling of debt securities of eurozone

---

[2] Naked short sales are short selling transactions in which the seller does not borrow or arrange to borrow the securities in order to deliver to the buyers within the required time frame. Market operators can then use them to fraudulently drive stock prices down to make profits because this practice is formally prohibited by laws and specific regulations.

Table 8.1 List of Short Selling-Banned Stocks in France and Germany

	France	Germany	
No.	Sept. 19, 2008	Sept. 19, 2008– Jan. 31, 2010	May 19, 2010– March 31, 2011
1	Allianz	Aareal Bank AG	Aareal Bank AG
2	April Group	Allianz SE	Allianz SE
3	AXA	ABM Generali Holding AG	Commerzbank AG
4	BNP Parbas	Commerzbank AG	Deutsche Bank AG
5	CIC	Deutsche Bank AG	Deutsche Börse AG
6	CNP Assuances	Deutsche Börse AG	Deutsche Postbank AG
7	Crédit Agricole	Deutsche Postbank AG	Generali Deutschland Holding AG
8	Dexia	Hannover Rückversicherung	Hannover Rückversicherung
9	Euler Hermes	Hypo Real Estate Holding AG	MPL AG
10	HSBC	MPL AG	Münchener Rückversicherung-Gesellschaft AG
11	Natixis	Münchener Rückversicherung-Gesellschaft AG	
12	NYSE Euronext		
13	Paris RE		
14	Scor		
15	Société Générale		

countries as well as credit default swaps (CDS) containing at least a liability of a eurozone country. BaFin also announced new temporary prohibitions on short sale transactions in the shares of 10 companies (Table 8.1). The prohibition period was initially set from May 19, 2010, to March 31, 2011. In France, short sales prohibitions by the French market authority (AMF) set in September 19, 2008, were maintained up until the time of this writing. Table 8.1 presents the list of shares restricted for both France and Germany, all of which are from the financial sector.

We analyze the volatility and volume behavior of 10 selected financial stocks subject to short selling bans by French and German market authorities (Table 8.2). Data used are daily closing prices and trading volume extracted from Datastream International. The entire study period from May 11, 2007, to January 29, 2010, is split into subperiods, with the break date being September 19, 2008: the normal period (May 11, 2007–September 18, 2008) and the ban period (September 19, 2008–January 29, 2010). Note that our analysis does not concern the ban on naked short

Table 8.2 Results of Z Test for Changes in Average Return and Volume

Company	Z Test for Mean Equalization		Z Test for Volume Equalization	
	Mean Change	p Value	Mean Change	p Value
France				
April Group	−0.0013	0.7542	−25560.1049	1.0000
AXA	−0.0002	0.5253	−2480548.8592	1.0000
BNP Paribas	0.0003	0.4490	−605424.6601	0.9999
Crédit Agricole	0.0016	0.2357	−2052750.2297	1.0000
Euler Hermes	0.0029	0.0630	−33857.7649	1.0000
Germany				
Aareal Bank AG	0.0039	0.1273	−9237.7500	0.7550
Allianz SE	0.0014	0.2608	−1012949.7186	1.0000
Commerzbank AG	0.0005	0.4377	3584401.2552	0.0000
Deutsche Bank AG	0.0021	0.2254	966721.9837	0.0000
Deutsche Postbank AG	0.0006	0.4003	−602251.9306	1.0000

sales imposed by Germany's financial market authority in order to get a homogeneous data set for two countries.

We first examine whether short sale restrictions have induced significant changes in observed average returns and trading volume using a right-side unilateral statistical test (Z test). Denoting average returns and average volume, respectively, over the periods before and after the ban on short sales by μ_0 and μ, respectively, null and alternative hypotheses are as follows:

$$H_0: \mu = \mu_0$$
$$H_1: \mu > \mu_0$$

The empirical statistics used to choose between H_0 and H_1 is

$$z^* = \frac{\bar{x} - \mu_0}{s/\sqrt{n}}$$

where $\bar{x}$ refers to average return and average volume, respectively, calculated over the ban period and n is the number of observations ($n = 344$ trading days). Under the assumption of the normality of stock returns, z^* follows a standard normal distribution under H_0. Considering, for example, a 5% level, H_0 is rejected if $z^* \geq Z$, where Z is a critical value resulting from the standard normal distribution table ($\text{Prob}(z^* \geq Z) = 0.05$). Because of the symmetry of the normal distribution, if $\mu < \mu_0$, the test will result in a p value larger than 0.95. Table 8.2 summarizes the results.

Several interesting facts can be noted. First, the null hypothesis of equality of average returns cannot be rejected at conventional levels for all stocks considered in view of the probability associated with the Z test. This leads us to conclude in favor of insignificant effects of a short sales ban on stock returns. Next, results of the Z test for changes in trading volume indicate heterogeneous behavior across stocks. Indeed, five stocks in France and two in Germany (Allianz SE and Deutsche Postbank AG) experienced significant decreases in volume (at the 1% level) over the ban period, while two German stocks (Commerzbank AG and Deutsche Bank AG) recorded significant increases over the same subperiod. However, no impact of short sales restrictions was found for the remaining stock (Aareal Bank AG). Finally, one should note that variations in trading volume are quite important for four financial firms largely involved in the commercialization of asset-backed securities (AXA, Crédit Agricole, Allianz AG, and Commerzbank AG).

The F test is then used to check for the statistical significance of return volatility changes for the sample of 10 stocks (Table 8.3). We assume that stock returns follow a normal distribution $N(\mu_1, \sigma_1)$ over the normal period prior to short sales restrictions and $N(\mu_2, \sigma_2)$ over the ban period. The comparison test of two subperiod variances is written as

$$H_0: \sigma_1^2 = \sigma_2^2$$

$$H_1: \sigma_1^2 \neq \sigma_2^2$$

Table 8.3 Results of F Test for Changes in Standard Deviation of Return Volatility

Company	F Test for Return Variance Equalization	
	Variance Change	p Value
France		
April Group	0.0007	0.0000
AXA	0.0014	0.0000
BNP Paribas	0.0012	0.0000
Crédit Agricole	0.0008	0.0000
Euler Hermes	0.0007	0.0000
Germany		
Aareal Bank AG	0.0029	0.0000
Allianz SE	0.0012	0.0000
Commerzbank AG	0.0025	0.0000
Deutsche Bank AG	0.0021	0.0000
Deutsche Postbank AG	0.0016	0.0000

The empirical statistics used to make decision between H_0 and H_1 is

$$F^* = \frac{s_1^2}{s_2^2}$$

where s_1^2 and s_2^2 are empirical variances of two subperiods, respectively. Under the null hypothesis, F^* follows a Fisher–Snedecor distribution with $(n_1 - 1)$ and $(n_2 - 1)$ degrees of freedom where n_1 and n_2 refer to the number of observations of two respective subperiods (i.e., 344 trading days in our case). The null hypothesis (H_0) is rejected when $F \leq c_1$ or $F \leq c_2$, where c_1 and c_2 are critical values of the unilateral F test on the left and on the right at a selected level of significance.

Upon inspection, results of the F test indicate that the null hypothesis is clearly rejected at the 1% level for all stocks (Table 8.3). When looking at sign changes, the return volatility of all selected stocks over the ban period is significantly higher than that in the normal period. Accordingly, a short selling regulation seems to have generated more repercussions on stock price volatility than on trading volume.

To further explore the dynamic changes in the volatility of stock returns, Figure 8.1 displays the 5-day rolling standard deviation over the study period. We note that the majority of financial companies under consideration experienced important peaks of volatility following the announcement of short sales bans by French and German market regulators.

For 9 of the 10 companies, 5-day volatility peaks attained more than 12% on a daily basis as compared to an average of less than 4% during the period preceding the short selling bans. These graphs also confirm the common tendency of increased financial volatility for almost all stocks reported in Table 8.3.

We also test whether the policy decision of prohibiting short sales on September 19, 2008, and the Lehman Brother bankruptcy filing on September 15, 2008, had a direct effect on return volatility of the 10 companies considered in this study (Table 8.4). We create two dummy variables corresponding to the two events, where one variable assumes a value of 1 at the event date and 0 otherwise. We then relate the 5-day rolling standard deviation of each company to two aforementioned dummy variables. Results obtained from regression analysis indicate short selling significantly affected stock returns in 6 out of 10 cases,[3] while the Lehman Brothers bankruptcy event, which marked the global stage of the recent financial crisis, induced significant changes in stock volatility of three French companies (AXA, BNP Paribas, and Crédit Agricole).

---

[3] AXA, Crédit Agricole, Aareal Bank AG, Allianz SE, Commerzbank AG, and Deutsche Bank AG.

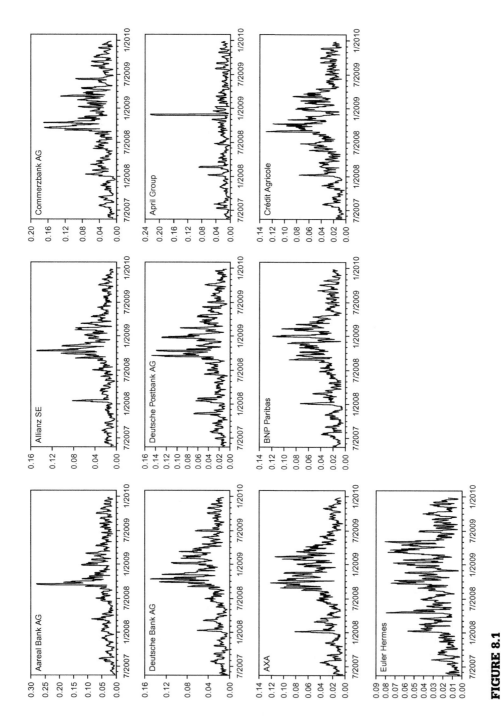

FIGURE 8.1

Five-day rolling standard deviation of stock returns over the period from May 11, 2007, to January 29, 2010.

Table 8.4 Return Volatility Reaction to Short Sales Restrictions and the Lehman Brothers Bankruptcy[a]

France	April Groupe	AXA	BNP Paribas	Crédit Agricole	Euler Hermes
Short sales restrictions	−0.0034 (0.0210)	0.0684*** (0.0231)	0.0485 (0.0196)	0.0752*** (0.0199)	−0.0010 (0.0163)
Lehman Brothers bankruptcy	0.0143 (0.0210)	0.0747*** (0.0231)	0.0633*** (0.0196)	0.0999*** (0.0199)	0.0197 (0.0163)
Constant	0.0203*** (0.0008)	0.0307*** (0.0008)	0.0287*** (0.0007)	0.0306*** (0.0007)	0.0262*** (0.0006)
R^2	0.07%	2.73%	2.36%	5.43%	0.22%

Germany	Aareal Bank AG	Allianz SE	Commerzbank AG	Deutsche Bank AG	Deutsche Postbank AG
Short sales restrictions	0.0682** (0.0322)	0.0517* (0.0203)	0.0853*** (0.0269)	0.0490** (0.0238)	0.0235 (0.0223)
Lehman Brothers bankruptcy	−0.0026 (0.0321)	0.0045 (0.0202)	0.0094 (0.0269)	0.0036 (0.0238)	0.0211 (0.0223)
Constant	0.0397*** (0.0012)	0.0252*** (0.0007)	0.0362*** (0.0010)	0.0304*** (0.0009)	0.0301 (0.0008)***
R^2	0.66%	0.95%	1.47%	0.62%	0.29%

[a] Results of the regression analysis relating stock volatility to two dummy variables representing short sales ban and Lehman Brothers bankruptcy events. Standard errors are in parentheses. Symbols *, **, and *** denote significance at the 10, 5, and 1% level, respectively.

As shown by our analysis of return volatility and trading volume, short selling prohibition contributed to a substantial increase in the volatility of the stocks affected by the regulation. It may also create more uncertainty for financial markets, in general, if we look at the volatility behavior of aggregate market indices over the same period. These facts are clearly in contrast to the initial objectives of the market regulators, which consisted of calming down the markets and avoiding speculative attacks against financial stocks.

The most recent example is the unilateral decision of Germany to prohibit naked short sales on debt securities and CDS involving eurozone countries that took effect beginning on May 19, 2010, and ending on March 31, 2011. The decision of prohibiting naked short sales is widely criticized by market authorities of numerous European countries because the lack of coordination by the German government generated important uncertainties for stock trading due to rising concerns about survival of the euro. The solution seems to have had only psychological and temporary effects during the crisis, as investors attempt to sell their shares of firms in distress and may bypass the restrictions through investing, for example, in short-biased funds and exchange-traded funds. By mainly trading options and futures instead of shorting stocks, these funds are able to achieve gains in down market periods. Finally, we may need appropriate regulations such as a permanent and harmonized regime of short selling practices at a global level to limit their harmful effects rather than prohibiting them explicitly.

8.3 COMMITTEE OF EUROPEAN SECURITIES REGULATORS INITIATIVE AND ITS IMPACTS ON PROFESSIONAL EQUITY INVESTMENTS

The initiative of the Committee of European Securities Regulators is to provide a model for a Pan-European short selling disclosure regime to improve the transparency of net short positions and market efficiency. Globally, this model imposes disclosure requirements for all shares admitted to trading on any European Economic Area (EEA)-regulated market or an EEA multilateral trading facility where all conditions and trading rules are defined exclusively by the stock exchange. The CESR determines disclosure obligations based primarily on the ratio of net short positions to the company's issued share capital. That is, a ratio of 0.2% net short positions would be disclosed to the relevant market regulator, in addition to the regulator, also to the market as a whole for 0.5% net short positions. All changes of positions would be reported at increments of 0.1% and disclosed first to the regulator for modifications from 0.3 until 0.4% and then to the regulator and to the market. One should note that the proposed model does not, however, treat naked short sales specifically.

In its current form, the CESR (2010) proposal may have several implications for market efficiency, investors, and professional equity investments. First, it is not sure that the expected effect of the proposed measures on market efficiency can be achieved because results of past studies regarding this issue still remain inconclusive. For instance, Bris (2008) shows that the efficiency hypothesis worsened after short sale restrictions, while Marsh and Niemer (2008) point out that the efficiency is not affected. Second, this disclosure requirement may lead to a long-term loss of liquidity and decrease in trading volumes, leading to a long-term fall of prices. Finally, excess volatility resulting from the application of this restriction can increase a gap *between share price and its fundamentals* and cause turbulences in stock markets. Excess volatility may also have dramatic effects on the psychology of investors, thereby reducing their confidence in the market.

Given that markets actually require new regulations that develop comprehensive and suitable rules that could reduce volatility and improve market transparency and efficiency, the appropriate solution would be to not prohibit short sales, but to regulate them, for example, setting trading bands in cases of extreme financial volatility (i.e., when a volatility threshold is reached) and/or limiting the trading amount. In addition, as stock markets are becoming more and more interdependent, any regulation should be global and coordinated internationally. The rationale behind this idea is that financial instability can increase substantially and transmit from one market to another if traders are allowed to shorten the same stock in different national markets with different levels.

8.4 CONCLUSION

Using data from a sample of 10 French and German companies whose shares have been subject to short selling prohibitions during the period from May 11, 2007, to January 29, 2010, we provided evidence of an excessive increase in volatility in almost all stocks under consideration in the follow-up of short sale ban decisions. Changes in trading volume, albeit heterogeneous, are significant in 9 out of 10 cases, and there is a general tendency toward a decrease in volume. Our analysis of rolling standard deviation reveals that the volatility of financial stocks is not much higher after the release of the U.S. subprime crisis in July 2007, but started to rise significantly after the French and German market authorities imposed a ban on short sales. These results lead us to believe that the appropriate solution for stabilizing stock markets in distress is not to prohibit short sales, but rather to introduce global rules for shorting stocks by setting trading bands and trading volume over a certain threshold of stock market volatility.

REFERENCES

Bris, A. (2008). *Short selling activity in financial stocks and the SEC July 15th emergency order*. Working Paper, New Haven, CT: Yale International Center for Finance.

CESR. (2010). *Model for a pan-European short selling disclosure regime* (March 2010 Report). Paris, France.

Diether, K., Lee, K-H., & Werner, I. (2009). It's SHO time! Short-sale price tests and market quality. *Journal of Finance, 64*(1), 37–73.

Lioui, A. (2009). *The undesirable effects of banning short sales*. Working Paper, Nice, France: EDHEC Business School.

Marsh, I., & Niemer, N. (2008). The impact of short sales restrictions. Working Paper, London, UK: Cass Business School.

CHAPTER 9

Short Selling, Clearing, and Settlement in Europe: Relations and Implications

Daniela Russo and Simonetta Rosati

CONTENTS

ABSTRACT

Disruptions that short selling, and naked short selling in particular, can bring to the settlement process in case it results in settlement fails is one important concern to the market and market authorities addressed by short selling regulation. This chapter describes the relationship between short selling and settlement risk. In particular it examines how short selling can impact the effectiveness of a settlement discipline regime, that is, the set of rules and mitigation measures that aim to prevent fails or protect the settlement layer. Furthermore, it explains how settlement systems can potentially support market discipline by monitoring the fails and enforcing additional regulatory restrictions.

KEYWORDS

Central counterparty; Delivery versus payment; Fails; International Organization of Securities Commissions; Securities settlement systems; Settlement risk; Short selling.

9.1 INTRODUCTION

The debate surrounding short selling focuses on the benefits and drawbacks of this trading practice and whether securities market regulators should ban it or introduce prudential requirements, such as having reporting and transparency requirements, or allow it without any specific restriction. While individual traders may have a variety of reasons to engage in short selling, there are two positive effects for the market as a whole associated with short selling: (1) its positive impact to ensure market liquidity and (2) its contribution to the timely processing of new market information for accurate price discovery by the market. At the same time, short selling presents some potential disadvantages, particularly if it turns out to be a means for market manipulation and/or when naked short selling leads to an inability to deliver the traded assets on the agreed settlement date (known as "settlement fail"). Settlement fails have the potential to degenerate into a systemic disruption of the settlement systems if parties not receiving the assets as expected cannot themselves fulfill a subsequent delivery obligation, which can undermine market confidence of the clearing and settlement infrastructure. This could lead to a wider disruption of financial markets served by those settlement infrastructures. Hence, the settlement risk potentially associated with short selling is an important reason to justify restrictions or to regulate short selling and, more importantly, naked short selling.

Regulators' assessment of the balance between the risks and the benefits of short selling varies from country to country because of the dependence on the size and the structure of the market as well as the type of investors [e.g., the number of institutional (wholesale) investors and retail investors operating in those specific markets]. Following the financial turmoil of 2008 and 2009, the relevant authorities of several member states of the European Union (EU) have enacted regulations on short selling. In September 2009 the European Commission published a proposal with the purpose of harmonizing the regulatory treatment of short selling in the EU and avoiding concentration of short selling in less (or non)regulated markets, while ensuring an adequate and common level of transparency in European financial markets.

These regulatory initiatives have revamped the debate on the risks of short selling, including the settlement risk dimension. Because of their systemic risk relevance, securities clearing and settlement systems are subject to oversight by central banks and securities markets regulators with settlement risk being addressed by a set of regulatory measures. A varied set of measures and rules, referred to as "settlement discipline," ensure that participants in clearing and settlement systems adopt behaviors conducive to an appropriate level of settlement efficiency. Because there are incentives to avoid fails and ensure prompt resolution, clearing and settlement systems have procedures to contain settlement fails contagion and avoid systemic risk.

This chapter contributes to the current debate by first describing the relationship between short selling and settlement risk via the potential materialization of settlement fails in Section 9.2. Section 9.3 describes the determinants and consequences of settlement fails and the settlement discipline framework in European securities settlement systems (SSSs) to contain disruptions due to fails, including those potentially due to short selling. This provides an important background for the subsequent discussion in Section 9.4 on how enforcing a strong settlement discipline can support market discipline relating to short selling. Section 9.5 deals with the impact of short selling on the effectiveness of some settlement discipline measures.

9.2 SHORT SELLING AND SETTLEMENT RISK

Settlement risk is the risk that settlement of a financial transaction will not take place as expected usually due to a party defaulting on one or more settlement obligations. Settlement risk can be the result of the materialization of operational risk, for example, a technical problem, a human error preventing the correct execution of settlement instructions, if assets due for delivery are not available on time, and finally credit risk/default. Problems of legal enforcement may also prevent a party from obtaining control of assets due to subsequent delivery and thus be a source of settlement risk (see Kokkola, 2010).

A financial transaction is said to "fail" if either the seller does not deliver the securities in due time or the buyer does not deliver funds in the appropriate form on the settlement. As explained in ECB (2011), in the context of securities settlement, the term fail is often employed to refer to the nondelivery of securities [although with the adoption of delivery-versus-payment (DVP[1]) settlement mechanisms, fails can also derive from nonsettlement of the cash leg of the transaction]. One reason why securities fails may be more difficult to resolve than cash fails is that cash, by nature, is fungible and the party failing to deliver the cash leg may rely on credit facilities. While securities need to

---

[1] Delivery versus payment are transactions where securities are delivered by the seller against a payment from the buyer. In particular, DVP facilities ensure that a money settlement does not take place if securities have not been delivered and vice versa.

be delivered in the specific agreed type, in some cases this may not be easily retrievable in the market for purchase or borrowing. This chapter focuses on securities fails as these are relevant for short selling.

9.2.1 Understanding Fails: Determinants and Consequences of Fails

A fail is called aged when it remains unsettled for more than a specifically prescribed period of time beyond the settlement date (the length of the period of time may be defined differently across settlement systems). Aged fails are often subject to specific measures aimed at protecting the settlement process (see Section 9.3).

Fails determinants and consequences are described in detail in ECB (2011). In particular, fails may be determined by various circumstances. First, *operational risk* exists where there is a miscommunication between traders or back offices, mistakes in manual processing, computer problems, or untimely processing of instructions. The effects of operational risks range from short-lived fails to more serious systemic disruptions. For example, the computer breakdown suffered by the Bank of New York in 1985 forced the bank to borrow more than $20 billion from the New York Fed, and September 11 operational disruptions led to massive settlement problems (Fleming & Garbade, 2002). Peaks in fails were reported in European SSSs while upgrading technical systems for the first few days when participants were less familiar with the new procedures, as well as in periods of high market volumes due to the operational challenge in processing a large number of transactions.

Second, liquidity problems due to the unavailability of assets due for delivery, may be the result of the following.

- Cascading fails when the nondelivery of securities causes its buyer to fail subsequent delivery to another party in back-to-back transactions.[2]
- Technical conditions in other market segments. For example, in correspondence with the deadlines for delivery in derivatives markets, should many players opt for physical delivery, this could cause a shortage of underlying securities in the cash securities market.

---

[2] "Back-to-back trades" refers to a pair of transactions that require a counterparty to receive and redeliver the same securities on the same day. The transactions involved may be outright purchases and sales or collateral transactions (repurchase agreements or securities loans). For example, a securities dealer might buy and sell the same securities for the same settlement date in the course of making markets for customers or it might buy securities for inventory and finance the position through a repurchase agreement see BIS (2003). Back-to-back trading has the major advantage of avoiding unnecessary funding costs by the party buying and on selling the securities. This practice poses no particular (settlement) risk when the delivery follows an actual final receipt of the securities. However, it may be challenging if more than one settlement system are involved, for example, in a cross-border context, due to differences in the timing of settlement cycles or of finality of the securities transfer.

- Naked short sales where short sellers have not managed to purchase or borrow the securities in time for delivery to the buyer. Short sales by broker/dealers that are market makers in a certain security help provide liquidity in fast-moving market conditions. However, abusive short sale practices (such as a series of short sales to create apparent active trading in a security or to manipulate a stock's price) are normally illegal.

Parties failing to deliver due to a liquidity problem normally try to obtain credit or borrow the securities due for delivery. In some cases, the specific securities due for delivery may be difficult or very expensive to borrow as a result of thin markets or illiquid stocks.

Third is the lack of incentives to avoid fails. The cost of delaying or failing delivery is typically determined by market practices that set the compensation to pay to indemnify the party who has not received the assets. Usually, it corresponds to the overnight deposit rate for each day of delayed delivery. When the cost of borrowing the assets is equal to or higher than the cost of failing to deliver, market participants may lack the incentives to take corrective measures to avoid fails. This can be due to different reasons. For example:

- Fails may be determined by the trade-off between the interest of the dealer back office to ensure early and smooth settlement (i.e., avoid the fails) and that of the same dealer front office to keep the liquidity for financing other trades. The final decision may be affected by the banks' internal policies, risk adversion, and budget constraints for the front office.
- Fails may also be derived from arbitrage strategies implemented on behalf of a dealer's customers in equity markets characterized by different "settlement cycles."[3] For instance, in some EU jurisdictions, equities transactions are settled 3 days after the trade day, whereas in others they are settled 2 days after the trade date. Customers operating in multiple jurisdictions may commit to deliver assets in jurisdictions where settlement occurs 3 days after the trade and purchase the same assets in jurisdictions where they expect to receive the assets 2 days after the trade. In this case, the lack of delivery in one jurisdiction will determine settlement fails also in the other jurisdiction. However, as long as these settlement fails only concern retail investors and their amount is limited compared to the business of the bank, the latter may not have strong incentives to adopt corrective measures.
- In certain cases, incentives can be such that a party may even find it preferable to fail [these are called "strategic fails," i.e., situations where the settlement fail is due to a decision to fail of the party, not to the lack

---

[3] The time span in days between trading and settlement is usually referred to as a "settlement cycle."

of assets; see, e.g., Fleming and Garbade (2005)]. Typically, strategic fails take place in situations where the cost of the fails turns out to be lower than the revenue stemming from the alternative use of the assets. Fleming and Garbade (2005) demonstrate that the U.S. government bond market tends to be characterized by persistently high fails in periods when costs for security borrowing are persistently lower than the general collateral repurchase agreements rate, which is closely related to the overnight Fed funds market rate. The potential role of incentives in a low or negative interest rate environment has been recognized by the European Repo Council of the International Capital Market Association (ICMA). The ICMA has issued a self-regulatory recommendation prescribing that in the event a repo seller failed to deliver in a repo transaction at a negative rate, the repo rate would immediately be reset to zero or the repo buyer could terminate the unsettled repo (ICMA-ERC, 2010).[4]

In general, settlement fails may imply three main consequences. First, the parties continue to be exposed to credit risk (in free of payment transactions) and replacement cost risk (in DVP transactions).[5] Second, the securities seller is exposed to liquidity risk on the settlement date because of lack of the expected cash. Third, the securities buyer is exposed to a liquidity risk because of the impossibility of using the expected (nondelivered) incoming securities for settling other transactions on the same day. If the fail is not resolved promptly, settlement problems may propagate to other transactions and potentially trigger a disturbance of the smooth settlement process. While a certain rate of fails can be considered "physiological," high settlement fail rates may result in "daisy chains," or a chain of cascading fails. A daisy chain may degenerate into a "round robin" when the last participant in the chain fails to deliver to the first participant in the chain, thereby creating circular gridlock situations. Under extreme circumstances, the entire settlement process may be seriously affected or impaired unless corrective measures are taken to break the fails chain. For an example of a U.S. experience with significant and persistent fail rates following September 11, 2001, see Fleming and Garbade (2002). In this perspective, it should be noted that the consequences of fails

---

[4] However, according to ICMA-ERC, currently "this recommendation needs to be agreed upon by parties before each transaction or incorporated into the documentation governing repo transactions between them. This would typically be the ICMA's global master repurchase agreement (GMRA), which is the most extensively used cross-border master agreement for repos. However, the recommendation is likely to be integrated into the standard GMRA when this is revised next year."

[5] Free of payment transactions are delivery of securities from the seller to the buyer. Delivery versus payment transactions are securities delivered by the seller against a payment from the buyer. In the first case, should the delivery of securities fail, the buyer will have to face a credit risk. In DVP transactions, if securities are not delivered, the buyer can keep the money for the payment. In this case, the only risk is that the cost for buying or lending the securities in the market is higher than the original cost of the assets. This risk is referred to as a "replacement cost risk."

can be different depending on the settlement model adopted in the relevant securities settlement system, in particular on the specific DVP model used. Using the BIS (1992) taxonomy, in DVP Model 1—where both legs[6] are settled on an individual basis—a delivery fail blocks only one transaction, which may still cause consequential fails if the trading parties have taken commitments to redeliver the incoming assets. However, there would be no impact on the settlement of trades where none of the counterparties of the original failed trade are involved. In contrast, if the settlement system adopts DVP Model 3, both legs are settled on a net basis in batches whereby a securities fail may impede the settlement of an entire settlement batch, which would include parties having no direct involvement in the failed trade. In DVP Model 2, securities are settled on a gross basis, whereas cash is settled on a net basis. However, a settlement fail can also impede the smooth settlement of the entire process, propagating to transactions unrelated to the original fail, if the gross settlement of all the individual securities transactions (the "securities leg") is designed to take place at the same time as the net settlement of the cash (the "cash leg"). For this reason, specific measures are usually in place to protect settlement in DVP Models 2 and 3 where often guarantee funds can be used in buy-in procedures.

Fourth, even securities lending markets for assets subject to a significant volume of fails could be affected negatively, as lenders may withhold collateral in the fear that the high fails in that security diminish the likelihood of the collateral being returned to them. Withholding scarce collateral may, in principle, contribute to increasing the fails rate and prolonging fails duration.

9.2.2 Short Selling as a Potential Cause of Settlement Risk

The potential for fails to trigger contagion of settlement risk is not unique to short selling as long selling could also result in fails in case of operational problems preventing timely delivery. However, this explains why short selling which starts with a sale where the assets are not yet in the availability of the seller, raises settlement risk concerns. While the settlement risk profile of covered short selling is not different from that of long and back-to-back transactions, naked short selling is often believed to be relatively more prone to settlement risk because of the limited time available to source the securities between trading date T and settlement date usually 2 or 3 days after T, depending on the asset type and local market practice. Nevertheless, it has been argued

---

[6] Most securities transactions require delivery of securities against payment of cash. The two components of a transaction are often referred as "legs." Delivery-versus-payment arrangements allow for ensuring that the delivery of securities (securities leg) does not occur without payment of the corresponding cash (cash leg).

(ICMA-ERC, 2010) that, at least in the European repo market, *unintentional* naked short selling does not automatically result in settlement fails. Because sellers manage to purchase or borrow the securities in time and, in most cases, under normal market conditions, only *intentional* naked short selling results in *strategic fails*. The debate over whether restrictions on short selling are justified to protect markets from settlement risk depends on how much short selling contributes to settlement fails and how much the market participants and regulators are willing to accept that source of risk.

The relationship between settlement failures and short selling has been investigated by a strand of research for the U.S. market. Using a data set on the entire cross section of U.S. equities, Boni (2006) argued that delivery failures were pervasive and "… consistent with the hypothesis that market makers strategically failed to deliver when borrowing costs were high." Analyzing actual transaction data of a major options market maker in the U.S. market, Evans, Geczy, Musto, and Reed (2006) show that under the exemption from short selling restrictions granted by Regulation SHO in the United States to hedging market makers in options, in the most hard-to-borrow market situation, this market maker chose not to borrow and instead failed delivery to its buyers. Furthermore, Stratman and Welborn (2010) studied the trading behavior of options market makers before and after the repeal of certain restriction waivers granted previously to them by the Securities and Exchange Commission (SEC) in September 2008. The authors conclude that the exceptions granted to options market makers before the recent review of Regulation SHO had led to increased fails and lower stock borrowing rates for optionable stocks when compared to nonoptionable stocks. There were more fails for optionable stocks when the stock borrowing price was high and that options market liquidity declined after the restriction waivers were eliminated. In addition, the authors quote two studies by the SEC's Office of Economic Analysis that investigated the impact of Regulation SHO amendments on fails to deliver. The SEC indicated that investors who failed previously to deliver in stock markets after the grandfathering clause that allowed exemption of pre-2005 fails from close-out requirements introduced in 2007 "have (…) moved to the options markets to establish a synthetic position. Given that option market makers benefit from an exception of the close-out rule and tend to hedge their positions in the equity markets, the fails may now be stemming from the options market makers instead of the equity investors themselves" (SEC OEA, 2008). In a subsequent study on the elimination of the options market makers exception to Regulation SHO on fails to deliver, the SEC finds "some evidence that optionable stocks experience larger declines in fails than non-optionable stocks."

Data on settlement fails and short selling in Europe are not widely collected and published. Fails monitoring and reporting are not harmonized methodologically, thus limiting the possibility for comparison of availability and data also because restrictions on short selling are not taking place in all markets (see EC, 2009). Therefore, it is not possible to empirically establish a relation between short selling and settlement fails. However, due to the reported low level of settlement fails in European securities settlement systems, we assume that short selling as only one potential source of fails tends to be limited. The potential for peaks in fails during periods of market stress and volatility cannot be ruled out, and it is possible that rules governing settlement in most of European SSSs minimizes incentives to strategic fails by raising its cost. The various settlement-enhancing measures adopted by the SSS to resolve aged fails limits the life span of outstanding fails. The relationship between settlement discipline and short selling market discipline is explored more in detail in the next sections.

9.3 SETTLEMENT DISCIPLINE IN EUROPE

A settlement discipline framework is the set of rules and measures in specific markets to ensure an adequate level of settlement efficiency. These measures, which can be implemented at various points along the trading and post-trading processing value chain, usually relate to the securities clearing and settlement systems and can be classified by before settlement, on the settlement day, or after the failed settlement. Settlement discipline includes measures aimed to prevent fails and to resolve them ideally on the intended settlement dates, as well as to mitigate their effects to avoid spillover of liquidity problems and settlement risk contagion. Some of these measures are relevant to address and contain settlement risk that can possibly arise from short selling. Several studies conducted by central banks on settlement efficiency measures in securities settlement systems revealed that the settlement discipline is not harmonized in Europe.[7] For a detailed description of the measures to prevent, discourage and mitigate fails see ECB (2011), on which this section draws. The regimes in force in various markets include a different combination of the following elements.

9.3.1 Measures to Prevent Fails
- A high level of automation of market transactions exists at the various levels of the financial transaction processing chain and reduction of manual intervention and decreasing the occurrence of mistakes in settlement instructions. For example, the automated transmission of settlement instructions from exchanges central counterparty (or CCPs) to the settlement systems.

---

[7] The European Central Securities Depositories Association (ECSDA) has also carried out a survey on the discipline measures adopted by its members [see ECDA (2009)].

- Existence of a CCP also contributes to diminishing fails rate (1) indirectly, because the CCP relieves the counterparties from taking and managing directly the risks vis-à-vis numerous counterparties of various standing, and (2) directly, by decreasing the value of cash and securities that must be settled to a net position when multilateral netting is generally used.
- Mandatory matching procedures whereby sometimes matched instructions are binding and cannot be cancelled unless bilaterally agreed. Unmatched transactions not corrected by the start of settlement are excluded from the settlement procedure and can either be cancelled or set aside.
- Presettlement informative processes are used to simulate settlement and provide customers with information about transactions likely to fail.[8] These reports may take the form of "alledgments"[9] reports or of "unmatched" reports (where both parties have submitted instructions that do not match) on the intended settlement date.
- Technical liquidity optimization measures, such as "sizing" or "shaping," whereby the SSS is allowed to split a transaction that would fail into a number of transactions of smaller value to attempt to settle as many parts of the transactions as possible. This would unblock the settlement of subsequent delivery instructions that would otherwise be ending in queues or fails. Queuing optimization mechanisms change the order of transactions within a queue to facilitate synchronization of incoming and outgoing flows of cash and securities.
- Regular publication of data regarding settlement fails, typically aggregated by the type of security and without the names of the failing participants, may also be useful in informing the market as to which instruments may be temporarily scarce.
- The SSSs may also provide a range of services that can facilitate settlement. These include securities lending and borrowing programs for the securities leg and intraday credit and self-collateralization services that refer to securities being delivered and are used as collateral to provide intraday credit enabling cash settlement for the cash leg. Another solution sometimes adopted in the last settlement cycle of the day is partial delivery. In partial delivery the nonfailing party is given the possibility to accept a partial delivery of cash or securities to receive the remaining assets as soon as they become available. Assets delivered later may be mark to market.

---

[8] For example, in one CSD, simulations run throughout the day and can be followed by the participants via an Internet application, and lists of simulated fails in securities are sent to participants via email.

[9] Alledgments reports are usually sent by an SSS and contain information on instructions sent from one party but for which the other party (the receiver of the report) has not entered corresponding instructions.

9.3.2 Measures to Discourage Fails

In this category we find measures aimed at increasing the cost of fails for the failing party, such as the application of margin requirements on fails, mark-to-market failed positions, and/or collection of fail penalties. Penalties should not be confused with fees. While *fees* are often paid to the SSS as a compensation for administrative costs, *penalties* may be collected by the SSS in favor of the damaged party as compensation for the loss suffered.[10] In one European country, penalties are applied by the SSSs only to fails of a certain impact. These penalties are charged to participants who have generated fails on the securities side only if the overall settlement performance of the system measured on a daily basis has fallen under a predetermined target as a result of the fails. Other measures aimed at discouraging fails are publication of data concerning chronic fails, including, in extreme cases, the identity of the failing participants. This is possible in several SSSs, but only a few of them enforce this right and suspension of the participant in extreme cases of reiterated fails. The possibility of applying this last measure may indeed discourage short sellers, causing them to lose access to the clearing and settlement infrastructure. In practice, this would block their trading activity and exclude them, at least temporarily, from the market altogether.

9.3.3 Measures to Mitigate the Adverse Effects of Fails

This category of measures typically includes special procedures for handling aged fails with the objective of avoiding spreading of liquidity risks due to fails by making sure that the innocent party receives the assets and can in turn fulfill its possible obligations. In a forced buy-in procedure, the SSS purchases the securities that could not be delivered on behalf of the failing party for the benefit of the buying party. The failing party may be required to provide collateral in cash to finance the purchase or the SSS may acquire a pledge on the cash and other assets held in accounts of the failing party. If a guarantee fund exists, the failing party may be required to advance the funds for the buy-in by making a payment to the fund.

---

[10] Normally, a scheme contains one or more of the following measures: (1) delay fee. These normally take the form of a flat fee (fixed amount per delay) and are not applied to parties that fail to deliver after having suffered a fail to receive (within a daisy chain). However, delay fees can be higher if the fail has resulted in subsequent fails by other parties and can increase in case of repeated fails. In some cases, delay fees are applied for each day of a delayed settlement. Usually they are not applied for intraday fails. (2) A compensation penalty, often collected by the SSS and paid to the innocent party, which is normally a percentage of the failed transaction. (3) A cancellation fee, which may be higher than the delay fee. (4) A cancellation penalty, which may also be higher than the compensation penalty. (5) Other penalties: if the fail is not resolved and measures to mitigate the effects of fails are activated (e.g., use of mutual funds or guarantee funds, buy-in or sell-out procedures), the failing party has to pay for the whole costs of the procedure.

A forced sellout is the opposite transaction, carried out by selling securities or other collateral of the party failing to deliver cash to complete the transaction in favor of the selling party. One important aspect of fails management that is not harmonized in Europe is the definition of aged fails, which is also a measure of the tolerance of systems and markets for keeping fails outstanding before activation of mandatory resolution measures.

Under extreme circumstances, fails may become chronic, and their effect on the liquidity of the entire market could be serious enough to require the adoption of ad-hoc measures. These measures would be aimed at lowering the cost of borrowing securities or increasing their supply by authorities and/or policy makers. This is similar to reopening the issuance of certain unexpectedly scarce government bonds or lending to the market scarce assets held by central banks or by the treasury (see Fleming & Garbade, 2002).

9.4 RELATION BETWEEN SHORT SELLING MARKET DISCIPLINE AND SETTLEMENT DISCIPLINE

Market discipline relating to short selling is usually designed around four main principles, as defined by the International Organization of Securities Commissions (IOSCO) (2009). For example, (i) short selling should be subject to appropriate controls to reduce or minimize the potential risks that could affect the orderly and efficient functioning and stability of financial markets. (ii) Short selling should be subject to a reporting regime that provides timely information to the market or to market authorities. (iii) Short selling should be subject to an effective compliance and enforcement system. (iv) Short selling regulation should allow appropriate exceptions for certain types of transactions for efficient market functioning and development. Detailed discussion of the various regulatory tools to ensure these objectives are fulfilled is outside the scope of this chapter, but for ease of comparison between settlement discipline measures and short selling regulatory measures, Table 9.1 lists general objectives of the main regulatory tools of short selling, and Table 9.2 compares the two sets of tools based on their contribution to regulatory objectives.

As shown in Table 9.2, both approaches are largely complementary, and the IOSCO 2009 report clearly states that "having an effective discipline for settlement of short selling transactions is the first pillar for an effective short selling regulatory regime. The technical committee recommends that regulation of short selling should, as a minimum requirement, impose a strict settlement (such as compulsory buy-in) of failed trades." Making reference to the Committee on Payment and Settlement Systems (CPSS) IOSCO recommendations for SSSs (BIS, 2001), IOSCO further notes that shortening

Table 9.1 Regulatory Balance and Approaches to Short Selling

Balance of Regulators Preference Regarding Positive and Negative Effects of Short Selling	Regulatory Approach	Purpose
Restrictive (risks concern prevail on expected benefits)	Ban	Eliminate settlement risk implications of short selling
Restrict with exemptions	Ban but exempt certain players	Minimize short selling drawbacks while making sure market makers can effectively provide liquidity to markets and hedge market-making positions
Allow subject to restrictions	Preborrow requirement	Minimize settlement risk in specific situations: make sure (certain) short sellers have borrowed securities they do not own before selling them
	Locate requirement	Minimize settlement risk in specific situations: make sure (certain) short sellers have entered into borrowing agreement or taken other measures allowing them to borrow securities before selling them
	Flagging[a]/reporting	Monitor short selling and fails and provide an audit trail to follow up on suspect cases. Support public disclosure
	Price restrictions/ "tick rule"	Prevent short sales at successively lower prices and thus might moderate the pace of market decline in extreme market conditions
Open (expected liquidity and market efficiency benefits prevail over risks concerns)	No restrictions	Fully benefit from positive impact on market liquidity, price discovery, and efficiency

[a]Refers to a system that requires putting a marker on each short sale that a broker sends to the exchange or alternative trading facility for execution.

the settlement cycle will make fails visible earlier and, following the application of settlement resolution measures, will counter building up of a large short selling position. At the same time, the decision to shorten the settlement cycle needs to be taken in light of a careful consideration of pros and cons, as a shorter time to instruct, match, and execute settlement may imply tighter operational conditions and less time to ensure funding of short positions in the securities lending markets for certain illiquid assets. At the European level, provisions similar to the CPSS-IOSCO recommendations but more specific for the European context are the ESCB-CESR recommendations (see ECB, 2009). More recently, some initiatives have been undertaken with a view to harmonize the settlement cycles at least in Europe by moving from T+3 to T+2.

The complementarities of both sets of measures also entail that some could be used as alternative tools to achieve a common objective. However,

Table 9.2 Short Selling Market Discipline and Settlement Discipline

Objective of Discipline	IOSCO Principles and Measures	Settlement Discipline
Minimize potential risks that could affect the orderly and efficient functioning and stability of financial markets	Strong settlement discipline framework Regulatory restrictions to short selling in order to avoid fails: locate requirement, preborrowing requirement in order to minimize undesirable impact on prices (tick rules)	Measures to prevent fails and to minimize their impact on settlement: technical measures ensuring early submission of correct settlement orders to clearing and settlement systems. Publication of aggregated data on (temporarily) scarce assets. Securities lending programs and facilities
Transparency toward market and authorities	Reporting short selling (flagging individual transactions or other reporting ways)	Monitoring and reporting fails (mandatory based on oversight principles, CPSS-IOSCO and ESCB-CESR RSSS3), but different modalities of data collection and frequency of reporting to authorities and/or disclosure to public
Compliance and enforcement	Penalties for illegal short selling activities	Measures to discourage fails and avoid strategic fails: elimination of failed transactions from the settlement cycle, activation of fails resolution procedures at the cost of the failing party (forced buy-ins and closeout of positions). The latter may be activated by the SSS or by a CCP if applicable but the first acting as agent for the innocent party, while the latter as principal in the transaction. Publication by the SSS of detailed fails data, including security and name failing party ("name and shame"). Suspension of chronic failers from clearing and settlement infrastructures
Preserving benefits of short selling	Exemptions to short selling restrictions for certain intermediaries (market makers) and/or markets (derivatives)	Settlement facilitating services that increase likelihood of settlement of *all* transactions (including bona fide covered and naked short selling, e.g., securities lending programs, automated lending facilities provided by some SSSs)

whether or not two specific measures are alternative or complementary is questionable and there is no clear-cut answer. In this regard, some measures in place at securities clearing and settlement systems place them in a good position to support the timely settlement of short-sold securities. In this regard, an important role can be played by the automated securities lending program operated by numerous European SSSs. By having full visibility of the allocation of securities held in custody, these SSSs can automatically select the missing securities from participants that join the program as securities lenders and lend to those participants that need them for settlement. The transaction can be reversed later according to the borrowing and lending terms of the program.

Securities lending as a means to avoid settlement failures is the object of ESCB-CESR (and CPSS-IOSCO) Recommendation 5 for securities settlement systems. The recommendation states that barriers that inhibit the practice of lending securities for this purpose should be removed. An efficient securities lending and borrowing market, coupled with automated lending facilities on the settlement date, makes a location requirement redundant if all short positions identified by the system can be covered in time. Should such a requirement or a preborrowing requirement be in force, participation in the automated lending facilities could serve to provide evidence of compliance and of bona fide short selling in case of unintentional fails due to operational reasons or in postevent investigations during a crisis.

The complementarities of both approaches also raise the question as to which is the most appropriate institution to be in charge of enforcing settlement discipline by charging and collecting penalties and initiating closeout or forced buy-in procedures. To the extent that sufficiently strong measures are in place and enforced effectively at the clearing and/or settlement layer for all transactions, including short sales, no additional or special penalties for short selling may be necessarily warranted. Which institution along the processing chain is better placed to carry out enforcement measures depends on the specific setup of the market, the level of sophistication of the various technical platforms, and whether they were designed by embedding the functionalities required to carry out the task. In at least one case (Malta) in Europe where naked short selling is prohibited, a securities prevalidation and blocking procedure is in place between the trading system and the securities registers held within the SSS. In Cyprus, there is a similar system, making sure securities to be sold are available prior to trade execution.

Securities settlement systems can, in principle, also contribute to ensuring transparency on short sales toward the market. In the United Kingdom, where short selling is allowed, the SSS provides a specific online service, providing information on stock loans. This enables the SSS to meet customers' demand for gaining a clearer view on short selling activity for specific securities. However, most SSSs are not able to provide the service, given the lack of all the necessary information. In particular, when an SSS receives instructions to deliver securities not yet available in the seller's account, the SSS has no element to judge whether the required securities were preborrowed or bought by the seller, as they could still be delivered later before or at the settlement date. Adapting systems to allow flagging of individual short sales may be operationally complex for certain types of infrastructures or overly costly compared to the expected benefits.

Finally, another point raised by the relation between market discipline and settlement discipline is the need for coordination among the relevant authorities. Securities clearing and settlement systems are subject to oversight by competent authorities and central banks. The central banks overseeing payment systems and with an interest in the smooth functioning of securities settlement systems that they use to receive the collateral required to secure their credit operations would need information on the level of fails and their significance in terms of broader systemic contagion. CPSS-IOSCO Recommendation 18 provides a framework for cooperation and exchange of information among relevant authorities on a cross-border level.

One limit to consider in assessing the mix of regulatory tools and their scope of application is the role of financial innovation, particularly the use of derivatives contracts to achieve the same economic effects of short selling positions in cash markets, including cases where the cash securities markets are subject to short selling restrictions and the derivative instruments are not.

9.5 IMPACT OF SHORT SELLING AND FAILS ON THE EFFECTIVENESS OF SETTLEMENT DISCIPLINE MEASURES

Some of the measures used to minimize and contain fails implemented by SSSs rely on the assumption of efficiently working markets, such as forced buy-in, securities lending, and liquidation of collateral pools to fund the purchase missing assets. Fails, for instance, could negatively affect securities lending markets and lead to more fails. A generalized fail problem could, however, impair markets and make it difficult, if not impossible, to enforce the measures quickly, even if mandatory. Massive or abusive short selling triggering or amplifying a downward price spiral could make it challenging to liquidate collateral or expose a CCP to substantial losses. Short selling in derivatives markets may also result in fails in the underlying cash instrument market. Because the systemic implications of fails and short selling are potentially great, it is important that authorities and market participants are able to monitor them in order to develop "early warning indicators" to adopt corrective measures before systemic propagation of contagion. In particular, it is of key importance that competent authorities have the powers to adopt extraordinary measures in case of need.

9.6 CONCLUSION

The systemic implication of settlement failures possibly resulting from short selling is one of the concerns underpinning short selling regulatory principles. Therefore, market discipline relating to short sales and settlement discipline rules are interconnected, and strong settlement discipline enforcement is key to preserving safe and efficient conditions in financial markets. However, as short selling is only one and reportedly not a significant source of fails potentially disrupting settlement, banning or restricting short selling does not eliminate all fails.

The short selling discipline and settlement discipline are largely complementary in achieving common, although distinct, objectives, and there is a need for a consistent approach in line with cost and benefits of the various specific measures and with the size and features of the market. To some extent, market discipline could rely on measures implemented at the clearing or settlement levels for achieving certain objectives, notably the avoidance and minimization of settlement risk under the condition that a strong and effective settlement regime is enforced. Where this is the case, fails levels are usually low, and fails derived from both long and short sale positions can be considered limited under normal market conditions. Developed securities lending markets are an important condition allowing prompt sourcing of securities needed for delivery and contribute to solving bona fide fails irrespective of their origin. The control and minimization of intentional fails through short selling practices may be obtained by a mix of mandatory fails resolution procedures (i.e., forced buy-ins) and enforcement of market abuse regulation. In crisis situations it is important that authorities have the power to investigate suspect cases and take extraordinary measures.

Due to lack of public data and nonharmonized monitoring and disclosure practices in Europe, there is a need to increase transparency on settlement fails and short selling to gain insight in market dynamics, intermediary behaviors, and incentives, particularly at times of crises. An improvement in this respect is expected from various market initiatives undertaken in view of harmonizing settlement discipline rules before the launch of the target-2-securities settlement platform that the eurosystem plans for 2014.

An increased level of cooperation among authorities in charge of overseeing and regulating clearing and settlement systems will be beneficial in ensuring the effective monitoring of settlement fails in both normal and crises times, including at the cross-border level.

REFERENCES

BIS. (1992). Committee on Payment and Settlement Systems, "Delivery Versus Payment in Securities Settlement Systems" retrieved from www.bis.org.

BIS. (2001). CPSS-IOSCO recommendations for securities settlement systems.

BIS. (2003). Committee on Payment and Settlement Systems, "A glossary of terms used in payments and settlement systems" retrieved from www.bis.org.

Boni, L. (2006). Strategic delivery failures in US equity markets. *Journal of Financial Markets*, 9, 1–26.

ECB. (2009). ESCB-CESR recommendations for securities settlement systems and recommendations for central counterparties in the European Union. Retrieved from www.ecb.europa.eu.

ECB (2011). "Settlement Fails – Report on securities settlement systems (SSS) measures to ensure timely settlement", retrieved from www.ecb.europa.eu.

ECSDA. (2009). *Market discipline regimes in Europe.* Retrieved November 2010 from https://www.ecsda.eu.

European Commission. (2009). *Proposal for a regulation of the European parliament and of the council on short-selling and certain aspects of credit default swaps.* Retrieved from http://ec.europa.eu.

Evans, R. B., Geczy, C. C., Musto, D. K., & Reed, V. (2009). Failure is an option: Impediments to short selling and options prices. *Review of Financial Studies, 22*(5), 1955–1980.

Fleming, M. J., & Garbade, K. D. (2002). When the back office moved to the front burner: Settlement fails in the treasury market after 9/11. *FRBNY Economic Policy Review,* 8(November), 35–57.

Fleming, M. J., & Garbade, K. D. (2005). Explaining settlement fails. *Current Issues in Economics and Finance, 11*(9), 1–7. Retrieved at www.newyorkfed.org.

ICMA-ERC. (2010). *A white paper on the operation of the European repo market, the role of short-selling and the need for reform of the market infrastructure.* Retrieved July 13 from www.icmagroup.org.

IOSCO. (2009). *Technical Committee of the International Organisation of Securities Commissions: Regulation of short selling* (Final Report, June).

Kokkola, T. (2010). *The payment system: Payments, securities and derivatives, and the role of the eurosystem.* Retrieved from www.ecb.europa.eu.

SEC, Office of Economic Analysis. (2008 and 2009). *Impact of recent SHO amendment on fails to deliver.* Retrieved from http://www.sec.gov/comments/s7-19-07/s7-1907-562.pdf and http://www.sec.gov/comments/s7-30-08/s73008-121.pdf.

Stratman, T., & Welborn, J. W. (2010). *Rules matter: Short-selling, stock lending, and settlement failures.* Unpublished, www.ssrn.com.

CHAPTER 10

The 2008 Emergency Regulation of Short Selling in the United Kingdom, United States, and Australia

Kym Sheehan

CONTENTS

ABSTRACT

Mid-September 2008 saw governments around the world initiating emergency regulatory action to ban short selling. This chapter examines the responses of regulators in three jurisdictions: the United Kingdom, the United States, and Australia. In analyzing the objectives of securities regulation, it finds that these initiatives are explained more readily by the need to ensure the stability of the banking sector. It also highlights the difficulties seeking to implement global solutions: perceived problems with short selling reflect local issues.

KEYWORDS

Australian Securities Investments Commission; Disclosure-based initiatives; Financial Services Authority; Immediate postban; International Organization of Securities Commissions; Managing settlement risk; Preban; Prohibition/ restriction initiatives; Securities and Exchange Commission; Temporary ban.

10.1 INTRODUCTION

Short selling is a practice that has existed for many years and is regarded as a valuable activity to aid price discovery by the market, enhancing both market liquidity and efficiency (Bris et al., 2007; Diamond & Verrecchia, 1987; FSA, 2009; Saffi & Sigurdsson, 2011). However, these benefits may be absent when the markets are turbulent or when the market can be characterized as lacking in confidence (IOSCO, 2008b): short selling might lead to credit squeezes and market manipulation (IOSCO, 2008a). Outright bans on short selling have been rare (Finnerty, 2005). Thus the responses of many governments in 2008 to the global financial crisis were unprecedented. Many took emergency regulatory action in respect of short selling: restricting naked short selling but permitting covered short selling or else banning short selling in the securities of financial institutions. However, if regulatory actions by securities regulators are to ensure an informed and efficient markets, actions to prohibit or limit short selling can prove to be out of line with the objectives and principles of securities regulation.

This chapter examines the emergency responses to short selling undertaken by the United Kingdom, the United States, and Australian governments during 2008. The "temporary ban" period was from around mid-September to late October 2008, representing the period when a ban on short selling financial institution securities was imposed in the United Kingdom and Australia, although the Securities and Exchange Commission (SEC) banned naked short selling in certain financial institution securities as early as mid-July 2008. The "preban" period was the period from January to September 2008, with the "immediate postban" period defined as November 2008 to March 2009. The discussion will typically focus on the actions of the securities regulator—the Australian Securities Investments Commission (ASIC), the Financial Services Authority UK (FSA), and the SEC.

Section 10.2 discusses the objective of securities regulation. Section 10.3 analyzes the responses of the three regulators during the temporary ban and immediate postban periods as defined in the previous paragraph. Section 10.4 examines three particular regulatory techniques deployed: disclosure-based initiatives, prohibition/restriction initiatives, and managing settlement risk.

10.2 OBJECTIVES OF SECURITIES REGULATION

The International Organization of Securities Commissions (IOSCO) sets three objectives for securities regulation: investor protection; the assurance of market efficiency, transparency, and fairness; and the reduction of systemic risk (IOSCO, 2003a). Full disclosure is the primary means of ensuring investor protection, although clearly other measures are deployed. However, IOSCO also states that entry to and exit from markets and products should not be subject to "unnecessary" barriers. Furthermore, markets are to be open to the widest range of participants who meet specified entry criteria for the particular market. Additionally, regulatory bodies should consider the regulatory impact of any policy initiatives. Finally, all participants should face the same regulatory burden, where the nature of the burden is based on the nature of the financial commitment or promise made rather than on the identity of the participant (IOSCO, 2003a).

These last four objectives translate into 30 principles of regulation. Of these, the most relevant for regulation of short selling are: that regulators should have adequate powers and should adopt clear and consistent regulatory processes (principle 6.1), the promotion of transparency (principle 27); the detection and deterrence of market manipulation and unfair trading practices (principle 28); proper management of default risk (principle 29), and the reduction of systemic risk via systems for clearing and settlement of securities transactions (principle 30).

10.2.1 Objectives of Individual Securities Regulators

In the three jurisdictions of interest, the primary functions of the securities regulator are settled by legislation. All three had some regulatory objective that related to financial systems generally, as well as objectives on promoting market integrity and the overall efficiency and development of the economy. The extent to which each regulator assumed responsibility for the financial system differs among the jurisdictions, with subtle differences in wording that make a difference. For example, the first of ASIC's objectives is to "maintain, facilitate and improve the *performance* of the financial system and the entities within that system." It shares responsibility for the financial system with the Reserve Bank and with the Australian Prudential Regulatory Authority. One of the FSA's policy objectives set out in the *Financial Services and Markets Act 2000* (UK) is "to *maintain confidence* in the financial system (defined to include financial markets and exchanges, regulated activities and other activities connected with financial markets and exchanges)." The SEC's objectives, discerned from necessity for regulation in Section 2 of the *Securities Exchange Act of 1934* (15 U.S.C. §78b), include an aim to *protect the national banking and Federal Reserve systems*. Protecting the financial system could involve taking action to regulate the securities markets. As shown later, this is crucial to understanding the temporary short selling measures in respect of financial institutions in 2008.

Market integrity is another common objective, that is, the fairness and transparency of markets, where transparency includes information about prices and available volumes of securities, and fairness focuses upon the ability of some traders to profit because of greater information or power to manipulate the market (Gibson, 2008). As Section 2 of the *Securities Exchange Act 1934* notes, regulation is also necessary to address the manipulation and control of markets, where excessive speculation results in "sudden and unreasonable fluctuations in security prices."

10.3 ANALYSIS OF EMERGENCY RESPONSES

Responding to the challenges posed by market volatility in 2008, the ASIC, the FSA, and the SEC found themselves in immensely diverse starting positions, especially the FSA, which had never directly regulated short selling until its first emergency response in June 2008. Table 10.1 summarizes the approaches to short selling in Australia, the United Kingdom, and the United States, respectively, by comparing the preban position with the temporary measures and the immediate aftermath (postban). Approaches to the regulation of short selling are not identical and reveal some fundamental differences in terms of two issues: (1) the definition of "short sale" and the ability to confer title on the buyer and (2) why short selling needs to be regulated.

10.3.1 Definition of Short Sale and Title Issues

With the emergency regulatory responses either prohibiting or restricting short selling and/or requiring disclosure of short selling, the definition of "short selling" is critical. The definitions of short sale, either in the relevant primary legislation/regulation or in secondary documents, differ across the three jurisdictions. The SEC's definition defines a short sale as any sale of a security that the person "does not own *or* any sale which is consummated by the delivery of a security borrowed by, or for the account of, the seller." This term, read in conjunction with the "locate rule" (the broker locates the securities to be "borrowed" before the short sale is made), allows for a looser arrangement to exist than permitted by the Australian approach. The Australian approach defines a short sale in terms of a sale by a person [either on their own account or as an agent for a principal (client)] who has (or their principal has) a presently exercisable and unconditional right to vest the securities in the buyer, that is, a legally enforceable right (ASIC, 2010, p. 9). The FSA's approach focuses on the existence of a "net short position" of a particular size, not the individual short sale, broadly defined in terms of having *economic interests in the underlying securities*.

Table 10.1 Regulation of Short Selling: Australia, the United Kingdom, and the United States

	Preban	Temporary Ban	Postban
Regulating Short Selling: Australia			
Prohibit short selling	Prohibited unless seller has a presently existing and unconditional right to vest products in the buyer	Ban all for period; Ban all in S&P/ASX 200 Financials Index + 5, but other short sales allowed if comply with s 1020B(2) + (3)	No change from (2) in temporary ban
Exceptions to prohibition	Odd lot; Arbitrage transactions; Prior purchasing of securities; Prior borrowing of securities; ASX approved short sales list	None initially then: Hedging; Exercise ASX ETOs	Prior purchasing; Exercise of ETO, unobtained financial products and certain bonds and debentures
Disclosure on T + 1 basis	✓	✓	✓ gross position
Client to advise financial services licensee who is to advise the market	Yes: if 2, 4, or 5 above	✓	✓ with market operator to publish
Inquiry obligation imposed on financial services licensee ("is this a short sale?")	✓	✓	✓
Regulating Short Selling: United Kingdom			
Prohibit short selling			
Deemed market abuse	Failing to make T + 1 disclosure of discloseable short position (DSP) in security subject to rights issue	Entering into or increasing a net short position in UK financial company; Failure to make T + 1 disclosure of DSP (thresholds)	Failure to make T + 1 disclosure of DSP (0.25, 0.35, 0.45, 0.55%, and then every 0.1%)
Regulation of Short Selling: United States			
Prohibit short selling	✓	Must preborrow for 19 financial institutions (FI) then banned for 799 FI	Return to preban situation
Exceptions	✓		✓
Disclosure on T + 1 basis	✓		✓
Tagging of order as a short sale	✓	No change	No change
Client–broker–market note	✓	No change	No change
Weekly report on gross short positions, including intraday positions		✓	✓
Locate rule (locate the security for settlement before entering the short sale)	✓ with an exception for options market maker	No exceptions	Same as temporary ban
Hard closeout (close out existing open positions before new positions can be taken)		✓ T + 4	
Deemed market abuse	✓	✓	✓

The seller's property or contractual rights in respect of the securities at the time of sale, combined with the existence of either a contractual or a property right that allows the seller to vest title in the buyer, are fundamental to any definition of "short sale" (IOSCO, 2003b). Many of the relevant factors noted by IOSCO are describing how the securities will be obtained so that the seller can deliver title at settlement. The Australian approach aims to distinguish covered from naked short selling to prohibit naked short selling. Under the Australian definition of a short sale, the focus is on the strength of the seller's right (or ability) *at the time of sale* to vest title in the buyer at settlement, determined at the time of sale. The SEC's position is different. The definition of a short sale (which includes a number of deemed ownership scenarios) seems to allow for persons who own the security to still enter a transaction that is a short sale because it is not the owned security, but rather a borrowed security that will settle the transaction. Read in conjunction with the locate rule, the level of legal rights that the seller has to have to enter into the short sale is far less than those required under the Australian approach. In other words, short selling that would be permitted by Regulation SHO would be illegal in Australia. The focus in Regulation SHO is on how the transaction will be settled, that is, the seller's right (or ability) *at the time of settlement* to vest title in the buyer. If an obligation to disclose or to tag a transaction as short is to be attached to entering the sale, the definition has to be able to define what makes it a short sale at the time of sale.

The FSA's approach is completely different again. In choosing to focus on a net short position, it focuses on the balance of the seller's economic interest amounting to ownership (its long positions) against its economic interests that create an obligation to deliver title (its short positions) at particular points in time (namely when the seller has to determine if it has a disclosure obligation). This is because the FSA had previously recognized a trend for sizable short sale positions in equities and equity derivatives to be used as hedges by investment banks to their pension fund and life insurance company clients (FSA, 2002). A similar approach is evident in the ability of ASIC to exempt or modify the application of the short selling provisions to transactions that have the same or similar effect to a short position in the underlying financial product.

10.3.2 Short Selling Is a Legitimate Practice But . . .

According to IOSCO, securities regulation aims to ensure that markets are fair, efficient, and transparent, while minimizing (or managing) systemic risk, while protecting investors (IOSCO, 2003a). All three securities regulators agreed that short selling was a legitimate activity because of the contribution it can make to market liquidity, price discovery, and market efficiency. This position was evident in the preban statements from each regulator, was maintained through the temporary ban, and persists into the postban period. However, all three regulators likewise had some issues with short selling that demanded a regulatory solution. A first key question for regulators and governments alike is *what is the regulatory objective*? The required rules will depend on how this is defined. Does short selling create difficult settlement problems, is short selling primarily a market/price manipulation problem, or are persistent settlement failures an indicator of likely market abuse?

Settlement problems are best addressed at the "scene of the crime," namely at the level of the relevant stock exchange. For example, the power to specify the content of the operating rules in the *Corporations Act* could be used to state that short selling must be addressed in such rules, although the regulations currently use more generic descriptions of outcomes. The SEC's rules on abusive naked short sales likewise suggest that short selling is a settlement problem.

Market abuse and market manipulation problems are more challenging. This is because the conduct that constitutes "market abuse" and "market manipulation" will not typically be restricted to one short sale trade, whereas settlement rules deal with trade by trade. To detect a pattern of conduct requires a clear picture of what is "bad" short selling, a rule(s) that can allow for market trades to be screened, and a way of containing the abuse and manipulation quickly. The FSA's temporary ban approach of deeming particular short selling "market abuse" (also adopted by the SEC) is an example of this alternative approach. However, if short selling is a "systemic risk problem"—large short sale positions can have significant pricing effects that create unacceptable systemic risk if settlement failures occur—then a different approach again, something akin to that adopted by the FSA during the temporary ban period, is warranted.

10.4 TYPES AND RANGE OF INITIATIVES

Three particular initiatives are evident in the approaches of the ASIC, the FSA, and the SEC: disclosure-based rules, prohibition or restrictions on short selling, and regulation to managing settlement risk.

10.4.1 Use of Disclosure-Based Initiatives

A goal of securities regulation is to achieve transparent markets, that is, the "degree to which information about trading (both pre- and post-trade) is made publicly available on a real-time basis" (IOSCO, 2003a, p. 43). This regulatory objective dictates the nature and form of disclosure information sought, and different techniques will achieve different objectives (IOSCO, 2003b). A number of disclosure-based initiatives are evident in the approaches shown in Table 10.1. Four aspects influence the rule choices made: whether to require disclosure of a position in a security or individual short sales (*short position cf short sales*); what size of short positions (*net cf gross position*)[1]; how timely must the disclosure be (daily, *T + 1 cf weekly time frame*), and how public should the information be (*confidential cf nonconfidential reporting*).

Satisfying the regulatory objective of having the processes to detect and deter manipulative and unfair trading practices requires different information to that needed by the market on price and to address settlement issues. Balancing these competing regulatory priorities is critical. If short selling is creating a market abuse/manipulation problem, the SEC's weekly reporting of daily short sales positions, including intraday positions, makes sense. Such an approach allows a regulator to track manipulative behavior to be used to check against trading data obtained from an electronic trading system. IOSCO cautions that disclosure requirements should have identified the types of information about short selling behavior that correlate with market abuse and seek that information (IOSCO, 2003b).

10.4.2 Prohibition/Restriction Initiatives

As noted earlier, prohibiting manipulative and unfair trading practices is a goal of securities regulation of secondary markets. Each jurisdiction deployed these types of initiatives during the temporary ban, but only Australia and the United States had a preban regulatory regime that prohibited (or at least attempted to prohibit) some forms of short selling and to restrict others. As with transparency, there are a variety of ways in which short selling can be proscribed, depending on the particular regulatory goal (IOSCO, 2003b). This is reflected in the definitions adopted for short selling and how the restriction or prohibition is imposed: a direct rule ("no short sales") or an indirect rule ("failing to disclose a net short position is deemed market abuse").

10.4.3 Managing Settlement Risk

As noted earlier, reducing systemic risk through settlement systems that are fair, effective, and efficient is a principle of securities regulation (IOSCO, 2003a). Significant short positions can raise questions of manipulative practices (IOSCO, 2003b), as well as settlement issues if the seller fails to deliver at settlement. Settlement risk is an appropriate concern of market exchange operators and is reflected in the extensive rules that exist at that level for settlements. Settlement risk varies among jurisdictions, making it difficult to make "mitigating settlement risk" the overarching regulatory goal. For example, settlement risk is not perceived to be a major problem in Australia due

---

[1] The net short position gives two types of information: whether short selling is likely to be driving observed price movements and whether any settlement issues due to overhang are likely.

to the low number of settlement fails (Reserve Bank of Australia, 2008),[2] although it lies behind the SEC's decision to implement Regulation SHO and also recent rules with respect to abusive naked short selling (SEC, 2008a,b).

Settlement failures may be best addressed via sanctions at the level of the market exchange and a range of regulatory options exists. A system of fines for deliveries that fail to meet the T + 3 time frame for settlement, coupled with disciplinary actions for repeated failures, is one option. A second approach is to aim to prevent settlement failures via use of a buy-in procedure. The LSE's rules include an optional buy-in procedure whereby the LSE buys in the securities (London Stock Exchange, 2009, Rules 5140-5153) to ensure that settlement and delivery occur, irrespective of the reasons for the seller's failure to deliver. A third approach is a close-out rule imposed by the securities regulator, such as the SEC's T + 3 close-out rule. This rule also prevents further short sale orders being executed by the broker or dealer until the open but overdue short sale positions are closed out.

10.5 CONCLUSION

All three regulators have a responsibility for maintaining an orderly market. While both the FSA and the SEC justified the ban on short selling in financial securities by reference to the need to ensure the stability of the financial or banking system,[3] not the securities markets, the rules as made were securities market rules, not financial institution or banking system rules. For reasons of political expediency, doing nothing in the 2008 financial crisis was not an option (Enriques, 2009). However, from a regulatory perspective, one real issue is that the objectives of securities regulation were invoked to undertake far-reaching and urgent rule making without resorting to the usual rule-making processes. Of the three regulators, only the SEC had specific "emergency powers" that could be invoked.[4] Responses to the 2008 crisis created precedents for managing future crisis. Perhaps we need "circuit breakers" instead of outright bans (Avgouleas, 2010).

The IOSCO's regulatory principles for the secondary market noted earlier—the promotion of transparency (principle 27), detection and deterrence of market manipulation and unfair trading practices (principle 28), and the

---

[2] Less than 1% of transactions in Australia "reportedly" fail to settle on T + 3 due to a participant's failure to deliver securities.

[3] The U.K. government has signaled a change to the system of financial regulation in the United Kingdom, which will change the role of the FSA dramatically (HM Treasury, 2010).

[4] The FSA has recently addressed this problem: *Financial Services Act 2010* (UK) c 28, s 8, inserting new section 131D in the *Financial Services and Markets Act 2000* (UK) c 8.

reduction of systemic risk via systems for clearing and settlement of securities transactions (principle 30)—are all reflected in the emergency responses to short selling examined in this chapter. These attempts seek to allow *just enough* short selling to occur to promote price efficiency *but not too much* so as to cause market abuse via market manipulation. A "just right" regulatory approach wants particular disclosures to facilitate market monitoring by supervisors, but not too much to prove a regulatory burden to market participants. It wants *just enough* real-time information in the market to promote price efficiency, but not too much so as to protect "proprietary research" and investment strategies, as well as avoiding copycat trading. It wants to ensure prompt settlement of trades but not necessarily involve the securities exchange via buy-in arrangements or impose a "locate rule" to resolve the problem. It wants information about securities lending, but who should supply that information and which regulator should compel and compile the information might be difficult in a multiregulator environment. Linking all the relevant pieces of information together to get an accurate picture of short selling may prove a goal that, ultimately, cannot deliver what the market wants (efficiency price discovery), what issuers want (identity of the holders of an interest in the issuer's securities), and what regulators want (swift detection of market manipulation and successful prosecution of manipulators to act as a deterrent to others).

Finally, the analysis in this chapter indicates substantial overlap and divergence in the primary motivation to regulate short selling (Table 10.1). Transnational initiatives by groups such as IOSCO and CESR to establish principles for short selling should not set regulatory consistency as the primary objective to be achieved when it is likely that different regulatory imperatives exist among countries.

REFERENCES

Australian Securities & Investments Commission (ASIC) (2010). *Short selling.* Regulatory Guide 196. Canberra, Australia.

Avgouleas, E. (2010). A new framework for the global regulation of short sales: Why prohibition is inefficient and disclosure insufficient. *Stanford Journal of Law, Business & Finance, 15*(2), 376–425.

Bris, A., Goetzmann, W. N., & Zhu, N. (2007). Efficiency and the bear: Short sales and markets around the world. *Journal of Finance, 63*(2), 1029–1079.

Diamond, D., & Verrecchia, R. (1987). Constraints on short selling and asset price adjustment to private information. *Journal of Financial Economics, 18*(2), 277–311.

Enriques, L. (2009). Regulators' response to the current crisis and the upcoming reregulation of financial markets: One reluctant regulator's view. *University of Pennsylvania Journal of International Law, 30*(4), 1147–1156.

Financial Services Authority. (2002). *Short selling.* Discussion Paper 17. London.

Financial Services Authority. (2009). *Temporary short selling measures: Consultation paper CP 09/1.* London.

Finnerty, J. (2005). Short selling, death spiral convertibles and the profitability of stock manipulation. Working Paper. Bronx, NY: Fordham University Graduate School of Business.

Gibson, B. (2008). Improving confidence and integrity in Australia's capital market. Presentation to the Committee for Economic Development of Australia, Sydney.

HM Treasury. (2010). *A new approach to financial regulation: Judgement, focus and stability.* London.

International Organization of Securities Commissions (IOSCO). (2003a). *Objectives and principles of securities regulation.* Madrid, Spain.

IOSCO. (2003b). *Report on the transparency of short selling.* Technical Committee. Madrid, Spain.

IOSCO. (2008a). IOSCO Technical Committee members' initiatives relating to restrictions on short sales. Media Release 014. Madrid, Spain.

IOSCO. (2008b). Statement by the international organization of securities commissions regarding efforts to enhance investor confidence during the credit crisis. Media Release. Madrid, Spain.

Reserve Bank of Australia. (2008). *Review of settlement practices for Australian equities.* Canberra.

Saffi, P., & Sigurdsson, K. (2011). Price efficiency and short selling. *The Review of Financial Studies 24*(3), 821–852.

Securities Exchange Commission. (2008a). *"Naked" short selling anti-fraud rule.* Exchange Release No. 34-57511, 73 FR 15376. Washington, DC.

Securities Exchange Commission. (2008b). *"Naked" short selling anti-fraud rule.* Exchange Act Release No. 34-58774, 73 FR 61666. Washington, DC.

CHAPTER 11

Reflections on Short Selling Regulations in Western and Eastern Europe

Jeannine Daniel and François-Serge Lhabitant

CONTENTS

Handbook of Short Selling

ABSTRACT

The 2008 financial crisis cast a spotlight on the roles played by short sellers, particularly in Europe where the regulatory approach to short selling has been fragmented. As a result, in various jurisdictions, ad-hoc temporary measures, such as banning or imposing conditions on short selling activities, have been introduced. Numerous academics have studied the impact of such restrictions and questioned the wisdom of imposing them. Nevertheless, in September 2010, the European Commission (EC) introduced a proposal for a new pan-European short selling regime. This chapter presents the background and main aspects of this new EC's draft regulation. It compares it to the existing national regulations and assesses the likely economic and financial consequences of its implementation, should this draft regulation become law.

KEYWORDS

Autorité des Marchés Financiers; Comissao do Mercado de Valores Mobiliarios; Commission Bancaire Financiere et des Assurances; Committee of European Securities Regulators; Contracts for difference; Covered short sale; European Commission; European Union; Financial Supervisory Authority; Naked short sale; Porsche versus VW; Undertakings for Collective Investments in Transferable Securities.

11.1 INTRODUCTION

For years, short selling has been at the center of an intense debate among regulators, politicians, the media, and academics. One of the key questions is whether short sellers' activity amplifies the fall of security prices below fundamental values. If the answer is positive, then short selling can potentially create disorderly markets and increase systemic risks. If the answer is negative, then short selling can be seen as a valuable complement to conventional financial market instruments for efficient price discovery, liquidity enhancement, and portfolio hedging and risk management.

Short selling is a concept that many investors and even regulators have trouble understanding. Consequently, its practice is among the most controversial activities in financial markets. Because it benefits from falling prices, short selling is regularly criticized, particularly during times of crisis or following major price declines. The general idea seems to be that short selling is malevolent, morally wrong, and even against the word of God (Proverbs 24:17: "Do not rejoice when your enemy falls, and do not let your heart be glad when he stumbles").

Not surprisingly, during the second half of 2008, short selling was criticized severely. Shareholders, managers, and employees have publicly blamed short sellers for the sharp price decline or even collapse of their company. Given the magnitude of the losses, some have even initiated legal actions and alleged market manipulation by short sellers. At the peak of the crisis, several stock exchange regulators around the world have imposed emergency measures to restrict or impose conditions on short selling. These hurried and noncoordinated interventions, which varied considerably in terms of intensity, scope, and duration, were aimed at restoring the orderly functioning of securities markets and limiting unwarranted drops in securities prices. The situation of Europe is particularly illustrative of the situation. Some countries imposed restrictions on the short selling of specific shares (typically financials); others restricted naked short selling; some also introduced disclosure obligations of different kinds; and others decided to do nothing.

These fragmented approaches, which vary in breath and detail and keep changing country by country, create difficulties and costs for market participants. They may also lead to competitive distortions and potential regulatory arbitrages, which are undesirable from a single market perspective. To limit the compliance nightmare, financial market trade bodies have united to urge the European Commission (EC) to harmonize its members' approach to short selling. After some consultation, the Committee of European Securities Regulators (CESR) has proposed to the EC a first draft regulation to establish a permanent and harmonized pan-European short selling framework. This chapter summarizes existing national short selling regulations in Europe and compares them to the main aspects of the new EC's draft regulation. It also assesses the likely economic and financial consequences of its implementation, should this draft regulation become law.

11.2 A REVIEW OF THE NATIONAL REGULATORY REGIMES IN THE EUROPEAN UNION (EU)

As mentioned previously, at the EU level, until now, the regulation and supervision of financial market activities have remained heavily fragmented. Short selling makes no exception, apart from abusive short selling activities, such as spreading false rumors or using insider information, which are prohibited under the Market Abuse Directive 2003/6/EC. For the rest, national regulations are in place. These are reviewed in this section, but before going into the details of the various regulations, it is important to discuss two technical aspects briefly.

A naked short sale is a situation where the seller neither owns the sold security nor has an unconditional and enforceable legal claim to obtain it.

The seller will therefore look for a security lender *after* the sale has been concluded. In contrast, in a covered short sale, the seller already owns the sold security or has prearranged the security lending agreement. The difference may look subtle, but it is fundamental. One of the major risks of a naked shorting transaction is that the seller may not be able to deliver the security at the predetermined date for clearing and settlement of the trade (typically, T+3). This should not happen with covered sales. Regulators therefore tend to treat naked short selling more severely.

In addition, short selling can be an inherent nonspeculative activity for some specific institutions that play a useful role for financial markets. A typical example is market makers who offer both firm "buy" and "sell" quotes for a market on an ongoing basis and may need to temporarily hedge the positions resulting from client dealings when there are a greater number of participants on one side of the market. These firms would be at a serious competitive disadvantage if they were not able to short or if their short positions were disclosed to other market participants. Regulators therefore tend to grant them reasonable exemptions from short selling restrictions so that they can continue their activity.

11.2.1 Austria

On September 22, 2008, the Austrian regulator (Austrian Financial Market Authority, FMA) prohibited naked short selling of shares in a series of "affected issuers." The list includes Erste Group Bank AG, Raiffeisen International Bank-Holding AG, UNIQA Versicherungen AG, and Wiener Stadtische Versicherung AG. In addition, the Wiener Borse and the Austrian central clearing counterparty, in consultation with the FMA, shortened the period in which a seller may cover delivery. The FMA restrictions have been extended in 3- and 6-month periods at various junctures and are currently in force until the end of May 2011. Only short-term naked short sale positions assumed by market makers or specialists within the range of their contractual obligations are excused from the ban.

Note that incurring or holding a net short position (including through derivatives) in excess of 0.25% of the market capitalization of an issuer can raise grounds for charges of criminal market manipulation under Austrian law. Illegal market manipulation carries a penalty of up to 50,000 euros, and illegal insider trading could carry a prison sentence of up to 5 years. In both cases, illegally earned profits are forfeited.

11.2.2 Belgium

As a result of the financial crisis, the Belgian financial regulatory authority (Commission Bancaire Financiere et des Assurances, CBFA) issued a series of restrictions regarding short selling on September 19, 2008. These restrictions, which were confirmed by the Royal Decree of September 23, 2008, are applicable for an indefinite period. They can be summarized as follows.

- Prohibition of naked short selling in a series of "affected issuers" listed on Euronext Brussels, covering both equities and equity derivatives. The "affected issuers" are essentially financial institutions, for example, Dexia SA, Fortis NV/SA, KBC Groep NV, and KBC Ancora Comm. VA. Until September 21, 2009, the list also included ING Groep SA/NV.
- Disclosure of net economic short positions in excess of 0.25% of the share capital of one of the aforementioned issuers to the CBFA by any appropriate means, as well as to the market through an internationally distributed press release. Note that disclosure is to be made to the market on a net basis and to the CBFA on a gross basis. The term "net economic short position" means any instrument (contracts for differences, spread bets, options, equities, etc.), giving rise to an exposure, whether direct or indirect, in the equity share capital of a company.
- Obligation for qualified intermediaries to take rational measures to determine that their clients have suitable coverage for their planned short transactions. Using derivatives is not considered a proper way of covering a position.

These rules are generally applicable to all transactions carried out on the stock exchange or off-exchange in Belgium or abroad. The CBFA also indicated that market participants should refrain from lending the aforementioned securities. Exemptions for these rules apply in the case of market makers, liquidity providers (as defined by the Euronext Rule Book), and block trade counterparties.

11.2.3 Denmark
In accordance with regulation laid out and effective by the Danish Financial Supervisory Authority (FSA) on September 22, 2008, there was a ban on naked short selling securities of Danish licensed banks whose shares are traded on a regulated market. No official list of the pertinent banks has been published. However, exclusion applies in the case of market-making activity and hedging exposures in applicable bank stocks, if the hedging remains in "rational proportion" to the risk.

11.2.4 Finland
Unlike most other EU countries, Finland has weathered the current financial crisis relatively well. In addition, it is not a country with a wide practice of short selling. As a result, in late 2008, the Finnish FSA expressly confirmed

that it did not consider any regulations or emergency measures relating to short selling necessary.

11.2.5 France

On September 22, 2008, the Autorité des Marchés Financiers (AMF) issued a series of emergency measures on short selling, with an initial application time of 3 months. These measures can be summarized as follows.

- Prohibition of naked short selling in the equities and equity derivatives of a series of 15 banks and financial institutions. Any seller in these 15 names must either have bought the securities or have borrowed them before the time of the sale. The list included the following names: Allianz, April Group, AXA, BNP Paribus, CIC, CNP Assurances, Credit Agricole, Dexia, Euler Hermes, HSBC Holdings, Natixis, NYSE Euronext, Paris Re, Scor, and Societe Generale.
- Disclosure of net economic short positions in excess of 0.25% of the share capital of one of the aforementioned issuers to the AMF within T+3 days.

The AMF also indicated that market participants should refrain from lending the aforementioned securities. Exemptions for these rules apply in the case of market makers, liquidity providers, or block trades counterparties.

The original provisions were due to expire on December 22, 2008, but were extended until the end of January 2010 and then subsequently until further notice. However, a law "for banking and financial regulation" was voted on October 28, 2010. It contains several provisions regarding the implementation of a permanent short selling regime in France. As a result, the measures taken by the AMF on September 19, 2008, to prohibit short selling of specified financial stocks will therefore no longer apply as of February 1, 2011. The new measures that will replace them are likely to require some harmonization once a European-wide regime is set up through the European Commission.

11.2.6 Germany

In the wake of the financial crisis, the German Regulator BaFin prohibited short selling in shares of 10 financial institutions, governmental bonds, and credit default swaps (CDSs) by general decree. On July 27, 2010, these decrees were repealed following adoption of the Act on the Prevention against Abusive Dealings in Securities and Derivatives, which essentially prohibits three types of short selling positions:

- Naked short sales in all shares admitted to trading on a regulated market in Germany.

- Naked short sales in debt securities of "central governments, regional governments, and local authorities" of EU member states trading on the regulated market in Germany.
- Naked CDSs referring to liabilities of EU member institutions. This includes CDS on indices and basket products that contain at least one liability of a EU member institution as reference liability.

The shares and debt securities prohibitions apply irrespective of the place where the transaction was concluded and therefore also cover transactions concluded abroad. The CDS prohibition only covers transactions that were actually concluded in Germany. In any case, credit institutions are also obligated to notify BaFin without delay in case of any suspicion of a violation.

These restrictions go far above and beyond average restrictions in the EU, but they have a limited impact in practice. First, apart from German government bonds, very few debt securities of EU member institutions are trading on regulated German markets. Similarly, most of the activity on credit default swaps on EU sovereign reference entities takes place in London. Second, these provisions do not cover intraday short positions. Traders can therefore initiate a naked short position if they cover it (i.e., borrow the corresponding shares) the same day. Third, these provisions do not apply to derivative financial instruments that refer to shares or debt securities such as futures, options, swaps, or transactions on index or basket products. Last but not least, other European countries have not followed Germany on that road.

German Chancellor Angela Merkel has indicated that the current ban would remain in place until the EU comes up with a comprehensive alternative. Note that in addition to the aforementioned rules, the German parliament adopted new disclosure obligations for net short selling positions. They require a notification to BaFin if a net short position reaches 0.2% of the share capital of a German-listed company, and each 0.1% thereafter. They also require publication in the electronic *German Federal Gazette* of any net short position above the 0.5% of the share capital of a German-listed company, and each 0.1% thereafter. These disclosure obligations will not come into effect until March 26, 2012.

11.2.7 Greece

In October 2008, the Greek regulator (Hellenic Capital Market Commission, HCMC) decided to ban short sales on the Athens bourse. The ban was renewed several times and was ultimately lifted in June 2009. However, on April 28, 2010, a day after Standard & Poor's downgraded Greece's credit rating to junk status, Greek stocks and bonds came under considerable selling pressure. The HCMC therefore decided to ban again short selling completely. On August 31, 2010, the short selling ban was lifted, but the ban on naked short selling was maintained. Under the most recent announcement, short selling is allowed under the condition that the seller has ensured, prior to the transaction, adequate shares at the settlement date (T+3) in order to fulfill settlement obligations. Disclosure requirements require the report of all net short positions in excess of 0.10% of issuance to the HCMC and publication in the HELEX daily official list. Exceptions are in place for market makers.

11.2.8 Ireland

On September 19, 2008, following a similar prohibition by its U.K. counterpart, the Irish Financial Regulator introduced provisions to prohibit short selling Irish quoted banking stocks. The ban applies to four companies: Bank of Ireland, Allied Irish Bank Plc, Irish Life and Permanent Plc, and Anglo Irish Bank Corporation Plc. It is applicable to shares or American depositary receipts in London and other international trading venues, as well as in Dublin, with exemptions in place for market makers. Disclosure requirements have also been introduced for economic interest totaling 0.25% or more of the issued share capital in the affected names. Note that the short selling ban has been reaffirmed in 2009 as well as in 2010, even after the banks receive fresh capital injections.

11.2.9 Italy

The regulation of short selling activities in Italy has varied over time. On September 22, 2008, the Italian regulator (Commissione Nazionale per le Società e la Borsa, CONSOB) banned the short selling of shares of Italian banks and insurance companies. Companies subject to this initial short selling ban were as follows: Banca Italease S.p.A, Class Editori S.p.A., Eurofly S.p.A, Giovanni Crespi S.p.A, I Viaggi Del Ventaglio S.p.A, Omnia Network S.p.A, Richard Ginori 1735 S.p.A., Safilo Group S.p.A, Unicredito S.p.A, and Unicredit RISP. On October 10, 2008, the CONSOB extended the ban to *all* shares listed and traded on the Italian regulated markets, regardless of their business sector. Exemptions for these rules applied in the case of market makers, liquidity providers, or block trades counterparties. On August 1, 2009, the CONSOB lifted its short selling ban except with regard to Italian-listed companies that declared a rights issue before November 30, 2009. The CONSOB then maintained the list of companies whose shares were subject to the ban. On August 25, 2010, the last two companies on that list were removed from it, therefore implying that there was no longer a short selling ban in Italy.

11.2.10 Luxembourg

In accordance with regulation laid out and effective by the Luxembourg regulator (Commission de Surveillance du Secteur Financier, CSSF) on

September 19, 2008, naked short selling was prohibited where the underlying assets are stocks of a credit institution or insurance undertaking traded on a regulated market. Market making is not covered by this ban.

11.2.11 The Netherlands

On September 22, 2008, the Netherlands regulator (Autoriteit Financiële Markten, AFM) introduced a ban to prohibit both covered and naked short selling in shares of publicly quoted financial companies. The list includes Aegon, Binck Bank, Delta Lloyd, Fortis, ING Groep, Kas Bank, SNS Reaal, Van Der Moolen, and Van Lanschot, both on spot and derivative markets. The Dutch short selling expired on June 1, 2009, and was replaced by new disclosure requirements for any net short position that reaches, exceeds, or falls below 0.25% and every subsequent 0.10% of the capital of a financial company. Disclosure must be made to the AFM no later than end of business on the next working day. These measures remain in place today.

11.2.12 Norway

In accordance with regulation laid out and effective by the FSA of Norway, Kredittilsynet, on October 8, 2008, there was a temporarily ban on the short selling of financial equities. On October 10, 2008, this was extended to cover short selling on primary capital certificates. This was subsequently lifted, although some disclosure requirements remain in place.

11.2.13 Portugal

On September 22, 2008, the Portuguese regulator (Comissao do Mercado de Valores Mobiliarios, CMVM) prohibited naked short selling of financial instruments related to a series of selected financial firms listed on Euronext Lisbon. The list includes the following issuers: Banco Comercial Portugues, Banco BPI, Banco Espírito Santo, Banco Popular, Banco Santander Central Hispano, Banif Sgps, Finibanco Holding, and Espirito Santo Financial Group. Subsequent to this, new regulation came into effect in July 2010, extending the mandatory reporting of short interest to all shares admitted to trading on a regulated market or trading in multilateral trading or operating in Portugal. Previously this only applied to shares of companies in the PSI-20 and financial institutions. The threshold for reporting is at 0.20% to the CMVM and at 0.50% to the market.

11.2.14 Spain

Naked short selling of any Spanish-listed security has been prohibited under Spanish stock market legislation since 1939—investors must hold the securities before introducing a sale order in the market. There are no exemptions, but the operating needs of market makers and liquidity providers are taken into account by the Spanish stock market regulator (Comisión Nacional Del Mercado De Valores, CNMV).

In accordance with regulation laid out and effective by the CNMV on September 22, 2008, investors are required to disclose in T+1 their short positions exceeding 0.25% of the listed stock capital in any member of a list of financial sector companies. This list includes the following names: Banco de Andalucía, Banco de Vasconia, Banco de Castilla, Banco Español de Crédito, Banco de Crédito Balear, Bankinter, Banco de Galicia, BBVA, Banco Guipuzcoano, Caja de Ahorros del Mediterráneo, Banco Pastor, Grupo Catalana Occidente, Banco Popular Español, Mapfre, Banco Sabadell, Inverfiatc, Banco Santander, Bolsas y Mercados Españoles, Banco de Valencia, and Renta. Note that for the disclosure rule, investors should consider all positions in financial instruments (including the relevant shares and derivatives) that provide the holder a positive exposure to downward movements in the price of the relevant shares. In the case of derivatives on a basket of shares, the weight of the relevant issuer in the basket of shares shall be taken into account in order to calculate the global position. In case of derivatives, positions should be delta adjusted. Long and short positions can be netted, provided that the person or entity that has made both investment decisions is the same.

Effective June 10, 2010, the regulator announced an extension of the disclosure requirements to cover all shares listed on Spanish official stock exchanges on short positions that exceed 0.2% of the listed capital. Once a position has been reported, updates will have to be made on any subsequent adjustment that represents an increase/decrease of more than 0.1%. If a short position represents more than 0.5% of the listed stock of an issuer, disclosure will be made to the market on the CNMV's Web site, including the identity of the holder, as well as for any subsequent increase/decrease of more than 0.1%.

11.2.15 United Kingdom

On September 22, 2008, the U.K. regulator (FSA) proscribed any transaction resulting in the creation of increase or a net short position in the share price of a list of 32 U.K. financial sector companies. The ban applied to both cash and derivatives markets and had a global reach regardless of the place of the trade. The FSA also required (i) daily disclose of all net short positions in the predefined list if the short position was in excess 0.25% of the ordinary share capital of a U.K.-listed company on a net delta-adjusted basis, with additional disclosure at 0.1% increments; and (ii) disclose on a one-off basis of net short positions of 0.25% or more in companies that undertake rights issues whose shares are admitted to trading on a prescribed market.

The ban on short selling expired on January 16, 2009, and the FSA has not proposed any new direct restriction nor has it expressed support for other constraints, such as new circuit breakers or uptick rules. The required disclosure for significant net short positions remains in place indefinitely, as the FSA's current position is that public disclosure is the most cost-efficient transparency option.

11.3 THE CASE OF EASTERN EUROPE

The largest category of short sellers in eastern Europe is hedge funds, which typically need to access the pool of securities of their prime brokers to borrow and sell short. The ability to sell short is therefore reliant on (i) the prime broker's pool having the desired stock and (ii) permission from the securities owners to lend out the stock. Alternatively, one may also defer to a third party to borrow the stock, but this can have the effect of creating additional fees and expenses.

For liquidity reasons, the ability to short in various eastern European jurisdictions is limited, and hence short selling regulation is less relevant in certain jurisdictions. A general guide for short selling in larger eastern European countries is provided here.

Turkey: Turkey has one of the more developed markets for shorting in eastern Europe. There is a stock loan market enabling one to short through physical, swap, custom index swap, MSCI swap, and via futures contracts on the Istanbul Stock Exchange National 30 (ISE 30 Index). Potential investors should note, however, that although the large constituents are fairly liquid, there is significant overlap among the various indices, with a heavy tilt toward financial services. For example, Turkiye Garanti Bankasi AS, Akbank, and Turkiye Is Bankasi constitute over 40% of the ISE 30 Index.

With reference to short selling regulation in Turkey, ISE members are allowed to short sell all equities traded in the ISE markets, except those listed on the watch list market. Currently there are no securities on the watch list.

Poland: Poland also has a reasonably deep market for shorting in comparison to its neighboring countries. Like Turkey, there is a stock loan market, mainly via physical, swap, custom index swap, MSCI swap, and via the future on the Warsaw Stock Exchange (WIG 20 Index, a capitalization-weighted index of 20 companies). The larger index constituents are fairly liquid and readily available for borrow. Again, there is a large degree of overlap between the regional MSCI and WIG indices and both are heavily weighted toward banks and utilities. By way of example, 30% of the WIG 20 Index is split between two bank names.

Effective July 1, 2010, Poland bucked the general trend by actually introducing a regulatory framework to permit, while governing, the naked short selling of positions. Jaroslaw Ziebiec, director of financial instruments at the Warsaw Stock Exchange, said "the new framework for naked short selling would narrow spreads and increase arbitrage opportunities on the exchange's derivatives market and stimulate greater liquidity on its cash market" (source: http://www.thetradenews.com). Regulations permit short sale transactions in the most liquid Polish securities, including, but not limited to, those blue-chip stocks in the WIG 20 exchange index and listed treasury bonds. The Warsaw Stock Exchange maintains and publishes a list of qualifying securities. Under the new regime, market makers and other liquidity providers will be able to short sell the 140 most liquid stocks on the WSE, as well as treasury bonds issued by the National Bank of Poland, but market participants will be restricted to a smaller list of securities when trading on behalf of clients or on a proprietary basis. In this case, constituents of the WIG 20 blue chip index, plus 16 other liquid stocks and 40 treasury bonds, will be available for short selling initially.

The Warsaw Stock Exchange may suspend short sale orders in certain cases. This consists of a circuit breaker ruling that occurs on all securities if the value of the WIG index decreases considerably (a fall of 3% or more) or affects a single stock if it drops by 10% or more. In each case, the suspension occurs only if the value of short sale transactions exceeds 20% of all sale transactions in the given securities.

Hungry, Cyprus, Israel, Russia, and Czech Republic: There is a stock loan market via physical, swap, custom index swap, and MSCI swap. Futures contracts are not liquid enough to trade, and while liquidity is usually reasonable within the respective country index, it can become tight in the tail end of the index. On the subject of short selling regulation in the latter, the Czech National Bank does not ban legitimate short selling techniques and has no plan to proceed with temporary action. Effective June 15, 2009, investors in the Russian market are permitted to execute short selling trades if the price is not more than 3% lower than the closing price of the previous day.

Of the stock-lending desks of those investment banks surveyed, very few provided the ability to short Kazakhstan, and they also commented that it can be difficult to go long stock there, indicating that the market is not yet developed enough. The same observation applies to Slovakia, Latvia, Estonia, Romania, and Slovenia. Kazakhstan may be tradable through synthetic securities, which is largely dependent on the inventory the provider has in-house, which is likely to also be limited. Depositary receipts may be an alternative way to gain access.

11.3.1 The Case of Undertakings for Collective Investments in Transferable Securities (UCITS)

The Undertakings for Collective Investments in Transferable Securities (UCITS III) directive was intended primarily as establishing a "passport" for collective investment funds, which would allow a fund approved in one EU jurisdiction to be approved automatically in all the others. In the rear view mirror of 2008 and amid fears of illiquidity and counterparty risk, UCITS III regulations have gained traction and their impact goes much further. In particular, there are now an increased number of UCITS-compliant European *hedge funds* for which short selling in the traditional sense is not possible— the UCITS regulation explicitly prohibits outright short positions. The usual workaround for UCITS to short is through the use of contracts for difference (CFD). A CFD is not a covered instrument and the broker does not necessarily have to hedge the position and so is considered a pure derivative.[1]

Providing that the regulator allows short selling in its market, it is theoretically possible for a broker to structure a CFD on any security globally that it can have access to or borrow via the stock-lending market. This extends theoretically to those eastern European jurisdictions where there is stock available to borrow. Pricing should be linked directly to the underlying equity with a wider spread to allow for the broker to close out the position without loss; therefore, the liquidity of the CFD is completely reliant on the underlying security and it is, of course, possible to create a short squeeze. If the local market has numerous taxes or capital gain on a position, this will also be factored into the overall price of a CFD and make the spread even wider as the broker would need to account all of this if he or she was to cover the position correctly.

11.4 THE NEW EUROPEAN COMMISSION'S DRAFT REGULATION

As a result of the disparity among the various regulations, the CESR had to issue a summary paper to market participants (see CESR, 2010a, 2010b). The market maker exemption was in particular a serious source of problems, as the member states did not share the same criteria to determine who could qualify as a market maker—a complete failure to achieve the "level playing field" goal of the EU securities regulation.

11.4.1 The Draft Proposal

After extensive dialogue and consultation with all major stakeholders, including securities regulators and market participants, on September 15,

---

[1] A similar conclusion applies to credit default swaps.

2010—the second anniversary of the collapse of Lehman Brothers—the EC released a legislative proposal to create a harmonized framework for short selling throughout Europe. Here are some of its key points.

- To ban naked short sales in equity securities. Short sales will only be permitted if the seller has borrowed the security, entered into an agreement to borrow it, or made other arrangements to ensure that the security has been located and reserved for lending.
- To increase transparency and disclosure standards for short positions in shares traded on a European exchange or trading facility. The proposal suggests in particular that any net short position of 0.2% (and all 0.1% increments above that level) will be disclosed to the relevant national regulators. Net short positions of 0.5%, and all 0.1% increments above that level, will be disclosed to the public. Note that this might be a serious problem and create short squeezes for small and mid-cap securities, as a short position of 0.5% of outstanding capital is reached quickly.
- To establish adequate processes and give regulators powers to restrict short selling entirely, limit entries into CDS transactions relating to an obligation of a member state, or require additional private notification or public disclosure in exceptional circumstances.
- To establish buy-in procedures and daily fines for late settlement of transactions. Regulated markets must also prohibit those who have failed to settle in the past from entering into further trades. This clause, in addition to the ban on naked short selling, should help reduce counterparty risk, another risk that could potentially undermine the stability of the financial system.
- To exempt market makers acting in their capacity as such in a uniform way across Europe.
- To establish the European Securities and Markets Authority as a central Paris-based authority to take and/or coordinate short selling measures in exceptional situations, for example, a threat to the orderly functioning and integrity of financial markets or the stability of the financial system.

Interestingly, the proposal also contains some provisions related to sovereign issuers and credit default swaps. New restrictions on entering into uncovered short sales of shares or sovereign debt instruments will be defined, but not as an outright ban, as is currently the case in Germany. Moreover, a net short position relating to the issued sovereign debt of a member state or an uncovered short position in a CDS referencing the member state should also be disclosed to the relevant national regulators, but the threshold levels have not yet been specified.

The devil, as always, remains in the detail. Numerous technical details must still be discussed and specified. Examples include methodologies for netting in corporations with various divisions and entities, handling of convertible bonds and warrants, clarification of which borrowing agreements are acceptable, and so on.

The commission's proposal is now being considered by the European Parliament and the Council of Ministers where the final text will need to be agreed. If adopted, the proposal may apply from July 1, 2012, but with a transitional period allowing member states to continue with their existing short selling regimes until July 1, 2013. The good news is that the final text is likely to be passed by way of regulation, as this would make it directly applicable in all member states without leaving inconsistencies in implementation or interpretation. Its potential benefits are a reduction of legal costs associated with individual regulations (either directly or indirectly as a result of decreased confusion among market participants), significant time savings for the legal body for each jurisdiction, less room for regulatory arbitrage, and more confidence against uncertainty for market participants. It is this confidence that is core to ensuring the stability of the financial system.

One of the objectives of the commission's proposal is to increase transparency and disclosure standards for short positions in shares. This measure of incremental position disclosure should help avoid sudden shocks to the financial system, which can result in sudden price moves. A case example of how the use of derivative instruments can lead to market disruption is well illustrated in the October 2008 study of the Porsche Automobil Holding SE ("Porsche") and Volkswagen AG ("VW") situation.

11.4.2 Case Study: Porsche versus VW

On October 26, 2008, Porsche announced that it had increased its stake in VW, a German automotive manufacturer, to 42.6%, from an earlier 31%, and that it held cash-settled call options to acquire an additional 31.5% stake. Porsche structured its options as "cash settled," as BaFin, Germany's financial regulator, ruled that firms were not forced to reveal positions where the derivatives were settled into cash rather than stock. Thus, Porsche's actions were not transparent to market participants and, therefore, the resulting impact on VW's stock price was significant.

The 74.1% stake, coupled with 20.1% ownership in the company by the German state of Lower Saxony, left just 5.8% of the company as free float. This compares to 12.9% of VW stock on loan as reported by Data Explorers, creating a significant mismatch and resulting in what is being cited as the largest short squeeze in history. In response, investors, including several hedge funds, have attempted to cover their short positions, with the owners of shares able to exercise discretion in the price at which they would sell their shares. As a result, the stock of VW soared 123.7% on Monday, October 27, and a further 94.9% the next day. Porsche subsequently announced their intention to settle hedging transactions in the amount of up to 5% of VW's ordinary shares, which was expected to result in an increase in the liquidity of the shares. As a result, VW stock lost 42.4% on the day.

Germany's largest market capitalization-based index, the DAX, was also affected, with a number of anomalies in terms of the car maker's absolute and relative valuations. Following the share price moves and according to Bloomberg, the company's respective weighting in the index increased from 4.8% on September 1, 2008, to a peak of 28% on Tuesday, October 27. This overweight position caused the region's index to meaningfully outperform its European peers on Tuesday, as the DAX appreciated 11.3% against the MSCI Europe Index, which fell 2.2%. On that Monday, the DAX rose 0.9%, despite a fall in all of the remaining 29 DAX companies. In an absolute sense, based on market capitalization, VW traded briefly at levels that made it the largest company in the world, ahead of Exxon, and, in a relative sense, the company was larger than the remaining U.S. and European automotive companies combined.

Implications were also felt outside of the automotive sector as certain banks were rumored to have been affected adversely by the trade, which market participants saw as potentially liable to lend substantial capital to Porsche in order for the company to exercise the right to buy VW stock at its inflated levels. This led to downward pressure on the share prices of Societe Generale, Goldman Sachs, and Morgan Stanley, companies that may, or may not, be associated with the transaction. This was against a backdrop of generally higher financial stocks over the same time period.

Although this situation involved the accumulation of naked call options (long) rather than naked puts (short), it highlights the potential risks when there is significant short interest in a stock, particularly naked (uncovered) shorts, which, when combined with small free float, can result in a short squeeze. This is due to a supply-and-demand imbalance as short sellers are forced to buy back the stock to cover their position, usually at the same time leading to upward pressure on the company's share price. A company's stock price can rise infinitely, but fall only to zero.

In the United Kingdom, new proposed FSA rules, which started in September 2009, obliged the disclosure of cash-settled derivatives. However, in Germany, cash-settled options will still not set off notification duties since they don't carry a right to obtain the underlying stock and time will tell if other European partners will pursue the FSA's footsteps.

11.5 CONCLUSION

In a few years, the short selling regulation in Europe has evolved dramatically, and this process is likely to continue over the near future until a unified framework ultimately replaces the piecemeal nation-by-nation approach. Most industry groups, including the Alternative Investment Management Association, the Managed Funds Association, and the International Securities Lending Association, are now trying to negotiate certain key aspects of the future European legislation.

REFERENCES

CESR. (2010a). *Model for a Pan-European short selling disclosure regime* (Report No. 10-088). Retrieved from http://www.cesr-eu.org.

CESR. (2010b). *Technical details of the Pan-European short selling disclosure regime* (Report No. 10-453). Retrieved from http://www.cesr-eu.org.

European Commission. (2010). *Proposal for a regulation of the European Parliament and of the Council on Short Selling and Certain Aspects of Credit Default Swaps*. Working Paper. Retrieved from http://ec.europa.eu.

CHAPTER 12

Regulating Short Selling: The European Framework and Regulatory Arbitrage

Giampaolo Gabbi and Paola Giovinazzo

CONTENTS

ABSTRACT

Short sellers speculate by driving the prices of financial assets below their fair value, which is frequently denounced as one of the reasons of high market volatility and market corrections. To prevent the risk of a meltdown, European regulators introduced short selling bans with dissimilarities. This chapter compares the main features of these regulations and explains their partial ineffectiveness and the risk to unlevel the playing field of large financial stocks.

KEYWORDS

Fundamental view; Market Disclosure; Financial Services Authority; Regulatory cooperation; Regulatory view.

12.1 INTRODUCTION

There are two points of view on short selling. First, financial literature suggests that short sellers provide an advantage by accelerating the alignment process of stock prices toward their fundamental value (Abreu & Brunnermeier, 2002; Beber & Pagano, 2010; Dechow, Hutton, Meulbroek, & Sloan, 2001). Second, regulators argue predominantly that the short selling practice drives stock prices below their fair value. This is the rationale of recent market regulations with additional restrictions, tougher stringent disclosures, and even complete bans on short selling to restrain the pressure on stock prices. However, there are various methods to introduce limits on short selling. According to the Financial Services Authority (2009), regulators can prohibit (i) short selling of all stocks, (ii) naked short selling of financial stocks, and (iii) firms engaging in rights issues.

Banning short selling of all stocks listed on a market brings about numerous indirect costs, such as pricing efficiency, liquidity shortage, foregone profits, and consequent trading reduction. Therefore, regulators usually prefer to focus the ban on specific types of stocks or capital market players to reduce the speculative risks, especially when speculation or market abuse affects only specific securities. Otherwise, arbitrage opportunities would arise. The risk is higher when regulations are managed by agencies with heterogeneous organizations and missions, which still occurs in Europe, even though there is at least one supervisory authority for each country.

This chapter examines and compares the European regulatory interventions after the 2008–2009 financial crisis to investigate their effectiveness and dissimilarities of policies. In addition, it shows how these policies affected the decisions of financial advisors, as well as the market processes among European countries. It further demonstrates that multinational banks and financial intermediaries could arbitrage regulatory asymmetries and unbalance the playing field.

The remainder of this chapter is organized as follows. Section 12.2 describes views on the regulation of short sellers and distinguishes between academic and regulatory approaches. Section 12.3 explains interventions in four of the largest European countries (the United Kingdom, France, Germany, and Italy). Section 12.4 presents an analysis of the effectiveness of these interventions and regulatory arbitrages.

12.2 THEORETICAL VIEWS OF SHORT SELLING REGULATION

Short sales can be aimed at speculating, hedging risk in pairs trading, and arbitraging assets (Boehmer, Jones, & Zhang, 2008; Desai, Krishnamurthy, & Venkataraman, 2006). Short sellers are often blamed for stock declines and market corrections. There are two main approaches to short selling and its impact on stock prices. The first is the *fundamental view* that short sellers use information to influence the convergence of asset market prices to their fair values (Dechow et al., 2001). This approach is substantiated by equilibrium models where short sellers estimate the fair value for stocks and bonds. A more sophisticated analysis adds to the fundamental view; the "timing puzzle," that is, when asset prices converge toward their fundamental values (Chen, Rhee, 2010). According to a landmark study, short selling limitations do not reduce stock return volatility (Beber & Pagano, 2010). A statement summing up this approach was presented before the Committee on Rules and the House of Representatives in 1917 by Bernard Baruch (a supporter of short selling), who stated "bears can only make money if the bulls push up stocks to where they are overpriced and unsound."

The second is the *regulatory view*, which amplifies price collapse when uncertainty and information asymmetries converge toward a negative scenario. According to this view, financial market regulation authorities introduced different types of bans in order to avoid speculative forces destabilizing European markets. The history of short selling bans in the United States began in 1812 and lasted until the 1850s (Taulli, 2004). However, prior to the 1929 crash, short selling was permitted (Jones & Lamont, 2002). The Pecora Commission of 1932 set out to investigate the reasons for the stock market crash in the United States and defined short selling as dangerous for stock market stability.

In 2009, the U.S. Congress gave the Financial Crisis Inquiry Commission the mandate to investigate potential causes of the crisis with short selling being one of the main themes (Public Law 111-21 Fraud Enforcement and Recovery Act of 2009). On July 15, 2008, the U.S. Securities and Exchange Commission (SEC) announced provisional restrictions on naked short sales of 19 financial stocks (SEC, 2008). In particular, the SEC was "concerned about persons that sell short securities and deceive specified persons about their intention or ability to deliver the securities in time for settlement, or deceive their broker-dealer about their locate source or ownership of shares, or otherwise engage in abusive naked short selling."

Boulton and Braga-Alves (2010) observed a positive market reaction to the announcement of short sale restrictions and vice versa when the ban expired. Their findings suggest that announcement returns were superior for companies having a higher concentration of naked short sale activity in days immediately prior to the announcement of the restrictions. The authors show that regulation reduced the activity of naked short sellers for restricted stocks. Chung and Lee (2010, p. 532) suggest that "the negative impact of this regulation can be listed as follows: (i) naked short selling increased for a number of financial firms during the restricted period and (ii) worsening of liquidity measures, such as bid–ask spreads and trading volumes."

The current broad view appeared to be that the deteriorating credit crisis was being magnified by short sellers. Numerous financial market regulators in Europe, Asia, and Australia intervened directly by banning short sellers from focusing on financial stocks. European interventions were partially coordinated but presented inconsistencies in some cases, thus creating opportunities for arbitrage (Duan, Hu, McLean, 2010).

12.3 EUROPEAN REGULATIONS AFTER THE LEHMAN BROTHERS COLLAPSE

A majority of European countries introduced restrictions on short selling activities during the months of September and October 2008. Their range and number of restricted assets were partly diverse with different durations. Some countries, such as the Czech Republic, Finland, Hungary, Poland, Slovenia, and Sweden, did not introduce any type of restriction. Table 12.1 compares several of the main features of short selling regulations in European countries displaying the start and end dates after the Lehman Brothers collapse.

The first countries to introduce restrictions on September 19, 2008 (i.e., 4 days after the bankruptcy) were Ireland, Luxembourg, Switzerland, and the United Kingdom, and the last country to introduce restrictions was Belgium on October 26, 2008. On average, restrictions were delayed by 13 days after the Lehman collapse, and the heterogeneity affected the European market equality as well as the opportunistic behavior of several financial players.

The largest European countries (United Kingdom, Germany, France, and Italy) enforced restrictions for short sellers with varying measures depending on the country, ranging from a ban on net short positions to the prohibition of both naked and covered short selling.

12.3.1 Short Selling Regulation in the United Kingdom
The idea of short selling regulation in the United Kingdom after the 2008–2009 financial crisis was stated by the Financial Services Authority (2008) as follows:

> While we still regard short-selling as a legitimate investment technique in normal market conditions, the current extreme circumstances have

Table 12.1 Timing of Short Selling Decisions in European Countries after the Lehman Brothers Collapse

Country	Start Date	End Date	Duration in Days
Austria	10/10/2008	06/07/2009	240
Belgium	10/26/2008	07/27/2009	274
Czech Republic			
Denmark	10/13/2008	06/23/2009	253
Finland			
France	09/22/2008	06/23/2009	274
Germany	09/20/2008	06/23/2009	276
Greece	10/10/2008	06/01/2009	234
Hungary			
Ireland	09/19/2008	06/23/2009	277
Italy	09/22/2008	06/01/2009	252
Luxembourg	09/19/2008	06/23/2009	277
Netherlands	09/22/2008	06/01/2009	252
Norway	10/08/2008	06/22/2009	257
Poland			
Portugal	09/22/2008	06/23/2009	274
Slovenia			
Spain	09/24/2008	06/23/2009	272
Sweden			
Switzerland	09/19/2008	01/16/2009	119
UK	09/19/2008	01/16/2009	119

Source: *Beber and Pagano (2010) from various financial market authority reports.*

given rise to disorderly markets. As a result, we have taken this decisive action, after careful consideration, to protect the fundamental integrity and quality of markets and to guard against further instability in the financial sector.

After the Halifax Bank of Scotland bailout in October 2008, the FSA agreed to introduce new provisions to the code of market conduct to forbid the formation or the increase of net short positions for both naked and covered short sales in publicly quoted financial stocks. In addition, the FSA stressed mandatory daily disclosure of all net short positions in excess of 0.25% of the ordinary share capital of the relevant firms held at market close on the preceding trading day. Furthermore, the FSA extended *sine die* the rules of transparency on short positions. In February 2009, the FSA extended the list to include all publicly traded U.K. firms to maintain a transparency regime of net short positions and recommended that the threshold of capital be increased from 0.25 to 0.50% for all listed firms incorporated in the United Kingdom.

12.3.2 Short Selling Regulation in Germany

The rationale of Germany's regulations was "to prevent certain types of short selling since these could give rise to excessive price movements. These in turn could jeopardize the stability of the financial system, resulting in serious disadvantages for the financial market."[1] The German Federal FSA (Bundesanstalt für Finanzdienstleistungsaufsicht, BaFin) banned naked short selling transactions on 11 listed financial stocks from October 20, 2008, until June 23, 2009. BaFin did not ban covered short selling. In addition, disclosure obligations had not been provided for short positions on financial stocks. On January 18, 2010, the ban for naked short selling on financial stocks was reintroduced for sovereign bonds issued by European countries and for credit default swaps brokers. The purpose was to support bond prices during the euro crisis and the speculative pressure against Greece. One of the main criticisms of this regulation was that it applied only to German operations. All banks outside Germany could continue taking short positions on sovereign bonds; however, most of the large banks decided to manage short selling operations from their foreign offices.

12.3.3 Short Selling Regulation in France

With the purpose to "provide as much consistency as possible between the Paris marketplace and major foreign financial centres, in particular those that are home to markets operated by Euronext,"[2] the French Financial Market Authority (Autorité des Marchés Financiers, AMF) banned naked short selling on September 19, 2008. The AMF requested that financial institutions abstain from securities lending transactions in financial stocks. Short positions generated through the use of derivatives, such as futures, were also banned. In terms of disclosure, the AMF imposed to communicate to the authority any net short positions exceeding 0.25% of the issued share capital of listed firms.

On February 23, 2009, the AMF published a document presenting measures that would discourage short selling by (i) introducing more penalties for parties not delivering the title sold on contractual dates, (ii) publicly disclosing net short positions that exceed 0.25% of capital of the listed companies, and (iii) forcing investors that engage in short selling to inform the AMF of the volume and price of securities lending transactions to prevent any pressure on the stock market.

---

[1] General decree of BaFin dated September 21, 2008, and expired by the end of January 28, 2010.
[2] AMF report, February 23, 2009.

12.3.4 Short Selling Regulation in Italy

With the aim of reducing speculative activities against financial stocks during the crisis on September 19, 2008, the Italian National Commission for Companies and Exchanges (Commissione Nazionale per le Società e la Borsa, CONSOB) preferred moral suasion as a means of intervention to reduce the activity of short selling. Three days later, naked short selling was banned (Act No. 16622). On October 1, 2008, for a period of 3 months, CONSOB adopted restrictive measures whereby naked and covered short selling on insurance and bank stocks were banned. However, futures and other derivatives were not banned. On October 10, 2008, CONSOB extended the list for all listed shares on Italian markets until December 31, 2008, and subsequently extended it until January 31, 2009. These restrictive measures applied for all financial players except market makers in order to let them quote both bid and ask prices.

12.4 REGULATORY ASYMMETRIES AND ARBITRAGE

The process followed by financial market authorities in Europe to initiate short selling restrictions brought about the primary question concerning the possible existence of cost asymmetries among heterogeneous financial firms. Authorities decided to avoid short selling bans for all stocks and chose different options under the general agreement to circumvent relevant differences among countries and restricted financial advisors from short selling.

When authorities need to supervise short selling, they can regulate their involvement by the following approaches.

1. The *direct approach* defines the restrictions on short selling by assets and market players. The regulatory ban options can be on covered and/or naked short selling; on all or several investors, depending on their specialization and their contribution to market efficiency (in this case, liquidity providers often are allowed to take short positions); or on all or several listed companies, which are subject to speculation. In numerous cases, authorities introduced the uptick rule requiring that short sales be made only in a rising market.

2. The *disclosure approach* requires more information on trading activity from financial firms in order to monitor short selling volume and enhanced disclosure. In this situation, information can be disclosed to the market or to regulators. In the first instance (market disclosure), information concerning the short selling entity is made public and is flagged. Consequently, it decreases asymmetric information, notwithstanding the numerous setup costs for developing a flagging regime, costs, and

monitoring, as well as enforcements costs. The second approach (authorities disclosure) of reporting to regulatory authorities reduces some weakness, but there is a limit in terms of market transparency and ability to reduce the information asymmetries between short sellers and retail investors.

3. The *mixed approach* combines the previous two approaches in order to minimize the negative short selling impact and to supervise financial speculation more effectively. Usually, this option includes reporting all net short positions and reprimands all noncompliance short sellers.

Even though European regulators managed to introduce limitations on short selling around October 2008 to minimize opportunistic behavior, their approach was significantly different from each other. Table 12.2 displays the difference in terms of approach and types of stocks banned during the period of short selling regulation.

The analysis of European regulation not only shows a relevant discrepancy in start and end dates (Table 12.1), but also a set of features where the rules could be bypassed by large financial firms by managing or placing short sale orders from different countries.

Table 12.2 Features of Short Selling Regulations in European Countries after the Lehman Brothers Collapse

Country	Approach	Typology of Stocks Banned
Austria	Direct	Financial
Belgium	Direct	Financial
Denmark	Mixed (market disclosure)	Financial
France	Mixed (authorities disclosure)	Financial
Germany	Mixed (authorities disclosure)	Financial
Greece	Direct	All stocks
Ireland	Mixed (authorities disclosure)	Financial
Italy	Mixed (authorities disclosure) then direct	Financial and then all stocks
Luxembourg	Mixed (authorities disclosure)	Financial
Netherlands	Mixed (market disclosure)	Financial
Norway	Mixed (authorities disclosure)	Financial
Portugal	Mixed (authorities disclosure)	Financial
Spain	Direct	All stocks
Switzerland	Mixed (authorities disclosure)	Financial
UK	Mixed (market disclosure)	Financial

12.5 CONCLUSION

Many recent empirical studies (Beber & Pagano, 2010; Devos et al., 2010; Fotaket et al., 2009; Gagnon & Witmer, 2009; Gruenewald et al., 2009; Grundy et al., 2009; Helmes & Henker, 2009) show how prohibitions introduced in many countries were not able to reduce volatility and price declines.

To summarize these conclusions, Beber and Pagano (2010) cite an interview where the chairman of the SEC, Christopher Cox, stated:

> While the actual effects of this temporary action will not be fully understood for many more months, if not years, knowing what we know now, I believe on balance the Commission would not do it again. The costs (of the short selling ban on financials) appear to outweigh the benefits.

Our study shows that European countries, particularly those within the euro area, suffered another disadvantage, as the implementation of various short selling regulations could induce opportunistic behaviors. The implication among regulators is that imperfect cooperation reduces the effectiveness of market players response. This increases the risk of competitive distortions and creates an advantage for a few players.

REFERENCES

Abreu, D., & Brunnermeier, M. (2002). Synchronization risk and delayed arbitrage. *Journal of Financial Economics, 66*(2), 341–360.

Beber, A., & Pagano, M. (2010). *Short-selling bans around the world: Evidence from the 2007–2009 crisis.* Working paper, University of Amsterdam, Amsterdam.

Boehmer, E., Jones, C. M., & Zhang, X. (2008). Which shorts are informed? *Journal of Finance, 63*(2), 491–527.

Boulton, T. J., & Braga-Alves, M. V. (2010). The skinny on the 2008 naked short sale restrictions. *Journal of Financial Markets, 13*, 397–421.

Chen, C. X., & Rhee, S. G. (2010). Short sales and speed of price adjustment: Evidence from the Hong Kong stock market. *Journal of Banking and Finance, 34*(2), 471–483.

Chung, W.-I., & Lee, S.-C. (2010). The impact of short-sales constraints on liquidity and the liquidity-return relations. *Pacific-Basin Finance Journal, 18*(1), 521–535.

Dechow, P. M., Hutton, A. P., Meulbroek, A., & Sloan, R. G. (2001). Short-sellers, fundamental analysis, and stock returns. *Journal of Financial Economics, 61*(1), 77–106.

Desai, H., Krishnamurthy, S., & Venkataraman, K. (2006). *On distinguishing between valuation and arbitrage motivated short selling.* Working paper, Southern Methodist University. Retrieved from http://ssrn.com/abstract=969432.

Devos, E., McInish, T., McKenzie, M., & Upson, J. (2010). *Naked short selling and the market impact on failures-to-deliver: Evidence from the trading of REITs.* Working paper, University of Texas at El Paso.

Duan, Y., Hu, G., & McLean, R. D. (2010). Costly, arbitrage and idiosyncratic risk: Evidence from short-sellers. *Journal of Financial Intermediation, 19*(4), 564–579.

Financial Services Authority. (2008). *FSA statement on short positions in financial stocks.* Retrieved from http://www.fsa.gov.uk/pages/Library/Communication/PR/2008/102.shtml.

Financial Services Authority. (2009). *Short selling.* Discussion paper. Retrieved from http://www.fsa.gov.uk/pubs/discussion/dp09_01.pdf.

Fotak, V., Raman, V., & Yadav, P. K. (2009). *Naked short selling: The Emperor's new clothes?* Working paper, University of Oklahoma.

Gagnon, L., & Witmer, J. (2009). *Short changed? The market's reaction to the short sale ban of 2008.* Working paper, Queen's University, Kingston, Canada.

Gruenewald, S., Wagner, A. F., & Weber, R. H. (2009). *Short selling regulation after the financial crisis: First principles revisited.* Working paper, University of Zurich.

Grundy, B. D., Lim, B., & Verwijmeren, P. (2009). *Do option markets undo restrictions on short sales? Evidence from the 2008 short-sale ban.* Working paper, University of Melbourne, Melbourne, Australia.

Helmes, U., & Henker, T. (2009). *The effect of the ban on short selling on market efficiency and volatility.* Working paper, UNSW, Sydney, Australia.

Jones, C. M., & Lamont, O. A. (2002). Short-sales constraints and stock returns. *Journal of Financial Economics, 66*(2–3), 207–239.

Securities and Exchange Commission. (2008). *Naked short selling anti-fraud rule; proposed rule.* Retrieved from http://www.sec.gov/rules/proposed/2008/34-57511fr.pdf.

Taulli, T. (2004). *What is short-selling?* New York: McGraw-Hill.

CHAPTER 13

Do Option Prices Reveal Short Sale Restrictions Impact on Banks' Stock Prices? The German Case*

Stefano Corradin, Marco Lo Duca, and Cristina Sommacampagna

CONTENTS

ABSTRACT

This chapter examines empirically the effect of naked short selling restrictions, introduced in September 2008, on the behavior of stock and option prices of 11 major European banks traded on Deutsche Borse. Investors can replicate long and short stock positions by accessing the options market and by simultaneously taking long and short positions on put and call options and lending cash. This chapter explores whether stock prices implied in synthetic positions are significantly different from the observed market price, before and during the ban. Our analysis focuses on intraday tick data on stock and option trades over the period of July 5, 2007–November 28, 2008. We find no evidence that naked short selling restrictions affected bank stock prices or option prices.

___

* The views expressed in this chapter are those of the authors and do not necessarily represent the views of the European Central Bank.

KEYWORDS

Call and put trades; Covered short selling; Intraday tick data; Naked short selling; Nelson–Siegel model.

13.1 INTRODUCTION

In mid-September 2008, regulatory authorities around the world adopted a series of restrictions on the short selling of financial stocks. The common objective of these measures was to restore confidence during the global financial crisis. On September 18, 2008, the U.K. Financial Services Authority (FSA) blocked covered short sales of 34 financial stocks and strictly enforced the requirement that stocks must be borrowed prior to a short sale to prevent naked short selling. To increase transparency, the FSA introduced rules requiring the disclosure of short positions that exceeded a certain threshold of a company's stock. The U.S. Securities and Exchange Commission (SEC) adopted similar measures and temporarily blocked the covered short sales of 799 financial stocks on the following day. Following the FSA and the SEC, European regulators introduced rules prohibiting the naked short selling of financial shares. Some evidence of a resulting decline in market efficiency for the affected stocks in the United Kingdom and the United States has been documented. For the German stock market, this chapter examines how the short selling restrictions introduced on September 22, 2008, by BaFin, the federal financial supervisory authority, affected the behavior of stock prices of financial companies. Specifically, BaFin prohibited naked short selling of 11 financial stocks.

Investors can replicate the price behavior of stocks in the options market by simultaneously taking long and short positions in puts and calls and lending cash. This chapter assesses whether the stock price as implied in the synthetic position is lower than the market price where restrictions on short sales apply, thereby making it difficult or expensive to short sell the stock. The analysis focuses on intraday tick data of stock and option transactions for 11 major European banks, traded on Deutsche Borse, during the period of July 5, 2007, to November 28, 2008. The data set includes 4 of the 11 financial companies subject to the BaFin's restriction: Commerzbank, Deutsche Bank, Deutsche Postbank, and Hypo Real Estate Holding. The other financial companies included in our sample are BNP Paribas, Credit Suisse, Credite Agricole, Fortis, UBS, Unicredito Italiano, and Société Générale.

We do not find any evidence that short selling restrictions, introduced on September 22, 2008, affected bank stock prices or option prices. We argue that results depend on the type of restrictions introduced. BaFin introduced rules prohibiting naked short selling on financial stocks, while both the British and the American regulators (FSA and SEC) prohibited covered as well as naked short selling. Covered short selling is the practice of selling stocks without owning them but rather borrowing them, hoping to buy them later at a lower price, thus making a profit. Naked short selling is the practice of selling stocks without having the stock nor a lending party, hoping to find it later. Prohibiting naked short selling may make the practice of short selling more costly, but it is a less severe restriction than prohibiting covered short selling. As a consequence, the impact on market efficiency is minimal.

The outline of the chapter is as follows. Section 13.2 provides a brief description of related literature. Section 13.3 describes the methodology implemented to calculate the stock price implied by option prices. Section 13.4 describes our data. Section 13.5 investigates the impact of naked short selling restrictions on stock and option prices.

13.2 LITERATURE REVIEW

Following the introduction of short selling restrictions in mid-September 2008, some researchers documented its impact on stock markets. In a landmark study, Bris (2008) is the first to document that market quality and stock liquidity of the U.S. market declined as investors found it increasingly difficult to hedge market risks. When examining the U.K. stock market, Clifton and Snape (2008) note that bid–ask spreads increased significantly for the banned financial stocks and registered a dramatic decline in volume and turnover.

More recently, Beber and Pagano (2010) confirm the first evidence reported for the United Kingdom and the United States. They look at the change in the short sale regime in 30 countries and find that short sale bans were detrimental for liquidity, especially for stocks with small market capitalization, high volatility, and no listed options. Moreover, they document that the restrictions slowed down price discovery, especially in bear market phases. Further, Battalio and Schultz (2009) and Grundy and colleagues (2010) examine the trading activity in options written on financial stocks subject to the SEC ban between September 19, 2008, and October 8, 2008, and compare it with trading activity on options written on nonbanned stocks. Both papers document that trading costs for options increased sharply when the ban was initiated and that option trading volume decreased during the period of the ban for stocks for which short sales were banned. In addition, they both show that the stock price implied in a position became inexpensive relative to the actual share price but the contemporaneous increased spreads in option prices mitigated the majority of these potential arbitrage profits.[1]

13.3 METHODOLOGY

Under the condition of no arbitrage, it is well known that, for European options on nonpaying dividend stocks, put–call parity holds:

$$S = PV(K) + C - P \tag{13.1}$$

where S is the underlying stock price, $PV(K)$ is the present value of the strike price, and C and P are the corresponding call and put price, respectively, of options with strike price K and equal time to maturity.[2] Let us define S^* as the stock price implied by the put–call parity, $S^* = PV(K) + C - P$, and let's assume the other variables' values are as observed on the market. If S^* is different from the stock price observed on the market, Equation (13.1) fails and two violations, or categories of arbitrage opportunity, can be identified:

> Violation 1: $S > S^*$—The stock price drifts above the price implied in the options market. To arbitrage between the stock and options market, one would buy S^*, the synthetic position, and sell S, the stock. Because short sales on the stock are banned or shorting the underlying stock may be costly, an arbitrage does not exist that leads to convergence of the two values.
>
> Violation 2: $S < S^*$—The stock price falls below its implied price in the options market. One could arbitrage by buying the stock, S, and selling the synthetic position, S^*.

We investigate Equation (13.1) empirically by taking the quoted prices of call and put option pairs (i.e., with same strike and time to maturity), the corresponding underlying stock price, and the prevailing market interest rate.

13.4 DATA

The analysis focuses on the period of July 5, 2007, to November 28, 2008. We collect tick data of American call and put option trades and of the underlying stock trades for 11 major European banks traded on Deutsche Borse. For each

---

[1] In the literature, the same type of analysis was conducted to examine whether difficulties in shorting Internet stocks during the run-up of Internet stock prices during the period of 1998–2000 meant that the prices reflected beliefs of optimistic investors only (see Battalio & Schultz, (2006); Lamont & Thaler, (2003); Ofek & Richardson, (2003); Ofek et al., (2004)).

[2] For American options on nonpaying dividend stocks, the put option is more valuable than implied by the put–call parity because there is a positive probability of optimal early exercise. Accounting for the early exercise premium on the American put option, the put–call parity becomes $S = PV(K) + C - P + EEP$, where EEP is the early exercise premium of the American put option.

Table 13.1 Summary of Trading Activity in the Considered Sample July 5, 2007, to November 28, 2008[a]

Stocks with Ban	ISIN	Call Option Trades	Put Option Trades	Call and Put Pairs	Call and Put Pairs Used
Commerzbank	DE0008032004	96,676	105,336	99,420[b]	9,008
Deutsche Bank	DE0005140008	107,258	118,026	58,700	7,919
Deutsche Postbank	DE0008001009	23,866	25,362	7,357	663
Hypo Real Estate	DE0008027707	45,822	49,062	33,884	5,560
Total		273,622	297,786	199,361	23,150

Stocks without Ban	ISIN	Call Option Trades	Put Option Trades	Call and Put Pairs	Call and Put Pairs Used
BNP Paribas	FR0000131104	17,552	16,912	6,520	384
Credit Suisse	CH0012138530	44,121	45,031	15,782	736
Credit Agricole	FR0000045072	5,744	6,110	1,420	20
Fortis	BE0003801181	4,861	5,721	827	61
UBS	CH0024899483	64,922	75,680	31,481	2,643
Unicredito Italiano	IT0000064854	4,530	6,732	1,636	104
Société Générale	FR0000130809	17,894	14,718	5,128	240
Total		159,624	170,904	62,794	4,188
Grand total		433,246	468,690	262,155	27,338

[a]Options used for the analysis are matched within an hour, have an exercise price within 20% of the matched market stock price, and have 5 to 90 days time to maturity.
[b]In this particular case, the same call option trade was matched with more than one put option trade.

option contract, we use the Nelson–Siegel model[3] in order to calculate the continuously compounded, zero-coupon, risk-free interest rate corresponding to the remaining time to maturity of the option and calculate the discounted value of the strike price, $PV(K)$. Table 13.1 lists the bank stocks we considered, along with their ISIN number and the number of trades of their call and put options as available in the data set.

The following exercise is conducted to match (i) call and put trades and (ii) call–put pairs with the corresponding stock trades. For each traded call, we identify the put, with the same strike price and same time to maturity, traded at the same time, with a precision of milliseconds. For call trades for which no put trade was conducted within milliseconds, trades conducted within the minute are selected; if more than one trade is then identified, the average trade price is taken. The same approach is taken for trades for which no put trade was conducted within the minute and 10 minutes are then

---

[3] Parameters of the Nelson–Siegel model are provided by ECB at http://www.ecb.int/stats/money/yc/html/index.en.html.

taken as the reference period. Finally, if no put trade is conducted within 10 minutes, those conducted within an hour are considered and their prices averaged. The call–put pairs so identified are then matched with the underlying stock price using the very same algorithm. Table 13.1 details the number of matches we could identify.

In order to calculate the value of the stocks, S^*, implied in the synthetic positions, we restricted the sample to options matched within an hour, with exercise price within 20% of the matched market stock price and with 5 to 90 days time to maturity. We limit our analysis to the options satisfying these conditions, as these are the contracts for which the highest liquidity is observed on the market. This resulted in 27,338 pairs being considered, as detailed in the last column of Table 13.1.

As the options are American in style, we calculate their early exercise premium to obtain the corresponding European price.[4] Calculation of the early exercise premium is based on the assumption that the Black–Scholes model holds. This is the only modeling assumption in our analysis. The early exercise premium is a very small portion of the value of the at-the-money, short time-to-maturity puts that we consider. Therefore, model misspecification and volatility misestimation are unlikely to cause a significant bias.

13.5 DO OPTIONS PRICES REVEAL SHORT SALE RESTRICTIONS?

We look for evidence of arbitrage opportunities by comparing the synthetic stock price, S^*, with the market stock price, S. We examine violations of Equation (13.1) separately, such that either (i) investors could seemingly profit by purchasing a synthetic position in the stock, S^*, and selling short the stock on the market, because $S > S^*$ (Violation 1), or such that (ii) investors could seemingly profit by selling a synthetic position in the stock, S^*, while buying the stock on the stock market, because $S < S^*$ (Violation 2). The first type of violation only can be due to a short sale ban, as in a market without a ban the violation would lead to an arbitrage opportunity that the market would exploit.

By matching at-the-money, short time-to-maturity options, we have 27,338 pairs of trades that can be used to generate synthetic stock prices.

---

[4] The early exercise premium is the difference between an American and a European option value. Because we assume that no dividend is paid to the underlying stock, it is only necessary to derive the early exercise premium for the put contract. First, we extrapolate the volatility implied in the put option price using the finite difference method to numerically solve the partial differential equation for American put options and then we calculate the corresponding European put price.

As restrictions on naked short selling were introduced on September 22, 2008, we split the sample in two subperiods, creating a preevent sample and a postevent sample: the first one going from July 5, 2007, to September 22, 2008, with 24,846 pairs of observations, and the second one going from September 22, 2008, to November 28, 2008, with 2492 observations.

Table 13.2 shows the number of times Violations 1 and 2 are observed by percentage of difference between S and S^*. The left half of Table 13.2 shows how many times the stock price, S, is higher than the synthetic price, S^*, by more than 1, 2, 3, or 4% (Violation 1). The right half of Table 13.2 shows how many times the stock price, S, is lower than the synthetic price, S^*, by more than 1, 2, 3, or 4% (Violation 2). The count for the postevent sample is reported in parentheses.

In the great majority of cases, Equation (13.1) is not violated and there are no arbitrage opportunities. Overall, we find the following:

> Violation 1: 1520 in the preevent sample and 101 in the postevent sample. These are cases in which it appears that an investor could buy synthetically in the options market and sell at a higher price in the stock market.
> Violation 2: 285 in the preevent sample and 165 in the postevent sample. These are cases in which it appears that investors could buy in the stock market and sell synthetically at a higher price.

A larger portion of stock trades leads to apparent arbitrage opportunities due to Violation 1 than to Violation 2. We observe that these apparent arbitrage opportunities do not belong exclusively to the postevent sample. As they involve short selling of stocks, they might have been impossible or too expensive to exploit. Second, these apparent arbitrage opportunities do not belong exclusively to the financial companies subject to the naked short sale ban (Commerzbank, Deutsche Bank, Deutsche Postbank, and Hypo Real Estate Holding). Overall, results suggest that introducing restrictions on naked short selling did not affect the behavior of stock and option prices as apparent in the preevent sample.

In addition, we estimate a probit model, similar to the one suggested by Battalio and Schultz (2009), to examine the marginal impact of the short sale ban on the frequency of apparent arbitrage opportunities. We estimate the model for banned and nonbanned stocks separately. The model is as follows:

$$
\begin{aligned}
PctArb_t = {} & \alpha_0 + \alpha_1 \, BanPeriod + \alpha_2 \, (S/K)_t + \alpha_3 \, (S/K)_t^2 + \alpha_4 \, (S/K)_t^{-1} \\
& + \alpha_5 \, ISDC_t + \alpha_6 \, ISDC_t^2 + \alpha_7 \, ISDC_t^{-1} + \alpha_8 \, ISDP_t + \alpha_9 \, ISDP_t^2 \quad (13.2) \\
& + \alpha_{10} \, ISDP_t^{-1} + \alpha_{11} \, (S/K)_t \, ISDC_t + \alpha_{12} \, (S/K)_t \, ISDP_t + \varepsilon_t
\end{aligned}
$$

Table 13.2 Matching Short-Term-at-the-Money Options[a]

Stocks with Ban	S > S* (Violation 1)				(S − S*)/S	S < S* (Violation 2)				Total
	4%	3%	2%	1%	0%	-1%	-2%	-3%	-4%	
Commerzbank	96 (8)	88 (0)	36 (4)	100 (28)	7,676 (864)	52 (32)	20 (4)	0 (0)	0 (0)	8,068 (940)
Deutsche Bank	143 (0)	37 (2)	17 (5)	26 (8)	6,703 (776)	93 (88)	8 (8)	1 (0)	2 (2)	7,030 (889)
Deutsche Postbank	0 (0)	0 (0)	7 (0)	17 (0)	599 (38)	2 (0)	0 (0)	0 (0)	0 (0)	625 (38)
Hypo Real Estate	0 (0)	8 (0)	200 (8)	472 (0)	4,756 (68)	32 (0)	12 (0)	4 (0)	0 (0)	5,484 (76)
Total	239 (8)	133 (2)	260 (17)	615 (36)	19,734 (1,746)	179 (120)	40 (12)	5 (0)	2 (2)	21,207 (1,943)

Stocks without Ban	S > S* (Violation 1)				(S − S*)/S	S < S* (Violation 2)				Total
	4%	3%	2%	1%	0%	-1%	-2%	-3%	-4%	
BNP Paribas	0 (0)	0 (0)	0 (0)	16 (16)	276 (76)	0 (0)	0 (0)	0 (0)	0 (0)	292 (92)
Credit Suisse	22 (0)	20 (0)	23 (1)	19 (7)	552 (64)	17 (11)	0 (0)	0 (0)	0 (0)	653 (83)
Credite Agricole	0 (0)	0 (0)	0 (0)	0 (0)	20 (0)	0 (0)	0 (0)	0 (0)	0 (0)	20 (0)
Fortis	0 (0)	0 (0)	2 (0)	2 (0)	53 (4)	0 (0)	0 (0)	0 (0)	0 (0)	57 (4)
UBS	25 (0)	31 (1)	14 (0)	39 (9)	2,182 (288)	35 (13)	3 (3)	0 (0)	0 (0)	2,329 (314)
Unicredito Italiano	0 (0)	0 (0)	0 (0)	0 (0)	88 (16)	0 (0)	0 (0)	0 (0)	0 (0)	88 (16)
Société Générale	0 (0)	0 (0)	0 (0)	60 (4)	136 (32)	4 (4)	0 (0)	0 (0)	0 (0)	200 (40)
Total	47 (0)	51 (1)	39 (1)	136 (36)	3,307 (480)	56 (28)	3 (3)	0 (0)	0 (0)	3,639 (549)
Sub totals	286 (8)	184 (3)	299 (18)	751 (72)	23,041 (2,226)	235 (148)	43 (15)	5 (0)	2 (2)	24,846 (2,492)
Grand total	1,520 (101)				23,041 (2,226)	285 (165)				24,846 (2,492)

[a] By matching short-term-at-the-money options, 27,338 pairs of trades are obtained from which the synthetic stock prices are extrapolated. The sample is split in preban (July 5, 2007–September 22, 2008) and postban (September 22, 2008–November 28, 2008) periods, with 24,846 and 2492 observations, respectively. Violations 1 and 2 of Equation (13.1) are counted and displayed in the right and left half of the table, respectively. The count for the postban sample is reported in parentheses.

where $PctArb_t$ is the proportion of apparent arbitrage opportunities due to Violation 1 during day t; $BanPeriod$ is a dummy variable taking a value of one on and after September 22, 2008; $(S/K)_t$ is the average ratio of the stock price over the exercise price on day t, $(S/K)_t^2$ and $(S/K)_t^{-1}$ are the square and the inverse of the same variable on day t; $ISDC_t$ is the mean call option implied standard deviation on day t, $ISDC_t^2$ and $ISDC_t^{-1}$ are square and inverse of the same variable on day t; $ISDP_t$ is the mean put option implied standard deviation on day t; and $ISDP_t^2$ and $ISDP_t^{-1}$ are square and inverse of the same variable on day t. As square and inverse of moneyness and implied standard deviations are included to control for nonlinear relations, their parameters' estimates are difficult to interpret and do not add value to our analysis. Therefore, we only report the coefficient of the $BanPeriod$ variable. We find the following: (i) for banned stocks, the coefficient estimate of α_1 is -0.309, with a standard error estimate of 0.59, and (ii) for nonbanned stocks, the coefficient estimate of α_1 is 0.176, with a standard error estimate of 0.911. Neither coefficient of the $BanPeriod$ variable is statistically significant. Probit results suggest that restrictions on naked short selling, introduced on September 22, 2008, had no impact on banking stock and option prices.

13.6 CONCLUSION

Following the introduction of short selling bans, some evidence of a consequent decline in market efficiency for the affected stocks in the United Kingdom and the United States has been documented in the literature. We find no evidence that the short selling restrictions introduced on September 22, 2008, in the German market affected stock prices and option prices for 11 major European banks. We argue that this result depends on the types of restrictions introduced. European regulators introduced a ban for naked short selling on financial stocks, while both covered and naked short selling were prohibited in the United Kingdom and the United States. Prohibiting naked short selling may make the short selling practice more costly, but it is a less severe restriction than prohibiting covered short selling. Based on our analysis, the impact of the naked short selling ban on German market efficiency was minimal.

REFERENCES

Battalio, R., & Schultz, P. (2006). Options and the bubble. *Journal of Finance, 61*(5), 2071–2102.

Battalio, R., & Schultz, P. (2009). *Regulatory uncertainty and market liquidity: The 2008 short sale ban's impact on equity option markets*. Working paper, University of Notre Dame, Notre Dame, IN.

Beber, A., & Pagano, M. (2010). *Short-selling bans around the world: Evidence from the 2007–09 crisis*. Working paper 241, Centre for Studies in Economics and Finance, Naples, Italy.

Bris, A. (2008, September 29). Shorting financial stocks should resume. *The Wall Street Journal*, p. 6.

Clifton, M., & Snape, M. (2008). *The effect of short-selling restrictions on liquidity: Evidence from the London stock exchange.* London Stock Exchange Policy Note, London, UK.

Grundy, B., Lim, B., & Verwijmeren, P. (2010). *Do option markets undo restrictions on short sales? Evidence from the 2008 short-sale ban.* Working paper, University of Melbourne, Melbourne, Australia.

Lamont, O., & Thaler, R. (2003). Can the market add and subtract? Mispricing in tech stock carveouts. *Journal of Political Economy, 111*(2), 227–268.

Ofek, E., & Richardson, M. (2003). DotCom Mania: The rise and fall of internet stock prices. *Journal of Finance, 58*(3), 1113–1137.

Ofek, E., Richardson, M., & Whitelaw, R. (2004). Limited arbitrage and short sales restrictions: Evidence from the options market. *Journal of Financial Economics, 74*(2), 305–342.

CHAPTER 14

Short Selling in France during the Crisis, the Bans, and What Has Changed since the Euro Correction

Emmanuel Fragnière and Iliya Markov

CONTENTS

ABSTRACT

In the wake of the stock market turmoil of 2008, market regulators all over the world started imposing restrictions on short selling. Although most regulators intervened during the period of September 2008–October 2008, the restrictions were of various lengths and intensities. We start by examining previous studies on short selling bans, which conclude that the bans were detrimental to price discovery and market liquidity. We continue by examining the restrictions in Europe and particularly France, which introduced a naked short selling ban and disclosure regime for financial stocks. Our study shows that restricted stocks in France did not perform better than the rest of the stocks. Moreover, comparisons with Switzerland and Sweden reveal that restricted French stocks performed similar to Swiss and Swedish stocks of the same type. We conclude by examining the most recent developments and trends concerning short selling bans in Europe and France, which prove that despite the overwhelming evidence against the bans, market regulators were being given even more power to curb short selling.

KEYWORDS

Bans; Bid–ask spreads; Disclosure regime; Naked short selling.

14.1 INTRODUCTION

The financial meltdown of 2007–2008 forced market regulators around the world to impose restrictions on short selling and naked short selling. Most of the world's major economies imposed their regulations around the same time—September and October 2008. The regulations, however, were of various lengths and intensities. In some cases, they only lasted for several weeks, whereas in others they are still in force. The intensity of the restrictions varied from disclosure regimes for short positions and restrictions on naked short selling to bans on short selling of financial stocks or outright bans on all short selling.

We start by examining previous studies on short selling bans, which conclude that the bans were detrimental to price discovery and liquidity. We continue by examining the restrictions in Europe and particularly France, which still maintains a naked short selling ban and disclosure regime for financial stocks. Our study suggests that French restrictions on short selling were ineffective. We base this conclusion on the finding that financial stocks, which were affected by the ban, did not perform better than the market as a whole or stocks unaffected by the ban. We also investigate Switzerland (which only had a 3-month-long ban) and Sweden (which did not impose any new regulations) only to find that Swiss and Swedish financial stocks performed similar to French stocks. The chapter concludes by examining the most recent developments and trends concerning short selling bans in Europe and France, which show that despite the overwhelming evidence against the bans, market regulators are being given more power to curb short selling.

This section continues with an explanation of the nature of short selling and why it is viewed by regulators as an unhealthy practice. Then we present our research question and the position we take, which we revisit at the end of the chapter. Section 14.2 conducts a review of academic literature in response to the regulatory changes. Section 14.3 outlines major points of the short selling ban in France in the context of the wider European economy. Section 14.4 presents our statistical analysis, which shows that the short selling ban in France was unproductive because it did not support the

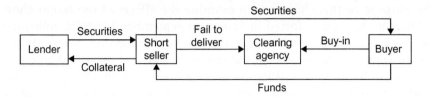

FIGURE 14.1
Short selling diagram (Gruenewald, Wagner, & Weber, 2010b).

value of financial stocks. Section 14.5 presents the latest developments and trends concerning short selling and a discussion of our findings.

In order to understand why short selling was targeted by regulators around the world, we need to understand what it is. In short selling, an investor borrows a security and sells it at the current market price. After a certain period of time, he buys an identical security and returns it to the lender. If in the meantime the price has decreased, he reaps a profit equal to the difference between the price at which he sold and the price at which he bought. Figure 14.1 is a simplified diagram of the process of short selling.

As shown in Figure 14.1, the short seller and the buyer are intermediated by a clearing agency. Gruenewald and colleagues (2010b) explain that after the short seller and the buyer of a security conclude a deal, the short seller typically has 3 market days to "locate" the security and deliver it to the buyer. In case he is unable to locate, he "fails to deliver." At that point the buyer "buys in," that is, orders the clearing agency to find the security within its system or buy it on the market. The buy-in may or may not be successful depending on whether the clearing agency is able to locate the stock. If it is successful, the clearing agency delivers the security to the buyer and charges the short seller's account.

Gruenewald and colleagues (2010b) also explain an even more controversial practice called "naked short selling." In conventional short selling, the seller must arrange to borrow the stock in order to deliver it. In naked short selling, the seller has no intention of borrowing the stock. Therefore, naked short selling always results in fails to deliver. This is the reason why the practice has been outlawed by most regulators around the world.

The main reason why short selling was restricted or banned in many countries is that in the opinion of market regulators it brings stock prices down to a level that does not reflect true demand and supply. Short sellers are accused of depressing stock prices and hurting innocent shareholders, the markets, and thus the economy as a whole. This opinion is shared by many economists and financiers as well.

The purpose of this chapter is to examine the effects of the recent short selling ban that was enforced in France on September 22, 2008, following the downturn of the stock market and the euro correction. We study the case of France in the context of the rest of Europe and the world and analyze the problem by consulting previous studies of short selling bans and conducting our own statistical study. While we admit that there could be certain short-term benefits of the short selling ban, we share the views of many researchers and analysts in saying that it was largely unproductive because it was detrimental to liquidity and price discovery and did not fulfill its main objective of supporting stock values and reducing volatility.

14.2 LITERATURE REVIEW

This section presents possible as well as confirmed effects of short selling bans from different points of view. We consult previous studies of the recent short selling bans and discover that the majority of them denounce the bans as unproductive and dangerous.

Economic theory dictates that stock prices in a competitive market are formed by taking into account all the available information, be it positive or negative. Therefore, a ban on short selling has a negative impact on price discovery. As Copeland (2010) explains, a ban on short selling excludes the no voter from having a say in the price formation. Government bans, aimed at supporting certain institutions, can prop up their stock prices above the market optimum and reduce their cost of capital. Thus the government hinders the optimal allocation of resources in the economy. Experience shows, however, that information will ultimately infiltrate the market through liquidation of existing positions and diversion of money away from suspect shares. Moreover, a ban on short selling can affect all targeted shares negatively, not just the ones that were initially suspicious.

By reducing the number of sellers, short selling bans effectively remove liquidity from the markets. Clifton and Snape (2008) conduct a detailed study of the Financial Services Authority's ban on short selling in the United Kingdom. They study market liquidity for a 30-day preban and a 30-day postban period and find out that the bid–ask spreads of the affected stocks widened 150% more than the bid–ask spreads of unaffected stocks. Trading volume of the affected stocks decreased by 10%, whereas trading volume of the unaffected stocks increased by an astonishing 50%. Unaffected stocks performed better also in terms of depth and turnover. Clifton and Snape's results are significant even after controlling for market-wide changes in volatility.

Boehmer, Jones, and Zhang (2009) discover that the short selling ban in the United States reduced short selling activity by 65% and had a negative impact on spreads, price impact, and intraday volatility. In addition, they explain that the price boost of the affected stocks cannot be attributed directly to the ban because of the various other initiatives that the Securities and Exchange Commission started. Beber and Pagano (2010) confirm the results of Boehmer and associates (2009). Beber and Pagano (2010) study the effect of the bans on bid–ask spreads and discover that in countries where the bans were introduced on all stocks, bid–ask spreads during the ban periods were higher than before and after the bans. Differences in the median bid–ask spreads during the bans and outside the bans are statistically significant at the 1% confidence level. Moreover, in countries where the bans were introduced on financial stocks only, the increase in bid–ask spreads of financial stocks was higher than the increase for the rest of the stocks. While it is true that bid–ask spreads in some cases started widening before introduction of the bans, ample evidence shows that bid–ask spreads of affected stocks widened much more than those of unaffected stocks. The median bid–ask spreads of affected stocks in the United States increased by 243%, whereas for unaffected stocks they increased by only 54%.

Gruenewald and colleagues (2010b) give several more reasons why bans on short sales or naked short sales are unproductive. First of all, because short sales can be replicated by futures and options, bans would be ineffective unless regulators impose the same restrictions on futures and options. Unlike options, however, economic interest, which expresses the percentage of short positions out of the total outstanding shares, is publicly available information. It helps investors make a more informed decision as to what position to take. The total amount of options replicating short selling strategies, however, is unknown.

Second, only minor economic differences exist between naked and conventional short selling, yet regulators have been much more aggressive toward naked short selling. In their opinion, naked short selling leads to an increased risk of delivery failures and gives false signals to market participants about a stock's real liquidity and price. In reality, however, clearing agencies have mechanisms of resolving delivery failures by sourcing the stocks and ultimately debiting the short seller's account. Therefore, the short seller bears the same risk of not delivering the stock on time. As to the practice where a short seller shorts a massive amount of a company's shares in an attempt to create "phantom shares" (Gruenewald et al., 2010b) and drive share prices down, this would constitute market abuse under most existing legislations. Therefore, regulating naked short selling only, as many market regulators did, is economically unjustified.

14.3 REGULATORY DEVELOPMENTS CONCERNING SHORT SELLING IN FRANCE

On September 19, 2008, the French market regulator, the Autorité des marchés financiers (AMF), issued a news release stating that following the example of the United States and the United Kingdom, France would introduce emergency measures regarding short selling (AMF, 2008). The measures were to come into force on September 22, 2008, and their main aspects were as follows.

- A naked short selling ban on the stocks of 15 banks and financial institutions: Allianz, April Group, AXA, BNP Paribas, CIC, CNP Assurances, Crédit Agricole, Dexia, Euler Hermes, HSBC Holdings, Natixis, NYSE Euronext, Paris Re, Scor, and Société Générale (Gruenewald et al., 2010a). The restriction applied to spot, forward, and option transactions (Gruenewald et al., 2010a).
- A disclosure regime for the concerned stocks. An investor who holds a net short position amounting to more than 0.25% of the share capital of one of the companies must disclose that information to the AMF.
- Financial institutions should abstain from lending securities of the concerned companies, except when the purpose is not the establishment of a short position.
- The AMF will take all measures to ensure compliance with the new rules, and any person who violates them will be considered likely to have committed market abuse.
- Market makers, liquidity providers, and block trade counterparties are exempt from the new regulations (Gruenewald et al., 2010a).

According to Theris (2010), France introduced the ban on short selling for an initial period of 3 months, which was later extended several times. In an effort to replace temporary bans with a permanent one, the AMF established a committee whose report, however, suggested that the bans should be replaced by disclosure regulations and more severe penalties in case of fail to deliver. The report was published on February 23, 2008. It was followed by a decision that the AMF should not impose a permanent ban before consulting with other European market regulators.

The AMF participated in the Committee of European Securities Regulators, which in March 2010 issued a report with a proposal of a European-wide short selling disclosure regime. According to the report, an investor with a net short position of 0.2% of the share capital of a company should disclose the position to the relevant regulator on the next market day. An investor with a net short of 0.5% of the share capital of a company should disclose this position to the market on the next market day. Subsequent changes in the short positions would also require disclosure. These regulations should apply to shares traded in the European Economic Area (EEA), unless the primary market of those shares is outside the EEA.

As explained earlier, the AMF committee suggested lifting the ban on short selling and replacing it with a series of strict regulations in the form of a disclosure regime. This led to altercation with Germany, which, on May 19, 2010, imposed a eurozone-wide ban on naked short sales for the stocks of 10 banks and insurers, as well as on naked credit–default swaps on eurozone government bonds (Chu, 2010). French finance minister Christine Lagarde said France was not considering such regulation and that she regretted Germany's unilateral approach. She added that Germany should have consulted other countries that use the euro before issuing the ban (France 24, 2010).

Germany's new ban on short selling sent stocks, commodities, and the euro into a downfall. Investors panicked and believed they would not be able to hedge their European positions or sell as the debt crisis in Europe reached new highs. Following the ban, the euro hit a 4-year low (Chu, 2010). In the words of Greg Gibbs of the Royal Bank of Scotland, "[if] you don't feel like you can sell bonds and equities in Europe, you're left with selling the euro to express a negative view" (Chu, 2010). The ban "[created] a view that the authorities sense bigger problems than what may appear on the surface, creating more nervousness and fear" (Chu, 2010).

By June 9, 2010, however, France and Germany seem to have reconciled their positions. They asked the European Union (EU) to explore the possibility of harmonizing the settlement and delivery of securities across the EU. Although France was not considering introducing a German-like ban, Angela Merkel and Nicolas Sarcozy agreed that the EU should accelerate the pace of financial reform, especially with regards to the regulation of short selling positions (Graham, 2010).

On June 10, 2010, the Assemblée nationale, the lower house of the French Parliament, voted in favor of a draft law for banking and financial regulation, which contained important provisions relating to the banking and financial sector. On the next day it was sent for examination by the Sénat (Theris, 2010), which later also voted positively (Fleury, Robé, & Seibt, 2010).

14.4 STATISTICS

This chapter employs statistical techniques to assess the efficiency of the naked short selling ban and the disclosure regime introduced in France. It examines the performance of restricted French financial stocks both in the context of the French stock market and in comparison to other European stock markets.

14.4.1 The Effect of the Ban in France

To assess the effect of the short selling ban in France, we built two portfolios: one composed of financial stocks with a ban on short selling and one composed of stocks with no ban on short selling. For both portfolios we used publicly available data from Yahoo Finance. The price developments of both portfolios were studied from August 1, 2008, to October 31, 2010. To assess the efficiency of the short selling ban, we had to examine the relative price developments of the portfolios. Therefore, we constructed them so that they both have the value of €1000 at the introduction of the ban—September 22, 2008. The stocks in both portfolios are weighted equally on September 22, 2008, with the weights equal to €1000 divided by the number of stocks in the respective portfolio. Weights are not readjusted as time elapses so that each stock can deliver the effect of its price development on its portfolio.

Portfolio 1: Stocks with a ban on short selling. Our portfolio consisted of 10 stocks affected by the short selling ban. Five of the affected financial stocks were not considered due to incompleteness or inconsistencies in available data. Our restricted portfolio is thus composed of April Group, BNP Paribas, CIC, Crédit Agricole, Euler Hermes, HSBC Holdings, Natixis, NYSE Euronext, Scor, and Société Générale. On September 22, 2008, each stock has a weight of €100.

Portfolio 2: Stocks with no ban on short selling. The following 31 stocks are constituents of France's CAC 40 index and were not affected by the ban on short selling. They represent a diversified portfolio of stocks with the exception of financials, which were affected by the short selling ban. The stocks are Accor, Air Liquide, Alcatel Lucent, Alstom, Bouygues, Capgemini, Carrefour, EADS, EDF, Essilor, France Télécom, Groupe Danone, L'Oréal, Lafarge, LVMH, Michelin, Pernod Ricard, PSA Peugeot Citroën, PPR, Publicis, Renault, Saint-Gobain, Sanofi-Aventis, Schneider Electric, Suez Environnement, Technip, Total, Unibail-Rodamco, Vallourec, Veolia Environnement, and Vivendi. On September 22, 2008, each stock has a weight of €32.258.

Figure 14.2 is a comparison of the price developments of our two portfolios, where the vertical line is introduction of the short selling restrictions on financial stocks in France.

We observe that the short selling ban appears to be efficient immediately after its introduction, with the restricted portfolio slightly outperforming the unrestricted one. Soon afterward, however, the unrestricted portfolio is above the restricted one. At the lowest point, the unrestricted portfolio falls to €596, whereas the restricted falls to €464. At that point the unrestricted portfolio outperforms the restricted one by almost 30%. Another period of significant divergence between the two portfolios is May–September 2010. This could be

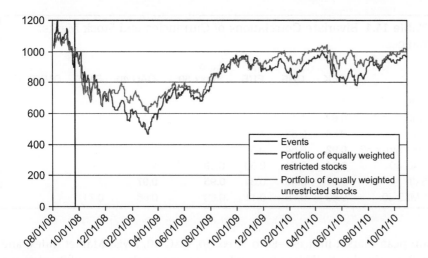

FIGURE 14.2
Comparison of restricted and unrestricted portfolios of French stocks.

attributed to the short selling ban issue being raised again and the shivers it sent through the markets. By the end of the study period, the unrestricted portfolio outperforms the restricted one 81% of the time.

The correlation between the two series is represented by a correlation coefficient of 0.93, which is extremely high. The volatility of the restricted portfolio since introduction of the short selling ban is equal to €129.15, as measured by the standard deviation. In comparison, the unrestricted portfolio had a slightly lower volatility, equal to €115.43. An interesting fact is that the CAC 40, normalized to have the value of €1000 on the day of the introduction of the ban, has a standard deviation of only €84.87. Therefore, the market as a whole is less volatile than the equally weighted restricted portfolio.

Up until now, there is no evidence that the short selling ban has had a positive impact on the affected stocks. Unfortunately, unlike in countries such as the United Kingdom, where the short selling ban was lifted, in France it is still in place, which means that we cannot study the effect of a lift of the short selling ban.

14.4.2 Comparison to Switzerland and Sweden

In order to better understand the inefficiency of the French ban, we need to make comparisons to other European countries. Table 14.1 calculates the bivariate correlations of three European currencies in terms of dollars—Swedish krona, Swiss franc, and euro (Exchange Rates Federal Reserve)—and four

Table 14.1 Bivariate Correlations of Currencies and Stock Market Indices

	SEK	CHF	EUR	Euro Stoxx 50	CAC 40	SMI	OMXS 30
SEK	1						
CHF	0.69	1					
EUR	0.68	0.53	1				
Euro Stoxx 50	**0.92**	0.54	0.55	1			
CAC 40	**0.91**	0.54	0.50	**0.99**	1		
SMI	0.84	0.49	0.34	**0.95**	**0.97**	1	
OMXS 30	0.60	0.75	0.11	0.63	0.66	0.71	1

European market indices—Euro Stoxx 50, CAC 40, Swiss Market Index, and OMX Stockholm 30 (Yahoo Finance). The reason for the choice of Sweden and Switzerland is that they are two major developed European economies outside the eurozone. They are useful for comparison with France because Sweden did not issue any new regulations regarding short selling and Switzerland only had a 3-month-long ban.

Two important results stand out in Table 14.1—high correlations of the European, French, and Swiss market indices (which is hardly surprising) and high correlation of the Swedish currency and the European and French markets.

The correlation coefficient of the exchange rates of the franc and the euro against the dollar is not very high but may be good enough so that a portfolio of French and Swiss stocks expressed in euros is well correlated. The krona and the euro, on the one hand, and the French and Swedish market indices, on the other hand, are not well correlated, which means that portfolios of French and Swedish stocks expressed in euros could be well correlated because a combination of two bad correlation coefficients could result in a good one. We examine our hypotheses by successive comparisons of the performance of the restricted portfolio of French financials with portfolios of Swiss and Swedish financials.

The Swiss market regulator imposed a ban on naked short selling, which lasted from September 19 to December 19, 2008. The ban affected seven financial stocks: Bâloise Holding, Credit Suisse Group, Julius Bär Holding, Swiss Life Holding, Swiss Re, UBS AG, and Zurich Financial Services (Gruenewald et al., 2010a). We used data from Yahoo Finance to build a portfolio of six of the aforementioned financial stocks. Julius Bär Holding was omitted due to incomplete data. The portfolio is expressed in euros (Exchange Rate ECB) and is equally weighted on September 22, 2008, to

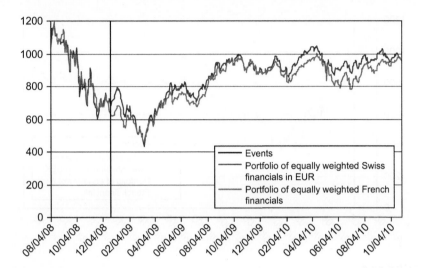

FIGURE 14.3
Comparison of Swiss (EUR) and French (EUR) financials.

allow comparison to the French stocks. On that day, each stock in the Swiss portfolio has a weight of €166.67.

Figure 14.3 plots the comparative movements of both portfolios, yielding a correlation coefficient equal to 0.97. The vertical line in Figure 14.3 represents the lift of the ban in Switzerland. It is followed immediately by a jump in the value of the Swiss portfolio, which is related to a short appreciation of the franc against the euro following the lift of the short selling ban in Switzerland. Although the Swiss portfolio drops slightly more at the lowest point, it is slightly higher than the French portfolio 83% of the time after September 22, 2008. For the same time period, the Swiss portfolio has a standard deviation of €135 compared to €129 for the French portfolio. The difference appears to be small.

The performance of Swiss financial stocks in terms of francs is similar because the franc-to-euro exchange rate does not change significantly during the entire study period. There is a slight appreciation of the franc in the last several months of the study period. During the lowest point, however, the comparison is not distorted by significant changes in the exchange rate.

Next we turn our attention to Sweden. We use data from Yahoo Finance to build a portfolio composed of the stocks of Sweden's four largest financial institutions: Nordea, SAB, Svenska Handelsbanken, and Swedbank. They are all constituents of the OMX Stockholm 30 market index. Figure 14.4 plots

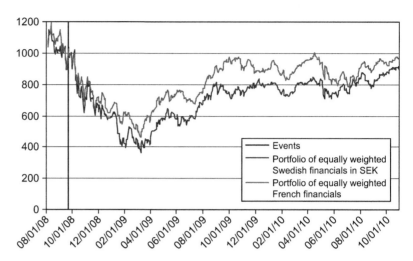

FIGURE 14.4

Comparison of French (EUR) and Swedish (SEK) financials.

the Swedish portfolio in terms of kronor to see if the price development of the portfolio relative to Sweden's currency is due to the high correlation of the krona and the CAC 40. The portfolio is constructed in the same way as the portfolios of French and Swiss stocks mentioned earlier. On September 22, 2008, its value is 1000 kronor and the four stocks have a weight of 250 kronor.

Figure 14.4 shows a striking similarity between the performance of the portfolio of the 10 restricted French financial stocks and the 4 Swedish financial stocks. The correlation coefficient between the two series is 0.94. Even though the portfolio of Swedish stocks is below the portfolio of French stocks most of the time, both portfolios move together as expressed by the high correlation coefficient. During the downturn period, both portfolios depreciate at a similar pace. Later the Swedish portfolio recovers more slowly but ultimately the portfolios converge again. Both portfolios have comparable volatilities, with the standard deviation of the Swedish portfolio being slightly higher.

If expressed in euros (Exchange Rate ECB) and normalized again to have the value of €1000 on September 22, the Swedish portfolio performs worse than the French one. Both portfolios are plotted in Figure 14.5. This result is related directly to depreciation of the Swedish krona relative to the euro. Even in euro terms, however, it is evident that the two portfolios ultimately converge. At the end of the study period, the krona-to-euro ratio is close to the one at the beginning of the period.

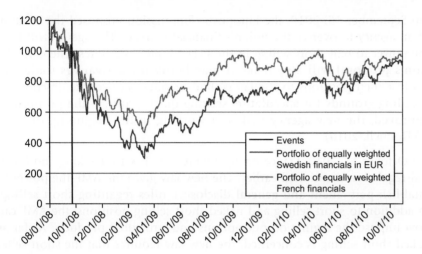

FIGURE 14.5
Comparison of French (EUR) and Swedish (EUR) financials.

14.5 DISCUSSION

We have seen so far that the overall effect of the short selling ban in France was not positive. Figure 14.2, nevertheless, shows that introduction of the ban was followed by a short period in which affected stocks slightly outperformed unaffected stocks. This could relate to certain short-term behavioral effects of the short selling ban. Whether this is the case still remains unknown. However, the statistical analysis presented earlier shows that the portfolios of restricted and unrestricted stocks evolve with only minor differences. The comparison of France and Switzerland reveals that Swiss financial stocks, which were affected by the ban for only 3 months, move in an almost identical manner as French ones both inside and outside the ban period in Switzerland. Swedish financial stocks denominated in euros perform worse than French stocks. Yet again, if we eliminate the distortive effect of the krona's depreciation, we still have a high degree of similarity.

Far from saying that governments should never intervene in the markets, we reaffirm our position that this should only be done after careful analysis of the advantages and disadvantages of the intervention. The recent bans on short selling, however, were imposed hastily and without consultation. Not surprisingly, their effects were not the ones that the market regulators hoped to achieve. We share the opinion of an array of researchers and analysts who say that the bans were unjustified and largely ineffective.

Even though there is overwhelming evidence to the contrary, short selling continues to be blamed for wreaking havoc in the financial markets.

On September 15, 2010, the European Commission proposed the creation of an agency to oversee the union's financial markets. The agency will have the power to ban short selling in the EU's 27 member states. The commission's proposal will also make it mandatory for derivatives traders to disclose their positions to regulators. Both trading practices are described as breeding grounds for speculators seeking quick profit. If the proposal is approved, the new agency will start working in the beginning of 2011 (O'Donnell, 2010).

On October 11, 2010, France finally adopted the law for banking and financial regulation mentioned earlier. The new law gives the AMF the power to establish permanent and general disclosure rules regarding short selling. In addition to short selling and naked short selling positions, the AMF can now impose the regime on put options and structured products. As far as naked short selling is concerned, the new law requires that the short seller must be in possession of the security he is selling or to have arranged to obtain it from a third party at the time of the short sale, thus effectively prohibiting this practice. The settlement period (between sale and delivery) will be reduced from 3 to 2 market days in line with EU harmonization (Fleury et al., 2010).

In conclusion, we mention SEC Chairman Christopher Cox's statement that the short selling ban in the United States was the "biggest mistake of his tenure" (Paley & Hilzenrath, 2008). However, on the other side of the Atlantic, Europe is stagnating and continues to believe that the short selling bans were and still are instrumental in the preservation of orderly market behavior. The evidence we presented points to the contrary. The short selling bans were detrimental to market liquidity and price discovery and did not reduce volatility. Moreover, the singling out of naked short selling was economically unjustified. The case of France, which still maintains a ban on naked short selling and a disclosure regime for short positions, shows that the restrictions were ineffective both in the context of France and in comparison to other countries.

Future research in the topic could study the change in the liquidity patterns of the affected stocks in France and how those compare to the patterns of unaffected stocks after introduction of the ban. An even more interesting subject would be the study of any possible short-term beneficial effects of the ban from a behavioral finance point of view. According to Cox, after the lift of the short selling ban in the United States:

> While the actual effects of this temporary action will not be fully understood for many more months, if not years, knowing what we know now, I believe on balance the commission would not do it again. [...] The costs appear to outweigh the benefits (Younglai, 2008).

REFERENCES

AMF. (2008). *Short-selling: Ban on unsecured transactions and transparency of short positions in financial sector securities. AMF.* Retrieved from http://www.amf-france.org/documents/general/8424_1.pdf.

Beber, A., & Pagano, M. (2010). *Short-selling bans around the world: Evidence from the 2007-09 crisis.* Working Paper, University of Naples, Italy. Retrieved from http://ideas.repec.org/p/sef/csefwp/241.html.

Boehmer, E., Jones, C., & Zhang, X. (2009). *Shackling short sellers: The 2008 shorting ban.* Working Paper, Cornell University, Ithaca, NY. Retrieved from http://papers.ssrn.com/sol3/papers.cfm?abstract_id=1412844.

Chu, P. (2010). *Stocks, commodities fall as euro hits 4-year low on german ban. Bloomberg Business-Week.* Retrieved from http://www.businessweek.com/news/2010-05-19/stocks-commodities-fall-as-euro-hits-4-year-low-on-german-ban.html.

Clifton, M., & Snape, M. (2008). *The effect of short-selling restrictions on liquidity: Evidence from the London Stock Exchange.* Working Paper, University of Technology, Sydney, Australia. Retrieved from http://img.iex.nl/iexprofs/images/2008-12-01ResearchEvidenceofShortSelling Restrictions.pdf.

Copeland, L. (2010). *Short sales bans: Shooting the messenger.* Working Paper, Cato Institute, Washington, DC. Retrieved from http://www.cato.org/pub_display.php?pub_id=12131.

Fleury, B., Robé, J., & Seibt, F. (2010). *French banking and financial regulation bill: Summary of main provisions.* Gibson Dunn & Cutcher LLP. Retrieved from https://www.lexology.com/library/detail.aspx?g=8ceeda6a-9750-42f6-9885-aba4a23be.

France 24. (2010). *French finance minister rejects Germany's short-selling ban. France 24.* Retrieved from http://www.france24.com/en/20100519-french-finance-minister-lagarde-germany-naked-short-selling-trading-clamp-eu.

Graham, D. (2010). *Germany, France urge EU to eye short selling ban. Reuters.* Retrieved from http://in.reuters.com/article/idINIndia-49167720100609.

Gruenewald, S., Wagner, A., & Weber, R. (2010a). *Emergency short selling restrictions in the course of the financial crisis.* Working Paper, Swiss Finance Institute, Zurich, Switzerland. Retrieved from http://papers.ssrn.com/sol3/papers.cfm?abstract_id=1441236.

Gruenewald, S., Wagner, A., & Weber, R. (2010b). *Short selling regulation after the financial crisis: First principles revisited.* Working Paper, Swiss Finance Institute, Zurich, Switzerland. Retrieved from http://papers.ssrn.com/sol3/papers.cfm?abstract_id=1439652.

O'Donnell, J. (2010). *EU unveils short-selling curbs, derivatives controls. Reuters.* Retrieved from http://www.reuters.com/article/idUSLAG00637020100915.

Paley, A., & Hilzenrath, D. (2008). *SEC chief defends his restraint. Washington Post.* Retrieved from http://www.washingtonpost.com/wp-dyn/content/article/2008/12/23/AR2008122302765.html?sid=ST2008122302866&s_pos=.

Theris, C. (2010). *Short selling regulations in France.* Herbert Smith. Retrieved from http://www.herbertsmith.com/NR/rdonlyres/BD2962FD-DD6E-4F84-B555-D5D5A3BB3E42/0/French ShortSellingRulesMain.htm.

Younglai, R. (2008). *SEC chief has regrets over short-selling ban. Reuters.* Retrieved from http://www.reuters.com/article/idUSTRE4BU3FL20081231.

Section 3

China, Japan, and Australia

CHAPTER 15

The Chinese Real Estate Bubble: Is It an Opportunity for Short Selling?

Peter T. Treadway and Michael C.S. Wong

CONTENTS

ABSTRACT

This chapter evaluates arguments on the emergence of the China real estate bubble. Because of the lack of data, it is hard for analysts to verify the arguments. However, evidence points to further problems in the Chinese banking and real estate sectors. If this is true, it is not too late to short Chinese banks and property stocks listed on the Hong Kong market in the form of H-shares and in the United States in the form of American depositary receipts.

KEYWORDS

American depositary receipts; Case–Shiller index; Exchange-traded funds; Minsky–Kindleberger model; Real estate bubble.

15.1 INTRODUCTION

In early 2010, certain prominent investors in the West, known as "global bears," were forecasting that China was undergoing a massive bubble in real estate similar to that already experienced by the United States. Notable among these short sellers is Jim Chanos, president of Kynikos Associates, and U.K. hedge fund manager Hugh Hendry. An influential negative report entitled *China's Investment Boom: Great Leap into the Unknown* on China produced by Monaco-based Pivot Capital Management (2009) received widespread attention in the investing community.

The basic arguments of Pivot are:

1. China's export model has stalled thanks to recession in the U.S. and European economies. Pressure to revalue the renminbi against the U.S. dollar will make things worse for China's exports.
2. China is overinvesting in real estate, basic materials, and infrastructure.
3. The 31% expansion of Chinese bank loans in 2009 was bound to result in a misallocation of capital, asset bubbles, and a rise in nonperformers.

Adding to the negative story, Northwestern University political science professor Victor Shih (2010) provided estimates of significant borrowings by entities controlled by local authorities. If Shih's estimates are correct—and the government now seems to be conceding that he is at least partly right—it would suggest that China's public debt to gross domestic product (GDP) ratio is probably 30% higher than conventional estimates and a definite problem for Chinese banks.

The global bears have advocated shorting stocks with exposure to China and Chinese real estate in particular. We make the following points.

1. The ruling Communist Party in China today bases its fundamental legitimacy on its success in producing an ever-increasing standard of living for its citizens. Current government policies taken to cool off the residential real estate sector have probably already gone too far and are likely to be partly reversed. Residential sales as of early June in 2010 have reportedly dropped dramatically as the result of restrictive government measures put in place. Restrictive policies were implemented not just for macro reasons of preventing overheating but also because of fears of discontent on the part of the average citizen who felt priced out of the market by speculators. The government faces a difficult tightrope of trying to cool the high end of residential housing without overly damaging the economy.
2. Despite its shift toward market economics, China is still a state-controlled economy. For example, monetary policy does not operate in China in

the same way as it does in the United States. In the United States, under quantitative easing the Federal Reserve has vastly expanded bank reserves. But the Fed has no way of forcing banks to lend, and bank lending has been declining (except at government-controlled Fannie Mae and Freddie Mac). However, in 2009, the Chinese government ordered by and large state-owned banks to increase lending as part of the government's stimulus program. Banks did not have to worry about capital ratios or nonperforming loans and now must raise additional capital.

3. When compared with the United States, Chinese statistics are scarce and of dubious reliability. National reliable statistics on real estate prices, vacancy rates, real estate inventories, mortgage loans outstanding, loan-to-value ratios, and nonperforming ratios are generally not available or not reliable. Moreover, the country operates in a language that non-Chinese cannot read or speak.

4. The lack of investment alternatives, low real estate carrying costs, and negative real interest rates on bank deposits have caused many wealthy Chinese to view owning real estate as they would tangible assets such as gold, which do not produce cash flows. This makes vacancy rates more difficult to interpret than in a U.S. context. Some residential unit purchasers do not expect to live in or rent out their properties. Anecdotal reports suggest a large number of high-end apartments without water and electricity in major cities. Vacancy rates as high as 40% have been reported for some of the major cities and resort areas. The threatened imposition of property taxes—unknown in China at present—would radically change the economics of luxury properties. The most likely scenario is that these taxes, if imposed, will be confined to the high end.

5. The bulls argue that the continuous migration of people from the country-side and China's recent record of rapidly increasing personal incomes may bail out real estate and infrastructure capacity that is put in place before demand actually materializes. China will "grow into" its current oversupply of real estate and infrastructure. Global bears are arguing that the number of Chinese yet to move to the cities is actually considerably smaller than is realized and that China is far more urbanized than is widely realized. They further argue that in any case the average Chinese cannot afford the high-end luxury apartments being built. Millions of in-migrant poor people do not make for solid demand for high-end properties.

6. It has been argued that comparisons of house price/income ratios can be misleading due to China's one-child policy. When a first-time home-buying couple buys an apartment, it is often said that six people are buying: the couple and both sets of parents. Global bears dismiss this type of "China is different" argument.

7. If the current residential market statistics are murky in China, those for commercial real estate are absolutely opaque. Global bears point to the existence of large amounts of empty office space in China based usually on personal observation (see, for instance, Hendry, 2009).

15.2 COMPARISON WITH THE UNITED STATES

Figures 15.1 and 15.2 provide a good snapshot of the U.S. residential real estate bubble and bust. Figure 15.1 displays the Case–Shiller index.

The U.S. Case–Shiller index is a very reliable indicator in that it adjusts for housing quality and size, the general level of inflation, and is a national home price index. As observed in Figure 15.1, U.S. housing prices began their upward trend in March 1998 and peaked in 2006.

Figure 15.2 displays the accompanying rise in mortgage financing. The unrestrained behavior in the U.S. bubble, including lax standards, overly complicated mortgage-backed securities, and excesses of Fannie Mae and Freddie Mac, is by now well known. However, the U.S. residential real estate bubble, significantly financed by debt, lasted approximately 8 years before peaking. The resulting debt deflation is likely to slow U.S. economic growth for years to come.

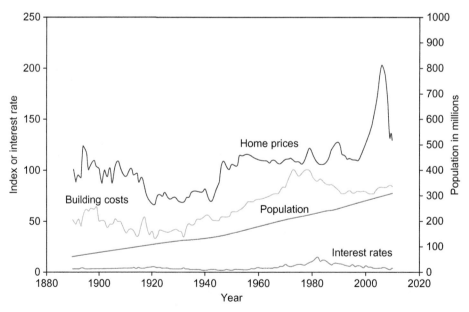

FIGURE 15.1
United States Case–Shiller index (data source: http://www.econ.yale.edu/~shiller/data.htm).

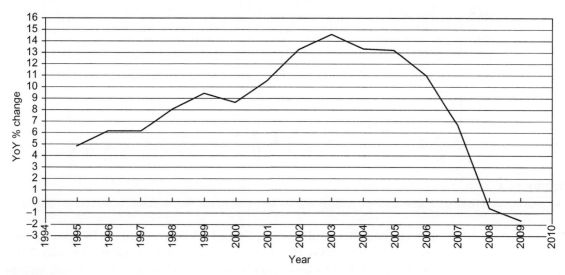

FIGURE 15.2

United States household home mortgage growth (data source: Federal Reserve).

15.3 THE BUBBLE IN CHINA

Figure 15.3 provides a somewhat less reliable snapshot of the Chinese real estate bubble. It is a graph of monthly year-over-year price increase data from a series called "Sales Price Indices of Buildings in 70 Medium-Large Sized Cities."

Data are not adjusted for inflation (Figure 15.3). These numbers, augmented by anecdotal evidence from major cities, suggest an unusual pattern. Although Figure 15.3 only begins in 2005, some acceleration of Chinese real estate prices apparently got under way in 2002. It should be remembered that the Asian crisis of 1997 and the severe acute respiratory syndrome (SARS) outbreak in 2003 had an inhibiting effect on real estate activity not just in China but in Hong Kong as well. Figure 15.3 depicts that the rate of increase accelerated into 2008 and then fell off dramatically. In addition, the global financial crisis in 2008 clearly interrupted price acceleration. Therefore, over the last 12 years, there were three interrupting factors, that is, the Asian crisis, SARS, and the global crisis of 2007–2008, which probably acted as a check on Chinese bubble formation, with real estate price acceleration resuming in 2009. Moreover, most observers believe the numbers upon which Figure 15.3 are based understate price appreciation in many areas of China. Newspapers in China report year-over-year price increases of 30–50% in major cities such as Shanghai, Beijing, Shenzhen, and Guangzhou, as well as in resort areas

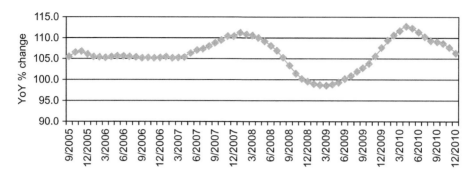

FIGURE 15.3

Sales price indices of newly constructed residential buildings in China (total) (data source: National Bureau of Statistics of China).

such as Hangzhou and Hainan. Figure 15.3 shows that price increase resumes quickly after June 2006. However, price begins to decrease starting May 2010. The change in the first four months of 2011 is close to 0. This means, around 100 in the same chart.

15.4 THE DEBT DEFLATION MODEL—DOES IT APPLY TO CHINA?

The general pattern of real estate bubbles has been one of a rapid rise in real estate values financed by bank debt. When asset values reach extreme values, bubbles burst due to some government action to restrain the process, resulting in a plunge of asset values. Borrowers suffer financial distress as they find themselves in a negative equity position as the value of their mortgages begins to substantially exceed the value of their houses. Banks in turn experience rising nonperforming loans and, in many cases, become insolvent with a significant recession always ensuing. Versions of this model have been put forth by economist Hyman Minsky and financial historian Charles Kindleberger and Aliber (2005).[1] Further research summarized by Rogoff and Reinhart (2009) provides examples of this boom–bust bank insolvency recession cycle for a number of countries. The model would appear to describe very well the experience of the United States from 1998 through the current real estate bust. Likewise, it would describe the Japanese real estate boom bust, which commenced in 1985 and peaked in 1990.

Data on Chinese bank mortgage lending and loans to real estate developers are not published by government sources. However, the managing director of

---

[1] The Kindleberger–Minsky framework explains the characteristics of financial crises and consists of five stages: (1) displacement, (2) boom, (3) overtrading, (4) revulsion, and (5) tranquility.

China equities and commodities at J.P. Morgan Jill Ulrich (2010) states in the *South China Morning Post* that the property sector accounted for 21% of Chinese bank loans in 2009. In the article she seems not to be unduly disturbed by real estate price increases in China, but loans classified as real estate may not be the entire story. Shih (2010) has estimated that banks have lent some RMB 11 trillion (US$1.4 trillion) to local government entities, most of this occurring in 2009. If a substantial portion of this has found its way into real estate, then the picture changes. These entities, rather than private individuals or companies, may be significant real estate borrowers.

Our tentative conclusion is that the Minsky–Kindleberger model does describe what is happening in China today, although it might make a difference from a macroeconomic perspective if a substantial portion of future defaulters are government entities rather than individuals. The bubble in China has come quickly, mostly during 2009 and the first 5 months of 2010. Most likely many observers are assuming that the government would bail out the banks if the need arose. From the perspective of a short seller, the crucial question is: where is China in the Minsky–Kindleberger model's time line? Is the peak still ahead or has China, in a relatively short time period, managed to produce a debt-driven real estate bubble that is now near its peak? Government authorities are aware of the bubble and, as mentioned, have taken measures to slow it down, something that Minsky and Kindleberger might have approved. However, have the authorities' actions come in time or are they the straw that is breaking the bubble's back? Are they ignoring the root cause of the problem, which lies in an excessively expansive monetary policy and negative real interest rates? What about a failure to revalue the renminbi in 2009? The revaluation in real terms is taking place via inflation, especially asset inflation, in China.

15.5 THE STOCK MARKET—FORECASTING THE BURSTING OF THE BUBBLE?

Since November 2009 the various Chinese stock markets have apparently been reflecting worries about a slowdown and possibly a real estate/banking correction in China. Figures 15.4 and 15.5 display the index value on the Shanghai and Shenzhen markets for banks and real estate companies, which are down 28 and 42%, respectively in 2010. The indexes have remained stable until May 2011.

A similar picture emerges on the Hong Kong Stock Exchange where major Chinese banks and real estate companies are listed. The stock prices of numerous banks and real estate companies displayed in Figures 15.6–15.11 show similar price patterns.

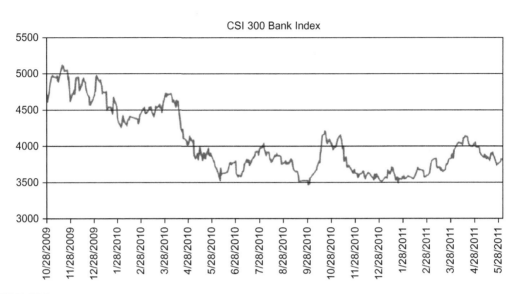

FIGURE 15.4

CSI 300 Banks Index (data source: http://finance.yahoo.com).

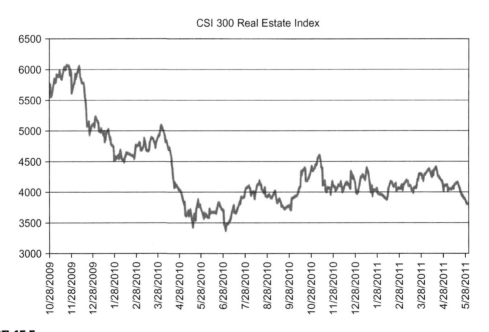

FIGURE 15.5

CSI Real Estate Index (data source: http://finance.yahoo.com).

FIGURE 15.6

China Construction Bank Index (data source: http://hk.finance.yahoo.com).

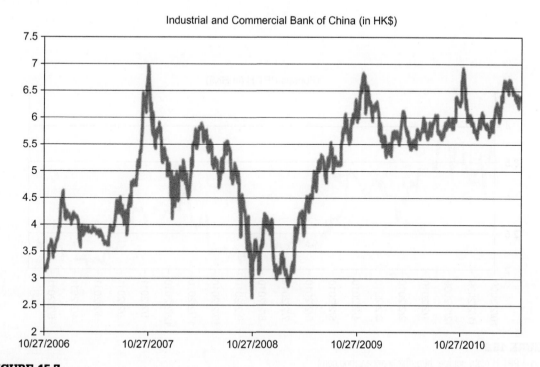

FIGURE 15.7

Industry and Commercial Bank of China (data source: http://hk.finance.yahoo.com).

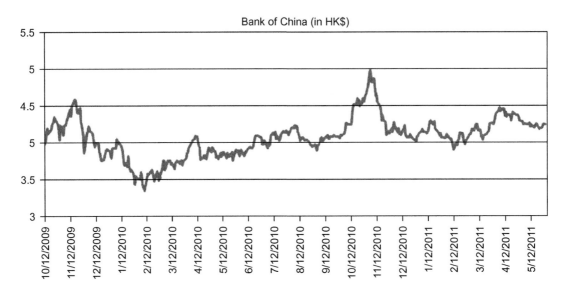

FIGURE 15.8

Bank of China (data source: http://hk.finance.yahoo.com).

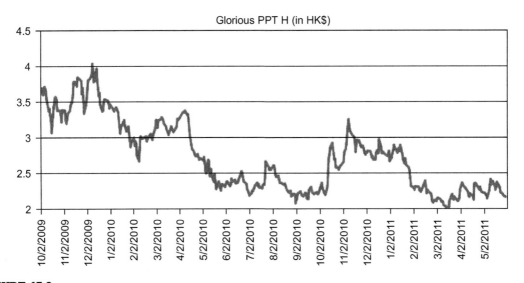

FIGURE 15.9

Glorious PPT H (data source: http://hk.finance.yahoo.com).

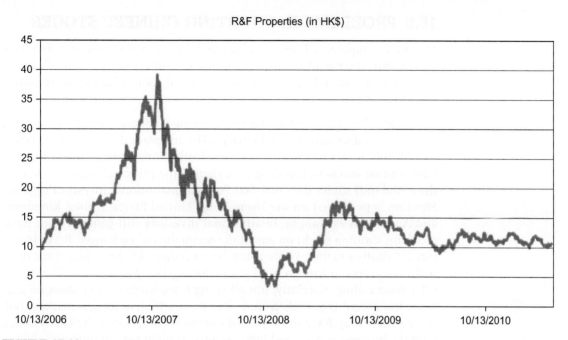

FIGURE 15.10

R&F Properties (data source: http://hk.finance.yahoo.com).

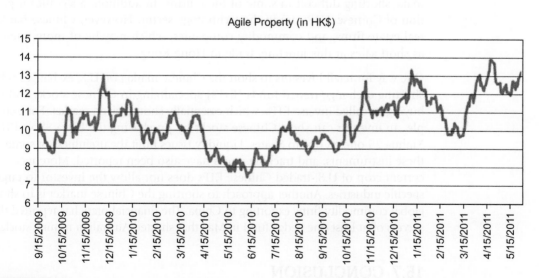

FIGURE 15.11

Agile Property (data source: http://hk.finance.yahoo.com).

15.6 PROBLEMS IN SHORTING CHINESE STOCKS

Thanks to computer technology, advanced telecommunications, and abundant bandwidth, the world is moving toward a seamless integration of capital markets. Unfortunately, partly because of capital controls in various countries and other restrictions, we are not there yet.

First of all, shorting of individual stocks on the Shanghai Stock Exchange was only approved in principle in January 2010 and started on March 31, 2010. In addition, under Chinese regulations, institutional foreign investors only have limited access to investing in A shares (the principal shares traded on the mainland) under the Qualified Foreign Institutional Investor Program. Shorting is permitted on the Hong Kong, United States, United Kingdom, and Australian exchanges. Institutional investors will generally not have problems shorting stocks on any of the nonmainland exchanges. Retail investors are another matter. While a number of online U.S. brokerage firms offer real-time access to foreign markets, including Hong Kong, not all of these offer short selling. Similarly, not all Hong Kong brokers offer short selling. Some traditional U.S. brokers may offer short selling in foreign markets, but these orders may have to be placed during the day when the U.S. market (and the brokers) is open and then executed at night eastern time.

Approximately 100 Chinese American depositary receipts (ADRs) trade in the United States and they can all be shorted, although liquidity issues may make shorting difficult in some of these firms. In addition, a significant portion of Chinese ADRs are in the technology sector. However, Chinese banks, real estate firms, and commodity companies, which may be of more interest as short sales at this juncture, trade in Hong Kong.

One way for retail investors to short the Chinese market on U.S. exchanges is by shorting exchange-traded funds (ETFs) specializing in Chinese stocks and by buying so-called inverse ETFs, which essentially short a given market. For example, an investor can short Chinese stocks by purchasing the Ultra Short FTSE Xinhua 25 offered by Pro Shares. Liquidity issues limit the usefulness of some of these instruments, and tracking errors have also been reported. Moreover, the current crop of U.S.-traded Chinese ETFs does not allow the investor to target specific industries. Another approach to shorting the Chinese market is to short global commodity firms exporting to China. The financial press has reported the success of at least one hedge fund in May that shorted Australian mining stocks.

15.7 CONCLUSION

While other factors, such as the Greek crisis, may have contributed to the decline of Chinese banks and property shares, it appears that both of these sectors have been selling off in anticipation of the problems in the Chinese real estate market. Investors have become sensitized to the bubble phenomenon. The question is whether it is too late to short the property market and whether global shorts have exaggerated the problem.

The lack of reliable data and the short operating history of China as a semicapitalist country make firm conclusions difficult. However, overall the evidence points to further problems in the Chinese banking and real estate sectors. If this is true, then it is not too late to short Chinese banks and property stocks.

Some investors predict that China's real estate bubble will soon burst. Property prices in China are relatively high with respect to GDP per capita. Also, the Chinese government took actions in April 2010 to regulate real estate prices. However, the bubble may not burst in a way that the U.S. market experienced in 2007–2009.

For residential mortgage loans in China, the loan–asset ratio is always kept below 50%. If the property price drops by no more than 50%, there is no such issue of negative worth and foreclosure. Further, due to the high savings rate of China's population, many residential properties are owned by families without having any mortgage. The declining property prices may hurt real estate speculators, property developers, or property investment companies but would not have much impact on the Chinese economy.

However, economic activities in China are controlled by central and municipal governments, sizable state-owned banks, and enterprises to a great extent. In 2010, the magnitude of bank lending has been reduced greatly following the change in monetary policy. In fact, bank lending on a large scale cannot be sustained any longer due to the potential risk from industry, as exports are severely affected by the European sovereign debt crisis. In 2011, the Chinese government will combat inflation and limit property-related personal and commercial loans. This will hopefully cool down the transaction volume of the real estate market. However, whether the real estate market will fall freely will be hard to say in such an economy with government interventions.

Even with the drop of property prices, the Chinese central government is taking measures to curb current real estate prices. A decline of 30% or more in real estate prices is widely accepted by the central government, but it is not certain that commercial banks can assume such big declines. Possibly a decline of over 50% in real estate prices would likely induce a new wave of financial crisis in China. Therefore, a rapid drop in real estate prices is hazardous to the banking system and the government expects a slow decline. In addition, if the yuan appreciates, then material costs will decrease. For example, if we assume that labor cost and land prices are the same, then property prices should be lower. However, if inflation is high and land prices are high, then property prices will be higher. We believe that the Chinese government will allow no more than a 5% change in the yuan per year; therefore, it is hard to make solid conclusions. The Chinese government has recognized that a bubble currently exists and has opted to contain real estate prices to maintain a "harmonious society." The above discussion while it may have practical implications should be regarded to be academic discussion. No explicit recommendation to buy or sell any security or fund should be implied.

REFERENCES

Hendry, H. (2009). *Chinese economy 2009. A YouTube video*. Retrieved from http://www.youtube .com/watch?v=ektMQGbW3wk.

Kindleberger, C. P., & Aliber, R. (2005). *Manias, panics, and crashes, a history of financial crises*. Hoboken, NJ: John Wiley & Sons.

Pivot Capital Management. (2009). *China's investment boom: Great leap into the unknown*. Retrieved from http://www.scribd.com/doc/21544021/PIVOT-CAPITAL-MANAGEMENT-China-s-Investment-Boom-the-Great-Leap-Into-the-Unknown.

Rogoff, K., & Reinhart, C. (2009). *This time it's different: Eight centuries of financial folly*. Princeton, NJ: Princeton University Press.

Shih, V. (2010). *China's hidden debt risks 2012 crisis. Bloomberg Businessweek*. Retrieved from http://www.businessweek.com/news/2010-03-02/china-s-hidden-debt-risks-2012-crisis-northwestern-s-shih-says.htm.

Ulrich, J. (2010). *Home truths. South China Morning Post, 18*(1), 1.

CHAPTER 16

Introduction of Margin Trading and Short Selling in China's Securities Market: The Case of Disordered Warrant Prices

Wei Fan, Qingbin Meng, Liu Yang, Lingqing Xing, and Sihai Fang

CONTENTS

ABSTRACT

Due to the lack of short selling in China's securities market prior to the implementation of margin trading and short selling on March 31, 2010, a low level of efficiency and completeness existed, impairing stock and derivatives prices. We find that the basic reason for the disordered warrant prices is abnormal high stock prices resulting from the lack of short selling prior to this period. Furthermore, this chapter focuses on introducing the rules and our opinions on margin trading and short selling launched in mainland China's stock market. To our knowledge, this is the first academic study to investigate margin trading and short selling of warrant prices in China.

KEYWORDS

Amount limits; Black–Scholes pricing model; Call warrants; China Securities Regulatory Commission; Disordered warrant prices; Duration limits; EGARCH model; Margin trading; Naked short selling; Tick rule; Warrants.

16.1 INTRODUCTION

With the introduction of margin trading and short selling, China's stock market officially entered the short selling era on March 31, 2010. As a necessity to improve market completeness and efficiency, margin trading and short selling will play a very important role in the stability of capital markets. In addition, it will also have far-reaching influences for capital market participants and for the market itself. For investors, it will provide diversified investment opportunities and a means of hedging risk, increasing market volume, and improving stock market liquidity and activity while reducing liquidity risk. For example, Woolridge and Dickinson (1994) find that short sellers provide liquidity to the market by increasing the trading volume in bull markets while reducing the volume in bear markets. Further, Anchada and Hazem (2003) observe that among the 111 stock markets around the world, emerging markets with severe short selling constraints showed significantly lower market liquidity than ones in developed countries with no such constraints, a finding further confirmed by Liao and Yang (2005) and Luo and Liao (2007). According to statistics, the amount of margin trading and short selling in foreign countries has accounted for more than 15% of total stock trading. For instance, the percentage in the United States is 16 to 20%, Japan 15%, and China and Taiwan 20 to 40%. Margin trading and short selling will also help improve the stock price formation mechanism, reduce market volatility, and provide price discovery.

Before the introduction of short selling and margin trading in China's stock market, the prices of certain stocks were in a disordered state. For example, a number of warrant prices were below their intrinsic value, and numerous closed-end fund prices were below 30% of their net asset value. In terms of research into warrants in other countries, Kremer and Roenfeldt (1993) investigated the U.S. warrant market using the Black–Scholes pricing model and the jump diffusion model. They concluded that both models undervalued warrant prices when continuous dividend payments were considered. Further, Schulz, and Trautmann (1989, 1994) examined the German warrant market and discovered that market prices were lower than theoretical prices using the constant elasticity of variance model. With regards to the Japanese warrant market, studies were conducted by Mikami (1990) and Kuwahara and Marsh (1992). The first study found that market warrant prices were above the Black–Scholes pricing model when warrants were out of the money and below the Black–Scholes pricing model prices when warrants were in the money. The second study used the generalized autoregressive conditional heteroskedasticity and exponential general autoregressive conditional heteroskedastic (EGARCH) models to fit the stochastic volatility and concluded that a significant discrepancy existed between market prices and theoretical (model) prices, predominantly when they were deep in the money and deep out of the money. Warrant pricing research for the Dutch market (see Veld, 1992) has also been conducted with mixed indications of whether warrant prices were undervalued or overvalued.

Because China's warrant market has just been developed, very few studies on warrants have used data from China's warrant market. Lin, Zheng, and Peng (2005) discuss the first warrant issued in China's market—the Baogang JTB1—and observed that the market price was significantly higher than the theoretical price obtained by the Black–Scholes model. Yuan, Fan, and Liu (2008) provide some particular descriptive statistics on China's warrant market and observe that the market price of warrants was also higher than the theoretical price of the Black–Scholes model.

In addition, Fan and Yuan (2010) studied call warrant prices in China's market and found that the market price of warrants was higher overall than the theoretical price using the Black–Scholes model, but as time passed the bias between them became smaller. This demonstrates that with the gradual improvement of the warrants market system and pricing efficiency, it has resulted in standard market prices of warrants.

This chapter begins with disordered warrant prices due to the lack of short selling and examines how short selling is important for a complete securities market. Finally, we introduce the rules of margin trading and short selling in China's securities market.

16.2 THE DISORDERED WARRANT PRICE IN CHINA'S SECURITIES MARKET

We study the price performance of call warrants[1] in China's securities market. These warrants are contingent claims issued by companies or financial institutions on their underlying stocks, which facilitate share

---

[1] A call warrant is a warrant that gives the holder the right to buy the underlying share for an agreed price on or before a specified date. In China's securities market, put warrants are also issued. A put warrant is almost the same as a put option in this market. This chapter does not examine them, and the term "warrant" in our analysis will be used to refer to a "call warrant" specifically.

reform.[2] On August 22, 2005, the first warrant (Baogang JTB1) was issued on the Shanghai Stock Exchange (SSE). As of January 2007, according to Goldman Sachs, China's warrant market became the largest in the world in terms of annual total trading volume, surpassing that of Hong Kong (see Mitchell, 2007). Nevertheless, as an emerging market, there are still some particular problems that need to be studied, with the most significant one being the disordered warrant price phenomenon.

In China's securities market, most of the warrants are nominally Bermudan (similar to American-style options), but European options can be exercised within 5 days of maturity. They are log dated with maturity of 1 or 2 years, which is particularly interesting, as 16 calls (our sample) traded below their intrinsic value, that is, $max(S-K,0)$ (see Hull, 2003; Merton, 1973). We plot daily prices of the Wuliang YGC1 warrant against the Black–Scholes theoretical price and the intrinsic value. The plot appears to violate the "no arbitrage" principle. From Figure 16.1, the warrant price is not only below the Black–Scholes pricing model, but also below the intrinsic value. However, this is not a special case in China's market, but rather a common phenomenon.[3] How can such a puzzling phenomenon exist in China's market for such a long time?

It appears that such phenomenon of warrants has not been reported for markets in the United States (Kremer & Roenfeldt, 1993), Germany (Schulz &

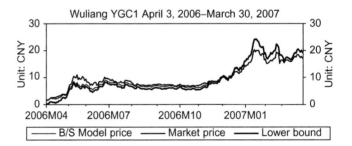

FIGURE 16.1
Wuliang YGC1[4] model price, market price, and intrinsic value from April 3, 2006, to March 31, 2007.

---

[2] According to Yuan and associates (2008), the China Securities Regulatory Commission (CSRC) launched a share reform in May 2005, when the A-share market was almost at an 8-year low. Reform plans for listed companies were proposed and approved by their shareholders, with minor government intervention. In order to carry out the reforms smoothly, holders of nontradable shares had to pay for the "right" to trade. As a result, holders of tradable shares were awarded additional shares, free warrants, or cash payments (or any combinations of these). A warrant is an important type of "right" payoff.

[3] Among the 17 warrants in China's securities market, 11 of them have experienced such a situation, and these 11 call warrants are Angang JTC1(030001), Wuliang YGC1(030002), Qiancheng HQC1(031001), Wugang JTB1(580001), Baogang JTB1(580002), Hangang JTB1(580003), Wanhua HXB1(580005), Yage QCB1(580006), Changdian CWB1(580007), Yili CWB1(580009), and Magang CWB1(580010).

[4] Wuliang YGC1 warrant (030002) is a call warrant, maturing on April 2, 2008, with an exercise price of 6.87 CNY.

Trautmann, 1989, 1994), Japan (Mikami, 1990), London OTC (Kuwahara & Marsh, 1992).[5] For warrants on closed-end funds on the London Stock Exchange, Gemmill and Thomas (1997) find that nearly 40% of more than 12,000 closing prices of warrants observed were below the standard intrinsic value. However, Gemmill and Thomas (1997) do not mention if any of the prices were far below the intrinsic value of the warrants.

We select a sample including all call warrants whose prices are below the lower bound since development of the share reform in 2005. For each warrant, we use the daily closing prices of warrants and their underlying stocks to compute the price gaps based on the Black–Scholes pricing model. We then attempt to explain this phenomenon.

The 16 warrants with market prices below their intrinsic value are listed in Table 16.1. All are Bermudan calls, except MagangCWB1[6] and GangfanGFC1,

Table 16.1 Terms of the 16 Warrants

Name	Derivative Type	Issuing Date[7]	Exercise Dates
WuliangYGC1	Long-dated call	06/04/03	08/03/27–08/04/02
QiaochengHQC1	Warrant	06/11/24	07/11/19–07/11/23
GangfanGFC1	Warrant	06/12/12	07/11/28–07/12/11
			08/11/28–08/12/11
BaogangJTB1	Long-dated call	06/03/31	07/03/26–07/03/30
HangangJTB1	Long-dated call	06/04/07	07/03/31–07/04/04
ShouchuangJTB1	Long-dated call	06/04/24	07/04/19–07/04/23
WanhuaHXB1	Warrant	06/04/27	07/04/20–07/04/26
YageQCB1	Long-dated call	06/05/22	07/05/17–07/05/21
ChangdianCWB1	Warrant	06/05/25	07/05/19–07/05/24
YiliCWB1	Warrant	06/11/15	07/11/08–07/11/14
MagangCWB1	Warrant	06/11/29	07/11/15–16,19–23,26–28
			08/11/17–21,24–28
ZhonghuaCWB1	Warrant	06/12/18	07/12/11–07/12/17
GuodianJTB1	Long-dated call	06/09/05	07/08/31–07/09/04
WugangCWB1	Long-dated call	07/04/17	09/04/10–09/04/16
JiangtongCWB1	Long-dated call	08/10/10	10/10/4–10/10/09
ErjiaoEJC1	Long-dated call	08/07/18	09/07/13–09/07/17

---

[5] Those are dual-currency, Japanese equity warrants with early exercise provisions (American-style options). Some were traded below their European exercise values when in the money but still above their intrinsic values.

[6] The exchange-assigned abbreviation for a warrant is used here, which has the following pattern: Pinyin of the first two Chinese characters, three (Roman) letters, and one digit.

[7] Data are in yy-mm-dd or yy/mm/dd format.

which could be exercised at the end of the first year; the rest are close to European in prices. Seven are typical warrants, which cause dilution effects upon exercise; nine are long-dated calls without dilution.

The previous section described call warrants in China's securities market. This section calculates the warrant model prices each day as a function of their underlying stock prices. In China's securities market, most call warrants are covered warrants. Therefore, they can be treated as long-lived stock options. Even if it is an equity warrant, Schulz and Trautmann (1989, 1994) demonstrated that it is not necessary to correct the option pricing formula for the dilution effect.[8] The reason for the success of this approximation is that it incorporates offsetting biases. On the one hand, there is an upward bias due to the dilution effect; on the other hand, there is a downward bias resulting from the use of stock prices, which serves as a substitute for the firm's value in the classical warrant pricing formula[9] (see Gemmill & Thomas, 1997; Veld, 2003). These biases can offset each other almost perfectly. Therefore, we use the Black–Scholes pricing model to compute daily warrant values. The formula is described as

$$C = SN(d_1) - Xe^{-r_f T}N(d_2)$$
$$d_1 = \frac{\ln(S/X) + (r_f + \sigma^2/2)T}{\sigma/\sqrt{T}}$$
$$d_2 = d_1 - \sigma\sqrt{T}$$

(16.1)

where C is the warrant price; S, X, σ, T, and r_f are, respectively, the underlying stock price, exercise price, volatility, time to maturity, and risk-free rate; and $N(d)$ is a cumulative normal distribution function. The model requires

---

[8] Schulz and Trautmann (1989) compared outcomes of the correct warrant pricing model with outcomes of the original Black–Scholes pricing model. From this investigation, these authors argue that even if an extremely high dilution factor is assumed, the bias resulting from simply using the Black–Scholes pricing model is very small. Schulz and Trautmann (1994) conclude that to obtain warrant prices with acceptable accuracy, adjustments to the Black–Scholes pricing formula are not needed.

[9] According to Galai and Schneller (1978), the classical warrant pricing formula can be described as

$$W = \frac{N}{N+n}[VN(d_1) - Xe^{-r_f T}N(d_2)]$$

$$d_1 = \frac{\ln(V/X) + (r_f + \sigma_V^2/2)T}{\sigma_V/\sqrt{T}}, \quad d_2 = d_1 - \sigma_V\sqrt{T}$$

where V is the value of the firm's asset, $V = NS + nW$. N is the number of shares outstanding and n is the number of new shares created if the warrant is exercised. We need to replace the stock price S by the firm value V and to replace the volatility of the stock price by the volatility of the firm value in the Black–Scholes framework. We then also multiply by the dilution factor.

five parameters, namely (a) price of the underlying stock, (b) strike price, (c) time remaining to maturity, (d) risk-free rate,[10] and (e) volatility of the underlying stock. The first four parameters can be observed directly. As for the last parameter, we consider the two kinds of volatility models here[11]: historical volatility and volatility derived from an EGARCH model (see Nelson, 1991).

First, for a single stock, the historical volatility model is described as

$$\sigma = \sqrt{\frac{1}{n-1} \sum_{i=1}^{n} [u_i - E(u)]^2} \qquad (16.2)$$

where u_i is the continuously compounded return for the ith interval, which can be expressed as

$$u_i = \ln(S_i/S_{i-1}), i = 1, 2, \ldots, n \qquad (16.3)$$

This chapter uses the 180-day historical volatility to estimate the volatility parameters.

Second, for a single stock, we fit the EGARCH (p,q) generation in which the stock volatility process is as follows:

$$r_{it} = \mu_i + \varepsilon_{it} \qquad (16.4)$$

$$\ln \sigma_{it}^2 = c + \sum_{i=1}^{q} \left(\alpha_i \left| \frac{z_{it}}{\sigma_{it}} \right| + \lambda_i \frac{z_{it}}{\sigma_{it}} \right) + \sum_{j=1}^{p} \beta_j \ln \sigma_{it-j}^2 \qquad (16.5)$$

In Equation (16.4), r_{it} is stock ith return over interval t with a constant mean μ_i and ε_{it} is described as

$$\varepsilon_{it} = \sigma_{it} Z_{it}, Z_{it} \sim N(0,1) \qquad (16.6)$$

In the variance Equation (16.5), α_i is the innovation term, λ_i is the asymmetry term, and β_j is the persistence term. The EGARCH model performs well in simulating stock price volatility and adds more weight on the impact of recent price changes on volatility. We also consider the asymmetric effect of volatility; in other words, the model considers the different effects between good news and bad news. For example, from daily returns of Dongererjiao

---

[10] Here, we use the central bank 1-year base interest rate issued by the People's Bank of China to measure the risk-free interest rate. The base interest rate is 2.25% before August 19, 2006, 2.52% during the period from August 19, 2006, to March 18, 2007, and 2.79% hereafter.

[11] At first, we also consider using implied volatility, but later we find that implied volatility of the deep-in-the-money warrants is sometimes negative so we do not use implied volatility in this chapter.

shares (the underlying stock of the Erjiao EJC1) during the July 18, 2008–July 10, 2009 period, we obtain the EGARCH (1,1) maximum likelihood parameter volatility:

$$r_t = 0.003 + e_t \tag{16.7}$$

$$\ln \sigma_{t+1}^2 = -0.678 + 0.291 \frac{|z_t|}{\sqrt{\sigma_t^2}} - 0.176 \frac{z_t}{\sqrt{\sigma_t^2}} + 0.892 \ln \sigma_t^2 \tag{16.8}$$

From the variance Equation (16.8) we obtain an α of 0.291 and an asymmetry λ of -0.176, which states that, when $z_{it} > 0$, the "good" information's impact on the conditional variance's logarithm is 0.115 [equal to $0.291 + (-0.176)$]; when $z_{it} < 0$, the "bad" information's impact is 0.467 [equal to $0.291 - (-0.176)$].

After selecting the eight warrants (Table 16.2) whose prices are lower than their intrinsic value (long term), we compare their market prices, the price according to the Black–Scholes pricing model, and the intrinsic value, respectively. First, we compare the bias between the market price and the Black–Scholes pricing model. By dividing the entire sample section into eight subsample sections, we calculate the daily warrant model prices using

Table 16.2 Comparison between Black–Scholes Pricing Model and Market Prices[a]

	First Half of 2006	Second Half of 2006	First Half of 2007	Second Half of 2007	First Half of 2008	Second Half of 2008	First Half of 2009	Second Half of 2009
Wanhua	−6.2%	−11.5%	−6.5%					
HXB1	−6.7%	−12.2%	−7.1%					
Hangang	38.0%	29.6%	−1.4%					
JTB1	49.7%	31.7%	−1.3%					
Wuliang	25.3%	−6.5%	−12.1%	−15.5%	−7.1%			
YGC1	26.4%	−7.4%	−12.4%	−17.4%	−8.4%			
Yili	4.7%	5.2%	−3.7%	−1.4%				
CWB1	3.8%	4.3%	−3.9%	−1.1%				
Magang	2.1%	−2.0%	−4.0%	4.7%				
CWB1	1.9%	−2.5%	−10.0%	−1.4%				
Qiaocheng	0.1%	4.8%	−7.6%	3.6%				
HQC1	−0.7%	3.9%	−8.2%	2.9%				
Jiangtong						−4.3%	−15.4%	−11.4%
CWB1						−2.9%	−14.8%	−11.9%
Erjiao						15.8%	−1.5%	−2.8%
EJC1						13.4%	0.9%	−2.6%

[a]Of all the biases between the Black–Scholes pricing model and market prices, the first row uses 180-day historical volatility and the second row uses volatility derived from the EGARCH model.

the Black–Scholes pricing model and describe the bias between model prices and market prices among the entire sample section and different subsample sections as follows:

$$\text{Bias1} = \frac{\text{Market price} - \text{Model price}}{\text{Model price}} \qquad (16.9)$$

Second, we compare the bias between market price and intrinsic value (Table 16.3):

$$\text{Bias2} = \frac{\text{Market price} - \text{Intrinsic value}}{\text{Intrinsic value}} \qquad (16.10)$$

Finally, we investigate the underlying reasons of the "below the intrinsic value" puzzle that has been faced by some recent warrants. This puzzle is not a result of illiquidity or of transactions costs in the warrant market. For example, the Wuliang YGC1 and the many other warrants that trade in China have good liquidity. In China's market, transaction costs (including the commission and the stamp duty) are less than 0.3%. When we remove transaction costs, the phenomenon still persists.

Table 16.3 Comparison between Black–Scholes Pricing Model and Intrinsic Value[a]

	First Half of 2006	Second Half of 2006	First Half of 2007	Second Half of 2007	First Half of 2008	Second Half of 2008	First Half of 2009	Second Half of 2009
Wanhua	−6.03%	−11.14%	−6.17%					
HXB1	−6.49%	−11.75%	−6.66%					
Hangang	38.47%	29.79%	−1.32%					
JTB1	49.74%	32.09%	−1.27%					
Wuliang	25.41%	−6.49%	−12.03%	−15.47%	−6.81%			
YGC1	26.65%	−7.33%	−12.33%	−17.19%	−8.31%			
Yili	5.09%	5.67%	−3.67%	−1.23%				
CWB1	3.88%	4.35%	−3.81%	−0.76%				
Magang	2.51%	−1.59%	−3.83%	4.73%				
CWB1	2.36%	−2.45%	−9.99%	−1.20%				
Qiaocheng	0.30%	5.07%	−7.19%	3.89%				
HQC1	−0.65%	4.25%	−7.95%	2.95%				
Jiangtong						−3.94%	−14.99%	−11.18%
CWB1						−2.49%	−14.70%	−11.90%
Erjiao						15.87%	−1.10%	−2.58%
EJC1						13.51%	1.01%	−2.15%

[a]Of all the biases between the Black–Scholes pricing model and market prices, the first row uses 180-day historical volatility and the second row uses volatility derived from the EGARCH model.

What other possible reason can cause the "below the intrinsic value" puzzle? We believe it is due to trading mechanism constraints, short-selling constraints, and the T+1 trading mechanism.[12] In China's securities market, stocks were not allowed to be sold short until March 31, 2010. The absence of short selling can prevent negative information or opinions from being reflected in stock prices, thus allowing stocks to be overpriced. In addition, investors cannot short the stock and go long in the underpriced warrant. Therefore, this regulation prevents rational investors from driving warrant prices to reasonable levels[13] (close to the price calculated by theoretical models). Moreover, the T+1 trading mechanism prevents shareholders from selling their shares by exercising them all at once.

16.3 DEVELOPMENT OF MARGIN TRADING AND SHORT SELLING IN CHINA

In 1999, the Chinese government enacted the "Securities Act," whose primary purpose was to control financial risks, and forbid brokerage firms from engaging in margin trading or short selling activities. In accordance with "Securities Act" requirements, China's financial institutions had to separate their operations and management activities such that the securities industry, banking industry, trust industry, and insurance industry should operate separately. As the capital market is developing, this practice of separate operation and management will gradually break down. State-owned groups in China began to establish banks, brokerage firms, and insurance companies.

To address the 15-year-old-long only mechanism, the new "Securities Act" was formally implemented on January 1, 2006. The act lifted the ban on margin trading and short selling as long as the activities were in accordance with the provisions of the state council. From June 2006 to September 2006, the China Securities Regulatory Commission (CSRC) created the following laws: "Regulations of Pilot Margin Trading and Short Selling," "Detailed Rules for Implementation of Pilot Margin Trading and Short Selling," "Detailed Rules for Implementation of Margin Trading and Short Selling Registry and Clearing Business," "Risk to Announce Book of Margin Trading and Short Selling," and numerous other laws marking the introduction of margin trading and short selling as a start-up phase.

In 2008, the financial crisis in the United States affected the global economy and the Chinese stock market; however, the market downturn did not halt the preparation for margin trading and short selling. The CSRC objectives of

---

[12] This implies that investors can only sell stocks purchased after 1 day rather than immediately.

[13] It is reasonable that warrant prices should not be lower than their intrinsic value.

implementing margin trading and short selling were to maintain stability in China's stock market, enhance investors' confidence, and avoid market turmoil. On April 25, 2008, the China State Council officially enacted the "Securities Supervision and Management Regulations." On October 5, 2008, the CSRC officially announced the launch of margin trading and short selling as a trial program. On December 1, 2008, the "Securities Business Scope Interim Provisions" allowed brokerage firms to apply for margin trading and short selling. On January 22, 2010, the CSRC issued the "Guidance on Implementing Margin Trading and Short Selling Business," listing the requirements for brokerage firm applicants. On February 12, 2010, the SSE and the Shenzhen Stock Exchange (SZSE) officially launched the "Notice on the Initial List of Underlying Securities and Range of Margin Collateral Securities." They released the list of underlying securities and the range of collateral securities, conversion rates, and related issues. On March 31, 2010, the SSE and SZSE formally accepted six pilot dealers' trading applications, and after 4 years of careful preparation, margin trading and short selling entered into an operational phase. On April 1, 2010, published transaction data showed that the total amount of the first trading day was 6.59 million RMB, of which 6.4956 million and 0.095 million consisted of margin trading and short selling, respectively.

16.4 INTRODUCTION AND INTERPRETATION OF CHINA'S KEY RULES ON MARGIN TRADING AND SHORT SELLING

The law entitled "Securities Supervision and Management Regulations" stipulates that margin trading and short selling refer to brokerage firms lending money to investors for the purchase of securities or lending securities to investors for selling and making sure investors deposit collateral with the dealers.

16.4.1 Dealer Limits, Investor Limits, and Account Limits

Dealer limits are specified in "Guidance on Implementing Margin Trading and Short Selling Business." For example, eligible dealers should have net capital over 5 billion RMB ($732 million) in the last 6 months and possess an "A" rank evaluation by the Chinese government to be part of the pilot project. In China, brokerage firms are ranked according to their risk management structure and are classified and evaluated by 27 indicators. The ratings affect the risk reserve funds ratio; in order to reinforce risk management, during the pilot phase, the ratio was raised from 10 to 50%. Under this provision, six pilot brokers were selected at this stage.

Investor and account limits are discussed in the "Detailed Rules for Implementation of Pilot Margin Trading and Short Selling" act. For example, eligible individual investors should only have one securities account for trading, with assets over 50 million RMB, and have an account for over 18 months. "Regulations of Pilot Margin Trading and Short Selling" outline that clients applying for margin trading and short selling should receive some form of professional education from brokers and pass exams to be more knowledgeable about the trading risks involved. Because this is the first time for individual investors in China to engage in short selling and margin trading, the government has relaxed many restrictions for investors.

16.4.2 Margin Trading and Short Selling with Brokerage Firms' Funds and Securities

To ensure the premise that the degree of trading can be controlled, the risk can be quantified and withstood. "Regulations of Pilot Margin Trading and Short Selling" state that in the pilot phase, brokerage firms should use their own funds and securities to provide margin trading and short selling services.

As for margin trading, the authorized capital available at this time is about 35 billion RMB. As the stock market needs time to adjust to these new innovations, the funds may be enough at this point; however, the lack of financing channels is a common problem. China's brokers are (1) the interbank lending market and (2) the short-term commercial bonds market. In the long run, this will affect the level of margin trading. As for short selling, dealers can only lend securities they own and also intend to hold over the long term. Due to the subprime mortgage crisis in 2008, brokers have limited numbers of securities at hand and, also due to limited financing channels, are bound to have an impact on short selling.

The Chinese government created a wall between the bank credit market and the stock market; hence, it is not possible to completely adopt American-style, decentralized, market-oriented credit transaction instruments for the time being. The primary business of China's commercial banks has consisted of deposit and lending operations for many years. Because the risk control departments are mostly responsible for real estate valuation and mortgages, they lack the related experience in volatile stocks and other virtual assets, particularly in securities valuation and risk assessment. Therefore, we believe that China should implement a two-tier system that would allow brokerage firms to provide services to exchange-listed firms and investors. Furthermore, China should implement a hybrid system like Taiwan that would allow brokerage firms eligible for short selling and margin trading to raise funds in two ways: (1) by lending securities to brokers wishing to engage in short selling and (2) by providing mortgages for purchasing real estate.

16.4.3 Underlying Stock Limits, Collateral Limits, and Margin Limits

"Detailed Rules for Implementation of Pilot Margin Trading and Short Selling" state that publicly traded stocks, investment funds, bonds, and other securities can be used as underlying securities in margin trading and short selling. In addition, the underlying stocks for margin trading should have more than 1 million shares or the market value in circulation should be more than 500 million RMB. The underlying stocks for short selling should have more than 200 million shares or the market value in circulation should be more than 800 million RMB; the number of shareholders should be more than 4000.

Investors can use underlying securities and other securities as collaterals to offset margin. Table 16.4 describes the detailed collateral conversion rates. During the pilot phase, the initial margin ratio is 50%, the maintenance margin ratio is 130%, the deadline to meet the margin call shall not exceed 2 days, and the additional maintenance ratio is 150%. When the margin ratio is over 300%, investors can withdraw the excess amount from the margin account or use the money to offset collateral securities until the maintenance ratio of 300% is attained.

At present, the "Securities Act" states that "securities" refer to stocks, corporate bonds, and other securities recognized by the state council according to law. Other securities mainly refer to investment fund shares, noncorporate bonds, government bonds, state bonds, etc. However, stock index futures, options, and depository receipts are not mentioned, narrowing down the scope of collaterals and underlying securities, thus reducing the trading volume. With the development of the domestic financial market and the globalization of capital investment, this will surely cause an increase in

Table 16.4 Detailed Collateral Conversion Rates

Collateral Type	Collateral	Highest Conversion Rate
A shares	SSE 180/SZSE 100 Index constituent stock	70%
	SSE 180/SZSE 100 Index constituent stock	65%
	ST/suspended stock	0%
Funds	Exchange-traded funds	90%
	Other traded funds	80%
Bonds	State bonds	95%
	Listed bonds	80%
Warrant	Warrant	0%

newly listed securities in China's stock market, and additional revisions to related laws and regulations are expected to follow.

The underlying securities released in the pilot phase are SSE and SZSE 50 Index constituent stocks. Because these stocks have a relatively larger market value, better liquidity and lower volatility, which reflects the government's attempt to try to avoid the unfavorable influence of short sales on smaller stocks due to the potential manipulation of prices.

Although the relevant laws and regulations have set a scope for margin trading and short selling securities, as well as their conversion rates, brokerage firms may have the liberty to determine the actual scope and conversion rates within the provisions. According to the customer's credit status, collateral value, contractual capacity, market situation, and other factors, brokerage firms can determine a credit line for a specific client. For brokerage firms, this flexibility requires superior market research and value assessment capability and it also reflects the market differentiation strategy to compete for market share. For now, based on margin trading and short selling information published by the six pilot dealers, the difference lies in the conversion rates. A number of conversion rates are determined in accordance with securities credit ratings and some by their own specific characteristics. However, the overall leverage of margin trading is no more than three times, and no more than two times leverage for short selling.

16.4.4 Certain Regulations of Trading: Tick Rule, Duration Limits, Amount Limits, and Naked Short Selling Limits

In "Detailed Rules for Implementation of Pilot Margin Trading and Short Selling," the SSE and SZSE stipulate that the declared selling prices for short selling securities should be higher than the last transaction prices, in essence the "tick rule." The agreed duration of a margin trade and a short selling transaction should be no more than 6 months. When the transaction balances of certain securities have reached 25% of their market capitalization, the exchange will suspend them from trading the second (next) day. When the balance drops to 20% or less, trading can be resumed on the second day. Furthermore, investors are forbidden to sell short securities that one does not own or exceed the number that one has, implying that naked short selling is restricted in China's securities market.

The uptick rule states that short selling is only allowed when stock prices are increasing, but when the market falls, short sale transactions are limited to avoid the spread of market risk caused by a wave of pessimism. This prudent consideration is important for this pilot phase; however, it also restricts price discovery from functioning perfectly. From practices in the United States,

Japan, and Taiwanese markets, restrictions on short selling prices are not applied to exchange-traded funds, warrant issuers, option market makers, and structured products issuers. This would give these institutions no limits on normal arbitrage or hedging, thus reducing the effects on the market mechanism. However, until now, regulators in China have not issued similar rules.

The duration restriction implies that investors must close one transaction within 6 months. For instance, investors should sell securities to raise money or, through direct payment, terminate the margin trading transaction within 6 months. This leads to more short-term and frequent operations, which in turn will cause large transaction costs. Amount limits and naked short selling limits are intended for better risk control and prevent stock price manipulation. In the pilot period, the SSE and the SZSE will pay close attention to the trading activities, disclose trading balances and other information on a daily basis, and detect and suppress unusual transactions when severe abnormal market transactions occur. The exchange has the power to suspend (1) certain underlying securities, (2) all margin trading, and (3) short selling market from trading to ensure stable operation of the stock market.

We believe that margin trading and short selling in the short term may exacerbate market volatility. However, in the long term, it will not increase volatility. Furthermore, it will make up the "long-only" institutional defects of China's stock market, improve the current market situation of high systemic risk, enhance the market price discovery mechanism, and be conducive to financial innovation. China's stock market will no doubt benefit from the introduction of margin trading and short selling.

On June 19, 2010, the People's Bank of China announced implementation of a flexible exchange rate policy, a move welcomed by the international community. Fluctuations of the RMB exchange rate may contribute to the free movement of capital in China's capital market and, in addition, will encourage overseas investment institutions to initiate margin trading and short selling on the Chinese stock market. The stock market reforms created by the Chinese government will no doubt develop and improve the financial environment in China.

16.5 CONCLUSION

This chapter examined the disordered warrants price market problem due to the lack of short selling and subsequently introduced the development of margin trading and short selling in China. In addition, we provided interpretations of key rules and regulations established by the reforms. We then analyzed the significance of margin trading and short selling in China's stock market and made policy recommendations for business development. Finally, we believe that short selling and margin trading will provide more completeness to Chinese markets and likely prevent abnormal high stock prices with the current reforms adopted on March 31, 2010.

ACKNOWLEDGMENTS

Professor Meng Qingbin (the corresponding author) thanks Professor Gregoriou for allowing us to revise the manuscript numerous times. This chapter was supported by funds from Renmin University of China (No. 2009030125, 2010030082). Work was supported by a National Natural Science Foundation of China grant (No. 71003012) and Fundamental Research Funds for the Central Universities in China (No. ZYGX2010X023).

REFERENCES

Anchada, C., & Hazem, D. (2003). *The world price of short selling.* Working Paper, Owen Graduate School of Management, Vanderbilt University, Nashville, TN.

Fan, W., & Yuan, X. (2010). Call warrants in China's securities market: Pricing biases and investors confusion. *New Mathematics and Natural Computation, 7*(2), 1–12.

Galai, D., & Schneller, M. (1978). Pricing of warrants and the value of the firm. *Journal of Finance, 47*(5), 80–81.

Gemmill, M., & Thomas, R. (1997). Warrants on the London Stock Exchange: Pricing biases and investor confusion. *European Finance Research, 1*(1), 31–49.

Hull, J. (2003). *Options, futures and other derivatives.* 6th Edition, Prentice Hall, New Jersey.

Kremer, L., & Roenfeldt, F. (1993). Warrant pricing: Jump-diffusion vs. Black-Scholes. *Journal of Finance and Quantitative Analysis, 28*(2), 255–272.

Kuwahara, H., & Marsh, A. (1992). The pricing of Japanese equity warrants. *Management Science, 38*(11), 1610–1641.

Liao, S., & Yang, C. (2005). Short selling, volatility and liquidity: Empirical research of Hong Kong stock market. *Management World, 12,* 6–13.

Lin, H., Zheng, Z., & Peng, B. (2005). *Stock volatility and the pricing of warrants.* Working Paper, Department of Finance, Xiamen University, China.

Luo, Y., & Liao, S. (2007). Liquidity effect of short selling: Experience evidence of Taiwan stock market. *Finance Research, 5*(2), 118–132.

Merton, R. (1973). The theory of rational option pricing. *Bell Journal of Economics and Management Science, 4*(1), 141–183.

Mikami, T. (1990). Investment strategy: Convertible bonds and equity warrants. Berkeley Program in Finance. In Asia Seminar, Tokyo.

Mitchell, T. (2007). *China warrants market is biggest in the financial times.* Retrieved from http://www.ft.com.

Nelson, D. (1991). Conditional heteroscedasticity in asset returns: A new approach. *Econometrica, 59*(2), 347–370.

Schulz, U., & Trautmann, S. (1989). *Valuation of warrants: Theory and equity tests for warrants written on German stocks*. Working Paper, University of Stuttgart, Germany.

Schulz, U., & Trautmann, S. (1994). Robustness of option-like warrant valuation. *Journal of Banking and Finance, 18*(5), 841–859.

Veld, C. (1992). *Analysis of equity warrants as investment and finance instruments*. Tilburg, Holland: Tilburg University Press.

Veld, C. (2003). *Warrant pricing: A review of empirical research. European Journal of Finance, 9*(1), 61–91.

Woolridge, J., & Dickinson, A. (1994). Short-selling and common stock price. *Financial Analysts Journal, 1*, 20–28.

Yuan, X., Fan, W., & Liu, Q. (2008). China's securities markets: Challenges, innovations, and the latest developments. *International Finance Research, 8*, 245–262.

CHAPTER 17

Impact of Short Selling on China Stock Prices

Kaiguo Zhou and Michael C.S. Wong

CONTENTS

ABSTRACT

This chapter investigates the impact of short selling on China stock prices. As short selling was approved in China on March 30, 2010, it provides a very unique data set to test the impact of short selling. With event study methodology and use of a control group for comparison, we find that stocks allowed for short selling tend to have worse performance than those not allowed for short selling. This may support the arguments that short selling provides a tool to informed investors to correct overpricing and that short selling helps mitigate the occurrence of a stock market bubble.

KEYWORDS

Abnormal return; China Securities Regulation Committee; Cumulative abnormal return; Event study methodology; Short selling; Stock market bubble.

17.1 INTRODUCTION

Before March 31, 2010, short selling had always been prohibited in the Chinese stock market. China regulators worried that short selling would exacerbate market volatility and cause severe instability to the stock market. Despite the global financial crisis of 2008/2009, the Chinese stock market remains actively traded in the postcrisis period. For instance, the Shanghai Stock Index increased around 80% per annum at the end of 2009, giving Chinese regulators reassurance to reform the stock trading environment in China.

On March 30, 2010, the China Securities Regulation Committee (CSRC) formally announced the permit of margin purchase and short selling. The CSRC approved a total of 90 selected stocks on the Shanghai and Shenzhen exchanges for a trial run of the new reform. The reform provides us with a new data set for studying the impact of short selling on stock prices. Findings show that by allowing short selling, stock prices go lower. With the presence of short selling, asset overpricing and stock market bubbles may be less pronounced.

17.2 LITERATURE REVIEW

17.2.1 Reasons for Securities Lending and Borrowing

It is generally argued that investors engage in short selling because of their belief that assets are overpriced (see, e.g., Dechow, Hutton, Meulbroek, & Sloan, 2001). Some sell short simply to hedge against the risk of their current asset holdings. Their hedges may be perfect hedges in which assets being short are the same as assets being held. In addition, some hedges may be imperfect hedges in which assets short and assets held are not the same. However, both are highly correlated. For instance, an investor may hedge his stock portfolios by selling short stock index futures. In some cases, short selling can be unrelated to any view on the market prices of the assets' short. D'Avolio (2002) provides detailed discussion on the market for securities borrowing and lending.

17.2.2 Impact of Short Selling on Asset Prices

Investors may be unwilling to sell short stocks because of tax reasons in some jurisdictions (see Fabozzi, 2004). Some may be reluctant to sell short stocks because short sellers may be required to cover their positions at short notices. All these arguments imply that short selling would have minor impacts on asset prices.

Some argue that short selling improves market efficiency because informed traders can correct mispricing easily (see Bris, Goetzman, & Zhu, 2004;

Jones & Lamont, 2002). This suggests that assets may be less volatile if short selling is allowed because mispricing will be less likely. Many studies on short selling activities find no evidence to support that short sellers are well informed (see Brent, Morse, & Stice, 1990; Figlewski, 1981; Figlewski & Webb, 1993; Woolridge & Dickinson, 1994). However, some studies find that short selling does result in excess negative returns (see Aitken, Frino, McCorry, & Swan, 1998; Angel, Christophe, & Ferri, 2003; Asquith & Meulbroek, 1996; Senchack & Starks, 1993). It seems that previous studies do not provide conclusive evidence on how short sales affect asset prices.

With the recent approval of short selling in China, this chapter is among the first batch of research examining the impact of short selling on the China stock market.

17.3 METHODOLOGY

This chapter applies a standard approach of event study as follows.

a. The relationship between returns of a stock and the market is estimated with 60-day data before the event date. The ordinary least-squares (OLS) regression method is used to estimate the beta coefficient.

b. The relationship is based on the following regression model:

$$R_{j,t-h} = a + b R_{m,t-h} + e_{j,t-h}$$

where $R_{j,t-h}$ is return of stock j at date $t-h$, $R_{m,t-h}$ is return of Shanghai Stock Index at date $t-h$, $e_{j,t-h}$ is the error term of stock j in the regression at date $t-h$, and $h = 1$ to 60.

c. After the event date (t), abnormal return (AR) of stock j at date $t+k$ is estimated by

$$AR_{j,t+k} = R_{j,t+k} - [a + b R_{m,t+k}]$$

where $k = 1$ to 20.

d. Cumulative abnormal return (CAR) of stock j at date $t+k$ (CAR$_{j,t+k}$) is obtained by

$$CAR_{j,t+k} = AR_{j,t+1} + AR_{j,t+2} + \ldots AR_{j,t+k}$$

In this chapter, day t is defined as the announcement date and start date (March 30, 2010) of short selling allowed by the CSRC. The estimation window for stocks' beta coefficients is 60 trading days before the announcement date. The time window investigated for abnormal return is 20 trading days after the announcement date, that is, from March 31, 2010, to April 28, 2010.

On calculating CAR, we consider the AR at day 1 and thereafter. This means that we count abnormal returns from March 31, 2010, onward. The market index selected for the OLS estimation is the Shanghai Composite Index, as most of the stocks allowed for short selling are from the Shanghai Stock Exchange. The Shanghai Composite Index is the most representative index for research. As for the risk-free interest rate, the yield on a 3-month China government bill is used.

17.4 SAMPLE AND HYPOTHESES

A total of 90 stocks are approved for short selling in the Chinese stock market. In general, stocks with a higher market capitalization are more active in short selling. Therefore, to mitigate bias from infrequent trading, we select the top 30 stocks in terms of market capitalization in our research. The list of sample stocks with market capitalization is displayed in Table 17.1. Market capitalization is calculated on the basis of day-end prices on May 24, 2010. These 30 stocks are grouped as the "test group."

Among the 30 stocks in the test group, 29 stocks are from the Shanghai Stock Exchange and only 1 (the code 000858) is from the Shenzhen Stock Exchange. Hence, we choose the Shanghai Composite Index as a proxy for the Chinese stock market.

In addition to the test group, we construct a control group for comparison, which includes stocks not permissible for short selling. We adopt the following criteria to construct the control group.

i. For each stock in the test group, we select a corresponding control sample from the same industry with the test sample.
ii. Market capitalization of the control sample is the closest to that of the test sample within the same industry. If one stock has been selected into the control group before, the next closest one in market capitalization is selected. The same procedure is used until one stock is selected to be a member in the control group.

The null hypothesis is: Short selling does not affect stock prices. If this hypothesis holds, we would anticipate the following empirical results:

a. Average (abnormal returns) $AR_{j,t+k}$ of the test group should be equal to 0.
b. Average (cumulative abnormal returns) $CAR_{j,t+k}$ of the test group should be equal to 0.
c. The line of the CAR of the test group should be flat.
d. There should be no difference between the test group and the control group in terms of CAR and AR.

Table 17.1 Top 30 Stocks in Market Capitalization among List of Stocks Approved for Short Selling (Test Group)

Code	Company Name	Capitalization (100 Million RMB)
601857	PetroChina	20315.33
601398	ICBC	15197.86
601939	China Construction Bank	11964.88
601988	Bank of China	10178.95
600028	Sinopec	7863.92
601628	China Life	7015.30
601088	China Shenhua	4954.50
601318	China Pingan	3584.34
601328	Bank of Communications	3410.01
600036	China Merchants Bank	3025.04
601601	China Pacific Insurance Company	1971.98
600000	SPD Bank	1743.05
600016	Mingsheng Bank	1527.19
601600	Aluminum Corporation of China	1409.25
601166	Industrial Bank	1403.00
600900	China Yangtze Power	1397.00
600030	Citic Securites	1391.74
601111	China Airlines	1379.50
601898	China Coal	1337.80
600519	Kweichow Moutai	1283.28
600019	Baoshan Iron & Steel	1175.06
600104	SAIC Motor	1144.50
601006	Daqin Railway	1135.47
601668	China State Construction Engineering	1119.00
600050	China Union	1100.10
601899	Zijin Mining	1076.06
601919	China COSCO	1053.30
601727	Shanghai Electric Group	1000.24
601390	China Railway Group	992.58
000858	Wuliangye	969.49

17.5 EMPIRICAL FINDINGS

Table 17.2 shows the AR and CAR of the test group. Clearly, its AR is negative in 15 out of the 20 days. Furthermore, its CAR is always significantly negative since the first day of short selling. The *t* statistics indicate that more than half of the CAR is significantly negative. The eventual CAR within the

Table 17.2 Abnormal Returns and Cumulative Abnormal Returns for 30 Selected Stocks Permitted for Short Selling

Day	AR (%)	t Statistic	CAR (%)	t Statistic
1	−0.1900	−1.48	−0.1900	−1.48
2	−0.1534	−1.42	−0.3433	−2.04**
3	−0.3990	−1.85*	−0.7423	−2.71**
4	−0.0523	−0.36	−0.7946	−2.57**
5	−0.0424	−0.26	−0.8370	−2.41**
6	−0.3788	−1.37	−1.2158	−2.73**
7	−0.0300	−0.24	−1.2458	−2.69**
8	−0.2947	−0.91	−1.5406	−2.72**
9	0.7812	2.54**	−0.7593	−1.18
10	−0.0430	−0.23	−0.8023	−1.20
11	0.1228	0.71	−0.6796	−0.98
12	−0.2747	−1.53	−0.9543	−1.33
13	0.1002	0.32	−0.8540	−1.09
14	−0.1331	−0.43	−0.9872	−1.17
15	−0.1995	−0.78	−1.1867	−1.35
16	−0.5945	−2.63**	−1.7812	−1.96*
17	−0.0373	−0.14	−1.8186	−1.92*
18	−0.6742	−1.73	−2.4927	−2.44**
19	0.2271	0.88	−2.2656	−2.15**
20	0.0690	0.31	−2.1966	−2.04**

*Significant at 10% level (two-tailed test).
**Significant at 5% level (two-tailed test).

test window is −2.20%, implying that in the first 20 days after short selling was allowed, the stock had a cumulative loss of 2.20%, on average. The CAR line of the test group displayed in Figure 17.1 illustrates that it is significantly downward sloping. Therefore, empirical results reject the null hypothesis that the test group has zero CAR and further support that short selling adds downward pressure on Chinese stock prices.

Next we study the AR and CAR of the control group. Results are shown in Table 17.3. There is no significantly negative CAR. Eleven out of the 20 days have positive AR and 9 days have negative AR. Only two ARs are significant but one is positive and another one is negative. For the purpose of illustration, the trend of the CAR is shown in Figure 17.2. We cannot find an apparent upward or downward sloping trend of the CAR for the control group. Furthermore, the magnitude of CAR fluctuations is relatively very low.

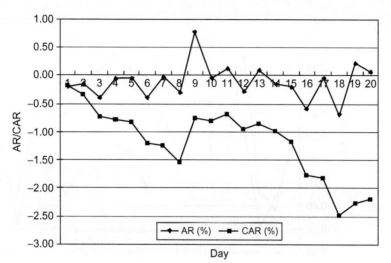

FIGURE 17.1
Trend of the cumulative abnormal return (CAR) within the test window for the 30 stocks in the test group.

Table 17.3 Abnormal Returns and Cumulative Abnormal Returns for 30 Stocks in the Control Group

Day	AR (%)	t Statistic	CAR (%)	t Statistic
1	0.0996	0.47	0.0996	0.47
2	−0.4272	−2.32**	−0.3276	−1.17
3	−0.2585	−0.99	−0.5861	−1.53
4	0.8808	3.80***	0.2947	0.66
5	0.0865	0.29	0.3813	0.71
6	0.1173	0.44	0.4986	0.84
7	−0.0074	−0.05	0.4912	0.80
8	0.0758	0.24	0.5670	0.82
9	0.3939	1.41	0.9609	1.29
10	−0.2549	−1.00	0.7060	0.90
11	0.0706	0.43	0.7766	0.97
12	0.1225	0.34	0.8991	1.02
13	−0.1414	−0.33	0.7577	0.78
14	−0.0878	−0.19	0.6699	0.62
15	−0.2827	−0.76	0.3872	0.34
16	−0.1628	−0.44	0.2244	0.19
17	0.0401	0.15	0.2645	0.21
18	−0.5394	−1.21	−0.2750	−0.21
19	0.0936	0.21	−0.1814	−0.13
20	0.2838	1.06	0.1025	0.07

**Significant at 5% level (two-tailed test).
***Significant at 1% level (two-tailed test).

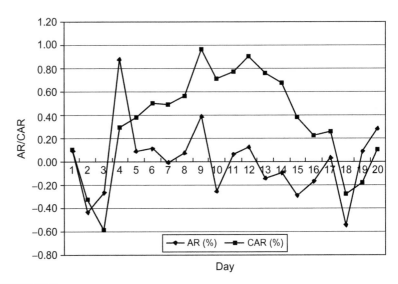

FIGURE 17.2

Trend of the cumulative abnormal return (CAR) within the test window for the 30 stocks in the control group.

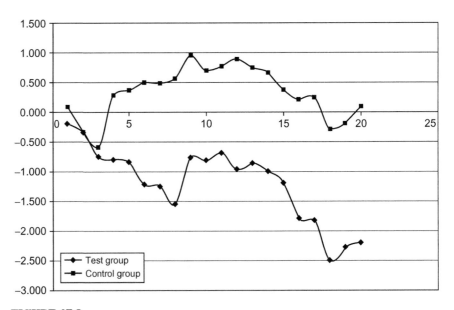

FIGURE 17.3

Trend of the cumulative abnormal return of both the test group and the control group.

Figure 17.3 compares the CAR between the test group and the control group. It is obvious that the CAR of the test group is consistently lower than that of the control group. We apply the t test to examine whether the difference in AR and CAR between the test group and the control group is significant. Table 17.4 displays the results. We find that the mean difference in AR between the test group and the control group is significantly negative at the 10% level and that the mean difference in the CAR between the two groups is significantly negative at the 1% level. Results indicate that the AR of the test group is significantly lower than that of the control group at the 10% level and that the CAR of the test group is significantly lower than that of the control group at the 1% level.

All of these empirical results reject our null hypothesis that short selling has no impact on stock prices. These findings support the premise that allowing short selling can cause stock prices to go lower.

Table 17.4 Difference in Abnormal Returns and Cumulative Abnormal Returns between Test Group and Control Group

	Difference in AR (%)	Difference in CAR (%)
Day	Test Group–Control Group	Test Group–Control Group
1	−0.2896	−0.2896
2	0.2738	−0.0157
3	−0.1405	−0.1562
4	−0.9331	−1.0893
5	−0.1289	−1.2183
6	−0.4961	−1.7144
7	−0.0226	−1.737
8	−0.3705	−2.1076
9	0.3873	−1.7202
10	0.2119	−1.5083
11	0.0522	−1.4562
12	−0.3972	−1.8534
13	0.2416	−1.6117
14	−0.0453	−1.6571
15	0.0832	−1.5739
16	−0.4317	−2.0056
17	−0.0774	−2.0831
18	−0.1348	−2.2177
19	0.1335	−2.0842
20	−0.2148	−2.2991
Average	−0.1150*	−1.5200***

*Significant at 10% level (two-tailed test).
***Significant at 1% level (two-tailed test).

17.6 CONCLUSION

This chapter investigated the impact of short selling on Chinese stocks. With short selling being approved recently in China, we anticipate that this will lead to additional research over a longer time period and provide new insight on this issue. With event study methodology and use of a control group for comparison, we find that stocks allowed for short selling tend to have worse performance than those not allowed for short selling. This tends to support the argument that short selling provides a tool for informed investors to correct overpricing. However, in the long run, short selling will likely help mitigate the occurrence of stock market bubbles in the Chinese stock market.

REFERENCES

Aitken, M. J., Frino, A., McCorry, M. S., & Swan, P. L. (1998). Short sales are almost instantaneously bad news: Evidence from the Australian stock exchange. *Journal of Finance, 53*(6), 2205–2223.

Angel, J. J., Christophe, S. E., & Ferri, M. G. (2003). A close look at short selling on NASDAQ. *Financial Analysts Journal, 59*(6), 66–74.

Asquith, P., & Moelbroek, L. (1996). *An empirical investigation of short interest.* Working Paper, Cambridge, MA: Harvard University.

Brent, A., Morse, D., & Stice, E. K. (1990). Short interest: Explanations and tests. *Journal of Financial and Quantitative Analysis, 25*(2), 273–289.

Bris, A., Goetzman, W. N., & Zhu, N. (2004). *Efficiency and the bear: Short sales and markets around the world.* Working Paper, New Haven, CT: Yale International Center for Finance.

D'Avolio, G. (2002). The market for borrowing stock. *Journal of Financial Economics, 66*(2–3), 271–306.

Dechow, P. M., Hutton, A. P., Meulbroek, L., & Sloan, R. G. (2001). Short sellers, fundamental analysis, and stock returns. *Journal of Financial Economics, 61*(1), 77–106.

Fabozzi, F. J. (2004). *Short selling: Strategies, risks and rewards.* Hoboken, NJ: John Wiley and Sons.

Figlewski, S. (1981). The informational effects of restrictions on short sales: Some empirical evidence. *Journal of Financial and Quantitative Analysis, 16*(4), 463–476.

Figlewski, S., & Webb, G. P. (1993). Options, short sales, and market completeness. *Journal of Finance, 48*(2), 761–777.

Jones, C. M., & Lamont, O. A. (2002). Short-sale constraints and stock returns. *Journal of Financial Economics, 66*(2–3), 207–240.

Senchack, A. J., & Starks, L. T. (1993). Short-sale restrictions and market reaction to short-interest announcements. *Journal of Financial and Quantitative Analysis, 28*(2), 177–194.

Woolridge, J. R., & Dickinson, A. (1994). Short selling and common stock prices. *Financial Analysts Journal, 50*(1), 20–28.

CHAPTER 18

Short Selling the Real Estate Bubble in China

Kaiguo Zhou

CONTENTS

ABSTRACT

This chapter investigates the real estate bubble in China by analyzing the recent trend of real estate prices, as well as comparing the relative financial costs of buying versus renting a house. Historical data depict that real estate prices in China have been growing rapidly in recent years and that current real estate price levels are beyond the affordability of urban residents. According to calculations, renting a home is preferred by urban residents rather than purchasing a new home. Evidence suggests an existing real estate bubble in China, and some ideas are proposed on how investors can short sell the Chinese real estate bubble.

KEYWORDS

Gross domestic product; Price index; Real estate bubble.

18.1 INTRODUCTION

The global financial crisis of 2008 is still causing ripple effects universally. Although there are many inducing factors contributing to the financial crisis, emergence of the subprime loan crisis in the United States in 2007 was due to the real estate bubble. For example, during the Asian financial crisis of 1997, Japan also experienced a real estate bubble.

According to Herring and Wachter (2002), real estate bubbles may induce financial crisis. The authors proposed a theoretical structure of interactions linking the real estate market and the behavior of banks. Banks, which own real estate indirectly through loans, play a significant role in the real estate market. Increases in real estate prices will increase the economic value of bank capital and also

> the value of loans collateralized by real estate. This increase may lead to a decline in the perceived risk of real estate lending. Consequently, an increase in real estate prices will increase the supply of credit to the real estate industry, which in turn, will lead to further increases in real estate prices (Herring & Wachter, 2002, p. 2).

A decline in real estate prices may diminish bank capital by decreasing the value of real estate assets owned by banks. A drop of this type may possibly shrink the value of bank loans collateralized by real estate, which in turn can result in additional defaults, thereby reducing the bank's capital. These factors will likely decrease the credit supply to the real estate industry. Furthermore, supervisors and regulators could respond to the ensuing deterioration of the capital positions of banks by augmenting capital requirements. Such a measure will further reduce the supply of credit to the real estate industry and place additional pressure on real estate prices (Herring & Wachter, 2002).

18.2 IS THERE A BUBBLE IN CHINA'S REAL ESTATE MARKET?

There is a consensus that speculation can fuel a real estate boom, which ultimately induces a real estate bubble (see Case & Shiller, 2003; Malpezzi & Wachter, 2002). In an early study, Carey (1990) developed a model of land prices explaining the role of optimists in real estate bubbles in a market with no short sales and a fixed land supply. Similarly, Krugman (1998) constructs a model based on moral hazard that produces comparable results. As long as fund providers evaluate land and homes at market prices when determining their values, the upward trend in house prices can continue. However, once buyers realize that housing prices are very high and exceed market value, sales will not continue to increase and consequently the real estate bubble will burst. In recent years, speculation has played an important role in development of the housing market in China. The direct impact of speculation has caused housing prices to increase rapidly since 2007. Although the gross domestic product (GDP) per capita and disposable income per capita are both increasing in China, the growth rate of housing prices is far greater than the GDP and disposable income. A majority of urban residents in China cannot afford a home or even a down payment in a city where they live and work according to the current level of their personal income.

Historical data on the price index of real estate sales are collected from the National Bureau of Statistics of China. The consumer price index and disposable income data are obtained from China's Center for Economic Research database developed by SinoFin Information Services. Figure 18.1 displays the monthly price index of real estate sales, which are calculated from the housing prices of 70 large and medium cities in China. Data cover the period from January 2007 through April 2010, a total of 40 months. The index is on a month-to-month basis and we can observe the continuous change of real estate prices. From Figure 18.1 we find that the trend of Chinese real estate price changes within this period can be divided into three ranges. The first range starts in January 2007 and ends in September 2007. During this period, real estate prices were growing rapidly with the index increasing from 100.6 in January 2007 to a peak of 101.7 in September 2007. Thereafter, the growth rate had declined slowly until November 2008 when the index reached its lowest point of 99.5, forming the second range. The third range starts in December 2008 and continues until April 2010, which is the second wave of rapid growth of real estate prices in China.

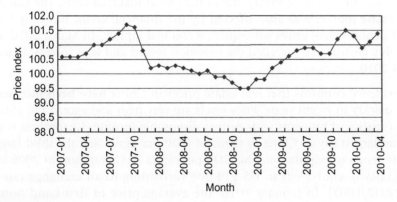

FIGURE 18.1
Monthly price index of real estate sales on a month-to-month basis.

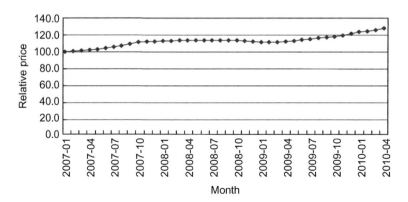

FIGURE 18.2
Relative price level of each month, with January 2007 as the basis month.

In order to investigate the price changes directly, we calculate the change in relative price level according to the monthly price index, with January 2007 as the basis month (Figure 18.2). First, during the entire period there is a long upward trend in the price level. Using a basis level of 100, the highest price level is 125.3, implying that average prices increased by 25.3% in 39 months. The equivalent annualized growth rate was 7.2%, which is significantly higher than the average inflation rate.[1] Second, in only 7 of the 40 months the price level decreased slightly. In a majority of the months, the price level was higher than that of the previous month.

Figure 18.3 displays the monthly price index of real estate sales with the index compared during the same period of the prior year with the price index increasing in most months. Of the 40 months, in only 6 consecutive months (from December 2008 to May 2009) did the price index display values less than 100, probably due to the global financial crisis. The Chinese real estate market was also affected by the financial crisis, but only for a short period where prices subsequently climbed rapidly. In March 2010, the monthly growth rate exceeded the historical record and kept increasing until April 2010.

All evidence confirms that real estate prices in China have been increasing very quickly in recent years. Price levels are very high and exceed the affordable capacity of residents with current disposable income. Guangzhou is the second largest city in China in terms of GDP per capita and the third largest city in terms of population. The GDP per capita in Guangzhou in 2009 was 88,834RMB, equivalent to US $13,006 (according to an exchange rate of 6.83RMB/USD). In January 2010, the average price of first-hand homes

---

[1] The inflation rate is 4.8 and 5.9% in 2007 and 2008, respectively.

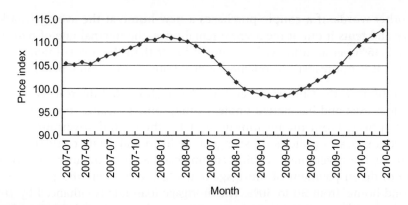

FIGURE 18.3
Monthly price index of real estate sales compared with the same period of the previous year.

(new homes) in the urban area of Guangzhou was 11,412RMB per square meter. In 2009, the disposable income per capita in Guangzhou was 27,610RMB, suggesting that if a couple uses all of its disposable income to purchase a home of 90 square meters in Guangzhou, it will cost them an equivalent of 19 years of salary (ignoring the time value of money). Thus, the current real estate price level is beyond the affordability of urban residents in China.

In order to prove that current real estate prices are very high, we perform a simple calculation. Assuming a couple purchases a home of 90 square meters with a price of 11,412RMB per square meter, they need to pay about 1.03 million RMB; however, if they rent their home, the rental price per month is 2500RMB according to current average rental prices. If we assume an annual interest rate is 5% for long-term deposits of 50 years,[2] then depositing that amount of money into a bank account, the couple can earn 4280RMB in interest. Oddly enough, the couple would never be paid back if they purchased the new home and rented it out when the time value of money is factored in. In other words, if a couple rents a new home for 70 years,[3] they must receive at least 4414RMB per month in order to break even. If the couple borrows money from a bank using a mortgage loan, the loan rate would be higher than the deposit rate. Consequently, the couple needs to receive even more than that amount in order to break even.

---

[2] Actually, we cannot observe the interest rate for such a long term. Instead, the longest term for deposits is 5 years with a corresponding rate of 3.60%. The yield on a 30-year government bond in China is 4.01%. Accordingly, it is assumed that the 50-year interest rate is 5% per annum. Even if the interest rate is assumed to be 4% per annum, the monthly interest on that amount of money is 3424RMB, much higher than the monthly rent price.

[3] The land usage period in China is 70 years.

In other words, if a couple purchases a new home at the average market price and rents it out at the average rental price, the internal rate of return is only 2.36% per annum, which is much lower than the 5-year interest rate. Hence, it is not realistic to purchase a new home—it is simply better to rent.

Up until now, the Chinese government has realized that the real estate bubble does exist and has started implementing some measures to suppress real estate prices. From the beginning of 2010, the central government completed a series of policies on stringent credit to real estate companies. For example, the government requires commercial banks to enhance the proportion of down payment of mortgage loans to a borrower who purchases a second home, from 30 to 50%. The mortgage loan rate is enhanced by 10% for the purchase of a second house. The purchase of a third house for a family is restricted in many cities. The required reserve ratio of commercial banks was also enhanced six times within 1 year (2010; effective dates are January 18, February 25, May 10, November 16, November 29, and December 20, respectively). Enhancement of the reserve ratio sent a very strong signal, suggesting that the government will eventually lower the high real estate prices.

Another measure taken by the government is house property tax levy. Since January 2011, two cities (Shanghai and Chongqing) have enforced the property tax levy. The direct purpose of this levy is to increase the cost of holding homes in order to suppress speculation in the real estate market. In other words, possessing several homes by speculators ever since the property tax levy was enforced makes the cost of owning more homes in inventory higher. Three months after the levy enforcement, the effect is significant. For example, real estate prices in Chongqing were reduced by 10% in the first quarter of 2011 and it is expected that the property tax levy will be extended to the entire country.

In addition, loans from commercial banks have been reduced significantly. In the author's point of view, the current real estate bubble will not last very long with real estate prices decreasing during 2011. If real estate prices still stay at a high level, or even increase, then speculators will not stay in the real estate market with the expectation that real estate prices will drop. The purpose of the aforementioned policies is to eliminate speculation and drive real estate prices down to a reasonable level. If the aforementioned policies are not met with success, then the Chinese government will issue more stringent polices. For example, the government may require real estate companies to maintain a higher proportion of their own capital. The government may call back vacant land sold to real estate firms after a certain period. According to the author's forecast, real estate prices will drop dramatically during the fourth quarter of 2011; by then, the real estate bubble will have contracted. In fact, real estate prices started dropping in several big cities during the second quarter of 2011. According to the latest policy of the central bank, the commercial banks' loan quota for real estate firms has been further shrunk since the second quarter of 2011. Therefore, it is foreseeable that real estate prices will be dropping gradually as of the third quarter of 2011.

18.3 HOW TO SHORT SELL THE REAL ESTATE BUBBLE

Short selling stocks in China started on March 31, 2010. Investors can now short sell stocks related to China's real estate industry. Currently, there are 113 real estate companies listed on the Shenzhen and Shanghai Stock Exchanges. Short selling real estate stocks directly is feasible; however, only a small part of stocks in China are selected by the government to be short sold. If investors believe that some stocks are overpriced and are not on the short selling list, then two choices exist. One is to hold a short position in index futures using the Shanghai and Shenzhen 300 index futures contract; the other is to short sell stocks that have a high positive correlation to real estate stocks. In the commodities market, there are opportunities for investors to short sell China's real estate bubble. Given that the real estate industry in China will continue in a downward channel until the near future, the demand for commodities such as steel, cement, and wood will decrease significantly. Investors may choose to short sell such kinds of commodities in the international market. In addition, the finance industry is closely related to the real estate industry, as major sources of funding for real estate companies are Chinese commercial banks. Moreover, because the decrease of housing prices will deteriorate the value of banks' assets, it would be profitable to also short sell bank stocks.

Overseas investors are not allowed to buy and sell Chinese stocks directly except qualified foreign institutional investors (QFII).[4] Instead, foreign investors have three alternative channels to short sell Chinese real estate. One of them is to simply short sell stocks on the Hong Kong stock market that are closely related to Chinese real estate firms, and the other is to short sell Chinese companies listed both in mainland China and in Hong Kong (called "A+H shares"). The other channel is to short sell American depositary receipts issued by mainland Chinese and Hong Kong firms in the U.S. market.

---

[4] QFII was set up in 2002 to permit licensed foreign investors to purchase and sell stocks (A shares) denominated in Yuan on the Shanghai and Shenzen stock markets. Under this program, approximately 80 qualified investors were sanctioned in early 2009.

18.4 CONCLUSION

China is an emerging market in terms of the real estate market since the reform on resident housing in urban areas was initiated in the late 1980s. Historical data depict a picture that real estate prices in China have been growing rapidly in recent years whereby the current real estate price level is beyond the affordability of urban residents. Compared with current rental price levels, purchasing a home is not a reasonable choice, whereas renting a home is preferred by urban residents. Evidence suggests a current real estate bubble in China. Finally, some suggestions on how to short sell the Chinese real estate bubble are provided for investors.

In June 2010, the People's Bank of China (the Central Bank of China) announced that flexibility of the renminbi exchange rate will be enhanced further, and it is anticipated that the range of daily changes in the renminbi exchange rate will be wider in the future; however, the process will be slow. It seems that expectation on the appreciation of renminbi may support the high price on real estate. However, it does not play an important role in determination of the future trend of real estate prices in China.

REFERENCES

Carey, M. S. (1990). Feeding the fad: The Federal Land Banks, land market efficiency, and the farm credit crisis. Ph.D. Dissertation. Berkeley, CA: University of California at Berkeley.

Case, K. E., & Shiller, R. J. (2003). Is there a bubble in the housing market? *Brookings Papers on Economic Activity, 2003*(3), 299–342.

Herring, R., & Wachter, S. (2002). Bubbles in real estate markets. Wharton Real Estate Center Working Paper, Philadelphia, PA: University of Pennsylvania.

Krugman, P. (1998). What happened to Asia? MIT Working Paper, Cambridge, MA.

Malpezzi, S., & Wachter, S. (2002). The role of speculation in real estate cycles. Wharton Real Estate Center Working Paper, Philadelphia, PA: University of Pennsylvania.

CHAPTER 19

Impact of Macroeconomic Indicators on Short Selling: Evidence from the Tokyo Stock Exchange

M. Nihat Solakoglu and Mehmet Orhan

CONTENTS

ABSTRACT

This study is an attempt to analyze the behavior of short selling due to changes in main macroeconomic indicators of output, interest rate (in terms of bond yields), and exchange rate, as well as the stock exchange index, namely the Nikkei 225. In addition, this chapter examines the existence of cointegration between short selling volume and the Nikkei 225 Index to investigate the permanent relation between the two. We have intentionally used monthly Japanese data from November 2005 to October 2009 to encompass the global financial crisis and differenced the series to attain stationarity. Our Granger test of causality concluded a bidirectional relation between short selling and the Nikkei 225. We could not verify causality between short selling and gross domestic product, as well as the exchange rate, but there is causality from the exchange rate to short selling.

KEYWORDS

Augmented Dickey–Fuller test; Bond yield; Consumer price index; Exchange rate; Granger test; Gross domestic product; Interest rate; Macroeconomic indicators; Nikkei 225 Index; Output.

19.1 INTRODUCTION

Short selling has received a lot of attention in the last decade by academicians, regulators, and investors. While some academicians argue that short selling leads to higher market efficiency, others argue that short sellers are investors with private information that aim to profit at the expense of naïve investors. If the second view is correct, then we should also expect to observe higher volatility in the markets due to short selling. Given the varying degrees of restrictions imposed on short selling in major markets starting in 2008 due to the global crisis, we can assume that regulators prefer to accept the second view over the first. For instance, in 2008, a wave of restrictions on short selling, some being temporary, was announced for more than 20 major markets.[1] In particular, for Japan, short sales of all stocks were prohibited until March 2009 and naked short selling was prohibited. Moreover, the threshold for disclosure obligation was set to 0.25% or more of outstanding stocks.[2]

Is there a strong relationship between short selling and abnormal returns? In other words, can short sellers predict a decline in share prices so that they can profit by short selling? Some studies' findings indicate that traders cannot profit through short selling strategies. For instance, Figlewski and Webb (1993) find no evidence between short selling and abnormal returns. Similarly, Brent, Morse, and Stice (1990) and Woolridge and Dickinson (1994) document no evidence between short selling and abnormal returns. Using the TA100 index of the Tel Aviv Stock Exchange, Cohen (2010) suggests that short sellers cannot outperform the market and hence contribute to market efficiency in the long run. However, Asquith and Meulbroek (1996) focus on firms with large short positions to examine whether short sellers are able to profit. Their finding shows a strong and consistent relationship between short positions and abnormal returns indicating the ability of firms with large short positions to profit. This should not be surprising, as firms with large short positions are expected to be more informed or

---

[1] Introduction of new regulations for short selling in the United States by the SEC in 2005, short-term ban of short selling in the United States in 2008, in the United Kingdom, and total ban in Australia can be used to show how regulators view short selling.

[2] For details, please see http://www.fsa.go.jp/en/news/2008/20081027-2.html page from Financial Services Agency of Japan.

have access to private information. This finding is consistent with Boehmer, Jones, and Zhang (2008) and Blau, Van Ness, and Van Ness (2010) as they both find evidence that traders with larger short sales are more informed than traders with smaller short sales. Blau and associates (2010) also document that, with greater market efficiency, short sellers will have difficulty in predicting future negative returns correctly using NASDAQ and NYSE short selling data.[3]

For the Australian Stock Exchange, Aitken, Frino, McCorry, and Swan (1998) provide evidence that short sales result in bad news for the market. Christophe, Ferri, and Angel (2004) and Christophe, Ferri, and Hsieh (2010) document that the majority of short sellers are informed traders and are able to target stocks with overvalued prices or potential downgrades. Moreover, Christophe and colleagues (2004) find some evidence of a higher level of short selling for firms with a negative earnings announcement. The Christophe and colleagues (2010) study suggests a similar finding for analysts' downgrade decisions. Both findings imply that short sellers are informed traders.

Prior studies assume short sellers either as informed traders or uninformed hedgers/speculators.[4] For uninformed traders, there should not be a consistent and significant relationship between short selling and abnormal returns. If short sellers are informed traders, then they should be able to select overpriced stocks or use the same set of information as stock analysts to come up with the same downgrade decision. An alternative could be acquisition of private information of a stock that is not publicly available. For example, short sellers may receive tips from a brokerage firm for a potential downgrade of a stock and then utilize this information to profit. The findings of Christophe and colleagues (2010) show some evidence that short sellers receive some private information, whereas Diether, Lee, and Werner (2007) argue that the tipping hypothesis[5] is highly unlikely to occur as there are strict regulations levied on corporate insiders. This is true with approximately 75% of short sellers being institutional investors in the United States (as implied by Boehmer & colleagues, 2008).

A third alternative is short sellers acting as voluntary market makers, as discussed by Diether and colleagues (2007) and Ko and Lim (2006). An exception to this alternative is short sellers in Japan. Approximately 10% of short sellers in Japan are exchange member firms, while the rest include customers such as foreigner investors, corporations, and individual investors, which consist of

---

[3] Specifically, they argue that NYSE is more efficient compared to NASDAQ and hence short selling is more predictive picking out stocks with a potential decline on NASDAQ than NYSE.

[4] Some informed traders will not participate actively in short selling due to legal or regulatory constraints (Christophe & colleagues, 2010).

[5] Prereleasing research to certain preferred investors before it is distributed widely.

the majority. As a result, it can be argued that short sellers in Japan do not have private information and have no obligation to provide market liquidity.[6] However, Ko and Lim (2006) document that a positive relationship exists between short interest and abnormal return; hence, even in the absence of market makers short sellers' actions provide liquidity to the markets.

In this study, we intend to analyze short selling in Japan using selected macroeconomic indicators of output, interest rate, and exchange rate. As indicated by Ko and Lim (2006), short sellers in Japan are mostly individual customers with no private information and hence we expect them to pay close attention to economic fundamentals as well as firm-related news. The sample we use includes monthly data of short selling volume from the Tokyo Stock Exchange and macroeconomic data including the Nikkei 225 Index for the period from November 1, 2005, to September 30, 2009. Our period of study is selected intentionally to encompass the global financial crisis.

After the introduction, the rest of the study is organized as follows: Section 19.2 reviews briefly the Japanese macroeconomic indicators. Section 19.3 is retained to data and methodology, where we start with unit root tests of variables. Given that we are working with time series data, we examine the stationarity of all the series at the beginning of the period using the augmented Dickey–Fuller test. We then investigate the existence and direction of causality, with the so-called Granger causality test, and the cointegrating relation between short selling volume and the Nikkei 225 Index.

19.2 DATA AND BRIEF OVERVIEW OF JAPANESE MACROECONOMIC INDICATORS

Monthly short selling figures come from the archives of the Tokyo Stock Exchange.[7] The data set is monthly and covers November 1, 2005, through September 30, 2009. All remaining macroeconomic data series are from Nikkei (www.Nikkei.com).

Figure 19.1 plots the real gross domestic product (GDP) index. The plot reveals that the Japanese economy was in recession during our sample period. The last decade of the Japanese economy was associated with a low growth rate, failure in attaining full employment, and persistent deflation. Export-led growth, existing before 2007, came to a standstill in 2008. In addition, the recession intensified as a consequence of the global financial crisis with less expectation for constant growth in the coming years due to an added uncertainty in forecasts. The continued quantitative easing of the

---

[6] In that case, we should assume that the "tipping hypothesis" does not hold in Japan.
[7] http://www.tse.or.jp/english.

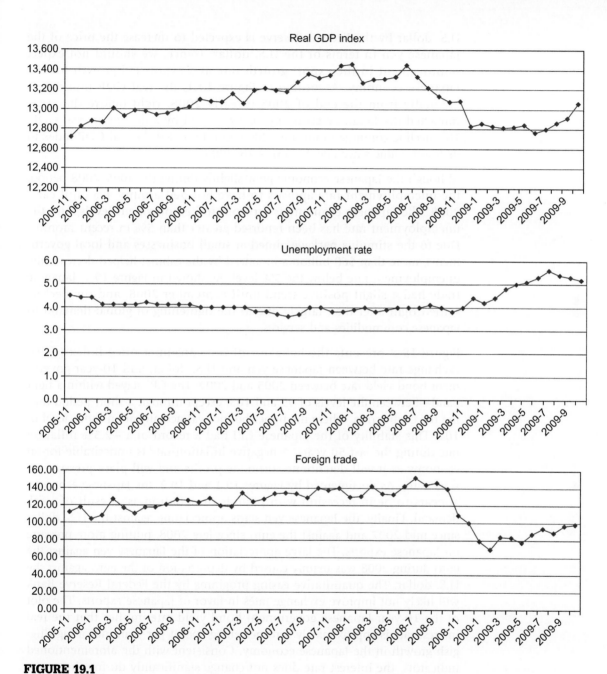

FIGURE 19.1

Main macroeconomic indicators in the Japanese economy.

U.S. dollar by the Federal Reserve is expected to increase the price of the Japanese yen in terms of the U.S. dollar. Hence, we should not expect improvement in the export growth rate and export-led growth for the Japanese economy. According to Figure 19.1, the real GDP index grew gradually from the end of 2005 to early 2008, right before the crisis impacted the Japanese economy, as evidenced by a decline in real GDP. This decline continued until mid-2009 and decreased the real GDP index to its lowest value since late 2005 or early 2006.

Although the Japanese economy grew slightly during the 2005–2008 period, the unemployment rate appears to have hovered around 4% until early 2008. The Japanese economy is far from full employment levels, and the unemployment rate has been reported greater than 5% in recent months. Due to the stimulus package aimed at small businesses and local governments, more than $60 billion announced by the cabinet helped decrease the unemployment rate below the 5% level. As shown in Figure 19.1, Japanese trade had a slight positive trend until September 2008, and the decline started right after that, largely due to the tightening of global demand to Japanese commodities and services.

Figure 19.2 presents the behavior of the consumer price index (CPI), exchange rate between Japanese yen and U.S. dollar, and 10-year government bond yield rate between 2005 and 2009. The CPI stayed within a tight band—between the levels of 99 and 103, except through a short period during the credit crisis, where the upper bound was actually at an index level of 101. This stability of the Japanese CPI had a record of a −2.5% inflation rate during the last 50 years. A negative inflation rate is undesirable for an economy as it will deteriorate corporate profits and will place pressure on wage rates. As documented by Figures 19.1 and 19.2, the Japanese economy appears to be in recession with periods of deflation as a result of weak demand. Finally, the Japanese yen starts appreciating against the U.S. dollar since mid-2007 and against the euro since late 2008, putting more pressure on Japanese exports. The large appreciation of the Japanese yen against the euro during 2008 was mainly caused by depreciation of the euro against the U.S. dollar. The quantitative easing programs by the Federal Reserve Bank will likely not improve exchange rates in favor of Japanese exports. The plot of the 10-year Japanese government bond yield rate implies that the real interest rate is approximately zero percentage point per year, indicating sluggish growth in the Japanese economy. Consistent with the aforementioned indicators, the interest rate does not change significantly during the examined period, and it was never reported more than 0.10% in 2010.

Figure 19.3 plots total volume of short selling volume and the Nikkei 225 Index. The movement of both variables over time appears similar, with the

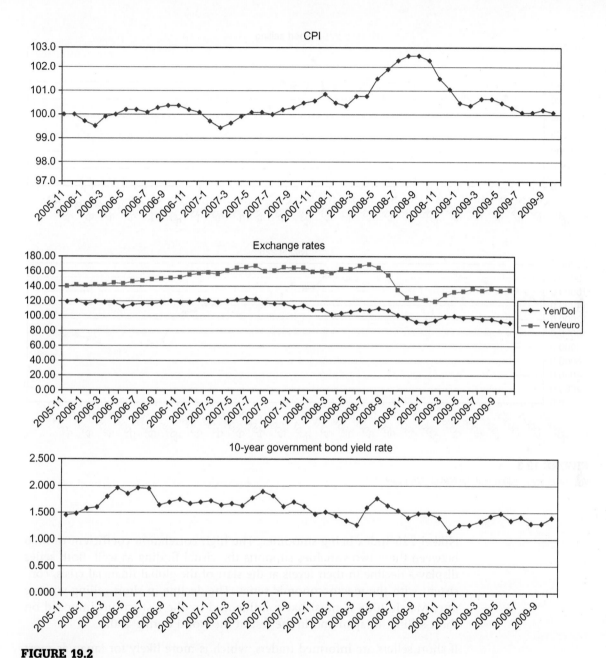

FIGURE 19.2

Consumer price index, exchange rate, and government bond yield.

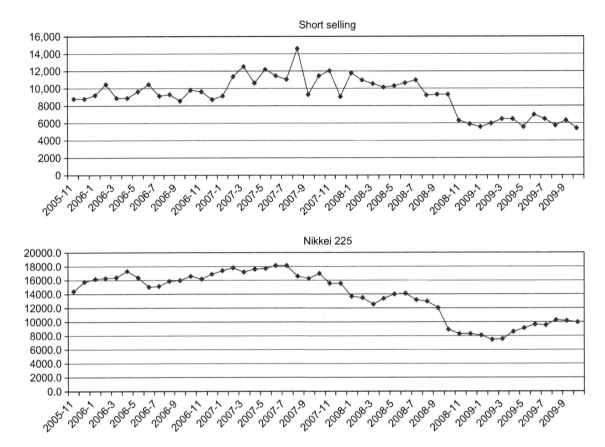

FIGURE 19.3
Volume of short selling and the Nikkei 225 Index.

Nikkei 225 Index being smoother. The high correlation coefficient of 0.76 between these two variables supports the visual finding as well. Both series display a decline in their levels at the start of the global financial crisis, consistent with the macroeconomic series. The decline in short selling volume after March 2008 is most likely influenced by the restrictions imposed on short selling in Japan and in the rest of the world during 2008.

If short sellers are informed traders, which is more likely for Japan as most short sellers are customers and not exchange member firms (Ko & Lim, 2006), they should follow macroeconomic series closely as well as firm-specific information to predict a decline in share prices. For our analysis, we consider the Nikkei 225 Index, the government bond yield rate, foreign exchange rates, and GDP as the relevant macro series.

19.3 DATA AND METHODOLOGY

Monthly short selling values are obtained from the archives of the Tokyo Stock Exchange[8] from November 2005 to September 2009. All macroeconomic data and stock index series are obtained from the Nikkei Web page (www.Nikkei.com).

19.3.1 Granger Causality between Macroeconomic Variables and Short Selling

We first check for the stationarity of the time series to avoid spurious regression. Dickey and Fuller (1979) designed a model to check for the existence of a unit root and subsequently use an improved model called the "augmented Dickey–Fuller (ADF) test" (Dickey & Fuller, 1981).

We make use of the ADF test, which suggests the following model:

$$\Delta y_t = \alpha + \beta t + \lambda y_{t-1} + \delta_1 \Delta y_{t-1} + \delta_2 \Delta y_{t-2} + \cdots + \delta_p \Delta y_{t-p} + \varepsilon_t \qquad (19.1)$$

In this model, β is the coefficient of time to account for trend and p is the lag order of the autoregressive process. The test checks whether $\lambda = 0$ or not, with the help of critical values, listed specifically for this test. We use E-Views software to execute the ADF test and report the results for both levels and first differences of the series in Table 19.1. According to the test results, all series, with the exception of "bond yields," have unit roots and are not stationary at levels, but the first differences of all series are stationary. Test results, as shown in Table 19.1, show explicitly that the series under examination have changing mean and/or autocorrelation over time. Although it is not necessary to attain stationarity, we take the difference of the "bond yields," as we would like to have all variables in differences. Table 19.1 indicates that all variables are stationary at their first differences.

Table 19.1 Unit Root Test Results at Levels, H_o Claims "No Unit Root"

Variable	Levels		First Differences	
	t Stat.[a]	Prob.	t Stat.[a]	Prob.
Short selling	−1.304	0.872	−8.645	0.0000
Nikkei 225	−2.27	0.441	−5.715	0.0001
GDP	−1.971	0.602	−7.039	0.0000
Bond yield	−3.702	0.032	−5.855	0.0001
Exchange rate (yen/dollar)	−2.195	0.481	−6.088	0.0000

[a]1, 5, and 10% critical values are −4.176, −3.513, and −3.187, respectively.

[8] http://www.tse.or.jp/english.

One approach in examining the relationship between interacting variables is to look at the causality among these variables. Granger (1969) designed a statistical test, called the "Granger causality test," using a series of t tests and F tests to determine whether one time series is useful in predicting another time series. The Granger causality test does not necessarily address the cause-and-effect relation between variables as it may not indicate true causality.[9] We assume that x_t and y_t are two stationary series; to determine whether x_t Granger causes y_t, first y_t is autoregressed on itself and the proper lag length is determined. In the next step the augmented autoregression of

$$y_t = \alpha_0 + \sum_{i=1,\dots,p} \alpha_i y_{t-i} + \sum_{j=1,\dots,q} \beta_j x_{t-j} + \varepsilon_t \tag{19.2}$$

is estimated. The null hypothesis of "no Granger causality" is tested with a version of the F test, which checks whether all coefficients of x_{t-j}, namely β_{t-j}, are equal to 0. If all β_{t-j} are found to be equal to 0, then x_{t-j} does not precede y_{t-j}.

Table 19.2 presents results for the causality test. To perform the test, we focus on the short selling volume and the macroeconomic variables considered as part of the short sellers' information set.

The null hypothesis of "no Granger causality" is rejected highly significantly for the relationship between the short selling volume and the Nikkei 225 Index with a p value of 0.242%. However, the causality test reveals causality from the short selling volume and the Nikkei 225 Index with a lower significance level of 1.163%. Thus, test results document bidirectional causality of Granger type between the Nikkei 225 Index and the short selling volume. We find no indication of causality between short selling volume and GDP, and the same is true for the bond yield return.

Table 19.2 Granger Causality Test Results of Variables with First Differences

Null Hypothesis	F Stat.	Prob.
Nikkei does not Granger cause short selling	5.77264	0.00242
Short selling does not Granger cause Nikkei	4.21475	0.01163
GDP does not Granger cause short selling	0.77179	0.51720
Short selling does not Granger cause GDP	1.10629	0.35886
Bond yield does not Granger cause short selling	1.06901	0.37403
Short selling does not Granger cause bond yield	1.00406	0.40187
Exchange rate does not Granger cause short selling	2.77537	0.05484
Short selling does not Granger cause exchange rate	1.70138	0.18353

[9] For example, if there is a third series that causes the first and second series to change, it is possible to find a casuality between the first and second series.

Although GDP is the most widely used indicator for the economic performance of a country, it does not appear as a variable that leads to short selling. Given the low levels of GDP growth rates in Japan and no big surprises for expected changes in the past for the Japanese economy, this should not be surprising. Finally, we find empirical evidence that documents causality from exchange rates and short selling volume.

19.3.2 Cointegration between Short Selling Volume and the Nikkei 225 Index

Following Table 19.3 results, we investigate the existence of a permanent relationship between short selling volume and the Nikkei 225 Index in this part of the study. Cointegration between variables is a convenient way to propose the long-run relationship between them. If there is a list of series, say $Y_t = (Y_{1t}, Y_{2t}, ..., Y_{nt})$, then this set of series is called "cointegrated" if coefficients exist, $\beta = (\beta_1, \beta_2, ..., \beta_n)$, to satisfy $\beta_1 Y_{1t} + \beta_2 Y_{2t} + \cdots + \beta_n Y_{nt} \sim I(0)$, where $I(0)$ denotes stationarity of the series. If cointegration is proven for a series, then there is a long run equilibrium, and occasional deviations from the streamline will be removed to restore the equilibrium.

We look for a cointegration relationship between short selling volume and the Nikkei 225 Index with the assumption of a linear deterministic trend. Cointegration test results are reported in Table 19.3. Findings indicate that

Table 19.3 Cointegration between Short Selling Volume and Nikkei 225 Index, Test Results

Trace Test				
Hypothesized		**Trace**	**5%**	**1%**
No. of CE(s)	Eigenvalue	Statistic	Critical value	Critical value
None	0.165754	8.807615	15.41	20.04
At most 1	0.010191	0.471180	3.76	6.65
Maximum Eigenvalue Test				
Hypothesized		**Maximum Eigen**	**5%**	**1%**
No. of CE(s)	Eigenvalue	Statistic	Critical value	Critical value
None	0.165754	8.336435	14.07	18.63
At most 1	0.010191	0.471180	3.76	6.65
Normalized Cointegrating Coefficients (Standard Error in Parentheses)				
Nikkei	Short sell			
1.000000	−1.650126			
	(0.30444)			

the null hypothesis of "at most 1 cointegration relation" is not rejected according to the values of both trace and maximum eigenvalue statistics. This implies that short selling volume and the Nikkei 225 Index have a permanent, long run relationship for the Japanese economy during the investigation period. Table 19.3 displays normalized cointegration coefficients as well as standard errors in the bottom rows.

19.4 CONCLUSION

We examined Japanese financial markets with monthly data from November 2005 to October 2009 to document if a causality relation exists between short selling volume and macroeconomic variables, such as GDP, bond yield, and exchange rate, as well as the Nikkei 225 Index. Given the characteristics of Japanese short sellers, we expect a causal relationship between macroeconomic variables and short selling volume, which indicates that Japanese short sellers are informed traders. Based on this finding, we can also assume indirectly that the tipping hypothesis does not apply to Japanese short sellers. In addition, we also investigated the existence of cointegration between short selling volume and the Nikkei 225 Index to determine whether a long run relationship exists between the two.

We found that the short selling volume, the Nikkei 225 Index, and the exchange rate have unit roots and are thus nonstationary; however, the bond yield rate is stationary. We achieved stationarity of the series at their first differences. Using the Granger causality test, we also showed bidirectional causality between short selling volume and the Nikkei 225 Index. However, there is no causality between short selling volume and GDP, as well as bond yield rate. However, our findings document that exchange rate Granger causes a short selling volume, but short selling volume does not Granger cause exchange rate. These findings indicate that the short sellers' information set contains the Nikkei 225 Index and exchange rate movements, but not macro fundamentals. Our results also document the permanent long run relationship between short selling volume and the Nikkei 225 Index.

We documented a cointegration relationship between short selling volume and the Nikkei 225 Index. Further research in this direction may continue with construction of an error correction mechanism to explore the duration of the regression toward the mean over the long run in case of a shock to the economy.

Money managers dealing with the Japanese market should concentrate on the two findings of this study. First, short sellers are informed traders and their information set does not include private information. Second, the information set contains information mostly from stock and currency markets and does not seem to be influenced by economic fundamentals. Hence, the prediction of stock price declines, instead of relying on tips, using the aforementioned information set with firm level information, may be a profitable strategy by short selling in the Japanese market.

DATA APPENDIX

	Real GDP Index	Unemp. Rate (%)	Trade	CPI	Nikkei 225	Yen/$	Yen/€	Gov. Bond Yield	Short Selling Total
2005-11	12,711	4.5	112.33	100.0	14368.1	118.41	139.54	1.445	8795
2005-12	12,825	4.4	117.66	100.0	15650.8	118.64	140.68	1.470	8830
2006-1	12,877	4.4	104.02	99.7	16085.5	115.45	139.99	1.560	9232
2006-2	12,865	4.1	107.89	99.5	16187.6	117.89	140.77	1.585	10,399
2006-3	13,006	4.1	126.89	99.9	16311.5	117.31	140.98	1.770	8902
2006-4	12,928	4.1	116.47	100.0	17233.0	117.11	143.56	1.920	8889
2006-5	12,984	4.1	110.51	100.2	16322.2	111.51	142.54	1.830	9611
2006-6	12,975	4.2	117.42	100.2	14990.3	114.53	145.14	1.920	10,386
2006-7	12,943	4.1	117.90	100.1	15147.6	115.67	146.72	1.915	9103
2006-8	12,958	4.1	120.89	100.3	15786.8	115.88	148.47	1.620	9244
2006-9	12,996	4.1	126.50	100.4	15934.1	117.01	149.11	1.670	8583
2006-10	13,017	4.1	125.82	100.4	16519.4	118.66	149.66	1.720	9722
2006-11	13,093	4.0	123.51	100.2	16101.1	117.35	151.13	1.645	9578
2006-12	13,072	4.0	128.09	100.1	16790.2	117.30	154.92	1.675	8716
2007-1	13,067	4.0	119.04	99.7	17286.3	120.58	156.56	1.695	9149
2007-2	13,149	4.0	118.71	99.4	17741.2	120.45	157.60	1.630	11,242
2007-3	13,053	4.0	134.23	99.6	17128.4	117.28	155.29	1.650	12,381
2007-4	13,187	3.8	123.64	99.9	17469.8	118.83	160.36	1.615	10,552
2007-5	13,211	3.8	127.40	100.1	17595.1	120.73	163.19	1.745	12,077
2007-6	13,185	3.7	133.26	100.1	18001.4	122.62	164.48	1.865	11,360
2007-7	13,175	3.6	134.44	100.0	17974.8	121.59	166.68	1.790	10,961
2007-8	13,273	3.7	133.26	100.2	16461.0	116.72	158.98	1.600	14,365
2007-9	13,357	4.0	129.02	100.3	16235.4	115.02	159.64	1.675	9298
2007-10	13,310	4.0	140.14	100.5	16903.4	115.74	164.74	1.600	11,399
2007-11	13,344	3.8	137.53	100.6	15543.8	111.21	163.28	1.460	11,920
2007-12	13,436	3.8	140.01	100.9	15545.1	112.34	163.50	1.500	9076
2008-1	13,452	3.9	129.23	100.5	13731.3	107.66	158.14	1.440	11,651
2008-2	13,264	4.0	130.12	100.4	13547.8	107.16	158.18	1.355	10,868
2008-3	13,300	3.8	142.67	100.8	12602.9	100.79	156.28	1.275	10,474
2008-4	13,303	3.9	133.20	100.8	13355.8	102.49	161.53	1.575	10,094
2008-5	13,325	4.0	132.73	101.6	13995.3	104.14	162.05	1.740	10,277
2008-6	13,447	4.0	142.00	102.0	14084.6	106.90	166.23	1.610	10,537
2008-7	13,324	4.0	151.67	102.4	13168.9	106.81	168.35	1.530	10,856

Continued...

(*Continued*)

	Real GDP Index	Unemp. Rate (%)	Trade	CPI	Nikkei 225	Yen/$	Yen/€	Gov. Bond Yield	Short Selling Total
2008-8	13,213	4.1	144.17	102.6	12989.4	109.28	163.75	1.405	9196
2008-9	13,132	4.0	146.32	102.6	12123.5	106.75	153.25	1.480	9270
2008-10	13,072	3.8	139.05	102.4	9117.0	100.33	133.49	1.480	9313
2008-11	13,080	4.0	108.75	101.6	8531.5	96.81	123.25	1.395	6432
2008-12	12,830	4.4	99.83	101.1	8463.6	91.28	122.79	1.165	5970
2009-1	12,855	4.2	79.24	100.5	8331.5	90.41	119.68	1.270	5706
2009-2	12,831	4.4	69.88	100.4	7694.8	92.50	118.33	1.270	6106
2009-3	12,816	4.8	83.73	100.7	7764.6	97.87	127.44	1.340	6597
2009-4	12,823	5.0	83.40	100.7	8768.0	99.00	130.50	1.430	6522
2009-5	12,846	5.1	77.59	100.5	9304.4	96.30	131.92	1.480	5714
2009-6	12,764	5.3	87.02	100.3	9810.3	96.52	135.46	1.350	7014
2009-7	12,805	5.6	93.20	100.1	9691.1	94.50	133.00	1.415	6590
2009-8	12,868	5.4	88.54	100.1	10430.4	94.84	135.31	1.305	5878
2009-9	12,912	5.3	97.01	100.2	10302.9	91.49	132.80	1.295	6429
2009-10	13,063	5.2	98.17	100.1	10066.2	90.29	133.87	1.405	5505

REFERENCES

Aitken, M., Frino, A., McCorry, M. S., & Swan, P. L. (1998). Short sales are almost instanta-neously bad news: Evidence from the Australian Stock Exchange. *Journal of Finance, LIII*(6), 2205–2223.

Asquith, P., & Moelbroek, L. (1996). *An empirical investigation of short interest*. Working Paper, Harvard University, Cambridge.

Blau, B. M., Van Ness, B. F., & Van Ness, R. A. (2010). Information in short selling: Comparing NASDAQ and the NYSE. *Review of Financial Economics*, doi:10.1016/j.rfe.2010.09.002.

Boehmer, E., Jones, C. M., & Zhang, X. (2008). Which shorts are informed? *Journal of Finance, 63*, 491–527.

Brent, A., Morse, D., & Stice, E. K. (1990). Short interest: Explanations and tests. *Journal of Financial and Quantitative Analysis, 25*, 273–289.

Christophe, S. E., Ferri, M. G., & Angel, J. J. (2004). Short-selling prior to earnings announce-ments. *The Journal of Finance, LIX*(4), 1845–1875.

Christophe, S. E., Ferri, M. G., & Hsieh, J. (2010). Informed trading before analyst downgrades: Evidence from short sellers. *Journal of Financial Economics, 95*, 85–106.

Cohen, G. (2010). Do short sellers outperform the market? *Applied Economics Letters, 17*, 1319–1322.

Dickey, D. A., & Fuller, W. A. (1979). Distribution of the estimators for autoregressive time series with a unit root. *JASA, 74*, 427–431.

Dickey, D. A., & Fuller, W. A. (1981). Likelihood ratio statistics for autoregressive time series with a unit root. *Econometrica, 49*, 1057–1072.

Diether, K., Lee, K.-H., Werner, I. (2007). *Can short-sellers predict returns? Daily evidence.* Fisher College of Business, Working Paper Series, Ohio State University.

Figlewski, S., & Webb, G. P. (1993). Options, short sales, and market completeness. *Journal of Finance, 48,* 761–777.

Granger, C. W. J. (1969). Investigating causal relations by econometric models and cross-spectral methods. *Econometrica, 37*(3), 424–438.

Ko, K., & Lim, T. (2006). Short selling and stock prices with regime switching in the absence of market makers: The case of Japan. *Japan and the World Economy, 18,* 528–544.

Woolridge, J. R., & Dickinson, A. (1994). Short selling and common stock prices. *Financial Analysts Journal, 50,* 20–28.

New Regulatory Developments for Short Selling in Asia: A Review

Jeannine Daniel and François-Serge Lhabitant

CONTENTS

ABSTRACT

Short selling in Asia has historically been relatively difficult, but the associated rules are increasingly being relaxed to allow the practice under certain circumstances. Certain countries allow covered short sales but not naked shorts, others impose an uptick rule, and some restrict the list of stocks that may be shorted and/or the mechanism by which the short sell may be executed. Last but not least, some countries allow short selling for retail investors but prohibit institutional investors. This chapter provides a comprehensive review of major Asian regulations on short selling. It also discusses the development of securities lending and short selling in mainland China—a likely evolution that will allow for the development of China-based hedge funds arbitraging away price inefficiencies in the China market.

KEYWORDS

Covered short sales; Naked short sales; Private disclosure; Public disclosure; Uptick rule.

20.1 INTRODUCTION

In the 17th century, the Dutch prohibited short selling after the price of tulip bulbs suddenly plummeted. In 1929, U.S. President Hoover blamed short sellers for the market crash and ordered stock exchange authorities to ban their activities. In 2008, following the turmoil created by the collapse of Lehman Brothers, many countries seriously restricted short selling and required additional disclosure of short positions. In the United States, for instance, the Security and Exchange Commission (SEC) provisionally prohibited short selling for nearly 1000 stocks related to the financial sector. A similar action was taken by the Financial Services Agency for U.K. financial sector companies. All these examples illustrate that serious market crashes in the Western world are usually followed by public attacks from governments and additional emergency regulation against short sellers—usually the perfect scapegoats because they profit from falling share prices.

Is the situation comparable in Asia? The general 2008 Western clampdown on short selling came almost exactly a decade after Asia suffered its own financial crisis. On the ground in Asia, short selling is far less prevalent than in the Western world. In fact, it has historically been a relatively difficult activity. Securities lending is not easily available everywhere, and when it is, the cost of borrowing securities is often much higher. In addition, the lower liquidity of many Asian markets opens the door to short squeezes and exacerbates the potential impact of massive short sales. It is therefore not surprising that Asian regulators monitor short selling very closely and do not hesitate to step in whenever needed to allow or restrict the practice based on circumstances.

This chapter provides a comprehensive review of major Asian regulations on short selling. Interestingly, many short selling constraints imposed in Asia are reminiscent of short sale regulations in the United States in the early 1930s. It also discusses the development of securities lending and short selling in Asia, particularly in mainland China—a long awaited evolution that will allow for the development of China-based hedge funds arbitraging away price inefficiencies in the China market.

20.2 TYPICAL SHORT SELLING CONSTRAINTS

Asian regulators willing to limit the short selling activity on their respective market typically have the choice of a variety of standard measures. Let us discuss some of them as well as their effectiveness.

- *Private disclosure*: most regulators believe that more short selling transparency should benefit market participants and improve market confidence. They may therefore require short sellers to mark and report their short transactions to an appropriate authority. This arguably serves two key purposes: facilitate the effective supervision of market activity and enhance market efficiency and price formation, if some consolidated statistics on short sales are published.
- *Public disclosure*: regulators may move one step further and force all short sellers to disclose their short positions publicly. Several studies in Europe and the United States have evidenced that public disclosure significantly decreases the short sellers' level of participation in equity markets, which is exactly what regulators want. However, as a consequence, markets typically became less liquid, more expensive, and more difficult to trade for all market participants.
- *Uptick rule*: this old rule states that one can only short a stock if it trades higher than its previous transaction price. Its impact varies as a function of the size of the investor. In particular, larger investors can work around the rule by placing a small buy order just prior to placing a heavier short for their real bets.
- *Banning naked short sales*: Banning naked short sales forces short sellers to borrow or arrange to borrow the stock they want to sell before trading rather than merely locating a potential lender after having concluded the transaction. This typically results in an increase of the fee charged by share lenders because it increases the overall demand for borrowing shares (see Culp & Heaton, 2008).
- *Banning covered short sales*: This is the most restrictive type of constraint, as it makes it impossible for most market participants to short sell financial shares.

Note that real impacts of the aforementioned restrictions need to be analyzed, particularly for stocks where traded options are available. A simple application of the put–call parity shows that it is possible to duplicate a short position by purchasing and selling a combination of options (a "synthetic short") from an options market maker. Because market makers are often exempted from short selling bans, they can easily short sell directly to hedge their position when assuming the other side of a synthetic short. Sophisticated informed traders could therefore be the only ones able to short in the presence of a short selling ban. If that is the case, any regulatory restrictions on short selling would be useless unless regulators would also be agreeable to limit options and futures trading.

20.3 EXAMPLES OF A FEW ASIAN COUNTRIES

This section summarizes the essential steps that some major Asian regulators have taken regarding short selling practices.

20.3.1 Hong Kong

Hong Kong has a long history of regulating short selling. In January 1994, the Hong Kong Stock Exchange introduced a pilot scheme for the regulated short selling of 17 securities. This scheme was revised in March 1996, with an abolition of the initial uptick rule and an increase of the number of eligible stocks to 113. In September 1998, following the Asian crisis, regulators banned naked short selling, reinstated the uptick rule, and strictly enforced the T+2 settlement period. All short sales must be identified by brokers at the time of the order, and exchange members must maintain a ledger of daily short sale transactions and make it available to the exchange at all times. More recently, the Securities and Futures Commission (SFC) had announced a short position-reporting regime for all constituent stocks of the HSI, the H-shares Index, financial stocks, and other stocks specified by the SFC, but not for derivatives. According to the regime, short positions higher than 0.02% of issued share capital or a market value of $30M HKD (whichever is lower) must be reported. Note that a well-developed stock lending market exists.

20.3.2 Korea

In South Korea, the Financial Services Commission (FSC) restricted covered and naked short selling of all Korea Exchange (KRX)- and KOSDAQ-listed stocks on October 1, 2008. The ban was lifted partially on June 1, 2009. As stipulated in the Financial Investment Services and Capital Markets Act, naked short selling is not allowed but covered short sales of nonfinancial shares are, subject to an uptick rule.

Short sales must be reported as such to the KRX and the Korea Financial Investment Association. Brokers are required to verify whether they have strictly followed the short selling regulations correctly. In particular, borrowed shares must be booked and time stamped prior to the short sell being executed. The Korea Securities Depository, a securities borrowing and lending intermediary, provides services that include system operation, trade intermediation, and collateral management. Investors must register to become securities borrowing and lending participants. Alternatively, short selling can be done via a total return swap.

20.3.3 Taiwan

In Taiwan, the FSC banned short selling of the constituents of three key indices (the Taiwan 50, the Taiwan Mid-Cap 100, and the Taiwan Technology Index) from September 2008 to January 2009. Today, naked short selling is still not allowed, but covered short selling is possible subject to an uptick rule and some size restrictions. First, the balance of securities borrowing and lending (used as a proxy for short sales) of any given security cannot exceed 10% of the total outstanding of that given security. Second, the balance of local securities borrowing and lending and margin short sales of any given security cannot exceed 25% of total outstanding shares of that given security.[1] Third, short selling orders of any given security per day cannot exceed 3% of the total outstanding shares of that given security. Exceptions for the uptick rule are in place for selling borrowed constituents of the Taiwan 50 Index, Taiwan Mid-Cap 100 Index, Taiwan Technology Index, ETFs, hedging by put warrants issuers, or simply by hedging stock options by market makers. A regulated stock loan market exists, but most shorts are done through total return swaps.

20.3.4 Japan

During a previous slump in the stock market in 2002, the Japanese Financial Services Agency (JFSA) introduced a series of measures to reinforce the restrictions on short selling of stocks. These included:

- Requirements for traders to validate and mark whether or not the transactions are for short selling.
- An uptick rule condition that forbids short selling at prices no higher than the last market price announced by the stock exchange.
- Request for exchanges to improve their disclosure on information concerning short selling. Exchanges are obliged to make daily announcements on their collective price of short selling vis-à-vis all securities and collective price of short selling by sector (33 sectors in total).

---

[1] If the limit is reached, short selling is banned until the short sold amount falls below 18% of the stock's total shares.

On October 27, 2008, following a drop of more than 18% of the Nikkei 225 stock average in 5 trading days, the JFSA added two additional restrictions:

- A temporary ban on naked short selling. Consequently, all market participants placing short sell orders must have the required borrow arrangement in advance to ensure delivery on the settlement date.
- A reporting requirement. All holders of a short position of more than 0.25% of the outstanding shares of a stock are required to report their position to exchanges through brokerage firms, and exchanges are required to disclose that information publicly.

These restrictions remain in place today. There are a few exemptions, such as selling when a long position is ensured, arbitrage and hedge transactions, bridge sales (or "Tsunagi Uri"), the short sale of odd lot stocks, and short sales at the volume-weighted average price (VWAP; limited to morning VWAP, afternoon VWAP, and all-day VWAP).

20.3.5 Singapore

On September 22, 2008, the Singapore Exchange (SGX) tightened its rules to discourage naked short selling. In particular, it imposed a penalty of 5% of the value of any trade that would ultimately result in nondelivery of the underlying shares, with a minimum fine of S$1000 (US$710). Naked short sellers must therefore cover their positions within the same day or face a buy-in by the SGX. Note that there is no uptick rule applicable.

In the summer of 2010, the SGX issued a consultation paper to propose new short selling disclosure rules and reporting of short sales volume to increase market transparency. The proposal essentially required investors to mark their sell orders as either short sell orders or normal sell orders. Brokers would then collect these data and provide it to the SGX, who would publish short sales statistics with a 1-day lag.

20.3.6 Australia

On September 19, 2008, the Australian Securities and Investment Commission (ASIC) took emergency measures to ban naked short selling in Australia and tightened disclosure rules on covered short selling. A few days later it banned covered short sales as well. Several subsequent clarifications exempted transactions hedging existing positions, dual-listed entities, exchange-traded options, index arbitrage transactions, and market makers.

The ban on covered short selling of nonfinancial securities was lifted on November 19, 2008. The ban on covered short selling of financial securities was lifted on May 25, 2009, but naked short selling remains prohibited.

Note that the reporting obligations currently in place include the reporting of short sale transactions to brokers and the reporting of short positions directly to the ASIC. There are exemptions from reporting short positions below a $100,000 size threshold and they represent less than 0.01% of the total quantity of securities.

20.3.7 Indonesia

On October 7, 2008, the Indonesia Stock Exchange strictly prohibited short selling, including intraday trades. In addition, the KPEI (central clearing) suspended its stock-lending facilities, thereby eliminating stock borrowing. As a result, short selling was no longer possible in Indonesia. Today, securities borrowing and lending are available from the KPEI but are restricted to local residents. Short exposure is generally facilitated via total return swaps.

20.3.8 China

Article 35 of the 1998 Chinese Securities Law implicitly prohibited short selling by mandating spot cash transactions, but the 2005 Chinese Securities Law lifted the prohibition on stock-lending mechanisms as well as the ban on margin-related trades. However, activity has remained very limited due to the lack of regulations or market rules dealing specifically with short selling and/or securities lending. More recently, in March 2010, after 4 years of preparation, the China Securities Regulatory Commission launched margin trading, securities lending, and index futures on the Shanghai and Shenzhen stock exchanges. Interestingly, Qualified Foreign Institutional Investors and other offshore investors were not able to participate at the program's inception. Eleven Chinese securities brokers competed for a license, but only six were ultimately approved to participate in the program: Guotai Junan Securities, Guosen Securities, CITIC Securities, Everbright Securities, Haitong Securities, and GF Securities. Initially, the inventory available for short selling was tight, as securities borrowing and lending, as well as margin lending, were limited to stocks in the China Security Index CSI 300, and only proprietary holdings of stock can be lent—no agency lending is allowed. Note that an investor must have been a client of one of these brokers for more than 6 months before that investor can trade on margin or short stock with that broker. Naked short selling is not allowed.

20.3.9 India

Short selling in India was originally quite common but it became broadly prohibited in March 2001 by the Securities and Exchange Board of India (SEBI) following a major stock market manipulation scam. In December 2007, covered short selling was reintroduced again for all types of investors (institutional and retail) under regulations similar to those developed in the

United States, but naked short selling remained banned. It was also decided at that time to put a proper securities lending and borrowing scheme in place to provide the necessary impetus for short selling.

All investors are allowed to borrow and lend securities via an approved intermediates (AI) platform through clearing members, which include banks and custodians. The maximum tenure of security borrowing and lending contracts is 1 year with AIs given the "flexibility to decide the tenure" within that period. The total security borrowing and lending position for an ultimate borrower in a single stock is limited to 0.1% of the free float; clearing intermediaries are limited to about $1 million in loans of a single name. However, the major difficulty in India is inactivity of the onshore stock loan market—total transactions reported by the National Stock Exchange in 2009 for security borrowing and lending were around US$5000.

For foreign investors, the situation is more complex. Practically, they have two entry routes to India:

- "Front door," which requires registration with the SEBI as a foreign institutional investor (FII). Once registered, FIIs are permitted to short sell, lend, and borrow equity shares of Indian companies.
- "Back door," which implies using offshore derivative instruments and synthetics such as participatory notes (PNs) issued by other registered FIIs. Note that the SEBI has indicated several times its "disapproval" of stock lending and borrowing overseas through PNs, as it is difficult to know the ultimate beneficiaries. In June 2010, the SEBI has therefore asked FIIs issuing participatory notes to disclose their short positions on a daily basis.

Note that there is no uptick rule for onshore/offshore borrows, but the SEBI is in discussions on whether to apply uptick to onshore borrows.

20.3.10 Malaysia

Malaysia amended its Securities Industry Act in 1995 to allow short sales. Regulated short selling started officially in September 1996 on the Kuala Lumpur Stock Exchange but was suspended in August 1997 due to the Asian financial crisis. Anecdotally, the finance ministry then proposed mandatory caning as the punishment for short sellers.

Today, short selling is authorized again, but is strictly regulated.[2] Market participants must open a new short selling account before engaging in short selling.

---

[2] Note that another topic that has been discussed regularly in Malaysia was whether short selling was Shariah compliant, as it seems to clearly violate the general Islamic rule of "Do not sell what you do not possess." Nevertheless, the Shariah Advisory Council of the Malaysian Securities Commission has recently legalized the use of short selling instruments in the Islamic Capital Market in Malaysia.

Shares must be borrowed first and have already arrived in this account before any short selling operation be initiated. Direct borrowing from lenders is not allowed. Instead, all borrowers and lenders must register with the Bursa, which operates a clearing system whereby all shares lent out are pooled. They can be recalled anytime. As a result of this system, most of the time, short exposure is facilitated via total return swaps.

20.3.11 Other Countries

The situation in other Asian countries varies greatly from one country to another. In Vietnam and Thailand, securities borrowing and lending exist but the market is not very liquid. In the Philippines, naked short selling is prohibited but covered short selling is possible with an uptick rule. The securities borrowing and lending market is very illiquid and extremely regulated. In Pakistan, naked short selling is prohibited and covered short selling is only allowed for members of the stock exchange but not for financial institutions and foreign investors. There is no securities borrowing and lending market. In Bangladesh, the SEC approved a short sale regulation in February 2006, but has not yet implemented it. In all these countries, short selling is facilitated via total return swaps.

20.4 RECENT DEVELOPMENTS IN CHINA

In stark contrast to its peers, China seems to be the only market going against the tide and plans to facilitate short selling in the near future. Surprisingly, it is also one of the few markets where no detailed operational guidance for short selling has been issued so far.

In the authors' opinion, opening the door to short selling and securities lending is likely to radically transform the structure and dynamics of the rapidly growing Chinese markets. So far, China has essentially been a one-sided relatively closed equity market where investors could only buy and less than 1% of overall market capitalization was open to foreign investors. Going forward, many new foreign market participants might be interested in trading Chinese equities once they have a proper mechanism to manage risk more effectively. Extremely high valuations and bubbles should become less frequent once investors have a way to play against them. More importantly, the ability to short should help in exploiting the massive price differentials among the various exchanges trading Chinese equities.

Let us recall that mainland China companies have various options to list their shares. Let us mention, for instance, (i) A shares, which are shares of Chinese companies listed in Shanghai or Shenzhen under Chinese law, denominated in renminbi. It is on this market that an index futures has been launched recently; (ii) B shares, a.k.a. renminbi special shares, which are registered shares listed and traded in securities exchanges inside China, with a face value denominated in renminbi but subscribed and traded in foreign currencies by foreign investors; (iii) H shares, which are shares in Chinese companies issued in China under Chinese law, but listed on the Hong Kong Stock Exchange and subject to its stringent listing and disclosure requirements, and denominated in H.K. dollars. They are available to international investors with minimal restrictions; and (iv) so-called N shares for companies listed on the New York Stock Exchange and, more recently, in Singapore (S shares) or in Australia. Most N shares are traded in the form of American depositary receipts with the underlying shares listed in Hong Kong. They are available to international investors with no restrictions. Since April 2006, qualified domestic institutional investors are also allowed to access foreign security markets.

Historically, shares of the same company were often traded simultaneously but at very different prices by segmented investor groups. More importantly, for the same company, the various share classes seem to have their own pricing dynamics and move independently of others in the long run (see, e.g., Kim & Shin, 2000; Tian, 2007). Because equity issuance and buybacks were severely constrained by the restrictive rules imposed by the government, companies could not profit from the misevaluation of their own stocks. Strict capital controls and the absence of short selling also prevented investors from arbitraging away the differences. With the ability to short sell or use derivatives, this should be passé.

Development of a domestic hedge fund industry within China is clearly the next stage. Interestingly, China's second-largest asset management company, E Fund Management Co., announced in September 2010 the creation of China's first officially registered hedge fund subsequent to the securities regulator, saying it would permit separately managed accounts at asset management firms to trade stock index futures based on their clients' needs.

20.5 CONCLUSION

When markets fall, it is popular to demand the heads of short sellers. In 1997, Malaysia's finance ministry reportedly proposed caning or legal corporal punishment for them, in complete violation with the basic principle that to avoid distortions a price on a financial market should reflect all kinds of views from optimistic buyers to pessimistic sellers.

Slightly more than a decade later, various countries in Asia have had different experiences with short selling regulation. Some are still dealing with emergency short selling bans and constraints—and the tendency of some regulators to retain them permanently. Others have understood that this was not very efficient in the long run and are trying to set up a new regulated framework to benefit from short selling in order to boost their domestic capital markets. Interestingly, none of them seem to go the European way suggested by the Committee of European Securities Regulators (2010) and try to harmonize their short selling regulations.

REFERENCES

Committee of European Securities Regulators. (2010). *Model for a Pan-European short selling disclosure regime* (Report 10-088). Committee of European Securities Regulators. Retrieved from http://www.cesr.eu.

Culp, C., & Heaton, J. B. (2008). The economics of naked short selling. *Regulation,* (Spring), 46–51.

Kim, Y., & Shin, J. (2000). Interactions among China-related stocks. *Asia-Pacific Financial Markets, 7*(2), 97–115.

Tian, G. G. (2007). Are Chinese stock markets increasing integration with other markets in the Greater China Region and other major markets? *Australian Economic Papers, 46,* 240–253.

CHAPTER 21

The Signaling of Short Selling Activity in Australia

Mathew J. Ratty, John L. Simpson, and Peter D. Mayall

CONTENTS

ABSTRACT

There is a perception among investors and the public that short selling, for example, by hedge funds, exacerbates the downward spiral of stock prices and rewards the participants. Large sales, combined with multiple sellers, almost guarantee a self-fulfilling fall in prices. As a consequence of the 2008 global financial crisis, financial regulators in the United States, the United Kingdom, France, Germany, Canada, and Australia banned naked short selling as well as, in Australia's case, the covered short selling of listed stocks, primarily in the financial sector. The Australian financial regulator, the Australian Securities and Investment Commission (ASIC), prohibitions on naked and covered short selling came into effect on September 21, 2008, and lasted until May 25, 2009, when a partial recovery in equity markets allowed lifting of the ban on covered short selling. As a consequence of this period of instability, ASIC requires daily reporting by market participants, to the Australian Stock Exchange, of gross short sales for the current and following day. The study in this chapter does not deal with actual short selling transactions, but demonstrates that part of the short selling problem may well have occurred as market players followed credible short sell profit opportunities in unregulated markets following sale decisions by company directors that first created profit opportunities for the selling directors.

KEYWORDS

Australian Securities and Investment Commission; Cumulative average abnormal return; Directors' sales; Director signaling; Market signaling; Selling announcements.

21.1 INTRODUCTION

The fundamental premise of this chapter is the intuitive thought that when directors buy and sell shares in their own company they are trading on the basis of having superior knowledge about the future prospects of the firm. For example, if directors are buying shares in their own firm they are communicating positive signals about the future value of the firm to the market (e.g., Fidrmuc, Goergen, & Renneboog, 2006). Selling would logically convey negative news about the company despite evidence provided by, for example, Lakonishok and Lee (2001) who argue that consideration needs to be made about the possibility that directors have liquidity needs and that there are certain diversification benefits associated with such sales. Personal preferences may be another reason why directors may want to sell. The question, however, remains as to whether or not sale completions by directors represent a signal of bad news, but also represent short selling profit opportunities in a bear market.

21.1.1 Australian Regulation

The Australian share market is regarded as being typical of that of an advanced country. It has a reasonable degree of informational efficiency and is quite well regulated. For example, Section 205G of (Australian) Corporations Act (2001) requires every director of a listed company to notify the Australian Stock Exchange (ASX) about holdings and changes in relevant interests in securities in their own firms. The notification must be within 5 business days of the change in interest. In order to satisfy this requirement, directors are obliged to complete an appendix, which is then recorded by the ASX. This reveals the director who trades, the amount traded, the price at which they bought or sold, and whether or not it was an on or off market trade. This information is then disseminated to the general public on the day the director lodges the appendix. In an examination by the ASX, its 2008 report revealed that over 13% of directors did not conform to the reporting requirement.

In March 2008, the ASX issued a report to all companies reminding them of their obligations and stating that, from July 1, 2008, they will be heavily scrutinizing directors' interest notices that are lodged late or incomplete. Breaches of Section 205G may result in criminal prosecutions by the Australian Securities and Investment Commission (ASIC). When ASIC identifies a breach, the director is sent a letter asking for an explanation. This explanation may not necessarily avoid prosecution being taken. However, the explanation will be taken into account when the ASIC is deciding criminal prosecution.

In September 2008, the practice of short selling became the focus of the Australian regulatory authorities. Company directors selling stocks in a bear market were not regarded as the major problem. After all, they were only selling shares that they already owned. Nevertheless, the position put in this chapter is that their decision to sell stock in their own company may have become a signal for those market players who wished to profit from a fall in the share price. The moral justification of short selling was again brought into the spotlight. Can we legally sell something that we do not own? Did selling directors contribute either innocently or deliberately to others short selling profits being generated on the basis of bad news? Did short selling exacerbate a fall in the Australian stock market? The regulatory authorities felt the latter activity did, and bans on uncovered and covered short selling were introduced on September 21, 2008. The ban on covered short selling was lifted on May 25, 2009, primarily on the basis of a partial recovery in the Australian stock market, but reporting requirements remained.

21.1.2 Signaling Theory

For the purpose of this chapter, market signaling is defined as actions taken by the agent of a company that may convey meaningful information about the true value of their organization and thereby have an effect on the stock price. Many information-signaling models that were formulated rely heavily on the concept of information asymmetry. The original asymmetric model was developed by Akerloff (1970) in his economic paper about "lemons," but since then has been extended into the finance world by Spence (1973), Leland and Pyle (1977), and Miller and Rock (1985). Noe (1999) argued that no matter what side of the deal the transaction is on, directors' trades signal long-term earnings growth information about the firm. Hamill, McIlkenny, and Opong (2002) studied the correlation between information content associated with the purchase and sales transactions of directors and how this is associated with future firm performance. They, like Noe (1999), deduced that directors' purchases are related positively to future firm performance and should be taken as a signal; however, there is no clear evidence of this with sales. The evidence presented in this chapter supports the notion of director signaling of short selling opportunities.

It has been argued (Anand, Brown, & Watson, 2002; Ke, Huddart, & Petroni, 2003) that directors get involved in "insider selling" well in advance of a break in their firm's earnings patterns to try and go "under the radar" and avoid the appearance of taking advantage of inside information. Ke et al. (2003) undertook their study in the United States and used a sample of 4179 firms between 1989 and 1997, the results of which suggest directors' sales signal their knowledge of a break in the earnings pattern. Furthermore, they argued that directors who are buying shares seem to purchase in lots instead of just one large block to avoid suspicion of insider trading.

Signaling does not just stop at directors buying and selling. It extends to the actions of the corporation as a whole. Many signaling theories extend to capital management initiatives such as secondary offerings, share buybacks, merger and acquisition announcements, dividend changes, sell-off announcements, initial public offerings, and earnings announcements. This chapter focuses on selling announcements by directors.

21.2 LITERATURE REVIEW

As discussed earlier, directors' decisions to issue equity or buy or sell shares in their company are thought to have a market-signaling effect. This chapter tests that effect and specifically tests whether director sales may be a signal for market sales and short selling profit opportunities as the share prices fall. It is assumed that director sales activity, which has increased director returns in a falling market, has also increased returns of others who may have engaged in short selling activity and who may have, with the directors' sales, exacerbated the fall in the share price.

The empirics in this chapter do not deal with actual short selling transactions per se. They do, however, deal with credible short selling signals by directors' sale decisions. It is useful to review some of the related literature. For example, Finnerty (1976) analyzed 30,000 individual transactions on the NYSE and found that directors earned above average returns when they traded securities in their own firm. The overall result for selling is that when directors decided to sell, the shares declined more than the general market over the same period. He deduced from his study that in the short run, directors are able to identify profitable as well as loss avoidable situations in their own companies because they can identify and quantify the information set to enable theirs to perform better than the market.

Hillier and Marshall (2002) find that buying occurs following a price fall and selling following a price rise, which again is consistent with the notion that directors time their trades perfectly. Their results indicate that there are significant positive abnormal returns on the buy side and some smaller but still significant abnormal returns in glamour stocks on the sell side. A more recent study carried out by Cheuk, Fan, and So (2006) examined the characteristics and price movements of over 23,000 directors' transactions in Hong Kong from January 1993 to December 1998. However, in contrast to the previous studies, they find that abnormal gains are larger when directors are selling as compared to buying. Research by Betzer and Theisen (2007) argues that companies with less liquid stocks, as measured by market capitalization or trading volume, are likely to be followed by fewer analysts. As a result, it is expected there would be stronger informational asymmetries between directors and the capital market, thus the impact on the share prices of insider trades in these firms would be larger.

The most comprehensive paper within Australia to date relating to directors' buy and sell decisions is that of Uylangco, Easton, and Farr (2010), who find, consistent with the majority of the studies in this field, that directors achieve abnormal returns through trading shares in their own company. Furthermore, these abnormal returns are highest for sales in resource companies where directors avoided losses by selling prior to a price fall.

Primary analyses on all trades irrespective of the value show a positive cumulative average abnormal return (CAAR) for purchases and negative CAAR for sales transactions for both large and small cap (capitalization) stocks (see Tables 21.1 and 21.2). However, with large sale trades as seen in Tables 21.3 and 21.4, the results for directors' sales are now reversed,

Table 21.1 Effects of Directors' Trades on CAARs for ASX 200 Companies

Event Window	Insider Purchases		Insider Sales	
	CAAR	t-Statistic	CAAR	t-Statistic
Preevent window (−30,−1)	−0.0356*	−2.724	0.0441*	−6.184
Event day (0)	−0.0004	−0.452	0.0011	−0.656
Postevent window (+1,+5)	0.0064**	−2.132	0.0083**	−2.192
Postevent window (+1,+10)	0.0130*	−4.002	0.0038	−0.872
Postevent window (+1,+20)	0.0190**	−2.038	0.0141**	−2.196
Postevent window (+1,+30)	0.0140**	−1.473	0.0275*	−3.703
Postevent window (+1,+90)	0.0779*	−6.173	0.0281*	−2.409
Postevent window (+1,+180)	0.1615*	−10.329	0.0841*	−4.122

denotes significance levels are at the 1% level.
**denotes significance levels are at the 5% level.*

Table 21.2 Effects of Directors' Trades on CAARs for Emerging Index Companies

Event Window	Insider Purchases		Insider Sales	
	CAAR	*t*-Statistic	CAAR	*t*-Statistic
Preevent window (−30,−1)	−0.0345*	−3.536	0.0876*	−4.651
Event day (0)	0.0001	−0.32	0.008	−0.07
Postevent window (+1,+5)	0.0158*	−3.84	0.0202*	−2.603
Postevent window (+1,+10)	0.0231*	−4.466	0.0153**	−1.869
Postevent window (+1,+20)	0.0338*	−4.947	0.0228**	−1.802
Postevent window (+1,+30)	0.0386*	−4.356	0.0321**	−1.949
Postevent window (+1,+90)	0.1497*	−6.729	0.0234**	−0.923
Postevent window (+1,+180)	0.2881*	−9.977	0.1127*	−3.274

* denotes significance levels are at the 1% level.
** denotes significance levels are at the 5% level.

Table 21.3 Value of the Trade on CAARs for ASX 200 Companies

Value Range	Directors' Purchases		Directors' Sales	
	30-Day Return	180-Day Return	30-Day Return	180-Day Return
$5000–$50,000	2.18%	21.10%	−2.41%	−9.41%
$50,000–$100,000	2.01%	13.84%	−3.85%	−11.63%
$100,000–$500,000	1.26%	12.41%	−0.41%	−9.54%
$500,000–$1,000,000	0.78%	9.19%	4.23%	0.83%
$1,000,000–$10,000,000	2.13%	13.20%	4.39%	2.85%
$10,000,000–$20,000,000	2.83%	10.93%	6.67%	3.62%

Table 21.4 Value of the Trade on CAARs for Emerging Index Companies

Value Range	Directors' Purchases		Directors' Sales	
	30-Day Return	180-Day Return	30-Day Return	180-Day Return
$5000–$50,000	4.28%	34.13%	−4.24%	−15.03%
$50,000–$100,000	3.56%	21.24%	−3.01%	−11.28%
$100,000–$300,000	1.72%	18.30%	−1.06%	−6.80%
$300,000–$1,000,000	0.78%	14.93%	4.92%	1.03%
$1,000,000–$3,000,000	2.13%	14.27%	5.82%	3.40%

meaning that directors who sell in large values are actually gaining from their trades as this action is followed by a fall in the share price. Thus the opportunity for short selling activity was created by the directors' decision to sell.

This study also finds that directors who sell small parcels of shares (less than $500,000 for ASX 200 and less than $300,000 for stocks in the Emerging Index companies) do not gain at all from their sales. However, when directors are selling in large amounts, above $500,000 for large cap and $300,000 for small cap, the market seems to take this as a negative signal for large and small cap stocks. Consequently, the stock price falls over the next month and the directors profit for both large cap stocks and small cap stocks, although most of the apparent gains occur within the first month. It is concluded that when the value of the trade is taken into account, directors' trades seem to be information revealing for both purchases and sales.

The results complement Anand et al. (2002) and Ke et al. (2003) who argue that directors seem to buy in small amounts and sell in large amounts when trading on the basis of inside information. Given what is known under the umbrella of modern financial theory and assuming that investors are risk averse in nature, they tend to feel a loss more than a gain. Hence, they will tend to sell in large volumes when they know unfavorable news is going to impact the stock price and tend to buy in small amounts when favorable news is approaching.

As noted previously, when directors are selling individually, they lose money from their trades in both short and long terms. However, results suggest that when multiple directors are selling, they can gain in large cap and in small cap abnormal returns when measured over a 30-day period. Can we safely say that directors know in the short term if the stock price is going down? It is concluded that the market seems to interpret directors' sales transactions as negative news when several directors are selling within a month of each other. It is further argued that if a single director sells, the market seems to act as if this transaction is due to liquidity needs rather than unfavorable news about the company.

In essence, results suggest that both directors' buying and selling transactions are credible signals to the market when multiple directors are transacting within a month of each other. All of these studies regarding directors' purchases and sales produce findings that may represent a signal to the market for short selling activity. Rational expectations would suggest that the higher the value of the trade, the more credible the signal to the market as directors are buying or selling a rather large proportion of their shares.

21.3 DATA AND METHODOLOGY

Information on directors' trades was obtained by confidential interviews from *The Insider Trader* (2010), who specifically record trades for all ASX companies. Data only include transactions bought and sold on the market at the discretion of the director and exclude such trades that were the result of dividend reinvestment schemes, employee share purchase plans, and the exercise of options and warrants. Data were filtered manually to obtain transactions of the companies listed on the ASX Index for large capitalization stocks (large cap) and those listed on the Emerging Markets Index for small capitalization stocks (small cap).

The returns for all companies were obtained from the ASX Web site. Data contain all directors' transactions reported to the ASX from January 2005 to June 2009. Data on pre- and postevent dividend-adjusted daily closing prices were obtained from the Datastream database. A survivorship criterion was imposed such that stocks not in either index in the full 5-year period were removed. In addition, any stock that had insufficient data for the 1-year pre- and postclean period was removed. Only trades greater than $5000 were included in the study. The final sample was 2481 transactions with the ASX 200 Index accounting for 1485 of these and the remainder from the Emerging Index. The final sample number of companies was 185 for the ASX 200 Index and 150 for the Emerging Index.

A standard event study methodology was used. The study used the methodology of Uylangco et al. (2010) whereby they find that returns to directors after the day they trade but before they announce the trade to the market are not significantly different from zero. Two different event periods are constructed. In the first event period, the event day is defined as being the actual date of the transaction. In the second analysis, the event day is taken as 5 days after the transaction date on the assumption that all information required by the ASX would have been supplied. An event window of −30 to +180 days is used around the event date. These periods are divided into subsample event periods in the preevent analysis and +5, +10, +20, +30, +90, and +180 days as the postevent analysis to capture whether the directors' transactions are associated with short- or long-term payoffs. The same is completed for the benchmark model required to calculate abnormal returns (i.e., return in excess of the benchmark needs to be isolated).

The study examines the CAAR from day t_0 to the ending event day, and the CAAR is the sum of average abnormal returns between event windows:

$$\text{CAAR}_t = \sum_{i=t_0}^{t} \text{AAR}_t \tag{21.1}$$

The t statistical tests for basic hypothesis testing for CAARs for pre- and postperiod analysis are calculated using the standard deviation (σ) of the CAAR at time t as follows:

$$t_{\text{CAAR}_t} = \frac{\text{CAAR}_t}{\sigma_{\text{CAAR}_t}} \qquad (21.2)$$

If persistent abnormal returns are found that are statistically different from zero for both event studies, then it is likely that outsiders can mimic directors to make abnormal returns.

21.4 FINDINGS

The findings are now reported in full in this section. Note that figures in percentages reported here represent positive or negative CAARs. When CAARs come up as a negative it is because this is the CAAR on the stock, and if it is a negative stock return after the sale, this represents a profit to the directors. The opposite is the case if CAARs are positive.

With regard to directors' buying and selling in general, irrespective of multiple trades or certain values, findings are that buying shares is profitable and selling shares is not profitable. As per Table 21.1, in the ASX 200, directors are selling when there is a 4.41% price run up, but after they sell and lock in at 4.41%, they start to lose on their sales as the share price keeps rising (up to 2.75% over 30 days and up to 8.41% over 180 days). Thus, in general, sales are not profitable to the directors or to those market players thinking of engaging in short selling.

Table 21.2 shows that selling in small caps is similar. Directors sell when there is an 8.76% price run up, but they lose after their sale as the share price keeps rising (i.e., with CAARs up 3.21% over 1 month and 11.27% over 180 days).

However, when taking the value of the trade into account (see Tables 21.3 and 21.4), directors' sales are now information revealing. It is noted that, in the ASX 200, when directors are selling over the $500,000 range there is a 4.23% profit over a 30-day period and when selling in the small cap stocks any sale over $300,000 yields a 4.92% profit. These are the critical thresholds for anyone looking to follow a directors' sale decision. The main point here is that directors may sell in small parcels for liquidity purposes or to perhaps pay private expenses, but when selling in large amounts they are selling to avoid large portfolio losses, which may be seen as a signal for short selling by some market players. If the directors profit, so will the short sellers as the signal is deemed to be credible.

Table 21.5 Effects of Multiple Directors Buying and Selling on CAARs for ASX 200 Companies

	Insider Purchases	Insider Sales
Event Window	CAAR	CAAR
Preevent window (−30,−1)	−0.042	0.0513
Event day (0)	−0.0002	0.0005
Postevent window (+1,+5)	0.0093	−0.0112
Postevent window (+1,+10)	0.0195	−0.0193
Postevent window (+1,+20)	0.0235	−0.0201
Postevent window (+1,+30)	0.0299	−0.0218
Postevent window (+1,+90)	0.0923	0.0212
Postevent window (+1,+180)	0.1829	0.0665

Table 21.6 Effects of Multiple Directors Buying and Selling on CAARs for Emerging Companies

	Insider Purchases	Insider Sales
Event Window	CAAR	CAAR
Preevent window (−30,−1)	−0.0392	0.0672
Event day (0)	−0.0001	−0.0001
Postevent window (+1,+5)	0.0198	−0.0192
Postevent window (+1,+10)	0.0291	−0.0261
Postevent window (+1,+20)	0.0368	−0.0318
Postevent window (+1,+30)	0.0527	−0.0326
Postevent window (+1,+90)	0.1591	0.0319
Postevent window (+1,+180)	0.3174	0.0928

When taking multiple directors' selling into account (see Tables 21.5 and 21.6), findings are that when directors are transacting more than once within a single month, they are now information-revealing events. They make up to 2.18 and 3.26% profit for large and small cap stocks sales, respectively. However, they lose over the long term on their sales for both large and small caps. That is, the highest gains from selling come from 30 days after the trade. Directors are making short-term profits from their sales, which is a credible signal for some other market players to short sell for profit.

The previous section on multiple directors' trades gives the average return to directors when two or more trades in the same direction (i.e., buy or sell) are completed within a single month of each other. This section breaks down the analysis to include the actual number of transactions within 1 month of each other (i.e., if one transaction happens within 1 month, or two transactions, or three...). The main idea here is that if there is heavy activity going on by directors, then this is likely to be a signal that something is going on.

Results are reported in Table 21.7. For sales, when there are three or more directors selling in the ASX 200, then directors start to earn a profit at 1.10% over 30 days. The highest return occurs when 19 selling transactions are transacted within a month of each other (4.34%), but because this only occurs once, it is argued that the signal is three directors selling, and such overselling is a signal for bad news, but also credible short selling for profit.

For small companies (Table 21.7, Panel B), the majority of directors were selling in multiples of three within a given month. This yields excess returns

Table 21.7 Effects on CAAR When a Certain Amount of Transactions Occur by Directors within a Single Month

Panel A: ASX 200		
Frequency of Directors' Transactions	30-Day Return	30-Day Return
1	0.60%	2.16%
2	0.83%	0.80%
3	1.37%	−1.10%
4	3.52%	−1.90%
5	3.10%	−2.34%
6	3.15%	−4.12%
7	3.19%	–
9	4.02%	–
12	–	−2.85%
19	–	−4.34%
Panel B: Emerging Index		
Frequency of Directors' Transactions	30-Day Return	30-Day Return
1	1.20%	4.12%
2	2.34%	2.93%
3	6.56%	−1.84%
4	4.48%	−4.19%
5	3.13%	−3.85%
6	3.20%	–
7	2.98%	–
9	3.85%	–

of 1.84% for the directors. It can also be seen that when four directors are selling in the small cap they earn 4.19%.

21.5 CONCLUSION

Findings for the Australian market in this study provide a contribution to sparse literature in Australia and capture data that include the period of the global financial crisis. Generally, the work of Uylangco et al. (2010) and others on the subject of director signaling is supported, updated, and expanded for the Australian market. On the surface, without the decomposition of trading transactions, director selling, irrespective of the size of the trade and whether multiple trades occur, results in a loss to directors (as the share price keeps rising after they sell). There is no signal to the market for short selling opportunities.

However, when the value of the trade is taken into account, directors' sales are now information revealing. It may be that directors sell in large parcels when they know there is imminent bad news. Also, when they sell in small parcels, it seems as though they are selling for private liquidity purposes. Either way, profits are made where share prices decline, and this must have represented a signal for other market players to short sell. In addition, when multiple directors are selling, sales are also information revealing. This means that when directors sell more than once within a single month, then it is likely to yield excess returns. This is higher in small cap stocks as these are less scrutinized by investors and perhaps regulators, but again short selling signals are generated.

Moreover, when the analysis is further decomposed into the actual number of directors selling (when directors sell two times in a month, three times in a month, etc.), it is noted that, in the ASX 200, four sales within a month is the most credible signal. However, in small cap stocks, three directors selling is the most credible signal (most directors in small cap stocks are selling in multiples of three within a single month). Again, this represents a credible short selling signal.

It needs to be made quite clear that director selling decisions are their decisions and their business. They are selling what they already own and may do so within the law. The study reported in this chapter provides Australian evidence that credible signals by selling directors, either intentionally or unintentionally, were provided to the Australian share market of short selling, profit-making opportunities. There seems no doubt that investors acting on these signals have influenced the downward slide of share prices during the global financial crisis and assisted in the prompting of legislation to ban uncovered positions and to later withdraw the ban for certain transactions, but to install short selling reporting requirements.

REFERENCES

Akerloff, G. (1970). The market for lemons: Quality uncertainty and the market mechanism. *Quarterly Journal of Economics, 84*(3), 488–500.

Anand, A., Brown, P., & Watson, I. (2002). Directors' trades as signals of their firms' future financial performance: Evidence from the Australian share market. Working Paper, Crawley, Australia: University of Western Australia.

Betzer, A., & Theissen, E. (2007). Insider trading and corporate governance: The case of Germany. *European Financial Management, 15*(2), 402–429.

Cheuk, M.-Y., Fan, D. K., & So, R. W. (2006). Insider trading in Hong Kong: Some stylized facts. *Pacific-Basin Finance Journal, 14*(1), 73–90.

Corporations Act. (2001). *Legal rules and regulations.* Canberra, Australia: Australian Commonwealth Government.

Fidrmuc, J. P., Goergen, M., & Renneboog, L. U. C. (2006). Insider trading, news releases, and ownership concentration. *Journal of Finance, 61*(6), 2931–2973.

Finnerty, J. E. (1976). Insiders and market efficiency. *Journal of Finance, 31*(4), 1141–1148.

Hamill, P., McIlkenny, P., & Opong, K. (2002). Directors' share dealings and company financial performance. *Journal of Management and Governance, 6*(3), 215–234.

Hillier, D., & Marshall, A. P. (2002). The market evaluation of information in directors' trades. *Journal of Business Finance & Accounting, 29*(1–2), 77–110.

Ke, B., Huddart, S., & Petroni, K. (2003). What insiders know about future earnings and how they use it: Evidence from insider trades. *Journal of Accounting and Economics, 35*(3), 315–346.

Lakonishok, J., & Lee, I. (2001). Are insider trades informative? *Review of Financial Studies, 14*(1), 79–111.

Leland, H., & Pyle, D. (1977). Information asymmetries, financial structure, and financial intermediation. *Journal of Finance, 32*(2), 371–387.

Miller, E., & Rock, K. (1985). Dividend policy under asymmetric information. *Journal of Finance, 40*(4), 1031–1051.

Noe, T. H. (1999). Insider trading and the problem of corporate agency. *Journal of Law, Economics and Organization, 13*(2), 287–318.

Spence, M. (1973). Job market signaling. *Quarterly Journal of Economics, 87*(3), 355–374.

The Insider Trader. (2010). www.theinsidertrader.com.au/. (accessed 03/31/2010).

Uylangco, K., Easton, S., & Farr, R. (2010). The equity and efficiency of the Australian market with respect to director trading. *Accounting Research Journal, 23*(1), 5–19.

CHAPTER 22

Sourcing Securities for Short Sales: The Proper Legal Characterization of Securities Loans

Paul U. Ali

CONTENTS

ABSTRACT

The regulatory constraints on short selling that were imposed in the aftermath of the global financial crisis have largely been concerned with the perceived negative impact of short selling on share prices, particularly the prices of shares in financial institutions. These constraints have been accompanied by greater regulatory scrutiny of securities lending, the chief means by which shares for covered short sales are sourced. This chapter considers the new regulatory framework for short sales in the United States and other major markets in the context of the practice of lending shares for the purposes of short sales. It also considers a recent decision of the Australian courts that has decisively answered the question as to the proper regulatory characterization of securities loans.

KEYWORDS

Beconwood Securities Pty Ltd. v. ANZ Banking Group Ltd.; Covered short sales; Dividend arbitrage; Securities lending; Securities loans; Voting rights.

22.1 INTRODUCTION

The regulatory constraints on short selling that were imposed in the major securities markets in the aftermath of the global financial crisis have largely been concerned with the perceived negative impact of short selling on share prices and thus on stability of securities markets. Less attention, however, has been paid to securities lending, the chief means by which securities for covered short sales are sourced. This chapter considers the operation of securities loans as well as a recent decision of the Australian courts that has addressed the question of the proper legal characterization of securities loans.

22.2 TRANSACTIONAL ATTRIBUTES OF SECURITIES LOANS

A securities loan, basically, involves the transfer of securities (shares or bonds) from a "lender" to a "borrower" in exchange for the borrower paying a fee to the lender. In a similar fashion to an actual loan of monies, the borrower of securities agrees to return securities equivalent to those borrowed on the cessation of the loan. (The attributes of securities loans, as described in this chapter, are based on the Global Master Securities Lending Agreement, the industry-standard template for securities loans.)

The label "loan" is a misnomer. While it does signify that the transfer of securities is temporary in nature, given the borrower's obligation to "repay" the securities borrowed, this so-called loan actually comprises two absolute transfers or sales of securities. Thus, on the inception of the loan, the borrower acquires full legal title to the securities being borrowed and, like any purchaser of securities, enjoys the full legal incidents of ownership. The borrower can on-sell the securities (as is the case when the borrower executes a short sale of those securities), relend the securities to another borrower, pledge the securities as collateral, or retain the securities and, in the case of shares, exercise the voting rights attached to the securities (Hu & Black, 2006).

Securities loans effectively separate the legal incidents of ownership of securities from the economic incidents of ownership. The initial transfer of securities that takes place under a securities loan vests clear title to the securities in the borrower and that title carries with it enjoyment of the economic incidents that ordinarily flow from title, but the borrower is obligated, under the terms of the loan, to pay to the lender amounts equivalent to any distributions received by the borrower during the term of the loan in respect of the securities. In addition, the lender remains exposed to price risk in relation to the securities since, under the terms of a securities loan, the borrower can "repay" the lender by transferring equivalent securities to the lender at a preagreed price. That preagreed price is constituted by the return to the borrower of the collateral (typically, cash collateral) posted by the borrower to support the securities loan.

The lender, having transferred title to the securities to the borrower, does not retain any entitlement in respect of the voting and other rights attaching to the securities. If, as in the case of shares, the lender wishes to vote the securities, it must "recall" the securities. This involves an early termination of the loan.

As mentioned earlier, securities loans are supported through the provision by the borrower of cash or other collateral to the lender as "security" for the performance by the borrower of its obligations under the securities loan; the principal obligation is the obligation on the borrower to repay the borrowed securities on the maturity of the loan or on an earlier recall by the lender. On termination of the securities loan, the borrower transfers to the lender equivalent securities to those borrowed against the lender's transfer of the collateral to the borrower.

22.3 SECURITIES LOANS AND SHORT SALES

Covered short sales involve selling securities that have been obtained under a securities loan, with the objective of buying back the securities at a lower price for return to the lender of the securities.

Admittedly, the level of securities lending activity in a market does not directly correspond to the level of short selling in the market. Apart from covered short sales, securities are borrowed for hedging purposes, dividend arbitrage, to raise funds on a secured basis, and, most controversially of all, to gain access to the voting rights that follow ownership of shares (D'Avolio, 2002; Duffie, Garleanu, & Pedersen, 2002).

Accordingly, many of the recent regulatory initiatives worldwide to increase the transparency of short selling activity have been accompanied by measures requiring the disclosure of securities lending activity. By having available information about both short sales and securities loans, market participants will be better equipped to gauge correctly market sentiment about securities and the extent to which, for instance, securities are being borrowed to create an inventory for future short sales, to protect against a recall of borrowed securities, or for dividend arbitrage. Perhaps, most important of all, investors and issuers will be able to assess the extent to which securities are being borrowed, on or about the announced cutoff date for determination by a listed issuer of voting entitlements at that issuer's upcoming general meeting for the purpose of obtaining votes to cast at that meeting (Christoffersen, Geczy, Musto, & Reed, 2007; Hu & Black, 2006, 2008).

Disclosure will also assist market participants in assessing settlement risks flowing from short sales. The inability of one market participant being unable to fulfill its settlement obligations may lead to significant delays in settlement. Thus, high levels of securities lending activity in particular securities compared to the market capitalization of the issuer or the average daily turnover of those securities can be important indicators of the increased potential for settlement delays or failure.

22.4 SECURITIES LOANS AND VOTING RIGHTS

One of the consequences of the separation of legal and economic rights in securities—apart from facilitating short sales—is that temporary access is obtained in respect of the voting rights attaching to borrowed shares. This is tantamount to vote buying (Christoffersen et al., 2007; Hu & Black, 2006).

Securities loans can therefore be used to distort the results of shareholder voting and may even determine the outcome of a meeting of an issuer where the matter under consideration is controversial or one on which the views of shareholders are finely balanced. A voting result that has been secured using votes attaching to shares, that have been borrowed for the purpose of gaining access to those votes, may not necessarily reflect the views of the majority of the company's other shareholders. This is of particular concern in the context of matters that affect operation of the market for corporate control.

Securities loans, when used to obtain access to votes, can also have an effect beyond the securities actually borrowed. The securities no longer form part of the free float of securities of the issuer. This has the potential to influence the outcome of a close contest by withdrawing shares and their votes from, for example, the opposition to a proposed transaction with control implications. Moreover, use of the shares to support a particular change of control transaction means that not only are the shares not available to opponents of the transaction or competing bidders, but also that the shares have actually been deployed (through the exercise of the votes attaching to them or by being sold into a takeover bid) against those parties.

22.5 LEGAL CHARACTERIZATION OF SECURITIES LOANS

As noted earlier, securities loans typically involve two coupled pairs of transfers: a transfer of securities against the delivery of collateral on the inception of the loan and a transfer back to the original transferor of equivalent securities against the return of collateral on the cessation of the loan.

Each of these transfers—whether of securities or collateral—is documented as an absolute transfer of title to the securities or collateral.

However, the coupling of these transfers raises the issue as to the proper legal characterization of the composite securities loan, as the combined transfers have, at the very least, a superficial resemblance to mortgages and other secured loans. Thus, the securities loan could well be viewed legally as an actual loan. The case for such a view of securities loans is strongest where cash collateral is employed to support the loan: the initial transfer of securities from the lender to the borrower against the delivery of cash collateral can be viewed functionally as an actual loan of that cash collateral from the borrower of the securities to the lender supported by the lender's transfer of the securities. The transfer of equivalent securities against the return of the cash collateral is consequently the effective redemption of the securities through the repayment of the cash collateral by the lender to the borrower.

This is not an anomalous result. There is a very long line of court decisions in common law jurisdictions (such as the United States, England, and Australia) dealing with the recharacterization of purported absolute transfers as secured loans. The recharacterization of a securities loan as a secured loan has significant consequences for the parties on the bankruptcy of the borrower and also on the borrower's ability to reuse the borrowed securities.

If title to the securities has passed to the borrower, then the lender has only a personal claim—no different to that held by the borrower's unsecured creditors—against the borrower should the borrower default in transferring equivalent securities to the lender on termination of the securities loan (hence the need for collateral). That personal claim ranks equally with the borrower's unsecured creditors and is subordinate to the claims of the borrower's secured creditors (Ali, 2009). However, if transfer of the securities to the borrower is by way of security only, the lender is entitled to redeem those securities by transferring back the cash or other collateral to the borrower. The borrower, in this second situation, never becomes the clear owner of the securities but is merely the holder of title to the securities less an equity of redemption in the securities retained by the lender (Ali, 2009). The borrower is thus the mortgagee, not the absolute owner, of the securities and, in that case, the securities would not form part of the pool of assets of the borrower available to the borrower's creditors and the lender would, in respect of the borrowed securities, enjoy a right superior to that of the borrower's creditors (whether secured or unsecured) (Ali, 2009).

The Australian case of *Beconwood Securities Pty Ltd. v. ANZ Banking Group Ltd.* (Federal Court of Australia, 66 ACSR 116, 2 May 2008) is one of the few cases from a major common law jurisdiction to consider the proper legal characterization of securities loans. The loans in question had been entered into by Beconwood with its broker, Opes Prime Stockbroking, and by the latter with ANZ. Opes Prime had advanced cash to Beconwood, under a securities loan, in exchange for the delivery of securities. That cash had been raised, in turn, by Opes Prime under a securities loan with ANZ. Beconwood contended that the securities loan between it and Opes Prime was, in reality, a loan from Opes Prime supported by Beconwood transferring securities by way of security only to Opes Prime. Thus, on Beconwood repaying the cash collateral to Opes Prime, Beconwood would, in common with any mortgagor, be entitled to redeem the securities. Moreover, the securities transferred by Beconwood to Opes Prime could not be transferred absolutely by Opes Prime to ANZ. Beconwood's rights to the securities would therefore have priority over any claim of ANZ against Opes Prime in respect of those securities.

The Australian Federal Court decisively rejected Beconwood's claims. The court decided that the securities loan had vested title to the securities absolutely in Opes Prime, and Opes Prime was therefore able, in turn, under its securities loan with ANZ, to vest those securities absolutely in ANZ. It was considered that three key attributes of a securities loan supported the characterization of such a loan as a sale of the securities, as opposed to a secured loan involving security over the securities (Ali, 2009; Legg, 2008):

i. The contractual terms of the securities loan provided for the absolute transfer of the securities being borrowed against the absolute transfer of collateral.
ii. There was no binding obligation on the borrower to return, on cessation of the loan, the very same securities that had been lent.
iii. The delivery obligations in relation to the borrowed securities and the collateral were capable of being netted against each other on early termination of the securities loan.

Of the aforementioned attributes, the one that influenced the court the most in deciding that a securities loan was not a secured loan was the inability of Beconwood, under the terms of the securities loan, to demand the return of the very same securities that had been transferred by it to Opes Prime. The court thus gave strong preference to the legal form in which the securities lending transaction had been clothed over the economic substance of that transaction. The economic substance of a mortgage, in contrast to that of a sale, is that the risk that the transferred property will not be sufficient to meet the transferor's obligations (in this case, the repayment of the cash collateral) to the transferee is borne by the transferor. The economic substance of a sale, however, is that the transfer of property passes all of the risks and benefits of that property to the transferee. Hence, under a mortgage, the transferee can recover any shortfall in the value of the transferred property from the transferor but is liable to account to the transferor for any surplus remaining once the transferor's obligations to the transferee have been discharged.

This is surprising when one takes note of the fact that in this case the securities loan between Beconwood and Opes Prime and also the securities loan between Opes Prime and ANZ had not been entered into to provide either of the borrowers (Opes Prime under the first-mentioned securities loan and ANZ under the other securities loan) with temporary access to the securities but had, instead, as their principal function the raising of funds by Beconwood and Opes Prime, respectively. Thus, the securities lent by Beconwood to Opes Prime were held by the latter as collateral to support the former's obligation to repay the cash transferred. This securities loan was, in fact, utilized by Beconwood as an in-substance margin loan (with Beconwood being required to maintain a certain ratio of securities to cash collateral by lending further securities to Opes Prime). The small- and mid-cap nature of the issuers of the securities the subject of the securities loan—and the relatively thin liquidity of some of those securities—meant that Beconwood had to resort to a securities loan to raise cash to finance its share dealings as that cash might not have been as readily obtainable or even obtainable at all via a conventional margin loan.

22.6 CONCLUSION

This chapter provided an overview of the operation of securities loans. It also discussed one of the few court cases anywhere in the world in which the proper legal nature of securities loans has fallen to be determined. While the court in that particular case clearly decided that transfers of securities under a securities loan were absolute transfers or sales and did not constitute an in-substance secured loan, the authority of that case is weakened by the court's seeming indifference to two related factors: the substantive differences between, as opposed to different legal forms of, sales of securities and mortgages of securities; and the use, in that case, of securities loans by the various participants as margin loans. The legal nature of securities loans cannot therefore be said to have been completely settled by that case.

REFERENCES

Ali, P. U. (2009). Short selling and securities lending in the midst of falling and volatile markets. *Journal of International Banking Law and Regulation, 24*(1), 1–12.

Christoffersen, S. E. K., Geczy, C. C., Musto, D. K., & Reed, A. V. (2007). Vote trading and information aggregation. *Journal of Finance, 62*(6), 2897–2929.

D'Avolio, G. (2002). The market for borrowing stock. *Journal of Financial Economics, 66*(2), 271–306.

Duffie, D., Garleanu, N., & Pedersen, L. H. (2002). Securities lending, shorting and pricing. *Journal of Financial Economics, 66*(3), 307–339.

Hu, H. T. C., & Black, B. (2006). The new vote buying: Empty voting and hidden (morphable) ownership. *Southern California Law Review, 79*(4), 811–908.

Hu, H. T. C., & Black, B. (2008). Equity and debt decoupling and empty voting II: Importance and extensions. *University of Pennsylvania Law Review, 156*(3), 625–739.

Legg, M. (2008). The Opes prime litigation: Securities 'lending' transfers legal title to securities. *Company and Securities Law Journal, 26*(6), 407–412.

SECTION

4

Emerging Markets

Short Selling in Emerging Markets: A Comparison of Market Performance during the Global Financial Crisis

Mario Maggi and Dean Fantazzini

CONTENTS

ABSTRACT

This chapter reviews short selling practices in emerging markets and market performances during the global financial crisis. In contrast to developed markets, many emerging countries do not permit short selling, which can pose severe limitations on market liquidity. We compare market volatility, the Sharpe ratio, maximum drawdown, and skewness across different countries from May 2002 to November 2010. Moreover, we show that a market crash impact is generally weak in countries where short selling is allowed.

KEYWORDS

Exogenous liquidity; Market liquidity; Market volatility; Maximum drawdown; Mean volatility; Sharpe ratio; Skewness.

23.1 INTRODUCTION

Short selling is a common practice in many developed countries. It is well known that short selling improves market liquidity and the efficient price discovery process. Stock market liquidity is a key variable for efficient market risk pricing and allocation, which is related to the rate of economic growth. Moreover, short selling prohibition poses limitations in derivatives market development and affects the pricing efficiency of even simple contingent claims (see Gupta & Jithendranathan, 2010). The importance of short selling as a source for exogenous market liquidity was emphasized by several studies (see, e.g., Bris, Goetzmann, & Zhu, 2007; Endo & Rhee, 2006). Market illiquidity is usually considered the consequence of a low demand for securities, high transaction fees, and limited supply of equity securities, inefficient market microstructures, and a low confidence in the local market due to poor regulation and the lack of good corporate governance.

Given these problems, an exogenous liquidity supply has been proposed as a way to develop local equity markets quickly. A possible source of exogenous liquidity is represented by foreign capital inflows, which explains why many emerging markets have pursued this strategy during the last decade. However, foreign investors can exit the market very quickly, thus causing market falls and liquidity shocks. An alternative form of exogenous liquidity is margin trading, intended both as short sales and as margin purchases, which has helped to accelerate the development of emerging equity markets as shown by Endo and Rhee (2006). The complete absence of regulated short selling or its restriction can seriously slow down market recovery. Instead, when short selling is allowed, the buying demand arising from short sellers covering their short positions has the potential to create upward pressures on stock prices.

Moreover, the absence of short sales makes the market microstructure asymmetric favoring buyers, making the market much more vulnerable to speculative bubbles. A biased market may push prices to extremely high levels, which can then result in a much more violent collapse. In addition, long positions cannot be hedged easily, and investors may either sell rapidly or hold their positions waiting for a market rebound, and the overall effect can be an amplification of market fluctuations raising the probability of extreme events.

Short selling and margin buying maintain market liquidity when the daily rolling method of trade settlement is implemented, as opposed to the periodic regular settlement method. The daily rolling settlement system verifies that trading positions do not increase uncontrollably; however, it may severely restrict market liquidity, unless margin trading facilities are allowed.

Reliable market regulation is required for short selling to be effective. For this reason, in many emerging countries, even though nonexplicitly prohibited, short selling cannot be practiced due to the lack of a suitable market infrastructure. To make short selling viable, regulators must perform higher supervisory and regulatory roles, as well as additional tasks in maintaining and updating customer accounting data and other information. Furthermore, short selling and margin trading require margin-lending facilities to perform daily rolling settlements. Without an efficient stock-lending system, when stock prices rise, short sellers rush to cover their short positions, thereby causing stock prices to increase further with more short sellers being forced to cover their positions, thus further pushing the price up to extreme levels (a phenomenon also known as "short squeeze").

A stock exchange regulator must avoid cumbersome and bureaucratic procedures that can make short selling basically impracticable. The most famous case is represented by the Colombo Stock Exchange, which introduced securities lending and borrowing in 1999 to stimulate short selling. For 2 years, no transactions materialized on the exchange due to the difficulty and time consumption for performing securities lending transactions.

Short selling requires a specific regulatory control over stocks eligible for short sales to avoid short squeezes and market manipulation practices such as "bear raids" (i.e., when traders attempt to push stock prices down by taking large short positions and spreading negative rumors) and so-called "cornering" (which involves buying a large amount of a stock to artificially create a short supply of it). In this regard, Fortune (2001) demonstrates that short sales may destabilize the market more often than margin purchases, and this effect is usually larger in small markets. Moreover, the reporting requirements for short sales should consider a cost–benefit analysis and avoid making short sellers vulnerable to squeezes by requesting excessive transparency. Similarly, order execution procedures have to be designed to prevent unstable market movements, which may damage market efficiency.

The remainder of this chapter is organized as follows. Section 23.2 reviews the main characteristics of short selling in emerging markets, whereas Section 23.3 compares the market performances of different emerging markets to see whether short selling has had an effect or not.

23.2 SHORT SELLING IN EMERGING MARKETS: MAIN CHARACTERISTICS

Many emerging financial markets suffer from a lack of liquidity. This is usually the effect of small markets, where a limited number of traders face an inefficient market structure, with high transaction costs and weak financial institutions. Moreover, in these countries, the income level cannot produce relevant savings and illiquidity is worsened further by prohibiting short selling or making its practice very difficult. Short selling is often prohibited due to cultural and/or religious reasons, and numerous regulators may fear that short selling can amplify market fluctuations via feedback trading (i.e., trading conduct based on historical data).

Countries are grouped into countries where short selling is allowed (*SS countries*) and countries where it is not allowed (*NSS countries*). Table 23.1 summarizes the status of short selling in different emerging countries where an exchange exists. We consider countries for which daily stock market data are available, and we retrieved data for the listed emerging markets from www.mscibarra.com, www.econstats.com, http://export.rbc.ru, and http://finance.yahoo.com. In the case of China, we consider both the Shanghai and the Hong Kong stock exchanges, due to their different history.

Short selling is currently practiced, even with limitations, in 13 out of 31 markets, but we observe that it is allowed in 22 countries. We also report whether a derivatives market is in place for two reasons: (1) derivatives trading allows speculation on falling prices even with short selling restrictions in place and (2) existence of an option market is a signal of a more developed market infrastructure. Short selling effects are difficult to disentangle from derivatives trading when there is an existing derivatives market and traders can find efficient instruments to hedge and speculate as an alternative to short selling. Short sales restrictions can also seriously affect the efficiency of no-arbitrage pricing and the hedging of derivatives (Diamond & Verrecchia, 1987; Gupta & Jithendranathan, 2010).

23.3 EMERGING MARKET MAIN INDICATORS

This section shows the recent evolution of emerging markets by analyzing some aggregate indicators of market risk and performance. We split the countries into two groups—SS and NSS—and display the effectiveness of short selling (see Table 23.1, third column). We compute various indicators on year-long rolling time windows. Our data set spans from May 30, 2002, to November 15, 2010, and recognizes the existence of missing data in the early years for a few countries.[1] We report some results in Figure 23.1 and Tables 23.2 and 23.3. Section 23.3.1 displays the behavior of indicators throughout the entire time period, while Section 23.3.2 focuses on the 2008 market crisis.

---

[1] We chose the starting date to minimize missing data; however, for the following countries, some data were not available. For Kuwait and Oman, data are available from May 31, 2005; for Sri Lanka, data are available from June 25, 2002; and for Tunisia, data are available from May 31, 2004.

Table 23.1 Short Selling Status in Various Emerging Countries and Information about Local Derivatives Market

Country	Is Short Selling Allowed? Practiced?		Remarks	Derivatives Market
Argentina	Yes	No	Strong limitations	Active
Brazil	Yes	Yes	Strong limitations	Active
Chile	Yes	Yes	Introduced, with restrictions, in November 2001	Developing
China (Hong Kong)	Yes	Yes		Active
China (Shanghai)	No	No		Active
Colombia	Yes	No	Rarely practiced	
Czech Rep.	Yes	Yes		Developing
Egypt	No	No		
Hungary	Yes	Yes	Low volume	Active
India	Yes	Yes	Only individual investors are allowed to do short selling. Very limited	Active
Indonesia	Yes	No		Developing
Jordan	No	No		
Kenia	No	No		
Kuwait	No	No		
Malaysia	Yes	Yes	Currently allowed, but banned many times during recent financial crisis. Very limited	Active
Mexico	Yes	Yes		Developing
Morocco	Yes	No		
Nigeria	No	No		
Oman	No	No		
Pakistan	Yes	Yes	Introduced in February 2002	
Peru	Yes	No		
Philippines	Yes	No	Lack of regulation	Active

Continued...

Table 23.1 Short Selling Status in Various Emerging Countries and Information about Local Derivatives Market *Continued*

Country	Is Short Selling Allowed? Practiced?		Remarks	Derivatives Market
Poland	Yes	No	Introduced in 2000, but rarely practiced	Developing
Slovak Rep.	No	No		Active
South Africa	Yes	Yes		Active
Sri Lanka	Yes	No		
Taiwan	Yes	Yes		Developing
Thailand	Yes	Yes	Low volume	Developing
Tunisia	No	No		
Turkey	Yes	Yes	Short selling volume 4.5% of total trading volume in 2008	Developing
Venezuela	Yes	No		

Source: Bris and colleagues (2007), Endo and Rhee (2006), Fikirkoca (2009), and Shah (1997).

23.3.1 Market Performance during the Last Decade (2002–2010)

Numerous studies demonstrate that short sales can have an effect on market performance, price dynamics, and market efficiency (e.g., see Bris et al., 2007). Figure 23.1 presents evolution of the average volatility, the Sharpe ratio, skewness and kurtosis, frequency of extreme events, and maximum annual drawdown.[2] The thick and the thin lines represent, for each date, the mean computed across SS and NSS markets, respectively.

Examining results by each country, we note that all indicators are more homogeneous among SS countries than among NSS countries. This homogeneity indicates a much more similar market structure for SS countries, while indicators' values are spread over a larger range of values across NSS countries.[3]

Empirical analysis highlights that the mean volatility of SS countries is smaller than that of NSS countries in the first part of the sample prior to 2008.

---

[2] We considered a return extreme if it differed from the mean by more than two standard deviations. The maximum drawdown is the maximum cumulative loss obtained buying at the peak price and selling at the following lowest price. We compute the maximum drawdown using an annual rolling window, and the reported value is the ratio between bottom and peak prices.

[3] For the sake of interest and space, these data are not reported here. However, they are available from the authors upon request.

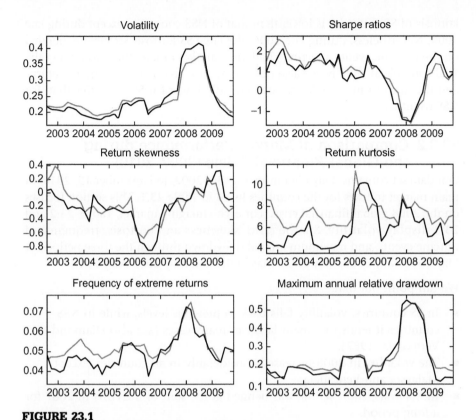

FIGURE 23.1
Time evolution of market risk and performance indicators.

During the 2008 crisis, the mean volatility of SS countries was higher than NSS countries, but returned to previous levels. In some NSS countries the volatility remained larger after the 2008 market crisis (see Table 23.2). We refer to Diamond and Verrecchia (1987) for similar results. Average Sharpe ratios for NSS countries are generally superior than those of SS countries. However, after the 2008 market drop, Sharpe ratios for SS countries recovered faster to previous levels than for NSS countries.

We further find that before 2008, the average skewness of returns of SS countries was often negative and lower than that of NSS countries. However, after 2008, the skewness of returns in SS countries was similar or slightly larger than that of NSS countries; we note that these results confirm (at least before 2008) the findings of Bris and co-workers (2007). For a similar analysis with Russian data and a review of short selling practices in Russia, see also Kudrov, Zlotnik, Dukhovnaya, and Fantazzini (2011). Furthermore, skewness tends to vary more in NSS countries than in SS countries. The average kurtosis of SS countries is lower than that of NSS countries, except during late 2006. Nevertheless, during late 2006, the large SS kurtosis strongly depended on the extreme events affecting Thailand's market in late 2006, following the Thai coup d'état. Finally, we also observe that the frequency of extreme returns and the maximum drawdowns are generally lower for SS countries than for NSS countries.

23.3.2 Comparison of Market Performance during the Global Financial Crisis (2007–2010)

Our data set contains daily data from May 30, 2002, to November 15, 2010, of main market indexes for the countries listed in Table 23.1. This section focuses on the 2008 global financial crisis. For each emerging market, Tables 23.2 and 23.3 display volatility, Sharpe ratio, skewness and kurtosis, frequency of extreme events, and maximum annual drawdown through the three periods of May 2007–May 2008, May 2008–May 2009, and May 2009–May 2010.

We can point out that:

- In SS countries, volatility falls back to previous levels, while in NSS countries it tends to remain larger in many cases (see also Diamond & Verrecchia, 1987).
- The volatility in 2008 increased considerably in all countries, except Malaysia and Venezuela.
- In Malaysia, short selling was banned at the start of the crisis in 2007 for a long period.
- China had high volatility in 2008 due the burst of its second large stock market bubble. See Jiang and colleagues (2010) for a detailed analysis of this bubble and Fantazzini (2010a,b) for a description of the global financial crisis in terms of log periodic power law models.
- Skewness tends to vary more in NSS countries than in SS countries. An exception of the latter group is Malaysia, which is probably due to the repeated ban of short selling during the global financial crisis.
- Finally, the frequency of extreme events appears to be higher in NSS countries than in SS countries, but no particular trend can be detected across individual countries.
- The relative rise in maximum annual drawdown is larger and more persistent for NSS countries.

23.4 CONCLUSION

This chapter reviewed the main characteristics of short selling in emerging markets, discussing how short selling restrictions can affect liquidity in emerging markets and considerably slow the market recovery after a

Table 23.2 Effects of 2008 Global Financial Crisis—SS Countries[a]

SS Country	Volatility		Sharpe Ratio		Skewness		Kurtosis		Extreme Returns (%)		Maximum Annual Drawdowns (%)	
Brazil	0.32	100	1.08	100	-0.37	100	4.04	100	3.83	100	20.95	100
	0.54	172	-0.68	-63	0.13	-33	5.64	139	6.90	180	61.58	294
	0.23	71	0.67	62	-0.19	50	4.81	119	5.36	140	12.35	59
Chile	0.22	100	-0.30	100	-0.19	100	5.04	100	4.98	100	29.94	100
	0.31	140	-0.23	77	0.78	-417	14.22	282	4.98	100	32.23	108
	0.15	66	1.83	-616	-0.08	44	4.50	89	4.60	92	9.22	31
China	0.35	100	0.65	100	-0.07	100	5.81	100	4.60	100	33.36	100
(Hong Kong)	0.50	141	-0.94	-144	0.31	-454	6.45	111	4.21	92	58.05	174
	0.25	70	0.87	134	0.03	-38	3.25	56	3.45	75	14.79	44
Czech Rep.	0.23	100	0.07	100	0.45	100	10.78	100	3.45	100	23.63	100
	0.49	208	-0.77	-1106	-0.45	-100	9.43	88	4.98	144	52.51	222
	0.20	87	0.36	515	-0.18	-41	4.30	40	4.98	144	11.11	47
Hungary	0.25	100	-0.65	100	0.09	100	3.64	100	7.28	100	32.97	100
	0.55	220	-1.21	187	0.08	85	6.43	176	6.90	95	66.96	203
	0.34	138	1.66	-256	0.04	39	3.09	85	2.68	37	15.32	46
India	0.32	100	0.74	100	-0.60	100	6.63	100	6.90	100	31.79	100
	0.45	140	-0.92	-125	-0.17	28	4.01	60	5.36	78	56.34	177
	0.28	87	1.36	184	2.98	-492	31.70	478	2.30	33	13.24	42
Malaysia	0.21	100	-0.39	100	-2.01	100	17.81	100	4.21	100	22.80	100
	0.21	99	-1.15	295	0.37	-18	4.50	25	6.90	164	37.66	165
	0.10	48	2.66	-682	0.07	-4	3.76	21	5.75	136	5.45	24
Mexico	0.27	100	-0.05	100	-0.06	100	4.51	100	4.98	100	24.38	100
	0.41	151	-0.74	1355	0.51	-928	5.41	120	7.28	146	48.12	197
	0.19	69	1.61	-2962	-0.34	623	3.89	86	4.60	92	8.92	37
Pakistan	0.22	100	0.66	100	-0.50	100	5.12	100	5.75	100	18.44	100
	0.45	204	-1.93	-294	-0.29	57	4.45	87	3.45	60	76.70	416
	0.22	102	1.62	246	0.14	-28	3.80	74	6.13	107	12.37	67
South Africa	0.22	100	0.13	100	-0.11	100	3.62	100	5.36	100	16.87	100
	0.35	157	-0.75	-564	0.11	-104	3.62	100	7.28	136	42.82	254
	0.16	71	1.29	971	-0.35	328	3.23	89	5.36	100	7.56	45

Continued…

Table 23.2 Effects of 2008 Global Financial Crisis—SS Countries[a] *Continued*

SS Country	Volatility		Sharpe Ratio		Skewness		Kurtosis		Extreme Returns (%)		Maximum Annual Drawdowns (%)	
Taiwan	0.25	100	0.37	100	-0.65	100	5.04	100	5.75	100	24.48	100
	0.35	139	-0.93	-256	0.06	-9	3.61	72	6.13	107	56.00	229
	0.19	78	0.97	265	-0.68	106	4.40	87	5.75	100	13.65	56
Thailand	0.25	100	0.79	100	0.22	100	3.39	100	5.36	100	21.94	100
	0.42	172	-1.17	-149	-0.62	-277	8.03	237	5.36	100	59.00	269
	0.28	112	1.61	203	-0.09	-39	4.06	120	4.21	79	13.75	63
Turkey	0.35	100	-0.15	100	0.02	100	4.17	100	6.51	100	33.96	100
	0.44	126	-0.66	433	0.30	1591	5.49	132	6.51	100	51.07	150
	0.25	73	1.95	-1288	0.17	898	3.22	77	5.36	82	12.60	37

[a]For each SS country, indicators are grouped in three rows: before (top), during (middle), and after (bottom) 2008. For each indicator, values (left columns) and relative values (right columns) are reported. Indicators are computed on year-long windows. Relative values are computed setting to 100 the "before" value.

Table 23.3 Effects of 2008 Global Financial Crisis—NSS Countries[a]

NSS Country	Volatility	Sharpe Ratio	Skewness	Kurtosis	Extreme Returns (%)	Maximum Annual Drawdowns (%)
Argentina	0.30 / 100	0.20 / 100	−0.24 / 100	4.23 / 100	5.36 / 100	29.45 / 100
	0.62 / 204	−1.28 / −644	−0.58 / 237	6.84 / 162	6.13 / 114	72.08 / 245
	0.31 / 102	1.68 / 845	0.28 / −113	6.02 / 142	4.21 / 79	17.22 / 58
China (Shanghai)	0.43 / 100	0.78 / 100	−0.17 / 100	4.77 / 100	6.13 / 100	44.12 / 100
	0.55 / 128	−0.82 / −104	0.26 / −151	5.64 / 118	5.36 / 88	64.78 / 147
	0.26 / 60	0.83 / 106	−0.03 / 19	3.11 / 65	3.83 / 63	14.40 / 33
Colombia	0.22 / 100	0.59 / 100	−0.88 / 100	10.43 / 100	4.21 / 100	26.17 / 100
	0.30 / 139	−0.47 / −80	−0.35 / 39	8.72 / 84	5.75 / 136	37.41 / 143
	0.15 / 71	2.73 / 464	0.14 / −15	4.55 / 44	4.98 / 118	9.69 / 37
Egypt	0.21 / 100	2.13 / 100	−0.86 / 100	8.40 / 100	5.36 / 100	12.89 / 100
	0.43 / 205	−1.89 / −89	−1.17 / 136	9.54 / 114	5.75 / 107	69.94 / 543
	0.30 / 145	1.19 / 56	−0.21 / 25	5.65 / 67	5.36 / 100	19.26 / 149
Indonesia	0.34 / 100	0.81 / 100	−0.32 / 100	5.89 / 100	5.36 / 100	23.70 / 100
	0.44 / 131	−0.76 / −94	−0.09 / 28	5.83 / 99	7.28 / 136	59.73 / 252
	0.25 / 75	1.72 / 213	0.02 / −7	3.94 / 67	4.98 / 93	9.97 / 42
Jordan	0.15 / 100	1.10 / 100	0.04 / 100	7.55 / 100	5.36 / 100	10.81 / 100
	0.34 / 224	−1.51 / −137	−0.67 / −1788	7.58 / 100	8.05 / 150	52.91 / 490
	0.18 / 119	−0.55 / −50	0.32 / 838	5.40 / 72	6.90 / 129	23.60 / 218
Kenya	0.21 / 100	0.61 / 100	−0.43 / 100	8.17 / 100	6.13 / 100	18.80 / 100
	0.28 / 137	−1.89 / −308	1.66 / −387	11.34 / 139	6.90 / 113	56.59 / 301
	0.14 / 68	2.78 / 453	0.88 / −204	7.01 / 86	3.45 / 56	12.48 / 66
Kuwait	0.15 / 100	0.81 / 100	−0.52 / 100	4.53 / 100	7.66 / 100	12.14 / 100
	0.44 / 296	−1.62 / −201	−0.61 / 117	6.45 / 142	7.28 / 95	63.20 / 521
	0.27 / 186	0.53 / 65	−1.03 / 199	9.46 / 209	4.21 / 55	26.35 / 217
Morocco	0.16 / 100	1.25 / 100	−0.31 / 100	6.95 / 100	4.60 / 100	12.89 / 100
	0.22 / 137	−1.32 / −106	−0.22 / 70	5.62 / 81	6.90 / 150	40.29 / 313
	0.15 / 94	0.35 / 28	0.50 / −163	5.43 / 78	5.75 / 125	21.99 / 171
Nigeria	0.16 / 100	1.12 / 100	1.01 / 100	7.27 / 100	4.60 / 100	9.58 / 100
	0.31 / 198	−3.04 / −272	0.08 / 8	3.28 / 45	11.88 / 258	71.49 / 746
	0.29 / 182	0.98 / 88	0.04 / 4	3.08 / 42	4.60 / 100	34.23 / 357

Continued...

Table 23.3 Effects of 2008 Global Financial Crisis—NSS Countries[a] *Continued*

NSS Country	Volatility		Sharpe Ratio		Skewness		Kurtosis		Extreme Returns (%)		Maximum Annual Drawdowns (%)	
Oman	0.18	100	3.36	100	-1.93	100	21.09	100	4.21	100	9.79	100
	0.45	249	-1.81	-54	-0.90	47	11.07	52	7.66	182	67.67	691
	0.16	86	1.58	47	1.22	-63	11.73	56	4.21	100	13.42	137
Peru	0.35	100	0.86	100	-0.56	100	4.22	100	3.07	100	30.32	100
	0.59	169	-0.88	-102	0.05	-9	5.31	126	7.66	250	67.14	221
	0.34	98	1.08	125	-0.11	19	3.89	92	3.07	100	20.31	67
Philippines	0.27	100	-0.76	100	0.17	100	6.75	100	5.75	100	32.94	100
	0.36	130	-0.52	69	-0.85	-501	9.27	137	6.51	113	39.69	120
	0.21	77	1.36	-179	0.10	59	4.48	66	5.36	93	11.78	36
Poland	0.26	100	-0.88	100	-0.09	100	4.10	100	4.60	100	30.93	100
	0.41	156	-1.20	137	-0.11	132	3.98	97	6.90	150	57.16	185
	0.28	108	1.01	-115	0.08	-87	3.91	95	4.21	92	12.77	41
Slovak Rep.	0.09	100	1.30	100	-0.84	100	9.02	100	5.36	100	4.45	100
	0.22	260	-1.25	-97	2.25	-269	27.69	307	4.60	86	37.19	836
	0.28	321	-1.58	-122	-4.11	491	30.58	339	3.83	71	40.42	909
Sri Lanka	0.11	100	-1.88	100	1.28	100	13.61	100	5.75	100	18.85	100
	0.32	293	-1.63	86	0.50	39	6.38	47	8.05	140	58.06	308
	0.29	258	2.87	-152	3.79	295	29.93	220	2.30	40	11.94	63
Tunisia	0.16	100	0.49	100	3.05	100	32.77	100	3.45	100	12.67	100
	0.20	126	0.40	81	-1.00	-33	8.96	27	5.36	156	16.42	130
	0.13	80	1.12	228	0.35	12	5.43	17	6.51	189	7.05	56
Venezuela	0.19	100	-0.62	100	1.07	100	7.68	100	4.60	100	23.45	100
	0.14	76	1.06	-171	0.96	90	7.07	92	4.98	108	17.03	73
	0.15	78	2.12	-340	0.32	30	4.90	64	4.60	100	7.41	32

[a]For each NSS country, indicators are grouped in three rows: before (top), during (middle), and after (bottom) 2008. For each indicator, values (left columns) and relative values (right columns) are reported. Indicators are computed on year-long windows. Relative values are computed setting to 100 the "before" value.

financial shock. Moreover, long positions cannot be hedged easily and, even in the case of a derivative market in place, derivatives cannot be priced efficiently. In general, short selling allows for efficient pricing information and a symmetric market microstructure, which makes the market more robust with respect to financial bubbles.

We then compared the market performance of different emerging markets to see whether short selling had an effect, with particular attention to the ongoing global financial crisis. Our work showed that the mean volatility of SS countries is, on average, smaller than that of NSS countries, except for the 2008 crisis: however, after 2008, volatility returned quickly to previous levels in SS countries, while this has not been the case for NSS countries. Interestingly, we also found that the average Sharpe ratios for NSS countries were generally better than those of SS countries before 2008, but after that year, the Sharpe ratios for SS countries have recovered much faster than those for NSS countries. Returns skewness tends to be much more variable in NSS countries than in SS countries, while the average kurtosis for SS countries returns is lower than that of NSS countries. Finally, we noted that the frequencies of extreme returns and average annual maximum drawdowns are lower for SS countries than for NSS countries.

This evidence makes us think of the famous anecdote of the "boiling frog," according to which "if a frog is placed in boiling water, it will jump out, but if it is placed in cold water that is heated slowly, it will not perceive the danger and will be cooked to death": short selling allows the market to react quickly to any information, even at the cost of some "temporary scalds" (in our case, high temporary volatility). Restricting or banning short selling practices condemns the market to a much slower recovery (lower Sharpe ratios, higher market drawdowns) and a lower liquidity, which can fatally limit its operation and slowly make it irrelevant for the local economy.

REFERENCES

Bris, A., Goetzmann, W. N., & Zhu, N. (2007). Efficiency and the bear: Short sales and markets around the world. *Journal of Finance, 52*(3), 1029–1079.

Diamond, D. W., and Verrecchia, R. E. (1987). Constraints on short-selling and asset price adjustment to private information. *Journal of Financial Economics, 18,* 277–311.

Endo, T., & Rhee, S. G. (2006). *Margin purchases and short sales in emerging markets: Their rationale and design variables.* World Bank Financial Sector Discussion Paper Series—May 2006.

Fantazzini, D. (2010a). Modelling and forecasting the global financial crisis: Initial findings using heterosckedastic log-periodic models. *Economics Bulletin, 30*(3), 1833–1841.

Fantazzini, D. (2010b). Modelling bubbles and anti-bubbles in bear markets: A medium-term trading analysis. In G., Gregoriou (Ed.), *The handbook of trading* (pp. 365-388). McGraw-Hill.

Fikirkoca, E. (2009). Short selling of securities in Turkey. TSPAKB Publication No. 39.

Fortune, P. (2001). Margin lending and stock market volatility. *New England Economic Review, 4*, 3–25.

Gupta, R., & Jithendranathan, T. (2010). Short sales restrictions and efficiency of emerging option market: A study of Indian stock index options. *International Journal of Finance and Economics, 46*, 99–109.

Kudrov, A., Zlotnik, A., Dukhovnaya, E., & Fantazzini, D. (2011). Short selling in Russia: Main regulations and empirical evidence from medium and long term portfolio strategies. In G. Gregoriou (Ed.), *Handbook of short selling*. Elsevier.

Jiang, Z. Q., Zhou, W. X., Sornette, D., Woodard, R., Bastiaensen, K., & Cauwels, P. (2010). Bubble diagnosis and prediction of the 2005–2007 and 2008–2009 Chinese stock market bubbles. *Journal of Economic Behavior & Organization, 74*(3), 149–162.

Shah, A. (1997). Derivatives in emerging markets. Appeared in *Economic Times* on 1 July 1997. Retrieved from http://www.mayin.org/ajayshah/MEDIA/index.html. (accessed date November 2010).

CHAPTER 24

Short Selling and the Problem of Market Maturity in Latin America

Miguel Díaz-Martínez and Emmanuel Fragnière

CONTENTS

ABSTRACT

This chapter presents practices and governmental policies regarding short selling in Latin America. By analyzing the characteristics of its equity, currency, and debt markets, our findings suggest that whereas regulators of developed countries have focused traditionally on the appropriateness of short selling bans to improve returns, efficiency, and financing costs in equity markets, short selling regulation in Latin America is rather a consequence of market development. This is supported by evidence found in currency and debt markets of Latin American countries, where liquidity is deeper than equity markets and agents have found mechanisms to short sell often in the absence of specific regulations on the topic.

KEYWORDS

Currency markets; Debt markets; Equity markets.

24.1 INTRODUCTION

Unlike developed economies where portfolio optimization techniques work well to assess the appropriateness of short selling strategies in stock markets, Latin American economies have particular structural features that complicate the regulatory environment of capital markets by affecting the effective execution of short sales. In developed countries, the structure of capital markets is highly efficient and therefore standard frameworks are applicable to evaluate the stability effects of short sale restrictions, irrespective of country-specific characteristics. However, Latin American financial markets are structurally different in terms of reduced liquidity, limited price formation, unavailability of information, and small economic size, making it difficult to assess the appropriateness of certain types of securities regulation and short selling norms. Furthermore, the existence of factors affecting country risk perception from the perspective of international investors trading emerging countries stocks in developed economies through American and Global depository receipts complicates the work of regulators. In addition, policies implemented to stabilize domestic emerging markets in an underdeveloped framework, which affects short- and long-term investments and their corresponding international capital flows, further burdens the job of regulators.

In this context, it is worth wondering if portfolio theory and optimization techniques are relevant when evaluating the integration of short positions in asset allocation strategies in Latin America. Similarly, it could be reasonable to assume that models are valid by adding variables related to country-specific imperfections. However, the question remains whether evidence from these markets supports the use of quantitative models. With this in mind, we examine how short sales are executed in Latin America and provide some reflections on the problem of market maturity.

The second section of this chapter examines the main regulations in Latin American countries where short sales are permitted. The third section examines main academic studies and their limitations. The fourth section presents the main features of short sales in Latin America, with special emphasis on currency, debt, and equity markets. The fifth section presents a discussion and draws some theoretical conclusions.

24.2 REVIEW OF NATIONAL REGULATORY REGIMES IN LATIN AMERICA

Legislation of short sales in Latin America is not only heavily fragmented, but also very incipient. We present the legal status and feasibility of short selling and describe the main regulations in Latin American stock markets where short selling is legal, even though legislation is limited and short selling is not widely developed in stock markets. The remaining sections extend this analysis to a wider range of securities where market actors have developed sophisticated mechanisms to short sell, often in the absence of regulation.

24.2.1 Legality and Feasibility of Short Sales

In order to analyze short sales in equity markets, Bris, Goetzmann, and Zhu (2007) classify countries in groups depending on whether short selling is legal and/or practiced. Based on the findings of Charoenrook and Daouk (2009), we classify countries according to these two aspects (see Table 24.1). Column 2 indicates the year short selling became legal, and column 3 is the year when short selling became feasible. "Yes" implies short selling has

Table 24.1 Legality and Feasibility of Short Selling in Latin America

Country	Legality	Feasibility
Argentina	1999	No
Bolivia	No	No
Brazil	1986	No
Chile	1999	2001
Colombia	No	No
Costa Rica	No	No
Ecuador	No	No
El Salvador	No	No
Guatemala	No	No
Honduras	No	No
Mexico	Yes	Yes
Nicaragua	No	No
Panama	No	No
Paraguay	No	No
Peru	2002	No
Uruguay	No	No
Venezuela	No	No

Source: Charoenrook and Daouk (2009).[1]

---

[1] The authors present these data for the year 2002. Changes after that year are not shown.

always been legal or feasible; "No" implies short selling has always been prohibited or not feasible.

Table 24.1 displays that short selling is not feasible in a large majority of markets. Even though legality is an issue that governements have focused on, it is not necessarily related to feasibility. Based on Table 24.1, we now examine the main rules and status of short selling in countries where it is legal.

24.2.2 Review of Regulatory Regimes in Latin America

i. Brazil

The rules in place do not allow naked short selling, and there are punitive rules that inhibit the nondelivery of stocks at settlement (T+3). According to Weguelin (2008), during the 2008 financial crisis, certain regulations were set forth to refrain from additional undesired volatility through short selling and maintaining market confidence through "covered" positions. While short selling is allowed in the Brazilian market (Bovespa), Weguellin argues that the rules in place have limited leveraged speculation, therefore avoiding the expansion of the crisis.

ii. Peru

Short selling can only be made with the shares listed at the Tabla de Valores Referenciales 1 and 2, two lists that include the most liquid securities traded on the Lima Stock Exchange (Bolsa de Valores de Lima). There are also price restrictions and brokers are not allowed to short sell at a price lower than the last quotation or at a price equal to the last quotation unless this is greater to the former (uptick rule).

Francke (2008) highlighted that the main effect of the financial crisis on Latin American stock markets was related to the "flight to quality" effect, whereby investors preferred to search for more "secure" investments in developed markets, as opposed to emerging markets. The flight to quality caused global capital to move from emerging to developed economies and stock prices to decline. The author also indicated that appropriate macreconomic policies in Peru were very successful in avoiding dramatic price declines in the local currency and stock prices. No changes were made in relation to short sales regulation.

iii. Mexico

Short selling is allowed but there is an uptick rule. The Secondary Legislation (Circular Única) establishes that short selling is only allowed through a stock exchange and for only highly liquid and semiliquid stocks. Even though the Mexican Stock Exchange (Bolsa Mexicana de Valores) is affected more easily by the crisis in the United States, no changes have been made in short selling regulation since the start of the subprime crisis.

iv. Chile

In terms of short selling regulation, this is probably the most advanced country in Latin America. The government has issued a manual that contemplates the mechanics, conditions, and restrictions of short selling operations, and stock brokers have developed standard formats to engage customers in short sales. However, short selling in the Santiago stock market (Bolsa de Comercio de Santiago) is not very developed and it is limited to a small number of stocks. Naked short selling is not allowed. Securities lending (which permits executing covered short sales) for short sellers is allowed for a maximum of 360 days. As was the case in other Latin American markets, no relevant changes in regulation were made after the financial crisis.

v. Argentina

With some specific restrictions subject to the companies or securities traded, nonnaked short selling is allowed. Even though stock prices have been particularly affected with the recent ban on short sales in Germany, regulation has not changed on the Buenos Aires Stock Exchange (Mercado de Valores de Buenos Aires or Merval).

24.3 PREVIOUS STUDIES ON SHORT SELLING IN LATIN AMERICA

Even though literature related to short sales is, in general, extensive, theoretical studies on Latin America are sparse. The main short selling studies in this part of the world are essentially derived from analyses conducted for the entire set of emerging countries but not specifically Latin America. In this respect, Bris and associates (2007) conducted a study in 46 equity markets around the world to consider whether short sales restrictions affect the efficiency of the market. The authors found evidence that prices incorporate negative information faster in countries where short sales are allowed and practiced. Similarly, based on short selling and put option trading data, Charoenrook and Daouk (2009) created a short selling feasibility indicator to analyze stock market indices around the world. Their findings suggest that aggregate returns and liquidity are better where short selling is possible and that short-sales restrictions do not affect the probability of a market crash. Also, Endo and Rhee (2006) demonstrated that margin trading is a vehicle that provides exogenous supply and liquidity, thus allowing the development of short selling frameworks according to country- and market-specific elements.

Although comparative analyses in developing markets are also very limited, there is a range of studies evaluating specific aspects in individual countries and governmental studies assessing short selling policies in Latin America. For example, Torres and Restrepo (2004) maintain that portfolio-building methods are based on hypotheses that are not realistic in emerging markets and comparatively tested portfolio optimization methodologies in the Colombian and New York stock markets, with important conclusions relating to imperfections (in short sales and other structural factors, such as market size, concentration, and informational inefficiencies) in Colombia.

Similarly, Agudelo, Gutierrez, and Munera (2010) undertook a comparative analysis of the Chilean and North American markets. The authors concluded that a suitable framework to implement short sales would involve a temporary stock transfer contract, which can operationalize this type of transaction in a context where legal frameworks do not allow them. Nevertheless, in some countries, financial services regulators have issued documents explaining how short sales should be undertaken (Chile and Peru) or interpreting if existing regulations allow short sales (Colombia and Brazil), or how regulations should be adapted to allow them.

Due to the academic inconclusiveness of short selling articles and the lack of research in less developed regions, we also examined general studies on financial markets and economic assessments from academicians and monetary authorities. In that respect, Feldstein (1999) investigated the actions of speculators and macroeconomic events during the 1997–1998 global financial crisis. The investigation was done to evaluate the most effective responses from emerging markets as opposed to the flawed programs of the International Monetary Fund, with significant conclusions for monetary policies related to the stabilization of local currencies. The Bank of International Settlements (BIS, 2002) published a series of papers on the development of bond markets, thus providing additional insight on the practical operation of debt securities in a number of emerging markets. Regarding equity market development, numerous studies provided an insight of stock market capitalization and emerging markets efficiency. For example, Bekaert and Harvey (2003) explored the effects of economic integration and liberalization policies in financial markets and demonstrated that such policies have effects in the microstructure of stock markets, thus reducing the cost of capital.

24.4 THE PRACTICE OF SHORT SELLING IN LATIN AMERICA

Given the complexities of emerging capital markets described in Sections 24.2 and 24.3 of this chapter and the lack of financial studies regarding short sales, we reviewed the relationship between global capital flows and a wide range of instruments traded in Latin America, including currencies, bonds, and stocks. Findings suggest that the most fundamental aspects permitting the development of short sale transactions are market liquidity and economic size, which provide the informational efficiency necessary to form reliable market prices and the consequent action of arbitrageurs to correct price anomalies (Blake, 2001). We thus undertake an analysis of short sales at three levels: (1) foreign currency markets, which are generally the larger and most liquid; (2) debt markets, which are relatively large and liquid due to the financing needs of governments; and (3) equity markets, which are often not as liquid as the others.

24.4.1 Currency Markets

We find three groups of countries in Latin America. First, countries whose currency floats freely[2] and is relatively easy to short sell (this group represents the vast majority of countries, e.g., Mexico, Chile Brazil, Bolivia, Colombia, and Peru, among others). Second, countries with fixed exchange rates where it is impossible to short sell (Venezuela and Cuba). Third, countries that have "dollarized" their economies (Panama, Ecuador, and El Salvador).

The political choice of a fixed or a floating currency regime depends on a variety of factors. For example, in 1991 the Argentinean government decided to fix the local currency at the time (the austral) at 10,000 australes per U.S. dollar to stabilize the economy and stop hyperinflation of the preceding decade. The policy was abandoned in 2001 following the events of the country's banking crisis and its consequent political and economic effects.

24.4.2 Debt Markets

The Latin American sovereign debt markets became relatively popular among international investors since implementation of the Brady plan in 1989, which was seen as a solution to the Latin American debt crisis of the 1980s. In fact, U.S. Secretary of the Treasury Nicholas Brady created the possibility to swap outstanding sovereign commercial loans for discounted debt bonds that would reflect the market value of debts from defaulted countries. The key innovation of those "Brady bonds" was to allow commercial banks to exchange their claims on Latin American countries into tradable instruments, allowing them to get the debt off their balance sheets, thus creating a secondary debt market.

More recently, Mohanty (cited by BIS, 2002) has compared the main bond markets in emerging markets and concluded that the main indicator of market liquidity (which facilitates short sales) is the bid–ask spread (the lower the spread, the higher the market liquidity). His analysis shows that Latin American public bond markets in Brazil, Chile, Mexico, Colombia, and Peru have deeper liquidity.

Due to the macroeconomic imbalances to which countries have been exposed to in Latin America, the main factors that lead speculators to short sell are related to sovereign risk. As is well known, when sovereign risk increases, local public finances deteriorate. For example, in 1994, Mexico did not have sufficient foreign reserves to maintain its fixed exchange rate[3] and therefore increased its risk perception among international investors. As a result of this,

---

[2] Also, there are countries controlling the fluctuation of their currencies within bands, but for purposes of this chapter we did not classify them in an additional group.

[3] Under a fixed exchange rate regime, governments sell or buy international reserves to increase or decrease demand for the local currency, therefore fixing its price.

the government was unable to issue new debt bonds, which reduced the availability of public funds. These events led investors to sell tesobonos,[4] which decreased the bonds' price and further increased sovereign risk, resulting in a self-reinforcing crisis known as the "tequila hangover."

24.4.3 Stock Markets

As highlighted in Section 24.2 of this chapter, short selling regulation is heavily fragmented and embryonic in the main Latin American stock markets. Also, the main literature and regulation regarding short sales are essentially focused on the inefficiency of equity markets. However, the liquidity and size of currency and debt markets have allowed the development of parallel financial transactions and contracts that permit short selling.

For these reasons, we believe that a comparison of short sales in Latin American markets should not only consider whether these are permitted or not, but also the underlying factors leading to an effective market operation. Where such operation is transparent and efficient, market agents normally find mechanisms to short sell, and regulation should come as a way to organize market activities. We analyze two issues: (1) factors that impel the trends of local stock markets and (2) concluding remarks related to market development.

24.4.3.1 Analysis of Latin American Stock Markets

The inexistent or very limited data of short sales in Latin American markets are different to over-the-counter markets and have not allowed us to draw sound statistical analyses on short selling practices. For this reason, we have developed a series of statistical analyses of stock index returns that could provide an indication of the behavioral patterns of investors and the main constraints of short selling in Latin American stock markets.

In the first analysis, we use monthly returns of nine stock market indices expressed in U.S. dollars—Dow Jones Latin America excluding Mexico, Dow Jones Venezuela USD, MSCI Argentina, MSCI Brazil, MSCI Chile, MSCI Colombia, MSCI Latin America, MSCI Mexico, and MSCI Peru. However, we use the first four indices for simplification purposes in Figure 24.1 and the entire set is displayed in Table 24.2. The data set ranges from January 1, 2000, to October 31, 2010.

Figure 24.1 plots the aforementioned series. It is obvious that some of the index returns, most notably the Dow Jones Venezuela USD, exhibit huge upward and downward swings—evidence of extreme volatility.

In our second analysis, Table 24.2 displays that the average returns of holding a long position in stock market indices are in the range of 1.19 to 2.66%. The

---

[4] This was the name of the Mexican treasury bonds.

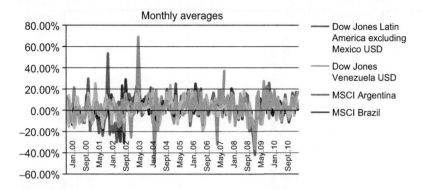

FIGURE 24.1

Monthly averages of Latin American market indices.

standard deviation ranges from 6.32% for Chile to 13.59% for Venezuela; however, higher standard deviations are not necessarily associated with higher returns.

Likewise, Table 24.3 gives bivariate correlations among nine series. Even though all indices are from the same geographical region, their percentage returns have surprisingly low correlations. Table 24.3 shows that Dow Jones Latin America returns are highly correlated with MSCI Latin America and MSCI Brazil indexes. The MSCI Latin America returns are highly correlated with MSCI Brazil and MSCI Mexico. Another interesting occurrence is the extremely low correlation between the Dow Jones Venezuela Index and all the other indices. A possible explanation could be that the Venezuela Index returns are the most volatile as a result of political instability and economic problems within the country.

These statistical analyses indicate that Latin American stock markets are largely driven by factors impacting the macroeconomic scenario and not by technical or idiosyncratic (i.e., firm-specific) issues, making it difficult to determine technical correlations between stocks. For this reason, it is not always possible to identify efficient portfolios in these countries; consequently, short sales cannot be necessarily associated with the optimization of stock portfolios. As highlighted earlier, some Latin American countries have higher volatilities with lower returns than others, which, in most cases, is due to economic and political instability.

In Latin America, local financial crises have determined the structure of capital markets. This was the case of the local debt markets after the Brady plan and the policies implemented in Argentina and Mexico after their local crises. To some extent, this is an explanation of why Latin American countries have not yet been successful in implementing clearer short selling legislation, as their main focus in the past was the development and stabilization of local markets.

Table 24.2 Mean and Standard Deviation (SD) of Latin American Indices

	Dow Jones Latin America	Dow Jones Venezuela	MSCI Argentina	MSCI Brazil	MSCI Chile	MSCI Colombia	MSCI Latin America	MSCI Mexico	MSCI Peru
Mean	1.91%	2.18%	1.29%	1.70%	1.24%	2.66%	1.41%	1.19%	2.27%
SD	9.44%	13.59%	12.33%	10.80%	6.32%	9.33%	8.24%	7.42%	9.19%

Table 24.3 Bivariate Correlations among Latin American Market Indices

	Dow Jones Latin America	Dow Jones Venezuela	MSCI Argentina	MSCI Brazil	MSCI Chile	MSCI Colombia	MSCI Latin America	MSCI Mexico	MSCI Peru
Dow Jones Latin America	1								
Dow Jones Venezuela	0.19	1							
MSCI Argentina	0.59	0.15	1						
MSCI Brazil	0.98	0.17	0.55	1					
MSCI Chile	0.72	0.12	0.48	0.64	1				
MSCI Colombia	0.48	0.26	0.35	0.43	0.48	1			
MSCI Lat Am	0.95	0.25	0.60	0.94	0.71	0.55	1		
MSCI Mexico	0.71	0.21	0.55	0.69	0.60	0.52	0.83	1	
MSCI Peru	0.63	0.08	0.45	0.61	0.44	0.39	0.67	0.58	1

In effect, the successful actions of governments in strengthening their economies are normally translated into reduced sovereign risk and improved ratings from risk rating agencies. These actions signify greater foreign investments and the possibility to construct better market infrastructure, including appropriate legislation, as well as mechanisms for short selling.

One of the authors of this chapter was a broker and trader on the Colombian Stock Exchange in recent years, and he asserts that stocks' short sales were practically inexistent in this market. Even though other Latin American countries have progressed with short selling, he highlights that short selling was not a practice for the average investor but rather for big institutional investors.

24.4.3.2 Market Development

There is a wide range of indicators that allow assessing stock market development. For example, Endo and Rhee (2006) have shown that the main factors of illiquidity in emerging equity markets are associated with five factors: short supply of equity securities, low demand for securities, high transaction costs, inefficient/defective market infrastructure, and low confidence in the market. Likewise, Bekaert and Harvey (2003) conducted a study of a sample of emerging economies that were liberalized and showed that the cost of capital in the economy decreased after liberalization. There is also a range of analyses from other authors comparing emerging countries' stock market capitalization, number of listed companies, and local stock correlations with international stocks and variables, among other variables. Our findings suggest that the assessment of short sales feasibility and regulation is highly correlated with market development.

Even though short sales are banned or not feasible in a big proportion of Latin American stock markets, it would be reasonable to expect that when such markets become better developed, regulators will need to regulate short selling as agents find mechanisms and utilize more sophisticated tools to short sell.

24.5 CONCLUSION

We found that global capital flows are one of the main drivers determining the depth of Latin American capital markets. Even in circumstances of underdevelopment, investors are interested in market liquidity, thus integrating the execution of short sales within their portfolio strategies. Although short sales may intensify the effects of financial crises, as was the case in the debt and currency markets of various Latin American countries in the past,[5]

---

[5] For example, during the Mexican crisis in 1994 (described earlier), the activity of short sellers in the debt and equity markets reinforced the price decline of the tesobonos and the Mexican peso.

the evaluation of bans should consider the practical effects of restrictions on investors' decisions. However, this is difficult where markets are typically inefficient, where infrastructure is defective, or where supply and demand are low, all of which are factors that complicate identifying the drivers of investor behavior.

International investors are interested in assessing Latin American market particularities as opposed to risks in developed markets, where liquidity is deep enough to individually evaluate companies on stock exchanges. However, in Latin America, correlations are often strongly biased depending on the political and economic events, and sovereign risk tends to become the most evident variable to evaluate against returns. Even though these conclusions are not decisive, further research could comparatively study concrete global portfolio-building strategies involving several sovereign instruments to increase the understanding of this topic. Also, there is a lack of public statistics to provide reasonable quantification of short selling in Latin America. We believe that the theory regarding short sales in emerging markets is not complete, but the evidence provides an understanding of the relationships among market maturity, short selling dynamics, policies, and investment decisions.

REFERENCES

Agudelo, D., Gutierrez, A., & Munera, N. (2010). *Ventas en Corto: Análisis comparativo y propuesta para su implementación en el Mercado de Valores Colombiano*. Medellín: Universidad Eafit.

Bank for International Settlements (BIS). (2002). *The development of bond markets in emerging economies*. Basel, Switzerland: Author.

Bekaert, G., & Harvey, C. (2003). Emerging markets finance. *Journal of Empirical Finance, 10*(1–2), 3–55.

Blake, D. (2001). *Financial market analysis*. Hoboken, NJ: John Wiley and Sons.

Bris, A., Goetzmann, W., & Zhu, N. (2007). Efficiency and the bear: Short sales and markets around the world. *Journal of Finance, 62*(3), 1029–1079.

Charoenrook, A., & Daouk, H. (2009). *A study of market-wide short-selling restrictions*. New York: Cornell University.

Endo, T., & Rhee, S. (2006, May). *Margin purchases and short sales in emerging markets: Their rationales and design variables*. World Bank Financial Sector Discussion Series, Washington, DC.

Feldstein, M. (1999). A self-help guide for emerging markets. *Foreign Affairs, 78*(2), 32–35.

Francke, P. (2008). Sexta Exposición Crisis Financiera Internacional. VII Encuentro de Red Informativa Agraria, RedGe, 28 Nov 2008.

Torres, C., & Restrepo, J. (2004). Selección de portafolios usando simulación y optimización bajo incertidumbre. *Dyna, 71*(141), 35–57.

Weguelin, S. (2008). Should we restrict short selling? *Capital Alberto Magazine, 6*(62), 64–65.

CHAPTER 25

Short Selling—The Ambrosia or Kryptonite of Emerging Markets?

Edward Pekarek and Maryam Meseha

CONTENTS

ABSTRACT

This chapter examines the nature of short selling in various emerging markets and explores the advantages and risks associated with short selling in an emerging market. The discussion extends to a survey of the leading emerging markets, including Brazil, Russia, India, and China (referred to as "BRIC" countries). This analysis is intended to educate the reader as to some of the essential basics of short selling in a foreign emerging equity market.

KEYWORDS

American depository receipt; Exchange-traded funds; Margin equity; Market liquidity; Quantitative easing.

25.1 INTRODUCTION

As discussed in far greater detail elsewhere in this text, traditional short selling involves a market transaction where a bearish investor sells borrowed securities in anticipation of a price decline and is required to return an equal number of shares at some point in the future (Endho & Rhee, 2006). Such an investor may profit from the speculation if the price of the security sold short experiences a subsequent decline in value. The ability to affect a traditional short sale hinges largely on the ability of an investor to borrow shares of a target security and commit capital sufficient to collateralize the securities loan that constitutes the bearish trading position.

A sound lending system of a country is a key component for successful short selling. However, regulations on lending can restrain an investor's capability to short sell. Securities borrowing and lending can directly establish the costs of short selling and therefore should be considered in conjunction with short sales constraints; even though short selling is permitted in numerous countries, securities borrowing and lending are so limited that short sales are not really possible (Bris, Goetzmann, & Zhu, 2003).

The difference between the price of the security sold short and the value of the collateral pledged by the short seller in his/her customer account with the lending broker is generally considered "margin equity." This difference must be financed with capital provided by the customer, and the total margin debt of all positions cannot exceed the trader's capital at any time (Brunnermeier & Pederson, 2007). While the lending broker has some discretion in terms of the acceptable ratio of margin equity, relative to the value of the borrowed securities, certain regulators, such as the Federal Reserve Bank in the United States, are empowered to establish margin equity minimums, designed to minimize system risk by establishing the maximum risk a lending broker can absorb in its customer accounts relative to margin debt.

A short sale offers the speculator an opportunity to exploit mispriced securities (Bris et al., 2003). The ability of short sellers to target overpriced stocks profitably is documented by Diether and colleagues (2009), who show that short sellers target overvalued stocks and, when successful, are able to predict price reversals (Blau, Van Ness, & Warr, 2010). Despite what might seem to be a negative effect, at least initially, it has been embraced by some emerging markets that have invited this form of exploitation. The benefits of short selling can greatly outweigh disadvantages of depreciating domestic securities, especially when securities prices are inflated artificially through "bubble" mania or fraud. Perhaps the most important benefits include smooth price fluctuations, increased asset pricing accuracy, and improved market liquidity (Brunnermeier & Pederson, 2007).

Despite the benefits identified by extensive literature and research, fewer than half of the world's recognized securities exchanges permitted short sales as of 2005. This lack of consensus on the benefits and detriments of short selling is most pronounced during an economic downturn (Charoenrook & Daouk, 2005). Most developed countries shift away from short selling during such instances because it is considered by regulators to be a destabilizing force that causes further financial panic (Charoenrook & Daouk, 2005). A stark example of this ends-justify-the-means policy is evidenced by the measures taken by United States and German regulators who, along with other developed nations, imposed heavy restrictions on short selling in the wake of the 2008 "Great Recession." In defiance of free market principles, these restrictions were used to insulate the very financial firms that were widely believed to have caused the economic crisis from free market price discovery for fear of an investor stampede to the exits at any price. Some emerging markets, however, continued to allow short selling despite these perceived fears. For example, China and Brazil refused to put restrictions on short selling in the wake of the 2008 financial crisis because they believed the benefits associated with the practice outweighed any potential risks.

This chapter explores various theories behind market movement away and toward short selling, including the benefits and risks an emerging market might encounter as a result of permissive short selling. Short selling in some key emerging markets, such as the "BRIC" nations (Brazil, India, Russia, and China), is surveyed. Finally, the benefits and risks for an investor who chooses to short sell in an emerging market are discussed.

25.2 EMERGING MARKET BENEFITS FROM SHORT SELLING

Short selling offers various benefits to the economic development of an emerging market. A permissive regime can foster capital raising because short selling frees up capital that may have been otherwise allocated to "long" positions during periods of market appreciation (Endho & Rhee, 2006). In addition, the authors state that a core function of short selling is the price discovery mechanism achieved through the trading of securities in the secondary market. In order for this price discovery mechanism to function effectively, capital must be available so that investors can properly determine the equilibrium price of a particular security (Endho & Rhee, 2006). The effectiveness of price discovery and its corollary capital raising, therefore, depend at least in part on the liquidity of an emerging market (Endho & Rhee, 2006). While this may seem like circular reasoning, short selling has been found to be a means by which an emerging market can facilitate efficient price discovery, thereby freeing more capital and allowing increasing liquidity, which in turn allows for further price discovery and a more efficient market in a virtuous cycle (Bris et al., 2003).

Permissive short selling also provides a means by which markets can segregate underperforming companies because the essence of short selling is the profit incentive of successfully identifying and exploiting overpriced securities (Bris et al., 2003). The ability of an investor to identify overpriced securities can reap handsome rewards. For example, in 2002, Bill Ackman, founder and chief executive of the hedge fund Pershing Capital Management LP, wagered aggressively that MBIA, the Armonk, New York-based insurer, would experience deteriorated financial results. By the end of 2002, the world's largest bond insurer had suffered an 84% loss. Bill Ackman's ability to identify the weak structural problems of MBIA generated more than $1B in short sale profits for Pershing over a 6-year span (Childs & Keene, 2010). Ackman's success is supported by various research models, which have determined that short sellers frequently correct stock mispricing. Research by Boehmer and Wu (2008) demonstrates that short sellers in U.S. markets have assisted in correcting mispricing. In particular, the authors report that short selling at the daily level reduced pricing errors and increased informational pricing efficiency (Blau et al., 2010). Moreover, Diether and colleagues (2009) report that short sellers are often contrarians who successfully predict negative returns, further suggesting that short sellers frequently target overvalued securities and consistently predict price reversals.

The correction of mispricing by short selling is directly related to the ability of bearish traders to facilitate information diffusion and transfer (Bris et al., 2003). The authors found that short selling restrictions result in an accumulation of unrevealed negative information. Such restrictions may aggravate subsequent market declines because the concealed information is not incorporated into prices by informed traders (BGZ, 2003). Information of this sort will not likely reveal itself in the market until prices begin to drop. Once previously concealed negative information is disseminated within the market, the prospect of more dramatic pricing shocks increases (BGZ, 2003). This may further aggravate market declines and could conceivably lead to market crashes (BGZ, 2003). These findings affirm the study of Hong and Stein (2002), which determined that prices of "protected" securities are slower to adjust to negative information than stocks that are unconstrained (BGZ, 2003).

Perhaps the most striking recent example of a short seller who pierced the asymmetry of concealed information is that of James S. Chanos. Well before any regulator took issue with the business operations and practices of Enron, Chanos discovered what he believed to be significant misconduct at the energy concern in connection with its "gain-on-sale" accounting and sought to profit from Enron's formerly well-concealed scheme (Chanos, 2010). Chanos realized a substantial profit as a result of his investigative and analytical diligence, which later led to public exposure of sweeping fraud at the hands of the Houston, Texas, company. A noted example of a sophisticated short seller who identified inaccurate "bubble" pricing was the Paulson hedge fund, which anticipated a "wipeout scenario" in the U.S. residential housing market and adopted a short position through the use of a synthetic short sale tool, the credit default swap (CDS), a topic discussed in greater detail in Chapter 2. CDS pricing has incidentally become a recent proxy of sorts for the expected performance of publicly held concerns, as well as sovereign nations, allowing for increasingly efficient dissemination of market information.

As noted earlier, short selling tends to increase market liquidity, which in turn has the potential to spur economic growth. In their 2005 study, Charoenrook and Daouk (2005) found that short selling also increases market volatility. Market liquidity created by short sellers typically depends on margin funding availability, and restrictions on lending requirements tend to impact negatively on liquidity (Jones, 2002). In turn, margin maintenance ratios are, to some extent, a function of the market liquidity of the collateral (Brunnermeier & Pederson, 2007). When funding liquidity tightens, short sellers become understandably reluctant to sell borrowed securities short; this tends to reduce market liquidity and has the potential to increase the risk of financing short sales, which often hikes margin maintenance ratios (Brunnermeier & Pederson, 2007).

The findings summarized earlier suggest overall that market-wide short sale restrictions can affect market quality adversely (Blau et al., 2010; Bris et al., 2003; Charoenrook & Daouk, 2005). From a regulatory perspective, the ability to short a stock in an off-shore different market, despite local restrictions, might render home market restrictions ineffective (Blau et al., 2010). An example of this is discussed at length in Chapter 2, when German regulators attempted to curtail the selling short of sovereign debt through CDS and sophisticated traders simply sought to circumvent the measures from other markets and continue the bearish trades against the debt of the so-called "PIIGS."

25.3 RISK OF SHORT SELLING TO AN EMERGING MARKET

Critics of short selling regimes propose various reasons why emerging markets should restrict the trading practice. Price manipulation is cited most typically as a disadvantage of short selling, and scandals such as that involving Amr Ibrahim ("Anthony") Elgindy provide ample fodder for such critics. Elgindy enlisted Jeffrey Royer, a corrupt former FBI agent, and a small army of Web denizen devotees to "attack" companies whose shares he had sold short, many of which became targets of his bearish trades because of information leaked to him by Royer (Stock Picker, 2006). Some critics charge that short selling creates violent price fluctuations and poses a systematic risk to financial systems that may lack the sophistication or information access necessary to withstand such movements in an orderly manner (Endho & Rhee, 2006). The underlying premise of this criticism is that short selling is believed to disrupt otherwise orderly markets through panic selling and resulting high volatility, which, according to these critics, can destabilize an economy (Charoenrook & Daouk, 2005).

Regulators who oppose short selling maintain that in a sizeable market decline, bearish speculators flock to the vulnerable market and increase sell-side volume by inciting panic, which, these critics contend, could create a larger market decline than if short sellers were not present (Charoenrook & Daouk, 2005). Some scholars deem short selling as the catalyst for various market crashes, particularly the 1987 "Black Monday" market crash and 1997 Asian currency crisis (Bris et al., 2003). Bernardo and Welch (2002) contend that constraints that hinder market participants from "front running" other sell-side investors can effectively prevent financial crisis. This theory finds support in the Allen and Gale (1991) study, which posits that short selling is a destabilizing influence in the economy.

This theory, however, has been roundly discounted in academic circles. Many scholars conclude that short selling is not responsible for causing market crashes. For example, Bernardo and Welch (2002) developed a model relating to how fear of financial crises, as an alternative to liquidity shocks, is the real origin of most financial crises. In addition, Bris and associates (2003) and Charoenrook and Daouk (2005) both found that short sale constraints do not prevent market crashes but rather inhibit price discovery, limit liquidity, and ultimately reduce market efficiency. Despite findings that dispel the myth that short selling causes financial crises, many regulators adhere to the notion that short sale restrictions prevent market crashes.

Short selling is seen as facilitating severe price declines in individual securities (Bris et al., 2003). However, the authors found that there was no compelling evidence to suggest that constraining short selling would prevent or mitigate severe price declines at the market level. Moreover, some companies rightfully should be shuttered and some securities deserve to go to zero. Nonetheless, short selling is disdained by some on moral grounds, perceived as exploitation of the misfortune of others and an exacerbating factor in times of crisis (Bris et al., 2003). Irrespective of moral judgments, there is always a seller for every buyer.

25.4 SHORT SELLING IN BRIC NATIONS

Many investors seeking "alpha" have ventured beyond the United States and other industrialized nations to invest in emerging markets due to the untapped potential of developing countries and the prospect of higher profits. The International Monetary Fund predicts the U.S. economy will grow in 2011 at an annual rate of 2.3% compared with 9.6% in China, 8.4% in India, and 6% in Chile (Lynch, 2010). Perhaps this trend has only been exacerbated by the recent decision by the Federal Reserve to buy $600B in long-term U.S. Treasury bonds in the hopes of stimulating a sluggish economy, a process known as "quantitative easing" (Lynch, 2010). In an apparent attempt to stoke inflation and equity prices, the Federal Reserve Bank has fueled a surge in emerging market investment, especially in commodity sectors, which underscores the difficulty of stimulating the economy through monetary policy with interest rates already at near record lows (Lynch, 2010).

Overseas investment by domestic corporations in the first half of 2010 exceeded the amount that foreign firms spent in the United States on factories and acquisitions at an annual rate of almost $220 billion, according to the Commerce Department. In the first half of 2006, the last year before the recent financial crisis, the net flow of funds favored the United States at an annual rate of roughly $30B (Lynch, 2010). U.S. Commerce Department data reveal that half of outbound investment dollars this year landed in Europe (Lynch, 2010). It is not unreasonable to conclude that BRIC nation securities markets are among the likely beneficiaries of a growing Federal Reserve balance sheet. "All the Fed can do is create liquidity… [it] has no control over how that liquidity is used" (Lynch, 2010).

25.4.1 Brazil

Brazil permits short selling but imposes specific restrictions based on the citizenry of the investor. Brazil imposes restrictions on foreign short sellers by requiring them to have a legal representative stationed in Brazil (Blau et al., 2010). The authors argue that this requirement has made short selling impracticable for retail investors. There is no indication that Brazil will lift this heavy restriction in the near future. However, it would be unremarkable if a Brazilian cottage industry developed to assist short selling, not unlike the use of nominees in a number of Caribbean island states, such as the Cayman Islands and Bahamas, to establish off-shore business entities.

25.4.2 Russia

Russia has explicitly regulated short selling since 2002. Such regulation stems from the default and collapse of the hedge fund Long Term Capital Management (LTCM) in 1998. LTCM employed heavily leveraged "black box" arbitrage trading strategies, and its managers expected bond spreads to narrow. LTCM was aggressively long Russian bonds and currency while short U.S. treasuries and the dollar when the yield spread between the bonds was historically very wide and LTCM managers speculated the spread would narrow (Laurenson et al., 2006). The bond spread only widened in a global "flight to quality" as investors fled the ruble and bought U.S. debt and currency. Russia eventually defaulted on its sovereign debt and the ruble collapsed while LTCM had more than $1T in foreign-exchange currency derivatives exposure and LTCM could not satisfy its margin calls but was absorbed by a bailout consortium led by the New York Federal Reserve Bank (De Borchgrave, 2010). The Russian collapse is a vivid example of the fragility of liquidity, as a relatively small shock had a disproportionately large impact. Compared to the total market capitalization of the U.S. debt and equity markets, losses due to the Russian default were arguably minuscule by comparison, but caused reverberations throughout financial markets worldwide (Laurenson et al., 2006).

Short selling was regulated actively until 2008 when Russia announced that it would ban margin selling and short selling altogether. Moscow was responding to the world's financial downturn and heralded the positions held by both the United States and Germany that constraining short selling would prevent further panic selling. Moscow affirmed its position by closing their two main exchanges for 2 days in order to stem a selling wave (Robinson, 2010). As of May 2010, these bans appear not to be lifted (Bentley, 2010).

In 2010 the Russian economy suffered from a depreciated ruble and significant oil stock decreases. Many blamed the country's depreciated currency on investors closing short arbitrage positions consisting of a European currency basket against the ruble as speculation grew that Irish banks would acquiesce to a European Union bailout. Sliding oil prices and concern over Russia's faltering economic growth caused an increase in short interest against the ruble and its oil producers (Corcoran & O'Brien, 2010).

Despite the bleak outlook, some have encouraged traders to cover their short positions go long based on valuations. Of course this view is dependent on a rebound for the Russian economy, which remains to be seen (Bentley, 2010).

25.4.3 India

India's regulatory system allows for short selling but it is rarely practiced. The Indian short selling regulatory regime distinguishes between various types of traders. Foreign institutions are prohibited from short sales but individual investors may make bearish wagers without restrictions (Blau et al., 2010). Foreign institutional investors are the primary sell-side players because they have the means by which to raise larger margins immediately. Because they are prohibited from the market, the practice is very limited in India.

Because India prohibits institutional investors from short selling, its market continues to experience pricing imperfections. According to a 2010 study conducted by Gupta and Jitherndranatham (2010), Indian restrictions cause market imperfections to persist because more informed institutional investors are precluded from taking advantage of the imperfections. The authors suggest that these restrictions, however, do not prevent the Indian market from reacting adequately to information arrivals as scholars have observed it absorbs new information as efficiently as developed markets. Furthermore, they hypothesize that this is a suggestion that the Indian investors are perhaps using derivatives to hedge risk efficiently.

25.4.4 China

Short selling was prohibited in Hong Kong prior to 1994. The Securities Exchange of Hong Kong allowed short selling to take place for a subset of 17 of the 33 stocks posted on the Hang Seng Index that year. These stocks were allowed to be shorted, albeit with heavy restrictions. Hong Kong only allowed short sales in securities designated specifically by the Hong Kong Exchanges and Clearing Ltd. (Bris et al., 2003). Chinese officials lifted these restrictions on March 25, 1996, and allowed all 113 Hang Seng stocks to be shorted without restriction (BGZ, 2003).

In the wake of the financial crisis of 2008, China did not follow in the footsteps of the United States. Instead of banning short sales, China permitted the practice in order to help develop Asia's second-largest market after prices and trading volumes slumped (Yidi & Shidong, 2008). China took this position, anticipating that it would increase trading without prompting further declines (Yidi & Shidong, 2008). Its decision to allow short sales is in line with various studies done on its stock exchanges. For example, Chen and Rhee (2010) found that short selling in Hong Kong actually speeds up the incorporation of new information and renders the market more efficient. It is worth noting that James Chanos is presently holding well-publicized short positions against a variety of Chinese securities and sees it as "the next domino to fall in the global meltdown" (Sherman, 2008).

25.5 SHORT SELLING IN OTHER KEY AREAS

25.5.1 South Korea

South Korea's Financial Supervisory Commission imposed a "temporary" ban on short selling in 2008, following in the steps of the United States. South Korean securities regulators have been cautious about foreign sell-offs because of the destabilizing effects on the local currency and the rest of the economy (Lim, 2009). Foreign investors, mostly hedge funds, were among the biggest short sellers in Seoul.

The announcement to ban short selling in South Korea came on the heels of its transition from emerging to developed market. The global index provider FTSE Group promoted South Korea to a developed market status from an advanced emerging market. MSCI Inc., another major provider of global financial information and indices, upgraded South Korea to a developed country from an emerging to developed market in June 2008 (MSCI Barra, 2008).

In May 2010, South Korean regulators commenced a review of short sale policies in an effort to attract foreign investor capital after Germany instituted a temporary ban on some trades designed to curb speculation (Hong, 2010). The author hopes that South Korea's regulatory reform will spawn trading and reduce the risk of capital flight. Further, he states that South Korea's 2010 gross domestic product is projected to expand by 5.9%. However, along with an increased tolerance for short selling, South Korean market regulators have indicated it will tighten short sale monitoring, designed to curb volatility (Hong, 2010).

25.5.2 Indonesia

Indonesia is the world's largest Muslim nation, with a population exceeding 200 million. It largely escaped the recent global economic crisis because of strong domestic consumption and is an increasingly vital part of southeast Asia. This trend shows no sign of slowing. Indonesia was a market standout in 2010, and its authorities are undertaking steps to smooth volatility in short-term instruments that might threaten market stability (Chatterjee, 2010). Loose monetary policy and profligate spending in the western hemisphere drove a flood of money to emerging markets such as Indonesia and contributed to an economic boom, where government bond yields are at record lows, its currency rests at 3-year highs, and its stock market has been launched into uncharted territory (Chatterjee, 2010).

Foreign holdings of Indonesian bonds have soared by almost 80% in 2010, according to Indonesian Finance Ministry data (Unditu & Bisara, 2010). Its central bank's key interest rate sits at a historic low of 6.5%, but still remains southeast Asia's highest, making Indonesia attractive for foreign investors seeking high-yield assets. By comparison, Malaysia's benchmark rate stands currently at 2.75%, Thailand's at 1.75%, and the Philippines' at 4% (Unditu & Bisara, 2010). The authors stress that despite the volatility risk of waves of "cheap" money flowing from overseas, the Indonesian government has indicated it has no plans to impose capital controls because its economic foundation is sound.

Despite its growth and optimism, Indonesia has acted at times far more like a developed market in terms of its treatment of short selling. The Indonesian Composite Index dropped more than 16% during the first quarter of 2008, and the Capital Market and Financial Supervisory Agency responded to the drop with a June 2008 short sale restriction and margin trading curb due to increased stock market volatility (Jakarta Post, 2008). The Indonesian Stock Exchange (IDX) had previously permitted investors to sell short approximately 50 major issues that trade on the bourse (Suhartono, 2008). It temporarily banned both covered and so-called "naked" short sales on October 1, 2008, for 30 days in response to the recent economic crisis (RBC Dexia, 2008). The IDX issued a letter on October 7, 2008, that emphasized (1) the ban of short sales was strict and (2) any day trade sale creating a short position covered by a buy trade is considered short selling for the purposes of the ban (Credit Suisse). The IDX also discontinued its monthly short sale securities list during the ban and suspended all stock-lending facilities (RBC Dexia, 2008). Any failure to deliver shares would be settled automatically by payment of the alternative cash settlement on the settlement date, including a 25% notional trade value penalty (RBC Dexia, 2008). Less than 1 week later, the Capital Market and Financial Supervisory Agency commenced an investigation into a dozen securities firms (11 foreign and one Indonesian) to determine if "illegal speculative practices in the market" precipitated the collapse (Jakarta Post).

The IDX lifted the ban in part on February 4, 2009, and revised its short sale and margin trading regulations with an effective date of May 1, 2009 (RBC Dexia, 2009). The 2009 IDX-relaxed short sale regulations pertain only to shares that meet certain criteria, such as (1) having been IDX listed for at least 6 months; (2) a 3-month trailing daily average minimum transaction value;

(3) regular trading of the security, with some exceptions; (4) a price-to-earning ratio (P/E) not in excess of three times the overall market P/E; and (5) a minimum of 600 shareholders who collectively own less than 5% ownership of the company's shares (RBC Dexia, 2009). Despite the booming economic prospects in Jakarta, Indonesian regulators possess something of a heavy hand and an itchy trigger finger, ready to impose conditions on short sellers in the event of signs of market turmoil on the horizon.

25.5.3 United Arab Emirates

The United Arab Emirates (UAE) Abu Dhabi Securities Exchange announced in October 2010 that it would introduce short selling in order to improve the country's prospects of gaining emerging market status under the MSCI, Inc. Index (Hankir, 2010). Hankir (2010) suggests that the UAE is currently ranked as a so-called "frontier" market. He also mentions that the ADS Exchange promised that new regulations would include trading by marking and the introduction of a delivery-versus-payment system.

25.5.4 Eastern Europe

Eastern Europe is widely known for its specializations in commodity trading. Although it has successfully traded in this area, it may be widely overlooked by investors. However, Driessen & Laeven (2004) have argued that Eastern Europe can be a profitable investment area and may not be widely affected by short selling constraints. They found that the regional diversification benefits appear largest on average for countries in Eastern Europe and can be substantial, even when allowing for short selling constraints. The increase in expected return for Eastern European countries of investing in the region is 0.3 percent per month on average, as expressed in U.S. dollars, even when short selling constraints are present. (Driessen and Laeven, 2004).

25.6 HELPFUL INVESTOR MECHANISMS

Investors who wish to short sell frequently encounter three typical structural problems. The first is an inefficient stock lending system. In order to sell a security short, an investor must first borrow the subject securities; without an efficient lending system, short selling can be highly impracticable. It is crucial therefore for investors who wish to adopt bearish strategies in emerging markets to identify those with well-functioning stock-lending systems. The second key problem is often cumbersome regulatory systems pertaining to securities lending rules. These rules severely restrict the ease and efficiency by which an investor may sell short, which can ultimately impede the probabilities of success.

Finally, investors must be aware of an emerging market's regulatory system. If a market utilizes a weak regulatory regime, there may be few, if any, protections afforded to an investor against bearish trades, such as "short squeezes," which potentially pose the risk of unlimited loss for short sellers. A recent example of this occurred with a number of U.S. hedge funds that suffered substantial losses in 2008 when they relied on public statements made by managers of Porsche Automobil Holding SE who commented publicly on its ownership interest in Volkswagen AG (Volkswagen), resulting in a massive squeeze that, according to some accounts, led to more than $1B in losses. The recent U.S. Supreme Court decision in *Morrison v. National Australia Bank Ltd.*, 130 S. Ct. 2869 (2010), portends for a dramatically higher risk environment for domestic investors, whether "long" or "short," who seek off-shore opportunities. The *Morrison* court expressly foreclosed private investor securities fraud claims before U.S. courts if the securities transaction(s) at issue, whether purchase or sale, occurred on a foreign exchange.

Investors need not be subjected to these three structural problems. There are mechanisms that an investor can use to circumvent or altogether avoid the aforementioned problems. The first mechanism is to purchase (or sell) an American depository receipt (ADR). ADRs are securities that represent a specific number of shares of foreign corporations but are traded in the United States (Blau et al., 2010) and can be used by short sellers to take advantage of constraint-induced overvaluation.

An investor may also be able to circumvent short sale constraints by shorting the ADR instead of the short sale-constrained stock (Blau et al., 2010). The authors find that the return predictability of short sellers is expected to be higher for unfeasible ADRs than for feasible ADRs. This study defined unfeasible ADRs as foreign stocks that face binding short sale constraints in their home market, whereas feasible ADRs were defined as foreign stocks with fewer home market constraints. Investors should note that ADRs can create risks in light of the recent *Morrison* decision, as the Supreme Court determined that the underlying shares were listed only nominally in the United States and declined to extend federal securities laws to cover such instruments.

Investors also have the option to invest in exchange-traded funds (ETFs). ETFs give investors, large and small, the opportunity to get exposure, long or short, to virtually every major market and asset class in the world (Bary, 2010). Bary (2010) notes that ETFs offer many benefits, including low fees, transparency of investments, and tax efficiency because of low portfolio turnover. For the purposes of this chapter, ETFs offer two key additional incentives: (1) short squeezes are dramatically less likely and (2) ETFs tend to reduce total portfolio risk (Sarkar & Li, 2002). These important benefits stem from composition of the ETFs themselves. Because the investor holds small pieces of various securities, and that exposure is often achieved via derivative products such as futures and options, the risk is spread out and thereby minimized to some extent.

Finally, investors may diversify their investments in order to minimize the risks associated with emerging markets. Roon, Nijman, and Werker (2001) found that diversification in emerging markets yields the same benefits as those found in the United States, Europe, and Japan. Moreover, Li, Sarkar, and Wang (2003) found that the lack of perfect correlation between foreign securities and U.S. securities allows domestic investors to gain from diversified international exposure. They did qualify the statement, however, by noting that the magnitude of diversification benefits in general depends on various portfolio constraints, such as an investor's ability to take short positions. It should also be noted that a counterargument exists among scholars that global market integration has decreased the benefits of diversification due to a high correlation of security prices worldwide (Sarkar & Li, 2002).

25.7 CONCLUSION

This chapter provides only a survey of various policy considerations regarding short selling in various emerging markets. It also identified some of the practical aspects of emerging market short selling. Various theories exist to support these movements against and for short selling. The benefits and risks vary by nation with regard to emerging market short selling, and investors would be well served to research the selected locales. Short selling policies in BRIC nations vary widely, often based on political events and climates, to such an extent that any investor considering such an investment strategy must become familiar with the market before accepting the risk of unlimited losses that short selling poses.

REFERENCES

Allen, F., & Gale, D. (1991). Arbitrage, short sales, and financial innovation. *Econometrica, 59*(4), 1041–1068.

Bary, A. (2010). ETFs everywhere. Retrieved from http://online.barrons.com/article/SB50001424052970204425904576605030063544648.html.

Bentley, E. (2010). Short-selling ban hits Russia. Retrieved from http://themoscownews.com/business/20100520/187832850.html.

Bernardo, A., & Welch, I. (2002). Financial market runs. NBER Working Paper No. W9251. Retrieved from http://ssrn.com/abstract=336367.

Blau, B., Van Ness, R., & Warr, R. (2010). Short selling ADRs and foreign market short-sale constraints. Retrieved from SSRN: http://ssrn.com/abstract=1619465.

Boehmer, E., Jones, C. M. & Zhang, X. (2008). Which shorts are informed? *Journal of Finance, 63*, 491–527.

Bris, A., Goetzmann, W., & Zhu, N. (2003). Short-sales in global perspective. *Yale ICF Working Paper No. 04-01.*

Bris, A., Goetzmann, W. & Zhu, N. (2003). Efficiency and the bear: Short sales and markets around the world. Working Paper, National Bureau of Economic Research, Cambridge, MA.

Brunnermeier, M., & Pederson, L. (2007). Market liquidity and funding liquidity. *Review of Financial Studies, 22*(6), 2201–2238.

Chanos, J. (2010). Anyone could have seen Enron coming: Prepared witness testimony given February 6, 2002 to the house committee on energy and commerce. Retrieved from http://www.pbs.org/wsw/opinion/chanostestimony.html.

Charoenrook, A., & Daouk, H. (2005). A study of market-wide short-selling restrictions. Working Paper, Cornell University, Ithaca, New York.

Chatterjee, N. (2010). Inflows prompt Indonesia to suspend 3-1mth SBI Sales. Retrieved from http://www.reuters.com/article/idUSSGE6A90CB20101110.

Chen, C. X., & Rhee, S. G. (2010). Short sales and speed of price adjustment: Evidence from the Hong Kong stock market. *Journal of Banking & Finance, 34*, 471–483.

Childs, M., & Keene, T. (2010). Ackman, who shorted MBIA, is long on equities. Retrieved from http://www.bloomberg.com/news/2010-05-20/bill-ackman-who-shorted-bond-insurer-mbia-is-long-on-equities-tom-keene.html.

Corcoran, J., & O'Brien, E. (2010). Russian stocks drop most in 12 weeks, ruble falls on oil, China. Retrieved from http://www.bloomberg.com/news/2010-11-16/russian-stocks-drop-most-in-12-weeks-ruble-falls-on-oil-china.html.

Credit Suisse report. (2008). Indonesia—short selling notice. Retrieved from https://www.credit-suisse.com/investment_banking/client_notices/en/indonesia_111308.jsp.

De Borchgrave, A. (2010). Stock market time bomb? Retrieved from http://www.washingtontimes.com/news/2010/may/10/stock-market-time-bomb/.

Diether, K. B., Lee, K. H., & Werner, I. M. (2009). Can short-sellers predict returns? Daily evidence. *Review of Financial Studies, 22*, 575.

Driessen, J., & Laeven, L. (2004). International portfolio diversification benefits: Cross-country evidence from a local perspective. Working Paper, University of Amsterdam.

Editorial: Watching the Irish crisis. (2010). Retrieved from http://www.thejakartapost.com/news/2010/11/22/editorial-watching-irish-crisis.html.

Endho, T., & Rhee, G. (2006). Margin purchases and short sales in emerging markets: Their rationales and design variables. The World Bank, Washington, DC.

Gupta, R., & Jithendranathan, T. (2010). Short-sales restrictions and efficiency of emerging market: A study of Indian stock index options. *International Research Journal of Finance and Economics, 46*(2), 99–109.

Hankir, Z. (2010). U.A.E. market regulator to implement short selling, ADX says. Retrieved from http://mobile.bloomberg.com/apps/news?pid=conewsstory&tkr=MXB:US&sid=afa.HFP5b6sA.

Hong, H., & Stein, J. (2002). Differences of opinion, short-sales constraints and market crashes, *Review of Financial Studies.*

Hong, J. (2010). South Korea may allow bond naked short-selling to lure foreign investors. Retrieved from http://www.bloomberg.com/news/2010-05-27/south-korea-may-allow-bond-naked-short-selling-to-lure-foreign-investors.html.

IDX bans short selling until January. (2008). Retrieved from http://www.thejakartapost.com/news/2008/12/27/idx-bans-short-selling-until-january.html.

Jones, C. M. (2002). Shorting restrictions, liquidity, and returns. Working paper, Columbia Univ.

Laurenson, E., Lustgarten, I., Nissim, M., & Fridman, F. (2006). Best practices for financial firms managing risks of business with hedge fund notes. *Securities Regulation and Law Report*, 38 Sec. Reg. & L. Rep. 1477 (LEXIS).

Li, K., Sarkar, A., & Wang, Z. (2003). Diversification benefits of emerging markets subject to portfolio constraints. *Journal of Empirical Finance*, *10*(1–2), 57–80.

Lim, J. (2009). South Korean securities group questions sell recommendations by foreign brokers. *Securities Regulation and Law Report*, 41 Sec. Reg. & L. Rep. 19.

Lui, P. (2010). Asian capital curbs may spur interest in Singapore government bonds. Retrieved from http://www.thejakartaglobe.com/bisindonesia/asian-capital-curbs-may-spur-interest-in-singapore-government-bonds/407944.

Lynch, D. (2010). Bernanke's 'Cheap Money' stimulus spurs corporate investment outside U.S. Retrieved from http://www.bloomberg.com/news/2010-11-17/bernanke-s-cheap-money-stimulus-spurs-corporate-investment-outside-u-s-.html.

Morrison v. National Australia Bank Ltd., 130 S. Ct. 2869 (2010).

MSCI Barra. (2008). MSCI Barra announces its conclusions from its recent market classification study. Retrieved from http://www.mscibarra.com/news/pressreleases/archive/20080618_pr.pdf.

Pepper pares initial gains on short selling. (2010). Retrieved from http://www.indiainfoline.com/Markets/News/Pepper-Pares-Initial-gains-On-Short-Selling/3379409803.

RBC Dexia Investor Services. (2008). Indonesia: Short selling suspended. Retrieved from http://gmi.rbcdexia-is.com/rt/GSS.nsf/News+Flashes+by+Date+Mini/EF68A3DEAC5199D5852574DA003B4471?opendocument.

RBC Dexia Investor Services. (2009). Indonesia: Short selling and margin trading regulations update. Retrieved from http://gmi.rbcdexia-is.com/rt/gss.nsf/0/fc96a66d76fcaa84852575a9003070e9?OpenDocument&Click=.

Review: All eyes on repo. (2010). Retrieved from http://www.businessday.co.za/articles/Content.aspx?id=127047.

Robinson, G. (2010). Russia bans short-selling, pledges $20bn boost. Retrived from http://ftalphaville.ft.com/blog/2008/09/19/16117/russia-bans-short-selling-pledges-20bn-boost/.

Roon, F., Nijman, T., & Werker, B. (2001). Testing for mean: Variance spanning with short sales constraints and transactions costs: The case of emerging markets. *Journal of Finance*, *56*(2), 723–744.

Sarkar, A., & Li, K., (2002). Should, U.S. investors hold foreign stock? *Federal Reserve Bank of New York Current Issues in Economics and Finance*, *8*(3), 1–6.

Sherman, G. (2008). The catastrophe capitalist. Retrieved from http://nymag.com/news/business/52754/.

Stock picker sentenced for extortion, fraud. (2006). Retrieved from http://articles.latimes.com/2006/jun/20/business/fi-wrap20.1.

Suhartono, H. (2008). Indonesia's bourse bans short selling for October. Retrieved from http://www.reuters.com/article/idINJAK15697520080930.

Unditu, F., & Bisara, D. (2010). Foreign inflows sustainable, controls unnecessary: Agus. Retrieved from http://www.thejakartaglobe.com/business/foreign-inflows-sustainable-controls-unnecessary-agus/404792.

Yidi, Z., & Shidong, Z. (2008). China allows short sales, margin loans to help market. Retrived from http://www.bloomberg.com/apps/news?pid=newsarchive&sid=aPW9M35ifzl8.

CHAPTER 26

Short Selling Consistency in South Africa

David E. Allen, Robert J. Powell, and Abhay K. Singh

CONTENTS

ABSTRACT

Throughout the global financial crisis (GFC), South Africa managed to maintain a consistent approach to short selling activity, thus minimizing trading disruption. That this was possible is largely attributed to a strong regulatory framework, as well as the rules, risk management systems, and surveillance capabilities of the Johannesburg Stock Exchange. This chapter explores environmental and regulatory factors that differentiated short selling activity in South Africa from global counterparts both prior to and during the GFC. The impact on South African share prices of short selling bans in global markets is also examined.

KEYWORDS

Financial Services Board; Global financial crisis; Johannesburg Stock Exchange; Regulation stability; Securities Services Act 2004; Share price index.

26.1 INTRODUCTION

Rules pertaining to short selling in South Africa remained the same over the preglobal financial crisis (Pre-GFC) and GFC periods. This included prohibition of naked short selling, with regulated covered short selling permitted. This chapter examines short selling practices in South Africa and the factors that contributed to regulation stability. The rules surrounding short selling are determined by the Johannesburg Stock Exchange (JSE) in consultation with the regulator, the Financial Services Board (FSB). This chapter commences by providing background on the JSE and financial markets regulation. This is followed by a discussion on trends in South African markets and how these were impacted by global events and by changes to global short selling practices. The rules governing short selling in South Africa are then examined, followed by conclusions.

26.2 JOHANNESBURG STOCK EXCHANGE AND FINANCIAL MARKETS REGULATION

The Johannesburg Stock Exchange has been operating since 1887. Through amalgamation with various other exchanges, most notably SAFEX (South Africa's Futures Exchange) in 2001 and BESA (Bond Exchange of SA) in 2009, the JSE offers a full range of services, including trading in equities, equities derivatives, commodities derivatives, currencies derivatives, and interest rate products. The equities fully automated trading system is operated by the London Stock Exchange according to world-class standards.

The JSE is regulated by the Financial Services Board, which oversees all nonbanking financial services, including insurers, intermediaries, friendly societies, unit trust schemes, management companies, and financial markets. The aim of the FSB is to promote and maintain a sound financial investment environment in South Africa. The JSE operates under the Securities Services Act 2004, overseen by the FSB. The aims of the act include increasing investor confidence in South Africa, protection of investors, reducing systemic risk and maintaining a stable securities market, and promoting international investor competiveness in South Africa. A key aspect of the act is that it allows the JSE to operate as a self-regulatory organization, which is expected to regulate their activities (and activities of users) by making and enforcing rules that comply with the act (Financial Services Authority, 2004; Müller, 2005).

26.3 SOUTH AFRICAN MARKETS PRIOR TO AND DURING THE GLOBAL FINANCIAL CRISIS

Figure 26.1 compares the JSE All Share Index to the S&P Euro and S&P 500 for the 5-year period from 2005 to 2009. We have rebased all indices to equal the S&P 500 at the start of the period, and all indices were based on

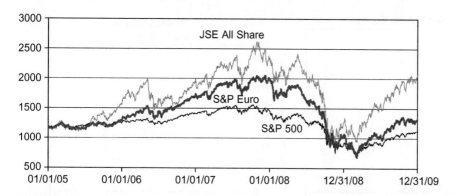

FIGURE 26.1
Share price index.

USD. Figures were obtained from Datastream. The JSE All Share Index closely mirrored turmoil in global markets during the GFC, plunging 66% from peak to trough over this period, which was the same percentage as the S&P Euro and higher than the S&P 500 at 57%.

In response to global bans on short selling, South African share market prices also followed global trends. For example, in the aftermath of the Lehman Brothers collapse, the Securities and Exchange Commission banned the short selling of certain U.S. financial institution stocks on September 18, 2008, in an attempt to stabilize financial markets, with the Financial Services Authority (FSA) following the same approach in the United Kingdom. On that day, as well as over the following 2 days, the impact on the JSE All Share Index was almost identical to that of the U.K. and U.S. markets—a marginal increase in share prices. On May 18, 2010, Germany temporarily banned naked short selling on euro area government bonds, sovereign credit default swaps, and the shares of 10 German banks and insurers in the wake of the European debt crisis. These announcements caused shock waves in global financial markets, with South African markets falling by approximately 3%, a very similar percentage to that experienced by key European share indices.

Figure 26.2 shows trading volumes for equities and for equities derivatives with figures obtained from the JSE (Johannesburg Stock Exchange, 2009). While equities trading volumes continued to increase during the GFC, equities derivative volumes dropped sharply (68%) from 2008 to 2009.

This fall has been ascribed by the JSE to a number of issues, including lack of investor confidence, particularly retail investors; the exit of Lehman Brothers as a major player in the JSE's equity derivatives market; and the increase in clearing margins by clearing members, particularly on small cap stocks.

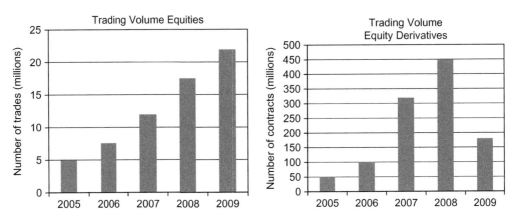

FIGURE 26.2
Johannesburg Stock Exchange trading volumes.

26.4 SOUTH AFRICAN SHORT SELLING RULES

South Africa's short selling rules effectively prohibit naked short selling. Covered short sales are permitted, whereby securities need to be borrowed or set aside prior to the instruments being short sold. This process can reduce the speed at which transactions take place, thus reducing settlement risk. Naked short selling, however, does not set aside or borrow such securities, placing reliance on the required number of securities being available in the market at the time of settlement, thus increasing settlement risk.

During the GFC, the JSE (2009), in consultation with the FSA, decided not to impose any changes or restrictions on their existing short selling rules, despite such action being implemented by many exchanges worldwide. The JSE wanted to avoid negative consequences associated with restrictions on short selling and changes to short selling rules. While short selling itself can have negative consequences, such as increased market volatility, there are benefits of short selling, and restrictions to short selling rules can have negative consequences. This can include aspects such as reduction of liquidity in the market by reducing the number of sellers (Hanson, Wanzare, Smith, & Gardner, 2008) and reduction in the speed at which negative information reaches the market (Hong & Stein, 2003). Given these potential negative impacts, globally there have been wide calls for better and consistent regulation rather than having to resort to bans during crisis times (see, e.g., Avgouleas, 2010; Masciandaro, 2010; Stone, 2009). South Africa has managed to achieve this consistency both pre-GFC and during the GFC. A key reason provided by the JSE (Johannesburg Stock Exchange, 2009) for the decision to maintain the status quo was the exchange's surveillance and risk management systems, which enable surveillance teams to see trades to beneficial holder level and to enforce the requirement for traders to cover short positions. The second reason the JSE was able to have a consistent short selling approach was existing rules prohibiting naked short selling. The decision not to change short selling rules was a vote of confidence by the FSA in the banking industry. South African banks were not as vulnerable to short selling activity as global counterparts, with South African banks remaining profitable and well capitalized during the GFC, with little exposure to subprime mortgages (South African Reserve Bank, 2009).

The rules that effectively prohibit naked short selling in South Africa include three key components. First, no member may enter any trade on the JSE trading system (STRATE) unless they have appointed a central securities depository participant, which is an institution (comprising mainly major South African banks) approved by the FSB. Second, the member must obtain evidence from the client that they own the securities, that another transaction has been concluded that will ensure sufficient securities will be available for settlement, or that a satisfactory borrowing arrangement has been entered into which will permit settlement to take place. Third, settlement must occur within 3 days of the trade date with rolling of settlements not permitted. These rules ensure that all short sales are covered.

26.5 CONCLUSION

South African financial markets have been impacted heavily by the turmoil in global financial markets during the GFC. Nonetheless, what has remained constant is the approach to short selling. The rules surrounding short selling imposed by the JSE in conjunction with the FSB, coupled with the surveillance ability of the JSE and the relatively sound financial stability of South African banks, have ensured the maintenance of this consistent approach across pre-GFC and GFC periods.

ACKNOWLEDGMENT

Allen and Powell thank the Australian Research Council for funding support.

REFERENCES

Avgouleas, E. (2010). A new framework for the global regulation of short sales: Why prohibition is inefficient and disclosure insufficient. *Journal of Law, Business & Finance, 15*(2), 376–425.

Financial Services Authority. (2004). Securities Services Act 36 of 2004, London.

Hanson, D., Wanzare, M., Smith, G., & Gardner, P. (2008). Has the short selling ban reduced liquidity in the Australian stock market? *JASSA, 4*(2), 14–20.

Hong, H., & Stein, J. (2003). Differences in opinion, short sales constraints and market crashes. *Review of Financial Studies, 16*(2), 487–525.

Johannesburg Stock Exchange. (2009). *Annual Report.* Johannesburg, South Africa.

Masciandaro, D. (2010). Reforming regulation and supervision in Europe: Five missing lessons from the financial crisis. *Intereconomics, 45*(5): 293–296.

Müller, N., Head of Capital Markets, FSB. (2005). *New Securities Services Act aligns South Africa with best international regulatory practice.* Johannesburg, South Africa.

South African Reserve Bank. (2009). *Financial Stability Review, March 2009.* Retrieved January 11, 2011, from http://www.resbank.co.za.

Stone, P. (2009). Regulators want short leash for short selling. *National Journal, 4 December 2009.* Retrieved January 11, 2011, from http://elibrary.bigchalk.com.

CHAPTER 27

Short Selling in Russia: Main Regulations and Empirical Evidence from Medium- and Long-Term Portfolio Strategies

Alexander Kudrov, Andrew Zlotnik, Elena Dukhovnaya, and Dean Fantazzini

CONTENTS

ABSTRACT

The main regulations of short selling in Russian stock markets are presented, and the importance of short selling practices is examined by comparing different asset allocation strategies. A new methodology based on the positive and negative potential for the price (or return) on the next day is presented, and its benefits are shown in an empirical exercise. The empirical analysis considers a list of shares traded on the Russian MICEX and RTS markets, including stocks allowed for short selling in the fourth quarter of 2010. Finally, the superiority of short selling-based strategies is highlighted.

KEYWORDS

Extreme events frequency; Federal Financial Markets Service; Generalized Pareto distribution; Kurtosis; Long–short trading strategy; Maximum annual drawdown; Sharpe ratio; Skewness; Volatility.

27.1 INTRODUCTION

The story of short selling in Russia has seen various ups and downs along the way, just as the classical stock market movements. Initially used only by large financial institutions, short selling has now attracted an increasing number of small investors, even during the crises of 2008 and 2009. In many world markets, short selling bans quickly followed after the start of the global financial crisis in the fall of 2007. This chapter discusses the most important regulations and common practices of short selling on Russian stock markets. Subsequently we then assess the importance of short selling by comparing different asset allocation strategies, including a new methodology based on the positive and negative potential for price on the next day. The comparison is performed by using a list of shares traded on the Russian MICEX and RTS markets, including stocks allowed for short selling in the fourth quarter of 2010 and the superiority of short selling-based strategies is highlighted.

The remainder of the chapter is organized as follows. Section 27.2 reviews the main Russian rules and practices, while Section 27.3 shows an empirical application comparing the different asset allocation strategies.

27.2 MAIN REGULATIONS AND PRACTICES

27.2.1 Current Situation

Short selling in Russia is regulated by a governmental body, the Federal Financial Markets Service (FFMS), and by specific rules set by the stock market. Rules for brokers wishing to provide margin accounts to their clients were approved in 2006 and then later modified in 2007 and 2009. Elaborated accounting systems are required by Russian authorities to ensure that short sales are accounted separately. In addition, each investor must provide his/her broker with collateral in the form of cash, cash equivalents, or other securities.

Brokers are entitled to short sell only quoted securities. Moreover, each exchange should form a list of the most liquid securities on a quarterly basis that can be traded in the next quarter according to the liquidity rating rules set by the FFMS. Only securities from this list are allowed for short selling. Brokers can further limit this list but are not allowed to extend it. Securities provided as collateral for short selling must satisfy the same liquidity requirements. Tables 27.1 and 27.2 list the securities

Table 27.1 Securities Allowed for Short Selling (as of Q4 2010) at MICEX[1]

No.	Issuer	Securities Type	Industry	Traded Volume in 3Q 2010, Million USD
1	Sberbank	Ordinary shares	Financial services	46,935
2	Norilsky Nikel	Ordinary shares	Metallurgy	20,514
3	Lukoil	Ordinary shares	Oil and gas	12,436
4	Rosneft	Ordinary shares	Oil and gas	12,489
5	Sberbank	Preference shares	Financial services	11,211
6	VTB Bank	Ordinary shares	Financial services	9,020
7	RusGidro	Ordinary shares	Energy and utilities	4,863
8	Transneft	Preference shares	Oil and gas	6,892
9	Severstal	Ordinary shares	Metallurgy	3,519
10	Government of Moscow	Bonds	State	17,980
11	Government of Moscow	Bonds	State	16,715
12	Uralkaliy	Ordinary shares	Metallurgy	1,647
13	FSK EES	Ordinary shares	Energy and utilities	2,588
14	Mobile TeleSystems	Ordinary shares	Telecommunications	4,156
15	Government of Moscow	Bonds	State	11,411
16	Rostelecom	Preference shares	Telecommunications	1,234
17	Inter RAO EES	Ordinary shares	Energy and utilities	1,607
18	MRSK	Ordinary shares	Energy and utilities	1,374
19	Polus Zoloto	Ordinary shares	Metallurgy	827
20	Uralsvyazinform	Ordinary shares	Telecommunications	1,124
21	Tatneft	Ordinary shares	Oil and gas	3,148
22	Government of Moscow	Bonds	State	11,328
23	Rostelecom	Ordinary shares	Telecommunications	449
24	OGK-6	Ordinary shares	Energy and utilities	499
25	OGK-1	Ordinary shares	Energy and utilities	901
26	Russian railroads	Bonds	Transportation	6,019
27	Mosenergo	Ordinary shares	Energy and utilities	406
28	Apotheks 36.6	Ordinary shares	Consumer goods	304
29	OGK-2	Ordinary shares	Energy and utilities	398
30	Novolipetsky metallurgic plant	Ordinary shares	Metallurgy	351
31	Sibmetinvest	Bonds	Metallurgy	7,827
32	Transneft	Bonds	Oil and gas	9,049
33	OGK-4	Ordinary shares	Energy and utilities	602
34	PIK	Ordinary shares	Construction	357
35	Raspadskaya	Ordinary shares	Mining	291
36	Avtovaz	Ordinary shares	Automotive	220
37	OGK-3	Ordinary shares	Energy and utilities	120
38	MMK	Ordinary shares	Metallurgy	214
39	Novatek	Ordinary shares	Oil and gas	421

Continued...

Table 27.1 Securities Allowed for Short Selling (as of Q4 2010) at MICEX[1] *Continued*

No.	Issuer	Securities Type	Industry	Traded Volume in 3Q 2010, Million USD
40	TGK-1	Ordinary shares	Energy and utilities	281
41	Sistema	Bonds	Diversified holding	3,327
42	Aeroflot	Ordinary shares	Transportation	204
43	TGK-2	Ordinary shares	Energy and utilities	33
44	Russian railroads	Bonds	Transportation	4,868

Table 27.2 Securities Allowed for Short Selling (as of Q4 2010) at RTS[2]

No.	Issuer	Securities Type	Industry	Traded Volume in 3Q 2010, Million USD
1	Sberbank	Ordinary shares	Financial services	14,895
2	Lukoil	Ordinary shares	Oil and gas	2,058
3	Rosneft	Ordinary shares	Oil and gas	1,415
4	Norilsky Nikel	Ordinary shares	Metallurgy	1,626
5	Sberbank	Preference shares	Financial services	914
6	Surgutneftegaz	Ordinary shares	Oil and gas	393
7	VTB Bank	Ordinary shares	Financial services	572
8	Polus Zoloto	Ordinary shares	Metallurgy	223
9	RusGidro	Ordinary shares	Energy and utilities	151

allowed for short selling, as of Q4 2010, on the Russian MICEX and RTS exchanges.

For risk management purposes, a broker must calculate the value of collateral and margin

- at the moment of short sale order execution
- 1 hour after the start of each trading day
- if the price of the asset changes more than 2%
- at the end of each trading day
- each time an investor's balance changes

and has to ensure that they satisfy all other official legal requirements (see citation later).

Limitations are set for short sales if the margin level falls below the minimum allowed, which is 50%, unless another level is stated in a separate contract between the broker and the investor. For more details, see "Rules of brokerage

---

[1] http://www.micex.ru/markets/stock/organization/margintrade.
[2] http://www.rts.ru/ru/oao/liquids.html?tid=872.

to be used for marginal deals" issued on March 7, 2006, n. 06-24/pz-n,[3] and "Rules of brokerage to be used for marginal deals for special categories of investors" issued on October 27, 2006, n. 05-53/pz-n.[4]

A broker cannot execute short sale orders if the price is less than the closing price for the previous trading day minus 3%. The broker may not follow this rule, if the price is not lower than the current quoted price at the moment of the sale.

27.2.2 The Short Selling Ban in 2008 and 2009

Due to the drop in stock prices on Russian stock markets, the FFMS banned short selling to prevent further speculations on September 18, 2008. During the last quarter of 2008, Russian regulators allowed short selling several times, but had to restore the ban on the same day or the next day because of sharp decreases of major Russian stock market indexes. Short selling was finally allowed again only on June 15, 2009, to improve market liquidity because many market operators and institutional investors abandoned the Russian market due to prohibition of short selling.

Some investors claimed that the short selling ban harmed not only speculators but also ordinary traders because it included market operations that were legally regarded as short sales, but in fact were not short sales. For example, consider the case of a trader who wants to buy a financial asset over the counter and then sell it on the stock exchange: unfortunately, it may take some time before he/she gets the legal ownership of the asset bought over the counter so that at the moment of the sell he/she may not have yet the ownership of the asset.[5]

Speculators can use complex arrangements to overcome the short selling ban, such as selling by third-party offshore intermediaries. Moreover, the association of stock exchange professionals claimed that some brokers used dangerous practices: for example, as supervisors of their clients' accounts, they are entitled to use clients' securities on behalf of clients and in the interest of clients; however, it happened that they traded the clients' securities (or used these assets in the calculation of the allowed margins/collaterals) as if those securities were belonging to the brokers in order to increase their allowed leverage for short selling and margin trading.[6]

In general, the effectiveness of the measures taken by the FFMS has resulted in mixed opinions. The repeated decision to stop trading has incurred criticism, as well as the extreme length of time for the short selling ban. These

---

[3] http://www.naufor.ru/tree.asp?n=6242&commtypes=22.

[4] http://www.naufor.ru/tree.asp?n=5077&commtypes=22.

[5] http://www.finansmag.ru/articles/5140.

[6] http://www.finansmag.ru/articles/5140.

measures had limited the liquidity of the Russian stock markets and led many operations to be redirected toward foreign markets, as well as to "gray" schemes aimed at circumventing and bypassing the established rules (see previous online articles for more details).

27.2.3 Brokers That Allow Short Selling and Average Costs

Not all brokers in Russia offer short selling due to its high risk. Brokers who want to start offering short selling practices to their clients have three options:

1. Buy securities *specifically* to be used for short selling on the spot market only
2. "Lend" these securities from other brokers or (cheaper) from their own clients who have these securities
3. Use securities from the broker's own long-term portfolio, which are used temporarily for short selling practices

Average costs for short selling in Russia, as of the end of 2008, are reported in Table 27.3.

According to a study carried out by Finam, one of the largest investment companies in Russia, 26.8%[7] of Russian investors employed short selling in 2008, and in July 2010, 41% of Finam's active clients used short selling. However, VTB24, another large investment company in Russia, reported that 25% of its active clients engaged in short selling.[8]

27.2.4 A Brief Summary of Russian Markets Risk and Performance Indicators

Figure 27.1 presents the evolution of numerous market risk and performance indicators for the Russian MICEX (the main stock market index): volatility, the Sharpe ratio, skewness and kurtosis, extreme events frequency, and maximum annual drawdown from June 1999 until November 2010 (for a similar analysis and a review of short selling practices in emerging markets, see Maggi & Fantazzini, 2011).

It is interesting to note that the previous indicators were rather similar, both during the periods when short selling was allowed and when it was banned. However, from September 18, 2008, to June 15, 2009, short sales were not permitted and volatility decreased considerably. Moreover, during this period of time, the Sharpe ratio was much lower, skewness was higher while

---

[7] http://www.finam.ru/analysis/ourating00018/default.asp.
[8] http://www.finansmag.ru/96160/.

Table 27.3 Brokers Allowing Short Selling and Average Costs (as of the End of 2008)

Broker	Number of Securities Available	Average Costs for Short Selling for 1 Day (Including REPO Deal and Loan Arrangement), % per Year
Absolut Bank (Абсолют-банк)	11	14.0
IT Invest (Ай Ти Инвест)	6	14.0–20.0
Alor (Алор)	13	12.7–14.7
Alfa Bank (Альфа-банк)	16	10.2
Aton (Атон)	13	10.5–16.8
Broker-Credit-Service (Брокеркредитсервис)	20	14.0–20.0
VTB24 (ВТБ24)	10	14.0
Dee Sea Capital (Ди Си Кэпитал)	14	18.0
East Commerce (Ист Коммерц)	N/A	16.1–18.0
KIT Finance (КИТ Финанс)	12	11.0
Nomos Bank (Номос-банк)	11	12.0
Opening (Открытие)	21	12.0–16.1
Renaissance Online (Ренессанс Онлайн)	21	15.0
Troika Dialog (Тройка Диалог)	16	10.0
Uralsib (Уралсиб)	12	12.0
Finam (Финам)	16	10.0–12.0
Zerich Capital Management (Церих Кэпитал Менеджмент)	13	15.0
Yutreyd.ru (Ютрэйд.ру)	10	14.0

kurtosis was lower, thus obtaining and confirming similar results in Bris, Goetzmann, and Zhu (2007).

27.3 EMPIRICAL ANALYSIS: A COMPARISON OF ASSET ALLOCATION STRATEGIES

This section presents a description of different asset allocation strategies and presents the results. Three types of portfolios are considered: (1) portfolios with long positions, (2) portfolios with short positions, and (3) portfolios with both long and short positions. The main idea of the asset selection decision process is the following: for a given asset, we use the closing quotes to estimate the positive and negative potential for the stock price on the next day (or the next period in case of a different frequency); if the positive effect is more than the negative effect, we go long and purchase the asset;

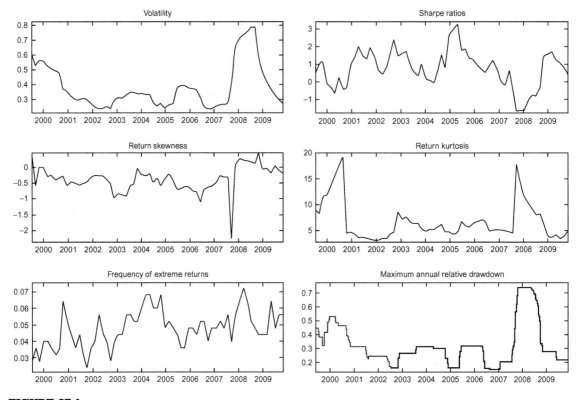

FIGURE 27.1

Time evolution of numerous market risk and performance indicators: volatility, Sharpe ratio, skewness and kurtosis, extreme events frequency, and maximum annual drawdown.

otherwise we go short. Calculations are performed using Russian stocks allowed for short selling in the fourth quarter of 2010. The entire asset allocation algorithm is described here.

■ Proposition 1

Estimation algorithm for positive and negative potentials for the asset price in the next period, with AR(1) -GARCH(1,1) filtration.

Step 1 (*sliding window AR(1)-GARCH(1,1) filtration*): For daily log returns X_t (calculated by using close prices), where $t \in [T-249, T]$, we estimate the following AR(1)-N-GARCH(1,1) model:

$$\begin{cases} X_t = \mu + \varphi X_{t-1} + \varepsilon_t \\ \varepsilon_t = \sigma_t \eta_t \\ \sigma_t^2 = \omega + \alpha \varepsilon_{t-1}^2 + \beta \sigma_{t-1}^2 \\ \eta_t \sim N(0,1), t \in [T-249, T] \end{cases} \tag{27.1}$$

and calculate the implied model's standardized residuals $(\hat{\varepsilon}_t)$, which can be interpreted as deviations from the trend.

Step 2: We separate extreme positive or extreme negative standardized residuals from the ones distributed in the center of the distribution using the 90% order statistics of the residuals for extreme positive standardized residuals and the 10% order statistics of the residuals for extreme negative standardized residuals. All the residuals between and are considered to be in the central part of the residuals' distribution.

Step 3: We assume that $(\hat{\varepsilon}_t)$ is stationary and has the following probability distribution (see McNeil & Frey, 2000):

$$
F(x) = \begin{cases}
1 - 0.1\left(1 + \xi_L \dfrac{L(T) - x}{\beta_L}\right)^{-1/\xi_U}, & \text{when } x < L(T) \\[3mm]
\dfrac{\#\{i: \hat{\varepsilon}_t \leq x\}}{N}, & \text{when } L(T) \leq x \leq U(T) \\[3mm]
1 - 0.1\left(1 + \xi_U \dfrac{x - U(T)}{\beta_U}\right)^{-1/\xi_U}, & \text{when } x > U(T)
\end{cases}
\tag{27.2}
$$

We fit separately the generalized Pareto distribution (GPD) to extreme positive and extreme negative residuals, respectively:

$$
G(y) = 1 - \left(1 + \xi \frac{y}{\beta}\right)^{-1/\xi}
$$

by using maximum likelihood methods. Denote $\hat{\xi}_U, \hat{\beta}_U$—the estimators of GPD for the positive residuals— $\hat{\xi}_L, \hat{\beta}_L$ the estimators of GPD for the negative extreme residuals.

Step 4: Finally, we calculate the negative $E_{0.1}^{-}(X_{T+1}|\Im_T)$ and the positive $E_{0.9}^{+}(X_{T+1}|\Im_T)$ potentials of the return X_{T+1}, given the information set $\Im_T = \{X_1, \ldots, X_T\}$:

$$
\begin{aligned}
E_{0.1}^{-}(X_{T+1}|\Im_T) &= \hat{\mu} + \hat{\varphi}X_T + (0.1x_{0.1} + 0.9y^{-})\sqrt{\hat{\omega} + \hat{\alpha}\hat{\varepsilon}_T^2 + \hat{\beta}\hat{\sigma}_T^2} \\[2mm]
E_{0.9}^{+}(X_{T+1}|\Im_T) &= \hat{\mu} + \hat{\varphi}X_T + (0.1x_{0.9} + 0.9y^{+})\sqrt{\hat{\omega} + \hat{\alpha}\hat{\varepsilon}_T^2 + \hat{\beta}\hat{\sigma}_T^2}
\end{aligned}
\tag{3.3}
$$

where

$$
x_{0.1} = L(T)\left[\frac{1}{1 - \hat{\xi}_L} - \frac{\hat{\beta}_U + \hat{\xi}_U L(T)}{(1 - \hat{\xi}_L)L(T)}\right]
$$

$$x_{0.9} = U(T)\left[\frac{1}{1-\hat{\xi}_U} + \frac{\hat{\beta}_U - \hat{\xi}_U U(T)}{(1-\hat{\xi}_U)U(T)}\right]$$

and

$$\gamma^- = \frac{\displaystyle\sum_t I_{(\hat{\varepsilon}_t < 0)}\hat{\varepsilon}_t}{\#\{\hat{\varepsilon}_t : \hat{\varepsilon}_t < 0, t \in [T-249, T]\}}$$

$$\gamma^+ = \frac{\displaystyle\sum_t I_{(\hat{\varepsilon}_t > 0)}\hat{\varepsilon}_t}{\#\{\hat{\varepsilon}_t : \hat{\varepsilon}_t > 0, t \in [T-249, T]\}}$$

I_A is the indicator function of the event A, while γ^- and γ^+ can be interpreted as means of negative and positive deviations, respectively. The inclusion of γ^- and γ^+ is justified by the possibility of using a poor-quality model for the trend, which systematically underestimates or overestimates the conditional mean, especially in the case of volatile markets. ∎

■ Proposition 2

Procedure for assets selection.

Let's assume that, for a given asset, we have $\Im_T = \{X_1, \ldots, X_T\}$ and we want to make a decision about the position for that asset at time $T + 1$ (see Marinelli et al., 2007):

1. If $E_{0.1}^-(X_{T+1}|\Im_T) + E_{0.1}^+(X_{T+1}|\Im_T) > 0$, we hold a short position for that asset.
2. If $E_{0.1}^-(X_{T+1}|\Im_T) + E_{0.1}^+(X_{T+1}|\Im_T) < 0$, we hold a long position.
3. If $E_{0.1}^-(X_{T+1}|\Im_T) + E_{0.1}^+(X_{T+1}|\Im_T) = 0$, we don't hold any position for that asset.

When we consider portfolios with short positions only, then we must consider only condition 1; if this condition is not satisfied, we don't hold any position. When we consider portfolios with only long positions, then we have to consider only condition 2; if this condition is not satisfied, we do not hold any position. Finally, if we consider portfolios with both long and short positions, then we have to consider conditions 1, 2, and 3, which cover the entire range of possibilities for short–long portfolios. ∎

■ Proposition 3

Weights for the portfolio assets.

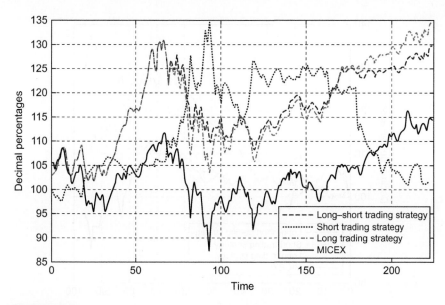

FIGURE 27.2

Cumulative returns of long, short, and long–short trading strategies in comparison with cumulative returns of the MICEX Index from January 11, 2010, to November 26, 2010.

For all portfolio types examined in this chapter, we consider the simple "1/N" rule (where N is the number of selected assets) so that we consider only equally weighted portfolios (for more details about the benefit of this simple portfolio rule, see DeMiguel et al., 2009).   ∎

Figure 27.2 denotes that the long and long–short trading strategies exceed the MICEX Index at the medium-term investment horizon. According to our expectations, the short trading strategy is very successful when the market falls and is usually ineffective when the market shows a positive trend. At a short time horizon (1 year), when the market grows up, results of the long strategy are slightly better than the MICEX Index, whereas results of the long–short strategy are slightly worse, see Figure 27.3.

Active portfolio strategies appear to provide the best results over a long investment horizon. When the market demonstrates sustainable growth, the long strategy outperforms others, while the short selling-based strategy is more suitable when the market is declining. However when the market changes directions many times over a 2-year period (or longer), the long–short strategy rises more than eightfold higher than the MICEX Index and twofold higher than the long trading strategy, see Figure 27.4.

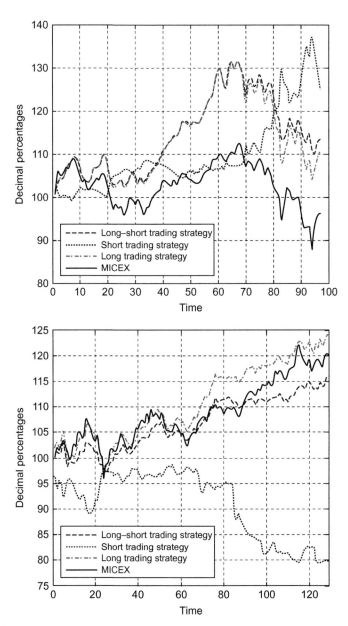

FIGURE 27.3

Cumulative returns of long, short, and long–short trading strategies in comparison with cumulative return of the MICEX Index from January 11, 2010, to May 28, 2010 (top), and from May 31, 2010, to November 26, 2010 (bottom).

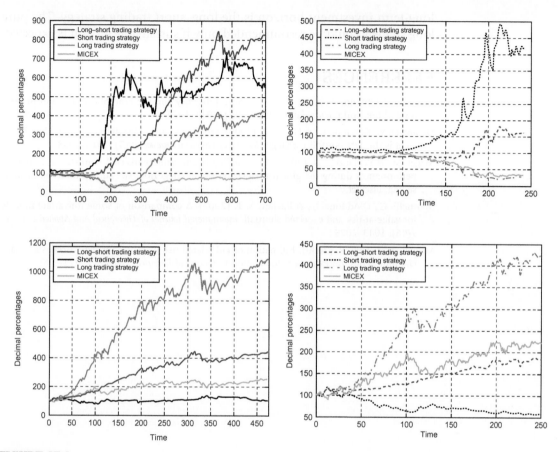

FIGURE 27.4

Cumulative returns of long, short, and long–short trading strategies in comparison with cumulative return of the MICEX Index from January 16, 2008, to November 26, 2010 (upper left), from January 16, 2008, to December 31, 2008 (upper right), from January 11, 2009, to November 26, 2010 (lower left), and from January 11, 2009, to December 31, 2009 (lower right).

27.4 CONCLUSION

This chapter discussed main regulations and common practices of short selling in Russian stock markets and then assessed its importance by comparing different asset allocation strategies, including a new methodology based on the positive and negative potential for the price (or return) on the next day. The comparison is performed using stocks allowed for short selling in the fourth quarter of 2010 in Russian stock markets. Research demonstrates advantages of using short selling in active portfolio management in Russian markets. The most preferable strategy on a long-term investment horizon is the long–short trading strategy. The pure long strategy could be recommended only if sustainable growth is expected.

REFERENCES

Bris, A., Goetzmann, W. N., & Zhu, N. (2007). Efficiency and the bear: Short sales and markets around the world. *Journal of Finance, 52*(3), 1029–1079.

DeMiguel, V., Garlappi, L., & Uppal, R. (2009). Optimal versus naive diversification: How inefficient is the 1/N portfolio strategy? *Review of Financial Studies, 22*(5), 1915–1953.

Maggi, M., & Fantazzini, D. (2011). Short selling in emerging markets: A comparison of market performances during the global financial crisis. In Gregoriou, G. (Ed.), Handbook of short selling. Elsevier.

Marinelli, C., D'Addona, S., & Rachev, S. T. (2007). A comparison of some univariate models for value-at-risk and expected shortfall. *International Journal of Theoretical and Applied Finance, 10*(6), 1043–1075.

McNeil, A., & Frey, R. (2000). Estimation of tail-related risk measures for heteroscedastic financial time series: An extreme value approach. *Journal of Empirical Finance, 7,* 271–300.

Portfolio Management and Performance

CHAPTER 28

Performance Persistence of Short-Biased Hedge Funds

Meredith Jones

CONTENTS

ABSTRACT

Shorting can be an effective hedge against market downturns, but is potentially costly during bull markets. This chapter examines the historical and future simulated performance persistence of short-biased hedge funds, as well as the diversification impact short-biased funds have on multimanager portfolios. Using a custom-constructed index of short-biased hedge funds, aggregated and individual historical performance will be examined and then projected forward using Monte Carlo simulations and other methodologies. Finally, using asset allocation models, recommended weightings to short-biased hedge funds based on varying risk–reward profiles will be examined.

KEYWORDS

Asset allocation models; Monte Carlo simulations; Multifactor stress testing; Net short; Risk–reward mandates; Short-biased hedge funds; Short-Biased Index; Stress-testing models.

28.1 INTRODUCTION

During financial meltdowns and bear markets, short selling can be an attractive option to many investors. Employing a short selling strategy, either on a single financial instrument or through investment in a short selling or short-biased fund, can provide a hedge against these market downturns and, if done correctly, can generate positive returns when other strategies are collectively failing. However, during a bull market, short selling is often perceived to be costly insurance against a potential market downturn and, as a result, many investors tend to shy away from permanent allocations to short selling strategies and managers. Instead, they prefer to "time" the market, often with fairly mixed results. With the recent increase in market volatility, the question of making a permanent allocation to short selling or short-biased strategies has again gained traction. To help determine the answer, this chapter examines the past performance of short-biased hedge funds to determine if there is performance persistence both across time periods and up-and-down market scenarios. Then, using Monte Carlo simulations and factor-based stress-testing models, the chapter attempts to ascertain whether the performance patterns of short-biased hedge funds will continue to persist. Finally, we look at asset allocation models to determine what role a short-biased hedge fund may have in a diversified portfolio.

28.2 WHAT ARE SHORT-BIASED HEDGE FUNDS?

To sell a stock short means that one borrows a share of a stock (generally from his or her broker) and sells it to another party. The hope is that before the short sale must be covered, which occurs when the number of borrowed shares are purchased on the market and returned to the broker, the price of the stock will have dropped. Thus, the short seller is able to pocket the difference in share price as profit. If, however, the price of the stock goes up before the short sale is covered, then the short seller posts a loss on the transaction. For this reason, short sales are generally more popular when markets, a market or geographic sector, or a specific stock is on the decline. In the world of hedge funds, short selling is a strategy whereby the manager of a hedge fund employs only short selling techniques as his or her investment strategy. However, given that the market has tended to go up more than it has gone down in the last two decades, pure short seller hedge funds have not been in strong supply.

A derivative strategy, often referred to as "short-biased" or "net short," has emerged as a more popular alternative to pure short selling hedge funds. In a short-biased hedge fund, the manager may maintain both long and short positions as part of his or her strategy. However, the fund generally must be "net short," meaning the manager has a larger percentage of the fund in short positions than in long positions. Thus, the downside risk to the fund during a bull market is somewhat mitigated by the presence of long positions, which may generate profits when the market is rising, while the fund can still go 100% short if a market or sector sell-off occurs.

Despite the emergence of this hybrid, somewhat more all-weather strategy, short-biased funds remain a very small segment of the overall hedge fund universe. In our research for this chapter, we never found more than 39 short-biased hedge funds operating in any given month out of a possible universe of up to 18,450 active funds (year end 2009). It is entirely possible that the number of short-biased hedge funds represented in this research is artificially low, however. Short sellers and short-biased managers have a well-known tendency to shy away from disclosure, whether it be their positions or their returns, for fear of a short squeeze (a situation in which the price of a stock rises rapidly, forcing short sellers to cover their position by buying the stock, which in turn pushes the stock price even higher). Regardless, we do believe that by using a combination of both currently operating and defunct short-biased hedge funds we have achieved a statistically significant sample on which to base our findings.

28.3 PAST PERFORMANCE OF SHORT-BIASED HEDGE FUNDS

To establish the past performance persistence of short-biased hedge funds, we created a monthly index using hedge funds categorized as either "short-biased" or "net short" from the BarclayHedge Graveyard Database, the BarclayHedge Global Database, the Eurekahedge Global Database, and the HedgeFund.net Database. The total number of funds in each month's index ranged from a low of 23 funds to a high of 39 funds. We collected approximately 10 years of historical performance (January 2000 through March 2010), choosing a time period that would encompass several different market conditions, including the "tech wreck," the bull market recovery that followed, the somewhat sideways trading of 2007, and, of course, the financial meltdown of 2008 and the market resurgence that followed in 2009. We compared the newly constructed Short-Biased Index (SBI) to the S&P 500, the Dow Jones Industrial Average (DJIA), and the MSCI World Equity Index (MSCI WEI), all three with dividends reinvested.

Yearly results for the SBI compared with the indices are indeed a mixed bag and seem highly correlated with the prevailing market conditions. In Table 28.1, one can see that during the history of the SBI it outperformed the market indices in 5 of the 10 full years represented, while it underperformed in the

Table 28.1 Annual Performance of SBI vs Market Indices

	2000	2001	2002	2003	2004	2005	2006	2007	2008	2009	2010 (3/10)
SBI	44.53%	5.85%	29.95%	−21.29%	−5.44%	1.50%	−5.35%	10.52%	36.64%	−19.65%	−5.71%
S&P 500 TR	−9.11%	−11.88%	−22.10%	28.68%	10.88%	4.91%	15.79%	5.49%	−37.00%	26.46%	5.39%
DJIA TR	−4.85%	−5.44%	−15.01%	28.28%	5.31%	1.72%	19.05%	8.88%	−31.93%	22.67%	4.82%
MSCI WEI	−12.92%	−16.52%	−19.54%	33.76%	15.25%	10.02%	20.65%	9.57%	−40.33%	30.79%	3.35%

other 5 years. Predictably, the SBI tended to outperform the indices primarily in bear market environments, although the somewhat sideways-trading 2007 also favored short-biased hedge funds. In periods of market recovery and bull markets, the market indices were, as expected, far and away the better performers.

Perhaps these trends are demonstrated more easily by looking at the monthly up-and-down market outperformance statistics for each index. In up markets, the SBI outperformed the market indices only a fraction of the time (Table 28.2). The SBI outperformed the DJIA in 13.04% of months when the latter was positive, while it outperformed the MSCI WEI and S&P 500 in only 8.57 and 5.56% of months, respectively, when each of those indices posted gains. However, in down market environments, the SBI easily outdistanced the market benchmarks, outperforming the DJIA in 85.19% of months when that index sustained a loss and outperforming the MSCI WEI and S&P 500 in 94.34 and 98.04% of months, respectively, when those market benchmarks fell (Table 28.3). Looking at these statistics, it is abundantly clear that the majority of the historical value of short-biased hedge funds has been generated in declining markets.

In Figure 28.1, it is possible to see a rather persistent performance differential between the SBI and the market indices, with the SBI outperforming all three indices through most of the period. While the SBI and indices have almost returned to parity at the end of 2006, the beginning of the market woes in 2007 derailed the indices' recovery and sent the SBI strongly positive once again. Given an initial starting value of $1000 for each at the outset of 2000, the VAMI chart shows a $500+ differential for the SBI over and above the three market benchmarks by the end of March 2010.

Table 28.2 Up Market Outperformance

SBI Up Market Outperformance	
vs S&P 500 TR	5.56% of months
vs Dow Jones Industrial Average TR	13.04% of months
vs MSCI World Index—gross	8.57% of months

Table 28.3 Down Market Outperformance

SBI Down Market Outperformance	
vs S&P 500 TR	98.04% of months
vs Dow Jones Industrial Average TR	85.19% of months
vs MSCI World Index—gross	94.34% of months

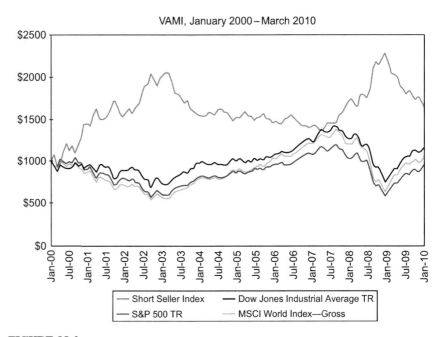

FIGURE 28.1

Value added monthly index chart for the SBI vs indices.

In fact, despite performing well only in negative market environments, the SBI demonstrated the highest annualized compound rate of return of the four indices over the full 123-month period, at 4.86%, while the S&P 500, Dow Jones Industrial Average, and MSCI WEI posted −0.42, 1.73, and 0.55%, respectively (Table 28.4). The annualized standard deviation was similar for the SBI and the DJIA, with the DJIA slightly edging the SBI in this measure (15.62% vs 15.83%). Meanwhile, the annualized standard deviation was similar for the S&P 500 and the MSCI WEI, at 16.11% and 16.55%, respectively. Of the four indices, only the SBI posted a positive Sharpe ratio (given a 5% risk-free rate of return) during this period, 0.07.

Looking at some of the individual managers who comprise the SBI, it is possible to see some of the reasons why the SBI has outperformed the market indices (Figure 28.2). In the data sample used to create the SBI, five managers had a 10-year or greater track record. Four of the five managers produced a greater compound annual return than the market indices, with one manager significantly outperforming over the period, while two of the five outperformed the market indices based on standard deviation.

In Table 28.5, note that in further comparisons to market indices over the full 123-month period, the SBI generates positive annualized alpha in all three cases. Looking at beta, or the degree to which the SBI's movement can

Table 28.4 Annualized Risk Reward Table for the SBI vs Indices

Annualized Risk Table	SBI	S&P 500	DJIA	MSCI WEI
Compound return on revenue	4.86%	−0.42%	1.73%	0.55%
Standard deviation	15.83%	16.11%	15.62%	16.55%
Semi deviation	14.21%	18.95%	17.12%	19.35%
Gain deviation	11.78%	8.81%	9.00%	8.53%
Loss deviation	8.56%	12.02%	11.52%	12.81%
Down deviation (10.00%)	11.02%	13.50%	12.65%	13.83%
Down deviation (5.00%)	10.22%	12.79%	11.94%	13.13%
Down deviation (0%)	9.43%	12.07%	11.23%	12.42%
Sharpe (5.00%)	0.07	−0.25	−0.12	−0.18
Sortino (10.00%)	−0.44	−0.74	−0.62	−0.65
Sortino (5.00%)	−0.01	−0.42	−0.27	−0.33
Sortino (0%)	0.5	−0.03	0.15	0.04

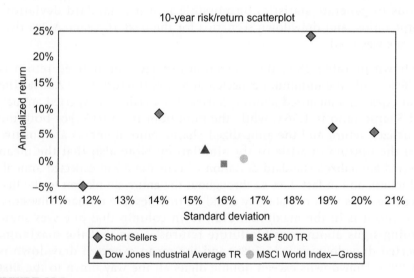

FIGURE 28.2
Individual short-biased managers vs market indices.

Table 28.5 Alpha, Beta, and Correlation of SBI to Market Indices

Short-Biased Index vs Benchmarks	Alpha	Annualized Alpha	Beta	R
S&P 500 TR	0.56%	6.87%	−0.763	−0.777
DJIA TR	0.66%	8.25%	−0.669	−0.661
MSCI WEI	0.62%	7.68%	−0.743	−0.777

be explained as a result of the market as a whole (represented by the three market indices), we see that the SBI's performance is largely an inverse function of the markets. The correlation of the SBI to the market indices is also negative, which, after a review of the historical performance, is probably not shocking.

28.4 FUTURE PERFORMANCE OF SHORT-BIASED HEDGE FUNDS

Of course, past performance is not necessarily indicative of future results. Therefore, we attempted to simulate the SBI forward to determine whether there is a possibility that its relatively stronger performance may persist in the future. One of the ways in which this was accomplished was by running Monte Carlo simulations on the SBI. We used bootstrap methodology to allow for non-normal distributions and ran 10,000 simulations to generate statistics on possible returns, standard deviation, Sharpe ratios, and drawdown scenarios for the next 10 years. A 3% risk-free rate was used.

As shown in Table 28.6, the maximum expected annualized return is 27.86%, while the minimum expected annualized return is −12.88%. The mean expected annualized return is 5.01%. The maximum expected annualized Sharpe ratio is 1.361, while the minimum is −1.015. For both the annualized return and the annualized Sharpe ratio, numbers are positive until the bottom quartile of the simulation. Note also that the mean expected annualized standard deviation exceeds the mean expected annualized return, and in fact does so throughout the entire simulation to the first percentile. This kind of volatility could be troublesome to many investors. However, it is in the maximum drawdown column that one sees some warning signs about possible future returns. Note that the maximum expected drawdown is −76.50%, and the mean expected drawdown is −31.99%. Drawdowns exceed double digits all the way down to the first percentile. For an investor who views risk as the possibility of losing money within a given time period, these kinds of drawdowns may be too much to bear, certainly as a single investment. However, as shown later, in a diversified portfolio, those drawdowns may be viewed as more "insurance premium" than risk.

Another way of looking at potential return scenarios is by using multifactor stress testing analysis. We ran stress tests to reveal what would happen to the value of the SBI (as a proxy for a single short-biased investment) if a particular crisis were to occur within the next month. Each crisis scenario reflects the maximum drawdown (or run up) of each factor in the selected

Table 28.6 Monte Carlo Simulation for the SBI

All Portfolio Statistics	Annualized Return	Annualized Standard Deviation	Annualized Sharpe (RF)	Maximum Drawdown
Number simulations	10,000	10,000	10,000	10,000
Mean	5.01%	15.70%	0.188	−31.99%
Median	4.84%	15.68%	0.191	−30.30%
Standard deviation	5.20%	1.32%	0.317	−10.70%
Maximum	27.86%	21.04%	1.361	−76.50%
Minimum	−12.88%	11.02%	−1.015	−10.83%
99th percentile	17.54%	18.87%	0.906	−62.09%
95th percentile	13.81%	17.91%	0.706	−52.30%
90th percentile	11.75%	17.43%	0.591	−47.13%
80th percentile	9.38%	16.80%	0.458	−40.57%
75th percentile	8.48%	16.57%	0.407	−38.41%
70th percentile	7.67%	16.37%	0.358	−36.39%
60th percentile	6.11%	16.02%	0.268	−33.12%
50th percentile	4.84%	15.68%	0.191	−30.30%
40th percentile	3.56%	15.36%	0.112	−27.79%
30th percentile	2.19%	14.99%	0.026	−25.23%
25th percentile	1.38%	14.79%	−0.025	−23.92%
20th percentile	0.61%	14.58%	−0.078	−22.67%
10th percentile	−1.53%	14.00%	−0.216	−19.61%
5th percentile	−3.20%	13.56%	−0.336	−17.58%
1st percentile	−6.46%	12.76%	−0.560	−14.28%

factor model over the period of time specified in Table 28.7. For purposes of this analysis, we used the financial crisis options listed in Table 28.7.

As would be expected from the historical performance, if any of the financial crises listed in Table 28.7 were to occur again in 1 month's time, the SBI would perform quite well. The best return would occur in a Black Monday scenario, where the SBI would be expected to generate a return of approximately 35% (Figure 28.3). Other disaster scenarios generated lower returns, but all stress test scenarios produced positive results. In general, the correlations of various investment vehicles tend to rise toward 1 during market meltdowns, regardless of past correlations, their investment strategies, or underlying instruments. However, looking at the SBI, it appears that short-biased hedge funds have the potential to provide the exception to the rule, maintaining their historical negative correlations in most market stress scenarios.

Table 28.7 Recent Financial Crisis Scenarios for Stress Testing

Black Monday
Maximum drawdown crisis period based on 18 observations from 10/1/1987 until 10/26/1987

September Crisis 2008—Lehman Blow up
Maximum drawdown crisis period based on 58 daily observations from 09/02/2008 until 11/20/2008

January Crisis 2008
Maximum drawdown period crisis based on 31 daily observations from 12/11/2007 until 1/22/2008

WTC Attack
Maximum drawdown crisis period based on 37 daily observations from 8/2/2001 until 9/21/2001

Market Downturn 2002
Maximum drawdown crisis period based on 104 daily observations from 5/17/2002 until 10/9/2002

August Crisis 2007
Maximum drawdown crisis period based on 20 daily observations from 7/19/2007 until 8/15/2007

Asian Crisis
Maximum drawdown crisis period based on 15 daily observations from 10/7/1997 until 10/27/1997

Kuwait Invasion
Maximum drawdown crisis period based on 29 daily observations from 7/16/1990 until 8/23/1990

Russian Crisis
Maximum drawdown crisis period based on 32 daily observations from 7/17/1998 until 8/31/1998

Katrina
Maximum drawdown crisis period based on 25 daily observations from 9/9/2005 until 10/13/2005

NASDAQ 2001
Maximum drawdown crisis period based on 21 daily observations from 3/7/2001 until 4/4/2001

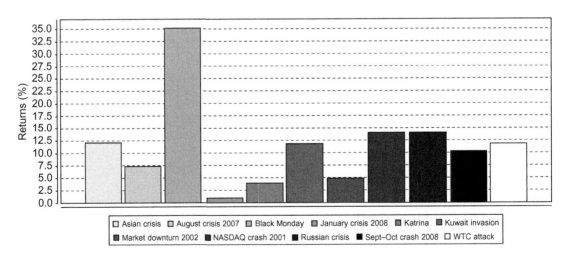

FIGURE 28.3
Expected returns during financial crises.

28.5 ASSET ALLOCATION AND SHORT-BIASED HEDGE FUNDS

Based on the strong historical pattern of the SBI outperforming in down market environments, combined with forward-looking simulations, it seems reasonable to ask the question "Where do short-biased hedge funds fit in with a diversified portfolio?" Based on our research, it seems the answer may depend on an investor's particular risk–reward mandate.

To help determine whether an allocation to short-biased hedge funds would be appropriate, we looked at three different portfolio mandate scenarios. Assuming a fictitious investor who is open to investing in both traditional and alternative investments (defined as short-biased funds, global hedge funds, and commodity trading advisors for the purposes of this study), we thought through three common risk–reward mandates. The first was an investor seeking the lowest risk portfolio, with risk defined as loss of assets and volatility. In the second scenario, we looked at a breakpoint portfolio, where the investor seeks higher returns and is willing to take a more balanced approach to risk versus return. In the third scenario, we simulated a portfolio with a mandate to produce maximum returns, regardless of risk.

As a proxy for the traditional portfolio, we used a 60% allocation to the S&P 500 with a 40% allocation to the Barclays Aggregate Bond Index. For the allocation to global hedge funds, the HedgeFund.net Global Hedge Fund Index was used as a proxy, while the HedgeFund.net Commodity Trading Advisor Index was used as a substitute for commodity trading advisors. Finally, the SBI was used to represent short-biased hedge funds in the portfolios. A standard mean variance optimization method was employed to create the portfolios.

The lowest risk portfolio generated an annualized compound rate of return of 5.65%, with a Sharpe ratio of 0.22 and a maximum drawdown of −6.58% (Table 28.8). To generate these returns, a portfolio allocation of 40.48% traditional, 21.7% SBI, and 37.77% global hedge funds was recommended (Figure 28.4).

When looking to generate higher returns while taking on some additional risk, the portfolio mix shifted radically. In this scenario, an allocation of 85.77% to global hedge funds and 14.23% to the SBI was indicated (Figure 28.5). This asset allocation mix yielded an additional 1.6 percentage points of annualized return over the lowest risk portfolio, while simultaneously increasing the Sharpe ratio to 0.56 and the maximum drawdown to −10.91% (Table 28.9).

Table 28.8 Lowest Risk Portfolio Characteristics

Compound rate of return	5.65%
Standard deviation	3.04%
Gain deviation	2.10%
Loss deviation	2.10%
Down deviation (10.00%)	2.88%
Down deviation (5.00%)	2.11%
Down deviation (0%)	1.51%
Sharpe (5.00%)	0.22
Sortino (10.00%)	−1.41
Sortino (5.00%)	0.29
Sortino (0%)	3.65
Sterling	0.19
Calmar	0.37
Maximum drawdown	−6.58%

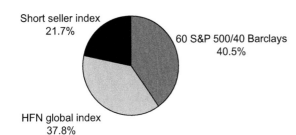

Exp return: 5.53%
Std dev: 2.87%

Short seller index 21.7%

60 S&P 500/40 Barclays 40.5%

HFN global index 37.8%

FIGURE 28.4

Asset allocation for lowest risk portfolio.

Exp return: 7.21%
Std dev: 3.78%

HFN CTA/Managed Futures 0.0%

Short seller index 14.2%

HFN global index 85.8%

FIGURE 28.5

Asset allocation for balanced portfolio.

Finally, we looked at the scenario that generated the highest return, regardless of risk. At this level, the asset allocation model was quite simple, with a recommended 100% allocation to commodity trading advisors (Figure 28.6). This portfolio would yield nearly one-and-a-half percentage points more than the breakpoint portfolio described earlier but would decrease the Sharpe ratio to 0.45 due to its higher volatility (Table 28.10). However, the maximum drawdown also improves by over one-and-a-half percentage points as well.

Of course, asset allocation models are fairly imperfect, but based on the observations of past performance and future simulations, they do seem directionally correct. If an investor wishes to purchase some level of "insurance" against market downturns, short-biased funds are a relatively cost-effective way of doing so. The "insurance premium" to the investor in these scenarios is approximately three percentage points in annualized return if they maintained a consistent allocation to short-biased hedge funds.

Further illustrating the "insurance premium" principle of including short-biased hedge funds in a diversified portfolio, we simulated a portfolio that doesn't include an allocation to short-biased

Table 28.9 Portfolio Characteristics for Balanced Risk–Reward Portfolio

Compound rate of return	7.25%
Standard deviation	3.95%
Gain deviation	2.37%
Loss deviation	2.89%
Down deviation (10.00%)	3.40%
Down deviation (5.00%)	2.73%
Down deviation (0%)	2.14%
Sharpe (5.00%)	0.56
Sortino (10.00%)	−0.75
Sortino (5.00%)	0.78
Sortino (0%)	3.28
Sterling	0.13
Calmar	0.17
Maximum drawdown	−10.91%

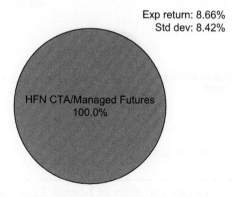

Exp return: 8.66%
Std dev: 8.42%

HFN CTA/Managed Futures
100.0%

FIGURE 28.6
Asset allocation for highest return portfolio.

hedge funds. For this portfolio, only traditional investments, global hedge funds, and commodity trading advisors were considered for allocations. In the lowest risk portfolio scenario based on this asset mix, the recommended allocations were 58.51% to global hedge funds, 28.05% to traditional investments, and 13.45% to commodity trading advisors (Figure 28.7). The compound rate of return for this portfolio improves slightly over the lowest risk portfolio, including the SBI (Table 28.11). However, the standard deviation increases by more than one-and-a-half percentage points and the maximum drawdown more than doubles. In this case, the insurance premium is a little more than a percentage point in exchange for lower volatility and drawdowns.

Table 28.10 Portfolio Characteristics of Highest Return Portfolio

Compound rate of return	8.66%
Standard deviation	8.42%
Gain deviation	6.08%
Loss deviation	3.94%
Down deviation (10.00%)	5.75%
Down deviation (5.00%)	4.96%
Down deviation (0%)	4.19%
Sharpe (5.00%)	0.45
Sortino (10.00%)	−0.21
Sortino (5.00%)	0.69
Sortino (0%)	1.99
Sterling	0.61
Calmar	1.83
Maximum drawdown	−9.35%

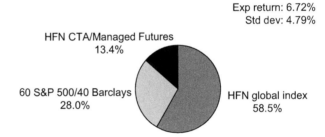

Exp return: 6.72%
Std dev: 4.79%

HFN CTA/Managed Futures
13.4%

60 S&P 500/40 Barclays
28.0%

HFN global index
58.5%

FIGURE 28.7

Asset allocation for lowest risk portfolio (ex-SBI).

Table 28.11 Portfolio Characteristics of Lowest Risk Portfolio (ex-SBI)

Compound rate of return	6.84%
Standard deviation	4.78%
Gain deviation	2.91%
Loss deviation	3.43%
Down deviation (10.00%)	4.02%
Down deviation (5.00%)	3.31%
Down deviation (0%)	2.69%
Sharpe (5.00%)	0.39
Sortino (10.00%)	−0.73
Sortino (5.00%)	0.53
Sortino (0%)	2.47
Sterling	0.18
Calmar	0.19
Maximum drawdown	−14.16%

28.6 CONCLUSION

The past performance of short-biased hedge funds has been remarkably uniform with patterns consistent with correlation and beta profiles. In addition, over the past 10 years and several different market scenarios, short-biased managers have been able to generate alpha over the market indices. Finally, it appears that short-biased hedge funds have the potential to perform in a similar manner going forward, based on both Monte Carlo simulations and multifactor stress testing. As a result, investors should perhaps reconsider their approach to short-biased hedge funds. Based on their individual risk–reward mandate and view of the market, it may make sense to maintain a permanent allocation to short-biased hedge funds, as the "insurance premium" for doing so is relatively low.

CHAPTER 29

An Empirical Analysis of Short-Biased Hedge Funds' Risk-Adjusted Performance: A Panel Approach

Greg N. Gregoriou and Razvan Pascalau

CONTENTS

ABSTRACT

This chapter investigates the risk-adjusted performance of hedge funds that follow a short-biased strategy. We use the Fung and Hsieh (2004a) approach to adjust for risk and compute short-biased funds' abnormal returns. The study uses rollover regressions of blocks of 4 years' worth of monthly observations by updating the sample at every 3 months over the January 2000–December 2008 period. The chapter documents that short-biased funds' alphas and appraisal ratios, respectively, deviate significantly over time from the long-run averages computed over the full sample. Using a panel approach, the chapter then investigates the sources of this time variation. Results in the chapter show that the causes are both market (macro) and fund related. Specifically, we find that market-based factors affect significantly the time variation in risk-adjusted returns, whereas short-biased funds' specific characteristics mainly determine the alphas' volatility. However, neither market-based nor fund-specific factors appear to have much explanatory power concerning the variation in appraisal ratios.

KEYWORDS

Fung–Hsieh alphas; Panel approach; Rollover regressions; Short-biased hedge funds.

29.1 INTRODUCTION

Short-biased hedge funds play an important role in spotting firms under duress (e.g., Enron,[1] Lehman, Tyco, and WorldCom) while providing liquidity and price discovery to financial markets in order to prevent market bubbles. In addition, short sellers can recognize frauds, find overvalued stocks, and expose unethical and deceptive accounting practices[2] reported in financial statements. Moreover, short sellers play an important role in asset allocation and portfolio diversification due to their negative correlation with traditional stock market indices. Although more complex than long-only investing, short selling requires meticulous precision and an extensive learning curve. However, their performance over time has varied significantly and some were short-lived. This study documents the time-varying performance of short-biased hedge funds and investigates some of the determinants of those time-varying patterns.

Traditionally, short-biased hedge funds are not representative of the classic hedge fund strategy developed by Alfred Winslow Jones in 1949 of selling short overvalued stocks and buying undervalued stocks, while using leverage to enhance returns in both up and down markets. The firms mentioned earlier were under the watchful eye of short sellers several months before their fraudulent practices became public.

Many U.S. publicly traded companies often come under pressure from short sellers, and these firms have expressed their views to the Securities and

---

[1] James S. Chanos, owner and founder of Kynikos Associates LP (1985), is a legendary short seller based in New York City. He predicted the collapse of Enron and sold short the stock from around $90 in November 2000 to $1 right up until the end of 2001. His trade has been viewed by many as the greatest trade of all time. Chanos also discovered and short sold infamous financial catastrophes, such as Baldwin-United, Commodore International, Coleco, Integrated Resources, Boston Chicken, Sunbeam, Conseco, and Tyco International. In addition, Barboza (2010) of the *New York Times* wrote an article entitled "Contrarian Investor Sees Economic Crash in China," stressing that Chanos' current bet is the crash of the Chinese real estate market.

[2] Briloff (1978, p. 1) refers to this as "the pervasive 'fakes' produced in the corporate accountability environment." In addition, Briloff (1972, p. 51) stresses the presence of a "gap in GAAP," which is frequently observed in corporate disclosures.

Exchange Commission (SEC) to apply a limit to the amount of trading short sellers can carry out. As a result, during the recent credit crisis (e.g., September 19, 2008[3]), the SEC ordered a ban on short selling of 989 banking stocks/financial firms to avoid the manipulation of markets. However, according to the SEC and the NYSE, the ban failed to stop short selling. Matsumoto (2009) states that

> throughout the period, short sales averaged 24.7 percent of the overall trading in Morgan Stanley, Merrill Lynch & Co. and Goldman Sachs on NYSE Arca and in 2008, short sales averaged 37.5 percent of the overall trading on the exchange in the three companies.

Even with the ban, during the credit crunch of 2008 and 2009, short-biased hedge funds as a group did very well. For instance, the $6 billion Kynikos Associates' Ursus Partners Fund and Ursus International short seller hedge funds produced 62% net of returns in 2008.[4]

Even more recently, short sellers have been blamed for the role played in Greece's financial crisis and its collapse in the international financial markets, as well as making big bets against the euro. It is well known and documented that when markets experience extreme negative events, short sellers and hedge funds are often the first ones to be blamed (Sloan, 2010). Furthermore, Chanos (2008) states that "short sellers keep the market honest" and "are guardians of our economy." Notables such as ex-SEC Chairman Cox and Ben Bernanke believe that short selling is a must to prevent market bubbles.

Given their strategies, short sellers will be inclined to perform well in bear markets and poorly in bull markets. For instance, in our sample, all short-biased hedge funds that died did so in the years prior to the crisis (i.e., four short sellers died in 2003, 2005, and 2007 or 22% of the funds in our sample), but none has died during the crisis (e.g., 14 funds or 78% of the short sellers in the sample). Similarly, the average monthly short-biased hedge fund return for the January 2000–July 2007 period was 0.28%, but 2.12% for the August 2007–December 2008 period.[5]

This study uses rollover regressions to obtain and document that the risk-adjusted performance of short-biased hedge funds and their respective volatilities vary over time. The study then asks and tries to answer the following questions. What macro and market-based factors influence the performance of short-biased hedge funds? Can size impact the performance of short-biased funds? Do large short-biased funds use less leverage than smaller ones?

---

[3] The ban ended on October 17, 2008.

[4] The Ursus Partners Fund and Ursus International are not included in the Barclay Hedge fund data set.

[5] We consider August 2007 as the start of the credit crunch/financial crisis.

Due to the small number of short-biased hedge funds in the Barclay Hedge database (e.g., 18 funds), their combined capital is estimated at $652 million. This chapter follows the standard approach in the literature and adjusts the raw returns for risk using the Fung and Hsieh (2004a) approach. The chapter then uses rollover regressions over the January 2000– December 2008 period to compare and contrast abnormal returns, their volatility, and respective appraisal ratios obtained on subsamples of data with those obtained for the full sample for each fund. Samples used in the rollover regressions are obtained by adding and subtracting 3 months at the end and the beginning of a 4-year period. Thus, each regression uses 48 monthly observations for each fund. Findings in the chapter indicate that for most short-biased funds, the risk-adjusted performance varies significantly over time. A visual inspection of Figures 29.1 and 29.2 supports this assessment. A panel approach using random effects is then employed to suggest that the determinants include both market-based and fund-specific factors. For instance, results show that the time variation of risk-adjusted returns depends mainly on the impact of market-based factors. In contrast, the volatility of short-biased Fung–Hsieh alphas varies mainly with the fund-specific factors.

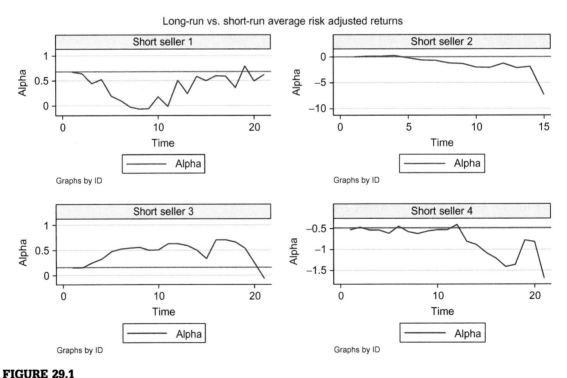

FIGURE 29.1

An example of short-run vs long-run Fung–Hsieh alphas. The horizontal line represents the average alpha for each full sample available.

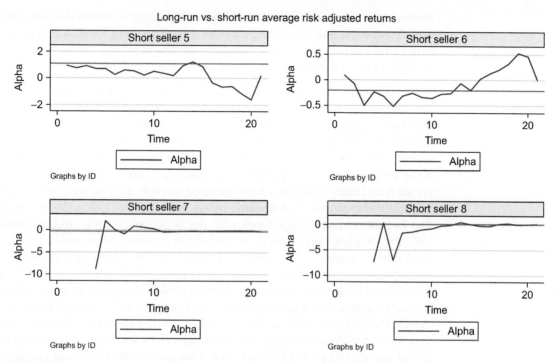

FIGURE 29.2

An example of short-run vs long-run Fung–Hsieh alphas. The horizontal line represents the average alpha for each full sample available.

The chapter is organized as follows. The next section discusses previous results in the literature, followed by a summary of data, and details the way in which dependent variables are constructed. The second to last section conducts the empirical analysis.

29.2 LITERATURE REVIEW

Studies involving the performance of short-biased hedge funds have been limited by the availability of data; however, a few studies have produced some sharp results of this category. For instance, short-biased hedge funds display better market-timing abilities and security selection when compared with other strategies in the hedge fund universe (Gregoriou, Rouah, & Sedzro, 2002). In addition, Gutfleish and Atzil (2004) suggest that short sellers have better analytical abilities, confirming the finding of Diamond and Verrechia (1987) who observe that short sellers, on average, possess better information than long-only investors. According to Christophe, Ferri, and Angel (2004), short sellers excel at fundamental analysis and abnormal short selling occurs prior to negative earnings surprises. Another noteworthy study by Lamont and Thaler (2002) further confirms that short sellers are better at finding overvalued stocks than other investment fund managers. More recently, Engelberg, Reed, and Ringgenberg (2010) detect that short sellers have an advantage that stems from their aptitude to evaluate information that is disseminated publicly.

Conventionally, short-biased funds sellers make money in down markets, and survival of this directional category is poor, with 50% of funds being reported as deceased in the Zurich Hedge fund database (Gregoriou, 2002a). Nevertheless, the second worst performance in terms of the last 12, 6, and 3 months of average monthly returns prior to liquidation of the fund is the short-biased category (Gregoriou, 2002b). However, notable short sellers such as James S. Chanos have survived the test of time with almost 25 years in the business. Past research by Gregoriou (2002a) has documented that live short-biased hedge funds with the largest assets under management have the smallest maximum drawdowns, the greatest compounded returns, the highest Sharpe ratios, and the lowest standard deviation than their smaller counterparts. Furthermore, Gregoriou (2002a) demonstrates that short-biased hedge funds have a median survival lifetime of 5.41 years, which is close to that of the aggregate hedge fund categories of 5.51 years. Using the Zurich Hedge fund database from 1990 to 2001, Gregoriou (2002a) finds that the short-biased strategy survives longer than sector, global-emerging, global macro, and global international strategies. When minimum purchase was examined, Gregoriou (2002b) observed that short-biased funds with less than $250,000 minimum purchase survived longer. Additionally, of the nine hedge fund strategies, short-biased funds with annual redemption survived longer than ones with shorter redemption periods.

The credit crunch of 2008/2009 affected nearly every type of investor, including well-known hedge funds and investment banks. Similarly, sophisticated investors watched their alpha evaporate during this period. In the past, prior to the credit crisis, academic studies had argued that hedge funds possessed performance persistence and produced alphas that were significant (Agarwal & Naik, 2004; Fung & Hsieh, 2004a; Kosowski, Naik, & Teo, 2007). However, it becomes inherently harder to generate steady alpha over the long haul. Therefore, can short-term alphas be prolonged to yield long-term alphas? This chapter investigates Fung and Hsieh (2004a) alphas of short-biased hedge funds during the January 2000–December 2008 period as well as during the crisis of 2007 and 2008. Although returns of long/short hedge fund managers stem from having net long or net short exposures (Agarwal & Naik, 2004; Fung & Hsieh, 2004b; Haglund, 2006, 2008), short-biased hedge funds such as Kynikos' Ursus Partners Fund and Ursus International shorts large cap firms, large financial firms with high likelihood of insolvency (Staley, 1996), as well as technology firms experiencing high levels of "technical obsolescence" (Chanos, 2010, p. 14).

29.3 DATA ANALYSIS

We use the Barclay Hedge database from January 2000 until December 2008 to investigate the performance of short-biased hedge funds using monthly net returns of all fees. We have 18 short-biased funds for which full information is available. All funds in the sample trade in the U.S. dollar and roughly half are onshore. Although not all funds in our sample provide full disclosure, it appears that in addition to a short portfolio exposure (i.e., 91% of the funds), most of them (i.e., 61%) also have a long portfolio exposure. Further, 94% (or 17 funds) of short-biased funds in our sample focus geographically on North America, while one fund has a global market focus with exposure to western and eastern Europe and Pacific Rim, respectively. In addition, while most funds do not disclose this information, it appears that a couple have the Barclay Equity Short Bias Index as the primary benchmark, while four more have the S&P 500 as the primary benchmark. One short biased fund further specifies NASDAQ as the secondary benchmark.

Table 29.1 details some summary statistics of our data, both in aggregate for all funds and separate based on their location (e.g., onshore vs offshore). The first column displays average, median, and average standard deviations of raw returns. However, as previous research has clearly documented (see Fung & Hsieh, 2004a), raw hedge fund data may suffer from several potential biases, including sample selection and incubation biases. To correct for those potential biases, we report sample results in parentheses after we have removed the first 12 observations from each series. Surprisingly, offshore funds display a performance (i.e., sample mean is 1.36%) three times higher than that of onshore funds (i.e., mean is 0.44%). Similarly, the median offshore funds return is also higher than the onshore median return (i.e., 0.48% vs 0.37%). In contrast, average volatilities appear quite similar for the two groups.

Further, bias-corrected raw returns suggest that offshore funds outperform onshore ones significantly according to both the mean (i.e., 1.85% vs 0.32%) and the median (0.78% vs 0.17%). However, as mentioned earlier, average volatilities appear roughly similar across the two groups. The typical short-biased fund in our sample has US$36.2 million under management, with the median size at US$17.9 million. Offshore short-biased funds, on average, have more assets under management, according to both the mean and the median. On average, a typical short-biased fund in our sample is around 4 years old, with offshore funds being, on average, 2 months older than onshore ones. In addition, the median lifetime of offshore funds is 9 months higher than that of onshore ones.

Management fees practiced by the two types of short-biased funds appear relatively similar. On average though, onshore funds charge management

Table 29.1 Short-Biased Hedge Fund Summary Statistics

	Return (Bias Correction)	AUM ('000)	Lifetime (Months)	Management Fee	Notice Period (Days)	Lock-up Period (Days)	Employees	Leverage
Average	0.85% (0.93%)	$36,200	49.42	1.45%	27.44	92.78	5.11	1.62%
Standard deviation	4.42% (4.39%)	$44,500	27.11	0.45%	19.53	152.44	7.28	0.96%
Median	0.37% (0.39%)	$17,900	45	1.35%	30	0	2.5	1%
Onshore Funds								
Average	0.44% (0.32%)	$31,700	45.6	1.48%	35.2	164	3.2	1.33%
Standard deviation	3.00% (3.80%)	$43,600	28.26	0.45%	17.96	176.43	2.39	0.65%
Median	0.23% (0.17%)	$10,200	33.5	1.50%	30	90	2.5	1%
Offshore Funds								
Average	1.36% (1.85%)	$44,800	47	1.34%	19.57	4.29	8.43	2%
Standard deviation	4.72% (4.85%)	$51,100	19.50	0.46%	18.46	11.34	10.95	1.16%
Median	0.48% (0.78%)	$19,700	54	1.20%	30	0	5	1.5%

Note: The bias correction of raw returns implies elimination of the first 12 months of observations from the sample.

fees 13 basis points higher than ones charged by offshore funds. Further, both the notice and the lock-up periods are higher for onshore funds. For instance, the average notice period for onshore funds is 35.2 days, while for offshore funds it is 19.57 days. Similarly, the lock-up period is 164 days for onshore funds relative to approximately only 4 days for offshore funds. In addition, the median onshore lock-up period is 90 days, while the median offshore one is zero. The average number of employees appears almost three times larger for offshore funds than for onshore ones; also, according to the median, offshore funds have twice as many employees than onshore short-biased funds. Finally, offshore funds appear more leveraged than onshore ones according to both the mean and the median.

Therefore, Table 29.1 suggests that while offshore and onshore funds have similar lifetimes and management fees, they appear to have a different performance, size, notice, and lock-up periods. Next, we want to investigate how the performance of short-biased funds has evolved over time. Two steps are required for this analysis. First, we adjust the raw returns for risk using the Fung–Hsieh (2004a) approach. Second, we employ rollover regressions over the analysis period to compute the short-biased abnormal returns (i.e., Fung–Hsieh alphas), their volatility, and appraisal ratios, respectively.

We calculate monthly Fung–Hsieh alphas or abnormal returns as fund excess returns minus factor realizations times loadings estimated sequentially over each sample period. Thus, we have:

$$\alpha_{it} = r_{it} - (\beta_{1i}PTFSBD + \beta_{2i}PTFSFX + \beta_{3i}PTFSCOM$$
$$+ \beta_{4i}(Equaity\,Mkt\,Factor) + \beta_{5i}(Bond\,Factor) \qquad (29.1)$$
$$+ \beta_{6i}(Credit\,Spread) + \beta_{7i}(Size\,Spread)$$

where $i = 1, \ldots, N$ funds, $t = 1, \ldots, T$ months, α_{it} is the abnormal return (Fung–Hsieh alpha) of fund i for month t, r_{it} is the fund return in excess of the risk-free rate (e.g., 1 month T-bill rate), PTFSBD is the return of the PTFS bond look-back straddle, PTFSFX is the return of the PTFS currency look-back straddle, PTFSCOM is the return of the commodity look-back straddle, Bond Factor is the change in the monthly market yield of the 10-year treasury constant maturity yield, Equity Mkt Factor is the Standard & Poor's 500 index monthly total return, Credit Spread is the monthly change in the Moody's Baa yield less 10-year treasury constant maturity yield, and Size Spread is the CRSP small decile return less the S&P 500 total return on CRSP.

Rollover regressions are using blocks of 4 years' worth of monthly observations (i.e., each sample has 48 observations) whereby the sample is updated every 3 months. Specifically, at every step we eliminate the first 3 months at the beginning of the sample and subsequently add three observations at the end of the sample. This process continues until the end of the sample period is reached for each fund.

Figures 29.1 and 29.2 display long-run and short-run risk-adjusted returns using the procedures described earlier. To economize on space, we show graphs only for the first eight short-biased funds in the sample. The horizontal line denotes the long-run risk-adjusted abnormal return or Fung–Hsieh alphas obtained using the full sample available for each fund. A quick inspection of the two figures shows that short-run alphas may or may not converge to the long-run value and that over time the short-run value may diverge significantly from the long-run mean. For instance, while for short sellers 1, 3, 7, and 8 it appears unambiguously that short-run alphas mean convert to long-run ones, this pattern does not appear sufficiently clear for the rest. For instance, graphs for short sellers 2 and 4 clearly suggest divergence from the long-run mean. Short sellers 5 and 6 appear to revert to the long-run mean, but the evidence is not very strong.

The mixed picture of Figures 29.1 and 29.2 requires a further investigation of those time-varying patterns. The next section performs this analysis.

29.4 EMPIRICAL ANALYSIS: A PANEL APPROACH

To increase the number of observations given the limited number of cross sections available we use a panel approach. We employ an extensive set of control variables in addition to fund-specific ones. Specifically, given that some short-biased funds have market indices such as the S&P 500 and NASDAQ as primary and secondary benchmarks, respectively, one would expect that macro and hedge fund-specific indices will be correlated with the evolution of short-run Fung–Hsieh alphas over time. Table 29.2 lists and discusses those variables.

We compute control variables in the same manner as our dependent variables. Specifically, we compute their moving averages by deleting the first three and subsequently adding three observations at the end of the 4-year period. We limit analysis to a panel regression under the assumption of random effects, as our fund-specific variables are constant over time. We believe that the extensive set of explanatory variables eliminates the possibility of omitted variable bias. However, inference needs to be performed with great care given the potential multicollinearity issues among the market and hedge fund indices used in the analysis. Table 29.3 displays results when dependent variables are Fung–Hsieh alphas. We have 226 observations corresponding to 14 funds for which we have full information.

First, results in Table 29.3 suggest that risk-adjusted returns vary with macro factors only. Thus, fund-specific variables do not appear to be significant at

Table 29.2 Variables

Barclay's Aggregate U.S. Bond Index	Previously known as the Lehman Aggregate Bond Index, it is a broad index maintained by Barclay's Capital and represents the investment grade bonds traded in the United States
CPI	Denotes monthly changes in prices paid by urban consumers for a representative set of goods and services
CITI 6-month T-bill	Rate of interest on Treasury bills and is the discount (i.e., the discount is effectively the interest earned by holding these instruments) expressed as a percentage of the issue price. NYSE, S&P 500, and NASDAQ measure the performance of the respective indices
Russell 2000 value index	Measures the performance of the small cap value segment of the U.S. equity universe. The index is revised annually to ensure that larger stocks do not distort the performance and characteristics of the true small cap ones and that the chosen companies continue to reflect value characteristics
Russell 2000 growth index	Measures the performance of the small cap growth segment of the U.S. equity universe
Fama-French HML (high minus low)	Average return on two value portfolios minus the average return on two growth portfolios [e.g., HML = 1/2 (small value + big value) – 1/2 (small growth + big growth)]
Fama-French SMB (small minus big)	Average return on three small portfolios minus the average return on three big portfolios [e.g., SMB = {1/3} (small value + small neutral + small growth) – {1/3} (big value + big neutral + big growth)]
CISDM-CASAM long/short index	Reflects the median performance of equity long/short hedge fund managers reporting to the CASAM-CISDM database. Its objective is to provide an estimate of the rate of return to equity long/short managers who take long and short equity positions, depending on the manager's view of the markets
CSFB/Tremont short dedicated short bias index	Represents a long position in undervalued stocks combined with a short position in overvalued stocks
CSFB/Tremont long-short index	Represents stock positions with a strategically net short bias, profiting from declining stock prices of companies suffering from fraud or deteriorating financial conditions
EDHEC long–short index	Summarizes long/short equity funds that invest in both long and short equity portfolios. Finally, EDHEC long/short summarizes short positions of overvalued stocks or stocks with anticipated disappointing earnings
Greenwich global short biased index	Greenwich Alternative Investments produces a global Short biased hedge fund index as part of their long short equity group of indexes
HFN short bias index	The Hedge Fund Net short bias index is based on 19 short biased hedge funds
HFN long-short index	The HFN long-short index consists of 1,632 long-short hedge funds.

Sources: U.S. Department of Labor, www.dol.gov; Professor Kenneth French's Web site, http://mba.tuck.dartmouth.edu/pages/faculty/ken.french/; www.russell.com; www.standardandpoors.com; www.nasdaq.com; www.nyse.com; www.hfr.com; www.edhec-risk.com; www.barclayhedge.com; www.pertrac.com; www.bnet.com; and www.wikipedia.org.

any of the conventional significance levels. In contrast, with few exceptions, macro and broad-based hedge fund indices are important for the time variation observed in short-run Fung–Hsieh alphas. Interestingly, with the exception of coefficients on the S&P 500, Russell 2000 Growth, CISDM-CASAM long–short, and HFN short indices that are positive, all the other variables

Table 29.3 Random Effects of Generalized Least Squares Regression-Dependent Variable: Fung–Hsieh Alphas[a]

Variable	Coefficient	(Robust Standard Error)	Variable	Coefficient	(Robust Standard Error)
Barclay's Aggregate U.S. Bond Index Bond Index	−1071.63**	(547.75)	Lifetime	−0.06	(0.05)
Unemployment rate	28.65	(32.35)	Domicile	0.72	(6.91)
CPI	−733.25*	(411.35)	Log (AUM)	0.81	(2.64)
CITI 6-month T-bill	−1567.24**	(782.11)	Open	2.98	(3.85)
U.S. Bond Index	102.72	(80.75)	Management fee	3.54	(5.74)
NYSE	−1048.54**	(502.21)	Performance fee	−0.25	(1.26)
S&P 500	1763.35**	(760.46)	Leverage	2.02	(4.69)
NASDAQ	−550.76**	(249.91)	Log (minimum investment)	−1.15	(5.59)
Russell 2000 value	−14875.89**	(5198.51)	Lock-up period	−0.01	(0.01)
Russell 2000 growth	377.22*	(231.22)	Redemption frequency	−0.35	(2.64)
Fama-French HML	−31.84**	(14.82)	Notice period	0.01	(0.25)
Fama-French SMB	66.90	(69.68)	Number employees	−1.06	(1.10)
CISDM-CASAM long/short index	1011.79**	(451.64)	U.S. investor	1.32	(6.39)
CSFB/Tremont dedicated short bias index	−114.80***	(27.72)	Intercept	83.02	(121.62)
CSFB/Tremont long-short index	−305.69***	(114.04)			
Greenwich global short biased index	−174.92***	(59.17)			
HFN long-short index	464.97	(361.72)			
HFN short bias index	1323.09**	(566.34)			
EDHEC long-short index	−291.46	(341.05)			
EDHEC short seller index	−114.46	(78.53)			
N	226				
R^2	0.238				

Significance levels: *10%; **5%; ***1%.
[a]The Barclay's Aggregate U.S. Bond Index represents investment grade bonds traded in the United States. CITI 6-month T-bill is the rate of interest on Treasury bills. The Russell 2000 Value Index measures the performance of the small-cap value segment of the U.S. equity universe. The Russell 2000 Growth Index measures the performance of the small-cap growth segment of the U.S. equity universe. Fama-French HML is the average return on two value portfolios minus the average return on two growth portfolios [e.g., HML = {1/2} (small value + big value) – {1/2} (small growth + big growth)]. Fama-French SMB is the average return on three small portfolios minus the average return on three big portfolios. The CSFB/Tremont dedicated short bias index reflects the median performance of equity long-short hedge fund managers reporting to the CASAM CISDM database. CSFB/Tremont long-short index short seller: bottom-up stock pickers that are long undervalue stocks and short overvalued stocks, with top-down views expressed with a net long or short bias. CSFB long-short: bottom-up stock pickers with a strategically net short bias, profiting from declining stock prices of companies suffering from fraud or deteriorating financial conditions. The HFN (Hedgefund.net) short bias index is based on 19 short-biased hedge funds and the HFN long-short index consists of 1,632 long-short hedge funds. EDHEC long short: long/short equity funds invest in both long and short equity portfolios. Short seller-specific independent variables include, among others, lifetime (short seller life measured in months), domicile (1 for onshore funds), log (AUM) (natural logarithm of assets under management), open (1 if the fund accepts new investors), management fee (measured in percentages), performance fee (measured in percentages), and U.S. investor (1 if investors are American residents).

have negative coefficients. For instance, the Barclay's Bond Index, the change in inflation, and the CITI 6-month T-bill rates, the returns on NYSE, NASDAQ, Russell 2000 Value, Fama-French HML, CSFB/Tremont dedicated short bias index short seller, CSFB/Tremont long–short index, and Greenwich global short biased index short, respectively, vary negatively with risk-adjusted returns. Those results are consistent either with strategies that long the market in boom economic times and/or short the market in bear markets. On average, it appears that in contrast with improvements of the Russell 2000 Value performance, which have a negative impact on short-biased funds' short-run alphas, increases of the performance of small-cap growth stocks impact positively short-biased funds' abnormal returns. Further, one can note that returns on the S&P 500 in contrast with those of NASDAQ and NYSE are associated positively with alpha returns. Thus, it appears that short-biased funds' risk-adjusted returns vary positively with smaller market indices such as S&P 500 and negatively with broader market indices (i.e., NYSE and NASDAQ). Higher inflation and interest rates, respectively, have a negative impact on short-biased funds' performance. Finally, the fact that most short-biased indices are correlated negatively with the risk-adjusted performance of short-biased funds in our sample suggests that increased competition reduces the returns of individual funds.

Second, Table 29.4 investigates determinants of time-varying patterns in the volatility of Fung–Hsieh alphas. Overall, the explanatory power of our control variables is much better in Table 29.4 than in Table 29.3 (e.g., the R^2 is 0.837 in Table 29.3 vs 0.238 in Table 29.3). This finding is consistent with previous research that has had more excess at explaining the volatility of returns than the returns themselves.

In contrast to findings in Table 29.3, results of Table 29.4 suggest that the volatility of the short-biased funds' performance is determined solely by fund-specific factors. Thus, none of the market or short-biased indices appear to have any significant impact. In contrast, coefficients on almost all of the fund-specific control variables appear significant at conventional significance levels. For instance, onshore short-biased hedge funds seem to have volatilities that are higher by 1.56 percentage points than those of offshore ones. The volatility of risk-adjusted returns increases with the size of the assets under management and is higher for funds that are still open (i.e., funds accept new investors). Those results make sense, as larger funds have a higher ability to pursue alpha, which may require riskier strategies. In addition, funds that are still open may want to lure new investors with higher returns, which in turn may require risk-enhancing strategies. Similarly, a higher required minimum initial investment increases volatility. This finding is consistent with the result that volatility increases with the size of short-biased funds. Both management and performance fees affect positively the volatility of Fung–Hsieh alphas. In contrast, a higher lock-up

Table 29.4 Random Effects of Generalized Least Squares Regression: Fung–Hsieh Alpha Volatility

Variable	Coefficient	(Robust Standard Error)	Variable	Coefficient	(Robust Standard Error)
Barclay's Aggregate U.S. Bond Index	−36.27	(40.23)	Lifetime	0.005	(0.003)
Unemployment rate	2.31	(2.37)	Domicile	1.56***	(0.51)
CPI	−28.88	(30.38)	Log (AUM)	−0.36*	(0.20)
CITI 6-month T-bill	−51.84	(57.47)	Open	−1.77***	(0.29)
U.S. Bond Index	4.96	(5.90)	Management fee	2.29***	(0.435)
NYSE	−38.15	(36.87)	Performance fee	0.16*	(0.09)
S&P 500	53.80	(55.88)	Leverage	−0.13	(0.35)
NASDAQ	−17.09	(36.87)	Log (minimum investment)	0.74*	(0.43)
Russell 2000 value	−210.13	(381.69)	Lock-up period	−0.002**	(0.001)
Russell 2000 growth	15.95	(16.99)	Redemption frequency	0.01	(0.19)
Fama-French HML	0.19	(1.09)	Notice period	−0.06***	(0.01)
Fama-French SMB	−3.15	(5.19)	Number employees	0.19**	(0.08)
CISDM-CASAM long/short index	23.84	(33.16)	U.S. investor	−1.70***	(0.48)
CSFB/Tremont dedicated short bias index	−0.58	(2.06)	Intercept	1.80	(8.99)
CSFB/Tremont long-short index	−3.35	(8.41)			
Greenwich global short biased index	−2.34	(4.37)			
HFN long-short index	21.42	(26.61)			
HFN short bias index	37.98	(41.60)			
EDHEC long-short index	−16.47	(25.09)			
EDHEC short seller index	−5.95	(5.72)			
N	207				
R^2	0.837				

*Significance levels: *10%; **5%; ***1%.*
[a]*The Barclay's Aggregate U.S. Bond Index represents investment grade bonds traded in the United States. CITI 6-month T-bill is the rate of interest on Treasury bills. The Russell 2000 Value Index measures the performance of the small-cap value segment of the U. S. equity universe. The Russell 2000 Growth Index measures the performance of the small-cap growth segment of the U.S. equity universe. Fama-French HML is the average return on two value portfolios minus the average return on two growth portfolios [e.g., HML = {1/2} (small value + big value) − {1/2} (small growth + big growth)]. Fama-French SMB is the average return on three small portfolios minus the average return on three big portfolios. The CISDM-CASAM long/short index reflects the median performance of equity long/short hedge fund managers reporting to the CASAM CISDM database. CSFB short seller: bottom-up stock pickers that are long undervalue stocks and short overvalued stocks, with top-down views expressed with a net long or short bias. CSFB long–short: bottom-up stock pickers with a strategically net short bias, profiting from declining stock prices of companies suffering from fraud or deteriorating financial conditions. The HFN (Hedgefund.net) short bias index is based on 19 short-biased hedge funds and the HFN long-short index consists of 1,632 long-short hedge funds. Greenwich Alternative Investments produces a global short biased hedge fund index as part of their long short equity group of indexes. EDHEC long–short: long/short equity funds invest in both long and short equity portfolios. Short seller-specific independent variables include, among others, lifetime (short seller life measured in months), domicile (1 for onshore funds), log (AUM) (natural logarithm of assets under management), open (1 if the fund accepts new investors), management fee (measured in percentages), performance fee (measured in percentages), and U.S. investor (1 if investors are American residents).*

period decreases volatility. A possible explanation for this result might be provided by the fact that a higher lock-up period limits the ability of short-biased funds to pursue riskier strategies. Similarly, a higher notice period decreases short-biased funds' returns volatility. Finally, if short-biased investors are U.S. residents, then the volatility of Fung–Hsieh alphas is lower. This result has the expected sign if one agrees that U.S. investors, on average, tend be more risk averse than non-U.S. investors. Note that the leverage amount does not appear to be significant.

Third, Table 29.5 shows results when dependent variables are appraisal ratios. Unfortunately, the explanatory power of this regression is small (e.g., R^2 is 0.271) and only one variable appears significant. Thus, in contrast to results in Table 29.4, we find that the lock-up period affects the appraisal ratio positively.

29.5 CONCLUSION

Given the limited data available on short-biased hedge funds, this study used rollover regressions and a panel approach to increase the number of observations to investigate the time variation of the short-biased funds' risk-adjusted performance. We used a data set provided by Barclay Hedge that covered the January 2000–December 2008 period. We have information on 18 hedge funds that followed a short-biased strategy. We adjusted the funds' raw returns for risk using the Fung–Hsieh (2004a) approach. Rollover regressions employed blocks of 4 years' worth of monthly observations, where at each step the sample was updated by eliminating and adding 3 months at the beginning and end of each sample, respectively. A comparison of short-run Fung–Hsieh alphas (obtained from rollover regressions) with their long-run average (based on the full sample available) indicates that the performance of short-biased funds in the short run deviates significantly from long-run behavior. This finding is not surprising given that short-biased funds are generally expected to perform better in negative market environments. Indeed, in our sample, short-biased funds registered an average monthly return of 0.28% during the January 2000–July 2007 period, but a 2.12% monthly return during the August 2007–December 2008 period.

This chapter then used a panel approach to investigate the causes of short-biased funds' change in performance over time. We proposed an extensive set of control variables that included not only both macro and market-based indices, but also fund-specific factors. The set of independent variables was constructed similarly to dependent variables using moving averages of 4 years' worth of monthly observations. Because fund-specific factors are fixed over time, the study was limited to a random effects panel regression. However,

Table 29.5 Random Effects of Generalized Least Squares Regression-Dependent Variable: Appraisal Ratio

Variable	Coefficient	(Robust Standard Error)	Variable	Coefficient	(Robust Standard Error)
Barclay's Aggregate U.S. Bond Index	55.97	(62.29)	Lifetime	−0.01	(0.01)
Unemployment rate	−5.19	(3.67)	Domicile	0.49	(0.79)
CPI	52.42	(47.04)	Log (AUM)	0.19	(0.31)
CITI 6-month T-bill	75.30	(88.98)	Open	0.51	(0.46)
U.S. Bond Index	−5.36	(9.14)	Management fee	0.16	(0.67)
NYSE	47.48	(57.08)	Performance fee	−0.07	(0.14)
S&P 500	−62.42	(86.52)	Leverage	0.26	(0.55)
NASDAQ	18.26	(28.43)	Log (minimum investment)	−0.36	(0.66)
Russell 2000 value	81.60	(590.95)	Lock-up period	0.002*	(0.001)
Russell 2000 growth	−19.15	(26.31)	Redemption frequency	−0.19	(0.31)
Fama-French HML	−0.45	(1.69)	Notice period	0.001	(0.029)
Fama-French SMB	8.61	(8.04)	Number employees	−0.092	(0.131)
CISDM-CASAM long/short index	−16.83	(51.33)	U.S. investor	−0.22	(0.75)
CSFB/Tremont dedicated short bias index	1.29	(3.19)	Intercept	−16.29	(13.92)
CSFB/Tremont long-short index	2.82	(13.02)			
Greenwich global short biased index	2.27	(6.76)			
HFN long-short index	−38.35	(41.20)			
HFN short bias index	−40.02	(64.41)			
EDHEC long-short index	18.51	(38.85)			
EDHEC short seller index	0.06	(8.86)			
N	207				
R^2	0.271				

Significance levels: *10%; **5%; ***1%.
[a]*The Barclay's Aggregate U.S. Bond Index represents investment grade bonds traded in the United States. CITI 6-month T-bill is the rate of interest on Treasury bills. The Russell 2000 Value Index measures the performance of the small-cap value segment of the U. S. equity universe. The Russell 2000 Growth Index measures the performance of the small-cap growth segment of the U.S. equity universe. Fama-French HML is the average return on two value portfolios minus the average return on two growth portfolios [e.g., HML = {1/2} (small value + big value) − {1/2} (small growth + big growth)]. Fama-French SMB is the average return on three small portfolios minus the average return on three big portfolios. The CISDM-CASAM long/short index reflects the median performance of equity long/short hedge fund managers reporting to the CASAM CISDM database. CSFB short seller: bottom-up stock pickers that are long undervalue stocks and short overvalued stocks, with top-down views expressed with a net long or short bias. CSFB long–short: bottom-up stock pickers with a strategically net short bias, profiting from declining stock prices of companies suffering from fraud or deteriorating financial conditions. The HFN (Hedgefund.net) short bias index is based on 19 short-biased hedge funds and the HFN long-short index consists of 1,632 long-short hedge funds. Greenwich Alternative Investments produces a global short biased hedge fund index as part of their long short equity group of indexes. EDHEC long–short: long/short equity funds invest in both long and short equity portfolios. Short seller-specific independent variables include, among others, lifetime (short seller life measured in months), domicile (1 for onshore funds), log (AUM) (natural logarithm of assets under management), open (1 if the fund accepts new investors), management fee (measured in percentages), performance fee (measured in percentages), and U.S. investor (1 if investors are American residents).*

we believe that the set of control variables was sufficiently large to eliminate the possibility of omitted variable bias.

Results of panel regressions suggest that market-based factors mainly affect Fung–Hsieh alphas, whereas fund-specific factors mainly influence the volatility of abnormal returns. Specifically, we found that higher interest and inflation rates affect short-biased funds' performance negatively. Further, evidence suggests that risk-adjusted returns vary negatively with broader market indices, such as NYSE and NASDAQ, but positively with smaller market indices, such as the S&P 500. In addition, individual short-biased funds' Fung–Hsieh alphas are influenced negatively by the increased competition reflected by the higher returns of hedge fund indices.

Regarding the volatility of Fung–Hsieh alphas, we found evidence that larger and open funds display lower volatility. Similarly, higher lock-up and notice periods have a negative impact on the short-biased funds' volatility of returns. In contrast, higher management and performance fees increase short-biased funds' risk. A descriptive analysis further strengthens the fact that results are different for onshore and offshore hedge funds. Unfortunately, our control variables have limited power to explain the variation of short-biased fund appraisal ratios.

ACKNOWLEDGMENT

We thank Sol Waksman, president of www.Barclayhedge.com, for providing live and dead hedge fund data. In addition, we would like to thank Francine English and Kim Shaw at PerTrac for providing the PerTrac 7.1 platform with indexes (www.pertrac.com).

REFERENCES

Agarwal, V., & Naik, N. Y. (2004). Risks and portfolio decisions involving hedge funds. *Review of Financial Studies, 17*(1), 63–98.

Barboza, D. (2010). Contrarian investor sees economic crash in China. *New York Times*, p. B1.

Briloff, A. J. (1972). *Unaccountable accounting*. New York: Harper & Row.

Briloff, A. J. (1978). *The truth about corporate accounting*. New York: Harper & Row.

Chanos, J. S. (2008, September 22). Short sellers keep the market honest. *The Wall Street Journal*, p. A23.

Chanos, J. S. (2010, May 18). The power of negative thinking. CFA Institute Annual Conference, Boston, MA.

Christophe, S. E., Ferri, M. G., & Angel, J. J. (2004). Short-selling prior to earnings announcements. *Journal of Finance, 69*(4), 1845–1875.

Diamond, D., & Verrechia, R. (1987). Constraints on short selling and asset price adjustments to private information. *Journal of Financial Economics, 18*(2), 277–311.

Engelberg, J. E., Reed, A. V., & Ringgenberg, M. C. (2010). How are shorts informed? Short sellers, news, and information processing. Utah Winter Finance Conference Selection, Salt Lake City, UT.

Fung, W., & Hsieh, D. A. (2004a). Hedge fund benchmarks: A risk based approach. *Financial Analysts Journal, 6*(3), 65–80.

Fung, W., & Hsieh, D. A. (2004b). Extracting portable alpha from equity long/short hedge funds. *Journal of Investment Management, 2*(4), 1–9.

Gregoriou, G. N. (2002a). Short-seller hedge funds. Working Paper, University of Quebec, Montreal.

Gregoriou, G. N. (2002b). Hedge fund survival lifetimes. *Journal of Asset Management, 3*(3), 237–252.

Gregoriou, G. N., Rouah, F., & Sedzro, K. (2002). On the market timing of hedge fund managers. *Journal of Wealth Management, 5*(1), 26–38.

Gutfleish, R., & Atzil, L. (2004). Spotting clues in Qs. In F. J., Fabozzi (Ed.), *Short selling strategies, and rewards.* 59-78). Hoboken, NJ: John Wiley and Sons, 259–278.

Haglund, M. (2006). Development of alpha in long/short equity hedge funds: Why selecting the right managers have become more important. Working Paper, Altevo Research, Stockholm, Sweden.

Haglund, M. (2008). Systematic factora driving the return of Swedish long short equity hedge funds: Separating betas and alpha. Working Paper, Altevo Research, Stockholm, Sweden.

Kosowski, R., Naik, N., & Teo, M. (2007). Do hedge funds deliver alpha? A Bayesian and bootstrap analysis. *Journal of Financial Economics, 84*(1), 229–264.

Lamont, O., & Thaler, R. (2002). Can the market add and subtract? Mispricing in tech stock carve-outs. Working Paper, Graduate School of Business, University of Chicago, Chicago, IL.

Matsumoto, G. (2009). Naked short sales hint fraud in bringing down Lehman. Retrieved March 19, 2009 from http://www.bloomberg.com/apps/news?pid=20601109&sid=aB1jlqmFOTCA. (accessed date March 19 2009).

Sloan, R. (2010). *Don't blame the shorts: Why short sellers are always blamed for market crashes and how history is repeating itself.* New York: McGraw-Hill.

Staley, K. F. (1996). *The art of short selling.* Hoboken, NJ: John Wiley and Sons.

CHAPTER 30

Short Selling by Portfolio Managers: Performance and Risk Effects across Investment Styles

Russell B. Gregory-Allen, David M. Smith, and Mark Werman[1]

CONTENTS

---

[1] We thank Audrey J. Moss for her significant contribution in the background and history of short selling in the first part of this chapter.

ABSTRACT

It has been suggested that if portfolio managers have the ability to short sell, they can improve investment performance. This chapter tests whether the effects of short selling are related to the portfolio manager's approach – i.e. bottom-up, top-down, quantitative, or fundamental. In particular, top-down and quantitative managers are likely to use short selling as part of a market neutral strategy, implying that restricting their use of this tool would be detrimental to performance. This study investigates over 5500 investment portfolios that used short selling between 2002 and 2009, comparing their performance as a function of their investment approach and controlling for the size and investment style (growth, value, or core). We find that prior to recent changes in short sale rules, quantitative managers who used short selling outperformed those who did not, with other managers exhibiting no differential performance due to short selling. After the latest short sell regulation change – removal of the uptick rule—quantitative managers who use short selling generally underperform those who do not.

KEYWORDS

Bear Stearns; Bottom-up analysis; Fama–French alphas; Fundamental analysis; Information ratio; Lehman Brothers; Naked short selling; Quantitative research; Top-down analysis; Tracking error; Uptick rule.

30.1 INTRODUCTION

This chapter examines the investment performance of portfolio managers who engage in short selling. In recent years, short selling as an investment strategy has moved into the mainstream, with the introduction of many hedge funds and even retail class mutual funds that follow a long–short approach. Still, the great majority of investment portfolios have long-only mandates, which restrict managers from taking full advantage of perceived overpricing.

Historically, short selling has been blamed by many commentators and governments for equity market declines and crashes. The ongoing financial crisis has seen many large, seemingly stable financial institutions fail in relatively short periods of time. Four such institutions were Northern Rock, HBOS, Bear Stearns, and Lehman Brothers. Each of these banks was an important global financial intermediary, but each had fundamental structural problems in their capital structures and investment portfolios. Their demises were preceded by a collapse of their stock price allegedly accelerated due to aggressive short selling of their shares by investors. The CEOs of each of these banks complained bitterly about two significant problems with short selling regulations. The first was the elimination of the "uptick" rule in 2007 and the second was the practice of "naked short selling."

30.1.1 What Is a Short Sale?

A normal investment scenario involves earning a profit by selling a security for more than its original cost or realizing a loss by selling the security for less than the original purchase price. A short sale is the sale of an asset that the investor does not currently own in hopes of buying it back at a lower price on some future date. Short selling allows the investor to profit from his belief that the price of a security will decline in price.

The mechanics of short selling are as follows. The investor borrows the security temporarily from a broker for a fee and then sells it at the current market price. Simultaneously, the investor agrees to return the security to the lender at some unspecified date in the future. The short seller must post margin equal to 150% of the value of the securities sold short. The investor then plays a waiting game. If the market price of the security declines, then the investor can buy it back at the lower market price, closing out the position, and return the security to the lender.

The gross profit equals the differential between the price at which he originally sold the borrowed security and the price at which he repurchased it. Additionally, the short sale and repurchase transactions precipitate brokerage fees. Another cost is the interest foregone on the margin funds that the investor must post. Institutional investors typically receive interest (the prevailing U.S. Fed funds rate) on the short sale proceeds, known as a "rebate rate." The short seller is responsible for covering cash dividends payable, if any, to the investor whose shares were borrowed. As a practical matter, borrowed shares are typically held in "street name"—that is, they are registered in the name of the brokerage firm. A final issue is stockholder voting rights. Two investors can rightly believe they have proxy voting rights for the same shares: (1) the investor whose shares were lent for the short sale and (2) the investor who bought the shares from the short seller. If shares are held in a street name, the lending investor has no ironclad guarantee of a voting right. Typically, the brokerage firm provides the client investor a voting proxy as a courtesy.

30.1.2 What Is a Naked Short Sale?

Naked short selling is the practice of selling a security without first borrowing it from a broker. Under Securities and Exchange Commission (SEC) regulations, when a security is sold short it must be delivered for settlement within 3 days. If the security is not delivered within 3 days, the trade does not settle because the seller "failed to deliver" the asset for settlement. The trade will usually remain open until the seller delivers the security. However, the unconsummated trade may affect the market price of the financial asset in question negatively, which could have been the short seller's intent all along. In 2005, the SEC, in an attempt to regulate naked shorts, required brokers to believe that financial assets were readily available for the ordered transaction and that the assets must be delivered for transfer within a short period of time (Regulation SHO). Rules regarding naked shorts are hard to enforce due to a lack of transparency and difficulty in tracking "failure to deliver" trades. In a further attempt to regulate naked shorts, in September 2008 the SEC required short sellers to deliver sold securities by the settlement date (3 days after the sale transaction date) and penalties were imposed for the failure to deliver within that time frame. These new regulations were designed to eliminate "naked shorts" because the SEC believed that these uncompleted trades could have been used to depress the price of a company's shares fraudulently.

30.1.3 What Is the "Uptick" Rule?

In the United States, the securities industry is regulated by the SEC pursuant to the broad authority granted to it under the Securities Exchange Act of 1934. This legislation was enacted during the Roosevelt administration and was part of his New Deal legislative package. The purpose of the legislation was to regulate secondary financial markets in the United States and to correct some of the practices that caused the stock market to crash in 1929. The "uptick" rule (Rule 10a-1) was added to the act in 1938, and its purpose was to limit how and when an investor could sell a financial asset short. In essence, an investor could sell a financial asset short only if the last quoted or bid price was not lower than the previously quoted or bid price. In other words, the asset must not be on a downward trend if a short sell is to be made.

In July 2007 the SEC amended its regulations by removing restrictions on the execution prices of short sales [i.e., "price tests" or "price test restrictions"—SEC (Release No. 34-55970; File No. S7-21-06), RIN 3235-AJ76 Regulation SHO and Rule 10a-1, page 1]. Investors were no longer constrained by the uptick rule when executing short sales. Therefore, the shares of Bear Stearns and Lehman Brothers were at the mercy of short sellers who could drive the share price of these companies down continuously without having to wait for an uptick. A review of the short selling of Bear Stearns and Lehman Brothers stock resulted in the SEC enacting a new uptick rule in February 2010 [SEC (Release No. 34-61595); File No. S7-08-09 RIN 3235-AK35 Amendments to Regulation SHO]. The new rule creates, in essence, a 2-day moratorium on the short selling of a company's shares if the price drops by more than 10% in 1 day.

30.1.4 Historical Perspective on Short Selling

Short selling is not a new investment strategy and it, in fact, dates back to the 1600s when the first stock exchange was created in the Dutch Republic. At that time Holland was a leading economic power in the world with a strong navy, adventurous explorers, and a global merchant fleet. Among the leading companies was the Dutch East India Company, known as the Vereenigde Oost-Indishe Compagnie (VOC), whose shares were traded on the Dutch stock market. In 1610 the Dutch stock market crashed and the price of VOC shares suffered dramatically as a consequence. Isaac Le Maire, a former board member of VOC and a large shareholder, was accused of manipulating the price of VOC shares by selling large blocks of shares short. Short selling was blamed for the market collapse and, as a consequence, the Dutch government placed a temporary ban on short selling.

Over 100 years later in 1720, a financial bubble broke in both France and England. The French share market collapsed due to overspeculation in shares of the Mississippi Company (the Mississippi bubble), which resulted in the collapse of its share price. Share prices in the Mississippi Company rose from 500 livres in May 1719 to 10,000 livres in February 1720 and then dropped back to 500 livres. Again, short sellers were blamed for the market crash and consequently short selling was banned temporarily by the French government. In fact, during the rule of Napoleon Bonaparte (1799 to 1814), short selling was banned entirely, as a treasonous activity, with violators arrested and imprisoned. Napoleon believed that it hampered his ability to raise the capital needed to finance his wars (Taulli, 2003). Meanwhile, in England, the financial bubble broke in 1720 because of dramatic fluctuations in the share price of the South Sea Company due to speculation when rumors circulated questioning the value of the company's trade in South America. Share prices of the South Sea Company suddenly rose from £128 in January to more than £1000 and then tumbled to under £150 in a matter of months. This resulted in the collapse of the British share market, and in response to the South Sea bubble the British government banned short selling (Elul, 2009).

30.1.5 Recent Crisis

During the recent financial crisis, there have been numerous examples of alleged abusive short selling of shares by some global financial intermediaries. In March 2008, Bear Stearns, an 80-year-old investment bank, collapsed due to rumors regarding its financial stability and liquidity. Within a 2-week period the market lost confidence in Bear Stearns: its customers withdrew their money from the firm, other financial firms refused to do business with Bear Stearns, and its share price disintegrated at a time of robust naked short selling of its shares (Taibbi, 2010). The U.S. Treasury and the U.S. Federal Reserve forced the sale of Bear Stearns to JPMorgan

Chase at a fire-sale price. The SEC is allegedly investigating the possibility of improper short selling of Bear Stearns shares, but no evidence of illegal activity has been proven to date.

Soon after the collapse of Bear Stearns, the share price of one of Britain's largest mortgage lenders, HBOS, dropped 20% on rumors regarding its financial condition. This led to an increase in short selling of HBOS shares, which caused its share price to be depressed even further. In March 2008 the Bank of England attempted to stabilize the financial markets and prevent a run on British banks by issuing a statement denying that any major High Street bank was in difficulty. This unprecedented statement by the Bank of England implied that HBOS was financially sound and was an attempt by the Bank of England to restore confidence in the British financial system (Goodway, 2008). In January 2009, HBOS was taken over by Lloyds TSB.

Six months after the Bear Stearns collapse, Lehman Brothers, a 150-year-old New York investment bank, filed for bankruptcy. On September 15, 2008, Lehman Brothers Bank failed because of the unwillingness of counterparties to trade with it, its inability to raise capital, and its rapidly declining share price. The CEO of Lehman Brothers, Richard Fuld, alleged that short selling was destroying the market value of the bank's shares (Sorkin, 2009). The SEC supported this contention when it reported that by September 11, 2008, as many as 32.8 million of Lehman Brothers' shares were sold but not delivered. The SEC linked those "failed to deliver" trades to naked short selling. It has been argued that those failed to deliver trades had a devastating effect on Lehman Brothers' share price and contributed to the demise of Lehman Brothers Bank (Matsumoto, 2009).

In response to this crisis, countries worldwide rushed to issue bans on short selling in an effort to protect investors. On September 19, 2008, a temporary ban on the short selling of 799 securities of U.S. financial institutions was announced by the SEC in conjunction with the Financial Services Authority (FSA) of the United Kingdom (SEC release 2008-211). This ban, originally scheduled to expire on October 2, 2008, was extended to October 17, 2008. Simultaneously, in the United Kingdom the FSA banned short selling on the shares of 29 financial institutions, which was later increased to 34. The U.K. ban expired on January 16, 2009. The Australian Securities and Investments Commission announced on September 19, 2008, that it was placing a total ban on naked shorts, it set forth a list of covered shorts that it would permit, and it established a reporting regime for covered shorts (ASIC 08-204). The ASIC bans and the reporting requirements were kept in place until June 1, 2009 (Williams, 2009).

More recently due to Greece's ongoing debt crisis, the Hellenic Capital Markets Commission banned both naked and covered short sales on the

Athens Stock Exchange and its related over-the-counter market from April 28, 2010, to June 28, 2010 (Petrakis, 2010). In a surprise move, the German government placed a temporary ban on naked short selling of bank and insurance company shares, credit-default swaps, and all euro-area government bonds because it believed that naked short selling of these securities was making the European debt crisis worse (Crawford, 2010). These bans remained in effect until March 31, 2011.

In general, economic policy makers and regulators worldwide seem inclined to restrict short selling in an attempt to decrease downward price cascades. For investors, short sale restrictions impose a constraint on their pursuit of alpha. There are potential market efficiency implications as well. In their empirical analysis of U.S. intraday data during 2005, Bardong, Bartram, and Yadav (2008) conclude that "short-sales provide an important stabilizing role by providing liquidity in periods of uninformed buying pressure." Restrictions on short sales decrease investors' ability to express often-legitimate negative sentiment about a stock, potentially decreasing pricing efficiency.

30.2 DATA DESCRIPTION

The PSN database provides a useful means by which to examine the effectiveness of short selling strategies. PSN, a survivor bias-free database, contains monthly performance information for over 13,000 portfolios offered by over 2000 firms. It also contains the results of portfolio manager surveys regarding each firm's, manager's, and portfolio's strategies and characteristics. Among the strategies is "short selling." For each strategy, respondents answer for their own portfolio according to a modified Likert scale: "very important," "important," "utilized," "not important," and "not utilized." We interpret any response other than "not important" or "not utilized" to indicate that the portfolio manager considers short selling to be a meaningful tool in implementing the firm's investment approach.

Other important characteristics available in the PSN database include the actual chosen benchmark for each portfolio, as well as monthly returns for each benchmark. As described later, we use this information to evaluate individual portfolios' performance. Among other variables in the database are fund size and asset allocation and the portfolio manager's primary investment approach.

The investment approaches identified include "quantitative," "fundamental," "top-down," and "bottom-up." Quantitative research involves making investment decisions based on mathematical and statistical models. Fundamental analysis involves making investment decisions based on market and financial statement ratios, such as price-to-earnings and price-to-book ratio and

Table 30.1 Summary of Sample Portfolios

Investment Approach	Number of Portfolios	Percent Using Equity Investment Style			Percent for Which Short Selling Is Utilized/Important
		Value	Core	Growth	
Quantitative	698	20	47	18	6
Fundamental	621	23	25	31	4
Bottom-up	3475	34	20	33	2
Top-down	212	17	22	21	2
Other	499	22	27	26	4
Totals	5505	29	25	30	3

dividend yield. Top-down analysis involves focusing first on the outlook for the economy, then a particularly attractive industry, and then the most attractive companies within that industry. Portfolio managers who do bottom-up stock selection emphasize prospects for the individual stock and give less weight to the outlook for the company's industry and the overall market. None of the approaches dominate the others a priori, but oftentimes a manager will find one approach to fit her capabilities and analytical preferences better than others.

In our sample, 13% of managers profess to follow a quantitative analysis approach, 63% are bottom-up managers, 11% use fundamental analysis, and 4% are top-down managers. Within each of those, the frequency of use of short selling ranges from 2 to 6%. Although the magnitude is lower than expected, at 6%, Quants are the biggest users of short selling (Table 30.1).

30.3 RESEARCH QUESTION/HYPOTHESIS

Dechow, Hutton, Meulbroek, and Sloan (2001) examine short-interest data and institutional holdings between 1975 and 1993. They find that professional investors held short positions in stocks with characteristics known to be associated with low future returns: where price-to-fundamentals ratios involving cash flow, earnings, book value, and sales were high. In retrospect, it is apparent that short sellers tended to exploit opportunities in stocks whose prices were temporarily high rather than in those for which fundamentals were temporarily low. Furthermore, the higher the short position on a stock, the more negative was the abnormal return in the subsequent year.

Due to the nature of how they invest, it is reasonable to expect that if quantitative managers are largely using long/short strategies (as in market neutral) that the short selling tool is not only important to them but, if restricted or changed, would hurt their performance.[2]

None of the other manager types would likely use long/short strategies as an integral part of their process, although top-down managers might be more likely to than bottom-up or fundamental managers, and any of the managers might use short selling as a specific target when a price drop is expected.

Therefore, we anticipate that quantitative managers will exhibit performance instability as the restrictions on short selling were changed, especially after short sales restrictions were removed completely in 2007. Not only would alterations in the rules likely upset the strategies used in their models, but it would change the way their models expect the rest of the market to use short sales. For the other manager types, we have no a priori expectations about the impact of the short sell restrictions.

30.4 METHODOLOGY

We examine the contribution of short selling to return of individual fund managers using a two-stage procedure. First, we estimate a performance alpha using two methods.

Active return is defined as return on the portfolio less the return on that portfolio's benchmark. The usual performance measure of active return is the information ratio, which is active return divided by the tracking error (best defined as the standard deviation of the active return):

$$r_{a,i} = r_i - r_{b,i}$$

where $r_{a,i}$ is the active return for fund i, r_i is the raw return for fund i, and $r_{b,i}$ is the return on the benchmark for fund i. Tracking error (TE) and information ratio (IR) are calculated as

$$TE_i = \sigma_{r_{a,i}} \quad IR_i = \frac{\bar{r}_a}{TE}$$

Commonly used risk-adjusted performance measurement methods are the CAPM-adjusted Jensen's (1968) alpha and an alpha extracted from the so-called "three-factor model" from Fama and French (1993)[3]:

$$r_i = \alpha_i^{FF} + \beta_1 r_{SP500} + \beta_2 SMB + \beta_3 HML + \varepsilon_i$$

---

[2] Lioui (2010) finds that the 2008 short sale ban increased market volatility significantly, over and above that of the financial crisis.

[3] Due to space constraints, we report only Fama–French results, but we also tested with Jensen's alpha, as well as the Carhart (1997) four-factor model, with qualitatively similar results.

where α_i^{FF} is the Fama–French alpha; R_i is the return for fund i, in excess of fees and the 90-day U.S. T-bill rate; R_{SP500} is the return on the S&P 500 index, in excess of the 90-day U.S. T-bill rate; and SMB and HML are Fama–French factors.

In a second stage, we examine the performance metrics against dummy variables representing the type of manager and their use of short selling. We do this in two parts: (1) to capture the overall impact of the use of short selling across all fund types, but controlling for the types, and (2) considering the combined use of specific management types and short selling.

For the first part, we model regressions of each performance metric on short selling, with control dummies for the fund type (quantitative, fundamental, bottom-up, and top-down). For each of these regressions (and those following), we examine with and without additional control variables. It has been well established in the literature that fund size can impact performance (see, e.g., Chen, Hong, Huang, & Kubik, 2004). Further, the manager's target universe (growth, value, core) can clearly impact raw performance (and is usually out of the control of the individual manager). Therefore, the equations for this first investigation have the form:

$$P_i = \beta_0 + \beta_1 SS_i + \beta_2 Q_i + \beta_3 F_i + \beta_4 B_i + \beta_5 T_i + \beta_6 LogSize_i + \beta_7 Gro_i + \beta_8 Val_i + \varepsilon_i$$

(30.1)

where for fund i, P_i is the performance metric for the equation (IR, Fama–French alpha); LogSize is the natural log of fund i's average size over the examination period; dummies for the most common investment style variables, growth and value (core omitted); dummies for the primary investment approach and use of short selling: SS = 1 if the manager uses short selling; Q = 1 if the manager is quantitative; F = 1 if the manager is fundamental; B = 1 if the manager is bottom-up; and T = 1 if the manager is top-down.

We estimate Equation (30.1), with and without control variables (last three terms in the equation), for each of the outperformance metrics.

In the second part of the investigation, we investigate whether short selling's impact on performance is different for specific fund manager types. For this, we create new dummy "interaction" variables, where SQ = 1 if the manager is quantitative *and* uses short selling (SQ = 0 otherwise). Similarly, for managers who use short selling: SF = 1 for fundamental managers and SB = 1 for bottom-up. We eliminate ST (top-down and short selling) because there were only four observations.

So, for the second part, our model regression equation looks like:

$$P_i = \beta_0 + \beta_1 SQ_i + \beta_2 SF_i + \beta_3 SB_i + \beta_4 LogSize_i + \beta_5 Gro_i + \beta_6 Val_i + \varepsilon_i \qquad (30.2)$$

where for fund *i*, P_i is the performance metric for the equation (IR, Fama–French alpha); LogSize is the natural log of fund *i*'s average size over the examination period; dummies for the most common investment style variables, growth and value (core omitted), and dummies for the primary investment approach and use of short selling: SQ = 1 if the manager is quantitative and uses short selling; SF = 1 if the manager is fundamental and uses short selling; SB = 1 if the manager is bottom-up and uses short selling.

Finally, we do all of the aforementioned for periods before and after two important regulation changes regarding short selling. Because naked short selling has been implicated as a prime suspect in several recent financial institution failures, the introduction of Regulation SHO may have had an impact. Perhaps even more dramatic was the removal of the nearly 70-year-old uptick rule and then several subsequent changes to regulations affecting some stocks. So, in our examination, we have:

Period 1: prior to Regulation SHO (July 2002–December 2004); period 2: from Regulation SHO to lifting of uptick rule (January 2005–July 2007); period 3: from uptick change to current (July 2007–December 2009), during which there were several changes to short selling restrictions; all: over the entire period July 2002–December 2009 (as periods 2 and 3 were each 30 months, we also use 30 months for period 1).

Risk impact:

In order to assess the impact of short selling on portfolio risk, we use two common portfolio risk metrics: tracking error and beta (from the CAPM), both as described earlier. We model these directly, using Equation (30.2), but substituting the risk metric for the performance metric.

30.5 RESULTS

30.5.1 Does Short Selling Have an Overall Impact on Return across All Managers?

When we examine the entire 90-month period, estimations for Equation (30.1) show that short selling is marginally beneficial to funds when performance is measured by the information ratio and has no impact when measured by Fama–French alphas. Period-by-period results reveal that all of that benefit came in period 1, before Regulation SHO. In period 1, short selling's impact on outperformance was significant by all metrics, but had no impact in periods 2 and 3 (see Table 30.2).

Table 30.2 Summary Results: Positive or Negative Significant Results

Performance Measure	Short Sells and Type		Period			All
			1	**2**	**3**	
			Before Reg SHO	**After Reg SHO and before Uptick Relaxed**	**After Uptick Rule Relaxed**	
IR	Short sells	All	+ +			
		Quantitative	+ + +		– –	
	Short sells and:	Fundamental				+
		Bottom up				+
FF	Short sells	All	+ + +			
		Quantitative	+ + +		–	
	Short sells and:	Fundamental				
		Bottom up				
TE	Short sells	All	+ + +	+ + +	+ + +	+ + +
		Quantitative	+		+ +	
	Short sells and:	Fundamental	+ +	+ +	+ +	+ + +
		Bottom up	+ + +	+ + +	+ +	+ + +
Beta	Short sells	All	– – –	– – –	– – –	– – –
		Quantitative	– – –	–	– – –	– – –
		Fundamental				
		Bottom up	– –		– – –	

"+" indicates positive impact: "+" significant at 10% level, "++" at 5%, "+++" at 1%.
"–" indicates negative impact: "–" significant at 10% level, "– –" at 5%, "– – –" at 1%.

30.5.2 Does Short Selling Have a Differential Return Impact for Specific Types of Managers?

Based on portfolios' information ratios over the entire period, we conclude that fundamental and bottom-up managers benefited significantly from the use of short selling. This is a notable result, given that many institutional and retail portfolios have long-only mandates. On average, portfolios that were granted the flexibility to use short sales outperformed their long-only peers over the long term. Surprisingly, information ratio results show no incremental benefit for Quants that use short selling. Fama–French alphas are not significantly different for short sellers versus nonshort sellers for any of the investment approaches.

In the period-by-period analysis, we see a different story. Before the introduction of Regulation SHO, Quants benefited from short selling, whether measured by information ratio or Fama–French alphas, but other managers did not. In period 2, no fund types benefited, and in period 3, quantitative managers were *hurt* significantly using short selling, again for both outperformance metrics.

In the interest of space, Table 30.2 contains only a representative sample of our regression runs. For all estimations, we ran regressions both with and without control variables. Results reported in Table 30.2 are robust to control variables: size, growth, and value (complete results available on request).

30.5.3 Does Short Selling Have an Overall Impact on Risk across All Managers?

Over the entire period, and for each subperiod, short selling has a consistent and very significant positive impact on tracking error and a very significant *negative* impact on beta.

Neither of these results is surprising. Equity performance benchmarks contain almost exclusively long positions. Hence, the returns for portfolios that use short selling will deviate from the benchmark more dramatically than returns of portfolios that hold only long positions. For the latter, the position that comes closest to shorting occurs when the portfolio maintains a decision not to invest in (or significantly underweight) a highly weighted index component, which is interpreted by analysts as an "active short position" (see Cremers & Petajisto, 2009).

As for the negative relation between portfolio beta and short selling, long positions will almost certainly have positive betas. Conversely, short positions themselves should have negative betas. The overall portfolio effect of a short component is to reduce beta, hence the strongly negative coefficient.

30.5.4 Does Short Selling Have a Differential Risk Impact for Specific Types of Managers?

When we look at the entire period, short selling increases TE clearly and very significantly and decreases beta. This result is not changed much when we examine the subperiods. In period 1, before Regulation SHO, Quants showed a marginally increased tracking error from short selling, with other managers' impacts all significant to very significant. Beta, however, is decreased significantly (by short selling) for Quants, a less significant but negative impact for bottom-up managers, and no impact for fundamental managers. In period 2, the beta impact is weak for all managers, but the tracking error impact is nil for Quants, and strongly positive for fundamental and bottom-up. In period 3, similar to period 1, all managers see tracking error increased, and Quants and bottom-up managers see their beta decreased.

30.6 CONCLUSION

Examining performance metrics as used most often in industry—active returns and the information ratio—we find, in general, that before Regulation SHO, quantitative managers benefited from short selling, but after the uptick restriction rule was relaxed quantitative managers were hurt using short selling. When using risk-adjusted measures, there was no impact. When performance is measured with the information ratio, fundamental and bottom-up managers benefited, but only if we take a long-term perspective; in each sub-period (and for other measures) there was no discernible impact for other measures.

Risk, whether measured by tracking error or by beta, is impacted significantly by short selling regardless of manager type. There was some variation across subperiods, but the overall result is very clear—short selling increases tracking error and decreases beta.

REFERENCES

Australian Securities and Investments Commission. (2008, September 19). (ASIC) 08-204. Retrieved from www.asic.gov.au/asic/asic.nsf/byheadline/08-204.

Bardong, F., Bartram, S. M., & Yadav, P. K. (2008). *Are short-sellers different?* EFA 2008 Athens Meetings Paper. Retrieved from http://ssrn.com/abstract=1101786.

Carhart, M. (1997). On persistence in mutual fund performance. *Journal of Finance, 52*(1), 57–82.

Chen, J., Hong, H., Huang, M., & Kubik, J. (2004). Does fund size erode mutual fund performance? The role of liquidity and organization. *American Economic Review, 94*(5), 1276–1302.

Crawford, A. (2010). Germany to ban naked short-selling at midnight (Update 2). Retrieved from www.bloomberg.com/apps/news?pid=2067001&sid=a06bs <http://www.bloomberg.com/apps/news?pid=2067001&sid=a06bs.

Cremers, M., & Petajisto, A. (2009). How active is your fund manager? A new measure that predicts performance. *Review of Financial Studies, 22*(9), 3329–3365.

Dechow, P. M., Hutton, A. P., Meulbroek, L. K., & Sloan, R. G. (2001). Shortsellers, fundamental analysis, and stock returns. *Journal of Financial Economics, 61*(1), 77–106.

Elul, R. (2009). Regulating short-sales. *Business Review, 2*(2), 11–18.

Fama, E., & French, K. (1993). Common risk factors in the returns on stocks and bonds. *Journal of Financial Economics, 33*(1), 3–56.

Goodway, N. (2008, March 19). HBOS crisis rumour denied as shares tank. *This Is Money.* Retrieved from http://www.thisismoney.co.uk/money/markets/article-1623270/HBOS-crisis-rumour-denied-as-shares-tank.html.

Jensen, M. C. (1968). The performance of mutual funds in the period 1945–1964. *Journal of Finance, 23*(2), 389–416.

Lioui, A. (2010, March). Spillover effects of counter-cyclical market regulation: Evidence from the 2008 ban on short sales. EDHEC Risk Institute, pp. 1–28. Retrieved from www.edhec-risk.com.

Matsumoto, G. (2009, March 19). Naked short sales hint fraud in bringing down Lehman (Update1). Retrieved from http://www.Bloomberg.com.

Petrakis, M. (2010, April 28). *Greek stocks regulator bans short selling. From Today to June 28.* Retrieved from http://www.bloomberg.com/apps/news?pid=2067001&sid=akAusD.

SEC Release No 2008-211. *SEC halts short selling of financial stocks to protect investors and markets.* Retrieved from www.sec.gov/news/press/2008/2008-211.htm.

Sorkin, A. R. (2009). *Too big to fail.* New York: Viking Press, Penguin Group.

Taibbi, M. (2010, April 10). Wall street's naked swindle. *Rolling Stone.* Retrieved from http://www.rollingstone.com/politics/news/;kw=[3351,11470].

Taulli, T. (2003). *The streetsmart guide to short selling: Techniques the pros use to profit in any market.* New York: McGraw-Hill.

Williams, R. (2009, May 27). Short selling ban had outlived its usefulness. *The Age.* Retrieved from http://www.theage.com.au/business/shortselling-ban-had-outlived-its-usefulness-20090526-bm34.html.

CHAPTER 31

Short Selling in an Asset Allocation Framework—The Search for Alpha

Nils S. Tuchschmid, Erik Wallerstein, and Sassan Zaker

CONTENTS

ABSTRACT

Introducing short selling in an asset allocation framework can enhance the performance of an investor's portfolio significantly. Short selling allows for separation of investments into beta and alpha exposure, which leads to better control of the asset allocation process. This chapter gives an intuitive example of how alpha–beta separation adds value and how it is implemented through short selling of market factors. The final section looks at a data set of funds of hedge funds to illustrate empirically the efficiency gains investors achieve through alpha–beta separation.

KEYWORDS

Active fund; Alpha–beta separation; Exchange-traded funds; Fund of funds; Hedge funds; Index fund; Policy portfolio.

31.1 INTRODUCTION

It has been heralded as the biggest revolution in portfolio management since Markowitz's (1952) mean-variance portfolio model. Portfolio managers should focus on separating their investment process into beta and alpha allocations and create an optimal allocation from these building blocks. Several articles, such as Kung and Pohlman (2004) and Clarke, de Silva, and Thorley (2009), have demonstrated the significant efficiency gains achieved through this approach. This demonstrates the necessity of short selling market exposure, or beta, in order to create pure alpha investment vehicles because alpha performance is most likely packaged in a suboptimal manner together with beta exposure. However, beta exposure is easily accessible through inexpensive index funds, futures, or exchange-traded funds (ETFs).

This chapter takes the view of institutional investors seeking optimal active and passive exposure to markets and the significant gains they can achieve through short selling. However, short selling market indices at an appropriate level to extract alpha is a complex process and requires skilled portfolio managers. There are three reasons for the complexity: (1) finding an active manager with consistent positive alpha, (2) estimating their beta exposure, and (3) implementing short selling of beta exposure.

The chapter is structured as follows. We begin with a stylized example that shows how portfolio performance is enhanced by alpha–beta separation through the help of shorting market indices. The next section is a more technical section on how short positions are estimated and managed. These techniques are illustrated with an empirical test on a fund of hedge funds (hereafter fund of funds) data set.

Also, we will mention some of the interesting literature on the importance and implications of allowing for short selling in an actively managed fund. For example, Clarke, de Silva, and Thorley (2002) show that under reasonable assumptions the long-only constraint induces a 42% loss of potential added value. Grinold and Kahn (2000) formalize and explain the conditions under which short selling adds value to an actively managed fund and highlight the fact that introducing short selling is a bet on the active management skills of the fund manager. They extend this analysis in Grinold and Kahn (2009).

31.2 A STYLIZED EXAMPLE

Central to the argument of shorting beta of an actively managed fund and creating a pure alpha portfolio is that the original active fund is most likely to have a suboptimal beta exposure when viewed in the asset allocation policy of the investor. To clarify this point, let us consider the following example.[1]

Assume a portfolio manager faces an investment set consisting of a market index fund, an active fund, and the risk-free rate. Their annual performance characteristics are presented in Table 31.1.

More precisely, the active fund operates in the same market as the index fund where they are able to deliver a 3% active performance, or alpha, on top of the 8% delivered by the market.[2] Furthermore, the alpha has a volatility of 5% and is uncorrelated with the market. From these last two assumptions, it is possible to derive the volatility of the active fund ($\sqrt{14^2 + 5^2} \approx 15\%$). The correlation between the active fund and the index fund is 94%.

The objective of the portfolio manager is to form a mean-variance efficient portfolio of these assets, or a policy portfolio. We are only interested in the portfolio formation of the risky part of the policy portfolio, as we know from portfolio theory (Tobin, 1958) that the investor's risk preference only changes the allocation between the risk-free rate and the risky asset. Table 31.2 presents mean-variance optimal portfolio weights for the tangent portfolio and the corresponding performance of the policy portfolio.

As seen in Table 31.2, in order to find the optimal risk/return profile as measured by the Sharpe ratio, the index fund is given nil allocation, as it has a similar risk exposure to the active fund. However, conjecture in this

Table 31.1 Annual Performance of Investment Opportunities

	Return	Volatility	Corr. w. Index Fund
Active fund	11%	15%	94%
Index fund	8%	14%	–
Risk-free rate	4%	–	–

Table 31.2 Performance and Formation of Policy Portfolio

				Weights	
	Return	Volatility	Sharpe	Active Fund	Index Fund
Policy portfolio	11%	15%	0.73	100%	0%

---

[1] For more extensive examples, see Kung and Pohlman (2004) and Clarke and colleagues (2009).

[2] A 3% active performance is a nontrivial assumption, as is shown by the rich literature on mutual fund performance; this is also discussed in a subsequent chapter.

Table 31.3 Alpha–Beta Opportunity Set

	Return	Volatility	Corr. w. Index Fund
Alpha fund	7%	5%	0%
Index fund	8%	14%	–

Table 31.4 Performance and Formation of Policy Portfolio

	Return	Volatility	Sharpe	Weights	
				Alpha Fund	Index Fund
Policy portfolio	6.4%	5%	1.32	82.5%	17.5%

simple setting that the active fund has a suboptimal allocation between alpha (or active) performance and beta (or market) exposure for our investor. Therefore, we separate the alpha performance in the active fund by taking a short position on the nominal amount of the fund and call this new fund the alpha fund. Proceeds from the short position are invested in the risk-free rate. Hence, the alpha fund will earn 11 − 8 = 3% from the long–short position and 4% from the risk-free rate. The volatility is 5%. The new investment opportunity set is presented in Table 31.3.

Solving for the optimal policy portfolio, we arrive at the results in Table 31.4. Compared to the results in Table 31.2, these results are strikingly different. Both assets are given allocation in the policy portfolio. Most significantly, the Sharpe ratio is increased by about 80% from 0.73 to 1.32 by forming the portfolio with pure beta and alpha sources.

The most important lesson from this example is that all the efficiency gains are achieved without using any additional sources of active management. By short selling beta and eliminating the suboptimal allocation of the active fund, we have added a degree of freedom to the portfolio optimization. However, in practice, there are several issues facing the portfolio manager of transporting active management to a market-neutral fund, which are discussed in more detail in the next section.

31.3 ALPHA TRANSPORTATION IN PRACTICE

Practical issues facing portfolio managers who wish to form their portfolio process around alpha–beta allocation are threefold: (1) finding skilled managers who consistently outperform the market, (2) estimating beta exposure successfully, and (3) implementing short selling of beta exposure.

Finding skilled managers is indeed very difficult. The investor makes a gamble that he or she can find a consistently outperforming fund manager. There is a wealth of academic literature evaluating the performance of active fund management. The fund performance literature is usually divided between long-only mutual funds and hedge funds, which are more flexible in terms of holding short positions, derivative investments, and imposing leverage. The literature on mutual funds mostly agrees that after fees, active long-only managers do not add value to investors (see Barras, Scaillet, & Wermers, 2010). With regards to hedge funds, the picture is somewhat more complex. However, a majority of empirical studies conclude that hedge funds (or funds of funds) do not deliver consistent outperformance to investors.[3]

However, assuming the investor has found an actively managed fund, there are large efficiency gains to be made, as the previous section showed, by transporting alpha performance to a market-neutral fund. This leads us to the second task of estimating outperformance (alpha) and market exposure (beta) of an actively managed fund. The most common approach is based on a multifactor linear regression. Formally, the return generating process of a fund is expressed as:

$$r_t = \alpha + \sum_{i=1}^{N} \beta_i f_{i,t} + \varepsilon_t$$

where r_t is the fund return, α is a constant, β_i is the exposure toward market factor $f_{i,t}$, and ε_t is the idiosyncratic variation of returns. In theory, we can extract the alpha of our fund by shorting each market factor ($f_{i,t}$) by the estimated exposure (β_i).

However, in practice, there are two major problems with using this model. First, estimations of market exposure, or beta, are made *ex ante* and there is no guarantee that this estimation will hold as the true *ex post* exposure. Many active managers switch between markets over time, which further complicates beta estimation. In the empirical section we mitigate the problem of estimating time-varying beta exposure by using only a 24-month rolling window to estimate beta exposure. Second, it is far from straightforward to select which assets best capture the risk and return structure specified in the $f_{i,t}$ in the aforementioned equation. Choosing the right

---

[3] A more complete picture of hedge fund performance is not in the scope of this chapter and the interested reader is referred to Fung, Hsieh, Naik, and Ramadorai (2008) for an example.

Table 31.5 Quarterly Returns of an Actively Managed Fund

	Returns	
	Q1	Q2
Active fund	−4%	−1%
Alpha	2%	1%
Market index	−6%	−2%

factors requires a careful analysis of the underlying funds, in which markets they operate and what strategies they employ. The choice of beta factors for equity and fixed-income markets has been influenced greatly over the years by the research of Fama and French (1993) and Carhart (1997). When selecting factors, is it crucial to bear in mind that they have to be investable, liquid, and possible to sell short and hold long. Otherwise they are useless from a practical point of view when implementing an alpha transportation program.

Short positions on broad market factors are accessed most commonly through instruments such as asset swaps, futures, short index funds,[4] or exchange-traded funds. However, short positions require additional risk management as compared to long positions. Short positions have unlimited loss possibilities, unlike long positions, which are limited to the nominal amount. Furthermore, the frequency with which short positions are readjusted to hedge some exposure is crucial to the performance of the market-neutral alpha fund. Table 31.5 displays quarterly returns for a sample actively managed fund.

From Table 31.5 we see that the manager is able to produce an alpha of 2 and 1% in the first and second quarter, respectively. For sake of simplicity, we assumed that the active manager has a unit nominal exposure toward the market. Consider an investor that forms a self-financed portfolio that holds a $100 million long position in the active fund and a $100 million short position in the market index. The investor sells off the portfolio at the end of the sample period. The evolution of this portfolio value is presented in Table 31.6.

Therefore, at the end of the period, the investor has earned an alpha of 2.92%. However, going back to Table 31.5, the compounded alpha of 2 and 1% is in fact 3.02%. The investor has lost out on 10bp of the alpha performance or $100,000 in real terms because the portfolio composition changed over the first quarter. At the beginning of the sample period there is a 100%

---

[4] It is not possible to short an index fund per se. Here we refer to fund providers who offer short market exposure in a fund.

Table 31.6 Value Evolution of Investor's Portfolio

	Portfolio Evolution (million $)	
	Q1	Q2
Long active fund	$96.00	$95.04
Short market index	$−94.00	$−92.12
Net value	$2.00	$2.92

long and 100% short position. However, at the end the portfolio composition has changed to being 101% long and 99% short. The shortfall would have been prevented by simply reweighting the portfolio by moving $1 million from the long to the short position at the beginning of the second quarter.

The effect that frequent reweighting has on short positions is also important to keep in mind when accessing short positions through short ETFs or short index funds, as they reweight their position at certain frequencies in order to keep the same weights as their underlying index. For an example, many short ETFs and index funds aim to keep the same individual security weights as their underlying index on a daily basis. This means that on a month-to-month basis the ETF will not deliver the exact opposite returns as the underlying index.

Finally, we mention some issues concerning short market positions through futures contracts. A long or short position in a futures contract, together with an equal position on cash at the risk-free rate, should, in theory, provide equal returns as the corresponding long or short positions in the underlying stocks composing the index. However, in terms of hedging, the length of the futures contract most likely will not coincide with the desired length of the beta exposure. Futures contracts are most often rolled over several times to cover the desired duration of the beta exposure; in addition, it is generally necessary to exit the final contract before its expiration date. These rollover and timing mismatches lead to various forms of tracking error risk between the actual evolution of the underlying index and the futures price. The tracking error risk stems from several sources. The risk-free rate is, in fact, not risk free and changes over time. Future dividends need to be estimated to price the contracts accurately and these are subject to forecasting errors. The interest rate yield curve is not flat, which induces friction when contracts are rolled over.[5]

---

[5] Several factors prevent perfect arbitrage between spot and futures markets, especially transaction costs, but also other constraints, such as limited capital, risk aversion, and various execution constraints, which may prevent arbitrage futures and spot prices to exact parity.

31.4 AN ILLUSTRATIVE EXAMPLE

A few years ago, when hedge funds were considered pure alpha managers, the idea of a portable alpha gained popularity and billions of assets were raised. The idea was to outperform an index such as S&P 500 by investing in the futures index on the one hand (requiring little capital) and using remaining capital to invest in a conservative fund of hedge fund (the alpha portfolio) on the other hand. This concept failed dramatically in 2008, as the alpha portfolio not only had a poor performance but became very illiquid. The assumption of alpha was wrong both with respect to considerable beta content and excessive illiquidity risk compared to the S&P 500. With this in mind, this section is dedicated to an empirical test on transporting alpha from a fund of funds. These represent actively managed funds with a high potential for alpha generation. The reason we have chosen a fund of funds is because these are accessed most easily by institutional investors.

The aim of our example is to compare the efficiency of the optimal risky allocation of a policy portfolio with respect to two cases. In the first case, the optimal portfolio, with respect to mean variance, is formed by a set of five general market factors plus a fund of funds. In the second case, we form an alpha portfolio, transported from the fund of funds, and again form the optimal portfolio based on the same set of five market factors and the new alpha portfolio.

31.4.1 Transporting Fund of Funds Alpha

We begin with describing our method of how the alpha is transported from the fund of funds. The method is based around a beta benchmark portfolio that is reweighted at the end of each month (t) over the sample period. Portfolio weights are estimated on a 24-month rolling window on *ex ante* data using a relaxed form of Sharpe's style analysis model (1992). An alpha fund is formed over the consecutive month on *ex post* data. The alpha fund has a unit long position in the fund of funds, a unit short position in the beta portfolio, and a unit long position in the risk-free rate. The model to estimate portfolio weights is defined as

$$r_t = \sum_{i=1}^{N} w_i f_{i,t} + \varepsilon_t$$

$$\text{s.t.} \sum_{i=1}^{N} w_i = 1$$

The constraint gives a natural portfolio interpretation. Unlike Sharpe's original model, this model allows for short selling, as it falls more in line with hedge fund strategies. Hedge funds report their monthly returns to data vendors with a delay of some weeks. To account for this, we lag *ex ante* data 1 month.

In terms of hedge funds, the selection of factors is somewhat more complicated. Hedge funds trade in equity, commodities, and bonds. However, many strategies are implemented through derivatives that will give nonlinear returns relative to the underlying asset. Therefore, the factor model should include derivative-based factors to overcome nonlinearities. However, this suddenly increases the possible set of factors enormously and makes the selection process increasingly complex. The influential paper by Fung and Hsieh (2004) suggests a seven-factor option-based model in performance attribution of hedge fund returns. Our approach to selecting factors that explain fund of funds beta exposure and help transport their active performance to our alpha fund differs somewhat from the literature. The factors should represent a plausible allocation of the fund of funds. In addition, the factors need to be liquid, be possible to short sell and be of plain vanilla type. The set of factors is, more precisely, (1) S&P 500, total return index; (2) RSL2000, the Russell 2000 index return; (3) EAFE, the MSCI EAFE (Europe, Australasia, and Far East) total return index; (4) BOND, the Barclays Capital U.S. Aggregate Corporate AA Bond total return index; and (5) CMDTY, the S&P Goldman Sachs Commodity total return index. S&P 500 and RSL2000 capture U.S. large and small-cap equity exposure, and EAFE captures equity exposure toward some parts of the developed world from an American investor perspective. The BOND and CMDTY both have natural interpretations and represent important exposures of hedge funds.

31.4.2 Data

The hedge fund data sample we use is collected from the Hedge Fund Research (HFR) database, January 1990 to December 2008. This covers a long period of financial bear and bull markets. We only collected funds of funds operating as of December 2008. Some funds of funds are filtered out from the sample based on the criteria that they have to be denominated in U.S. dollars, report returns net of all fees, report assets under management, and have a track record longer than or equal to 37 months. For funds with the same share class, the one with the longest history or domiciled in the United States is selected. These filters leave a sample of 885 funds of funds. The HFR categorizes each fund of funds in their database as either (sample size in parentheses) conservative (224), diversified (351), market defensive (29), or strategic (281).[6]

---

[6] Conservative refers to a fund of funds that invests in low volatility strategies as equity market neutral, fixed income arbitrage, and convertible arbitrage. A diversified fund of funds invests in a broad range of strategies. A market defensive fund of funds invests in short-biased and managed futures funds. Strategic is the most volatile category and is exposed primarily toward emerging market, sector-specific, and equity hedge funds.

31.4.3 Empirical Results

We consider an institutional investor that faces two different investments opportunity sets. The first set consists of the five market indices described earlier plus a fund of funds from the data set. The second opportunity set consists of the same five market indices plus the alpha fund of a fund of funds from the data set. Based on these two opportunity sets, a mean-variance optimal portfolio is estimated on the full sample period from February 1992 to December 2008. Table 31.7 presents the average performance of these six-asset portfolios of all 885 funds of funds and is organized according to subcategories. The cross-sectional standard deviation of performance is presented in parentheses. The left part of Table 31.7 presents performance when the fund of funds is the alternative asset in the portfolio, and the right part of Table 31.7 presents performance when the alpha fund is the alternative asset. The Sharpe ratio increases two times when the alpha fund is used as an alternative asset. This stresses the significant efficiency gains that can be made through an alpha–beta program. The volatility column in Table 31.7 shows that the alpha fund in particular increases the risk–reward ratio through reducing the risk level of the portfolio. Market defensive categories seem to benefit the least from alpha transportation. However, this should not be a surprise, as a market defensive fund of funds is focused on commodity trading advisors and short-biased hedge funds. The alpha of managed futures hedge funds should not be expected to be transported that well by a linear beta factor model.

Table 31.8 presents a cross-sectional average of mean-variance optimal portfolio weights over the two investment opportunity sets. The top part of Table 31.8 shows average weights when the alternative asset is the fund of funds. Interestingly, the fund of funds is not given the major allocation, often only half of that given to the bond index, implying that it does not

Table 31.7 Average Annualized Performance of Mean-Variance Portfolios

	Fund of Funds as Alternative Asset			Alpha Fund as Alternative Asset		
	Mean	**Volatility**	**Sharpe**	**Mean**	**Volatility**	**Sharpe**
All funds of funds	0.0493	0.0640	1.00	0.0572	0.0321	1.94
(std)	(0.0277)	(0.0485)	(0.6931)	(0.0255)	(0.1249)	(0.9314)
Conservative	0.0480	0.0606	1.14	0.0539	0.0305	2.36
	(0.0258)	(0.0521)	(0.8560)	(0.0252)	(0.0315)	(1.2826)
Diversified	0.0495	0.0625	0.99	0.0554	0.0329	1.95
	(0.0264)	(0.0520)	(0.6293)	(0.0195)	(0.0223)	(0.7348)
Market defensive	0.0801	0.0616	1.51	0.0667	0.0366	2.01
	(0.0385)	(0.0347)	(0.6932)	(0.0242)	(0.0155)	(0.8401)
Strategic	0.0469	0.0689	0.84	0.0613	0.0319	1.60
	(0.0277)	(0.0413)	(0.5665)	(0.0312)	(0.2186)	(0.6479)

Table 31.8 Portfolio Weights in Mean-Variance Portfolios

	Fund of Funds as Alternative Asset					
	SP500	RSL2000	EAFE	CMDTY	BOND	Alt. Asset
All funds of funds	0.1	0.8	3.1	5.7	60.7	29.6
(std)	(0.5)	(2.6)	(9.6)	(17.0)	(33.1)	(33.4)
Conservative	0.0	0.7	2.2	6.9	53.3	36.9
	(0.1)	(2.9)	(6.9)	(20.6)	(34.5)	(35.8)
Diversified	0.1	0.7	3.9	5.2	60.0	30.1
	(0.5)	(2.2)	(11.0)	(15.4)	(31.9)	(32.7)
Market defensive	0.4	1.3	1.9	4.1	42.6	49.8
	(1.2)	(3.1)	(5.7)	(10.3)	(27.2)	(33.0)
Strategic	0.1	0.8	2.9	5.7	70.2	20.3
	(0.5)	(2.8)	(9.9)	(16.2)	(31.5)	(29.3)

	Alpha Fund as Alternative Asset					
	SP500	RSL2000	EAFE	CMDTY	BOND	Alt. Asset
All funds of funds	0.4	1.9	2.0	3.0	43.4	49.4
(std)	(1.0)	(2.3)	(4.3)	(8.1)	(19.6)	(21.7)
Conservative	0.5	1.1	1.1	2.5	39.8	55.0
	(1.2)	(1.5)	(3.1)	(9.7)	(18.1)	(19.7)
Diversified	0.4	1.9	2.0	2.6	42.8	50.2
	(0.9)	(2.2)	(4.3)	(6.5)	(17.6)	(20.0)
Market defensive	0.8	2.5	3.9	4.2	54.0	34.6
	(1.9)	(3.1)	(6.6)	(3.5)	(15.3)	(17.0)
Strategic	0.2	2.4	2.4	3.8	45.7	45.5
	(0.8)	(2.7)	(4.8)	(8.6)	(22.7)	(24.2)

contribute many new sources of uncorrelated returns. The bottom part of Table 31.8 shows average weights when the alternative asset is the alpha fund. In this case, the alternative asset is given a much more central role with an increased portfolio weight of approximately 20–30%. Again, this stresses efficiency gains achieved through shorting beta exposure from the fund of funds to create an optimal portfolio composition for the end investor.

There are obvious look-ahead biases in the aforementioned test, as mean-variance portfolio weights are estimated on the same data sample as the performance is calculated. In order to examine the effect of the look-ahead bias, we conduct a test where the portfolio is estimated *ex ante* and performance evaluated *ex post*.[7] However, because all funds of funds differ on inception

---

[7] More precisely, the *ex ante* sample period is February 1992 to June 2000, and the *ex post* period is July 2000 to December 2008.

Table 31.9 Annualized Performance of Mean-Variance Portfolios Held *Ex Post*

	Fund of Funds as Alternative Asset			Alpha Fund as Alternative Asset		
	Mean	Volatility	Sharpe	Mean	Volatility	Sharpe
All funds of funds	0.044	0.042	1.06	0.052	0.021	2.45
Conservative	0.037	0.035	1.06	0.051	0.017	2.91
Diversified	0.044	0.041	1.07	0.050	0.021	2.37
Market defensive	0.063	0.042	1.48	0.050	0.028	1.82
Strategic	0.046	0.048	0.95	0.048	0.040	1.20

date and a large share has less than 15 data points, a cross-sectional *ex post–ex ante* test leads to unreliable test statistics. To overcome this, we have constructed equally weighted, monthly rebalanced portfolios of funds of funds and of alpha funds over the full sample period. The result from this test is presented in Table 31.9. The Sharpe ratio has, on average, more than doubled compared between the two investment opportunity sets. Again, least gains are observed for the market defensive category for reasons explained previously.

31.5 CONCLUSION

This chapter highlighted the central role short selling can play in an institutional investor's portfolio. An investor wishing to invest into active managers may want to address the need to short undesirable beta exposures because the active manager provides beta exposures in a suboptimal configuration to the investor's policy portfolio.

Our empirical section demonstrated on a large data set that transporting alpha from a fund of funds to a separate alpha fund implies large efficiency gains in the portfolio formation. The empirical test also shows that a fund of funds seems, to a large degree, to provide inexpensive beta exposure at a high fee. However, short selling investable market factors to transport alpha requires skilled portfolio managers. The investor needs to find an active manager with a consistent positive alpha. He or she needs to estimate *ex post* beta exposure with only *ex ante* information and successfully implement short selling of market indices. This begs for the institutional investor to demand well-designed and robust products.

REFERENCES

Barras, L., Scaillet, O., & Wermers, R. (2010). False discoveries in mutual fund performance: Measuring luck in estimated alphas. *Journal of Finance, 65*(1), 179–216.

Carhart, M. (1997). On persistence in mutual fund performance. *Journal of Finance, 52*, 57–82.

Clarke, R. G., de Silva, H., & Thorley, S. (2002). Portfolio constraints and the fundamental law of active management. *Financial Analysts Journal, 58*(5), 48–66.

Clarke, R. G., de Silva, H., & Thorley, S. (2009). *Investing separately in alpha and beta.* Charlottesville, VA: The Research Foundation of CFA Institute.

Fama, E., & French, K. (1993). Common risk factors in the returns on stocks and bonds. *Journal of Financial Economics, 33,* 3–56.

Fung, W., & Hsieh, D. (2004). Hedge Fund Benchmarks: A Risk-Based Approach. *Financial Analysts Journal, 60*(5), 65–80.

Fung, W., Hsieh, D. A., Naik, N. Y., & Ramadorai, T. (2008). Hedge funds: Performance, risk, and capital formation. *Journal of Finance, 63*(4), 1777–1803.

Grinold, R. C., & Kahn, R. N. (2000). The efficiency gains of long-short investing. *Financial Analysts Journal, 56*(6), 40–53.

Grinold, R. C., & Kahn, R. N. (2009). The efficiency gains of long-short investing. *Journal of Portfolio Management, 35*(4), 12–24.

Kung, E., & Pohlman, L. (2004). Portable alpha. *Journal of Portfolio Management, 30*(3), 78–87.

Markowitz, H. (1952). Portfolio selection. *Journal of Finance, 7*(1), 77–91.

Sharpe, W. F. (1992). Asset allocation: Management style and performance measurement. *Journal of Portfolio Management, 18*(2), 7–19.

Tobin, J. (1958). Liquidity preference as behavior towards risk. *Review of Economic Studies, 25*(1), 65–86.

CHAPTER 32

Machine Learning and Short Positions in Stock Trading Strategies

David E. Allen, Robert J. Powell, and Abhay K. Singh

CONTENTS

ABSTRACT

Investors may profit from either upward or downward movements in asset prices depending on whether they are long or short. To achieve immediate gains on their position they need to be able to predict the direction of short-term future price movements. The prediction of the direction of a price change is a classification problem. Customary statistical methods, such as linear logistic regression and discriminant analysis, are applied frequently to this problem. The development of more flexible methods, such as support vector machine classification, offers practitioners potentially better and more powerful solutions. This chapter applies support vector machines (SVM) to predict the direction of price changes for a small set of Dow Jones Industrial Average stocks and tests them against the predictions obtained from logistic regression analysis. SVM appear to dominate the results. The investment returns and Sharpe ratios are higher for SVM.

KEYWORDS

Book-to-market ratio; Dividend yield; Hyperplane; Investment returns; Logistic regression; Price-to-earnings ratio; Radial basis function; Sharpe ratios; Support vector machines; Traded volume factor.

32.1 INTRODUCTION

Any investment strategy requires some form of asset evaluation, that is, determination of the price or fundamental value, and the prediction of likely future price movements using financial, technical, or fundamental indicators. The decision to adopt a long or short position in an asset requires a view on its immediate future price movements, a complex task that has remained at the heart of investment and empirical finance for many years. Early statistical work suggested that prices move randomly (for a collection of work on the topic, see Cootner, 1964). Fama's (1965) early work promoted the concept of market efficiency (for a survey, see Fama, 1976). Tests of the various forms of market efficiency appeared to imply that passive diversification and buy and hold were the optimum investment strategies. However, the tests were not as robust as first thought, and Summers demonstrated (1986) that they had little power in rejecting the null hypothesis of market efficiency against plausible alternative hypotheses.

Technical analysis has remained a persistent feature of investment behavior, and short selling is a common and controversial feature of financial market behavior. (However, it was banned in various forms by a number of regulatory authorities at the height of the global financial crisis.) Short selling has been a source of controversy in recent months and has been featured in the U.S. Senate investigation of Goldman Sach's behavior. The chairman of Goldman Sachs, Loyd C. Blankfein, (2010), stated that

> We didn't have a massive short against the housing market and we certainly did not bet against our clients. Rather, we believe that we managed our risk as our shareholders and our regulators would expect.

Germany brought in a ban on naked short selling in May 2010 prompted by fears of further market reactions to the sovereign debt crisis.

A typical short seller would have to assess the potential future behavior of the asset price using different available factors, such as past returns and market effects, and technical indicators, such as market ratios. Many past studies favored the use of factors such as beta, book-to-market ratios, and earning-to-price ratios for return predictions (Blume, 1980; Fama & French, 1995; Lakonishok, Shleifer, & Vishny, 1994).

Financial forecasting involves a huge data processing exercise, which may be noisy, nonstationary, and unstructured in nature. Support Vector Machines (SVM), (Vapnik, 1998) is a machine learning algorithm, which is characterized by its particular decision functions and ability to apply linear and non linear transformations using different kernel functions. As SVM is established on structural risk minimization, it is more resistive to overfitting than other learning methods used for empirical risk minimization and may perform better. SVM performs well in comparison to other forecasting methods commonly used, such as (ARIMA), Artificial Neural Networks, etc. (Cheng et al., 1996; Van and Robert, 1997; Huang et al., 2004; Cao and Tay, 2001; Tay and Cao, 2001; Burges, 1998; Wei et al., 2005). SVM can be implemented in two different ways, as a regression analysis or for solving classification problems, which is the area investigated in this chapter.

We use support vector machine classification to predict the direction of price changes for a sample of five stocks from the Dow Jones Industrial Average Stock Exchange and evaluate this technique against linear logistic regression. We classify the price change into a binomial class (+1, −1) and take fundamental measures (beta, book-to-market ratio, price-to-earnings ratio, traded volume, and dividend yield) for each stock as independent variables or predictors of price change along with past returns. We compare SVM classification directly with logistic regression as a tool for short trading. We use a simple single stock trading strategy to get the final return from the testing period and evaluate both methods (SVM and logistic) using Sharpe ratios.

Section 32.2 explores previous work and explains SVM classification along with logistic regression. Section 32.3 outlines basic data and methodology, and results are discussed in Section 32.4.

32.2 LITERATURE REVIEW

The tests of stock return predictability typically involve a dual-hypothesis problem: a model of the stock pricing or return setting behavior has to be adopted and then a secondary hypothesis featuring a test of predictability is erected on the back of the pricing model adopted. Common choices in the literature have involved tests of stock price predictability using factor-based models; the capital asset pricing model (Lintner, 1965; Mossin, 1966; Sharpe, 1964; Treynor, 1961, 1962), the Fama–French factor model (Fama & French, 1992, 1993), and other arbitrage pricing theories are good examples here, but the jury is still out on whether any of these pricing models are satisfactory. Another common way of modeling and predicting financial time series behavior is by use of historical stock prices; examples would be ARIMA, autoregressive conditional heteroskedasticity, and generalized autoregressive conditional heteroskedasticity. Various studies argue that price behavior should be consistent with both historical and anticipated financial fundamentals (Banz & Breen, 1986; Ferson & Harvey, 1993; Jaffe & Westerfield, 1985; Jung & Boyd, 1996). Indeed, the whole market rationality literature triggered by the early work of Shiller (1981) is built around such issues.

Fama and Schwert (1977), Rozeff (1984), Keim and Stambaugh (1986), and Fama and Frech (1988, 1990) suggested that macroeconomic variables such as dividend yield, lagged price-earning ratios, and lagged returns have some predictive power. Traditional statistical techniques used for forecasting use linear models. Machine learning or artificial intelligence systems, which are nonlinear, are useful and attractive. Various studies showed the efficiency of SVM (Cao & Tay, 2001; Mukherjee, Osuna, & Girosi, 1997), neural networks (Donaldson & Kamstra, 1996; Refenes, Zapranis, & Francis, 1994; Zirilli, 1997), random forests, and other methods relative to linear methods. Unlike the present work, most previous studies have employed support vector regression, not support vector classification, to predict the directions of future price change.

32.2.1 Support Vector Machines in Classification

Support vector machines come from a family of generalized linear classifiers, with the special properties of minimizing empirical classification error and maximizing the geometric margin simultaneously while following structural risk minimization. In classification problems, linear separating functions, however, generalized with an error minimization rate, are not suitable for real-world applications. SVM maps the input vectors into a higher dimension feature space to find an optimal separating hyperplane in the feature space.

In a classification problem (here a two class classification) the goal is to separate the two classes by a function that is induced from available training data. The objective is to produce a classifier that will work on unseen data or testing data. For example, in Figure 32.1, there are many possible linear classifiers that separate data, but only one that maximizes the margin of separation (distance between nearest data point of each class). This generalized linear classifier is called an "optimal separating hyperplane."

More formally, SVM classification looks for this optimal separating hyperplane with maximum margins between the classes closest point, the margin points are called as support vectors, and the middle of the margins

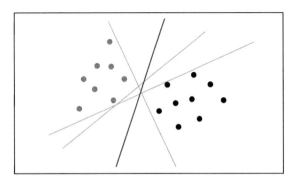

FIGURE 32.1
General idea of optimal separating hyperplane.

gives the optimal separating hyperplane (Figure 32.2).

Mathematically, consider the problem of classifying the set of training vectors into two classes, $\{-1,1\}$,

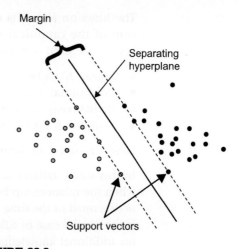

$$G = \{(x_i, y_i), i = 1, 2, ..., N\} \qquad (32.1)$$

with a hyperplane

$$y = f(x) = w^\tau \varphi(x) + b = 0 \qquad (32.2)$$

where $x_i \in R^n$ is the ith input vector and $y_i \in \{-1,1\}$ is the binary target. The SVM classifier satisfies the following conditions:

FIGURE 32.2

Optimal separating hyperplane in SVM.

$$w^\tau \varphi(x) + b \geq 1 \quad \text{if } y_i = 1 \qquad (32.3)$$

$$w^\tau \varphi(x) + b \leq -1 \quad \text{if } y_i = -1 \qquad (32.4)$$

where $\varphi: R^n \rightarrow R^m$ is the feature map, which maps this input space into a high dimensional feature space, making data points linearly separable. The values of w and b in the support vector machine (Boser, Guyon, & Vapnik, 1992; Cortes & Vapnik, 1995) are obtained from the following optimization:

$$\min_{w, b, \xi} \frac{1}{2} w^\tau w + C \sum_{i=1}^{l} \xi_i$$

given

$$y_i(w^\tau \varphi(x_i) + b) \geq 1 - \xi_i \qquad (32.5)$$
$$\xi_i \geq 0$$

Here C is the regularization constant determining the trade-off between the empirical error $(C \sum_{i=1}^{l} \xi_i)$ and the regularization term $(\frac{1}{2} w^\tau w)$, and ξ is called the "tube size" of SVMs. These parameters are selected empirically by the user.

Support vector machines use kernel functions for nonlinear separable cases, as follows:

$$Y = b + \sum \alpha_i y_i K(x_i x_j) \qquad (32.6)$$

The function $K(x_i x_j)$ is defined as the kernel function, which is a convolution of the canonical inner product in the feature space. The following kernels are used commonly in SVM:

- Linear: $K(x_i x_j) = x_i^t x_j$.
- Polynomial: $K(x_i x_j) = (\gamma x_i^t x_j + r)^d, \gamma > 0$.
- Radial basis function (RBF): $K(x_i x_j) = \exp(-\gamma \|x_i - x_j\|^2), \gamma > 0$.
- Sigmoid: $K(x_i x_j) = \tanh(\gamma x_i^T x_j + r)$.

Here γ, r, and d are kernel parameters.

In this study, radial basis function is used as this kernel can handle the case when the relationship between class labels and attributes is nonlinear, which occurs most of the time with financial time series data. Also, the linear kernel is the special case of RBF kernel (Keerthi & Lin, 2003). It is also useful when no additional knowledge of data is available (Smola, 1998). For implementation, the Libsvm tool is used with Weka; data mining software was developed at the University of Waikato.

32.2.2 Logistic Regression

Logistic or logit models are used commonly when modeling a binary classification. Logit models take a general form of

$$P(Y_i = 1 | X_i) = F(X_i \beta)$$

where the dependent variable Y takes a binomial form (in present case $-1,1$). P is the probability that $Y = \{-1,1\}$, and β is the known regression coefficient. X represents the independent or predictor variables and $F(.)$ is the density function for logistic distribution of the model. We use Weka to implement the logistic regression model, with dependent variables set to $-1,1$.

32.3 DATA AND METHODOLOGY

We use Dow Jones Industrial Average (DJIA)-traded stocks; out of the 30 stocks, a sample of 5 is taken for demonstrating the techniques used. Daily data for these stocks for a period of 5 years (January 3, 2005 to September 3, 2010) are used for calculating daily returns, direction of price change, beta, and other financial indicators. Table 32.1 gives the dependent or the predictor variables used for the same period. As discussed earlier, these factors influence the future price of the stocks.

We use daily log returns for past returns, a market beta calculated using the past 6-month rolling window of daily stock, and market returns. The past

Table 32.1 Factors Used for Prediction

Factor	Underlying Rationale
Previous 2-day daily log returns	Indicator of the historical performance, which is widely used in time series analysis
Beta (6-month rolling window)	Return dependence on the market return in the long run
Price-to-earnings ratio	Indicator of the current company value that affects the price movement.
Book-to-market ratio	Fama–French (1992, 1993)
Traded volume	Indicator of the performance of the stock in the market
Dividend yield	Indicator of company performance (Blume, 1980)

5-day (a week trading period) moving average is used for book-to-market ratio, price-to-earnings ratio, dividend yield, and traded volume factors.

32.3.1 Methodology

The main objective of this study is to test the applicability of SVM in forecasting the direction of stock price movements as a short selling tool. We evaluate SVM classification in comparison with logistic regression classification using the final accuracy of the forecasted and actual values.

As SVM can suffer from overinfluence of input vectors having higher magnitude, data are first standardized in range $(-1,1)$ using the following relation:

$$y' = \frac{y - \min(y)}{\max(y) - \min(y)} \Big(\text{new}(\max(y)) - \text{new}(\min(y))\Big) + \text{new}\min y \quad (32.7)$$

where $\min(y)$ and $\max(y)$ are the minimum and maximum values of attribute y. This standardization maps the values of attribute y to y' in $\text{new}(\min(y))$ to $\text{new}(\max(y))$, which is -1 to 1 in our case.

The direction of price change is classified into two classes based on present and previous day prices:

$$\text{if } p(t) \geq p(t-1) \to 1 \text{ else} -1 \quad (32.8)$$

As we are looking for downward price direction in this study, the aforementioned classification rule is all we need. After standardization and creating a classification class, data are divided into training and testing samples; we use the last 6 months of data as testing and the rest as the training sample. Two parameters, C (cost) and γ, for the RBF kernel in SVM require tuning to get the best possible forecasting SVM model; mostly a trial-and-error method is used to get these two values, but here we use a grid search algorithm, as proposed in the Libsvm package with Weka to search for the best parameters. We use a two-step grid search, a coarse grid search followed by a fine grid search using 10-fold cross validation, on training data to select the best C and γ parameters.

Generally, a low value of γ and a high value of C is suited for building the model, hence the parameters are searched in powers of 2 for C and powers of 10 for γ. Finally, using the parameter values that give the highest cross-validated accuracy, obtained from the grid search, the SVM model is built on training data, and forecasts are tested on the next 6 months of testing data.

Logistic regression is also done with the same training and testing data, and the two methods are evaluated and compared based on total accuracy. We use Weka with the Libsvm package for generation of our empirical results.

32.3.2 Investment Strategy

A simple trading strategy based on the predicted direction of price movement, from both classification routines, is applied in the testing period. As the direction indicates whether the price of a stock will increase (1) or decrease (-1), the trading strategy also follows the same direction for keeping a short or long position with the stock, that is, if the first prediction is positive, the investors buy a stock and keep it until the price doesn't go down (negative prediction). This strategy results in cash flow at the point of time when the stock price moves down and the investor shorts his or her position in the market (ignoring all transaction costs). If at time t the direction is positive, the investor buys \$1 of the stock and doesn't change his or her position as long as the prediction is not negative. On a negative prediction (-1) indicating a decline in price at time $t + n$, the return for the investor would be $\frac{log(p(t+n))}{p(t)}$. A generalization of this strategy gives the profit at time T as

$$\text{Total Return}(t) = \sum_{t=1}^{T-1} d_t r_{t+1} \tag{32.9}$$

where d_t is the direction of price change at time t.

We apply this strategy to our sample stocks to calculate the total return for the testing period (130 days) and evaluate them using Sharpe ratios. The 3-month U.S. Treasury bill rate is used as the interest rate in the Sharpe ratio calculation.

32.4 EMPIRICAL RESULTS

Table 32.2 gives the sample prediction results obtained from both classification methods, with testing data of 130 days. Column 1 in Table 32.2 gives the cost and γ values obtained from the grid search on training data; Table 32.2 also gives values for correctly and incorrectly classified instances in testing data, along with the mean absolute error for both techniques.

Table 32.2 Results from SVM and Logistic Regression Classification Methods

Stock		Result	SVM	Logistic Regression
Stock 1		Correctly classified instances	77 (59.2308%)	67 (51.5385%)
C	γ	Incorrectly classified instance	53 (40.7692%)	63 (48.4615%)
724	0.1	Mean absolute error	0.4077	0.5015
Stock 2		Correctly classified instances	112 (86.1538%)	109 (83.8462%)
C	γ	Incorrectly classified instance	18 (13.8462%)	21 (16.1538%)
1024	0.12	Mean absolute error	0.1385	0.316
Stock 3		Correctly classified instances	76 (58.4615%)	67 (51.5385%)
C	γ	Incorrectly classified instance	54 (41.5385%)	63 (48.4615%)
1448	0.003162	Mean absolute error	0.4154	0.4962
Stock 4		Correctly classified instances	76 (58.4615%)	69 (53.0769%)
C	γ	Incorrectly classified instance	54 (41.5385%)	61 (46.9231%)
724	3	Mean absolute error	0.4154	0.4963
Stock 5		Correctly classified instances	80 (61.5385%)	59 (45.3846%)
C	γ	Incorrectly classified instance	50 (38.4615%)	71 (54.6154%)
1448	0.56	Mean absolute error	0.3846	0.5091

Table 32.3 Investment Strategy Results

	Final Return		Sharpe Ratio	
	SVM	Logistic	SVM	Logistic
Stock1	20.10167056	−12.0362	17.42748	−13.0499
Stock2	7.246199093	6.009645	4.356055	3.369538
Stock3	16.33556329	15.30477	14.78509	13.72405
Stock4	14.33568424	5.611437	14.83901	4.495077
Stock5	18.27861273	−5.49125	14.62362	−6.39905
DJIA	10.12379524	8.10426878		

Table 32.2 shows that SVM classification is better than logistic regression and gives better forecasts. We apply it in short selling strategies, out of sample, and results of this investment strategy are reported in Table 32.3.

Table 32.3 shows the total final return for the testing period of 130 days for SVM and logistic regression and the performance of the market in this period. The price directions predicted by SVM clearly outperform those suggested by logistic regression. Figures 32.3, 32.4, and 32.5 display the direction of stock price as predicted by SVM, the actual return on that particular stock for the testing period, and the return obtained from the testing investment strategy, respectively. These results, although crude (as they ignore all other costs), strongly suggest the supremacy of SVM in price direction forecasting.

FIGURE 32.3
Stock trading direction.

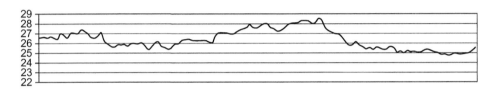

FIGURE 32.4
Actual stock return (testing period).

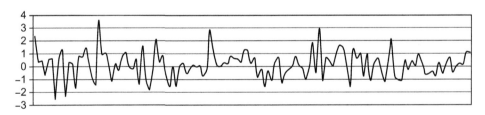

FIGURE 32.5
Investment strategy return (testing period).

32.5 CONCLUSION

This study used SVM classification and logistic regression to forecast the future price direction of a group of five stocks from the DJIA and then compared their results. Results show that SVM improves on simple logistic regression and provides more accuracy in predicting price changes. We show that SVM is a better tool than logistic regression for the prediction of stock prices and a better guide for adopting short positions.

ACKNOWLEDGMENT

Allen and Powell thank the Australian Research Council for funding Support.

REFERENCES

Banz, R., & Breen, W. (1986). Sample-dependent results using accounting and market data: Some evidence. *Journal of Finance, 41*(4), 779–793.

BlankFein, L. C. (2010). Prepared remarks by Lloyd C. Blankfein, Chairman and Chief Executive Officer, The Goldman Sachs Group, Inc. Retrieved from http://www2.goldmansachs.com/our-firm/on-the-issues/psi-folder/psi.html. (accessed 25/10/2010).

Blume, M. E. (1980). Stock returns and dividend yields: Some more evidence. *Review of Economics and Statistics, 62*(4), 567–577.

Boser, B. E., Guyon, I., & Vapnik, V. (1992). A training algorithm for optimal margin classifiers. In *Proceedings of the fifth annual workshop on computational learning theory* (pp. 144–152). New York: ACM Press.

Burges, C. (1998). A tutorial on support vector machines for pattern recognition. *Data Mining and Knowledge Discovery, 2*(2), 121–167.

Cao, L., & Tay, F. E. H. (2001). Financial forecasting using support vector machines. *Neural Computing and Applications, 10*(2), 184–192.

Cheng, W., Wanger, L., & Lin, C. (1996). Forecasting the 30-year US Treasury bond with a system of neural networks. *Journal of Computational Intelligence in Finance, 4*(2), 10–16.

Cootner, P. H. (1964). *The random character of stock market prices*. Cambridge, MA: MIT Press.

Cortes, C., & Vapnik, V. (1995). Support-vector network. *Machine Learning, 20*(1), 1–25.

Donaldson, R. G., & Kamstra, M. (1996). A new dividend forecasting procedure rejects bubbles in asset prices: The case of 1929 stock crash. *Review of Financial Studies, 9*(2), 333–383.

Fama, E. F. (1965). The behaviour of stock market prices. *Journal of Business, 38*(1), 34–105.

Fama, E. F. (1976). *Foundations of finance*. New York: Basic Books.

Fama, E., & French, K. (1988). Dividend yields and expected stock returns. *Journal of Financial Economics, 22*(1), 3–25.

Fama, E., & French, K. (1990). Business conditions and expected returns on stocks and bonds. *Journal of Financial Economics, 25*(1), 23–49.

Fama, E. F., & French, K. R. (1992). The cross-section of expected stock returns. *Journal of Finance, 47*(2), 427–486.

Fama, E. F., & French, K. R. (1993). Common risk factors in the returns on stocks and bonds. *Journal of Financial Economics, 33*(1), 3–56.

Fama, E. F., & French, K. R. (1995). Size and book-to-market factors in earnings and stock returns. *Journal of Finance, 50*(1), 131–155.

Fama, E., & Schwert, W. (1977). Asset returns and inflation. *Journal of Financial Economics, 5*(2), 115–146.

Ferson, W. E., & Harvey, C. R. (1993). The risk and predictability of international equity returns. *Review of Financial Studies, 6*(3), 527–566.

Jaffe, J., & Westerfield, R. (1985). Patterns in Japanese common stock returns: Day of the week and turn of the year effects. *Journal of Financial and Quantitative Analysis, 20*(3), 261–272.

Jung, C., & Boyd, R. (1996). Forecasting UK stock prices. *Applied Financial Economics, 6*(3), 279–286.

Huang, K., King, I., Lyu, M. R., & Yang, H. (2004). Improving Chow-Liu tree performance based on association rules, In *Neural Information Processing: Research and Development. Series: Studies in Fuzziness and Soft Computing*, Springer-Verlag, 152; 94–112.

Keerthi, S. S., & Lin, C. J. (2003). Asymptotic behaviours of support vector machines with gaussian kernel. *Neural Computation, 15*(7), 1667–1689.

Keim, D., & Stambaugh, R. (1986). Predicting returns in the stock and bond markets. *Journal of Financial Economics, 17*(2), 357–390.

Lakonishok, J., Shleifer, A., & Vishny, R. W. (1994). Contrarian investment, extrapolation, and risk. *Journal of Finance, 49*(5), 1541–1578.

Lintner, J. (1965). The valuation of risk assets and the selection of risky investments in stock portfolios and capital budgets. *Review of Economics and Statistics, 47*(1), 13–37.

Mossin, J. (1966). Equilibrium in a capital asset market. *Econometrica, 34*, 768–783.

Mukherjee, S., Osuna, E., & Girosi, F. (1997). Nonlinear prediction of chaotic time series using support vector machines. In *Proceedings of the IEEE workshop on neural networks for signal processing* (pp. 511–520). Amelia Island, FL.

Refenes, A. N., Zapranis, A. S., & Francis, G. (1994). Stock performance modeling using neural networks: Comparative study with regressive models. *Neural Networks, 7*(2), 375–388.

Rozeff, M. (1984). Dividend yields are equity risk premiums. *Journal of Portfolio Management, 11*(1), 68–75.

Sharpe, W. F. (1964). Capital asset prices: A theory of market equilibrium under conditions of risk. *Journal of Finance, 19*(3), 425–442.

Shiller, R. (1981). Do stock prices move too much to be justified by subsequent dividend changes? *American Economic Review, 71*(3), 421–436.

Smola, A. J. (1998). *Learning with kernels*. Ph.D. Thesis. Birlinghoven, Germany: GMD.

Summers, L. (1986). Does the stock market rationally reflect fundamental values? *Journal of Finance, 41*(3), 591–601.

Tay, F. E. H., & Cao, L. (2001). Application of support vector machines in financial time series forecasting. *Omega, 29*(4), 309–317.

Treynor, J. L. (1961). *Market value, time, and risk*. Unpublished Manuscript Subsequently published in Treynor, J. L. (2007). Treynor on Institutional Investing. Hoboken: Wiley Finance.

Treynor, J. L. (1962). *Toward a theory of market value of risky assets*. Unpublished Manuscript. Subsequently published as Chapter 2 of Korajczyk, R. A. (1999). Asset Pricing and Portfolio Performance: Models, Strategy and Performance Metrics. London: Risk Books.

Van, E., & Robert, J. (1997). *The application of neural networks in the forecasting of share prices*. Haymarket, VA: Finance & Technology Publishing.

Vapnik, V. N. (1998). *Statistical learning theory*. New York: John Wiley and Sons.

Wei, H., Nakamori, Y., & Wang, S.-Y. (2005). Forecasting stock market movement direction with support vector machine. *Computers and Operations Research, 32*(10), 2513–2522.

Zirilli, J. (1997). *Financial prediction using neural network*. London: International Thompson Computer Press.

CHAPTER 33

Short Selling Stock Indices on Signals from Implied Volatility Index Changes: Evidence from Quantile Regression-Based Techniques

David E. Allen, Abhay K. Singh, Robert J. Powell,
and Akhmad Kramadibrata

CONTENTS

ABSTRACT

An investor requires a prediction of the direction of the underlying asset price movements to devise a profitable trading strategy. In most of the techniques used for forecasting, a point estimate of the expected return or its volatility is calculated. The point estimate, although useful, does not give the extremes of the estimate, which can be useful in evaluating the possible losses or gains for the asset. This chapter uses machine learning-based methods for quantile regressions to calculate an extreme interval estimate for the expected volatility in index return and uses the inverse relationship between volatilities and index levels to generate a directional signal. We use the interval estimate to devise a trading strategy based on the expected direction of change in the

480 CHAPTER 33: Short Selling Stock Indices on Signals from Implied Volatility

interval to trade the underlying price index and compare results obtained from linear quantile regressions to machine learning-based methods.

KEYWORDS

Implied volatility; Kernel-based quantile regression; Linear quantile regression; Machine learning-based methods; Ordinary least squares method; Quantile regression random forests.

33.1 INTRODUCTION

This chapter investigates the profitability of a strategy based on short selling indices. It is constructed on the principle of the importance of leverage effects. This phenomenon relates to the fact that increases in volatility are linked with falls in stock prices and vice versa for decreases in volatility. One way of extracting information about market consensus views of changes in volatility is to appeal to the implied volatility changes implicit in option prices. This chapter employs changes in implied volatility derived from options on two indices: the S&P500 and the FTSE100. We utilize the history of the implied volatility series with quantile regression (QR) and machine-learning techniques to forecast changes in the quantile intervals of volatility. We use these forecast changes in volatility quantile intervals to set up two profitable short selling strategies featuring the two indices. Short selling has attracted quite a lot of attention in the context of the recent financial crisis. The authors find some of the debate about short selling quite puzzling, as explained later.

The process of investing involves two basic positions: buying and selling. If you purchase a security or asset in the belief that its price will subsequently rise, you have a long position in that security. To realize any ensuing gains from any price rise, you would subsequently have to sell the security to achieve the gains. You would then have a zero net position as both trades would have cancelled out.

Short selling is the reverse of going long. If you thought that a security was likely to fall in price, you could sell it, or go short, in the belief that the price would fall so that you could subsequently close out your position and realize a gain equal to the difference between the two reference prices: that at which you sold and that at which you subsequently purchase to close out the position. The main difference between the two strategies, which are reverse sides of the same coin, is that if you purchase a security, you have to come up with the money for the purchase immediately or it will not be delivered to you. If you sell something, you could perhaps already have a position in the security; in this case, this would be engaging in "covered" short selling, or you could sell a security you do not possess in the hope that you could subsequently purchase it for delivery at a lower price; in this case, this would be undertaking "naked" short selling. In the case of "naked" short selling, there is a potential risk that you might fail to deliver if market circumstances changed and the price went up or if your circumstances changed and you did not have the wherewithal to purchase the security you had sold for delivery.

Typically, markets have institutional frameworks and architectures that help guarantee delivery. Securities markets have margin calls if you have borrowed money to trade, and futures markets have both margin calls and marking to market to guarantee delivery. This leads to the next important point: short selling can be done in the cash market for the basic instrument or in derivative or futures markets based on the same underlying instrument. More recently, you could sell short by taking the appropriate position in contracts for the difference based on the same instrument. Thus, there are many different ways in which you can profit from the projected change in the price of an asset or security by taking appropriate positions in cash or derivative markets.

Short selling received much misguided criticism at the height of the global financial crisis (GFC). On February 24, 2010, the Securities and Exchange Commission adopted a new rule that places certain restrictions on short selling when a stock is experiencing significant downward price pressure. Rule 201 imposes the following, among other conditions:

Short Sale-Related Circuit Breaker: The circuit breaker would be triggered for a security any day in which the price declines by 10% or more from the prior day's closing price. The duration of the price test restriction is as follows: once the circuit breaker has been triggered, the alternative uptick rule would apply to short sale orders in that security for the remainder of the day, as well as the following day. It was argued that once the circuit breaker is triggered it will enable long sellers to stand in the front of the line and sell their shares before any short sellers. The uptick rule will permit short selling in a security if the price is above the current national best bid.

A 2009 IOSCO report on the regulation of short selling noted that in some jurisdictions, such as Hong Kong, short selling is only permitted in stocks that meet certain eligibility criteria, while in others there is a requirement to preborrow the stocks before they can be short sold. Other jurisdictions, such as the United States, previously had a "locate" requirement. Short selling in Canada, Hong Kong, and Japan is subject to trading controls such as price restriction rules. Furthermore, some jurisdictions such as Australia, Canada, Japan, Hong Kong, and the United States require the "flagging" of short sales when orders are submitted to the exchange markets for execution. Another tool employed is the use of margin requirements to control short selling, as is the case in Japan. Finally, in most jurisdictions, for transactions where stocks are not delivered within the standard settlement cycle, there is some form of mandatory buy-in or close-out requirement designed to cover the failed delivery of the stocks. IOSCO (2009) recommended the implementation of four broad principles in relation to short selling:

- The First Principle: Short selling should be subject to appropriate controls to reduce or minimize the potential risks that could affect the orderly and efficient functioning and stability of financial markets.
- The Second Principle: Short selling should be subject to a reporting regime that provides timely information to the market or to market authorities.
- The Third Principle: Short selling should be subject to an effective compliance and enforcement system.
- The Fourth Principle: Short selling regulation should allow appropriate exceptions for certain types of transactions for efficient market functioning and development.

These recommendations appear sensible and noncontroversial, but in the authors' view it is ironic that the report tries to sidestep the issues involving derivatives, stating that "the Technical Committee understands that the reporting of short positions might not provide a full picture if the data excludes derivatives." However, it leaves this up to the discretion of the local market authorities and, in the process, fails to heed Fischer Black's observation that net positions in derivatives must balance out to zero: given that for each writer there must be a counterparty. This leaves one wondering why the position in derivatives would matter?

A further dilemma is related to the following observation about market expectations: if stock market prices are modeled as a strict random walk, then upward or downward movements are equally likely. To impose short selling restrictions imposes restrictions on one side of the expected price path. However, if stock market prices are modeled as a random walk with drift, then short selling restrictions impose a condition on the price path that is in the reverse direction to the long-term trend. However, prices are stochastic, and presumably price paths can take marked deviations from the long-term trend. Short selling restrictions appear to sit awkwardly with considerations of the processes involved in price discovery and the stochastic nature of stock price changes.

However, this chapter does not dwell further on this controversy, but focuses instead on two related synthetic products for two markets: a pair of major indices and a short trading strategy constructed around the implied volatility of option contracts written on these underlying index contracts.

The rest of the chapter is constructed as follows: a brief literature review and an introduction to quantile regression, kernel quantile regression (KQR), and quantile regression forests (QRF) follow in Section 33.2. Data and research method and modeling utilized to construct a trading strategy are introduced in Section 33.3, followed by a presentation of results in Section 33.4.

33.2 LITERATURE REVIEW

33.2.1 Quantile Regression

In simple linear regression, a bivariate normal distribution is assumed between dependent and independent variables. The simple assumption of bivariate normality in a regression model may not be an appropriate assumption when the variables have some arbitrary joint distribution, in which case linear regression fails to describe the conditional distribution of the dependent variable.

Quantile regression (Koenker & Basset, 1978) is an alternative technique that can be used as a substitute for simple linear regression as characterized by the ordinary least squares (OLS) method. Through quantile regression, we can get different quantile relationships for different quantiles of the conditional distribution of the dependent variable. Quantile regression is less susceptible to the influence of outliers and hence is useful in quantifying the relationship between dependent and independent variables across the distribution in the domain of the desired quantiles. Koenker (2005) discusses the asymptotics of quantile regression methods and comments that score tests for quantile regressions are, in effect, a class of generalized rank tests. He notes that the works of Spearman (1904), Hotelling and Pabst (1936), Friedman (1937), and Kendall (1938) are generally given credit for initiating the rank-based approach to statistical inference.

Equation (33.1) gives the expression for a simple linear (OLS) regression, where X is the independent variable, Y is the dependent variable, α is the intercept, β is the coefficient, and e is an i.i.d. error term.

$$Y = \alpha + \beta X + e \qquad (33.1)$$

This regression model works on the assumption of bivariate normality of the variables, but if the variables are not bivariate normal then we need a more sophisticated regression method to model the conditional distribution $F(Y|X)$ (Alexander, 2008).

Quantile regression is modeled as an extension of classical OLS estimates of conditional mean models to the estimation of quantile functions for a distribution (Koenker & Bassett, 1978). The central case in quantile regression is the median regression estimator that minimized a sum of absolute errors as opposed to OLS, which minimizes the sum of squared errors. Other quantiles are estimated by minimizing an asymmetrically weighted sum of absolute errors. Taken together, the ensemble of estimated conditional quantile functions offers a much more complete view of the effect of covariates on the location, scale, and shape of the distribution of the response variable.

In quantile regression, α_q and β_q (q is the quantile of interest) can be estimated as a solution to the following optimization problem (Alexander, 2008)

$$\min_{\alpha,\beta} \sum_{t=1}^{T} (q - 1_{Y_t \leq \alpha + \beta X_t})(Y_t - (\alpha + \beta X_t)) \tag{33.2}$$

where

$$1_{Y_t \leq \alpha + \beta X_t} = \begin{cases} 1 & \text{if } Y_t \leq \alpha + \beta X_t \\ 0 & \text{otherwise} \end{cases} \tag{33.3}$$

For a more comprehensive discussion of mathematical details, see Koenker (2005) or Alexander (2008).

As quantile regression provides inference in quantiles, it can be used to build an interval prediction using extreme quantiles as the boundary intervals. If we predict the two boundary quantiles using quantile regression, for example, 1 and 99%, it gives us an interval estimate for our prediction and the value is expected to lie between these two boundary estimates. Instead of using point estimates from OLS, which are around the mean, we can use quantile regression to get an interval estimate, which gives us the expected extreme loss or expected extreme gain in stock returns; based on this estimate, a trading strategy can be constructed. The strategy here is to predict the next-day quantile interval estimate using quantile regression and position the direction of the trade based on it. We predict [1%–99%] and [5%–95%] estimates for the next day using a moving window of the last 250 days of observations. The last 6-day returns are used as independent or predictor variables and the present-day return as the dependent variable. The choice of intervals is based on the mostly commonly used value at risk quantile levels.

33.2.2 Kernel Quantile Regression

Kernel quantile regression is an evolving quantile regression (Takeuchi, Le Quoc, Sears, & Smola, 2006; Youjuan et al., 2007) technique in the field of nonlinear quantile regressions. As kernel quantile regressions are capable of modeling the nonlinear behavior of time series data, they prove to be more efficient in forecasting risk than other methods, including linear quantile regression. KQR is more efficient over nonlinear quantile regression as proposed in Koenker's (2005) monograph on quantile regression (Takeuchi et al., 2006).

Youjuan and colleagues (2007) also did some work on KQR in developing an efficient algorithm for their computation. The obvious advantage of KQR is the use of kernel functions (weighting functions) to model dependence, which allows modeling of both Gaussian and non-Gaussian data. Kernel quantile regression can be used to forecast value at risk, using past return levels as a training set (Wang, 2009).

For a training data set $(x_1, y_1), (x_2, y_2), ..., (x_n, y_n)$, where input $x_i \in \mathbb{R}^d$ and output $y_i \in \mathbb{R}$. Assuming the mapping function to be $f: \mathbb{R}^d \rightarrow \mathbb{R}$, the general formula for calculating the $\tau\%$ quantile is given by

$$\min_{f \in H_K} \left\{ \sum_{i=1}^{n} \rho_\tau(y_i - f(x_i)) + \lambda \|f\|^2_{H_K} \right\} \tag{33.4}$$

where H_K is a Hilbert space (Youjuan et al., 2007) and $\rho(\cdot)$ is defined as

$$\rho_\tau(r) = \begin{cases} \tau r & \text{if } r > 0 \\ (1 - \tau)r & \text{otherwise} \end{cases} \tag{33.5}$$

Point x_1 in the input space is mapped at a point $\phi(x_i)$ in the feature space by mapping function $\phi()$. An optimal linear quantile regression function in the feature space can be located by the following:

$$f(x_i) = b + w^T \phi(x_i) \tag{33.6}$$

The quantile hyperplane reproduced in kernel Hilbert space will be non-linear in original space.

Quantile regression is given by the following optimization problem:

$$\min_{b,w} C \sum_{i=1}^{N} \rho_\tau(y_i - b - w^T \phi(x_i)) + \frac{1}{2} w^T w \tag{33.7}$$

where C is the regularization parameter. A larger C gives greater emphasis on the empirical error term. The aforementioned minimization can be transformed into a quadratic programming problem (for more details, see Takeuchi et al., 2006; Wang, 2009; Youjuan et al., 2007).

We use KQR to predict the interval estimate using the last 250 days' moving window of training data as a sample consisting of the last 6-day daily returns as the input and present day's return as the output. This will be compared to linear quantile regression-based estimates and final returns based on the trading strategy (as described in Section 33.3).

33.2.3 Quantile Regression Forests

Random forests (Breiman, 2001) are one of many (support vector machines, neural networks, etc.) popular machine learning tools for regression and classification-based problems. Random forests provide inference about the conditional mean of the distribution in a random forest regression. Meinshausen (2006) generalized random forests and showed that they can provide information about the full conditional distribution of the response variable and can be used to forecast interval estimates. According to Meinshausen (2006), QRF give a nonparametric and accurate way of estimating conditional quantiles of high dimensional predictor variables.

Random forests, as the name suggests, is an ensemble of trees of n independent variables (Y_i, X_i), $i = 1, ..., n$. For each tree and each node in a large number of trees generated in random forests, variables are spit at random. Random forests have a single tuning parameter, which is the size of the random subset (subset of predictor variables at each node used for split point selection). In regression random forests they give the average of all tree responses as a prediction for a new data point (Breiman, 2001).

The random forests method approximates the conditional mean by a weighted mean over the observations of the response variable

$$\hat{\mu}(x) = \sum_{i=1}^{n} w_i(x) Y_i \tag{33.8}$$

where $w_i(x)$ is given by

$$w_i(x) = k^{-1} \sum_{t=1}^{n} w_i(x, \theta_t) \tag{33.9}$$

where θ is a random parameter vector, which determines how a tree is generated.

In quantile regression forests, trees are created with the same algorithm as in random forests. The weighted distribution (not the mean) of observed response variables gives the conditional distribution for quantile regression forests.

The conditional distribution of Y, given $X = x$, is given by

$$F(y|X=x) = P(Y \leq y | X = x) = E(1_{\{Y \leq y\}} | X = x) \tag{33.10}$$

Drawing analogies with the random forest approximation of the conditional mean, an approximation to $E(1_{\{Y \leq y\}} | X = x)$ can be defined by the weighted mean over the observations of $1_{\{Y \leq y\}}$:

$$\hat{F}(y|X=x) = \sum_{i=1}^{n} w_i(x) 1_{\{Y_i \leq y\}} \tag{33.11}$$

This approximation acts as the basis for the quantile regression forests algorithm. For further theoretical and mathematical details, see Meinshausen (2006).

33.3 DATA AND METHODOLOGY

The basic intuition in this study is to use the value or level (of implied volatilities) changes transformed into returns from the FTSE100 and S&P500 volatility indices as the basis for the decision on the position of a directional trade (short or long) in their respective underlying price indices (FTSE100 and S&P500). We use the last 4 years of daily logarithmic returns for these four indices, starting from January 2007 to October 2010. These are forward-looking estimates of volatility; for example, the S&P500 volatility is an average of the expected 30-day variance of the index estimated from a strip of options on the index.

Simple linear regression methods, which forecast the conditional mean, give a point estimate for the future value of the dependent variable, which may or may not be significantly close to the actual value. The predictions can be lower or higher than the actual value or can lie in an interval of lower and upper quantiles. A prediction interval for the future value can prove to be a better estimate when dealing with extreme value prediction, such as predicting extreme low and extreme high next-day return levels for a volatility index return as in the present case. We can form a prediction interval by forecasting the two extreme quantiles, for example, a 90% prediction interval for the value of Y is given by

$$I(x) = [q_{0.05}(x), q_{0.95}(x)]$$

There is a high probability of a future prediction lying within this prediction interval. These interval estimates can be forecasted using quantile regression, kernel quantile regression, and quantile regression forests.

When forecasting financial time series return quantiles, lower and upper quantile estimates are equivalent to predicting value at risk for short and long positions in the market. Based on two extreme quantile estimates, we can devise a trading strategy that changes our directional position, whether we go long or short, depending on the degree of change in the estimated extreme values. We predict two interval estimates, [1%–99%] and [5%–95%], using linear quantile regression, kernel quantile regression, and quantile regression random forests. We use the last 6 days of returns calculated from the FTSE100 volatility index and S&P500 volatility index as independent variables and the present-day return as the dependent variable. A moving window data set of the last 250 days is taken as a training sample to predict the next day's observation. We trade the underlying FTSE100 price index and S&P500 price index based on the directional signal generated from the trading strategy. We predict daily interval estimates for years 2008, 2009, and 2010 (until October 26, 2010) using previous years' (250 days) data as the training sample in a daily moving window.

We use the Quantreg, Kernlab, and Quantregforest packages in R to do the empirical exercise; data are collected from the Thomson Reuters Datastream database. We used all the default optimization settings in calculating the interval estimates. KQR estimates are obtained by means of a radial basis function kernel (which is useful when no prior information is available about training data), which has two parameters, namely cost (C) and sigma (s); C is taken to be 1 (default) and s is optimized by the automatic optimization provided in the Kernlab package. Quantile regression forest results are obtained using all the default parameters as in the QuantregForest package.

33.3.1 Trading Strategy

We use two sets of interval estimates to predict the direction of return, that is, 1 if the return is increasing and −1 if it is decreasing, which are used to decide and to predict when to short the underlying price index. If (l_t, u_t) represents an interval estimate for time t where l_t is the estimated lower quantile and u_t is the estimated upper quantile, the direction of returns can be decided based on the following algorithm:

- If $l_{t+1} \geq l_t + T$ and $u_{t+1} \leq u_t$ where T is a threshold (5% in present case) then −1
- If $l_{t+1} \leq l_t$ and $u_{t+1} \geq u_t$ then 1
- If $l_{t+1} > l_t, u_{t+1} > u_t$ and if $l_{t+1} - l_t > u_{t+1} - u_t$ then −1, else 1

The aforementioned rules use the absolute value of the predictions. The threshold is incorporated to avoid changing position on a minor increase in the lower quantile.

As the direction indicates whether the price of a stock will increase (1) or decrease (−1), the trading strategy also follows the same direction for keeping a short or long position in the stock, or index in this case; that is, if the first prediction is positive, investors adopt a long position (buy) and keep it until the price doesn't goes down (negative prediction). This strategy results in cash flow at the point of time when the stock price moves down and investors short their position in the market (ignoring all transaction costs). If at time t the direction is positive, the investor buys $1 of the index and doesn't change his or her position as long as the prediction is not negative. Once a negative prediction occurs (−1), indicating a decline in price at time

$t + n$, the return for the investor would be $log\frac{p(t+n)}{p(t)}$. A generalization of this strategy gives the profit at time T as

$$\text{Total Return}(t) = \sum_{t=1}^{T-1} d_t r_{t+1} \qquad (33.12)$$

where d_t is the direction of price change at time t.

33.4 RESULTS

Figures 33.1 and 33.2 give a confidence interval plot of the first 50 [5%–95%] interval estimates for FTSE100 volatility index returns and S&P500 volatility index returns obtained from linear QR, KQR, and quantile regression forests (QuantregForests). Dots in the graphs represent the actual return and the bar the predicted interval estimate, which shows that most of the actual returns lie within the estimated interval.

Tables 33.1 and 33.2 give final returns from the FTSE100 price index and S&P500 price index, after applying the trading strategy (as discussed earlier) on the interval estimates. They also give the hold-out return on these indices if the position is closed at the end of the testing (estimation) period for comparison. We can see that as the year 2008 suffers from GFC, none of the models tested gives a positive return, but the KQR method improves on the negative hold-out return for both of the markets. Results for year 2008 show that KQR [1%–99%] interval estimates outperform the other estimates, which can be accounted for by the increased volatility in the markets during this period and hence the returns are lying more in the extremes than the other relatively normal market periods.

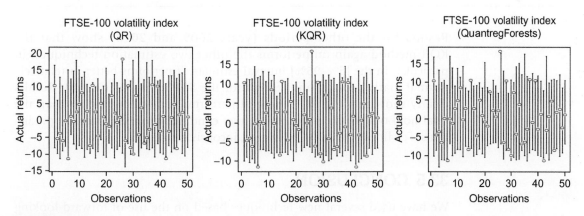

FIGURE 33.1

The first 50 [5%–95%] interval estimates and actual returns for the FTSE100 volatility index (year 2008).

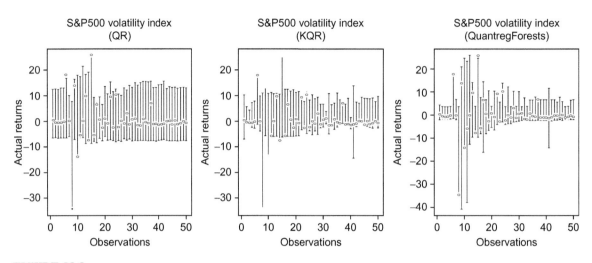

FIGURE 33.2
The first 50 [5%–95%] interval estimates and actual returns for the S&P500 volatility index (year 2008).

Table 33.1 Returns Observed with Trading Strategy Applied on FTSE100 Price Index

	Trading Strategy Returns					
	2008		2009		2010	
Year	[1%–99%]	[5%–95%]	[1%–99%]	[5%–95%]	[1%–99%]	[5%–95%]
QR	−54.2255	−23.8469	39.53271	5.229167	18.29091	11.51107
KQR	−24.9358	−46.2419	29.4114	30.91785	18.4969	23.37544
QRF	−46.9848	−36.1911	20.14434	−5.99551	−0.14102	−1.26365
Actual hold-out return	−36.6482427		23.53985451		7.022388286	

Results for the other periods (years 2009 and 2010) show that the KQR method again outperforms the other two estimation techniques; in particular, in the [5%–95%] interval estimate, it performs better in relatively normal market conditions (except for the S&P500 in year 2010). Results clearly show that the KQR method performs consistently better than the final hold-out return in normal market conditions for both interval predictions. For linear QR and QRF we get inconsistent results.

33.5 CONCLUSION

We have used several new techniques based on the use of forward-looking implied volatilities on two indices, the FTSE100 and the S&P500, to generate short and long trading strategies in the two indices. These strategies employ

Table 33.2 Returns Observed with Trading Strategy Applied on S&P500 Price Index

Year	Trading Strategy Returns					
	2008		2009		2010	
	[1%–99%]	[5%–95%]	[1%–99%]	[5%–95%]	[1%–99%]	[5%–95%]
QR	−62.7601	−61.9122	13.98154	20.32935	−11.59	6.456039
KQR	−41.5446	−56.4594	15.53714	30.62247	20.88832	18.41588
QRF	−44.5796	−51.7369	8.040667	16.19486	−4.92525	14.55047
Actual hold-out return	−48.58952303		24.98511848		6.66617096	

variants of quantile regression-based techniques, including linear quantile regression, kernel-based quantile regression, and quantile regression random forests, to predict quantile intervals and employ changes in these to generate a trading strategy. Kernel-based quantile regression methods appear to generate the greatest returns in our hold-out sample periods and dominate buy and hold returns. We ignore transactions costs in this exercise but it is clear from the results in Tables 33.1 and 33.2 that the deduction of realistic transaction costs would not change the order of the results.

ACKNOWLEDGMENT

Allen and Powell thank the Australian Research Council for funding support.

REFERENCES

Alexander, C. (Ed.). (2008). *Market risk analysis: Practical financial econometrics (Vol. II)*. Hoboken, NJ: John Wiley and Sons.

Breiman, L. (2001). Random forests. *Machine Learning, 45*(1), 5–32.

Friedman, M. (1937). The use of ranks to avoid the assumption of normality implicit in the analysis of variance. *Journal of the American Statistical Association, 32*(3), 675–701.

Hotelling, H., & Pabst, M. (1936). Rank correlation and tests of significance involving and assumption of normality. *Annals of Mathematical Statistics, 7*(March), 29–43.

IOSCO (International Organisation of Securities Commissions). (2009). Final report on regulation of short-selling. Retrieved from http://www.iosco.org/library/pubdocs/pdf/IOSCOPD292.pdf (21/10/2010).

Kendall, M. (1938). A new measure of rank correlation. *Biometrica, 30*, 81–93.

Koenker, R. (2005). *Quantile regression*. Econometric Society Monograph Series: Cambridge University Press.

Koenker, R. W., & Bassett, G., Jr. (1978). Regression quantiles. *Econometrica, Econometric Society, 46*(1), 33–50.

Meinshausen, N. (2006). Quantile regression forests. *Journal of Machine Learning Research, 36*(7), 983–999.

Spearman, C. (1904). The proof and measurement of association between two things. *American Journal of Psychology, 15*(1), 72–101.

Takeuchi, I., Le Quoc, V., Sears, T. D., & Smola, A. J. (2006). Nonparametric quantile estimation. *Journal of Machine Learning Research, 7*(2), 1231–1264.

Wang, Y. (2009). Value at risk estimation based on generalized quantile regression. Paper presented at the IEEE International Conference on Intelligent Computing and Intelligent Systems, Shanghai.

Youjuan, L., Liu, Y., & Zhu, J. (2007). Quantile Regression in Reproducing Kernel Hilbert Spaces. *Journal of the American Statistical Association, 102*(477), 255–268.

Modeling, Earnings, and Announcements

CHAPTER 34

Short Selling and the Equity Premium Puzzle

Jørgen Vitting Andersen

CONTENTS

ABSTRACT

Using growth theory it is argued that the worlds financial markets since the mid 19'th century have been in a state of "broken symmetry" which favours long term bull phases of growing financial markets, thereby also giving one possible explanation of the so called equity premium puzzle. The possibility of a "broken symmetry," leading to bull markets, arises as a combination of wealth effects, as well as the bias of investors taking predominantly long instead of short positions. With the arrival of the 21st century there is an increasing fraction of market players using short positions, which has slowly started to restore the "broken symmetry." As a result of this, the wealth effect could lead to long-term bear markets. The first signal of such long-term bear markets would be disappearance of the equity premium puzzle that began at the turn of the 21st century.

KEYWORDS

Agent-based modeling; Bull market; Equity premium puzzle; Growth theory; Investment bias; Wealth effects.

34.1 INTRODUCTION

It is probably not unfair to say that short selling has a somewhat mixed, if not a directly disputed, reputation, often being named as a contributing factor for market crashes. The U.S. Securities and Exchange Commission has often imposed restrictions (banning short sales of certain bank stocks during the subprime crisis) where the suspicion that short selling could damage markets, even though this has been very difficult to prove in practice. However, the argument often heard against this view is that short sellers, on the contrary, help find the accurate price of an asset (Lamont & Thaler, 2003). Therefore, it seems that the impact of short sellers on pricing in financial markets is lacking. One possible reason is that the tools and thinking used in traditional finance rarely consider the case of a heterogeneous population of investors. This heterogeneity is at the core of the problem with investors using short selling versus traditional fund managers, who are, in many cases, prohibited from short selling.

This chapter examines the origins behind the rise of very long-term trends in financial markets, with "long-term" implying examining trends over decades. In many aspects the long-term bull market since the very origin of the financial markets could be an anomaly that constitutes more the exception than the rule of what we should expect to occur during the following decades. We will argue that the reason for such an anomaly is mainly due to two factors: (1) during the 20th century and the early part of the 21st century there was an investment bias with investors heavily inclined in long positions and (2) as a result of the wealth effect implying a spillover from financial markets into the economy; such an investment bias had a nontrivial long-term positive feedback effect on the financial markets.

This chapter shows how these two aforementioned factors led to the equity premium puzzle (see, e.g., Mehra, 2003) that existed throughout the 20th century. In addition, this chapter also demonstrates how the exponential growth of hedge funds and banks using short selling could lead to a disappearance of this puzzle, as well as how short selling could have a nontrivial long-term effect on markets with a higher likelihood of extreme volatility coupled with more bear markets in the decades to come.

34.2 THEORY

This section examines the bull market of the 20th century from a growth phenomenon point of view. The wealth effect, as well as investor bias in long positions, will allow for sustainable long-term growth of financial markets, thereby creating an equity premium. The wealth effect is a mechanism between the performance of the stock market and the general economy, where rising prices in the stock market leads to higher consumer confidence and thus higher consumer spending. Higher consumer spending implies higher earnings for companies and hence gives rise to higher dividends.

In order to study how the century long bull market of the 20th century could be made, consider for a moment the common action of all investors in a given stock market. Over time this would signify a fluctuating pool of investors having different wealth while entering and exiting the market at different times, depending on the different moments each investor finds as an opportune time to be invested in the market. In reality, such a pool of different investors clearly would lead to highly fluctuating markets. However, examining only long-term trends poses a question on how the aggregate action of investors could lead to the long-term bull market witnessed in the last century. To study this let us call $W(t)$ the total aggregate wealth of the pool of investors who hold a given number $n(t)$ of market shares in a stock market at time t:

$$W(t) = n(t)P(t) + C(t) \tag{34.1}$$

Here $P(t)$ is the price of a market share and $C(t)$ is the cash possessed by the aggregate pool of investors at time t.[1] Given that we are considering the dynamics of financial markets over decades, the question to be asked is whether it is possible for long-term investors to continue accumulating shares and profiting from dividends while holding an increasing amount of shares over time. Here the prototype investor would be an investor making lifetime investment in a pension fund. At each time step the aggregate pool of investors purchases new shares with the result of pushing up the price of the market, thus creating an excess demand of market shares, $A(t)$. Now $A(t)$ gives rise to the following equation for the return $r(t)$ of the market (Bouchaud & Cont, 1998; Farmer, 2002):

$$r(t) \equiv \ln\left(P(t+1)\right) - \ln\left(P(t)\right) = \frac{A(t)}{\lambda} \tag{34.2}$$

Here, λ is the liquidity of the market. The fact that the price goes in the direction of the sign of the order imbalance $A(t)$ is intuitively clear and well documented (Holthausen, Leftwich, & Mayers, 1987; Chan & Lakonishok, 1993; Maslov & Mills, 2001; Challet & Stinchcombe, 2001; Plerou, Gopikrishnan,

---

[1] Market share here is a portfolio of stocks from which the market index is composed.

Gabaix, & Stanley, 2002). Since we are interested in the long term sustainability of investors to push up the market to their own benefit, fluctuations will be ignored and $A(t)$ will be considered as a constant, $A(t) \equiv A$, that is, we have

$$r(t) \approx \frac{d \ln (P(t))}{dt} = \frac{A}{\lambda}; \ P(t) = e^{\frac{At}{\lambda}} \tag{34.3}$$

and

$$\frac{dn(t)}{dt} = A; \ n(t) = At \tag{34.4}$$

Aside from the trading fees associated with purchasing shares, the pool of investors also receives income from dividends, $d(t)$, and from interest, $r(t)$, from the cash supply, $C(t)$.

This results in the following equation for the cash supply of the pool of investors as a function of time:

$$\frac{dC(t)}{dt} = -\frac{dn}{dt}P(t) + C(t)r(t) + n(t)d(t) + C_{flow}(t, r(t), d(t), P(t), \ldots) \tag{34.5}$$

$$= Ae\frac{At}{\lambda} + C(t)r(t) + Atd(t) + C_{flow}(t, r(t), d(t), P(t), \ldots) \tag{34.6}$$

The term $C_{flow}(t, r(t), d(t), P(t), \ldots)$ in Equation (34.6) is simply meant to describe all additional inflows/outflows of money into the pool of investors and can depend on time, dividends, interest rates, and price of the market, as well as many other factors, such as tax cuts.

It is preferable to express Equation (34.6) in terms of the growth rate of the financial market, $\alpha \equiv \frac{A}{\lambda}$, and cash in terms of market liquidity, $\overline{C} \equiv \frac{C}{\lambda}$. For a general description of the solutions to Equation (34.6), see Andersen (2005). In the following, $C_{flow} \equiv 0$. Assuming a wealth effect at play, dividends will grow proportionally to the price $\frac{d(t)}{d_0} = \frac{P(t)}{P_0}$ so that Equation (34.6) becomes

$$\frac{d\overline{C}}{dt} = -ae^{\alpha t} + \overline{C}(t)r + \alpha te^{\alpha t}d_0 \tag{34.7}$$

with the solution (Andersen, 2005):

$$\overline{C}(t) = \alpha e^{\alpha t} [\frac{td_0 - 1}{\alpha - r} - \frac{d_0}{(\alpha - r)^2}] + e^{rt} [\frac{-r\alpha + \alpha^2 + \alpha d_0}{(\alpha - r)^2} + C_0] \tag{34.8}$$

34.3 DATA

Underlying Equation (34.8) is the crucial assumption that $\frac{d(t)}{d_0} = \frac{P(t)}{P_0}$; therefore, empirical data are first presented to verify this hypothesis. Figure 34.1 depicts dividends as a function of the S&P 500 Index during the January 1,

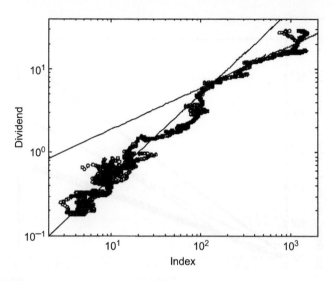

FIGURE 34.1
Dividend vs index value. Dividend as a function of the S&P 500 Index value in the time period January 1, 1871–December 31, 2009. Solid lines correspond to linear, respective square root growth of the dividends versus the index value.

1871, to December 13, 2009, period.[2] Solid lines correspond to linear (small values of the S&P 500 Index) square root growth of the dividends (large values of the S&P 500 Index) versus the index value. The linear relationship between $d(t)$ and $P(t)$ holds up to index values on the order of a few hundred corresponding approximately to the value of the S&P 500 Index at the end of the 1980s. For larger market index values, dividends appear to grow in a sublinear fashion with the price of the market.

Figure 34.2 illustrates the solution for the price of the market $P(t)$ (heavy solid line), Equation (34.3) as a function of time t for $\alpha = 0.0472$, $d_0 = 0.005$, $r = 0.472$, and $P_0 = 1$. The values of α and d_0 correspond to the empirical values of the performance of the S&P 500 Index over the time period of January 1, 1871, to December 31, 2009, whereas the value of r corresponds to the annual average long-term interest rate during the same period. In addition, two different values of the initial amount of cash available for the aggregate pool of investors are illustrated by two different thin solid lines. As can be seen from Figure 34.2, without enough cash at the start of the period (corresponding to $C_0 = 1.1$), the growth of the market is not sustainable, because at some point in time there is not enough cash available to keep on purchasing new shares, corresponding to an unstable solution of

---

[2] Data obtained from http://www.econ.yale.edu/~shiller/data.htm.

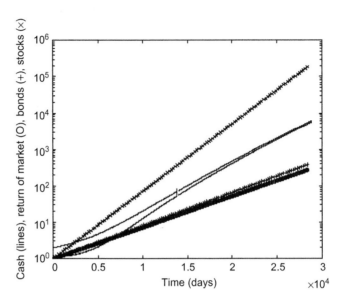

FIGURE 34.2

Cash of investors and return of the market vs time. Price of the market $P(t)$ (thick solid line) of (3) as a function of time t for $\alpha = 0.0472$, $d_0 = 0.055$, $r = 0.472$, $P_0 = 1$, and $C_0 = 1.1$, 1.3 (corresponding to the two different solid thin lines, with $C_0 = 1.3$ above $C_0 = 1.1$). Values of α and d_0 correspond to the annually averaged values obtained from the S&P 500 Index, whereas r corresponds to the annually averaged long-term interest rate over the time period of January, 1 1871–December 31, 2009. Crosses (upper curve) correspond to return from holding a stock, whereas plusses (curve above thick solid line) correspond to the return from holding a bond.

Equations (34.3) to (34.8).[3] However, for a larger initial amount of cash among the aggregate pool of investors, super interest growth (i.e., $\alpha > r$) is likely (corresponding to $C_0 = 1.3$). Figure 34.2 illustrates that it is possible for the aggregate pool of investors with enough cash initially ($C_0 = 1.3$) to ensure long-term growth of a market for their own benefit. Concurrently, growth of the market creates the equity premium puzzle, which is clearly present and can be observed by the difference in the performance of holding a stock (x's) compared to holding a bond (+'s). The case where dividends follow a sublinear growth, $\frac{d(t)}{d_0} = \frac{P(t)^\beta}{P_0}$, with $\beta < 1$ is discussed in Andersen (2005). Keeping all other parameters fixed and decreasing $\beta < 1$ will eventually reduce the super interest growth of the market and thereby also prevent the equity premium puzzle. Indication of a crossover occurring at the end of the 1980s and at the start of the 1990s, from $\beta = 1$ to $\beta = \{1/2\}$, is

---

[3] For a general discussion about stable versus unstable solutions, see Andersen (2005).

seen in Figure 34.1, suggesting the end of the equity premium puzzle. One possible origin for such a crossover is discussed in the next section.

The discussion so far has been on a pool of investors trying to benefit by creating a constant growth of a given stock market. However, one should notice that Equations (34.1) to (34.8) also describe the more ill-natured situation where a pool of investors (e.g., hedge funds) could strive to profit from a long-term constant decline in a stock market by short selling. This situation is simply described by making d_0 negative, as a short seller has to pay the dividend to the owner from which the stock was borrowed.[4]

34.4 IMPACT OF SHORT SELLING IN A HETEROGENEOUS GROUP OF INVESTORS

The situation described by eq. (34.1)–(34.8) was meant as a study to get an overview of what would be the main ingredients/variables that could explain the long term growth of the financial markets that we experienced in the last century. In reality, we face a much more complex setting with long-term financial market price dynamics determined by the volatile combinations of changing economic fundamentals as well as fluctuating investment strategies and the mood of investors. One way to allow for such a diversity of attributes of investors is to use agent-based models to study price dynamics (Andersen & Sornette, 2003; Challet, Marsili, & Zhang, 2004).

We now consider some sample results from agent-based modeling. The outcomes presented summarize simulation results that are robust across a broad range of parameter values. Simulation results shown in Figure 34.3 were performed with an agent-based market model where the selection of strategies was determined by a payoff function maximizing profit, consequently called the "$-game" in Andersen and Sornette (2003). The heavy solid line in Figure 34.3 illustrates the price history of such an agent-based model, the $-game with $N = 20$ investors (agents), $r = 10\%$, and $d_0 = 8\%$. The assumption $\frac{d(t)}{d_0} = \frac{P(t)}{P_0}$ is a condition that was incorporated in the game.

Randomness was introduced via the initial strategies held by the agents as well as by N additional "noise" agents who at each time step made a random decision to either buy or sell one market share.[5] Thin dotted lines in Figure 34.3 represent 5, 50, and 95% quantiles of the price of the market (from bottom to top), respectively. At every time t out of the 1000 different initial configurations, only 50 price trajectories were below the 5% quantile line, 500 price trajectories were below the 50% quantile, and 950 price trajectories were below

---

[4] This case is not discussed in this chapter; instead the interested reader is referred to Andersen (2005).

[5] For further details on simulations, see Andersen (2005).

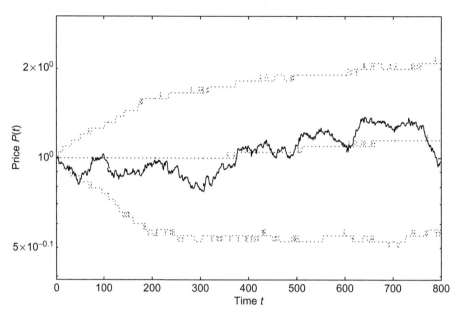

FIGURE 34.3

Price trajectory from simulations of the agent-based model without short sellers. Price trajectory $P(t)$ (fat solid line) from one configuration of the $-game [DG] with $N = 20$ agents, $r = 10\%$, and $d_0 = 8\%$ [assuming dividend $d(t)=d_0P(t)/P(t=0)$]. Parameter values used were $s = 4$, $m = 8$, and $C_0 = 50$. Randomness was introduced via N additional "noise" agents. The fraction of agents allowed to take short positions $\rho = 0$. Liquidity parameter $\lambda = 0.0025$. Thin dotted lines represent 5, 50, and 95% quantiles (from bottom to top), respectively, that is, at every time t out of the 1000 different initial configurations, only 50 got below the 5% quantile line and similarly for the other quantile lines.

the 95% quantile. The average behavior of an agent can now be understood using the analysis of Equations (34.1) to (34.8). All the N agents in Figure 34.3 are long only and never employ short selling, that is, they correspond to the case represented in Figure 34.2. As predicted, the price $P(t)$ is, on average, tilted toward positive returns. Figure 34.4 represents simulations with the same parameter values as in Figure 34.3 except that to study the impact of short selling a fraction, $\rho = 0.20$ of the agents can be both short and long. As can be seen from the 5% quantile, the introduction of agents that can take short positions (but don't necessarily do so) clearly increases the probability significantly for a long-term bearish trend. Increasing to $\rho = 0.4$ as seen in Figure 34.5 amplifies this tendency.

Another remarkable trend is the large increase in volatility seen by the moving frontiers of the 5 and 95% quantiles as a function of increasing ρ. Given that the setting of a wealth effect is imposed by the $\frac{d(t)}{d_0} = \frac{P(t)}{P_0}$ condition in

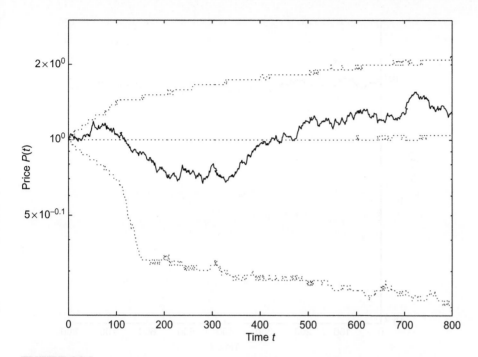

FIGURE 34.4

Price trajectory from simulations of the agent-based model with 20% short selling allowed. Price trajectory $P(t)$ (fat solid line) from one configuration of the \$-game [DG] with $N = 20$ agents, $r = 10\%$, and $d_0 = 8\%$ [assuming dividend $d(t)=d_0P(t)/P(t=0)$]. Parameter values used were $s = 4$, $m = 8$, and $C_0 = 50$. Randomness was introduced via N additional "noise" agents. The fraction of agents allowed to take short positions $\rho = 0.2$. Liquidity parameter $\lambda = 0.0025$. Thin dotted lines represent 5, 50, and 95% quantiles (from bottom to top), respectively, that is, at every time t out of the 1000 different initial configurations, only 50 were below the 5% quantile line and similarly for the other quantile lines.

the simulations, Figures 34.3 to 34.5 illustrate that removing the investment bias in the market, by allowing a small percentage of short sellers, is sufficient to make the equity premium puzzle disappear.

34.5 DISCUSSION

Using growth theory, the combination of wealth effect and investor bias with investors only taking long positions could lead to long-term bull phases of growing financial markets, giving a possible explanation for the equity premium puzzle. We then showed how the gradual removal of wealth effects with dividends that increase only in a sublinear fashion as a function of the price of the market will eventually inhibit super interest growth of the market and thereby also stop the equity premium puzzle.

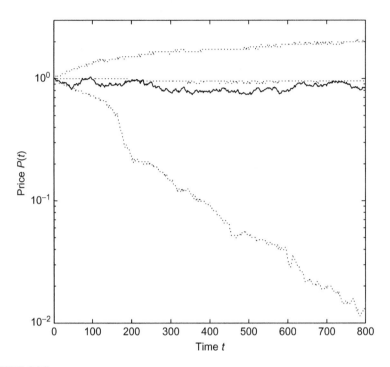

FIGURE 34.5

Price trajectory from simulations of the agent-based model with 40% short selling allowed. Price trajectory $P(t)$ (fat solid line) from one configuration of the $-game [DG] with $N = 20$ agents, $r = 10\%$, and $d_0 = 8\%$ [assuming dividend $d(t)=d_0 P(t)/P(t=0)$]. Parameter values used were $s = 4$, $m = 8$, and $C_0 = 50$. Randomness was introduced via N additional "noise" agents. The fraction of agents allowed to take short positions $\rho = 0.4$. Liquidity parameter $\lambda = 0.0025$. Thin dotted lines represent 5, 50, and 95% quantiles (from bottom to top), respectively, that is, at every time t out of the 1000 different initial configurations, only 50 were below the 5% quantile line and similarly for the other quantile lines.

Finally, computer simulations of price dynamics in markets created by agent-based models showed the impact of an increasing percentage of investors using short selling. In addition, removing the investment bias in the market by allowing a small percentage of investors the possibility to go short—all investors were allowed to go long—is a sufficient condition to make the equity premium puzzle disappear.

34.6 CONCLUSION

These findings suggest that the arrival of an increasing fraction of market players using short positions since the start of the 21st century has slowly altered the investment bias, which led to the long-term bull markets of the last century. Because of the wealth effect, this could lead to unseen long-term or prolonged bear markets. The first sign of such long-term bear markets would be disappearance of the equity premium puzzle, something that seems to be currently materializing.

ACKNOWLEDGMENT

The author thanks the "Collége Interdisciplinaire de la Finance" for financial support.

REFERENCES

Andersen, J. V. (2005). Could short selling make financial markets tumble? *International Journal of Theoretical and Applied Finance, 8*(4), 509–521.

Andersen, J. V., & Sornette, D. (2003). The $-game. *European Physical Journal B, 31,* 141–145.

Bouchaud, J.-P., & Cont, R. (1998). A Langevin approach to stock market fluctuations and crashes. *European Physical Journal B, 6,* 543–550.

Challet, D., Marsili, M., & Zhang, Y. C. (2004). *Minority games: Interacting agents in financial market.* Oxford, UK: Oxford University Press.

Challet, D., & Stinchcombe, R. (2001). Analyzing and modelling 1 + 1d markets. *Physica A, 300,* 285–289.

Chan, L. K. C., & Lakonishok, J. (1993). Institutional trades and intra-day stock price behavior. *Journal of Financial Economics, 33*(2), 173–199.

Farmer, J. D. (2002). Market force, ecology and evolution. *Industrial and Corporate Change, 11*(5), 895–953.

Holthausen, R. W., Leftwich, R. W., & Mayers, D. (1987). The effect of large block transactions on security prices: A cross sectional analysis. *Journal of Financial Economics, 19*(2), 237–267.

Lamont, O. A., & Thaler, R. (2003). Can the market add and subtract? Mispricing in tech stock carve-outs. *Journal of Political Economy, 111*(2), 227–268.

Maslov, S., & Mills, M. (2001). Price fluctuations from the order book perspective empirical facts and a simple model. *Physica A, 299,* 234–246.

Mehra, R. (2003). The equity premium: Why is it a puzzle? *Financial Analyst Journal, 59*(1), 54–69.

Plerou, V., Gopikrishnan, P., Gabaix, X., & Stanley, H. E. (2002). Quantifying stock price response to demand fluctuations. *Physical Review E, 66,* 027104.

CHAPTER 35

Affine Term Structure Models and Short Selling: The Liberal Case against Prohibitions

Vicente Jakas[1]

CONTENTS

ABSTRACT

Current government bond prices are not only the net present value of expected future surpluses. Yield curve movements are a function of a country's macroeconomic risks, and bond prices reflect exactly that. Governments should understand these risks as well as ensure that these are managed actively in advance in order to avoid speculative attacks, as failure to do

---

[1] This chapter expresses solely the author's opinion and not that of Deutsche Bank AG or DB Research.

so will give rise to multiple equilibrium, thus when the probability of a risk-free bond to become a risky asset rises. The prohibition of naked short selling of government bonds during times of financial distress is unlikely to be addressed within a global perspective, as short-term incentives to violate the ban more than outweigh the long-term benefits for individual participants to behave otherwise. An affine term structure model in absence of arbitrage is used for estimating European government bond yields. Unfortunately, in a competitive economy and during times of financial distress, a representative investor is left with no other choice but to "short" government bonds that exhibit a higher probability of becoming a risky asset and "long" those securities that are less likely to become risky.

KEYWORDS

Affine term structure models; European Union; Macroeconomic risks; Market-making activities; Unemployment rate.

35.1 INTRODUCTION

This entry is motivated by recent developments on southern European sovereigns and the resulting controversial "Merkel" prohibition on naked short selling on certain stocks and European Union (EU) members' issuances.[2] As investors saw that governments failed to address macroeconomic risks affecting their surplus, they were left with no other choice but to short similar paper in order to hedge losses in long positions that could not be disposed of. The reason is that the country's inherent macroeconomic risks affect the yield curve because they also affect governments' expected future surpluses.

In addition, the deterioration of sovereign spreads has shown the need of governments to address these issues as soon as possible in order to restore confidence. In the process of doing so, they will need to cut down on government spending with the subsequent negative effects on growth, as government spending comprises way more than 40% of total gross domestic product (GDP) in Europe and private expenditure is unlikely to grow enough to compensate for the fall in government spending.

Government securities have the property of acting as hedging instruments for times of low consumption growth, hence in times of financial distress. This is because they perform better in times when aggregate marginal utility is valued most. When governments fail to address their macroeconomic

---

[2] "Merkel prohibition" on naked short selling: the name stems from German Head of State Angela Merkel.

risks they give way to the possibility of a run on their issuances, which has a magnifying effect in times when bad news for consumption growth arrives.

Government securities are only optimal when inflation is low and the probability of deterioration in its present value is virtually zero. However, if there is asymmetric information and there are doubts about the capacity or ability of the government to manage its inherent macroeconomic risks and hence ensure its ability to generate funds via either tax revenues, issuing new debt at a low cost or adjust deficits in the future will result in investors categorizing the debt as risky. An investment that was once seen as a risk-free asset and that—unexpectedly—turns out to be riskier forces the representative investor to reassess the portfolio and adjust accordingly.

For those not familiar with the jargon, "short selling" refers to investors borrowing an asset from the lender and selling it to another market participant with the expectation that the price of the asset will fall. In the process of doing so, the investor will make a profit from the margin between the sell price, the cost of borrowing the asset, and the buy price at a later point to return it to the bond–lender.

The representative investor has a variety of reasons for shorting a security, not only for speculative purposes as depicted earlier. Representative investors are generally financial intermediaries, which within its investment banking operations offer clients so-called "market-making" activities. Market-making activities refer to the service whereby a financial intermediary ensures that clients' issuances will exhibit enough trading activity in order to continue to be attractive to investors. This is to ensure that investors are able to find active prices or quotes, either for trading purposes or for valuation. Investors prefer to acquire those assets where they can track their performance, as this brings more transparency and reduces information asymmetries. In order to do this, the financial intermediary necessary quotes bid-offer prices with the risk of increasing its balance sheet in case of sell-off or result in a short position in case of rallies. If financial intermediaries expect a sell-off, they will hedge this risk by initially shorting a position in line with their expectations on what the demand size will be so that at the end of the session they are left—ideally—with no position on their balance sheet.

35.2 AFFINE TERM STRUCTURE MODELS

A representative investor will try to anticipate changes in bond yields, which is done by observing interdependencies in macroeconomic variables. Moreover, macroeconomic risks are the drivers of changes in yields because yields are part of a network of economic variables and because macroeconomic risks also affect governments' current and future surpluses. Macroeconomic risks also affect market expectations on yields because they also reflect market expectations on governments' expected future primary surpluses.

"Affine term structure models" refers to models that explain changes in asset values due to changes in macroeconomic variables; see, for example, Piazzesi (2003). Hence, if changes in macroeconomic variables are the foundations for changes in asset prices, the resulting sensitivities of these explanatory variables reflect a kind of "beta" coefficient to a certain macroeconomic risk. For example, a change in unemployment can result in more than proportional changes in a government's yields, thus reflecting the risk the government issuance has as a result of a shock to the unemployment variable.

Equation (35.1) shows a simple affine term structure model for a yield curve with N different maturities,

$$y_t^{(N)} = A(N) + B(N)^T x_t + \varepsilon_t^{(N)} \tag{35.1}$$

for x_t being the state space vector with macroeconomic data comprising, for example, unemployment, consumer confidence index, production price index, and monetary aggregate (possibly M3). $y_t^{(N)}$ is an $N * 1$ column vector of observed yields, $A(N)$ is an $N * 1$ vector of constants, and $B(N)$ is an $N * K$ matrix of parameters "betas." The assumption is that the disturbance term of $\varepsilon_t^{(N)}$ is distributed independently and normally with zero mean and constant variance.

The model is simple: the greater the $B(N)$ term, the greater the risk. Depending on the sign and the size of the asset's beta—hence the $B(N)$ term—a representative investor will arrange the portfolio in order to hedge macroeconomic risks accordingly by selecting assets that exhibit an opposite relationship.

For instance, a government bond that should act as a hedge in times of low consumption growth will exhibit a negative $B(N)$ with respect to changes in unemployment rate. Hence, an increase in unemployment rate should exhibit a fall in government bond yields because an increase in unemployment will result in a fall in future consumption growth.

However, the aforementioned only works as long as the government security is seen as a risk-free asset. If the government fails to address the macroeconomic risks affecting its surplus, it will result in reverting from its issuance from risk free to risky. This is because it will imply a change in the sign of the $B(N)$ term. Thus using the example just given, the negative $B(N)$ term will become positive, as an increase in unemployment will result in a deterioration of the government's deficit and thus an increase in the size of its debt with even further deterioration of its deficit.

Hence, an increase in the unemployment rate would instead result in an increase in the bond yields with subsequent deterioration in the value of the asset. Unless the government is able to address the macroeconomic risk affecting its deficits/surpluses, there is no reason to believe that the investors will still be willing to lend at a lower price/yield. Government securities that change from a "good" equilibrium to a "bad" equilibrium will experience a change in the sign of its $B(N)$ term. In fact, if investors believe that government securities will change from "good" equilibrium to "bad" equilibrium, they will run on the government's debt, as investors will believe that the market will do so, and they do not know where they are standing on the queue to convert their bonds into cash. Thus, this further increase yields even above their fundamental values and attracts speculative attacks on weaker budgetary sovereigns. Moreover, those investors not being able—or not willing to sell at a low price—to avoid realizing losses will engage in shorting similar sovereigns that exhibit similar behavior in order to hedge their investment. In the process of doing so they spread contagion to other sovereign issuances, even if these actions are fundamentally not justified. All these give rise to self-fulfilling prophecies and herding behavior or bandwagon effects typical of bank runs or credit crises.

35.3 MACROECONOMIC SHOCKS AFFECTING GOVERNMENT SURPLUSES ARE AFFINE

Governments face the risk of a decrease in their tax revenues due to output shocks. Thus an unexpected fall in GDP could result in a decrease in government tax revenues, as businesses and individuals experience a fall in their taxable income. For example, an increase in unemployment results in a decrease in expected aggregate consumption and expected aggregate investment. As a result, there is not only a decrease in expected tax revenues but also an increase in expected government spending, which further deteriorates government finances.

Another shock affecting government surpluses can be derived from the fiscal theory of the price level. The fiscal theory of the price level was first developed by Leeper (1995), Sims (1994), Woodford (1995, 1996), and Dupor (1997) and says that the price level is determined by the ratio of nominal debt to the present value of real primary surpluses; in simple terms, the present value of outstanding debt equals the present value of real surpluses, thus as in Cochrane (2001) review of the theory suggested

$$\frac{B}{\pi} = \frac{s}{(1+\gamma)}$$

Making it formally and accounting for several periods:

$$\frac{B_{t-1}^{(N)}}{\pi_t} + \sum_{N=0}^{\infty} \beta^N E_t \left(\frac{1}{\pi_{t+N}}\right) B_{t-1}^{(t+N)} = E_t \sum_{N=0}^{\infty} \beta^{(N)} s_{t+N} \qquad (35.2)$$

For $B_{t-1}^{(N)}$ denote a zero coupon bond outstanding at the end of period $t-1$ that matures in N. $\beta^{(N)}$ is the discount factor and $\beta^{(N)} = 1/\gamma_t^{(N)}$, for $\gamma_t^{(N)}$ is affine as derived from Equation (35.2). π_t denotes the price level and s_t is the real primary surplus, and the real primary surplus is also affine:

$$s_t^{(N)} = A(N) + B(N)^T x_t + \varepsilon_t^{(N)} \qquad (35.3)$$

From Equations (35.1) to (35.3) we have determined how macroeconomic variables depicted in the state-space vector x_t affect both yield curve and expected future primary surpluses. In fact, Equation (35.2) shows that an expected deterioration in government finances would, *ceteris paribus*, result in an increase in the price level. The increase in the price level is expected to result in a subsequent increase in the yields to compensate investors for their loss in purchasing power with the expected increase in the discount factor and thus further falls in the net present value of future surpluses. From this point it is clear that fiscal discipline is unavoidable and that governments, in order to be able to smooth shocks on their surpluses, require accumulating resources for times when consumption growth is low so that they can compensate for the fall in private sector consumption and still be able to attend budgetary obligations without resulting in a deterioration in the country's welfare. Failure to do so will have no choice but to undertake the difficult and always unpopular measures of reducing deficits by cutting expenditure or increasing distortionary taxation.

35.4 SOME EVIDENCE ON AFFINE TERM STRUCTURE MODELS

This empirical work is based on monthly European macroeconomic data particularly from the European Central Bank and Eurostat available in Bloomberg. The author compares coefficients of 10-year European government bonds. Coefficients are calculated using the affine model presented in Equation (35.1). Most of the data series is only available since 1998, which makes this analysis difficult, hence for lack of longer time series. Data points for macroeconomic data are assumed to be released at every end of month. The day of the month at which data are released is not relevant on a monthly basis analysis. The period considered is from December 1999 until December 2009. This results in 121 observations and four regressions for each of the issuers being Germany, Spain, Italy, and Portugal (Table 35.1).

Table 35.1 Macroeconomic Risks—Coefficients for Germany, Spain, Italy, and Portugal

Macroeconomic Variable	Germany	Spain	Italy	Portugal
EU consumer confidence index	0.0134	0.0087	0.0065	0.0076
EU unemployment rate	−0.2605	−0.2980	−0.3184	−0.3038
EU producer price index	0.0046	0.0042	0.0037	0.0037

Note: All coefficients are very significant with a 5% confidence level.

All coefficients are very significant and show that the unemployment rate is the most important macroeconomic risk common to all of the aforementioned countries. The sign of the coefficient for unemployment shows that an increase in the unemployment rate would, *ceteris paribus*, reduce the 10-year yield on 26 to 32 basis points. However, following our analysis in Equations (35.2) and (35.3), if the issuance became risky due to changes in expected future surplus, the yield would change signs, having the opposite effect. Coefficients show that Germany is less sensitive to changes in the unemployment rate compared to Italy, which exhibits higher sensitivities to these macroeconomic data.

35.5 RISKS OF SOVEREIGN DEBT ROLLOVER

Governments face time inconsistencies in the process of issuing debt. In an optimal scenario, governments would not need to increase total debt outstanding and the roll of new debt would only be used to pay back the old maturing one. However, governments issue debt to increase budget deficits in order to compensate for the fall in private consumption in times of economic crises. In other words, governments engage in countercyclical interventions in order to smooth the decrease in aggregate consumption growth. In the process of doing so they avoid increasing taxes and alternatively increase long-term debt. The increase of long-term debt has the property of acting as a hedge for distortionary taxation and innovations in aggregate consumption growth. Another benefit is that it allows governments to trade current inflation for future inflation and spread the effects stemming from surplus shocks across maturities. However, from Equations (35.1) to (35.3), we know that if the government engages in such a policy it will need to convince investors that the current deficit is only temporary and that the government still has the ability to generate funds in order to repay debt servicing.

This is simple; why would you lend someone any money if you don't believe that repayment is a rather likely scenario? The less likely it becomes to investors that government actions signal a probable repayment of the debt the less keen they will be on buying government debt—in real terms—unless they are compensated for this risk.

The problem is that in times of financial distress, hence when financial resources are more valuable, these conditions become stronger to countries exhibiting less credible financial capacity. It is in these very moments that governments need to repay maturing debt and reissue new one at a higher cost, as the financial markets do not believe that governments will have the ability or political will of engaging in sometimes unpopular measures, particularly for those whose macroeconomic risks have been a pending homework.

Generally, in times of financial distress, those governments that have kept an acceptable budgetary surplus will be able to benefit from low yields, as in time of low consumption growth government bonds are valued most and thus exhibit low interest rate levels. However, for the case of risky assets the opposite occurs, as in times of economic distress there is no appetite for investors for risky assets as they pay off poorly. Only under a "compensation" for risk taking are investors going to be willing to take this risk into their balance sheets. In order to be successful, government ministers of finance should ask themselves: what if financial crises took place at this very moment, with the subsequent fall in consumption growth with a severe increase in unemployment rates? What is the outlook for the government expected future surplus? Has the government the capacity to smooth consumption while maintaining low costs of financing or has the government not done the homework all these years and will now face financial distress? How are tax revenues going to be affected by a severe fall in GDP growth? How are yields going to move as a consequence of innovations on these macroeconomic variables? Are the new issuances still going to be attractive to markets at a low price? The answer to all this is: depending on how macroeconomic risks affect their expected future surpluses.

35.6 HOW MULTIPLE EQUILIBRIUM WORKS AND HOW IT COULD RESULT IN "RUNS" ON GOVERNMENT ISSUANCES

Equations (35.1) to (35.3) have shown a competitive equilibrium, with uncertainty and absence of arbitrage. Now it is necessary to introduce an additional aspect: How can a risk-free asset become risky under financial distress? A possible answer is: this is the case when Equation (35.2) becomes an inequality as follows:

$$\frac{B_{t-1}^{(N)}}{\pi_t} + \sum_{N=0}^{\infty} \beta^N E_t\left(\frac{1}{\pi_{t+N}}\right) B_{t-1}^{(t+N)} > E_t \sum_{N=0}^{\infty} \beta^{(N)} s_{t+N} \qquad (35.4)$$

This equation simply explains the case when a representative agent's expectations are that there are higher chances that the expected future surpluses will not suffice to cover the government's future financing obligations. In fact, the representative investor believes that the government might fail to roll over debt successfully and will require to further increase debt outstanding with the subsequent increase in its cost of financing.

Note that for the case of a risk-free asset, when Equation (35.4) becomes a probable scenario, the sign of the coefficients in Equation (35.1) [the $B(N)$ term] changes so that the covariance now moves in the same direction as for the case of risky assets, hence correlated positively to consumption growth.

35.7 PROHIBITION IN NAKED SHORT SELLING: A POOR WORKAROUND WITH LITTLE EFFECTIVE CONSEQUENCES

There are several reasons that make the prohibition of naked short selling counterproductive.

First, the prohibition in naked short selling is market distortionary with the potential of collateral damage effects. This is because short selling is also a source of financing, as financial intermediaries are able to access cash to finance other trading assets by shorting positions. Prohibition in naked short selling can only result in further shrinking access to funds with the subsequent overall increase in the cost of financing.

Second, markets have the capacity to enforce discipline to the issuer, penalizing those who do not attend their own financial weaknesses. Markets would short sell if they believe that prices are too high, thus correcting and ensuring market values. When markets do not work, there is no trading, and then it is also not possible to short sell either.

Third, short selling is used in hedging strategies. For example, if two securities exhibit similar market behavior then they could be used in a hedging strategy by shorting one and leaving a long position on the other. This is a common government trading strategy, particularly when illiquidity in the market makes it difficult for the investor to dispose of a long position. The investor can instead hedge the long position by shorting on another similar security. The prohibition on naked short selling will force investors to acquire credit default swaps (CDSs) instead. One of the arguments against naked short selling was to make it more difficult for financial intermediaries and hedge funds to speculate or issue this kind of derivative. However, this could result in actually expanding even more the use of CDSs, as investors will be left with less hedging alternatives available.

Fourth, it is the mere existence of information asymmetries the true cause of market inefficiencies and not the sole existence of widespread short selling practices. Regulators and governments should concentrate efforts in improving transparency in order to reduce market imperfections instead, as these informational shortcomings are the true cause of the so-called herding behavior or bandwagon effects with the subsequent self-fulfilling prophecies. Governments, like any other issuers, should not exercise power simply because they are not happy on how the markets are reacting or treating their issuances. They should understand that markets are signaling weaknesses that need to be addressed. Governments should not reduce markets' ability to punish poor policy making.

Fifth, a ban in naked short selling cannot be implemented or monitored easily. Regulators or governments would require determining an infinite number of special cases such as how to treat the short positions before the ban was in place or even started or what are the roles of unconsolidated subsidiaries in overseas locations. Along these lines, another aspect that requires attention is the fact that intermediaries take short positions within the scope of their market-making activities and for which they require to undertake short positioning in order to fulfill this service; this gives way to a number of cases where prohibition cannot be implemented, as it would result in forcing intermediaries in not fulfilling their obligations as market makers with the subsequence decrease in liquidity in the market.

Sixth, it is also necessary to establish a general policy framework to ensure transparency. This policy framework will need to determine controversial issues such as eligibility criteria and the temporary horizon of the prohibition as to ensure transparency and reduce information asymmetries and, hence, avoid speculation. There should be clear arguments on why certain issues are eligible under the prohibition and others are not. As these give way to inefficiencies, moral hazard issues and for the case of banks, increases systemic risk in the long run. In addition, protection for certain eligible stocks would give rise to competitive disadvantages to those not being part of the program, giving further way to speculative attacks on who is and who is not eligible under such criteria.

Summarizing, all these unresolved issues can only make it worse before it can make it any better, as lack of transparency in the matter can only raise speculation even further, contrary to the effect that was originally wanted.

Such a ban can only work under an effective international policy coordination environment, not by empowering an international regulator with the possibility to sanction any noncomplaint institution or governments, as this is not only unlikely to happen, it will also involve governments giving up on an important part of their sovereign powers to an international agency, not to mention that it will produce a bureaucratic monster. In fact, there would be significant incentives for weaker governments to fail to comply, as noncompliance will attract financial institutions to the region of concern in exchange of an improvement their access into the international capital markets. A unilateral ban on naked short selling can only be understood as a mere declaration of intentions. This is only a populist measure that distracts from the main underlying issues: the diligent and responsible management of a country's macroeconomic risks.

35.8 CONCLUSION

An affine term structure model in absence of arbitrage is presented. This model is used for estimating sensitivities of some EU member nations. The model predicts that Germany exhibited lower sensitivities and thus less risk compared to other EU member states. Macroeconomic shocks to government surplus were discussed, and the model explained how these shocks affect government budget constraints. The analysis led to an inevitable conclusion: in a competitive economy and during times of financial distress, a representative investor is left with no other choice but to "short" government bonds that exhibit a higher probability of becoming risky and "long" those securities that are less likely to become risky. Affine term structure models can be used to assess a country's macroeconomic risks. It has been shown how macroeconomic risks affect government bond yields and that they are also the cause of surplus shocks. In order to avoid speculative attacks, governments should address these macroeconomic issues and hence improve their risk profiles instead of pursuing ineffective and distortionary prohibitions on short selling. Prohibitions on naked short selling are only another desperate attempt by politicians to do "too-little-too-late" improvisations. Governments should be held accountable for their mismanagement of macroeconomic risks.

Governments should understand these risks as well as ensure that these are managed actively in advance in order to avoid speculative attacks, as failure to do so will give rise to so-called multiple equilibriums, thus when the probability of a risk-free bond to become a risky asset rises. The prohibition of naked short selling of government bonds during times of financial distress is unlikely to be addressed adequately within a global perspective, as the short-term incentives to violate the ban more than outweigh the long-term benefits for individual participants to behave otherwise.

ACKNOWLEDGMENT

The author thanks Professor Dr. Ashok Kaul (University of Saarland) for his input. Any feedback is very welcomed at vicente.jakas@t-online.de or at vicente.jakas@db.com.

REFERENCES

Cochrane, J. H. (2001). Long term debt and optimal policy in the fiscal theory of the price level. *Econometrica, 69*(1), 69–116.

Dupor, B. (1997). Exchange rates and bank notes: The fiscal theory of the price level. *Journal of Monetary Economics, 45*(3), 613–630.

Leeper, E. (1995). Equiliria under active and passive monetary policies. *Journal of Monetary Economics, 27*(1), 129–147.

Piazzesi, M. (2003). Affine term structure models. Working Paper, UCLA and NBER. Los Angeles, CA.

Sims, C. (1994). A simple model for the determination of the price level and the interaction of monetary and fiscal policy. *Economic Theory, 4*(1), 381–399.

Woodford, M. (1995). Price level determinacy without control of a monetary aggregate. *Carnegie-Rochester Conference Series on Public Policy, 43*(1), 1–46.

Woodford, M. (1996). Control of public debt: A requirement for price stability. NBER Working Paper 5684.

BIBLIOGRAPHY

Ang, A., & Piazzesi, M. (2003). A no-arbitrage vector auto-regression of the term structure dynamics with macroeconomic and latent variables. *Journal of Monetary Economics, 50*(1), 745–787.

Barro, R. J. (1999). Notes on optimal debt management. *Journal of Applied Economics, 2*(1), 281–289.

Barro, R. J. (2003). Optimal management of indexed and nominal debt. *Annals of Economics and Finance, 4*(1), 1–15.

Blanchard, O. J. (1981). Output, the stock market and interest rates. *American Economic Review, 1*(1), 132–143.

Missale, A. (1997). Managing the public debt: The optimal taxation approach. *Journal of Economic Surveys, 11*(1), 235–265.

Missale, A. (1999). *Public debt management.* Oxford, UK: Oxford University Press.

Missale, A., Giavazzi, F., & Benigno, P. (1997). Managing the public debt in fiscal stabilizations: The evidence. Working Paper, University of Milan. Retrieved from www.SSRN.com (accessed May 2010).

Piazzesi, M. (2005). Bond yields and the Federal Reserve. *Journal of Political Economy, 113*(2), 311–344.

Piazzesi, M., & Schneider, M. (2006). Equilibrium yield curves. Working Paper 12609. National Bureau of Economic Research, Cambridge, MA. Retrieved from http://www.nber.org/papers/w12609 (accessed May 2010).

CHAPTER 36

Short Sale Constraints in the Equity Market and the Term Structure of Interest Rates

Abraham Lioui

CONTENTS

ABSTRACT

The September 2008 ban on the short selling of financial stocks had a great impact on U.S. equity markets. This chapter shows how the ban affected key term-structure variables, such as default spread, term spread, and inflation-related spread. The impact of the ban was substantial on the higher moments of innovation in variables related to the term structure. The main lesson from this study is that any regulatory move in the credit default swap market (such as banning short sales) should take into account the collateral impact of the measure.

KEYWORDS

Augmented Dickey–Fuller; Daily volatility; Default spread; Equity market; Inflation-related spread; Innovations; Kurtosis; Skewness; Term spread.

36.1 INTRODUCTION

The second semester of 2008 was characterized by regulatory uncertainty surrounding short sales. In the summer of 2008, short selling was banned on a small sample of stocks; the ban was overturned a few weeks later. In September 2008, once again, short selling of a very large sample of financial institutions' stocks was banned and then, 2 weeks later, the ban was overturned. These episodes had a substantial impact on the markets of the stocks placed off limits by the ban (see Bris, 2008; Lioui, 2009; Marsh & Niemer, 2008). Our aim in this chapter is to assess the potential spillover effects of these events on the bond market. This issue is of particular interest now, as questions are arising about the debt issued by sovereign nations—Greece, above all. The main lesson from this study is that any regulatory move in the credit default swap market (such as banning short sales) should take into account the side effects of the move.

We select variables characterizing the term structure such as nominal term spread and inflation spreads (defined as difference between a nominal yield and a real one). In our empirical investigation, we control for ongoing events, such as the subprime crisis.

Our main findings could be summarized as follows. Short sale constraints in equity markets have an impact on the term structure of interest rates (the two short sale-related dummies are statistically significant in our regressions). Both real and nominal term structures are affected by restrictions on short sales. Finally, regulatory uncertainty has an impact on the term structure as well.

We start by describing data used in this chapter as well as our empirical method. We then report our empirical results and offer some thoughts on policy implications.

36.2 DATA AND METHOD

36.2.1 Data Description

Our sample period starts on January 3, 2006, and ends on January 29, 2010. Key indicators of the term structure that have been used are the slope at different maturities for nonindexed bonds, the spread between nominal and real bond yields, and a measure of interest rates and of the default spread (DS). Bond yields were downloaded from FRED at the Federal Reserve Bank of Saint Louis Web site.

The DS is the difference between Moody's seasoned Baa and Aaa corporate bond yields. Moody's includes bonds with remaining maturities as close as possible to 30 years and drops bonds if the remaining life falls below 20 years, if the bond is susceptible to redemption, or if the rating changes.

To measure the slope of the nominal term structure, we use the difference between the yield of a long-term constant maturity Treasury bond and the yield on a 1-month Treasury bond. We use constant maturity yields corresponding to 10, 20, and 30 years. The term spread for the 10-year constant maturity bond (TS10) is equal to the difference between the yield on the 10-year constant maturity bond and the yield on the 1-month Treasury bond. The 20-year (TS20) and 30-year (TS30) spreads are defined in an analogous way.

To assess the expected inflation and the inflation risk premium in the bond market, we built an inflation spread for a term to maturity of 10 years, a spread that is the difference between the (nominal) yield of the 10-year constant maturity bond and the yield on the Treasury inflation-indexed security with a 10-year constant maturity. We denote this inflation spread IS10 and define analogously the 20-year spread, which we denote IS20. We use only 10- and 20-year inflation-indexed bonds.

Our aim is to assess the impact of the ban on short sales on the term structure; therefore, we need to control for other relevant events. In our regressions, we use several control variables. One is the return on the S&P 500, as the equity and the bond markets are likely to have common factors and this index is therefore likely to purge the term structure from these factors. This approach is conservative in that the S&P 500 itself is likely to incorporate the impact of the ban and therefore may already purge the term structure variables from the effects of the ban. The second control variable that we use is the log of the trading volume of the S&P stocks. The purpose of this variable is to apprehend the liquidity shortage that threatened the financial markets. We then use the 1-month Treasury bond yield that controls for the level of the term structure.

To control for the ban on short sales, we built three dummy variables. To distinguish between the effects of the subprime financial crisis, which began in the summer of 2007, and those of the ban, which began in September 2008, we proceeded as follows. "Crisis" is a crisis dummy (equal to 0 from January 3, 2006, to June 30, 2007, and to 1 until January 29, 2010). Its aim is to capture the impact of the ongoing subprime crisis. The first short dummy (short 1) is equal to 0 from January 3, 2006, to July 14, 2008, and from August 16, 2008, to January 29, 2010; it is equal to 1 from July 15, 2008, to August 15, 2008. The second dummy (short 2) is equal to 0 from January 3, 2006, to September 17, 2008, and from October 9, 2008, to January 31, 2010; it is equal to 1 from September 18, 2008, to October 8, 2008. We thus have a dummy that covers the exact ban period starting on September 18, 2008 (short 2), and an additional short dummy that covers the ban episode following the emergency order of July 15, 2008 (short 1). Because the two short ban episodes were close, it seemed to us useful to isolate the impact of the first ban on short selling from that of the second one.

36.2.2 Summary Statistics

Our sample period starts on January 3, 2006, and ends on January 39, 2010. Table 36.1 provides some summary statistics on the level as well as the innovation (first difference) in the treatment variables. Figures 36.1 and 36.2 provide information on the time series of these variables as well.

The average 1-month interest rate was 2.55% over the sample period with a large standard deviation (2.10%). This substantial volatility reflects mainly the continuous fall in the short-term interest rate, starting especially in summer 2007, with the subprime crisis (see Figure 36.1). The default spread averaged 1.41% over the sample period with a substantial positive skewness. The maximum of 3.5% was reached precisely during the ban period of September 2008; one wonders if there is causality. Nominal term spreads range, on average, from 1.52 to 2.04%, with sizable volatility. They increased continuously from the onset of the subprime crisis and became less correlated at the end of the sample period. The rise in investors' risk aversion is probably part of the story in this case, as the level of the term structure was clearly on a negative shape. The spread between nominal yields and their corresponding real yield was relatively stable over the period at around 2%, although it fell during the ban and then recovered the level and stability that characterized this spread before the ban.

On the whole, thus, something must have happened to the variables related to the term structure during the ban. Our purpose is to see whether one can explicitly relate part of this dynamic to the ban on short selling. In empirical investigations, we are not using the level of the variables but rather their innovations defined as the first difference. The reason is simply that the levels of these variables are highly persistent, which may bias our statistical inference. Table 36.1B shows the summary statistics of the innovations; their time series are shown in Figure 36.2. The notable characteristic of these

Table 36.1 Summary Statistics[a]

A: Summary Statistics of Levels							
	1 MTB	**DS**	**TS10**	**TS20**	**TS30**	**IS10**	**IS20**
Mean	2.55	1.41	1.52	2.04	1.97	2.08	2.33
St. dev.	2.10	0.74	1.48	1.74	1.76	0.57	0.48
Min.	0.00	0.75	−0.78	−0.57	−0.68	0.04	0.67
Max.	5.27	3.50	4.01	4.64	4.73	2.72	2.93
Skewness	−0.02	1.50	0.06	0.02	0.04	−1.71	−1.62
Kurtosis	1.26	3.92	1.46	1.37	1.39	5.29	5.07

B: Summary Statistics of Innovations							
	SP500	**DS**	**TS10**	**TS20**	**TS30**	**IS10**	**IS20**
Mean	0.0351	0.0000	−0.0038	−0.0045	−0.0048	0.0002	0.0004
St. dev.	1.64	0.03	0.13	0.13	0.13	0.05	0.04
Min.	−9.74	−0.35	−0.96	−0.97	−0.97	−0.33	−0.25
Max.	9.93	0.13	0.85	0.82	0.83	0.36	0.33
Skewness	0.71	−2.90	−0.01	−0.12	−0.10	0.32	0.71
Kurtosis	10.46	32.45	12.91	13.29	13.65	13.64	12.87

C: Correlation Matrix of Innovations							
	SP500	**DS**	**TS10**	**TS20**	**TS30**	**IS10**	**IS20**
SP500	1						
DS	−0.17	1					
TS10	0.06	−0.05	1				
TS20	0.04	−0.04	0.99	1			
TS30	0.03	−0.05	0.98	1.00	1		
IS10	0.29	−0.17	0.10	0.08	0.08	1	
IS20	0.24	−0.15	0.13	0.14	0.14	0.78	1

[a]This table shows summary statistics for the treatment variables. All numbers are in percentages and are annualized. "1MTB" stands for the yield on a 1-month constant-maturity Treasury bill. DS is the default spread measured as the difference in yields on a Baa and an Aaa long-term corporate bond. TS10, TS20, and TS30 are nominal term spreads for 10, 20, and 30 years. They are the difference in yields on bonds with 10, 20, or 30 years to maturity and yield on the 1-month Treasury bill. IS10 and IS20 are inflation spreads, as measured by the difference between the yield on a nominal bond and the corresponding yield on an inflation-protected bond. SP500 corresponds to the daily return on the S&P 500. (A) Summary statistics of the level of the variables, (B) summary statistics of the innovations (first difference) in the variables, and (C) correlations of the innovations. The sample period starts on January 3, 2006, and ends on January 29, 2010.

innovations is that their volatility is much greater than that of the corresponding variables. Another indicator worth looking at is the kurtosis of the innovations: it was, during a few days, more than 10 times the kurtosis of the levels. The extreme volatilities and values occurred around the short ban period.

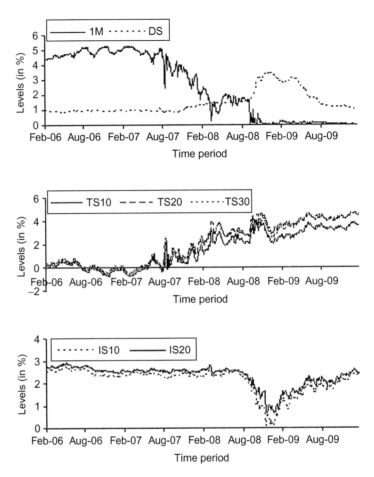

FIGURE 36.1

Time series of levels of term structure-related variables.

Figure 36.2 shows the correlation of the innovations in term structure variables. Nominal term spreads are highly correlated but the correlation with other variables is less than 0.3 in absolute value.

36.2.3 Empirical Method

A glance at the time series of term structure variables makes it clear that the short ban period was a particular period. Our aim is to isolate the impact of the short ban from that of other events that may have had an impact on these variables during the ban or after the ban was overturned.

Our method uses multivariate regressions in which independent variables are the log of the daily trading volume on the S&P 500 (liquidity), daily

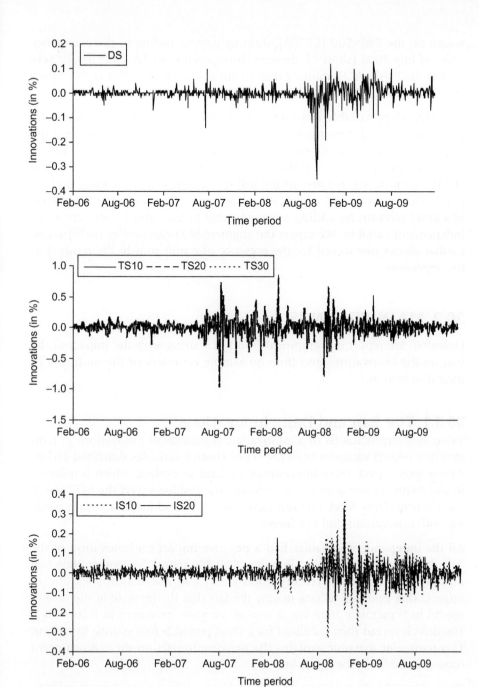

FIGURE 36.2

Time series of innovations in term structure-related variables.

return on the S&P 500 (SP500), dummy corresponding to the emergency order of July 2008 (short 1), dummy corresponding to the short ban of September 2008 (short 2), dummy that accounts for the subprime crisis (crisis), and the 1-month Treasury bill rate (1 MTB).

The dependent variable is either an innovation or a sample estimate of a moment of the distribution of the innovation. We thus investigate the impact of the ban on innovations themselves as well as on their volatility, skewness, and kurtosis. A 100-day rolling window is used to compute the last three moments. Because of the rolling windows, there is some built-in persistence in the sample estimates, for which we correct in the regressions whenever relevant by adding a lagged value of the sample estimate as an independent variable. We report the augmented Dickey–Fuller (ADF) statistic that allows one to test for the presence of a unit root in the residual of the regression.

36.3 MAIN FINDINGS

Hereafter, we report our empirical findings starting with the impact of the ban on the innovations and then on sample estimates of the moments of their distribution.

36.3.1 The Ban and Daily Innovations

Table 36.2 shows results of a multivariate regression of innovations in term structure-related variables onto the set of control variables described earlier. As one may expect, these innovations are hard to explain, which is reflected in the relatively low adjusted R^2. Because the residuals pass the ADF test at the 1% confidence level, one can view this as a sound justification for working with innovations and not levels.

All the independent variables had a negative impact on innovation of the default spread: four variables (liquidity, S&P 500 return, September 2008 ban dummy, and 1-month Treasury bond yield) had a statistically significant impact. This evidence reflects mainly the fact that the increase in the default spread in September 2008 was a one-off increase, as shown in Figure 36.1. The default spread then stabilized for a short period before starting to narrow. This particular dynamic explains the negative impact on the innovation of control variables in the regressions.

Short dummies had no impact on innovations in nominal term spreads. The reason is that these spreads have undergone a continuous increase since summer 2007 and the ban does not seem to affect the slope of this increase.

Table 36.2 Ban on Short Selling and Daily Innovations[a]

		Constant	Liquidity	SP500	Short 1	Short 2	Crisis	1 MTB	Adj. R^2	ADF
DS	Coefficient	**0.1512**	**-0.0065**	**-0.0029**	-0.0002	**-0.0269**	-0.0033	**-0.0022**	0.0420	-18.9609
	t statistic	1.7446	-1.6608	-4.9109	-0.0388	-3.4032	-0.9294	-2.5189		
TS10	Coefficient	**0.7913**	**-0.0364**	**0.0055**	0.0236	-0.0180	0.0130	-0.0009	0.0053	-22.7724
	t statistic	2.0764	-2.1187	2.1634	0.8668	-0.5159	0.8409	-0.2325		
TS20	Coefficient	**0.7492**	**-0.0343**	0.0032	0.0242	-0.0081	0.0086	-0.0016	0.0012	-22.8248
	t statistic	1.9716	-2.0031	1.2355	0.8937	-0.2345	0.5543	-0.3996		
TS30	Coefficient	**0.7626**	**-0.0349**	0.0027	0.0244	0.0085	0.0091	-0.0014	0.0009	-22.8418
	t statistic	2.0110	-2.0460	1.0490	0.9012	0.2446	0.5890	-0.3709		
IS10	Coefficient	0.1068	-0.0049	**0.0079**	**0.0168**	**0.0243**	0.0005	0.0000	0.0861	-21.7500
	t statistic	0.8348	-0.8487	9.1780	1.8451	2.0799	0.0944	-0.0355		
IS20	Coefficient	-0.0058	0.0003	**0.0057**	0.0098	0.0163	-0.0009	0.0002	0.0543	-19.0289
	t statistic	-0.0504	0.0489	7.3744	1.1930	1.5608	-0.1910	0.1800		

[a]This table reports results of a regression of daily innovation of a term structure-related variable on a set of control variables. Dependent variables are daily innovation in the default spread (DS), 10-, 20-, and 30-year nominal term spreads (TS10, TS20, and TS30), and finally 10- and 20-year inflation spreads (IS10 and IS20). Control variables are the log of the daily trading volume on the S&P 500 (liquidity), daily return on the S&P 500 (SP500), dummy corresponding to the emergency order of July 2008 (short 1), dummy corresponding to the short ban of September 2008 (short 2), dummy that accounts for the subprime crisis (crisis), and the 1-month Treasury bill rate (1 MTB). We report the coefficient from an OLS regression, as well as the corresponding t statistics. Coefficients that are statistically different from 0 at a 10% confidence level or less are shown in bold. We also report the adjusted R^2 of the regression, as well as the augmented Dickey–Fuller statistic that allows one to test for the presence of a unit root in the residual of the regression. The threshold for this statistic at a 1% level is –3.97. The sample period starts on January 3, 2006, and ends on January 29, 2010.

Finally, inflation-related spreads have been impacted positively by short dummies. As with default spreads, inflation-related spreads experienced a one-off fall when the September 2008 ban was instituted and then started to increase to their previous level (i.e., their innovation became positive).

We turn now to an in-depth analysis of the impact of the ban on the volatility of the innovation.

36.3.2 The Ban and Daily Volatility of Innovations

A large volatility of the innovation would indicate a great dispersion of opinion in the market since the market would not have any clear direction. The time series of volatilities are provided in Figure 36.3.

The volatility of the default spread and of inflation-related spreads clearly increased when the ban was instated; the dynamics formed an inverse U. Volatility increased by a factor of more than five over the period. The reaction of nominal term spreads is different. Their volatility increased substantially at the beginning of the subprime crisis and was very high in the summer and fall of 2007. This volatility then decreased up to the ban periods (summer 2008 and September 2008). Then, once again, the volatility started increasing but did not reach the highs of the beginning of the subprime crisis. On the whole, thus, the behavior of volatility was different during the ban from what it was before the ban. A key question, of course, is whether this differing behavior can be imputed to the ban. Results of the regression analysis that attempts to answer this question are found in Table 36.3.

Results shown in Table 36.3 shed light on the role of the ban in the dynamics of the volatility of the innovation. The crisis dummy had a positive and statistically significant impact on nominal term spreads but not on the default spread or on inflation-related spreads. Because we have controlled for several other variables, it is fair to impute the substantial increase in the volatility of these spreads over the summer of 2007 to the subprime crisis. The two successive bans of the summer of 2008 and September 2008 had statistically significant and opposing effects on the spreads. The September 2008 short ban had a positive impact on daily volatility, whereas the earlier ban had a negative impact. The impact of the September 2008 ban was greater than that of the summer ban.

There are several explanations for these results. First, the number of companies subject to the ban in summer 2008 was less than 10% of the number of companies subject to the ban in September 2008. Although the summer ban probably signaled some welcome regulatory activism, it may well be that the September ban was interpreted as signaling that regulatory authorities were panicking. Second, all the spreads are forward looking and, as a consequence, increased volatility also reflects increased dispersion of opinions. Although

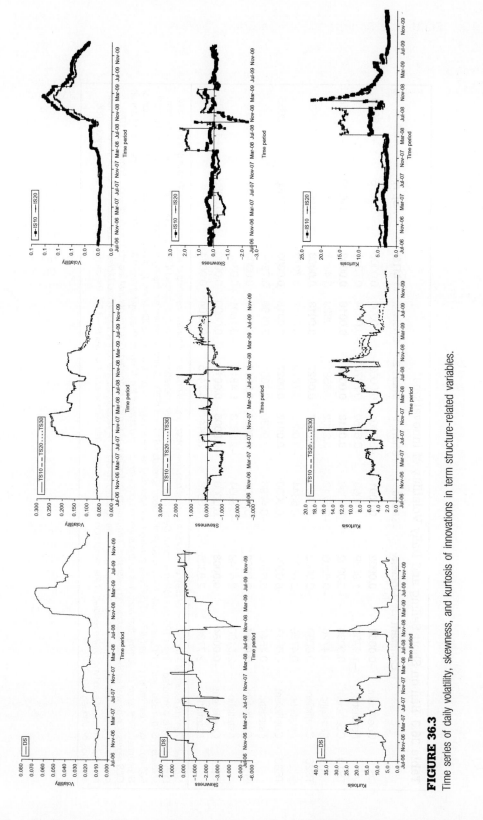

FIGURE 36.3

Time series of daily volatility, skewness, and kurtosis of innovations in term structure-related variables.

Table 36.3 Ban on Short Selling and Daily Volatility of Innovations[a]

		Constant	Liquidity	SP500	Short 1	Short 2	Crisis	1 MTB	Adj. R^2	ADF
DS	Coefficient	**-0.0053**	**0.0002**	**0.0001**	-0.0001	0.0002	0.0000	0.0000	0.9975	-14.6319
	t statistic	-1.9759	1.9889	4.4095	-0.6550	0.7270	-0.0634	0.7312		
TS10	Coefficient	0.0039	-0.0002	0.0000	**-0.0018**	**0.0026**	**0.0016**	**0.0003**	0.9979	-16.7558
	t statistic	0.4726	-0.6295	-0.6712	-3.2302	3.5581	3.2829	3.4357		
TS20	Coefficient	0.0039	-0.0002	0.0000	**-0.0017**	**0.0027**	**0.0018**	**0.0003**	0.9980	-16.2836
	t statistic	0.4789	-0.6507	-0.5344	-3.0558	3.7870	3.6477	3.7372		
TS30	Coefficient	0.0038	-0.0002	0.0000	**-0.0017**	**0.0027**	**0.0018**	**0.0003**	0.9980	-16.3665
	t statistic	0.4547	-0.6262	-0.4798	-2.9980	3.7051	3.6266	3.7259		
IS10	Coefficient	**-0.0064**	**0.0003**	0.0000	**-0.0004**	**0.0014**	0.0000	0.0000	0.9990	-16.2730
	t statistic	-2.5120	2.5549	-0.3994	-2.2623	6.4818	-0.1801	0.0347		
IS20	Coefficient	**-0.0064**	**0.0003**	0.0000	**-0.0005**	**0.0010**	0.0000	0.0000	0.9988	-17.4905
	t statistic	-2.7736	2.8325	1.3618	-3.0441	4.7445	-0.2704	0.0084		

[a]This table reports results of a regression of daily volatility of a term structure-related variable on a set of control variables in addition to lagged value of the volatility. Daily volatility is computed using a 100-day rolling window. Dependent variables are daily innovation in the default spread (DS), 10-, 20-, and 30-year nominal term spreads (TS10, TS20, and TS30), and finally 10- and 20-year inflation spreads (IS10 and IS20). Control variables are the log of the daily trading volume on the S&P 500 (liquidity), daily return on the S&P 500 (SP500), dummy corresponding to the emergency order of July 2008 (short 1), dummy corresponding to the short ban of September 2008 (short 2), dummy that accounts for the subprime crisis (crisis), and level of the 1-month Treasury bill rate (1 MTB). We report the coefficient from an OLS regression as well as the corresponding t statistics. Information for the lagged variable is omitted. Coefficients that are statistically different from 0 at a 10% confidence level or less are shown in bold. We also report the adjusted R^2 of the regression, as well as the augmented Dickey–Fuller statistic that allows one to test for the presence of a unit root in the residual of the regression. The threshold for this statistic at 1% level is -3.97. The sample period starts on January 3, 2006, and ends on January 29, 2010.

the lack of visibility on the stock market should foster some transfer of funds to the bond market, it doesn't seem that this was the case, as the return on the stock market had no significant impact on volatilities.

On the whole, the empirical investigation suggests three main messages: (i) short sale constraints in equity markets impact the term structure of interest rates (the two short sale-related dummies are statistically significant); (ii) both real and nominal term structures are affected (short dummies were affected to the same extent as nominal term spreads and inflation-related spreads); and (iii) active regulation may be associated with multiple equilibria—one short dummy had a positive impact while the other had a negative one.

We turn now to the impact of the short ban on the skewness of the innovations.

36.3.3 The Ban and Daily Skewness of Innovations

Figure 36.3 also shows the time series of the skewness of the innovations in term structure-related variables. It seems that skewness became more negative starting with the September 2008 ban. This means that decreases in these innovations are more frequent in the sample period than increases. Although most of the term or inflation-related spreads widened substantially after the ban, they returned only slowly to their preban values. A similar dynamic is also reflected in the inverse U shape of the daily volatility. Was the ban responsible for any of these features? Table 36.4 shows results of the empirical investigation. We ran the regressions without adding the lagged variable in the multivariate analysis since the model passes the ADF test without the lagged variable at 1 or 5% confidence levels.

Results are drastically different from those shown for daily volatility. The short ban of summer 2008 had a negative impact on skewness of the innovations, whereas the ban of summer 2008 had a positive impact. The crisis dummy was statistically significant in the vast majority of cases and with a positive sign.

This empirical evidence is hard to understand. We expect a period of turbulence to be followed by an increase in spreads (term spreads or inflation-related spreads). The impact of the short 1 ban falls into line with this expectation because it was positive. Combined with the impact on volatility, it seems that the first ban strengthened the belief that the term spread had to increase. But how then do we interpret the negative impact of the second ban? Volatility increased substantially during this period, which reflects a high dispersion of opinions. Still, spreads decreased. A tentative explanation could be related to market overreaction. Looking at the graph of the time

Table 36.4 Ban on Short Selling and Daily Skewness of Innovations[a]

		Constant	Liquidity	SP500	Short 1	Short 2	Crisis	1 MTB	Adj. R^2	ADF
DS	Coefficient	**28.0361**	**-1.3033**	-0.0223	**1.6966**	-0.3863	**0.4746**	**-0.1640**	0.1315	-4.0730
	t statistic	8.0129	-8.2978	-0.9788	7.0847	-1.2599	3.3229	-4.6963		
TS10	Coefficient	-1.6342	0.0659	-0.0047	**0.9829**	**-1.3411**	**0.4239**	**-0.0470**	0.2875	-4.8593
	t statistic	-0.9130	0.8200	-0.4070	8.0229	-8.5505	5.8022	-2.6334		
TS20	Coefficient	0.9577	-0.0647	0.0012	**1.1278**	**-1.3252**	**0.5474**	0.0041	0.3142	-5.6983
	t statistic	0.6251	-0.9403	0.1252	10.7551	-9.8723	8.7538	0.2692		
TS30	Coefficient	0.3894	-0.0401	0.0034	**1.1846**	**-1.3468**	**0.5690**	0.0072	0.3185	-5.6437
	t statistic	0.2468	-0.5660	0.3329	10.9670	-9.7396	8.8331	0.4591		
IS10	Coefficient	-1.0512	0.0543	-0.0044	-0.0390	**-1.6991**	**-0.1057**	**0.0215**	0.4292	-6.9395
	t statistic	-1.2605	1.4514	-0.8053	-0.6830	-23.2521	-3.1062	2.5818		
IS20	Coefficient	**3.6325**	**-0.1598**	-0.0010	**1.1147**	**-2.1653**	**0.3187**	**-0.0780**	0.2605	-3.8114
	t statistic	1.7358	-1.7007	-0.0767	7.7822	-11.8087	3.7310	-3.7355		

[a]This table reports results of a regression of daily skewness of a term structure-related variable on a set of control variables. Daily skewness is computed using a 100-day rolling window. Dependent variables are daily innovation in the default spread (DS), 10-, 20-, and 30-year nominal term spreads (TS10, TS20, and TS30), and finally 10- and 20-year inflation spreads (IS10 and IS20). Control variables are the log of the daily trading volume on the S&P 500 (liquidity), daily return on the S&P 500 (SP500), dummy corresponding to the emergency order of July 2008 (short 1), dummy corresponding to the short ban of September 2008 (short 2), dummy that accounts for the subprime crisis (crisis), and level of the 1-month Treasury bill rate (1 MTB). We report the coefficient from an OLS regression, as well as the corresponding t statistics. Coefficients that are statistically different from 0 at a 10% confidence level or less are shown in bold. We also report the adjusted R^2 of the regression, as well as the augmented Dickey–Fuller statistic that allows one to test for the presence of a unit root in the residual of the regression. The threshold for this statistic at a 1% level is -3.97. The sample period starts on January 3, 2006, and ends on January 29, 2010.

series of nominal spreads, one clearly observes the jump in spreads, which is followed immediately by a decrease.

A multiple equilibria story find itself supported by this evidence: the impact of the ban on short sales on skewness of treatment variables depends on market configuration. Regulation of short sales that takes into account swings of the business cycle is thus called for.

We turn now to the impact of the short ban on kurtosis of the innovations.

36.3.4 The Ban and Daily Kurtosis of Innovations

Figure 36.3 shows the time series of kurtosis of the innovations of treatment variables. The reaction of the spreads to the September 2008 short ban was identical across the spreads: we observe a substantial increase in the extreme market movements. Interestingly, it seems that the summer 2008 ban had a similar effect on nominal term spreads, as well as on inflation-related spreads. However, the default spread was not affected by this ban. The last thing to note is the reaction of these spreads to the subprime crisis: the default spread reacted strongly to the subprime crisis but less than the September 2008 ban. The nominal spread reacted more strongly to the subprime crisis than to the September 2008 ban. The inflation-related spread, finally, did not react to the subprime crisis at all.

To what extent is the ban responsible for this behavior of term structure-related variables? The regression analysis in Table 36.5 goes some way to providing an answer. We run the regressions without adding the lagged variable in the multivariate analysis, as the model passes the ADF test without the lagged variable at the 1 or 5% confidence level.

The two bans had a positive and significant impact on nominal term spreads. This impact is present after the ongoing financial crisis (the dummy crisis is significant for all the spreads) is controlled for. A similar conclusion holds for inflation-related spreads: both short bans had a positive impact on the kurtosis of these spreads. We fail to document a systematic impact of the ban on the default spread.

Banning short sells thus generated extreme market movements in markets other than equity markets.

36.4 CONCLUSION AND POLICY IMPLICATIONS

This chapter made explicit the effects of regulation in one sector of the financial market that spill over into another. Because stocks and bonds are part of diversified portfolios of any average institutional investor, constraining the positions on the stocks will clearly have an impact on the demand

Table 36.5 Ban on Short Selling and Daily Kurtosis of Innovations[a]

		Constant	Liquidity	SP500	Short 1	Short 2	Crisis	1 MTB	Adj. R^2	ADF
DS	Coefficient	**-86.9257**	**4.0420**	0.1317	**-4.5344**	1.3834	**2.6918**	**2.4071**	0.2511	-3.9350
	t statistic	-5.0675	5.2492	1.1814	-3.8620	0.9204	3.8443	14.0595		
10y TS	Coefficient	**-20.5368**	**1.0503**	-0.0094	**4.9025**	**3.6529**	**2.5106**	**0.4798**	0.2483	-5.1941
	t statistic	-3.0146	3.4345	-0.2131	10.5140	6.1195	9.0282	7.0559		
20y TS	Coefficient	**-20.2954**	**1.0001**	0.0352	**4.8564**	**5.3722**	**2.6468**	**0.6779**	0.2824	-5.6584
	t statistic	-3.0501	3.3482	0.8136	10.6631	9.2142	9.7448	10.2068		
30y TS	Coefficient	**-21.9866**	**1.0727**	0.0533	**4.9997**	**5.9559**	**2.7017**	**0.7022**	0.2725	-5.3730
	t statistic	-3.0634	3.3296	1.1420	10.1779	9.4708	9.2221	9.8023		
10y ITS	Coefficient	**-20.0996**	**1.1321**	0.0194	**2.2250**	**13.0910**	**-0.4631**	**-0.2649**	0.5451	-4.5644
	t statistic	-3.5963	4.5123	0.5332	5.8163	26.7316	-2.0298	-4.7490		
20y ITS	Coefficient	5.7651	-0.0437	0.0263	**5.9982**	**11.6129**	0.7144	-0.0726	0.2311	-3.5807
	t statistic	0.5555	-0.0939	0.3905	8.4444	12.7707	1.6863	-0.7009		

[a]This table reports results of regression of daily kurtosis of a term structure-related variable on a set of control variables. Daily kurtosis is computed using a 100-day rolling window. Dependent variables are the daily innovation in the default spread (DS), 10-, 20-, and 30-year nominal term spreads (TS10, TS20, and TS30), and finally 10- and 20-year inflation spreads (IS10 and IS20). Control variables are the log of the daily trading volume on the S&P 500 (liquidity), daily return on the S&P 500 (SP500), dummy corresponding to the emergency order of July 2008 (short 1), dummy corresponding to the short ban of September 2008 (short 2), dummy that accounts for the subprime crisis (crisis), and level of the 1-month Treasury bill rate (1 MTB). We report the coefficient from an OLS regression, as well the corresponding t statistics. Coefficients that are statistically different from 0 at a 10% confidence level or less are shown in bold. We also report the adjusted R^2 of the regression, as well as the augmented Dickey–Fuller statistic that allows one to test for the presence of a unit root in the residual of the regression. The threshold for this statistic at a 1% level is −3.97. The sample period starts on January 3, 2006, and ends on January 29, 2010.

for bonds and thus on their prices. More broadly, the bond market didn't escape the greater uncertainty in the financial markets.

Regulatory uncertainty clearly has an impact on market prices and leads to some types of multiple equilibria. This is an interesting lesson from the great regulatory uncertainty surrounding short selling. It is well understood that short sellers are useful for information processing and, as a consequence, any attempt to keep them out of the market is in itself already a valuable signal to the market. It is obviously true for the stocks concerned (the ban didn't relieve the downward pressure on stocks placed off limits) but also for other financial assets.

In a recent move, the Securities and Exchange Commission introduced so-called circuit breakers on short sales if markets fall too much (10% was the threshold). The impact of this measure on other segments of the market will be worth studying. Financial institutions such as pension funds depend heavily on the liquidity of bond markets. If the liquidity of these markets is dried up by regulation, there will be a price to pay.

REFERENCES

Bris, A. (2008). *Short selling activity in financial stocks and the sec July 15th emergency order.* Working Paper, Lausanne, Switzerland: IMD.

Lioui, A. (2009). *The undesirable effects of the short sale ban.* Working Paper, Nice, France: EDHEC-Risk Institute.

Marsh, I., & Niemer, N. (2008). *The impact of short sales restrictions.* Working Paper, London, UK: CASS Business School.

CHAPTER 37

Short Selling Assessment Where Consumer Prices Involve Both Currency Trades and Weather Shocks

Jack Penm and R. Deane Terrell

CONTENTS

ABSTRACT

Research has been conducted in short selling decisions where consumer prices involve both currency trades and weather shocks using new sparse patterned forgetting factor inclusive time-series approaches. In order to maximize forex trading opportunities and diversify a currency investment portfolio, results indicate that an investor can buy one short-term bullish currency and short sell another short-term bearish currency.

KEYWORDS

Currency trades; Forex trade strategy; Forgetting factor; Granger causality; Modified Hannan–Quinn criterion; Sparse patterned time-series modeling; Vector error-correction modeling; Weather shocks.

37.1 INTRODUCTION

In October 1987, a global stock market crash occurred of the magnitude of 30%, impacting simultaneously on most of the stock markets of the world, leading to an almost instantaneous reduction in share values of trillions of dollars. In today's dollar value, this market crash would correspond to an absolute loss of more than 15 trillion dollars. Stock market crashes can decimate years of funds accumulated for pensions and super-annuation savings almost in an instant. Therefore, the financial services industry, in particular investment funds, should not be complacent in expecting an uninterrupted massive growth in the resources managed by this industry. In particular, in Australia, 60% of Australian adults currently hold direct share investments in the stock market. The substantial risks in the investment industry, and the increasing complexity of financial services markets, including both stock and forex markets, create an urgent research need to better understand, assess, and manage risk in the financial services industry.

As significant advances in powerful concurrent computing equipment have made for major innovations in investment approaches, more increasingly sophisticated industry-oriented approaches to forex trade assessment and short selling decisions for capturing trading opportunities are now of central importance, driven by applications of increasing scale and complexity. As a result, the refinement of these approaches becomes essential, providing finance researchers with a window of opportunity to make a significant contribution to the frontier of industry-oriented and academic investment research. In this chapter, research has been conducted in short selling decisions where consumer prices involve both currency trades with respect to foods. To achieve this goal, it is necessary to use new sparse patterned forgetting factor inclusive time-series approaches. In order to maximize forex trading opportunities and diversify a currency investment portfolio, results indicate that an investor can buy one short-term bullish currency and short sell another short-term bearish currency. While forex trade and environmental investment decisions still have to operate in an uncertain market, and human judgment can never be fully replaced, sparse patterned time-series modeling has a significant role to play in guiding effective forex trade strategy and short selling decisions.

This chapter tests two hypotheses. The first hypothesis is that significant price indices will cause exchange rate movements under the conditions of weather shocks. We will undertake a causality test of the significant relevant finance variables involved in the causal relations. The absence of stable long-term relationships would indicate that, over a long period, exchange rate movements are less dependent on the levels of prices. If stable long-term relationships are identified among exchange rates and price indices, then, after temporary deviations in the short term, the levels of exchange rates would revert to their conventional long-term relationships with price indices. The second hypothesis is that the levels of significant price indices under weather shocks lead to a change in the same direction as exchange rate movements, if comovements in the same direction exist in cointegrating relationships. Such identified "unidirectional" comovements indicate increased currency values from higher price indices, or decreased currency values from lower price indices. Identification of such long-term and unidirectional comovements is essential in forecasting exchange rate movements, which affects buying and selling trade behavior and thereby suggests effective forex trade strategy and short selling decisions.

We test these two hypotheses using recent developments in cointegration theory. The tests are undertaken within the framework of sparse patterned vector error-correction modeling (VECM) and associated cointegrating vectors, with allowance for possible zero entries in coefficient matrices, as proposed in Penm and Terrell (2003). This method is particularly useful for analyzing cointegrating relationships between exchange rates and prices in forex trade markets. Its special attraction is that, by permitting zero coefficients in the patterned VECM, it allows for a highly insightful financial interpretation of the cointegrating relationships and their readjustment following deviations from equilibrium. New sparse patterned VECMs for linear and nonlinear modeling are helpful in explaining and interpreting certain aspects of causal links between price behavior and exchange rate movements. The patterned cointegrating vectors in the VECM are valuable not only in taking short sell trading opportunities but also in forecasting price changes.

Several other concerns must also be tackled before we set out the full complexity of the pattern of linkages being investigated. Significant price variables may differ from country to country and at different points in the sequence of events. Thus we investigate consumer prices, wholesale prices, and export and import prices in order to fully understand the strength and direction of certain causal linkages. We also consider whether such causal links are short or long term in nature and whether it is possible in a complex sequential process to detect feedback loops. We design a system model to investigate the following two causal chains.

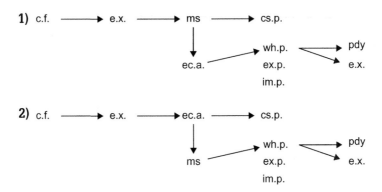

where c.f. is capital flows, e.x. is exchange rates, ms is money supply movements, ec.a. is economic activities, cs.p. is consumer prices, wh.p. is whole prices, ex.p. is export prices, im.p. is import prices, and pdy is productivity changes.

We also adopt a forgetting factor approach in the estimation of sparse patterned VECMs. The forgetting factor has been widely used to capture nonstationarity through patterned VECM modeling, including full-order models. A VECM model, which works well in explaining the behavior of a process over a small sample in a given time period, may have to be augmented for a longer data span when it evolves slowly over time due to economic, political, or other structural changes. Consequently, forecasts obtained by allocating greater weight to more recent observations and "forgetting" some of the past are likely to outperform alternatives in which such an allocation is not adopted. With a forgetting factor approach we are able to properly analyze complex systems where relevant data have been generated from structures subject to evolutionary change in their environment. This enhancement has taken place for data series, which may include a mixture of stationary and nonstationary elements, a most likely situation in economic, financial, and environmental series. This has led to new developments in dealing with cointegration, particularly where the underlying model structure involves sparse patterned matrices. Our forgetting factor approach improves the estimated parameter profile, model structure, and performance reliability for assessing complex relationships involving slowly evolving long-term effects. These qualities are not found in conventional time-series approaches involving only full-order models.

We investigate the causal relationships among exchange rates, price indices, other financial variables, and the exchange rate forecasting in Taiwan using monthly data over the period January 2001 through January 2010 in order to illustrate the practical use of the proposed forex forecast and short sell approaches. Weather shocks in Taiwan include changes in seasonal temperature variation and rainfall patterns; variations in soil moisture and water resources; and increases in the incidence of severe weather events such as earthquakes, typhoons, and floods. Financial variables are expected to be impacted negatively where outcomes relate to agriculture. For instance, negative changes in the availability and quality of land, soil, and water resources will be reflected in poorer crop performance, which leads to rising prices. Weather-related changes in agricultural conditions will most likely increase Taiwan's reliance on imported food. Those increased price indices will reflect changes over time in the long-term effects of weather shocks and their impacts on the production, use, and disposal of items purchased each year by consumers.

This chapter is organized as follows. Section 37.2 describes the forgetting factor approach and demonstrates patterned VECM modeling, showing "presence and absence" restrictions on the coefficients of time-series systems. Section 37.3 illustrates causal linkages among significant price indices and relevant exchange rates between the Taiwanese dollar and European euros. Forex forecasting results are presented to indicate significant exchange rate movements, and the total absolute error (TAE) criterion is used to examine prediction performance.

37.2 METHODOLOGY

37.2.1 The Fixed Forgetting Factor

In time-series modeling, the forgetting factor method assesses each incoming observation and applies appropriate weights to update the model structure and parameters. Use of a fixed forgetting factor in time-series analysis has attracted considerable interest in recent years. For example, Brailsford, Penm, and Terrell (2002) report the use of the forgetting factor in modeling and simulation of financial time series, while Penm and Terrell (2003) utilize a forgetting factor in subset autoregressive modeling of spot aluminum and nickel prices on the London Metal Exchange.

Consider a vector autoregressive (VAR) model of the following form:

$$z(t) + \sum_{\tau=1}^{p} A_\tau z(t - \tau) = \varepsilon(t) \tag{37.1}$$

where $z(t)$ is a sx1 vector of wide-sense stationary series. $\varepsilon(t)$ is an sx1 vector of independent and identically distributed random processes with $E\{\varepsilon(t)\} = 0$ and $E\{\varepsilon(t)\varepsilon'(t - \tau)\} = \Omega$ if $\tau = 0$ and $= 0$ if $\tau > 0$. A_τ, $\tau = 1,\ldots, q$ are sxs matrices of coefficients. The observations $z(t)$ $\{t = 1,\ldots, T\}$ are available.

Let $\delta(t) = [\delta_1(t) \; \ldots \; \ldots \; \delta_n(t)]$ denote a 1xs vector associated with time t. Following O'Neill, Penm, and Penm (2007), a strategy for determining the value of the forgetting factor $\delta(t)$ is as follows:

$$\delta_i(t) = \delta^{\lambda - t + 1} \text{ if } 1 \leq t \leq \lambda \text{ and } = 1 \text{ if } \lambda < t \leq T \text{ for } i = 1, \ldots n \qquad (37.2)$$

Equation (37.2) means that "forgetting" of the past occurs from time λ. No forgetting is involved from time $\lambda + 1$ to time T. If $\delta = 1$ for every t, then we obtain the ordinary least squares solution. If $0 < \delta < 1$, the past is weighted down geometrically from time λ. In theory, the value of δ could be different between $\delta(t)$ (a so-called variable forgetting factor). For simplicity, we only consider the fixed forgetting factor case in which the value of δ is constant for $\delta_i(t)$.

This means that the coefficients in Equation (37.1) are estimated to minimize:

$$\sum_{t=1}^{T} \delta(t)[z(t) - \sum_{\tau=1}^{p} A_\tau z(t - \tau)][z(t) - \sum_{\tau=1}^{p} A_\tau z(t - \tau)]' \qquad (37.3)$$

One important issue relating to the use of the forgetting factor in estimation is how to determine the value of δ in applications. The conventional method is based on arbitrary or personal choices. Penm and Terrell (2003) propose to determine the value of δ using the bootstrap. In this paper, their suggested method is adopted for determination of the value of δ. While Brailsford and colleagues (2002) also propose a procedure to determine the value of dynamic forgetting factor for nonstationary processes, we have focused on the use of a fixed forgetting factor in this chapter, as applications of a fixed forgetting factor to currency trading market movements is expected to be more predictable.

37.2.2 VECM Modeling for an $I(1)$ System

In constructing VECM modeling for an $I(1)$ system, from Equation (37.1) we have

$$A^p(L) = I + \sum_{\tau=1}^{p} A_\tau L^\tau$$

where L denotes the lag operator and $Lz(t) = z(t-1)$. It is assumed that the roots of $|A^p(L)| = 0$ lie outside or on the unit circle to ensure that $z(t)$ can contain $I(1)$ variables. Of note, $z(t)$ is integrated of order d, $I(d)$, if it contains at least one element that must be differenced d times before it becomes $I(0)$. Further, $z(t)$ is cointegrated with the cointegrating vector, η, of order g, if $\eta'z(t)$ is integrated of order $(d-g)$, where $z(t)$ has to contain at least two $I(d)$ variables.

Following Penm and Terrell (2003), the equivalent VECM for (37.1) can then be expressed as

$$A^p(1)z(t-1) + A^{p-1}(L)\Delta z(t) = \varepsilon(t) \qquad (37.4)$$

where $z(t)$ contains variables of the types $I(0)$ and $I(1)$. Note that $\Delta = (I - L)$, $\Delta z(t) = z(t) - z(t-1)$, and $\varepsilon(t)$ is stationary. Equation (37.4) can be rewritten as

$$A^* z(t-1) + A^{p-1}(L)\Delta z(t) = \varepsilon(t) \qquad (37.5)$$

where $A^* = A^p(1)$, $A^* z(t-1)$ is stationary, and the first term in Equation (37.5) is the error correction term. The term $A^{q-1}(L)\Delta z(t)$ is the vector autoregressive part of the VECM.

Because $z(t)$ is cointegrated of order 1, the long-term impact matrix, A^*, must be singular. As a result, $A^* = \psi\eta'$ and $\eta' z(t-1)$ is stationary, where the rank of A^* is j $(0 < j < s)$, and ψ and η' are matrices of dimensions $s \times j$ and $j \times s$, respectively. The columns of η are cointegrating vectors, and the rows of ψ are loading vectors.

In vector-integrated time-series analysis, model development is more convenient using VECMs instead of the equivalent VARs. VECMs have become an important means of detecting Granger causal relations and cointegrating relations. Commonly employed full-order VECM models assume nonzero entries in all their coefficient matrices. However, applications of VECM models to economic and financial time-series data have revealed that zero entries are indeed possible. The existence of zero entries has not been fully explored in causality and cointegration theory. Specifically, if indirect causality or Granger noncausality exists among the variables, the use of "overparameterized" full-order VECM models may weaken the power of statistical inferences. Penm and Terrell (2003) argue that the sparse patterned VECM is a more straightforward and effective means of testing for both indirect causality and Granger noncausality. The same benefits will be present if a sparse patterned VECM is used to analyze cointegrating relations. A VECM that makes allowance for possible zero entries in coefficient matrices is referred to as a "sparse patterned VECM."

In cointegrated time-series systems reported in Penm and Terrell (2003), the VARs in first difference will be misspecified, and the VARs in levels will ignore important constraints on the coefficient matrices. Although these constraints may be satisfied asymptotically, efficiency gains and improvements in forecasts are likely to result by imposing them. Comparisons of forecasting performance of VECMs compared to VARs for cointegrated systems consistently indicate that, in the short term, there may be gains in using the unrestricted VAR models. However, VECMs produce long-term forecasts with smaller errors when variables used in the models satisfy cointegration conditions. As described in Penm and Terrell (2003), in applications of VECM models to financial market data, it may be assumed a priori that zero entries are required. In such cases the use of *full-order* VECM models may lead to incorrect inferences. Specifically, in conducting causality and cointegration analysis, if entries assigned a priori to be zero were ignored and full-order VECM models were utilized, the power of statistical inferences would be weakened. Also, if the underlying true VECM and the associated cointegrating and loading vectors contained zero entries, the resultant specifications could produce different conclusions concerning the cointegrating relationships among the variables.

Cointegration theory is associated with "error correction" and has important implications for forecasting. If cointegration is found to exist among certain variables, then such long-term relationships should be explicitly identified when forecasting, which is very important in capturing trading opportunity and setting trading strategies. Recent empirical studies have demonstrated that imposing such restrictions in forecasting would benefit the forecasts significantly, especially in the longer term. Further, the development course of climate change is a long-term, slowly evolving underlying weather shock process, and the effects of climate change will be exhibited in the long-term patterned cointegrating relations, which are detected in the error-correction term of the patterned VECM.

In addition, one difficulty encountered in empirical research using cointegration theory is to provide satisfactory financial and economic interpretation for estimated cointegrating vectors. As emphasized by Penm and Terrell (2003), it is important to introduce a priori information, usually to produce sparse patterns. To address this issue explicitly, Penm and Terrell presented a search algorithm in conjunction with model selection criteria to identify the optimal specification of a sparse patterned VECM for an $I(1)$ system. Given the optimal sparse patterned VECM, the number of cointegrating vectors can be confirmed. Once the sparse patterned impact matrix has been determined, along with the number of cointegrating vectors in the system, a tree-pruning procedure is then undertaken to search for all acceptable sparse patterns of the cointegrating and loading vectors. After this, the dynamic ordinary least squares method reported in Penm and Terrell (2003) is utilized to estimate the acceptable patterned cointegrating vectors, and the regression method with linear restrictions as recommended in Penm and Terrell is conducted to estimate the acceptable patterned loading vectors. Model selection criteria are again employed to determine optimal sparse patterned cointegrating and loading vectors. This algorithm leads to a neat and effective analysis of the cointegrating relations in any vector time-series system and can be extended to higher order integrated systems.

A search algorithm proposed by Penm and Terrell (2003) to select the optimal sparse patterned ψ and η is described.

1. To begin this algorithm, we first identify the optimal sparse patterned VECM using model selection criteria.
2. After the optimal sparse patterned VECM is identified, the rank of the long-term impact matrix is then computed using the singular value decomposition method so that the number of cointegrating vectors in the system will be identified.
3. A leaps-and-bounds tree-pruning search algorithm that avoids evaluating all candidates is then implemented for selecting all acceptable sparse patterns of the loading and cointegrating vectors.
4. Identified candidates of the sparse patterned cointegrating vectors are estimated using a triangular error-correction modeling mechanism proposed in Penm and Terrell (2003).
5. Estimation of the associated candidates for sparse patterned loading vectors is carried out by the regression method with linear restrictions.
6. Optimal sparse patterned loading and cointegrating vectors are finally selected by model selection criteria.

37.3 DATA AND EMPIRICAL APPLICATION

This chapter uses monthly observations of exchange rate variables and economic price indices over the period January 2001 through January 2010 ($T = 109$). These data are obtained from the Taiwanese Economic Database. The year 2000 is selected as the base year for all indices involved. Table 37.1 presents those variables that are tested simultaneously in a stochastic vector system.

All variables, excluding BOPCF, are log transformed, such that $z_1(t) = \log(\text{UED})$, $z_2(t) = \text{BOPCF}$, $z_3(t) = \log(\text{ECP})$, $z_4(t) = \log(\text{EWP})$, $z_5(t) = \log(\text{EMP})$,

Table 37.1 Brief Description of Economic Variables Tested Simultaneously in a Stochastic Vector System

Variable	Brief Description
UED	Exchange rate (E): Taiwanese dollar per European (EU) euro
BOPCF	Taiwanese capital inflow
ECP	Ratio of price levels (P): Taiwanese CPI relative to EU CPI
EWP	Taiwanese WPI relative to EU WPI
EMP	Taiwanese import price index relative to EU import price index
EXP	Taiwanese export price index relative to EU export price index
EM2	Taiwanese M2 relative to EU M2
EPDY	Taiwanese industry production index relative to EU industry production index

$z_6(t) = \log(\text{EXP})$, $z_7(t) = \log(\text{EM2})$, and $z_8(t) = \log(\text{EPDY})$. We then undertake unit root tests. The outcome indicates that all transformed z series are $I(1)$. Using the approach proposed in Brailsford and co-workers (2002), we utilize a fixed forgetting factor with the value 0.99 to the stochastic system involved. We then conduct the identification procedures proposed in Penm and Terrell (2003) to obtain the optimal sparse patterned VECM model over the period January 2001 through July 2009 ($T = 103$).

We adopt the enhancement approach used by Penm and Terrell (2003) to select the optimal lag order (p) for the autoregressive part of the VECM system. That is, we test whiteness for the residual vectors from the VECM selected under the Akaike information criterion. If the residual vector process results in being nonwhite, we sequentially increase p to $p + 1$ and then examine the resultant residual vector process until the residual process becomes a vector white noise process. An optimal value 5 has been identified for p, as the resultant residual vector process for $p = 5$ confirms a white noise process. The optimal sparse patterned VECM with the lags 1, 4, and 5 for the autoregressive part, and the modified Hannan–Quinn criterion (MHQC), are used to select optimal α and β. Subsequently, we use MHQC as an abbreviation for the modified Hannan–Quinn criterion, which is defined by

$$\text{MHQC} = \log|\widehat{\Omega}| + [2\log\log f(T)/f(T)]N$$

where $f(T) = \displaystyle\sum_{t=1}^{T} \delta_{T-t}$ is the effective sample size, N is the number of functionally independent parameters, and $\widehat{\Omega}$ is the sample estimate of Ω.

Using the procedure for testing Granger causality proposed in Penm and Terrell (2003), the patterned VECM selected confirms the two Granger causality chains, which are shown in Figure 37.1.

Further, the Taiwanese dollar to European euro equation specified in the VECM modeling at $T = 103$ is presented in Table 37.2. The t statistics are shown in parentheses.

We undertake a one-step-ahead forecast using this patterned VECM at $T = 103$. We then utilize the model specification selection approach to select the optimal patterned VECM models at $T = 104, 105, 106, 107$, and 108. An identical VECM specification with the lags 1, 4, and 5 for the autoregressive part is selected by the MHQC at all times. One-step-ahead forecasts based on each optimal VAR are carried out, and the associated forecasts are calculated. The forecast trend criterion, $\text{TAE}_i = \displaystyle\sum_i \left[\frac{\text{forecast} - \text{actual value}}{\text{actual value}}\right]$, is then used to assess whether the predicted exchange rate of Taiwanese dollars against 1 euro is bullish or bearish in this forecast period. Our outcome of TAE = 3.1% over

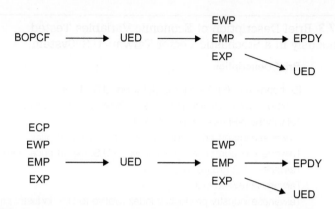

FIGURE 37.1
Two Granger causal chains confirmed in VECM modeling.

Table 37.2 Exchange Rate Equation Specified at $T = 103$ in the VECM

$DUED_t = 0.11852 \times DUED_{t-1} - 0.21787 \times \text{Error Correction}_{t-1}$
        (1.81)   (−2.37)

$\text{Error Correction}_{t-1} = .26331\, UED_{t-1} - 1.12830\, EWP_{t-1} - 0.01211\, ECP_{t-1}$
                    (1.97)   (−2.58)   (−3.12)

$- 4.17331\, EMP_{t-1} + 7.81 * 10^{-6} \times BOPCF_{t-1}$
        (2.23)   (−3.71)

where $DUED_t$ denotes $UED_t - UED_{t-1}$

the period August 2009 through January 2010 indicates that the predicted euro values against Taiwanese dollars have a bullish trend.

Analogously, we use the aforementioned approach to predict the exchange rate of the Taiwanese dollar per U.S. dollar over the period January 2001 through January 2010. Table 37.3 presents those variables, which are tested simultaneously in a stochastic vector system.

Figure 37.2 shows two Granger causal chains confirmed in the VECM modeling. The outcome is a negative TAE = −2.7%, which indicates that the trend of the predicted euro values against Taiwanese dollars is bearish.

Results indicate that an investor can buy one short-term bullish currency, the euro, and short sell another short-term bearish currency, the U.S. dollar, in order to maximize forex trading opportunities and diversify a currency investment portfolio.

Table 37.3 Brief Description of Economic Variables Tested Simultaneously in a Stochastic Vector Taiwan–U.S. System

Variable	Brief Description
USD	Exchange rate (E): Taiwanese dollar per U.S. dollar
UCP	Ratio of price levels (P): Taiwanese CPI relative to U.S. CPI
UWP	Taiwanese WPI relative to U.S. WPI
UMP	Taiwanese import price index relative to U.S. import price index
UXP	Taiwanese export price index relative to U.S. export price index
UM2	Taiwanese M2 relative to U.S. M2
UEA	Taiwanese revised GDP
UPDY	Taiwanese industry production index relative to U.S. industry production index

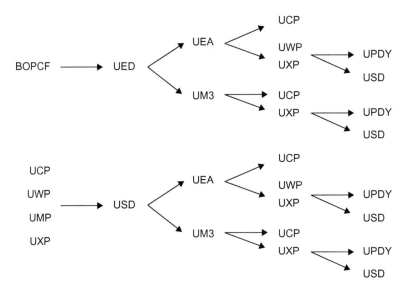

FIGURE 37.2
Two Granger causal chains confirmed in VECM Taiwan–U.S. modeling.

37.4 CONCLUSION

Research has been conducted in short selling decisions where consumer prices involve both currency trades and weather shocks using new sparse patterned forgetting factor inclusive time-series approaches. This chapter presented the Granger causality between macroeconomic price indices and exchange rates in a relevant and complex currency short selling environment using sparse patterned VECM modeling and simulations with the fixed forgetting factor.

In order to maximize forex trading opportunities and diversify a currency investment portfolio, results indicate that an investor can buy one short-term bullish currency and short sell another short-term bearish currency. This chapter provided a simple short sell example.

At the end of January 2001, a U.S. dollar was valued at 32.63 Taiwanese dollars, and a euro was valued at 30.61 Taiwanese dollars. An investor borrowed a million U.S. dollars to exchange for Taiwanese dollars, received 32.63 million Taiwanese dollars, and then exchanged those Taiwanese dollars to receive 1.066 million euros. At the end of January 2010, a euro was valued at 45.50 Taiwanese dollars and a U.S. dollar was valued at 31.87 Taiwanese dollars. This investor sold 1.066 million euros in exchange for Taiwanese dollars, received 48.503 million Taiwanese dollars, and then exchanged those Taiwanese dollars to receive 1.5219 million U.S. dollars. After returning the borrowed 1 million U.S. dollars, this investor gained 0.5219 million U.S. dollars.

The example just given using sparse patterned time-series forecasts indicates the usefulness of short selling to hedge fund managers. Our goal is to develop and apply excellent quantitative tools: sparse patterned time-series forgetting factor inclusive models allow hedge fund managers to improve their decision making with respect to risk management and asset allocation. Hedge funds are nontraditional in various ways and, in a strict sense, seek to protect against risky price movements, thereby maximizing the expected return-risk of the portfolio. Moreover, traditional hedge fund managers employ various strategies designed primarily to lower risk. These strategies are not always obvious and do not always fit within standard frameworks. Examples include short selling. Using sparse patterned time-series forgetting factor inclusive models, we argue that the right strategies can protect investors and even allow for positive returns in falling markets.

The alternative approach to investment performance using the sparse patterned time-series forgetting factor inclusive modeling suggested here is important to individual short selling investors, who can benefit from being able to better understand risk management and dynamic selection decisions. Those effective and efficient decisions can ultimately assist in improving returns to short selling investors.

REFERENCES

Brailsford, T., Penm, J., & Terrell, R. D. (2002). Selecting the forgetting factor in subset autoregressive modelling. *Journal of Time Series Analysis, 23*(6), 629–650.

O'Neill, T., Penm, J., & Penm, J. S. (2007). A subset polynomial neural networks approach for breast cancer diagnosis. *International Journal of Electronic Healthcare, 3*(3), 293–302.

Penm, J., & Terrell, R. D. (2003). *Collaborative research in quantitative finance and economics.* ACT, Australia: Evergreen Publishing.

CHAPTER 38

Aggregate Short Selling during Earnings Seasons

Paul Brockman, Andrew Lynch, and Andrei Nikiforov

CONTENTS

ABSTRACT

This chapter examines aggregate short selling during earnings seasons and shows that hedging is an important determinant of aggregate short selling activity around these highly volatile periods. Using a database made available through Regulation SHO of the Securities and Exchange Commission (SEC), we find that over 25% of all earnings season-related trading volume is attributable to short selling. We find that aggregate short selling increases sharply in the first 2 weeks of the earnings season and that aggregate short selling displays different patterns on different stock exchanges. Results show that aggregate short selling is independent of analyst following, suggesting that information motives do not explain aggregate short selling trading patterns during earnings seasons. Finally, we examine the effect of recent SEC curbs on short selling and find little impact on our empirical results.

KEYWORDS

Aggregate interest ratio; Aggregate short selling; Earnings seasons; Hedging; Short interest ratio; Short sales fraction.

38.1 INTRODUCTION

The issue of short selling company stock has recently attracted considerable controversy in the business and popular press. Commentators and regulators blame short selling for increased volatility, whereas short sellers (mostly banks and hedge funds) and academics maintain that short selling improves pricing efficiency and helps monitor corporate managers. Historically, short selling research relied on monthly short interest data, which seriously limited the precision of its conclusions. Recent studies utilize high-frequency transaction data to more thoroughly examine the effect of short selling on market quality, price informativeness, corporate decision making, and new regulatory proposals.

This study investigates aggregate short selling activity during earnings seasons. We find that the main driver of aggregate short selling around these highly volatile periods is not the informational advantage of short sellers, but the hedging activities of institutional investors. Empirical findings suggest that curbing short selling activity will contribute to lower market quality and increase the riskiness of trading around earnings seasons.

Previous studies provide two fundamental reasons for the existence of short selling. The first and by far the most widely investigated motive is the possession of some informational advantage on the part of short sellers. In an early theoretical paper, Diamond and Verrecchia (1987) argue that investors will not short sell for liquidity purposes, as short selling is costly (e.g., margin requirements, price risk, and other constraints), and will therefore short sell only if they have private information. Thus, these authors argue that short selling is informative. This view was later corroborated by numerous empirical studies. For example, others (Boehmer, Jones, & Zhang, 2008; Diether, Lee, & Werner, 2009) show that short selling helps incorporate information into stock prices. Dechow, Hutton, Meulbroek, and Sloan (2001) show that firms will be less susceptible to overvaluation when short selling is permitted, and Boehmer and Wu (2009) find that short selling improves overall market quality.

This information hypothesis posits implicitly that most short selling is based on private information. Researchers have tested this conjecture by investigating the link between short selling and contemporaneous or future returns. For example, Boehmer and co-workers (2009) show that individual short selling is correlated positively with stock returns, suggesting a contrarian strategy on the part of short sellers. Looking deeper into the composition of investors, Boehmer and colleagues (2008) find that this informed trading is limited to large institutional investors or to stocks with high short selling constraints. In contrast, Lamont and Stein (2004) look at the monthly short interest ratio and find negative correlations. This result implies that investors short sell in the aggregate when the stock market is already falling. Yu, Lynch, Nikolic, and Yan (2010) find similar results, showing that aggregate short selling is informed only over a few years of their 78-year sample.

No previous study has addressed the issue of aggregate short selling during earnings seasons. Earnings seasons are unique time periods (45 days at the beginning of each quarter) when thousands of firms flood the market with firm-specific announcements. If short selling is based predominantly on information, then we should see more of this activity just before or during the earnings season—all else equal. This clustering of information releases will thereby create aggregate patterns in short selling even if it is based purely on firm-specific information.

The activity of short sellers around an individual firm's earnings announcement has been examined in previous studies. For example, Christophe, Ferri, and Ang (2004) show that short sellers can correctly predict large negative surprises just before such earnings announcements. Francis, Venkatachalam, and Zhang (2005) show that increases in short selling activity is related inversely to analysts' downgrades. Desai, Hogan, and Wilkins (2006) find that short sellers can predict earnings restatements correctly. Finally, Diether and colleagues (2009) investigate whether short sellers make profits because of their ability to analyze available information or from analyst tips who are about to downgrade the stock. They find that analyst tips seem to drive their results.

The second fundamental motive for short selling is more technical and is not based on the possession of private information. The explosive growth of hedge funds in the last decade led to increases in shorting activity for hedging reasons. For example, shorting is an important part of such popular strategies as merger arbitrage, convertible arbitrage, and index arbitrage. Because many hedge funds use similar strategies and analyze the same public information, their short selling activities might amplify each other and result in what appears to be herding. In addition, market makers short shares routinely as part of their buffering activity (see Boehmer et al., 2008). Some investors might use short selling to provide liquidity during times of high market imbalances. If buy orders exceed sell orders substantially, the pressure will move the price higher. An investor who steps in and short sells will relieve this pressure and cause prices to settle lower, thus earning a small profit (see, e.g., Campbell et al., 1993; Chordia, Roll, & Subrahmanyam, 2002; Stoll, 1978).

In summary, short selling can be driven by informational motives and non-informational motives (e.g., hedging, arbitrage trading, liquidity provision). It is important to distinguish between these two motives, as each has different implications for financial markets and regulators. To investigate the relative importance of the two motives, this chapter looks at the aggregate short selling activity during earnings seasons, the regular intervals during which all public companies are required to file their quarterly earnings.

First of all, we expect to see strong patterns in aggregate shorting activity. Informational motives will result in more aggregate shorting just before the peak of announcements because that is the time when the majority of short sellers can take advantage of their private information. Hedging motives will result in higher short selling because earnings seasons are highly volatile. Because many types of arbitrage strategies become more attractive in the presence of increased volatility, we can expect herding-like increases in short selling during this time period. In addition, because trading in options increases sharply during the earnings seasons (Roll, Schwartz, & Subrahmanyam, 2010), market makers in the options market will simultaneously increase their hedging via short selling (Boehmer et al., 2008).

Second, we separate the two motives by looking into the composition of the sample. By controlling for factors that correlate strongly with the informational content of the firms' earnings announcements (e.g., size, exchange listing, analyst following, liquidity, and volatility), we are able to show that the hedging motive dominates aggregate short selling during the earnings seasons. Specifically, empirical results show that (1), on average, more than 25% of all volume is attributable to short selling, (2) aggregate short selling increases sharply in the first 2 weeks of earnings seasons but only for medium-sized portfolios, (3) aggregate short selling exhibits different patterns on different exchanges, and (4) aggregate short selling is independent of analyst following and, therefore, of the informational content of earnings releases.

Finally, we also examine the effect of the 2010 rule change of the Security and Exchange Commission (SEC) that seeks to curb short selling. The new rule restricts short selling activity whenever the firm's stock price falls by 10% or more in a single day (*Economist Magazine*, February 27, 2010). Further short selling is permitted only if the sales price is higher than the best available bid price. After applying this rule to our data set, we find that our empirical results are unchanged, as there is a relatively low fraction of firms with daily returns less than negative 10% during our sample period.

Section 38.2 describes data and methodology, and Section 38.3 presents and discusses empirical findings.

38.2 DATA AND METHODOLOGY

This study utilizes a unique data sample made available through SEC Regulation SHO, which required all major exchanges [NYSE, NASDAQ, American (AMEX), Archipelago (ARCA), Boston (BSE), Chicago (CHX),

NASD, National (NSX) and Philadelphia (PHX)] to disclose all short sales between January 3, 2005, and July 6, 2007. For each stock/day, we calculate short transactions and then merge these data with Center for Research in Security Prices (CRSP) daily pricing, volume, and returns information.

The two most widely used measures of short selling activity are short sales turnover [the ratio of shorted shares to the total shares outstanding (Yu et al., 2010)] and short sales fraction [the ratio of short sales to total trading volume in shares (Diether et al., 2009)]. Because the turnover changes dramatically around earnings seasons [Brockman and Nikiforov (2010) and references therein], short sales turnover is not suitable for our study. The second measure is more appropriate because it controls for changes in total turnover and is therefore our measure of choice. This measure has been used extensively in the short sales literature and is referred to commonly as "SIR" for "short interest ratio" (Boehmer, Huszar, & Jordan, 2010). Following the literature, we define daily SIR for every stock (i) traded during day (t) as follows:

$$SIR(i, t) = \frac{\# \text{Shares Sold Short}}{\text{Total} \# \text{Shares Traded}} \qquad (38.1)$$

Because we concentrate on aggregate short selling activity, we define aggregate SIR (ASIR) as the cross-sectional, equal-weighted average of all stocks shorted during a day. ASIR on day (t) is defined as follows:

$$ASIR(t) = \frac{\# \text{Shares Sold Short}}{\text{Total} \# \text{Shares Traded}} \qquad (38.2)$$

To capture the behavior of short selling during earnings seasons, we use several dummy variables to identify various periods in and around these information periods with periodicity of one quarter. Thus we look at the aggregate SIR 2 weeks prior to the beginning of each quarter, 2 weeks after the start of the quarter, the next 2 weeks, and finally the 2 weeks at the end of each quarter.

To investigate the unconditional impact of the various stages of earnings seasons on aggregate shorting activity, we run a simple regression (OLS) model where the aggregate short interest (ASIR) serves as the dependent variable and time period dummies (one by one) serve as independent variables as follows:

$$ASIR(t) = \text{Time Period Dummy}(j) + \varepsilon(t) \qquad (38.3)$$

where j stands for different time period dummies. Thus, WK00 stands for the 2 weeks before the beginning of the fiscal quarter, WK12 refers to the first and second week of the earnings season (quarter), WK34 refers to the third and fourth week of each quarter, WK56 refers to the fifth and sixth week of each quarter, and so on.

Because the size of a firm affects the short selling activity in a particular stock (Boehmer et al., 2010), we split our initial sample into 10 NYSE deciles. We run the same regression model [Equation (38.3)] for each decile. We repeat this exercise for different exchanges presented in our sample. We expect the listing to matter, as stocks from different exchanges possess different characteristics (size, age, liquidity, etc.).

To address the issue of whether short sellers have private information around earnings seasons we look at the changes in short selling activity for stocks with different information content. We measure information content by the dispersion of forecasts. Following Diether, Malloy, and Scherbina (2002), we define dispersion as the standard deviation of analysts' "1-year-ahead" forecasts. At the beginning of each quarter we sort stocks into five portfolios based on this measure and then run the regression model [Equation (38.3)] for each time period dummy.

Finally, we run the regression model [Equation (38.3)], while controlling for many factors shown to affect short selling activity. Thus we include the log of size, the exchange dummy, analyst dispersion, an illiquidity measure, and stock return volatility. The illiquidity variable is constructed following Amihud (2002) as the ratio of absolute returns to volume (in millions of dollars). To reduce noise, we average this ratio over half-month periods. Volatility is calculated as the squared return on that day.

38.3 EMPIRICAL RESULTS

Table 38.1 provides summary statistics for the total sample. Firms in the sample correspond to the SEC's Regulation SHO. This regulation requires all exchanges to report all short selling activity in all stocks during the period of January 2005 through June 2007. Transaction level short sale data disclosed under Regulation SHO are acquired directly from each of the nine exchanges used in our sample, except for the NYSE, which is obtained through WRDS. We report means, minimums, medians, maximums, standard deviations, and the number of observations (N) for each variable of interest (i.e., short ratio, short turnover, market capitalization, stock return volatility, analyst dispersion, and price level). The short ratio is the cross-sectional and time-series average of the volume of shares shorted relative to the total trading volume for all stock days. Short turnover is the volume shorted relative to total shares outstanding. Return volatility is found by squaring daily returns. Analyst dispersion is the standard deviation of the

Table 38.1 Summary Statistics[a]

Variable	Mean	Min	Median	Max	St. Dev.	N
Short ratio	0.2643	0.0000	0.2394	269.24	0.2417	3,747,325
Short turnover	0.2537	0.0000	0.0851	16,908	8.8785	3,747,656
Market cap	2802	0.009	346	486,489	13,170	4,119,831
Return volatility	0.0008	0.0000	0.0001	12.96	0.0173	4,118,351
Analysts' dispersion	0.0938	0.0000	0.0450	15.60	0.1828	2,180,061
Price	24.76	0.02	17.45	2675.00	34.93	4,119,831

[a]This table summarizes statistical characteristics of the total sample. Stocks in the sample come from SEC REG SHO, which required that all exchanges report all short activity in all stocks in 2005–2007. REG SHO data available from WRDS were updated manually to include stocks from exchanges beyond the three main ones: NYSE, NASDAQ, and AMEX. The short ratio is the cross-sectional and time-series average of the volume of shares shorted relative to the total trading volume for all stock days. Short turnover is the volume shorted relative to total shares outstanding. Return volatility is found by squaring daily returns. Analysts' dispersion is the standard deviation of the next fiscal period analysts' forecasts averaged over the last 6 months. The market cap is price times the number of shares outstanding in millions, and the price is the absolute value of CRSP variable PRC.

next fiscal period's analyst forecasts averaged over the last 6 months. The market cap is price times the number of shares outstanding (in millions), and price is simply the absolute value of the CRSP variable PRC.

The summary statistics in Table 38.1 represent a large sample of over four million observations across a wide range of firms. Market capitalizations range from a small firm worth $90,000 to a large firm worth $486 billion. Stock prices range from penny stocks ($0.02) to high price firms in the thousands of dollars per share ($2675). We also note considerable variation in our short selling variables, short ratios, and short turnovers. The mean (median) short ratio is 0.2643 (0.2394), with a minimum of zero and a maximum of 269.2418. The mean (median) short turnover is 0.2537 (0.0851), with a minimum of zero and a maximum of 16,908.

Table 38.2 regresses short ratios on time-period dummies that correspond to various time intervals both before and during the earnings season. WK00 corresponds to the 2-week period before the start of the earnings season; WK12, WK34, and WK56 correspond to the first, second, and third 2-week intervals during the earnings season, respectively; WK1234 and WK3456 correspond to the first and last 4-week (overlapping) intervals during the earnings season, respectively; and WK123456 refers to the entire earnings season. We report short ratio values for full sample regressions, as well as for decile portfolios based on firm size.

Full sample results in Table 38.2 show a statistically significant increase in short selling during the first 2 weeks (WK12) of the earnings season. This increase occurs in the midsize portfolios (i.e., deciles 3 through 7) and not

Table 38.2 Aggregate Short Ratio by Size Deciles[a]

	Full	Smallest	p = 3	p = 5	p = 7	Largest
WK00	−0.0016	−0.0009	0.0013	−0.0009	−0.0052*	−0.0076**
	0.56	0.73	0.71	0.78	0.06	0.00
WK12	0.0070**	−0.0004	0.0112**	0.0116**	0.0103**	0.0025
	0.01	0.88	0.00	0.00	0.00	0.32
WK34	−0.0019	−0.00331	−0.0014	−0.0022	−0.0022	−0.0015
	0.48	0.20	0.68	0.51	0.44	0.51
WK56	0.0001	0.00425*	−0.0023	−0.0032	0.0013	0.0032
	0.98	0.10	0.50	0.34	0.63	0.17
WK1234	0.0029	−0.0024	0.0056*	0.0054*	0.0046*	0.0005
	0.19	0.25	0.04	0.05	0.04	0.81
WK3456	−0.0012	0.000613	−0.0024	−0.0034	−0.0005	0.0011
	0.58	0.77	0.38	0.20	0.82	0.56
WK123456	0.0025	0.000351	0.0036	0.0029	0.0048*	0.0022
	0.21	0.86	0.16	0.25	0.02	0.20

[a]This table presents the effect of different time periods around earnings seasons on the aggregate short ratio. The aggregate short ratio is calculated as the cross-sectional average of individual short ratios for each stock day. We regress the aggregate short ratio on time-period dummies, which correspond to half-month, 1 month, or the whole season. WK00 is the half-month period before the start of the earnings seasons. WK12 corresponds to the first half-month. WK34 is the second half-month, and WK56 is the last half-month of a 45-day earnings season. WK1234 is the first month, WK3456 is the peak of the season, and WK123456 is the whole 45-day season. The second column corresponds to results for the total sample, and the next five columns are for different size deciles. Size deciles were obtained using NYSE decile breakpoints. $p = 1$ corresponds to the smallest stocks and $p = 10$ to the largest. Values shown are estimates of the regression coefficients with p values shown below the estimates. *Significance at 10% and **significance at 5% or better.

in the largest or smallest deciles. No other period yields statistically significant results for the full sample. We also find that the largest decile portfolio experiences a significant decrease in short selling activity during the 2-week period (WK00) prior to the release of aggregate earnings announcements. Finally, the smallest decile portfolio shows a significant increase in short selling activity at the end of the earnings season (WK56).

Table 38.3 examines the relationship between short selling and the stock exchange on which the short sold stock trades. Part A of Table 38.3 shows that 47.73% of sample observations are from NASDAQ, 39.42% are from NYSE, 8.81% are from AMEX, and the remaining 4.04% come from all other exchanges combined. In part B, short ratios on time-period dummies for each exchange grouping are regressed. Results show that the decrease in short selling activity for large firms in the preannouncement period (WK00), as shown in Table 38.2, is confined to stocks trading on NYSE. We also find that the increase in short selling activity during the first 2 weeks of the earnings season (WK12), as shown in Table 38.2, is confined to stocks trading on NASDAQ. This is an interesting result that requires additional research—no other exchange is

Table 38.3 Aggregate Short Ratio by Trading Venue (Exchange)[a]

A		
Exchange	**Number of Observations**	**Percent**
NYSE	1,623,838	39.42
AMEX	362,909	8.81
NASDAQ	1,966,499	47.73
Other	166,585	4.04
Total	4,119,831	100

B				
	NYSE	**AMEX**	**NASDAQ**	**Others**
WK00	−0.0054**	−0.0008	0.0015	0.0051
	0.03	0.39	0.72	0.11
WK12	0.0028	−0.0041	0.0126**	−0.0042
	0.20	0.23	0.00	0.22
WK34	−0.0033	−0.0024	−0.0005	−0.0060*
	0.14	0.32	0.90	0.06
WK56	0.0070**	0.0087**	−0.0080**	0.0061**
	0.00	0.03	0.05	0.05
WK1234	−0.0005	−0.0040	0.0070**	−0.0064**
	0.39	0.17	0.03	0.01
WK3456	0.0024	0.0040	−0.0054*	0.0001
	0.17	0.16	0.09	0.96
WK123456	0.0036**	0.0015	0.0015	−0.0020
	0.05	0.35	0.62	0.40

[a]The aggregate short ratio is calculated as the cross-sectional average of individual short ratios for each stock day for different exchanges. Smaller regional exchanges (Arca, Boston, Philadelphia, Chicago, NSX, and OTC) are grouped into "other." (A) Composition of the sample with respect to the trading venue. For each group, we regress the aggregate short ratio on time-period dummies, which correspond to half-month, 1 month, or the whole season. WK00 is the half-month period before the start of the earnings seasons. WK12 corresponds to the first half-month. WK34 is the second half-month, and WK56 is the last half-month of a 45-day earnings season. WK1234 is the first month, WK3456 is the peak of the season, and WK123456 is the whole 45-day season. Values shown are estimates of regression coefficients with p values shown below the estimates. *Significance at 10% and **significance at 5% or better.

susceptible to this increase in short selling activity at the start of the earnings season. Finally, we show that stocks trading on NYSE, AMEX, and all others experience a significant increase in short selling activity at the end of the earnings season (WK56), whereas stocks traded on NASDAQ experience a significant *decrease* over the same period. Again, these patterns warrant additional research.

Table 38.4 examines the relationship between short selling activity and the dispersion of analysts' forecasts. We find that the significant increase in short selling at the beginning of the earnings season (WK12) documented in Tables 38.2 and 38.3 is consistent across all dispersion-based portfolios.

Table 38.4 Aggregate Short Ratio by Analysts' Dispersion[a]

	Q = 1 (Low Dispersion)	Q = 3 (Medium)	Q = 5 (Large Dispersion)
WK00	0.00201	–0.00031	–0.00436
	0.62	0.92	0.14
WK12	0.01204**	0.00902**	0.00903**
	0.00	0.01	0.00
WK34	–0.00072	–0.00369	–0.00068
	0.86	0.23	0.82
WK56	–0.00662*	–0.00192	0.000826
	0.09	0.54	0.78
WK1234	0.00660**	0.00289	0.00486**
	0.04	0.25	0.04
WK3456	–0.00465	–0.00354	9.6E–05
	0.14	0.15	0.97
WK123456	0.00198	0.00143	0.00473**
	0.51	0.54	0.03

[a]The aggregate short ratio is calculated as the cross-sectional average of individual short ratios for each stock day for different levels of analysts' dispersion. For each stock that has forecasted earnings from at least two analysts on I/B/E/S, we calculate the average standard deviation of analysts' year-ahead forecasts over the last 6 months. Using this measure, we break the sample into five quintiles. For each quintile, we regress the aggregate short ratio on time-period dummies, which correspond to half-month, 1 month, or the whole season. WK00 is the half-month period before the start of the earnings seasons. WK12 corresponds to the first half-month. WK34 is the second half-month, and WK56 is the last half-month of a 45-day earnings season. WK1234 is the first month, WK3456 is the peak of the season, and WK123456 is the whole 45-day season. Values shown are estimates of regression coefficients with p values shown below the estimates.
*Significance at 10% and **significance at 5% or better.

Short sellers increase their short positions at the beginning of the earnings season regardless of the degree to which analysts disagree about the content of earnings announcements. Differences of opinions do not seem to be a driving force behind short selling behavior. Overall, these results show that analyst dispersion does not exert much influence over short selling patterns, that is, short selling activity does not appear to be a function of the precision of the market's information set.

Finally, we extend these results by regressing short ratios against time-period dummy variables and a set of control variables [i.e., PRIM, volatility, log (size), analyst dispersion]. PRIM is Amihud's (2002) illiquidity ratio, and all other variables are the same as defined earlier. We also include interaction terms for an additional set of four regressions. We report results for eight separate regressions in Table 38.5. The first four regressions (i.e., for WK00, WK12, WK34, and WK56) do not include interaction terms, whereas the second four regressions include interaction terms.

Results in Table 38.5 confirm the same general patterns shown in the sorted portfolio results in Tables 38.2 through 38.4. The strongest change in short

Table 38.5 Multivariate Analysis

	1	2	3	4	5	6	7	8
WK00	−0.0002				0.0217*			
	0.47				0.00			
WK12		0.01159*				0.02591*		
		0.00				0.00		
WK34			−0.002*				−0.018*	
			0.00				0.00	
WK56				−0.004*				−0.004*
				0.00				0.01
PRIM	−0.0001	−0.0001	−0.0001	−0.0001	0.0000	0.0000	−0.001*	−0.0001
	0.14	0.14	0.15	0.13	0.66	0.86	0.00	0.31
Volatility	0.39511*	0.40145*	0.39982*	0.39926*	0.43984*	0.40918*	0.31977*	0.45223*
	0.00	0.00	0.00	0.00	0.00	0.00	0.00	0.00
Log (size)	−0.0063*	−0.0063*	−0.0063*	−0.0063*	−0.0059*	−0.0060*	−0.0065*	−0.0065*
	0.00	0.00	0.00	0.00	0.00	0.00	0.00	0.00
Analysts' dispersion	0.00129*	0.00135v	0.00124	0.00125	0.00211*	0.00099	0.00100	0.00042
	0.05	0.04	0.06	0.06	0.00	0.18	0.18	0.57
WK**xPRIM					−0.0009*	−0.0014*	0.0008*	−0.0002
					0.01	0.00	0.00	0.36
WK**xVol					−0.2497*	−0.0621*	0.4025*	−0.2699*
					0.00	0.01	0.00	0.00
WK**xLogSize					−0.0024*	−0.0019*	0.0010*	0.0008*
					0.00	0.00	0.00	0.00
WK**xAn. Disp					−0.0056*	0.0021	0.0019	0.0046*
					0.00	0.24	0.27	0.01

[a]We regress stocks' individual short ratio on time-period dummies and various stock characteristics. PRIM is the Amihud's illiquidity ratio, volatility is the standard deviation of returns, and analysts' dispersion is the standard deviation of analysts' forecasts averaged over the past 6 months. WK00 is the half-month period before the start of the earnings seasons. WK12 corresponds to the first half-month. WK34 is the second half-month, and WK56 is the last half-month of a 45-day earnings season. WK1234 is the first month, WK3456 is the peak of the season, and WK123456 is the whole 45-day season. The last four variables are interaction coefficients of variables with the appropriate time-period dummies. Values shown are estimates of regression coefficients with p values shown below the estimates.
*Significance at 5% or better.

selling activity is the significant increase during the first 2 weeks (WK12) of the earnings season. The coefficient on this time-period dummy variable is positive and significant in both regression (38.2) and regression (38.6), that is, both with and without interaction terms. We find weaker evidence of increased short selling during the preannouncement period (WK00) with an insignificant coefficient in regression (38.1) but a positive and significant coefficient in regression (38.5). In contrast, short selling activity decreases significantly as we move through the earnings season. Coefficients on time-period dummy variables are negative and significant for both WK34 and WK56 (with and without interaction terms). The overall story that emerges from these results is that short selling increases at the beginning of the earnings season and then tapers off over time. The significant decrease in short selling toward the end of the earnings season suggests that short sellers are buying to offset their earlier short sales.

As an additional test, we implicitly incorporate the SEC's 10% rule as approved in early 2010. This trading rule restricts short selling activity whenever the firm's stock price falls by 10% or more in a single day. Under this condition, further short selling is permitted only if the sales price is higher than the best available bid price. After applying this rule to our data set, we find that our empirical results are essentially unchanged. The main reason that our results are unaffected is the very low fraction of firms with daily returns less than negative 10% (0.34% of all firms) during our sample period. This low incidence of large negative returns is due to the strong market performance over our sample period. The S&P500 increased steadily from 1185 to over 1500 with historically low volatility. In later periods, however, the fraction of stocks with daily returns less than negative 10% increases sharply. During the second half of 2008, 4.5% of all firms experienced negative returns of at least 10%. During the worse period of the 2008–2009 crisis, almost 6% of all firms experience such negative returns. This fraction changed again in the second half of 2009 when markets rallied, and less than 1% of all firms experienced such negative returns. Our analysis suggests that the degree to which the SEC short selling rule is binding depends to a great extent on underlying market conditions. Although the new rule is not binding during our sample period, this finding does not suggest that it will be ineffective during sharp market downturns.

38.4 CONCLUSION

Previous studies suggest two main motivations for short selling. The first motive is possession of an informational advantage on the part of short sellers. This view has found support in several empirical studies (Boehmer et al., 2008; Boehmer and Wu, 2009; Diether et al., 2009). The second motive for short selling is for hedging and arbitrage purposes. Hedge funds and other market participants use short selling in such strategies as merger arbitrage, convertible arbitrage, and index arbitrage. In addition, market makers use short selling to manage their inventories while providing liquidity. It is important to distinguish between these two short selling motives, as each has different implications for financial markets and regulators. To investigate the relative importance of the two motives, we looked at the aggregate short selling activity during earnings seasons.

Although earlier studies have examined short selling around earnings announcements of individual firms (e.g., Christophe et al., 2004; Francis et al., 2005; Desai et al., 2006; Diether et al., 2009), no previous study has addressed the issue of aggregate short selling during earnings seasons. Earnings seasons are unique periods during the year (45 days at the beginning of each quarter) when thousands of firms flood the market with firm-specific announcements. If short selling is motivated predominantly by the possession of private information, then we should find a significant increase in short selling just before the start of the earnings season.

We examined short selling trading patterns using a unique data sample made available through SEC Regulation SHO. This regulation required all major exchanges [NYSE, NASDAQ, American (AMEX), Archipelago (ARCA), Boston (BSE), Chicago (CHX), NASD, National (NSX), and Philadelphia (PHX)] to disclose short sale trades between January 3, 2005, and July 6, 2007. Our main empirical results showed that (1) over 25% of all trading volume is attributable to short selling, (2) aggregate short selling increases in the first 2 weeks of earnings seasons but only for medium-sized portfolios, (3) aggregate short selling exhibits different patterns on different exchanges, and (4) aggregate short selling is independent of analyst following. Overall, results suggested that short selling during the earnings season is motivated more by the needs of hedgers and arbitrageurs than by the possession of private information.

REFERENCES

Amihud, Y. (2002). Illiquidity and stock returns: Cross-section and time-series effects. *Journal of Financial Markets, 5*(1), 31–56.

Boehmer, E., Huszar, S., & Jordan, B. (2010). The good news in short interest. *Journal of Financial Economics, 96*(1), 80–97.

Boehmer, E., Jones, C., & Zhang, X. (2008). Which shorts are informed? *Journal of Finance, 63*(2), 491–527.

Boehmer, E., & Wu, J. (2009). *Short selling and the informational efficiency of prices*. Working Paper, Texas A&M University, College Park, TX.

Brockman, P., & Nikiforov, A. (2010). *Earnings clustering, liquidity shocks, and returns*. Working Paper, Lehigh University, Bethlehem, PA.

Chordia, T., Roll, R., & Subrahmanyam, A. (2002). Order imbalance, liquidity and market returns. *Journal of Financial Economics, 65*(1), 111–130.

Christophe, S., Ferri, M., & Ang, J. (2004). *Short selling prior to earnings announcements. Journal of Finance, 59*(4), 1845–1875.

Dechow, P., Hutton, A., Meulbroek, L., & Sloan, R. (2001). Short-sellers, fundamental analysis, and stock returns. *Journal of Financial Economics, 61*(1), 77–106.

Desai, H., Hogan, C., & Wilkins, M. (2006). The reputational penalty for aggressive accounting: Earnings restatement and managerial turnover. *Accounting Review, 81*(1), 83–112.

Diamond, D., & Verrecchia, R. (1987). Constraints on short-selling and asset price adjustment to private information. *Journal of Financial Economics, 18*(2), 277–311.

Diether, K., Malloy, C., & Scherbina, A. (2002). Differences of opinion and the cross section of stock returns. *Journal of Finance, 57*(5), 2113–2141.

Diether, K., Lee, K., & Werner, I. (2009). Short-sale strategies and return predictability. *Review of Financial Studies, 22*, 575–605.

Economist Magazine. (2010). Short-selling rules: Shackling the scapegoats. *February 27*, 83.

Francis, J., Venkatachalam, M., & Zhang, Y. (2005). *Do short sellers convey information about changes in fundamentals or risk?* Working Paper, Duke University, Durham, NC.

Lamont, O., & Stein, J. (2004). Aggregate short interest and market valuations. *American Economic Review, 94*(2), 29–32.

Roll, R., Schwartz, E., & Subrahmanyam, A. (2010). O/S: The relative trading activity in options and stock. *Journal of Financial Economics, 96*(1), 1–17.

Yu, H., Lynch, A., Nikolic, B., & Yan, X. (2010). *The information content of aggregate short selling.* Working Paper, University of Missouri, Columbia, MO.

CHAPTER 39

The Information Content of Short Selling before Macroeconomic Announcements

Paul Brockman and (Grace) Qing Hao

CONTENTS

ABSTRACT

This chapter examines short sale transactions in exchange-traded funds during a 2-day window prior to the release of 10 key macroeconomic announcements. A negative and significant relation between prerelease abnormal short selling and postrelease stock returns would suggest the presence of informed short selling. Previous studies suggest that some reports (e.g., the Employment Situation Report) are more important than others. Empirical results provide affirmative evidence of informed trading in prerelease short selling for the Employment Situation Report. This finding suggests that short sellers are able to predict the content of this important macroeconomic announcement. In contrast, we find no evidence of informed short selling for the other nine economic data releases.

KEYWORDS

Abnormal short selling; Employment Situation Report; Exchange-traded funds; Intraday short sale transaction data set; Macroeconomic reports; Regulation SHO; Self-regulatory organizations.

39.1 INTRODUCTION

Key economic indicators inform market participants and the public at large about general economic conditions. The related macroeconomic announcements are generally scheduled to be released at predetermined times. For example, the Employment Situation Report, the Manufacturing Institute for Supply Management Report, Manufacturers' Shipments, Inventories, and Orders (M3) Survey, and the New Residential Construction Report are released every month. While all of these economic reports can move the market significantly, some reports are more important than others. For example, the first Friday of every month, when the Employment Situation Report is released, is said to be the most important trading session of the month.

> The employment report is so crucial to financial-market participants that dealers, brokers, and economists plan their vacations around its release. Many traders can "make their month" (that is, earn a month's salary in a single trading session) on the day the report is released. People have actually been fired for missing the 8:30 a.m. (ET) release (Yamarone, 2007).

Investors with private information about the contents of these macroeconomic reports can establish short positions in exchange-traded funds (ETFs) when they expect a negative data release or, equivalently, can refrain from shorting shares when they expect a positive release. This study uses a comprehensive data set of daily short selling to explore key features of short sale transactions in equity ETFs prior to the release of key economic indicator data.

This chapter examines whether short sellers are generally able to predict the content of key economic indicator announcements. If short sellers are, on average, informed, then short selling activities should experience abnormal increases before the release of negative announcements and abnormal decreases before the release of positive announcements. Our empirical results can be summarized as follows: we find evidence of informed trading in prerelease short selling for the Employment Situation Report, but not for the other nine economic indicator data releases, including the Manufacturing Institute for Supply Management Report, Manufacturers' Shipments, Inventories, and Orders (M3) Survey, New Residential

Construction Report, gross domestic product, producer price index, consumer price index, consumer confidence, consumer sentiment, and retail sales.

These results are robust to alternative methods of computing standard errors. In particular, for the Employment Situation Report (arguably the most influential economic announcement), a 1% decrease in the announcement day return is associated with a 27% increase in abnormal short selling in the 2 days prior to the release of the report. Using a related measure, we show that a 1% decrease in the announcement day return is associated with a 10% increase in abnormal *relative* short selling. These findings increase our understanding of short sale transactions and informed trading in ETFs around major economic information releases. It also raises an interesting question for future research of how short sellers are able to predict the stock market reaction to the Employment Situation Report.

This study is distinguished from previous research on the informativeness of short selling in two ways. First, while many short sale empirical studies are based on monthly short interest (see, e.g., Arnold, Butler, Crack, & Zhang, 2005; Asquith, Pathak, & Ritter, 2005; Brent, Morse, & Stice, 1990; Chen & Singal, 2003; DeChow, Hutton, Meulbroek, & Sloan, 2001; Desai, Thiagarajan, Ramesh, & Balachandran, 2002), this chapter uses an intraday short sale transaction data set, which is made possible by Regulation SHO of the Securities and Exchange Commission (SEC). Prior to the SEC's promulgation of Regulation SHO, publicly available information on short sales only included the total number of shares sold short in individual stocks on a specific day of each month. Because of Regulation SHO of the SEC, we are able to obtain an intraday short sale transaction data set from 2005 through mid-2007.

Second, and more importantly, most other studies use daily short sales data to examine the informativeness of short selling on abnormal returns of individual stocks (Boehmer, Jones, & Zhang, 2008; Brockman & Hao, 2010; Diether, Lee, & Werner, 2009) around corporate events such as earnings announcements (Christophe, Ferri, & Angel, 2004), analyst downgrades (Christophe, Ferri, & Hsieh, 2010), initial public offerings (Edwards & Hanley, 2010), and seasoned equity offerings (Henry & Koski, 2009). However, this chapter focuses on more broad-based stock market movements by examining ETFs. There is considerable evidence that macroeconomic news affects aggregate stock returns (see, e.g., Flannery & Protapapadakis, 2002). To be profitable from aggregate stock price movements, ETFs would be a convenient trading vehicle. ETFs are popular because of their flexibility and because they combine easy diversification effects, low expense ratios, and tax efficiency of index funds with the features of ordinary stocks, including the use of limit orders, short selling, and options. ETFs provide a convenient way for investors to make profits from more broad-based stock market movements.

Broad-based stock market movements often occur during the release of key economic indicator data. Such releases can create quite a stir in financial markets, which creates a strong incentive for investors to acquire information prior to the releases. Although studies show that short sellers are informed prior to individual firms' earnings announcements and analyst downgrades (Christophe et al., 2004, 2010), we know little about whether short sellers possess private information about macroeconomic conditions. This study is the first attempt to fill this gap.

Bear market ETFs and put options on long market ETFs provide alternative ways for investors to profit from negative macroeconomic information. Thus, our empirical results on short selling ETFs are biased against showing any informed trading before economic data releases. Nevertheless, we find supporting evidence that a significant portion of short selling in long market ETFs is informed before the release of the Employment Situation Report.

This chapter is organized as follows. Section 39.2 describes the sample and its main characteristics. Section 39.3 explains the methods, and Section 39.4 presents results. Section 39.5 summarizes and concludes the study.

39.2 DATA SOURCES AND SAMPLE DETAILS

Daily short sale data are obtained for the American Stock Exchange (AMEX), Archipelago, Boston Stock Exchange, Chicago Stock Exchange, National Association of Securities Dealers, National Association of Securities Dealers Automated Quotations (NASDAQ), National Stock Exchange (formerly known as the Cincinnati Stock Exchange), Philadelphia Stock Exchange, and New York Stock Exchange (NYSE). Pursuant to the SEC's Regulation SHO adopted in 2004, all the aforementioned self-regulatory organizations (SROs) made tick data on short sales available publicly starting January 2, 2005. While short sale data for NYSE are available through the TAQ database, all the other SROs only make short sale data available at their own Web sites. The ending date for available Regulation SHO data varies from May 2007 to August 2007 across the SROs. Therefore, we chose the sample period during which short sale data are available for all the SROs (i.e., January 2005–May 2007).

This study focuses on U.S. equity ETFs. Our initial sample of U.S. ETFs includes all ETFs that appear in both of the following databases during the sample period of January 2005–May 2007: (1) the Center for Research in Security Prices (CRSP) daily stock file (with share code 73) and (2) the CRSP mutual fund database (an ETF/ETN flag value equal to "F"). There are 517 ETFs in this initial sample. We obtain fund information from the CRSP mutual fund database. We exclude ETFs that invest primarily in commodity, currencies, bonds, and non-U.S. stocks. We also exclude bear market ETFs. This leaves 193 ETFs in the sample. We then merge daily short sale data with daily return and trading volume data from CRSP. We exclude stock days where there is zero or missing volume reported by CRSP. If short sales in an ETF are missing from Regulation SHO data on a day, we set short sales as zero on that day. We then exclude ETFs whose median short sales are zero for two reasons. First, this excludes ETFs that are rarely shorted for practical reasons. Second, this is required by computing the abnormal short selling measures, which use median short sales as the denominator. The final sample has 154 ETFs.

Although most of the key economic indicators are usually released on fixed dates, there are rare exceptions. For example, the Employment Situation Report is typically released on the first Friday of each month. However, in 3 months during our sample period (i.e., March 2006, December 2006, and March 2007), the report was actually released on the second Friday of the month. Therefore, we obtain the specific dates for the key economic indicators' data releases from the Web site, briefing.com. To examine macroeconomic news surprises, we obtain actual data and forecasted data from briefing.com. We also obtain information about the availability of put options on ETFs from Yahoo! Finance ETF center.

39.3 MEASURES AND METHODS

If short selling is informed before key economic indicator data releases, we expect that abnormal short selling in the days prior to the release is related significantly to the share price reaction to the release. Following the literature, we define abnormal short selling as follows:

$$ABSS(-2, -1) = \frac{SS(-2, -1)}{AVESS} - 1 \qquad (39.1)$$

where $SS(-2, -1)$ is the daily average number of shares sold short during the 2 trading days prior to the release of the macroeconomic report of interest, and $AVESS$ is the daily average number of shares sold short over the full sample period. In a similar fashion, we define the abnormal trading volume for an ETF as follows:

$$ABVOL(-2, -1) = \frac{VOL(-2, -1)}{AVEVOL} - 1 \qquad (39.2)$$

where $VOL(-2, -1)$ is the daily average trading volume during the 2 days prior to the release of the macroeconomic report of interest, and $AVEVOL$ is the daily average trading volume during the full sample period.

Similar to the models given elsewhere (Christophe et al., 2004, 2010), our model for testing whether abnormal short selling is linked to information about upcoming economic data releases has the following form:

$$ABSS(-2,-1) = \beta_0 + \beta_1 RET0 + \beta_2 RET(-2,-1) + \beta_3 ABVOL(-2,-1)$$
$$+ \beta_4 Log(mktcap) + \beta_5 MOM + \beta_6 PUT \qquad (39.3)$$
$$+ \beta_7 VOLSTD + \beta_8 RETSTD + \varepsilon$$

where $RET0$ is the percentage return on the ETF on the announcement date (day 0), $RET(-2,-1)$ is the return on the ETF from the closing prices of day -3 to -1, and $ABVOL(-2,-1)$ is the mean daily abnormal volume for the ETF over the interval of day -2 to -1. In addition, $Log(mktcap)$ is the mean natural logarithm of market capitalization of the ETF over the interval of day -2 to -1. MOM is defined as the ETF's 5-business-day cumulative return over the interval of day -7 to -3. PUT is an indicator variable that equals 1 if the ETF has put options available and 0 otherwise. $VOLSTD$ is the standard deviation of the daily trading volume (million shares) of the ETF over the sample period. $RETSTD$ is the standard deviation of daily returns for the ETF over the sample period.

Our main independent variable of interest is $RET0$. This variable serves as a proxy for the unexpected information content of the macroeconomic data release. A positive (negative) return on the release day suggests a positive (negative) surprise. Alternatively, we could use the difference between actual and forecasted data to proxy for the announcement surprise. However, market returns on information release dates can better capture the profitability of short selling. If short selling prior to data release is indeed informed, then we expect a negative and statistically significant β_1 in Equation (39.3).

As a robustness check, we also define an alternative measure of abnormal short selling as follows:

$$ABRELSS(-2,-1) = \frac{SS(-2,-1)/VOL(-2,-1)}{AVESS/AVEVOL} - 1 \qquad (39.4)$$

where $SS(-2,-1)$, $VOL(-2,-1)$, $AVESS$, and $AVEVOL$ are defined the same way as in Equations (39.1) and (39.2). We refer to this measure as abnormal *relative* short selling. Using this alternative definition of abnormal short selling, we estimate the regression model in Equation (39.5) to examine whether the abnormal relative short selling is informed prior to data release. If short selling is informed in the prerelease period, then we expect a negative and statistically significant γ_1 in Equation (39.5).

$$ABRELSS(-2,-1) = \gamma_0 + \gamma_1 RET0 + \gamma_2 RET(-2,-1) + \gamma_3 Log(mktcap)$$
$$+ \gamma_4 MOM + \gamma_5 PUT + \gamma_6 VOLSTD + \gamma_7 RETSTD + \theta \qquad (39.5)$$

39.4 RESULTS

Table 39.1 summarizes the 10 macroeconomic announcements examined in this study. We provide the report code, brief description, source institution, and typical release date (and time of day) for each macroeconomic announcement (for additional descriptions, see Yamarone, 2007).

Part A of Table 39.2 presents summary statistics for the ETFs in our sample and their daily short selling data. On average, short selling represents 20% of share volume. Roughly one in five domestic equity ETF shares traded involves a short seller. Part B of Table 39.2 reports the mean announcement surprise, which is defined as actual economic data minus forecasted data provided by briefing.com. Column (4) shows the correlation between the announcement surprise and the announcement day return. Some of the relations are consistent with intuition. For example, a positive surprise for durable orders and consumer sentiment is related to a positive announcement day return. However, some of the relations are inconsistent with intuition.

Table 39.1 Ten Key Economic Indicators

Report Code	Indicator	Institute	Typical Release Date and Time (ET) during the Sample Period
EMP	Employment situation	Bureau of Labor Statistics, Department of Labor	8:30 a.m. on the first Friday of each month
ISM	Purchasing Managers' Index (PMI)	Institute for Supply Management (ISM)	10:00 a.m. on the first business day of each month
M3	Manufacturers' Shipments, Inventories, and Orders	Census Bureau, Department of Commerce	The advance report on durable goods is released at 8:30 a.m. between the 22nd and 29th of each month
CPI	Consumer price index (CPI)	Bureau of Labor Statistics, Department of Labor	8:30 a.m. between the 14th and 23rd of each month
GDP	Gross domestic product (GDP)	Bureau of Economic Analysis, Department of Commerce	8:30 a.m. on the third or fourth week of the month
HOS	Housing starts and building permits	Department of Commerce's Census Bureau & Department of Housing and Urban Development	8:30 a.m. between the 16th and 20th of each month
CON	Consumer confidence	The Conference Board	10:00 a.m. on the last Tuesday of each month
PPI	Producer price index (PPI)	Bureau of Labor Statistics, Department of Labor	8:30 a.m. between the 11th and 22nd of each month
MIC	Consumer sentiment index	University of Michigan	The preliminary report is released at 9:45 a.m., 9:50 a.m., or 10:00 a.m. on the second to last Friday of each month
RET	Retail sales	Census Bureau, Department of Commerce	8:30 a.m. between the 11th and 16th of each month

Table 39.2 Descriptive Statistics[a]

A. Descriptive Statistics of Sample ETFs and Short Selling in These ETFs

	Mean	Median	Maximum	Minimum	Std. Dev.
Market cap ($ billion)	1422	153	55,539	18	5053
SS (thousands of shares)	582	9	39,681	0.5	3742
RELSS	20%	20%	51%	3%	12%

B. Deviation from Market Forecast and ETF Return

Report Code	Economic Indicator	(1) Actual	(2) Actual Forecast	(3) RET0	(4) Std. Dev. of RET0	(5) Correlation between (2) and (3)
EMP	Nonfarm payrolls	139,069	−15,069	0.02%	0.76%	−0.03*
	Unemployment rate	4.84%	−0.05%	0.02%	0.76%	−0.01
ISM	ISM index	54.43	−0.53	0.17%	0.89%	−0.16***
M3	Durable orders	0.28%	−0.53%	−0.17%	1.07%	0.25***
CPI	Consumer price index	0.25%	−0.01%	0.05%	0.97%	0.00
GDP	Gross domestic product	3.01%	−0.07%	0.38%	0.98%	0.00
HOS	Building permits	1,906.34	0.14	0.31%	0.98%	−0.25***
	Housing starts	1,876.34	3.41	0.31%	0.98%	−0.17***
CON	Consumer confidence	103.50	1.04	−0.29%	1.06%	−0.17***
PPI	Producer price index	0.30%	0.04%	0.14%	0.89%	−0.00
MIC	Michigan sentiment	88.23	−0.35	0.00%	0.82%	0.19***
RET	Retail sales	0.37%	−0.05%	−0.00%	1.01%	−0.05***

[a]*This table presents descriptive statistics on 154 U.S. equity ETFs over the period 1/2005–5/2007. We obtain our sample of ETFs using the CRSP Mutual Fund database and the CRSP stock database. (A) SS is the number of shares sold short in a trading day. RELSS is the number of shares sold short divided by the trading volume in a trading day. We first take a time-series average for each ETF. We then report the cross-sectional average of these time-series averages. (B) Both actual and forecasted data are obtained from briefing.com. Columns (1)–(3) report the sample average. Column (4) reports the standard deviation of announcement day returns. In Column (5), correlations with significance at the 1, 5, and 10% levels are denoted with ***, **, and *, respectively.*

For example, a positive surprise for nonfarm payrolls, Institute for Supply Management (ISM) index, building permits/housing starts, consumer confidence, and retail sales is related to a negative announcement day return. While results can be consistent with several alternative explanations, the most important message is that the actual data's deviation from the market's forecast would not be a good proxy for the profitability of short selling.

Table 39.3 presents results from the multivariate analysis of estimating Equations (39.3) and (39.5). Specifically, we analyze short selling in the 2 days prior to the announcements. In parts A and B of Table 39.3,

Table 39.3 Results of OLS Regressions: Abnormal Short Selling and Abnormal Relative Short Selling in ETFs during the 2 Days prior to Key Economic Indicator Data Releases[a]

A. Estimation Results for the Employment Situation Report and the PMI by the ISM

| | EMP | | ISM | |
| | Equation (39.3) | Equation (39.5) | Equation (39.3) | Equation (39.5) |
Dependent Variable =	ABSS	ABRELSS	ABSS	ABRELSS
Intercept	4.97*** (4.17)	3.56*** (6.84)	5.40*** (3.37)	3.31*** (7.77)
RET0 (%)	−0.27*** (−2.77)	−0.10** (−2.04)	−0.96 (−1.39)	−0.10 (−1.45)
RET(−2, −1)(%)	−0.55 (−0.06)	−2.13 (−0.63)	−12.52 (−0.77)	4.48 (1.29)
ABVOL(−2, −1)	0.74*** (3.49)		0.99 (1.44)	
Log(mktcap)	−0.56*** (−3.11)	−0.40*** (−5.99)	−0.81** (−2.51)	−0.38*** (−7.00)
MOM(%)	10.43 (1.02)	5.02* (1.47)	39.35 (1.07)	−0.09 (−0.02)
PUT	0.12 (−0.19)	−0.02 (−0.12)	0.90 (1.14)	0.04 (0.20)
VOLSTD	0.03* (1.92)	0.03*** (4.92)	0.05 (1.18)	0.03*** (5.02)
RETSTD	−64.10 (−1.01)	−60.76** (−2.09)	45.67 (0.40)	−48.20* (−1.70)
N	3752	3752	3652	3652
Adj. R^2	8.20%	5.12%	4.34%	4.81%

B. Coefficient Estimate on RET0 (%) for Eight Economic Indicators

| | Equation (39.3) | Equation (39.5) | | Equation (39.3) | Equation (39.5) |
Dependent Variable =	ABSS	ABRELSS	Dependent Variable =	ABSS	ABRELSS
M3	0.16 (0.84)	−0.01 (−0.19)	GDP	0.22 (1.54)	0.13** (2.08)
HOS	0.08 (0.83)	0.04 (0.67)	CON	−0.15 (−1.00)	−0.07 (−1.42)
CPI	0.17 (1.35)	0.04 (0.64)	PPI	0.12 (0.68)	−0.04 (−0.69)
RET	0.12 (0.65)	0.14*** (3.42)	MIC	−0.30* (−1.85)	−0.02 (−0.46)

[a]This table reports estimation results for the following two regression equations. The sample period is 1/2005–5/2007.

$$ABSS(-2, -1) = \beta_0 + \beta_1 RET0 + \beta_2 RET(-2, -1) + \beta_3 ABVOL(-2, -1) + \beta_4 Log(mktcap)$$
$$+ \beta_5 MOM + \beta_6 PUT + \beta_7 VOLSTD + \beta_8 RETSTD + \varepsilon \qquad (39.3)$$

$$ABRELSS(-2, -1) = \gamma_0 + \gamma_1 RET0 + \gamma_2 RET(-2, -1) + \gamma_3 Log(mktcap) + \gamma_4 MOM + \gamma_5 PUT + \gamma_6 VOLSTD + \gamma_7 RETSTD + \theta \qquad (39.5)$$

$ABSS(-2, -1) = \frac{SS(-2, -1)}{AVESS} - 1$, where SS(−2,−1) is the mean daily number of shares sold short during the 2 days prior to economic data release, and AVESS is the median daily number of shares sold short during the entire sample period.

$ABRELSS(-2, -1) = \frac{SS(-2, -1)/VOL(-2, -1)}{AVESS/AVEVOL} - 1$, where VOL(−2,−1) is the mean daily trading volume during the 2 days prior to economic data release, and AVEVOL is the median daily trading volume during the entire sample period. RET0 is the percentage return on the ETF on the announcement date (day 0), RET(−2,−1) is the percentage return on the ETF from the closing prices of day −3 to −1. ABVOL(−2,−1) is the mean daily abnormal volume in the ETF over the interval of day −2 to −1. Log(mktcap) is the mean natural logarithm of market capitalization of the ETF over the interval of day −2 to −1. MOM is defined as the ETF's 5-business-day cumulated percentage return over the interval of day −7 to −3. PUT is an indicator variable that equals to one if the ETF has put options available. VOLSTD is the standard deviation of the daily trading volume (million shares) in the ETF over the sample period. RETSTD is the standard deviation of daily returns in the ETF over the sample period. In A and B, t statistics are adjusted by the Newey and West (1987) method and are reported in parentheses. Statistics with significance at the 1, 5, and 10% levels are denoted with ***, **, and *, respectively.

t statistics are computed based on standard errors adjusted by the Newey and West (1987) method, which allows for the presence of heteroscedasticity and autocorrelation. Part A reports estimation results for the release of the Employment Situation Report and the Manufacturing ISM Report. Of primary interest is the coefficient on the announcement date return, $RET0$. For the Employment Situation Report's release, the coefficient estimate on $RET0$ in Equation (39.3) is −0.27 and is highly significant at the 1% level (t statistic = −2.77). This implies that a 1% decrease in the Employment Report announcement day return is associated with a 27% increase in abnormal short selling, $ABSS(−2, −1)$, in the 2 days prior to the announcement. The coefficient estimate on $RET0$ in Equation (39.5) is −0.10 and is statistically significant at the 5% level (t statistic = −2.04). This implies that a 1% decrease in the Employment Report announcement day return is associated with a 10% increase in abnormal relative short selling, $ABRELSS(−2, −1)$, in the 2 days prior to the announcement. The relationships are not only statistically but also economically significant.

In addition, the size of an ETF also significantly affects abnormal short selling in the ETF. While Diether and colleagues (2009) find that large cap stocks have greater short selling on average than small cap stocks, we find that smaller cap ETFs have greater *abnormal* short selling prior to the economic data release.

For the Purchasing Managers' Index (PMI) released by the ISM, the coefficient estimate on $RET0$ in Equation (39.3) is −0.96. Although the magnitude of the coefficient for the PMI is larger than for the employment report, the coefficient for the PMI is not statistically significant at conventional levels (t statistic = −1.39). In untabulated results, we obtain standard errors directly from OLS regressions without adjusting them by the Newey–West method; the estimated coefficient −0.96 appears to be highly significant at the 1% level. The difference in the statistical significance highlights the importance of computing standard errors that are robust to heteroscedasticity and autocorrelation. Similarly, the coefficient estimate on $RET0$ in Equation (39.5) is −0.10; again, it is insignificant at conventional levels (t statistic = −1.45).

Part B of Table 39.2 reports estimation results for the following eight economic indicators: Manufacturers' Shipments, Inventories, and Orders (M3) Survey, New Residential Construction Report, gross domestic product, producer price index, consumer price index, consumer confidence, consumer sentiment, and retail sales. For brevity, we only report the estimated coefficients on $RET0$. None of the coefficient estimates is statistically negative, suggesting that short selling in the 2 days prior to these eight economic data releases is not informative.

As a robustness check, we also compute standard errors of the coefficient estimates by the bootstrap method using 5000 simulations. Results, which are untabulated for brevity, are qualitatively similar to the results in Table 39.2, suggesting that our results are consistent across these alternative methods of computing robust standard errors.

Because we obtain the information on the availability of put options on ETFs from Yahoo! Finance after our sample period (2005–2007) in 2009, it is possible that some of the ETFs that had put options in 2009 did not have the put options during our sample period. As a robustness check, we omit the indicator variable *PUT* from both Equations (39.3) and (39.5). The main results remain very similar (untabulated).

As an attempt to gain further insight into short selling before economic data releases, we examine whether short selling in the 2 days prior to data release can be explained by deviation of actual data from the market's forecast. However, in untabulated results, we find no evidence for this relation. This is consistent with two nonmutually exclusive explanations. First, the market constantly updates its expectation of soon-to-be-released data, making previously forecasted data stale. Data forecasted by briefing.com, as well as many other sources, are typically made available well in advance of the actual data release. Therefore, it is not surprising that a stale forecast does not represent the market expectation when it is close to the data release. Second, whether a particular data release is considered good or bad news may depend on the specific economic condition at the time of the data release. For example, a rising number of new housing starts may not always be good news. Such an announcement could suggest that the economy is overheating and that the Federal Reserve is more likely to raise interest rates.

39.5 CONCLUSION

This study investigated whether short sellers are generally able to predict the content of key economic indicator announcements. If short sellers are, on average, informed, then short selling activities should experience abnormal increases before the release of negative information announcements. Similarly, short selling activities should experience abnormal decreases before the release of positive information announcements. We specifically analyzed the short selling of ETFs, as these investment vehicles typically represent a diversified portfolio of stocks, bonds, and commodities. We expect that informed investors who trade equity ETFs will pay particular attention to the release of prescheduled key macroeconomic reports.

Our tests found evidence of informed prerelease short selling for the Employment Situation Report, but not for other economic indicator data releases, including the Manufacturing Institute for Supply Management Report, Manufacturers' Shipments, Inventories, and Orders (M3) Survey, New Residential Construction Report, gross domestic product, producer price index, consumer price index, consumer confidence, consumer sentiment, and retail sales. Perhaps because the Employment Situation Report is arguably the most influential economic report, traders spend more resources in an attempt to predict its content. How exactly short sellers are able to predict the content of this report (and not the content of other reports) is an interesting question for future research.

REFERENCES

Arnold, T., Butler, A., Crack, T., & Zhang, Y. (2005). The information content of short interest: A natural experiment. *Journal of Business, 78*(4), 1307–1335.

Asquith, P., Pathak, P., & Ritter, J. (2005). Short interest, institutional ownership, and stock returns. *Journal of Financial Economics, 78*(2), 243–276.

Boehmer, E., Jones, C., & Zhang, X. (2008). Which shorts are informed?. *Journal of Finance, 63*(2), 491–527.

Brent, A., Morse, D., & Stice, E. (1990). Short interest: Explanations and tests. *Journal of Financial and Quantitative Analysis, 25*(2), 273–289.

Brockman, P., & Hao, Q. (2010). *Short selling and price discovery: Evidence from American depository receipts.* Working Paper, Leigh University and University of Missouri.

Chen, H., & Singal, V. (2003). Role of speculative short sales in price formation: The case of the weekend effect. *Journal of Finance, 58*(2), 685–705.

Christophe, S., Ferri, M., & Angel, J. (2004). Short selling prior to earnings announcements. *Journal of Finance, 59*(4), 1845–1875.

Christophe, S., Ferri, M., & Hsieh, J. (2010). Informed trading before analyst downgrades: Evidence from short sellers. *Journal of Financial Economics, 95*(1), 85–106.

DeChow, P., Hutton, A., Meulbroek, L., & Sloan, R. (2001). Short sellers, fundamental analysis, and stock returns. *Journal of Financial Economics, 61*(1), 77–106.

Desai, H., Thiagarajan, S., Ramesh, K., & Balachandran, B. (2002). An investigation of the informational role of short interest in the NASDAQ market. *Journal of Finance, 57*(5), 2263–2287.

Diether, K., Lee, K., & Werner, I. (2009). Short-sale strategies and return predictability. *Review of Financial Studies, 22*(2), 575–607.

Edwards, A., & Hanley, K. (2010). Short selling in initial public offerings. *Journal of Financial, 98*, 21–39.

Flannery, M., & Protapapadakis, A. (2002). Macroeconomic factors do influence aggregate stock returns. *Review of Financial Studies, 15*(3), 751–782.

Henry, T., & Koski, J. (2009). *Short selling around seasoned equity offerings.* Working Paper, University of Georgia, Atlanta, GA.

Newey, W., & West, K. (1987). A simple, positive semi-definite, heteroskedasticity and autocorrelation consistent covariance matrix. *Econometrica, 55*(3), 703–708.

Yamarone, R. (2007). *The trader's guide to key economic indicators* Updated and expanded edition. New York: Bloomberg Press.

Index

Printed and bound by CPI Group (UK) Ltd, Croydon, CR0 4YY

08/05/2025

01864770-0003